Aspects of the Canadian Evangelical Experience

Canadian evangelicalism, a powerful religious impulse in the nineteenth century, continues to be a powerful force, with evangelicals making up fifty per cent of practising Protestants in the mid-1990s. *Aspects of the Canadian Evangelical Experience* explores Canadian evangelicalism in the nineteenth and twentieth centuries, placing it within historical, cultural, and theological frameworks.

An impressive list of specialists in the field examines the evangelical impulse in various denominations, from mainstream Methodists, Presbyterians, Anglicans, and Uniteds, through Baptists, Mennonites, and Lutherans, to the more sectish groups, including Holiness, Christian Mission Alliance, and the Pentecostals. Also included are comparisons between Canadian and American, British, and Australian evangelicalism and essays on evangelical networks, leaders and revivals, women, and evangelicalism in the 1990s.

Growing out of a conference sponsored by the Pew Charitable Trusts in 1995 at Queen's University, the essays elaborate a variety of important themes in the study of historical and contemporary evangelicalism and weave them together to provide an informative and challenging exploration of aspects of the evangelical experience in Canada.

The late G.A. RAWLYK was professor of history, Queen's University.

McGill-Queen's Studies in the History of Religion

Volumes in this series have been supported by the Jackman Foundation of Toronto.

SERIES ONE
G.A. Rawlyk, Editor

1 Small Differences
  Irish Catholics and Irish Protestants, 1815–1922
  An International Perspective
  Donald Harman Akenson

2 Two Worlds
  The Protestant Culture of Nineteenth-Century Ontario
  William Westfall

3 An Evangelical Mind
  Nathanael Burwash and the Methodist Tradition in Canada, 1839–1918
  Marguerite Van Die

4 The Dévotes
  Women and Church in Seventeenth-Century France
  Elizabeth Rapley

5 The Evangelical Century
  College and Creed in English Canada from the Great Revival to the Great Depression
  Michael Gauvreau

6 The German Peasants' War and Anabaptist Community of Goods
  James M. Stayer

7 A World Mission
  Canadian Protestantism and the Quest for a New International Order, 1918–1939
  Robert Wright

8 Serving the Present Age
  Revivalism, Progressivism, and the Methodist Tradition in Canada
  Phyllis D. Airhart

9 A Sensitive Independence
  Canadian Methodist Women Missionaries in Canada and the Orient, 1881–1925
  Rosemary R. Gagan

10 God's Peoples
   Covenant and Land in South Africa, Israel, and Ulster
   Donald Harman Akenson

11 Creed and Culture
   The Place of English-Speaking Catholics in Canadian Society, 1750–1930
   Terrence Murphy and Gerald Stortz, editors

12 Piety and Nationalism
   Lay Voluntary Associations and the Creation of an Irish-Catholic Community in Toronto, 1850–1895
   Brian P. Clarke

13 Amazing Grace
   Studies in Evangelicalism in Australia, Britain, Canada, and the United States
   George Rawlyk and Mark A. Noll, editors

14 Children of Peace
   W. John McIntyre

15 A Solitary Pillar
   Montreal's Anglican Church and the Quiet Revolution
   Joan Marshall

16 Padres in No Man's Land
   Canadian Chaplains and the Great War
   Duff Crerar

17 Christian Ethics and Political Economy in North America
   A Critical Analysis of U.S. and Canadian Approaches
   P. Travis Kroeker

18 Pilgrims in Lotus Land
   Conservative Protestantism in British Columbia, 1917–1981
   Robert K. Burkinshaw

19 Through Sunshine and Shadow
   The Woman's Christian Temperance Union, Evangelicalism, and Reform in Ontario, 1874–1930
   Sharon Cook

20 Church, College, and Clergy
   A History of Theological Education at Knox College, Toronto, 1844–1994
   Brian J. Fraser

21 The Lord's Dominion
   The History of Canadian Methodism
   Neil Semple

22 A Full-Orbed Christianity
   The Protestant Churches and Social Welfare in Canada, 1900–1940
   Nancy Christie and Michael Gauvreau

23 Evangelism and Apostasy
   The Evolution and Impact of Evangelicals in Modern Mexico
   Kurt Bowen

24 The Chignecto Covenanters
   A Regional History of Reformed Presbyterianism in New Brunswick and Nova Scotia, 1827 to 1905
   Eldon Hay

25 Methodists and Women's Education in Ontario, 1836–1925
   Johanna M. Selles

26 Puritanism and Historical Controversy
   William Lamont

SERIES TWO   In memory of George Rawlyk
Donald Harman Akenson, Editor

Marguerite Bourgeoys and Montreal, 1640–1665
Patricia Simpson

Aspects of the Canadian Evangelical Experience
Edited by G.A. Rawlyk

Aspects of the Canadian Evangelical Experience

EDITED BY G.A. RAWLYK

McGill-Queen's University Press
Montreal & Kingston · London · Buffalo

© McGill-Queen's University Press 1997
ISBN 0-7735-1547-X

Legal deposit second quarter 1997
Bibliothèque nationale du Québec

Printed in Canada on acid-free paper

This book has been published with the help of a grant from the Evangelical Fellowship of Canada. Funding has also been received from the Pew Charitable Trusts.

McGill-Queen's University Press is grateful to the Canada Council for support of its publishing program.

Canadian Cataloguing in Publication Data

Main entry under title:
  Aspects of the Canadian evangelical experience
  (McGill-Queen's studies in the history of religion)
  Includes bibliographical references and index.
  ISBN 0-7735-1547-X
  1. Evangelicalism – Canada. I. Rawlyk, George A., 1935–
  1995. II. Series
  BR1642.C3A85 1997   270.8'2   C96-901070-2

Typeset in Sabon 10/12
by Caractéra inc., Quebec City

Contents

Preface xi

Introduction, G.A. RAWLYK xiii

PART ONE   VIEWS FROM OUTSIDE AND INSIDE

1 Canadian Evangelicalism: A View from the United States   3
   MARK A. NOLL

2 "Up from Downunder": An Australian View of Canadian Evangelicalism   21
   MARK HUTCHINSON

3 Canadian Evangelicalism: A View from Britain   38
   DAVID W. BEBBINGTON

4 "Who Whom?": Evangelicalism and Canadian Society   55
   JOHN G. STACKHOUSE, JR

PART TWO   EVANGELICAL IMPULSE IN THE METHODIST, PRESBYTERIAN, ANGLICAN, AND UNITED CHURCHES

Methodists/United Church

5 "A March of Victory and Triumph in Praise of 'The Beauty of Holiness'": Laity and the Evangelical Impulse in Canadian Methodism, 1800–1884   73
   MARGUERITE VAN DIE

6 Condensation and Heart Religion: Canadian Methodists as Evangelicals, 1884–1925   90
PHYLLIS D. AIRHART

7 "We Will Evangelize with a Whole Gospel or None": Evangelicalism and the United Church of Canada   106
DAVID PLAXTON

Presbyterians

8 "Crackling Sounds from the Burning Bush": The Evangelical Impulse in Canadian Presbyterianism before 1875   123
DUFF CRERAR

9 From Preaching to Propaganda to Marginalization: The Lost Centre of Twentieth-Century Presbyterianism   137
BARRY MACK

Anglicans

10 Evangelical Anglicans and the Atlantic World: Politics, Ideology, and the British North American Connection   154
RICHARD W. VAUDRY

11 Redefining Evangelicalism in the Canadian Anglican Church: Wycliffe College and the Evangelical Party, 1867–1995   171
WILLIAM H. KATERBERG

PART THREE   BAPTISTS, MENNONITES, AND LUTHERANS

Baptists

12 "The Footprints of Zion's King": Baptists in Canada to 1880   191
DANIEL C. GOODWIN

13 "Shelter from the Storm": The Enduring Evangelical Impulse of Baptists in Canada, 1880s to 1990s   208
P. LORRAINE COOPS

Mennonites

14 Living with the Virus: The Enigma of Evangelicalism among Mennonites in Canada   223
BRUCE L. GUENTHER

Lutherans

15 Lutheranism and Evangelicalism: Travelling in the Same Circle of Influence 241
BRYAN V. HILLIS

PART FOUR HOLINESS, CHRISTIAN AND MISSIONARY ALLIANCE, AND PENTECOSTALISM

16 Sailing for the Shore: The Canadian Holiness Tradition 257
MARILYN FÄRDIG WHITELEY

17 Towards a Fourfold Gospel: A.B. Simpson, John Salmon, and the Christian and Missionary Alliance in Canada 271
DARREL R. REID

18 Canadian Pentecostalism and the Evangelical Impulse 289
RONALD A.N. KYDD

PART FIVE EVANGELICAL NETWORKS, LEADERS, AND REVIVALS

19 The Winnipeg Fundamentalist Network, 1910–1940: The Roots of Transdenominational Evangelicalism in Manitoba and Saskatchewan 303
D. BRUCE HINDMARSH

20 "The Heavenly Railroad": An Introduction to Crossley-Hunter Revivalism 320
KEVIN KEE

21 "The World of the Common Man Is Filled with Religious Fervour": The Labouring People of Winnipeg and the Persistence of Revivalism, 1914–1925 337
MICHAEL GAUVREAU and NANCY CHRISTIE

22 The Transplanted Mission: The China Inland Mission and Canadian Evangelicalism 351
ALVYN J. AUSTIN

23 Evangelical Bible Colleges in Twentieth-Century Canada 369
ROBERT K. BURKINSHAW

PART SIX WOMEN, SPIRITUALITY, AND THE
EVANGELICAL IMPULSE

24 "Canada's Gift to the Sawdust Trail": The Canadian Face of Aimee Semple McPherson 387
EDITH L. BLUMHOFER

25 Beyond the Congregation: Women and Canadian Evangelicalism Reconsidered 403
SHARON ANNE COOK

26 The Awakened and the Spirit-Moved: The Religious Experiences of Canadian Evangelicals in the 1990s 417
ANDREW S. GRENVILLE

Notes 433

Selected Bibliography 525

Preface

This monograph was substantially complete at the time that George Rawlyk died in late 1995. As literary executor, all I had to do was shepherd *Aspects* through the final stages of editing and checking page proofs – a minor task when one considers the work involved in the writing and compiling of this substantial volume. But even these final tasks would not have been possible without the assistance of a number of individuals. Douglas Hessler input my final editing and Maureen Garvie carefully copy-edited the manuscript. As important was the encouragement and support of my colleagues and particularly the folk at McGill-Queen's, notably Joan McGilvray and Donald Akenson. I know how important the evangelical project and this collection of articles were to George, and I can only hope that he would have been pleased with the final product.

E.J. Errington
Kingston
August 1996

Introduction

G.A. RAWLYK

Aspects of the Canadian Evangelical Experience is a collection of invited papers which, with one exception, were originally presented at a conference held at Queen's University, Kingston, Ontario, in May 1995. The conference was made possible because of a very generous grant from the Pew Charitable Trusts. Without this financial support, the conference would not and could not have taken place.

In the summer of 1992 conference participants were asked to use "as a very rough guide" for their various papers dealing with "the evolving Canadian evangelical experience in the so-called mainstream *and* non-mainstream Protestant denominations" the Bebbington "quadrilateral."[1] In his very influential *Evangelicalism in Modern Britain*, David Bebbington has argued that there have been during the past two centuries "four qualities that have been the special marks of evangelical religion – *conversionism ... activism ... biblicism ... and ... crucicentrism.*"[2]

It was also suggested to the conference presenters that they "might want to consult the various essays in D.W. Dayton and R.K. Johnston, eds., *The Variety of American Evangelicalism* (Knoxville: University of Tennessee Press, 1991)" in order to become more familiar with the ongoing American debate regarding the difficulties involved in actually trying to define the term "evangelical." Apart from these two bibliographical references, and a strong suggestion that the authors should "both summarize existing scholarship and also include new research findings,"[3] no explicit or implicit instructions were given concerning the actual approach to be taken. Each author, in other words, was given complete freedom to develop her or his overall thesis within an elastic conceptual and organizational framework.

It was understood from the beginning that papers would be presented not only by established scholars but also by younger ones. Moreover, the planning committee[4] felt strongly that a number of Ph.D. students working on dissertations about the Canadian evangelical experience should be invited to share their findings at the conference. The planning committee attempted to match its demand with the existing scholar supply in early 1992. A wide net was thrown out into the academic community – but, of course, some individuals and many themes were not brought in. Other conferences, and other volumes, will, I am certain, provide opportunities for other scholars of Canadian evangelicalism to have their voices heard. *Aspects of the Canadian Evangelical Experience* is very much a preliminary probe, one taken at a crucially important and strategic moment in Canadian social and cultural history.

From its late eighteenth-century beginnings, Canadian evangelicalism was shaped by its quadrilateral ideology of conversionism, biblicism, activism, and crucicentrism, as well as by what Ronald Knox once called its "peculiar enthusiasm." Evangelicalism, for me, has always been a complex kaleidoscope, constantly changing its shape and its colours, but never its core essence. By the late nineteenth century, conversionism, as a manifestation of ecstatic self-expression – which had been *the* key evangelical characteristic for over a century – was for a growing number of Canadian evangelicals no longer the central defining moment or the litmus-test experience at the centre of the kaleidoscope. Rather, it was merely one of four key doctrines establishing what one authority has argued are a "set of 'minimalist' criteria for evangelical membership."[5] And as the twentieth century unfolded, the New Birth was increasingly for evangelicals merely one of the fundamentally significant evangelical doctrines – displaced at the centre by a growing preoccupation with an inerrant and inspired Bible. By the late twentieth century, it may be argued, for a remarkable number of Canadian evangelicals the charismatic movement had become the leading edge of both evangelical belief and experience. If the New Birth defined the essence of evangelicalism during the first century of the history of the movement, and a preoccupation with an inerrant Bible the early part of the twentieth, the charismatic movement, including Pentecostalism, may be at the centre of the evangelical kaleidoscope in the early twenty-first century.

Two major groups of Canadian evangelicals in the late eighteenth century inhabited a wide spectrum of belief and practice. The first of these was what may be referred to as the "radical evangelicals," most of whom were Baptists and Methodists, who "sought an *emotional* faith that could not be controlled or manipulated by their well-educated 'social betters.'"[6] The Baptists and Methodists, it should be pointed out, had major theological differences, including radically different views of the nature of baptism; moreover, not all of them were radical evangelicals. Then there were the formalists – ranging from the formal extreme to the verge of informality – who all placed more stress on evangelicalism of the head than on evangelicalism of the heart.[7] Usually Presbyterians and Anglicans, this group stressed "an *orderly* faith" based upon "consistent doctrine, decorum in worship, and biblical interpretation through a well-educated ministry."[8]

Because of the remarkable success of a number of charismatic preachers like Henry Alline, Freeborn Garrettson, and Hezekiah Wooster, what is now Canada experienced a series of widespread religious revivals during the three decades following the end of the American Revolution.[9] When the War of 1812 broke out, the population of Maritime Canada (present-day New Brunswick, Nova Scotia, and Prince Edward Island) had grown to approximately 120,000, that of present-day Ontario to 80,000 and that of Quebec to around 300,000. In the Maritimes, despite large numbers of Roman Catholics and Anglicans, the radical evangelical groups – the Baptists and Methodists – set the religious tone of the region. This was also the case in Ontario, or Upper Canada as it was then called. Indeed, it may be argued that radical evangelicalism was the Protestant norm in pre-1812 English-speaking British North America.

By 1812 close to half of all Canadian Protestants were either self-confessed radical evangelicals, or else adherents of radical evangelical congregations.[10] There were also hundreds of formal evangelicals – Presbyterians and Anglicans – in British North America. Never again would radical *and* formal evangelical strength reach such a remarkable level of support in Canada. The evidence suggests that during the period spanning the end of the American Revolution and the War of 1812, evangelicalism was in fact a far more powerful force in what is now Canada than in contiguous regions of the United States. Moreover, it was more radical, more anarchistic, and more populist than its American counterpart. Unlike the new American evangelicalism, described so perceptively by Nathan Hatch, the Canadian variant did not have to carry the heavy American non-spiritual baggage of "civic humanism, republicanism, the covenant ideal, and possessive individualism."[11]

The worst fears of some Canadians about the evils of American republicanism and extreme religious enthusiasm seemed to be confirmed by the outbreak of the War of 1812. This negative view of Americans and the American republic helped to strengthen considerably a pro-British bias in what is now Canada – a bias further consolidated by the influx of hundreds of thousands of British immigrants after the war. Anti-Americanism triggered by the War of 1812, especially in Central Canada, and the demographic transformation of British North America in the post-War of 1812 period meant, among other things, that radical evangelicalism no longer would be the evangelical norm and the predominant strain in Canadian Protestantism. Rather it would be quickly pushed to the periphery of Protestantism by a burgeoning formal evangelical movement and by non-evangelical Protestantism, both of which owed a great deal to a growing middle class preoccupied with order, respectability, and a growing suspicion of democratic evangelical enthusiasm.

Despite the weakening, but certainly not the eradication, of radical evangelicalism, the nineteenth century in Canada has been called, with some justification, "the Evangelical Century."[12] But this was a moderate, accommodating evangelicalism, as Goldwin French perceptively observed in 1968, shaped by a "creed" – a loosely constructed yet pervasive body of Christian beliefs and assumptions – rather than by a common, collective, traumatic, religious conversion experience.[13] Before the War of 1812 in particular, but also during the third and fourth decades of the nineteenth century, even though there "was an evangelical element in the Anglican and Presbyterian churches," French has observed, there were still "real differences between them and the genuine evangelical churches – the Methodists and the Baptists."[14] By the latter part of the nineteenth century, however, these so-called genuine evangelical churches, whether in Atlantic Canada, central Canada, or the West, had become more like the accommodating evangelical Anglicans and Presbyterians. This new leadership, which joined together in the Evangelical Alliance, put more stress on the religion of the head and less on the religion of the heart – and easily "succumbed ... to the materialist delights" of late Victorian Canada.[15] This did not mean, of course, that evangelical pietism was dead or that there were no longer any radical evangelicals in the land – yet there was a growing gap between elite and rank-and-file religiosity.

And increasingly, as Canadian society changed in the so-called progressive milieu of the late nineteenth century, evangelicalism also was transformed. The old religious language about the New Birth and revivalism no longer defined the changing experience *and* practice of a growing number of Canadian Protestants. In an attempt to find new wineskins for the old evangelical wine, key members of the denominational elites began to articulate an altered evangelicalism – one that down-played traditional conversionism and placed more emphasis on the "spread of scriptural holiness by reforming the nation."[16] Middle-class values had begun to transform the old evangelicalism. And, for a growing number of Canadian Protestant leaders, and for some of their followers, evangelicalism, even with its new reformist priorities, had become something of an embarrassment. Many of these spiritual seekers, having lost faith in themselves and having altered and in some cases abandoned the priorities of the faith of their fathers and mothers, increasingly sought salvation in the gospel of "inhibited scientific inquiry."[17] Others turned to what has been called "the insidious antithesis to essential Christianity"[18] – the gospel of narcissistic, therapeutic self-realization underpinning North American consumerism. Though many still continued to follow the paths of traditional evangelical piety, at the turn of the century the seeds of an altered Canadian Protestantism had been sown widely in ecclesiastical and national life.

Evangelicalism in the nineteenth century exerted a far greater impact on all aspects of Canadian life than it did in the United States – always considered to be a far more Christian nation. But by the early twentieth century, the kaleidoscope of evangelical ideology was shifting, so that the centrality of the New Birth and the crucial importance of being directly involved in efforts at sharing the faith were being pushed towards the periphery by many, to be replaced by biblicism, by an almost rational approach to crucicentrism, or by a formal code of Victorian ethics. Moreover, the largely populist and radical evangelical ideology, so important in the early nineteenth century, was being challenged by a respectable middle-class movement that explicitly downplayed extreme emotionalism.[19] Cultural and theological accommodation to the exigencies of an expanding and rapidly developing nation soon became the twentieth-century norm. It was not long before the seeds sown by the elites' attempts to redefine evangelicalism bore fruit, and the "evangelical consensus" in Canada was replaced, first at the leadership level in the interwar years, then increasingly at the more popular level in the post–World War II period, by a largely "liberal" one.[20] The new liberal consensus was preoccupied with three issues – first, "the conscious, intended adaptation of religious ideas to modern culture"; second, the immanence and not only the transcendence of God; and third, the fact that "human society" was actually moving towards "the realization of the Kingdom of God."[21]

Canadian evangelicalism, of course, did not disappear from the religious landscape during the 1920s and 1930s. It merely moved from the leading edge of Protestantism to the periphery (but not necessarily the dark and distant periphery) where it would remain until the late 1980s. (How and why this happened is now being looked at by a myriad of Canadian scholars.) Then during the last decade of the twentieth century, perhaps because of the remarkable decline of Canadian liberal

Protestantism, and the fact that the charismatic movement and the so-called cultural wars have brought many Roman Catholic conservatives and Protestant conservatives together, evangelicalism has once again, almost by default, emerged as a formidable religious force. But in the 1990s, one-third of all evangelicals in Canada, in an ironic twist of past patterns, are practising Roman Catholics, and the Roman Catholic percentage will probably continue to grow if the evangelical percentage of the Canadian population moves beyond its present 16 per cent.

In late 1991 when I began to organize the Aspects of the Canadian Evangelical Experience Conference, I expected to see a rather small residue of evangelicalism left in Canadian Christian belief and practice in the 1990s. I certainly never anticipated finding any evidence of evangelicalism within Canadian Roman Catholicism. In fact, in our original introduction to *Amazing Grace*, written late in 1992 before the results of the Angus Reid surveys were analysed – surveys I had commissioned using some of the Pew grant – I persuaded my co-editor, Mark Noll, that it would be accurate to say that "between 5 and 10 per cent of Canadians were evangelicals in the early 1990s." This figure had to be changed, when the page proofs arrived, to "approximately 15 per cent."[22] Then in February 1995, when Andrew Grenville and the Angus Reid Group came up with a new "Christian evangelicalism scale," the Canadian evangelical percentage edged up to 16 per cent.[23] This figure was almost twice as high as I had originally thought. With an evangelical percentage of something between 5 and 10 per cent, it would have been relatively easy for me to have fitted my views about the sad state of contemporary Canadian evangelicalism into a straightforward declension thesis. But then the new data compelled me to look at all the new evidence in a far more open-minded manner. Or, at least, this is what I think happened. The survey results certainly raised some disconcerting questions about many of my preconceived views. But they did more than that – they confirmed my almost primitive belief that there has always been a gap between elite and popular Christianity in Canada. Moreover, the new data seemed to undermine the position of those influential advocates of secularization who have dominated Canadian scholarly discourse in recent years,[24] especially since the same polling data revealed also a substantial majority of "traditional" or "conservative" Christians – Catholics and Protestants – who did not share the evangelical traits.

It is noteworthy that one in six Canadians in the mid-1990s may be considered evangelical. And on most Sundays, 50 per cent of those who are worshipping in Protestant churches would be evangelicals. One hundred years ago perhaps one in four Canadians could be regarded as evangelicals, and 200 years ago fewer than one in twenty. Within the time frame of the past century, Canadian evangelicalism seems to have declined, at least in terms of the percentage of the total population. But if the time frame is stretched back to the 1790s, the prevailing authorized version of declension and secularization appears to be a completely wrong-headed explanatory device.

As the following essays clearly show, the irony of history, including the history of Canadian evangelicalism, is energized by the complex mingling of the forces of change and continuity. Contemporary Canadian evangelicalism cannot be and should not be severed from its past. And Canadian evangelicalism, whether in the late-eighteenth century or in the 1990s, must always be contextualized within a sophisticated, historical, cultural, and theological framework.

What follows is not an uncritical, triumphal story of the rise, fall, and rise of Canadian evangelicalism. Nor is this a pessimistic and gloomy study of inevitable declension and decline. *Aspects of the Canadian Evangelical Experience* is both – and much more. It is an attempt to understand in a critical yet empathetic manner a powerful religious impulse in Canada's past and present. It is my conviction that one cannot understand Canada's past or present without coming to grips with the richly textured nature of Canadian religion in general, and Canadian evangelicalism in particular.

There are six sections in this volume. The first, entitled "Views from Outside and Inside," contains four chapters, three of which explicitly introduce an important comparative dimension to the book. According to Mark Noll's perceptive view from the United States, Canadian evangelicalism is meaningfully different from its American counterpart, largely because the total Canadian environment is different from the American. For Noll the essential plasticity and adaptability of the evangelical impulse means, among other things, that even as it gathers strength in a certain society, it is likely to take on a specific colouring from that same society. This complex symbiotic relationship thus shapes the contours of the evolving evangelical experience whether in Canada, the United States, or Nigeria. And for Noll, the irenic, accommodating Canadian variety is, in certain respects, superior to that of its American neighbours.

Mark Hutchinson, in a ground-breaking chapter, stresses that there are all sorts of exciting opportunities for scholars interested in Canadian-Australian comparative religious history. He persuasively contends that too many Canadian historians are obsessed with things American and that the time has come for a return to a neo-Commonwealth approach. Hutchinson argues that Canadian evangelicalism, especially in the twentieth century, has suffered because of the lack of strong, vigorous leadership – a contention that is controversial, probably accurate, and raises a fundamental question about the role of charismatic leadership within Canadian evangelicalism. Why were there so many extremely gifted evangelical leaders in Canada in the century and a quarter following the American Revolution – people like Henry Alline, Egerton Ryerson, Harris Harding, Donald McDonald, George Grant, and A.B. Simpson? And why were there so few, apart from leaders like J. Oswald Smith, in the post-World War I period? Moreover, what is the real link between the evangelical movement and effective evangelical leadership?

David Bebbington, whose *Evangelicalism in Great Britain* has become a benchmark study, does not explicitly answer these questions in his "View from Britain." But what he does show convincingly is that both British Protestant order *and* British dissenting fragmentation affected Canadian evangelicalism. Noting the many and varied British influences, Bebbington challenges the "standard view" that Canadian evangelicalism absorbed from Britain primarily "decorum, restraint, and moderation," and from the United States "enthusiasm, innovation, and extremism." Bebbington's British corrective is absolutely essential in understanding Canadian evangelicalism, whether in the nineteenth or the twentieth century.

In "Who Whom?" John Stackhouse, building upon his already influential *Canadian Evangelicalism in the Twentieth Century* (1993), presents an anything but rosy picture of twentieth-century Canadian evangelicalism. This tough-minded realism – provoked by a vain quest for visible signs of the evangelical quadrilateral in contemporary Canadian society – should act as a powerful brake on any manifestation of Canadian evangelical triumphalism.

Part Two is concerned with the evangelical impulse in the Methodist, United, Presbyterian, and Anglican churches. In each of these denominations, over a period of 200 years, the evangelical impulse was at work – sometimes of major importance and influence, sometimes of less consequence, but always present. For Marguerite Van Die, during the nineteenth century the Canadian Methodist laity were remarkably successful in revitalizing evangelicalism by, among other things, adjusting their piety to meet the new demands of middle-class life. In her boldly conceived thesis, Van Die is especially sensitive to women's religious experiences and to the complex way in which religious change and continuity intertwine.

A somewhat different picture of evangelicalism within Methodism, at least for the 1884 to 1925 period, is painted by Phyllis Airhart, who uses "neutral zone" theory to try to understand the disorienting transition experienced by Canadian Methodism during these years. She also discusses the tension between Methodist denominational bureaucracy and localism – as it affected the evangelical impulse.

It is David Plaxton's contention that at both the leadership and rank-and-file levels evangelicalism has since 1925 been a force of some considerable consequence within the United Church. In this revisionist essay Plaxton forces the reader to reconsider the authorized version of United Church history with its emphasis upon change, rampant liberalism, and secularization.

As was the case with Van Die and the Methodists, Duff Crerar is eager to rediscover the evangelicalism of the Presbyterian grass roots – what he refers to as the "crackling noises from the lower branches of the burning bush." His emphasis on Presbyterian populist piety is a most welcome historiographical corrective. Crerar, in every sense, describes the Golden Age of Canadian Presbyterianism. Barry Mack, on the other hand, presents a disconcerting descriptive analysis of the remarkable decline and marginalization of what less than a century ago was the largest Canadian Protestant denomination. The creation of the United Church was, it is clear, a disaster for Canadian Presbyterianism and its once powerful evangelical engine. Mack's sad chapter title says it all; and his generational hypothesis will, I would wager, trigger some serious scholarly responses.

It is sometimes forgotten that since the late eighteenth century there has been an evangelical presence within Canadian Anglicanism. Richard Vaudry, stressing the Anglo-American and "political" nature of Canadian Anglicanism, examines its evangelical tradition, especially during the half-century preceding Confederation. He explains the Irish character of central Canadian Anglican evangelicalism, and its strong anti–high church bias. And Vaudry chronicles how, although a minority within Canadian Anglicanism, evangelicals were eager to use all means at their disposal, including violence, to protect their beliefs and their practices.

In a companion chapter dealing with the post-Confederation period, Will Katerberg shows how Canadian Anglican evangelicals took full advantage of strong British connections as well as the evangelical temper of Victorian Canada to exert an increasingly large influence on their denomination. Wycliffe College played a key role in what Katerberg calls the "redefining" of "evangelicalism in the Canadian Anglican Church." Evangelicalism within Anglicanism, it is clear, has been profoundly shaped by the irenic evangelicalism of the English variant. But this dependence also stunted Canadian evangelicalism's development and appeal to non-Anglophile Canadians.

Part Three, "Baptists, Mennonites, and Lutherans," provides a transition from the Canadian mainline denominations dealt with in Part

Two, to what have been referred to as the more "sectish groups" – holiness, the Christian and Missionary Alliance, and the Pentecostals – considered in Part Four. The two Baptist chapters by Dan Goodwin and Lorraine Coops are nicely integrated. Since the vast majority of Canadian Baptists have always been evangelicals, Goodwin and Coops sensitively permit the various groups of Canadian Baptists to tell their own evangelical stories. It is Goodwin's contention that during the century following the American Revolution, the heartland of the Baptists was to be found in the Maritimes where Baptist evangelicalism was significantly influenced by a radical populist tradition – an influence that permeated the entire Maritime Baptist experience. For Coops, Canadian Baptists, despite their often bitter internecine battles, have since 1880 continued "to focus [on] conversionism and activism," and in the last decades of the twentieth century, a weakening of the more liberal or accommodating Baptist impulse in all Canadian regions has resulted in a conservative revival that may eventually bring hitherto warring factions – the "Convention" and the "Fellowship" – together.

While Mennonites may have a great deal in common with Baptists, the Mennonites have for decades had a sometimes bitter love-hate relationship with evangelicalism. As Bruce Guenther persuasively argues in his most aptly titled chapter, "Living with the Virus," a growing number of Canadian Mennonites are becoming evangelicals, and he explains why. He also explains why some are not. The Canadian Mennonite world from a distance seems so uniform, but through the lens ground by Guenther, significant differences emerge that help to explain the Mennonite ambivalence towards evangelicalism.

There has been, and there is, an even greater degree of ambivalence towards evangelicalism among Canadian Lutherans than there is among Canadian Mennonites. But as Bryan Hillis shows, though there may not be any organizational links, there is an increasingly important "shared circle of influence." In drawing clear distinctions between Lutheran "evangelicalism" and Canadian evangelicalism, Hillis succeeds in explaining the existence of the chasm between these two worlds, as well as some of the bridges that have been and are being built, especially at the local level.

At the beginning of the twentieth century most Canadian evangelicals regarded holiness, Pentecostal, and Christian and Missionary Alliance believers as irrational fanatics whose aberrant behaviour brought embarrassment and disgrace to "the cause of Christ." At the end of the century, however, these once-despised "fanatics" have become the leading edge of Canadian Protestant evangelicalism and threaten to marginalize the formerly powerful mainstream. Marilyn Whiteley cogently describes the fascinating careers of Nelson Burns, Ralph Horner, Frank

Goff, and Albert Mills, and their links to a variety of small holiness groups – especially in Ontario. These men frontally challenged Canadian Methodism, and it may be argued that by attacking Methodism and attracting disillusioned Methodists they helped to weaken the evangelical impulse within Methodism at a critical time in the denomination's history.

A.B. Simpson and his followers, together with the Pentecostal movement, may have assisted in not only weakening evangelicalism within Canadian Methodism but also within Presbyterianism, Anglicanism, and among the Baptists. Darrel Reid tells two stories, one about A.B. Simpson, the Canadian-born, Presbyterian-trained founder of the Christian and Missionary Alliance (CMA), and the other about John Salmon, a former Methodist, Adventist, and Congregationalist, who played a formative role in the Canadian branch of the CMA. Reid convincingly shows that the CMA gospel of Christ as "Saviour, Sanctifier, Healer, and Coming King" had a surprisingly wide appeal. But its appeal would not be as wide as Pentecostalism, its bitter early foe.

Ron Kydd's chapter on Canadian Pentecostalism, sympathetically yet critically written, shows how various groups of Canadian Pentecostals, despite often bitter attacks from some evangelical leaders, became integral parts of the twentieth-century Canadian evangelical movement over time. There has been within the Pentecostal-evangelical world what Kydd calls an "oscillation between 'intra-' and 'extra-dependence.'" This vacillation helps to explain "the various shifts within Pentecostal history" and "Pentecostalism's present-day tentative bond with evangelical groups."

Part Five begins with Bruce Hindmarsh's study of the Winnipeg fundamentalist network from 1910 to 1940. At the centre of these connections, which stretched from Manitoba to Saskatchewan, was the influential Elim Tabernacle. Hindmarsh convincingly argues that the Winnipeg-based fundamentalist network had a greater influence on emerging Prairie evangelicalism than did any institution or centre in Alberta. It provided an "evangelical identity which transcended denominational and ethnic loyalty."

Kevin Kee reminds us that Canada once had two remarkable revivalists in the Crossley-Hunter team. As far as Kee is concerned, they preached a "cheap-grace" gospel permeated by bourgeois respectability and a concern about buttressing the power of the "middling classes." Caught up in their image as "evangelist-celebrities," the "manipulation" of the "divine" became a means for disconcerting "temporal ends."

Nancy Christie and Michael Gauvreau tell a somewhat different story about the nature of revivalism in working-class Winnipeg during the

1914–1925 period. Their contention is that many Anglo-Saxon working-class Winnipegers had a much greater affinity for conservative evangelicalism than for either socialism or the social gospel. The Christie-Gauvreau thesis is a provocative one, especially within the context of recent Canadian working-class historiography.

Alvyn Austin's chapter on the China Inland Mission and Canadian evangelicalism perceptively traces the amazing number of lines of communication connecting the CIM and Canadian evangelicalism in the late-nineteenth and early-twentieth centuries. Here is another example of an evangelical network at work in Canada, one that was more irenic and accommodating than its American counterpart.

It is interesting that Robert Burkinshaw's chapter on "Evangelical Bible Colleges in Twentieth-Century Canada" is the first general overview of this crucial topic. For as he explains, one cannot really understand twentieth-century Canadian evangelicalism without coming to grips with the formative role played by Bible schools and Christian colleges. But as he also points out, dramatic changes are taking place both at the demand and supply level, changes that are bound to alter fundamentally the essential nature of the formative relationship between these institutions and Canadian evangelicalism.

The final section of the book is made up of three rather different chapters. In the first, Edith Blumhofer argues that "Canada's Gift to the Sawdust Trail," Aimee Semple McPherson, was significantly influenced by her Canadian roots – especially the Canadian Salvation Army and early Canadian Pentecostalism. In her revisionist chapter on "Women and Canadian Evangelicalism," Sharon Cook uses the Woman's Christian Temperance Union to underscore the central importance of Canadian women in Canadian evangelicalism. She shows that women have all too often been written out of Canadian religious history in general and the history of Canadian evangelicalism in particular. And in the final chapter of the book, Andrew Grenville maintains that far too little has been written about the spirituality of evangelicals and their actual religious experiences. While developing this theme, Grenville introduces a potentially divisive contention for Canadian evangelical studies – that about one in three Canadian evangelicals in the 1990s is a Roman Catholic.

If any point stirred the 1995 conference waters, it was this one about these so-called Catho-evangelicals. Without question, this issue, and others raised in this collection, will be dealt with by a variety of scholars interested in Canadian evangelicalism. And other scholars will, of course, study themes not dealt with directly in this volume. For it must be kept in mind that, as its title indicates, this collection of essays considers "aspects of the Canadian evangelical experience." There are without question many other aspects still to be studied. And it is my hope that this book will encourage both new and more senior scholars to make their contributions to this expanding field, for although the authors presented here have made a start, "the fields are truly white unto harvest."

PART ONE
Views from Outside and Inside

1 Canadian Evangelicalism: A View from the United States

MARK A. NOLL

Two widely separated incidents can serve to introduce a portrait of evangelicalism in Canada as it looks from the United States. The first, which I take from fine recent books by William Westfall and John Webster Grant, concerns two of Ontario's great religious leaders of the nineteenth century, the Methodist Egerton Ryerson (1803–1882) and the Anglican John Strachan (1778–1867).[1] Strachan, who eventually became the bishop of Toronto, was Ontario's most active proponent of an Anglican establishment as the necessary vehicle for creating a Christian civilization in the Canadian wilderness. Ryerson came to public attention in 1826 when he published a fierce rebuttal to a statement of such principles from Strachan.

During a funeral address for the first Anglican bishop of Quebec, Strachan had denounced the Methodists. In his opinion they were "uneducated itinerant preachers, who leaving their steady employment, betake themselves to preaching the Gospel from idleness, or a zeal without knowledge, by which they are induced without any preparation, to teach what they do not know, and which from pride, they disdain to learn." Ryerson responded immediately and stressed what was wrong with Strachan's idea of religion. "Our savior," wrote Ryerson, "never intimated the union of his church with the civil polity of any country." Anglican ritual, to Ryerson, was "all pompous panegyric." What Canadians needed was passionate "preaching the gospel" for repentance and conversion. To Strachan the establishment of religion was the secret to creating a Christian society; to Ryerson it was the camp meeting. From a modern angle, Strachan was a representative of mainline Protestantism; Ryerson was an evangelical of the evangelicals.

Yet between the mid-1820s and the incident I wish to describe in the early 1840s, significant shifts took place in Upper Canadian religion. As the Methodists grew by leaps and bounds and as a never-ending series of complications impeded Strachan's push for an Anglican establishment, tempers cooled, and former antagonists began to drift closer to each other. This confluence of Methodist and Anglican interests set the stage for the first face-to-face meeting between Strachan the mainliner and Ryerson the evangelical. It took place in February 1842 when Ryerson, returning from Kingston to Cobourg, found himself unexpectedly thrown together in a coach with Bishop Strachan. As Ryerson and Strachan chatted during their long ride, they were surprised to discover how well they got along. The Methodists, under Ryerson's leadership, had just obtained provincial approval for transforming their denominational academy into Victoria College. During the journey Strachan offered Ryerson some advice on how to tap proceeds from the Clergy Reserves to fund the Methodists' new college. Neither Strachan nor Ryerson wanted to give up the distinctive contribution of their respective traditions, but each found it relatively easy to integrate his own concerns with those of a former opponent, while together promoting the place of religion in Ontario society.

For one who studies evangelical history in the United States, several things are striking about this Canadian incident from 1842.

First, and most obviously striking, is how easily the antagonisms of the 1820s were set aside for the common Protestant purposes of the 1840s. This was especially so in the way in which Ryerson's spiky evangelicalism mellowed, which illustrated an evolutionary, pacific, ameliorative response to challenges in church and society that stands in contrast to the polemical, sectarian, and all-or-nothing tendencies that have often characterized evangelicalism in the United States.

Second, from an American angle, it is notable that Strachan and Ryerson even met at all. Though Canada is geographically larger than the United States, its inhabited zone, as well as the size of the population in that zone, has always been much smaller. Thus it is not too surprising that, somewhere in the course of their long lives, the Canadian evangelical leader would encounter the leader of establishment Protestantism. In the United States, such face-to-face meetings of key leaders of various church factions have always been less frequent. To the best of my knowledge, for example, I do not think that Francis Asbury, the dynamic leader of evangelical Methodism early in the nineteenth century, ever met with his contemporary John Henry Hobart, the leader of American high-church Anglicanism.

5 A View from the United States

Third, even when American church leaders did meet face to face, they have almost never – at least since the early nineteenth century – spent even a single moment discussing how to use government money for the support of their distinctly religious enterprises. Yet that is the very subject that Strachan and Ryerson talked about in 1842, and it is a subject that still engages various sorts of Canadian evangelicals to this very day.

The second incident is much more recent and much less historically important. In the fall of 1994 I was asked to take part in the taping of a television program west of Toronto near Burlington. The program was *Cross Currents*, hosted by Brian Stiller (executive director of the Evangelical Fellowship of Canada) and sponsored by the EFC. Evangelical television efforts are by no means uncommon in the United States, but this Canadian venture seemed different. It was, for example, immediately obvious from the informal gatherings on the evening before the taping that Stiller (who is a Pentecostal minister) was being assisted – in chatting up the guests as well as in planning the general direction of the interviews – by Gerald Vanderzande, public-affairs director of the Citizens for Public Justice, a political-interest group with roots in the Christian Reformed community. Such cooperation between two of the more widely separated branches on the Protestant tree is not unprecedented in American evangelical history. It took place to some degree, for example, in the preparation of the New International Version of the Bible, and it sometimes occurs in connection with Billy Graham's activities. Nonetheless, it has not been all that common.

For another thing, the various interview segments that I was able to witness on the day of the taping were reasonably intelligent, and "intelligent evangelical television" are three words that one simply does not get to put together too often in the United States.

Yet a third observation concerns the relative casualness about boundary-marking that characterized the programs. Stiller and many of his evangelical guests made no effort to hide their own religious convictions, but the shows also included several guests from non-evangelical Christian traditions, and at least a few who made no religious profession at all. For the program I appeared on, Stiller had enlisted three historians to talk about whether religion in Canada was more than an export from the United States. The other two guests were a professor who studies the United Church and a historian who happens to be a socialist Baptist. Quite apart from the fact that there probably are no socialist Baptists of any sort in the entire United States, the panel's make-up was simply far too careless about theological and ecclesiastical boundaries ever to have been sponsored by a national evangelical body in the United States.

Finally, a comparison is in order with the National Association of Evangelicals (NAE), which is the rough American equivalent to the Evangelical Fellowship of Canada. The NAE is now over fifty years old, and was in fact a kind of inspiration for founding the EFC. As explained in John Stackhouse's recent survey of twentieth-century Canadian evangelicalism, the EFC is a much more recent effort. Founded only in 1964, it did not become a significant force until the early 1980s. But here is the contrast: even though the EFC is a considerably younger organization than the NAE, its television program has reached a level of sophistication and attained a degree of what can only be called theological-intellectual self-confidence unlike any similar activity ever promoted by the NAE in the United States.[2]

If we can generalize from the shape of these two incidents – the one of historical significance from 1842 and the other more ephemeral, my appearance on a television program sponsored by the EFC – we are alerted to what may be telling differences between the nature of evangelicalism in Canada and in the United States. They can be summarized quickly:

- Canadian evangelicals inhabit a much smaller world with respect to each other than do American evangelicals.
- Canadian evangelicals have experienced a different set of expectations for relations between church and state, especially with respect to education, than have American evangelicals.
- Whether or not Canadian evangelicals have self-consciously focused more on intra-evangelical cooperation, they nonetheless seem to manifest more of that cooperation than have American evangelicals.
- Canadian evangelicals may not be more intelligent than American evangelicals, but they seem to have succeeded at providing better forums for displaying whatever intelligence they do possess than have American evangelicals.
- Finally, Canadian evangelicals seem at least slightly less concerned about ideological boundary-marking than do American evangelicals.

QUALIFICATIONS

It is, of course, dangerous in the extreme to move from a pair of isolated incidents to large-scale generalizations about themes as broad as "American evangelicalism" and "Canadian evangelicalism." In the first place, categories such as "America," "Canada," and "evangelicalism" invite the paralysis of essentialism, the danger of abstractions taking over for careful attention to particulars. It is a particular mistake when speaking of Canada and the United States to forget how very important regional differences are. It is, in fact, possible to draw some meaningful regional comparisons – the Maritimes, for example, function for the history of Canadian religion somewhat as the South does for the history of American religion; the Canadian-American "left coast" that stretches from San Diego to far north of Vancouver is certainly a distinct region very different from the mountain and prairie communities to the east. But to generalize even about *the* Maritimes, *the* South, or the peculiarities of *the* West Coast is a risky enterprise indeed.[3]

It is just as risky to forget the meaningful differences within the general evangelical network. In the United States, for example, evangelicals in the Southern Baptist Convention and in the Wisconsin Lutheran Synod differ significantly in theological accent, attitudes toward the sacraments, styles of preaching, expectations for Christian engagement with culture, and many other matters.[4] So it is in Canada when comparing evangelicals within the United Church with Christian and Missionary Alliance evangelicals, Anglican evangelicals, Presbyterian evangelicals, Reformed evangelicals, Pentecostal evangelicals, Mennonite evangelicals, and so on.[5] So significant is intra-evangelical diversity that it would be difficult to identify even a single characteristic supposedly unique to Canadian evangelicalism that would *not* apply to some Canadian evangelicals, but that *would* characterize at least some American evangelicals. The same could be said for any conclusion supposedly identifying a unique quality of American evangelicalism.

Historiographical problems also beset the effort to interpret the evangelical presence in both countries. Methodism, for example, was immensely influential in setting the tone for nineteenth-century evangelical spirituality throughout all of North America, and it played a significant role as well in evangelical thought, social action, and worship. Yet for different reasons, at the end of the twentieth century historical attention to Methodism is only a shadow of the learning now shining down upon other evangelical groups. In the United States, Methodist historiography has fallen foul of internal theological changes and of divisions between a Methodist mainline and sectarian holiness bodies. In Canada the absorption of Methodism into the United Church has left it without a visible constituency. In both cases the result is the same: for lack of a vibrant historiography during the last forty years, when history-writing for other evangelical traditions has flourished, Methodism remains the unknown X-factor in general assessments of North American evangelicalism.

Another conceptual danger for a Canadian-American comparison is the tendency to downplay significant commonalties that have always bound Canadian and American churches together. Scholars like George

Rawlyk and Nancy Christie have shown how significant were the religious border crossings in the eighteenth and early nineteenth centuries.[6] Other scholars – among them, Phyllis Airhart, Edith Blumhofer, Robert Burkinshaw, David Elliott, Ian Rennie, and William Westfall – have done the same service for the religious history of the twentieth century.[7] If so many religious figures – such as Henry Alline, A.B. Simpson, Aimee Semple McPherson, or Leighton Ford – and so much shared religious experience – as represented by hymns like Joseph Scriven's "What a Friend We Have in Jesus" and Margaret Clarkson's "We Come O Christ to Thee" – have moved so easily from Canada to the United States, and if an even larger number of persons and a larger amount of religious baggage has moved so effortlessly across the border from south to north, it should be obvious that a very great deal links the evangelical histories of the two nations.

Another significant difficulty in comparing American and Canadian evangelicalism is what might be called the grass-is-greener effect. Particularly Americans with easily jaded temperaments have been known to magnify the difficulties in their own country at the same time as they romanticize the virtues of Canada. Fred Matthews of York University expressed this danger trenchantly in a thoughtful review of Seymour Martin Lipset's recent book, *Continental Divide*. According to Matthews, Lipset "overstates a familiar and cherished picture of Canada as benevolent bourgeois 'Other,' orderly, peaceful, sharing, and caring – a morally superior model for a United States seen as disorderly, violent, and selfish. Canada, one might say, is Starbuck to the American Ahab."[8] As a warning to what follows, let me say that this rosy-tinted view of Canada is a vision to which I also fall prey.

Finally, there are significant problems in comparing Canadian and American evangelicalism posed by the periodization of Canadian history. In more general historical terms, Canada's economic modernization lagged behind that of the United States. Census figures for the two countries show the population shifting from rural to urban only slightly faster in the United States than in Canada, but the broad influence of Canadian industrial and urban development lags by perhaps a generation. For religious history, this difference is important, because rural, small-town, pre- and early-industrial America was where evangelicalism flourished. Similarly, the transition from rural to urban and from early industrial to fully industrial marks the crest of evangelical self-confidence in American history. If, therefore, some aspects of Canadian evangelicalism look more attractive than their American counterparts, part of the reason may be that Canadian developments should really be compared to American circumstances of a generation earlier rather than to American developments of the same generation.

A different sort of problem posed by periodization concerns the general question of American influence in Canada. A feature noted by many observers is that Canada – at least from the early nineteenth century through the mid-twentieth century – was oriented more towards Britain (with different British regions exerting special influence in different Canadian locales) than toward the United States. American evangelical patterns profoundly influenced Canadian Protestant history in its early decades, until, that is, the War of 1812 convinced most Canadians that republicanism at the point of a gun was not for them.[9] Again, once Canada was absorbed into the American economic and media spheres in the twentieth century, evangelical influences from the United States have been very strong north of the border.[10] But in between – from the early decades of the nineteenth century through the middle of the twentieth century – British religious influences (as well as indigenous adaptations to the Canadian environment) seem to have been stronger in Canada than were American influences. As late as the run-up to World War II, for example, it was a matter of instinct for a young Canadian scholar like George Parkin Grant to seek graduate education in Britain rather than the United States. And it is not coincidental that this instinct was nurtured by the fact that Grant's own grandfather had been charged with the task of setting up the Oxford scholarships funded by Cecil Rhodes.[11] Much Canadian literature of the post–World War II period – for example, the narratives of Farley Mowat or the novels of Robertson Davies – continues to be written against the backdrop of British imperial influence, even though these authors realize that Canada has passed, in Davies's memorable phrase, from "the British connection … as the Brits grew weary under Imperial greatness," toward "the American connection … under the caress of the iron hand beneath the buckskin glove."[12]

As early as 1923, Canadian trade with the United States surpassed volume of trade with Britain, and in the 1920s radio stations from the United States already reached more listeners in Canada than did Canadian radio stations.[13] But this expansion of American economic and media influence northward was significantly checked by the traumas of the Second World War, which not only brought British refugees and tens of thousands of RAF personnel to Canada but also re-focused Canadian public opinion on ties to the empire. (A note of some significance to the intellectual history of twentieth-century evangelicalism, an American career for philosopher Arthur Holmes, originally from Bristol, England, was made possible only because this young English dissenting Protestant was in Canada long enough with the RAF during World War II to marry a Canadian and then to pursue advanced theological training at Wheaton College. Arthur's promotion of philosophy at Wheaton has been an important contribution to the recovery of orthodox

Christian philosophy in recent North America history.) Digressions aside, the important chronological point is that Canadian Protestant life was more heavily influenced from Britain than from the United States for about the century and a half before 1950. What this means for a comparison of Canadian and American evangelicalism is that characteristics seeming to divide Canadian and American evangelicals may often reflect the historically stronger British influence in Canada. It also means that, if American-Canadian contrasts are in fact due to that British influence, we should assume that recent American and Canadian evangelicalisms will appear increasingly similar as British influences in trade, education, and the media fade away in favour of the cultural juggernaut from the south.

These are the matters – forgetting the danger of large-scale categories like Canada, America, and evangelicalism; underestimating internal variations related to region and denomination; allowing romantic visions of a True North Strong and Free to overwhelm careful research; and dismissing the important changes in Canada's relations to both the United States and Britain – that prevent easy comparisons between Canadian and American evangelicalism.

COMPARISONS

Yet the attempt at comparison is still worth the effort.[14] Evangelicalism is an unusually adaptable form of Protestant pietism. In categories I have tried to explain elsewhere, one of the chief defining characteristics of evangelicalism is its experiential biblicism.[15] That is, English-speaking evangelicals have affirmed with particular earnestness the historic Protestant attachment to Scripture, and they have shared a conviction that true religion requires the active experience of God – especially in conversion, in appropriating the cross, and in lives of active service. This biblical experientialism lies behind three of evangelicalism's most prominent characteristics. First is a bias – it could be a slight prejudice, it could be a massive rejection – against inherited institutions. Second, evangelicalism, as a matter of principle, though often an inarticulate principle, is extraordinarily flexible in relation to theological, political, social, and economic ideas. Third, evangelicals practise "discipline," to borrow a well-considered phrase from Daniel Walker Howe.[16] Their experiential biblicism might lead along many different paths to principles of conduct for self and others, but, however derived, those principles embody a common evangelical conviction that the gospel compels a search for social healing as well as personal holiness.

The key thing for our purposes is that the basic thrust of evangelicalism – experiential biblicism pushing out against tradition, in myriad forms, and with discipline – has been chameleon-like in its ability to adapt. Thus, more than with many other Christian movements, to study the way that evangelicalism takes flesh in a particular culture reveals much about the character of that form of evangelicalism. The very plasticity of the pietist impulse means that, even as it gathers strength in a society, it is likely to take on colouring from that society. This, in turn, affects the internal quality of the experiential biblicism itself.

Nowhere is the environmentally shaped character of evangelicalism more obvious than in a comparison between black and white evangelicals in the United States.[17] A large portion of white Protestants, along with an overwhelming majority of African-American Protestants, share the four evangelical characteristics identified by David Bebbington – conversionism, biblicism, activism, and crucicentrism.[18] Yet in the United States it has mattered greatly whether these evangelical traits took root in black or white communities.

The relevance here is that to study the contexts of Canadian and American evangelicalism – to assess the respective evangelical interactions with history, culture, ideology – is to do more than simply find variations of one common story for an essentially identical evangelical faith. It is, rather, to see how the propensity of all pietist movements to adapt to local colouring actually creates somewhat different varieties of evangelicalism. Although Lamarckianism may not be in favour with biologists, it does seem to work historically where, in this case, the evolution of varieties of evangelicalism since the eighteenth century arises from the inheritance of characteristics acquired by different evangelical species in the course of their interaction with environment.

If this reasoning about adaptation to environment is correct, then one way to discuss differences between Canadian and American evangelicalism is to ask (a) what makes Canada different from the United States? and (b) do these Canadian-American differences play out in noticeable differences between Canadian and American evangelicalism? It would be wrong to forget the full measure of similarities between the two societies: the same European-based forms of Christianity facing many of the same perils and opportunities in an open new world; the same heritage of British political ideals; the same participation in revival; the same commitment to moralistic social reform; the same investment in doxological, Baconian science; and the same fear of Roman Catholicism. Yet that full range of shared historical circumstances is not complete. Canadian civilization has developed differently from American civilization in a number of particulars.

Where the United States' most serious social tension has involved blacks and whites, Canada's has been between speakers of French and speakers of English. Where the Catholic church was a late force in

American development, it was there from the start in Canada. Most importantly, where Americans find social and political axioms in the principles of their revolutionary break with Britain, Canadians find social and political axioms in the practice of loyalty and a commitment to peaceful, evolutionary change. Differences like these, moreover, are played out on two very different landscapes. Canada remains, by the standards of Asia, Europe, or even the United States, a scarcely inhabited land. (Quebec, for instance, is bigger than Alaska, but even as Canada's second most numerous province, it has considerably fewer people than New Jersey. Seven Canadian provinces are larger than California, but the population of California is roughly equivalent to the population of all Canada.)

If, therefore, evangelicalism in the two nations has absorbed some of the cultural colouring of the respective areas, we could only expect that the forms of evangelicalism would have significant differences as well.

What are those differences?

1 *Flexibility and Rapid Deployment*. A first concerns the possibilities opened up by Canada's relatively small population. I have mentioned already how rapidly the EFC sprang from almost nowhere during the last fifteen years to become a significant force. It is hard to imagine anything so substantial taking place so rapidly in the United States. In this same regard, it is also worth noting that Brian Stiller's double marginalization as a Pentecostal and as a native of Saskatchewan did not keep him from making a major contribution to all Canadian evangelicals as it might have done in the United States.

Canadian evangelicals reap the same sort of benefit in other spheres as well. The Mennonite Brethren, at best a speck on the religious landscape of the United States, have greatly assisted evangelicalism in Canada as a whole, nowhere more noticeably than through the *Christian Week*, which the vision of only a small number has made into an extraordinary national religious paper.

Similarly, Canada now enjoys fuller polling and interview data on its evangelical population than does the United States, because one person, Professor George Rawlyk of Queen's University, was able to parlay a modest amount of grant money and his personal connections with the Angus Reid Group into a major, on-going effort in opinion research.

The opposite side of this same coin is also worth considering. If effective evangelical projects require less time and bureaucracy in Canada, Canadians often seem stubbornly unwilling to be impressed with anything happening in their own nation. William Westfall has observed that "The first canon of Canadian historiography may well be the doctrine that important things happen elsewhere, that Canada receives from Clio [the goddess of history] only those things that are dull and second hand."[19] Canada's relatively small population means that good things can happen among evangelicals in a hurry but also that most Canadians may not be too impressed. I note in this regard that Canadian assessment of the "Toronto Blessing" seems only to have gotten off the ground once stories about this phenomenon began to appear in the United Kingdom, the United States, and even Australia.

2   *Myths of National Origin.* A second way in which differences between Canadian and American history are played out cuts closer to the heart of the faith. I am speaking of the two societies' founding myths, which have been as powerful in the United States since its break from Britain as they have been feeble north of the border. Canada has always lacked the sort of compelling national mythology that fuels American ideology. South of the border we have a wealth of inspiring slogans like "Give me liberty or give me death" or "With malice toward none, with charity toward all." North of the border there have been no civil wars worthy of the name and certainly no violent political revolution. (The few local skirmishes in 1837 that are sometimes styled "rebellions" are significant mostly for how thoroughly Canadian leaders repudiated the spirit that inspired them.)[20] The mythic pull exerted by Canada's founding fathers – railroad magnates and hard-drinking politicians meeting behind closed doors in the wake of the American Civil War to wheedle a hasty piece of legislation from the British Parliament in order to keep their defenceless provinces from falling into the maw of the rising American empire – is not exactly overwhelming.

The contrasts resulting from this difference may be less now than formerly. But at least to a historian, the kind of comparisons drawn by Seymour Martin Lipset's *Continental Divide* remain persuasive. Lipset's main argument is that Canadian society "has been and is a more class-aware, elitist, law-abiding, statist, collectivity-oriented, and ... [group-oriented] society than the United States."[21] The antistatism, individualism, populism, violence, and egalitarianism that characterize American history have been decidedly less prominent in Canada. Where Canada has stressed the state and community values, the United States has featured the individual and laissez faire. In contrast to the United States's embrace of classical liberalism (in the nineteenth-century, individualistic sense of the term), Canada has fostered a public attitude stressing communalities, whether "Tory-statist" on the right or "social democratic" on the left. The reasons for these systematic differences are both geographical and historic. Canada's vast space and sparse population have required a more active government and have placed a premium upon cooperation. Historically, the rejection of the American

Revolution, the presence of Quebec as a distinct community, the loyalism strengthened by American invasions during the War of 1812, and the prosaic understatement of the Dominion's founding slogan ("Peace, order, and good government") have all tended to enforce organic as opposed to individualistic arrangements in Canadian life.

Lipset does recognize that contemporary Canada is changing, and he stresses the new Charter of Rights as a main vehicle accelerating the pace of change.[22] Yet developments in the 1980s do not shake him from his basic conclusion. A preponderance of social indicators continues to convince him that the historic differences between Canadian and American society are still present. These differences include, for example, a far lower Canadian murder rate, fewer police per capita, a relative absence of civil disorder, a higher tolerance for taxes and government regulation, and a willingness to support tight gun control.

Subtle but important religious differences have arisen from the social and ideological contrasts that Lipset outlines. In both the United States and Canada anti-Catholicism has been one of the most stable elements of Protestant self-definition. (It is welcome indeed that some of that residual antagonism has broken down in recent decades.) Yet American anti-Catholicism has often differed from Canadian anti-Catholicism precisely because of the settings in which attacks on Rome took place. In American Protestant history, anti-Catholicism was fuelled by a distinct sense of American messianism. Lyman Beecher and countless other evangelical leaders of the nineteenth century, for example, attacked Roman Catholics because of their threat to America's rising role in the Kingdom of God.[23]

In Canada, by contrast, anti-Catholicism more directly replicates English, Scottish, or Ulster polemics. Many examples could be cited of Canada's virulent brand of British anti-Catholicism, but one of the most telling occurred at Bay Roberts on Conception Bay, Newfoundland, in 1883. A successful mission by Catholic Redemptorists inspired a Protestant reprisal that led to rioting, the death of five people, and an international incident eventually put to rest by the arrival of a British battleship. Significantly, the Protestant attacks had been spearheaded by the local chapter of the Orange Order, an Ulster-inspired fraternity that carried on in the New World right where it had left off in the old.[24]

In more general terms, the widespread acceptance in the United States of the liberalism of the American Revolution led not only to institutional differences with Canada (like the rigid American separation of church and state) but to many differences in tone. The exalted role for the language of freedom in general, the tendency to equate tradition with corruption, the suspicion of inherited institutions, the confidence in entrepreneurial innovation – all are traits flowing from American liberalism of the late eighteenth and nineteenth centuries that have affected the churches as well as American society as a whole.[25] Canada – and the Canadian churches – have traditionally presented a contrast to these American ways, not by affirming absolute antitheses but by moderating individualistic liberalism with various forms of traditionalism, corporatism, communalism, and deference to authority. If that resistance to American liberalism has faded in the decades since World War II, it still exists. At least it can still seem to be present from an American angle, even if important Canadian prophets like George Parkin Grant think that the historic cultural contrast has passed away altogether.[26]

3 *Politics.* Again in very general terms, the historical result of these contrasting ideals is that American evangelicals maybe have gotten more done, but at a cost. Political participation is a major case in point. Outstanding historians have recently spotlighted the contrasting ways in which evangelicals contributed to the political history of their respective countries in the mid-nineteenth century. I cite first the English historian Richard Carwardine, whose recent book, *Evangelicals and Politics in Antebellum America,* is the finest account ever written of its subject. Carwardine uses a contrast with the British situation during the same period to summarize his research on the evangelical contribution to American politics:

American evangelicals' optimistic postmillennialism, their Manichaean perception of the world as a battleground between good and evil, their moral absolutism, and their weak sense of institutional loyalty to political parties all acted to destabilize the American polity in the middle decades of the nineteenth century, at the very time that British evangelicals and their fellow citizens were entering an "age of equipoise," a period of mid-Victorian peace and good order for which evangelicals themselves have been given considerable credit. American evangelicals killed each other in a fight over slavery and the Union, while their British counterparts, deeply divided among themselves only over the more containable issue of disestablishment, sought as Christian soldiers to advance Christ's kingdom by less murderous means.[27]

If evangelical political behaviour in America contrasts sharply with British evangelical politics, the contrast with Canada may be even stronger. According to McMaster's Michael Gauvreau, currently doing some of the best work in all North America on nineteenth-century connections among theology, political theory, and practical political outcomes, the model of evangelical voluntarism was fundamental to the peculiar reconciliation of monarchy and republicanism which occurred in British North America after 1815, and ... the notions of "responsible government" undergirding the political system and the competition of parties could not have been accepted without the evangelical notion of the "responsible" individual and the "voluntary" model of society ... [M]ore speculatively ... evangelicalism, by underpinning this common culture, and by polarizing the politics of the colonies around religious issues between 1850 and 1864, provided an essential stimulus to those movements of colonial union which culminated with the ... Confederation of 1867, which rested upon a delicate balance of local and federal power.[28]

A similar contrast might be drawn concerning evangelical contributions to politics earlier in the twentieth century. In each nation, evangelicals played major roles in shaping important political visions – in the United States especially for the populist Democrats led by William Jennings Bryan, and in Canada with several different political movements west of Ontario. For a complicated set of reasons, Bryan's vision of populist communalism faded rapidly in America, while the rightist Social Credit of fundamentalist preacher William Aberhardt and the leftist Cooperative Commonwealth Federation (CCF) led by the Baptist minister Tommy Douglas both survived with considerable effect. Questions may be asked about the continuation of Christian values in the later history of Social Credit as well as in the evolution of the CCF into the New Democratic Party. For the Canadian-American comparison, however, it is significant that political movements with evangelical inspiration lasted longer and exerted broader effect than comparable efforts in the United States.

Another contrast may be relevant even for the most recent national elections in the two countries. While recognizing that polling information is not exactly equivalent for the two countries and realizing that party configurations were complicated for both countries in the most recent elections, nonetheless, as the following table indicates, in both nations a strong bond was forged between evangelical or conservative Protestant churches, on the one hand, and, on the other hand, a political body – the American Republicans and the Canadian Reform – that came to be perceived as "God's party." The point of contrast is that American evangelical support for the Republican presidential candidate was considerably stronger than conservative Protestant support for Reform parliamentary candidates in Canada.

In sum, where in Canada evangelical connections with politics have often moderated extremes, in the United States they have more regularly exacerbated political extremes.

"God's Party" Vote[29]

	Republican or Reform %*	Regular Church Attenders %
U.S. self-identified fundamentals and evangelicals	62	72
Canadian conservative Protestant denominations	34	41

* U.S. = Republican presidential 1992
Canada = Reform parliamentarian 1993

4 *Liberal Evangelicalism.* A final contrast concerns the relatively large place in Canadian Protestant history of what is often called "liberal evangelicalism" – although "mediating evangelicalism" may in fact be a better term. That is, instead of militant or combative forms of evangelicalism which have flourished in the United States, Canadian evangelicalism has featured somewhat less polemics and a somewhat more accommodating spirit. It is difficult to define this mediating evangelicalism specifically, even if it is a central feature in much of the great upsurge of scholarship on the Canadian churches that has appeared in the last decade. Even a partial review of such work shows the central place of a mediating evangelical spirit.

John Webster Grant's magisterial account of nineteenth-century Ontario highlights the ability of evangelical Protestants to harness both the social gospel and new intellectual forces while retaining the substance of historic evangelical convictions.[30]

William Westfall's description of Methodist and Anglican culture in nineteenth-century Ontario finds both of them maintaining a full measure of evangelical conviction along with a culture-embracing sense of social propriety.[31]

Michael Gauvreau's history of nineteenth-century evangelical intellectual life depicts a relatively pacific accommodation between genuinely evangelical beliefs and some modern intellectual habits.[32]

Richard Vaudry's account of the Presbyterian Free Church tradition in the nineteenth century stresses its irenic adjustment to both other Presbyterians and the realities of Canadian life.[33]

Marguerite Van Die's intellectual biography of the nineteenth-century Methodist leader Nathanael Burwash reveals him as both doctrinally conservative and yet unflustered by the great intellectual changes at the end of the nineteenth century.[34] Much the same can be said about the equipoise of other important evangelical theologians, like the Presbyterians George Monro Grant and W.W. Bryden, or from the conservative side of the spectrum, John McNichol, long-time head of the Toronto Bible College.[35]

Phyllis Airhart's book on the evolution of the Methodists in the half century before the creation of the United Church in 1925 notes that Methodist revivalism in Canada retained its vigour and postponed compromise with modernism at least for a generation longer than was the case in the United States.[36]

Edith Blumhofer's biography of Aimee Semple McPherson shows how the influence of the Canadian Salvation Army kept her ministry much more positive and much less polemical than comparable ministries of early twentieth-century Pentecostal itinerants.[37]

George Rawlyk's history of twentieth-century Maritime Baptists helps explain why a divisive fundamentalist-modernist battle did not occur in that body despite the presence of many of the same ingredients that led to such a showdown in the States.[38]

Robert Burkinshaw's descriptions of conservative evangelicals in western Canada show why they merited the label "fundamentalist" in some particulars yet avoided some of the most polemical excesses of their American colleagues.[39]

And John Stackhouse's recent book is notable, from an American perspective, especially for his argument that the feistier sort of polemicists, like T.T. Shields, did not in fact define the central concerns of Canadian evangelicalism.[40]

Whether called "liberal" or "mediating," this form of evangelicalism has been much more important in Canada than in the United States. By contrast to the Canadian situation, American evangelicals in the nineteenth century featured a great deal more enthusiasm for sectarian causes. In the early twentieth century, American evangelicalism divided much more clearly than its Canadian counterpart into a militant evangelical conservatism (i.e., fundamentalism) and an accommodating evangelical inclusivism (verging toward modernism). Precisely what differentiated Canadian liberal or mediating evangelicalism from American varieties (whether the Reformed-Baptist doctrinal variety, the holiness-Pentecostal experiential type, or hybrids) was its resistance to nineteenth-century "liberalism." That is, against an unrestrained focus on the spiritual freedom and the moral prerogatives of the individual, Canadians retained more respect for tradition. They did not divorce social concern quite so easily from the need for regeneration, and they were somewhat less prone to think of piety as an alternative to intellectual endeavour.[41]

Canadian evangelicalism, in sum, has differed from American evangelicalism because Canada differs from the United States. Geography matters, but differences in ideology, attitudes toward history, and conceptions of national culture matter even more.

In the perspective of this paper, *the* American evangelical problem in comparison with Canadian evangelicals has been to believe the ideology that justified the American Revolution. The mistake of American evangelicals has been to let that ideology, and the practices flowing from it, exert so much force in shaping Christian faith and life. The distinction of Canadian evangelicalism has been the space it offered for less nationalistic renderings of Christianity to shape faith and life.

Of course, the comparison is much more complicated than that. Canadian evangelicals – even Canadian mediating evangelicals – have never attained perfection. To cite just one example showing that the effects of The Fall linger north of the border too, it is possible to find Protestant leaders early in this century falling prey to racial stereotyping almost as easily as religious leaders did in the United States. In 1910, S.D. Chown, later a general superintendent of the Canadian Methodist Church, asked belligerently: "Shall the hordes of Southern Europe overrun our country as the Huns and Vandals did the Roman Empire?" His contemporary, the Rev. C.W. Gordon, who wrote immensely popular novels under the name Ralph Connor, pointedly compared the sober Anglo-Saxons of Winnipeg with the "steaming, swaying, roaring dancers ... all reeking with sweat and garlic" at a Ukrainian wedding. And an assistant superintendent of the Baptist Home Mission Board of Ontario and Quebec wrote in 1913: "We must endeavour to assimilate the foreigner. If the mixing process fails we must strictly prohibit from entering our country all elements that are non-assimilable. It is contrary to the Creator's law for white, black or yellow races to mix together."[42] Such lapses could be cited nearly without end. If Canadian evangelicalism has been superior to American evangelicalism, the superiority has been relative.

But at best, Canadian evangelicals have embodied qualities all too rare in the United States. They have preferred a degree of ecumenicity to ecclesiastical polemics; they have highlighted the virtues of peace over war; they have taken pretensions (whether religious or national) with a grain of salt; and they have made more rather than less of the ways in which Canadian Christianity fits into broader world patterns of the faith.

A final question is by now inevitable: If Canadian evangelicalism can be compared favourably with American evangelicalism in so many ways, why is it that the American varieties now seem to be so much more vigorous than their Canadian counterparts? The answer – at least in the terms stressed here – may be simple. If standards for success are not sought from an expanding cultural liberalism, then it is possible that criteria other than simply size or rampant energy deserve more attention. Since for a Christian it is always appropriate to ask what the Scriptures teach, I have a suspicion that, once fundamentally biblical standards are applied, it can be seen that evangelicalism may not in fact be better off today in the United States than in Canada.

2 "Up from Downunder": An Australian View of Canadian Evangelicalism

MARK HUTCHINSON

Historians are always interested in asking "what if" questions: What if Theodosius had not been thrown from his horse, or if Napoleon had not invaded Russia, or if the late and, in some circles, not so lamented Conservative government in Canada had not been so interested in the North American Free Trade Act (NAFTA). This, you might say, is our voyeurism coming out. What ancient historian, for instance, would not have liked to have had the sort of coverage for the assassination of Julius Caesar that Oliver Stone had for JFK. One could imagine it – "Big Julie" walks into the Senate House, the cameras pan in, and suddenly there is a movement off to the side. The camera swings, there is confusion as a group of toga-clad notables close in (all portly except, of course, for Cassius of the proverbially lean and hungry look). The camera jerks as the operator is jostled, but he persists and pushes in just in time to see the first length of steel spring from a hidden place and draw blood. In the background, over the sound of screaming and the flapping of leather sandals escaping across marble, a stentorian voice is yelling "Caesar is down, Caesar is down ..." Fade to black, run title screen.

Unfortunately we are not usually given either so much detail or the ability to run the film back and review the evidence, let alone the scientist's ability to re-run the experiment and change the constituent elements to see if the end result would be the same. What we do have, however, is comparative history. It may be argued that just as Canadian and Australian cultures have shifted away from their British roots over the past half century, so have the respective literatures describing the national experience. The consequence of this is that, whereas Canada and Australia during their colonial experience were invisible to one another as both looked back to Britain, this mutual invisibility has continued into their post-colonial experience by the emergence of the United States as a defacto replacement "metropolis" to two middle-sized powers. Religious historiography has followed this development in line with national literatures generally. It is important to tease out the wider contexts in which the religious life of these two post-colonial countries has developed, pointing out that, for the evangelical cultures of these countries, that life has remarkable similarities and indeed an unexpected amount of mutual influence.

Given the possible range of comparisons between the Canada and Australia, not to mention their direct links, a series of examples will have to suffice. In her overview of Canadian Protestantism from 1760 to 1815, Nancy Christie, a Canadian scholar of considerable Australian experience, typifies the early religious experience of Canada as a sort of eighteenth-century religious El Salvador – where rationalist establishment latitudinarians held the cities and the guerilla forces of experiential evangelicalism controlled the countryside. She notes that the Protestant religious elite during the years immediately following the American and French Revolutions were fully aware that evangelicalism, as a popular expression, was the dominant vehicle by which established notions of an orderly, stable, and hierarchical society were being challenged and transformed.[1] But one may ask "what if?" What if the roles were reversed, and the evangelicals held the cities and the Anglo-Catholics were wandering around in the bush? How would this change national character and the integration of religious life into that character? In fact, by transferring our gaze south of the equator, a comparative historical study of Australian and Canadian evangelicalism offers precisely this sort of "what if."

For the first forty years of Australia's existence, in which it was variously called Botany Bay (in England), New South Wales (in the colony itself), or, by its less voluntary inhabitants, simply Hell, there was no clergyman in the colony licensed to practise who was not an Anglican evangelical. Several interesting things result from this. First, it does not seem to matter that the people holding the cities are either Anglican or evangelical – they show the same tendency to develop close relationships with power and the same suspicion of "methodist" enthusiasm. This is despite the fact that some of these people, such as the senior chaplain, Samuel Marsden, came from what many people considered to be methodistical backgrounds. Secondly, when sufficient numbers of clergy became available in New South Wales to provide real diversity of opinion, Anglican evangelicalism and Methodist evangelicalism diverged from their early unity of spirit, with the former taking up the establishment position and the latter tending to go into opposition. It is not possible for Australian religious historians to simply speak, as Christie does, of "evangelicalism" as the party of change and the High Church as the party of reaction. This is more on the English pattern of divergent development within a churchish state rather than the American model of fragmentation within a pluralising society. The question, therefore, is whether Canadian experience can in fact be so starkly drawn, or whether it needs to be seen within a larger compass.

An overview of the Canadian model is an interesting exercise for an Australian religious historian. One quickly comes to the conclusion that if Canada stands (as John Stackhouse has suggested) between Britain and the United States in terms of its evangelicalism,[2] then Australia stands somewhere between Canada and Britain. This is so geographically as well as religiously – Canada is certainly "more than a hyphen," to quote Stackhouse and before him, Alvyn Austin, but it is also on the way to somewhere. The view of Canada provided to Australians has generally been conditioned by the fact that Canada is situated between England and the United States, and if the US was something to see on the way to England, Canada was something to see on the way to England from the United States.

The itinerary of Australian visitors to North America in the nineteenth century is instructive. For Henry Hussey, an Australian visiting the United States on his way to England in 1854, the itinerary was shaped by his religious fervour. His stop-off points included American churches, American voluntary societies such as the Bible Society, a lengthy interview with Alexander Campbell, a quick bit of spiritualized sight-seeing at Niagara, tacked onto which was a visit to Toronto, preparatory to taking ship for England. His conclusions were also indicative – Canadian hotels reminded him more of English inns than did hotels in the United States, and Toronto reminded him more of his home city, Adelaide, than did the cities he had just been in (though "Canada appeared to have adopted many practices which prevailed in the States").[3] That his observations were culturally shaped rather than direct, however, is observable by the fact that, despite having relatives in Canada (his aunt lived in Toronto), the great poles of his attention were Britain and the United States.

Canada and Australia, despite having close links, have thus always appeared to have been invisible to one another. The presence of such a cultural lens between the two countries is important, because our mutual invisibility has caused us to overlook one another as potential ways of seeing ourselves. How do we compare? While Canadian evangelicalism is less obviously revivalistic than American evangelicalism,

George Rawlyk's work on New Light revivalism and other studies indicate that Canada is probably more revivalistic than Australia has been. Simplistically put, churchish British national revivals compare to semi-churchish Australian revivals, to semi-churchish regional Canadian revivals, and un-churchish American national revivals. Such a typification of four distinct national experiences onto a continuum is an oversimplification, but this argument is merely a tool enabling us to gain some perspective on our national experiences.

COMPARISONS

What then does an Australian point of view offer historians of Canadian evangelicalism? First, as noted above, there is comparison. A growing body of evidence now suggests that Canada should be viewed not so much within the strait-jacket of the existing Canadian-American polarity but within the wider context of European expansion and societies of new settlement. This is not new – it is rather the natural consequence of now venerable and somewhat undermined theories offered by people such as Louis Hartz and the various proponents of frontier theory that commonality of origins has some force in determining the cultural mix that results. So it is not surprising to note that Australia and Canada have much in common. English Christianity was imported into both countries towards the end of the eighteenth century and settled among a scattered immigrant society, few of whose members "chose the province for religious reasons, and a fair number [of whom] came from areas where indifference, even hostility to religion were common."[4]

Further, both countries were typified by climatic and geographic characteristics that marked the development of religious practice – Canada as "a cold and insignificant backwater," Australia as a hot and harsh one. The great size of both countries and their immigrant nature meant that both have relied on governments more than their enterprising cousins in the United States. This produced a meliorism in religion and a conformity in social conduct that affected the nature of Christianity in both countries. Reinforcing this respect for authority (which has been reflected in the relative absence of schism and dissension) has been the continued impact of English pietism, which produced an irenic approach to potential religious disputation. In Australia and Canada the liberalizing process has rarely been aggressive, and the national temperament has inhibited the development of doctrinal controversy. Also because of their perceived backwater status, both countries found it difficult to attract ministers at all, let alone the best and most educated, and this cannot but have affected the image of religion that became current in the two societies.⁵ In these geographical realities the churches had to build from scratch.

Also part of the environment that shaped church life were population characteristics such as the difference in the quantity of immigrants. As Robert Burkinshaw suggests, British Columbian evangelicals have tended to be more British than American in character, despite the fact that some 20 per cent of the residents of their neighbouring province, Alberta, and up to 50 per cent of farmers in the southern part of the province were United States citizens.⁶ A low population, he suggests, reinforced their British tendency to be institutional rather than individualist evangelicals of the American mould. It is an observation applicable as well to New South Wales, where the population was even more scattered. Such tendencies also defended these societies against the inroads of modernism. The First World War made the passionately pro-British ex-colonies eschew all that was tainted with Germanic influence, in this case the Higher Critical methods that underlay modernist theological method. The United States, with many German settlers and a late entry to the war with a more fragmented religious profile, proved more prone to such influences, leading to the turbulence of the fundamentalist/modernist debates of the 1920s and 1930s. In Canada and Australia this bellicosity was tempered by the pietism implicit in Keswick holiness, despite the similarities in many of the formal doctrinal positions of the American fundamentalism and British proto-fundamentalism.⁷

The ability, or rather inability, of the two countries to call on ministerial support had a significant effect on the nature of the respective churches. The requirements were strenuous. To deal with the vast distances involved, J.B. Polding in New South Wales and Alexander Macdonell in Upper Canada led their clergy in becoming "galloping pastors" to the scattered settlements on the frontier.⁸ For this reason the Methodists in both countries proved to be more adept at founding churches and providing them with clergy. The circuit system and an Arminian passion for saving souls saw them make the best use of sparse manpower.

In turn, the Methodists' class system and revivalism converted and retained people who were not previously members. The ability to study under the guidance of a local supervisor for a lay preacher's licence obviated the immediate need for a sophisticated clerical-training establishment and provided some training where much training was not a possibility. Methodism in the United States expanded "with unprecedented rapidity during and after the revolution."⁹ Canada and Australia, both places with large frontiers like that to be found in the United

States, also witnessed speedy Methodist growth. In 1822, for instance, R.C. Gourlay noted that there were "Methodists everywhere."[10] One reason might be that in the United States after the Revolution the Episcopal Church was in tatters, causing American Methodists to break away completely and establish their own forms and structures. Canada and Australia retained a viable Church of England for much longer, leaving the Methodists to flourish in rural areas but with strong competition in the population centres.

Canada, as would be expected of a country that had pre-revolutionary links with both the United States and Britain, had a longer period in which its Methodism was seen as an auxiliary of mainstream Anglicanism. If one can trace an intellectual meliorism to Methodism's roots in Anglicanism, this may be one reason why in later periods Canadian Methodists did better in founding colleges and taking a leading role in higher education than did Australian Methodists. The more direct effect of the First Great Awakening on Atlantic Canada than Australia (through Henry Alline and William Black, a Methodist) also suggests an important difference between the two, though it is not true, as most Australian historians have suggested, that the First Great Awakening had no effect on Australia. Wesleyans and Congregationalists in particular had been affected by Wesley (John West and John Crooks, for example, were children of Wesley's close acquaintances), and Neil Gunson has noted the influence of Welsh Calvinist Methodism on Australia's early Anglican chaplains in particular, who carried the voice of Whitefield into Australia. Australia, however, received the First Great Awakening as a fading "coo-ee!" Canada received it as a close "halloo!" across the border.

In Upper Canada as in New South Wales, some ethnic groups such as the Irish brought their ministers with them. As Campion has pointed out, there were Irish priests and tertiaries among the lay and convict populations of New South Wales who organized church life even though their activities were officially suppressed.[11] The Scottish Glengarry Catholics did the same in Upper Canada. Evangelicals, depending on a pure "call" system without central mechanisms to attract ministers, found it more difficult: "The limitations of the efforts from within the province made it clear that external initiative was necessary."[12] The Congregationalists and Baptists could rely on only comparatively small amounts of external help in their adaptation to conditions in New South Wales, and both remained small, if influential. The Anglicans and Methodists in both continents could rely on missionary organizations like the Society for the Propagation of the Gospel in Foreign Parts, the Church Missionary Society and the Wesleyan Missionary Society to supply their pulpits, though even these were stretched by the need.

Presbyterians had no minister at all in New South Wales until 1823, and he, John Dunmore Lang, was to be instrumental in procuring almost all new ministers for the Kirk until the mid-1830s.[13] At least in the case of the Church of England, as Ken Cable has suggested, this procedure meant that Australia developed a much more clerically dominated church life than did Britain.[14]

It is not surprising given this that even before it happened in the home culture, there grew up in the colonies the idea that religion was something that happened in churches. For all that, Upper Canada (at least according to Grant's account) seems to have received a slightly better quality of ministerial candidate. Allowing for different denominational experiences, accusations of drunkenness and philandering in New South Wales were not the isolated incidents that he suggests they were in Upper Canada. It is, of course, an assessment based on sketchy data, but in all it appears as if the Canadian rough diamond Richard Pollard, who returned home after ordination swearing to "make his charges the finest damn parishes in all Upper Canada," would have been more at home in an Australian pub than he was amongst his Church of England confreres in the future Ontario.

A marked note of both Australian and Canadian evangelicalism is a defensiveness not found in, for instance, Britain. This is not surprising when one considers that at the time of their new settlement evangelicalism in both countries was on the defensive – from Enlightenment attacks on orthodox bases of faith, and from the sorts of disturbances to faith that occur when people are uprooted from their traditional family and social structures. They were also faced with moral and social conditions which militated against the sort of settled, parish Christianity they had practised in the Old World. For example, in its early years New South Wales faced a famine that nearly extinguished it, and for at least three decades more attention was paid to the harvest than the pulpit. Samuel Marsden and Richard Johnson, evangelical Anglican clergy, were probably more successful in farming than they were in making conversions and have since reaped a crop of criticism for it. Canada had a similar experience, for even when the circumstances of arrival were less unsettling than in the loyalist refugee camps, the task of rendering operative a farm or business called for an expenditure of time and energy that left little surplus for prayer and religious instruction and little incentive for distinguishing the days of the week.[15]

There was also the dislocation effect on immigrants: loosed from traditional ties and small-town moral oversight, for many immigrants to both colonies "their passions and appetites assume the reins," even after "many of their most pressing difficulties are removed."[16] Asahel Morse, a Baptist missionary who toured Upper Canada in 1807, for instance, described it as a "dismal region of moral darkness and the shadow of death," while the Church of England minister at Kingston, John Stuart, described the bulk of his congregation as "men not remarkable for either Religion, Industry or Honesty."[17] Their despair was matched by Presbyterian pope John Dunmore Lang's reaction to the colony of New South Wales: "The climate is delightful, the country is highly productive, but its people – O generation of vipers! Will they never be warned to flee from the wrath to come? I scorn to be the pensioner of thieves and adulterers. I shall stay here only till I get our Scots kirk finished and till I can leave the place honourably."[18] Lang's sense of humour over the state of colonial society was not improved when a prostitute mistook her mark while he was walking home from service one night in 1834, and propositioned him.[19]

Just as New South Wales was settled by a convict population with few religious commitments and a free population with many more commercial and material ones, Upper Canada was largely settled out of the American northeast, where church attendance had dropped to as low as 10 per cent of the population.[20] Though Canada profited more than Australia from the Second Great Awakening, the War of 1812 undermined some of this influence. The result of all this was, for many, to push religion to the side, and for others, to make religion captive to a sense of Victorian respectability that robbed it of much of its early fire. Material need became the central organizing principle of Canadian and Australian societies, with a certain socialized religion being imposed from above through the operations of the state and manifested through the building of churches and schools as the architectural expression of this imposition. Out on the frontier in suburban homes and even in the great edifices of the church in the major cities, individuals kept the flame burning, waiting for the tide to turn. The picture of one Mr Harris of Long Point, Upper Canada, for instance, reading the church service every Sunday to his household and to "any hired men who could be persuaded to attend," calls to mind the New South Wales Baptist bush worker who would, on gathering a group of fellow workers around a fire, read a prayer or a sermon out of Spurgeon's magazine, *The Sword and the Trowel*.[21] The examples could be multiplied – Christianity continued among the people even when it lacked support from the formal structures of society. But it was no longer the sort of Christianity envisaged by T.H. Scott or John Strachan, where church meshed with state and moulded the model citizen.

Both countries had to deal with the fact that the new country was less homogenous, socially, than the countries of origin. Differences of ethnic background, ecclesiastical affiliation, and length of residence ensured that no single approach would suit everyone. The inevitable result was not only competition but conflict.[22] Despite this, both countries were, by massive British immigration, established with a central ballast of the Anglican and Presbyterian churches, with a ginger element introduced by the undeniable size and strength of Catholicism and Methodism. Given the time of establishment, both Anglicanism and Presbyterianism were first represented by their most officially "respectable" forms, broad Anglicanism and the Church of Scotland (or Kirk).[23] These were quickly followed, however, by members of splinter groups – for the Anglicans, the Methodists and evangelicals; and for the Kirk, the Seceders and later the Free Church. Establishment in both countries thus arises as a problem of the timing of settlement and the religious constitution of the early governing class, followed quickly by diversification, the importation of sectarianism, and squabbles over authority. It is interesting to note that, therefore, in both Canada and Australia the questions and tensions over Anglican establishment are essentially the same, often being worked out at the same time by the same kinds of people.[24]

The establishment of Anglicanism in new colonies was seen by conservatives in England as essential for the retention of the Empire, a point that became particularly marked after the American Revolution. In 1813, for instance, Bishop Huntington declared that the American colonies would not have been lost if the Church of England had been established. (He seems to have forgotten that fear of episcopal domination was one of the causes of the rebellion!) He drew the lesson for the newer colonies, such as Upper Canada and New South Wales, suggesting that it was necessary to secure "the affections of the rising generation in New South Wales by establishing an Episcopal Church before the separatists had prejudiced their minds against our constitution, civil and religious ... The strongest means through which you can secure any real attachment to this country will be through the Episcopalians."[25] Until 1815 in Canada, the British Government paid the stipends of Church of England missionaries, a situation paralleled in Australia by the payment of military chaplains out of the Police Fund. The differences are apparent as well: one set were an arm of the military, the others expressing a call to duty which, while supported by the state, had been conceived by groups like the Society for the Propagation of the Gospel. In this, perhaps, may be seen part of the reason why Christianity became more marginalized in the southern continent than it did in Canada. In Australia it had to overcome the image of being an alien, oppressive force outside of civil society, while in Canada it was always a part of civil society, however militarized the governorships were in the different colonies.

Yet both countries were constantly being fed by and compared to the establishment of Anglicanism in Britain. Consequently, in both societies, particularly among conservatives, a strong theme held that church establishment and political stability were necessary to one another. So close were they that one could argue that not "religion" but rather the "religionized" state was the primary issue. By the same logic, people like John Morphett in South Australia and W.C. Wentworth in New South Wales drew from the example of Pitt's Canada Bill of 1791 in arguing for an upper chamber in the state legislature peopled with titled land-holders. Such importations on the model of Great Britain's organic constitution would, it was hoped, ensure that the tone of colonial societies was raised, loyalty to the crown repaid, and the forces of democratic excess curbed. In Wentworth's case, the suggestions were laughed at as the establishment of a "Bunyip Aristocracy," smacking too much of the privilege entrenched in the old country. There was long a strong sense, however, that the Church of England was the embodiment of "all the values that were held to qualify England to an unusual degree as a Christian nation," and the Empire as the means of spreading the light of civilization.[26]

Just as conservative groups in Australia drew on the Canadian experience to support their case, so did reformers. By the early 1820s the reformers could point to the rising opposition to clerical reserves and Establishment in Canada. The Colonial Office slowly came to the same conclusion. Paul Knaplund has pointed out that James Stephen switched from an earlier support of the Establishment of Anglicanism to a late-1820s position that it was impossible to do so. On a note on a Nova Scotian Act of 1828, for instance, he stated, "It is, I presume, vain to attempt to secure to the Church of England on the North American Continent, the species of monopoly of secular privileges which it enjoys in this Country, nor does it seem probable that the real interest of that Church would be promoted by maintaining any such exclusive principle."[27] This was something that was extended to Australia. Under the Grey ministry of 1830–1, Lord Goderich was secretary of state for the Colonies. He was advised by a House of Commons report which condemned the "Clergy and Schools estates" in all colonies as an example of the evil of unworked and unproductive lands, the reserve of which forced settlers to go further out to acquire land. Goderich wrote to both Australian and Canadian governors in this regard, institutionalising the Wakefieldian idea that populations should be concentrated to encourage stable social institutions.[28]

If Anglicanism could not be formally established, however, at least it could become the religion of the ruling class, and there were those in both countries who felt that the principle of working out the creation of a controllable society was more important than the denominational labels applied. Denominations were given piecemeal assistance through the late 1820s as the projects that arose appealed to the government. In 1835 Richard Bourke, the Irish liberal governor of New South Wales, decided to break the deadlock over how the Church and Schools Corporation lands should be distributed by commuting all payments to churches to allocations from a civil list.[29] Effectively, all major denominations were now established, something that Methodists in both countries found themselves ambivalent about but ended up becoming involved in. In Canada in 1840 a suggestion of Canadian Governor-General Charles P. Thompson saw a similar development: lands were broken up among the different denominations with priority given to the Anglicans and the Kirk, so establishing all the major lines of Christian belief.

Thus, if we are looking for a reason why Canadian and Australian evangelicals are different from British and American evangelicals in their meliorism and their reference to the state and/or private wealth, we can find an explanation in this common experience of establishment, of geography, of colonial new settlement and massive British immigration through the nineteenth century which relativized the contributions of other European cultures such as the Russian Dukhobors and German Mennonites. It is interesting to note that it is in Australia's states of highest European immigration that religious innovation seems to be at its peak – in South Australia and Queensland, for instance. Can we say the same for the Prairie provinces in Canada? It is at least a thesis worth investigating.

DIRECT LINKS

Due partially to our mutual invisibility, little has been written comparing the religious history of Australia and Canada, and what little has been written tends to be comparative, along the lines of the arguments sketched above. The leg-work to find actual links between the countries is only just beginning, and it would be impossible to untangle the vast web of family interconnections which, redolent with the common religiosities of families, link the two countries. (One thinks here of the Fry and Hammond families of Somerset, whose members scattered to Canada, Australia, New Zealand, and South Africa, or the Mackay brothers, one in Toronto and one in Melbourne, who formed the original link across which Presbyterian defence against church union was coordinated between Australia and Canada.[30]) Even now, however, the importance of the links is apparent. Our count of clergy who have spent significant time in both countries is up to 140 and still climbing, while in the standard biographical reference work for Australia, the *Australian Dictionary of Biography*, there are some eighty-seven non-clergy in the nineteenth century alone for whom religious affiliation and the Canadian connection are both important. Interestingly, it is much harder to find parallel references in the *Canadian Dictionary of Biography*, indicating, as previously suggested, Australia's position on the end of the colonial line.

While it is impossible to detail all the connections, among the more significant might be the following. In great part, Australians and Canadians have contributed to one another's evangelicalism through joint participation in the missionary movement. In an important sense this followed imperial lines in the nineteenth century and the lines of internationalist western culture in the period since World War II. Just as Australia was in one sense a reflection of and an important base for Britain's nineteenth-century expansion into the South Pacific and Asia, so Canadian evangelical missions tended to point towards Asia, the South Pacific, and Africa. Vancouver and Sydney in this sense played similar roles for missionary organizations such as the China Inland Mission, whose staff used these cities as the last Europeanized staging points for work further out. This is a role that has continued to the present. Indeed, in the New Hebrides, Australia and Canada shared a Presbyterian mission station, before the Australians took over completely towards the end of the century. Both countries supported the mission financially, leading to regular visits to Australia by Canadians John Geddie and Joseph Copeland.[31] While under the auspices of the Canadians, there was a "fair bit of give and take,"[32] as Australia was the nearest European-style country suitable for furlough and the raising of support. Geddie eventually settled in Melbourne, and other Canadian ministers may have visited at this time.

Other leaders of churches also kept up fraternal visits between continents. The Anglo-Canadian Methodist leader Morley Punshon became renowned for his travels, and it is clear that after the shattering loss of his wife, Australia was a real possibility for his resettlement.[33] The story about the death of Punshon's wife, Maria Ann Vickers, was replayed in the Australian press with the pathos which only the nineteenth century could support, and this sort of martyrology provided a definite link between the two countries long after Punshon moved to Canada.[34] That these links were continued into the twentieth century can be seen by the close ties between the South Seas Evangelical Mission, based in Australia, and the Sudan Interior Mission located in Toronto, which led to the exchange of mission families prior to World War II and the cross-publishing and mutual distribution of each other's books. A standing witness is the continuing involvement of the Austro-New Zealand-Chinese-Canadian leader of the Overseas Missionary Fellowship (OMF) in Canada, David Michel. Michel represents the sort of trans-national citizenship that Empire and evangelical missions provided for their personnel, yea, unto "a thousand [generations] of those who love me and keep my commandments," as the Book of Exodus reminds us.

Likewise, Canadian evangelicalism was deeply influenced by the early secretariat with the Canadian InterVarsity movement of that encourager of student missions, Englishman Stacey Woods. Woods's attachment to low Anglican liturgy and hymns, as well as his abhorrence of things American, strengthened the internationalist and British perspectives of the Canadian InterVarsity Fellowship (IVF). After his presence in Canada, the number of Australians who have wandered through or done short stints with Canadian institutions such as Prairie Bible College and Regent College is too many to count.

The number of New Zealanders and Australians in Canada is easily explicable by their cultural position at the end of the colonial line: Canada is on the way out of the Antipodes, and many stopped at the wells in Sinai while others continued on to the promised land of Oxford and Cambridge. Yet to be explored, however, is why Canada has needed to hold on to so many Antipodean refugees as leaders of interdenominational evangelical causes. This question was put to David Michel at the Overseas Missionary Fellowship, and his response contributes to our understanding of Canadian evangelical leadership:

It's harder to find people [who are Canadian and can lead] – and yet on the other hand you get people like Brian Stiller, head of the EFC [Evangelical Fellowship of Canada], and some of our pastors. But there is a sort of thing – I don't know whether inferiority complex is the word or what. But, you see, Americans have "big guys" – they act as such strong leadership and voice and so on. Unfortunately, there is a kind of reaction, and therefore there is a kind of diffidence. And Canadians certainly do best in supportive roles – whether it is as dorm parents, or mission home hosts and hostesses, you know, we have quite a lot of those in the mission. We also have some field leaders as Canadians, but in OMF we haven't attracted the strong leader type that we have in England, though we haven't done it too well in the States either. We probably have stronger leadership types from Australia and New Zealand, though I do believe in recent years we've got some people – I can think of three straight off – who would make good leaders of OMF in Canada. They're young in their service, some of them. However, there is a sort of a diffidence in reaction to the American style which colours the way that Canadians rise to initiative and activity, on the whole.[35]

Michel was not the only one to strike this problem. In 1944 Stacey Woods wrote to Paul White in Australia informing him that he had been called back to Canada because there was no one there to replace the now-drafted Melvin Donald, and that the IVF had been forced to take over both Scripture Union and the Canadian Sunday School Mission, as they were collapsing because of lack of leadership.[36]

Typically both ends of the evangelical world attempted to use their international contacts to gain leverage in the politics of church and university at home. When the position for principal of Women's College at the prestigious University of Sydney came up in 1945, Paul White wrote to Stacey Woods asking him to suggest a good female Canadian academic of an evangelical persuasion who could, with the glamour of international experience and the imperial network, capture the position for evangelicalism. Woods wrote back sadly: "I wish that I could write of someone sufficiently mature and well-trained to apply for the position of Principal of Women's College. We seem to be too young over here to have produced this sort of thing."[37] Four years later he could report back that the IVF had finally found a Canadian leader – "Wilber [sic] Sutherland, a science grad from the University of British Columbia. I think he is the real thing, and I hope that ultimately he will be able to assume the leadership of the Canadian work. It badly needs a Canadian at the helm."[38]

In the same decade that Woods went south to seek the wider fields in American university work, we find the IVF acting as a conduit for Australians into Canada – the future Archbishops of Sydney Donald Robinson and Marcus Loane, Vincent Craven heading up the Pioneer Camps movement, Northcote Deck and his son who moved backwards and forwards between Toronto and Sydney, Don Campbell, John Davies, Phyllis King, Constance Knox, Irene Young, and others equally recognizable as members of the Sydney Anglican evangelical nobility, such as David Grant. In the opposite direction there are fewer names, but important ones – Maurice Murphy, for instance, who tragically only served in parish ministry for a year before passing away, and most notably, the American Charles Troutman. Both Troutman and Murphy are interesting cases of Australia providing a British colonial place of refuge which was yet within the evangelical world for people like Murphy, who had run up against church authorities in Toronto for his brash evangelicalism, and Troutman, who left the United States rather than follow his convictions into open conflict with Stacey Woods in the American IVF. Interestingly, Troutman provided an important source of counterbalance to his great friend Wilbur Sutherland, whom he counselled "not to follow the American pattern too closely," and with whom he discussed plans for a Tyndale House model of intellectual action on university campuses.[39]

In their mutual anti-Americanism, Australian and Canadian evangelicals found a common interest. There are many other points that could be made about the Australian contribution to Canadian evangelicalism – the input by the "Commonwealth evangelist" Lionel Fletcher, for instance, or the Open Air Campaigners Movement, or the writings of people such as F.W. Boreham, but these will have to await another occasion. It is important to note, however, that, though Australia's gift to Canada has been leadership, Canada's gift to Australia has been equally important.

While Canada has had movements that have needed leading, Australia has developed leading figures without having sufficient population or cultural outlets for religious divergence to develop. Canada has been a superb bridge to the United States and Britain for Australian leaders, but the reverse also occurs – Canada has been the halfway house for some of North America's more interesting religious developments. I have already mentioned the tie between Canadian and Australian anti-union movements within Presbyterianism, and two other particular examples spring to mind: the Hornerite holiness movement after World War I and Latter Rain Pentecostalism in the 1950s. The Latter Rain, with its stress on "end times" and "signs and wonders," was introduced to Australia in 1952 when Ray Jackson brought the Latter Rain teaching from Saskatchewan to Australia. While his personal influence has largely been through the Associated Mission Churches in Asia, Jackson's teachings have been mediated and moderated in two of Sydney's largest churches – Christian City Church in Brookvale and the Hills Christian Life Centre in Baulkham Hills. As these churches dominate the music and liturgy of Australian Pentecostalism and even mainline charismatic churches, the influence has been and continues to be significant.

Many other examples could be given – the impact of Wycliffe College in Toronto on Sydney, via the agencies of Howard Mowll and Charles Venn Pilcher, for example, or the influence of J. Oswald Smith of the Peoples Church in Toronto on E.G. Telfer and the United Aborigines Mission. But these few will suffice to indicate that the flow back across the Pacific has been a vital one. It is important to think of Canada not only as more than a hyphen between the United States and Britain but also as more than a hyphen in the shaping of international religious culture through the fading ties of British Empire and the strengthening ties of the global market of ideas.

The mainstream literature about Canadian evangelicalism is a second-stage literature. It has emerged from the interest in Aunt Nellie's collection of prayerbooks into a healthy post-colonial attempt to draw a tension between the two largest objects in the epistemological landscape – the thriving evangelical cultures of Britain and the United States. It is a natural conclusion (reinforced by literary tropes that assume a sort of organic growth to nations, and therefore to national cultures) that Canadian evangelicalism begins as a form of dependency, grows up through a tangled web of international cultural influences, and slowly emerges as a late adolescent, early adult figure demonstrating some bracing self-assertiveness. These emphases are not wrong, but they are limited, and, I would suggest, limiting.

Canada's increasing assertiveness is at least in part a myth. Comparisons with, and a bit of digging around in, countries outside the UK-USA axis demonstrates the fact that cultural influence is a subtle thing. It is at least a two-edged sword, if not a multi-pointed flail. Australia's influence on Canada, and vice versa, indicates that cultures do not develop in axes but within fields of influence and intellectual hierarchies which appear bipolar but are in fact multi-faceted.

Such hierarchies can be made evident by reference to two depictions from the first quarter of this century, one Canadian and the other Australian. The first voice is that of Dr E. Scott, who, speaking on the issue of Church Union in 1925, noted that "the Presbyterian Church may be in Britain, Canada or the USA – in Australia, South Africa, or New Zealand – in India, China or Korea – or in any other country. Whatever it may be, it is 'The Presbyterian Church' in that country."[40] Such clumpings of countries tell us something of the fields of perception current among Canadians of the time. "Britain, Canada or the USA" were a different sphere to "Australia, South Africa or New Zealand." Geography clearly plays a part, but much stronger is the "mission field concept" common to the Asian countries, as opposed to the Commonwealth concept common to the dominions grouped together. I suggest that an account of Canadian evangelicalism cannot be allowed to remain trapped in the first level of explanation – the field embracing "Britain, Canada or the USA." The other fields effectively condition and alter the development of the national religious culture, though (by their very otherness) they threaten to do so invisibly.

The second voice is that of the chief justice of Tasmania, who on Empire Day in 1915 noted that "Right now [on the fields of France] South African, Canadian, and Australian soldiers were preaching great sermons ... in the cause of liberty, that would never be forgotten." It was, said the judge, a baptism of fire, of blood, the beginning of nationhood: "Through the sacrifices they had made Australia springs unto a realisation of nationhood such as could have come in no other way."[41] In each of the nations mentioned, war has had a similar effect – something Granatstein and Morton point out in their history of Canada during the Second World War, *A Nation Forged in Fire*.[42] For the readers of the *Presbyterian Record*, and others, then, religion was the other side to a categorization of the world dominated by the structures of Empire and factors such as the growing industrial giant to the south of the Canadian border.

We should not, however, impose a bipolarism on nineteenth-century and early twentieth-century Canadian evangelical thought which may not have been so evident to the actors themselves. British North America long lived in the full noon light of the "Westward Course of Empire," in its day a religio-political ideology quite as strong as America's Manifest Destiny. If it does anything, an Australian view of Canadian evangelicalism provides scholars with a standpoint much more approaching pre-war Canadian assumptions than is evident in much contemporary historical literature and allows them not to be quite so overcome by the power of detail and proximity as to forget the power of history and paradigm.

3 Canadian Evangelicalism: A View from Britain

DAVID BEBBINGTON

Evangelical Protestantism in Canada is commonly seen as poised between its American and British counterparts. The United States, according to this standard view, has promoted enthusiasm, innovation, and extremism while Britain has encouraged decorum, restraint, and moderation. Over the whole period between the eighteenth century and the present, it is believed, ebullient Americans have urged populist techniques on their northern neighbours, whereas Great Britain, at least until the decay of its influence during the twentieth century, has exported the values of decency and order. In a recent and most persuasive book, Nathan Hatch has argued that between the American Revolution and about 1830 the religious experience of the new United States was shaped by the dismissal of elite authority, the spread of popular devotional zeal, and the rise of untrained outsiders to positions of leadership. American Protestantism, he contends, has remained thoroughly democratized ever since.[1] Britain, by contrast, is known to have retained traditional ways and a deferential society. The two contrasting approaches, it is often held, vied for the ascendancy in Canada, a land long constitutionally bound to Britain but always inconveniently close to the United States.

The rivalry for the Canadian soul, it has been suggested, was reinforced by other polarities. The rural areas attracted footloose American revivalist preachers, but the rising cities acquired a taste for British respectability.[2] The more sectarian expressions of twentieth-century evangelicalism have been linked with areas of recent settlement, in part from the United States, but its more churchly expressions with places of long-standing British immigration.³ Again the radical evangelicalism of the late eighteenth century flourished in denominations with strong American links, the Baptists and the Methodists; but a more formal or orderly variant was usually found in the Presbyterianism and Anglicanism that were deeply rooted in the established churches of the British Isles.⁴ In these various dichotomies – rural/urban, sectarian/churchly, and radical/formal – the element associated with Britain was always on the side of sobriety. Wildfire was likely to fly northwards across the border rather than westwards across the ocean.

Canada, then, has been depicted as an experimental laboratory in which substances from America and Britain have been brought together, sometimes with explosive force. The early nineteenth century, for example, was marked by a sharp collision over jurisdiction in Canada between the Methodist Episcopal Church of the United States and the British Wesleyan Conference. The Canadian stations, the British Missionary Committee told the American Bishop Asbury in the wake of the War of 1812, must be ceded to its authority – Montreal especially, it explained, "as a considerable part of the money for building the chapel and house was raised in this country."⁵ The Americans simply refused, and rival preachers were supplied by the two sides for several years. Similarly in 1850 a disgruntled English Baptist minister who had taught in Montreal commented on the "ignorance and fanaticism" abounding in the two Canadian provinces. The explanation was not far to seek: "The country," he wrote, "is deluged with the cheap, trashy publications which daily issue from the presses of the United States."⁶ At other times the cultural influences could mingle more harmoniously. In Newfoundland Methodism during the 1880s, for instance, the lay readers who could not rise to composing their own sermons instead turned equally to those by the American D.L. Moody and to those by the Englishman C.H. Spurgeon.⁷ Again, the best informed commentator on mid-twentieth-century Pentecostalism observed that the outward characteristics of Canadian meetings tended to occupy "about a midway position between the British and the American, possessing some features of both."⁸ It is undoubtedly the case, for good or ill, that the two other countries have done much to mould Canadian evangelicalism.

Yet it has rightly been emphasized that Protestantism in Canada has gradually evolved a character of its own. John Moir and John Webster Grant have related the development of Canadian religion to the emerging national consciousness.⁹ George Rawlyk has pointed to the intensity of Christian experience cultivated by Henry Alline, his followers, and successors as a distinctive feature of religion in the Maritimes.¹⁰ Others have argued that theology in Canada was less speculative than in Britain or the United States, that evangelicalism in Ontario retained its cultural dominance longer than in the other two countries and that such features as indigenous institutions and a particular denominational balance have differentiated the Canadian movement from its equivalents elsewhere.[11] Evangelicalism in Canada has possessed characteristics that do make it unique. Nevertheless, features that might at first sight be labelled Canadian often turn out to be simply un-American. What marked off Canada from the United States was commonly shared with Britain. Although it is true that the prominence of Mennonites in late twentieth-century evangelicalism was unparalleled outside Canada, the significance of Anglicans and Brethren in the Canadian movement, which distinguished it from its American counterpart, was also a striking feature in Britain.[12] The weakness of fundamentalism and the late polarization of Protestantism between conservatives and liberals, both features of Canada as against the United States, were equally true of Britain.[13] Canadian evangelicalism was much more distinctive in a North American context than in a transatlantic comparison. So three related questions arise for consideration: How similar were the British and Canadian versions of evangelical Protestantism? How is the degree of affinity to be explained? And is it true that the British connection operated uniformly in favour of order and restraint?

The geophysical setting in which the movement functioned in the two countries was markedly different. The difficulties imposed by extremes of temperature and the immense terrain made heavy demands on Christian workers in Canada. During eighteen months in 1869–70, W. Carpenter Bompas, in charge of the Athabasca district and soon to be a bishop, travelled the enormous distance of 4,700 miles, chiefly by canoe or on foot, in the course of his duties.[14] As late as 1937 Bishop Taylor Smith, on a visit from Britain, was dismayed to discover that two clergy from the West had to travel more than a hundred miles each Sunday to take three services.[15] Yet, apart from limiting contact with ordained ministers, the huge extent of the country did have significant consequences. In Manitoba the two Presbyterian churches were forced to pool their resources in order to sustain a single college serving the scattered population even before the competing bodies merged in 1875. The environment of the West, it was explained at the time, allowed them to put aside their denominational rivalries "in advance of the churches in the mother-land and even in the go-ahead United States."[16] When, in 1924, the Presbyterians voted on the proposal for a United Church of Canada, whereas in Ontario only 62 per cent of congregations supported it, in the four western provinces the proportion was as high as 95 per cent.[17] The great open spaces made for ecclesiastical cooperation and eventual union. Geography modified the pattern of Canadian church life, creating contrasts with Britain.

So did the inhabitants of the land. The French-speaking communities, outside as well as inside Quebec, were a constant challenge to evangelicals because of their Roman Catholic allegiance. More successful were the missions to the aboriginal peoples. When, in 1879, the Anglicans founded Emmanuel College at Prince Albert, Saskatchewan, its languages curriculum included English, Latin, Greek, and Hebrew, as an Englishman might expect of a theological college, but also Sioux and Cree.[18] All these missions within the Canadian landmass helped keep sharp the evangelistic edge of the churches. There were also other consequences, particularly for the Church of England. The North-West was staffed largely by missionaries under the auspices of the evangelical Church Missionary Society (CMS). Hence as dioceses were gradually carved out of the wilderness, CMS men received the lion's share of preferment. The result was a hierarchy with a far stronger evangelical presence than in England. Cyril Bardsley, one of a tiny handful of evangelical bishops at home in the Church of England, was struck in 1937 that the procession at the Diamond Jubilee Service of the evangelical Wycliffe College in Toronto contained the primate and no fewer than fourteen Canadian bishops.[19] The Indian mission was also expensive. For mid-nineteenth-century Methodists, that consideration was a major factor inducing them to favour ecclesiastical links with Britain, then able to channel funds into the cause, rather than independence.[20] A Baptist writing in 1850 blamed the desire of emigrants to better themselves for their reluctance to contribute to church work: "In Canada generally," he remarked, "preaching must be cheap in order to be enjoyed."[21] A just reply had already been offered in 1825 by Thomas McCulloch, principal of the Presbyterian Pictou Academy, Nova Scotia: settlers had to travel far to buy goods, necessarily spent all their money on large stocks, and so had cash flow problems that prevented them from contributing much for the support of the gospel.[22] There was consequently a need for funds from elsewhere, and in the nineteenth century that normally meant Britain. It is clear that the straitened circumstances of many early settlers, together with the ethnic mix of the population, impinged on the character of evangelicalism in Canada.

If the land and the people moulded the movement in distinctive ways, there was nevertheless an underlying commonality between its members in Canada and Britain. They shared the basic qualities of evangelicals throughout the world. The atonement, as the Canadian Wesleyan Conference assured its British counterpart in 1861, was central to their faith: "We shall continue to preach peace through the blood of the everlasting covenant."[23] The favourite hymn of a female Indian convert at Asisippi in Saskatchewan on her deathbed began "Alas! and did my Saviour bleed / And did my Sovereign die?"[24] The proclamation of the cross was rooted in the message of the Bible, which evangelicals revered. The confidence in the power of scripture was expressed, for example, in the work of a Bible Women's Mission in Montreal between 1861 and 1874. Women sold copies of the Bible from door to door, reading passages in any house that would admit them.[25] The scriptures would lead their hearers to conversion, on which evangelicals insisted. "I tell 'em," declared Captain William Beaver, an Indian Methodist lay preacher, "they must all turn away from sin; that the Great Spirit will give 'em new eyes to see."[26] The quest for conversions induced an intense activism. One of the Montreal Bible women, for instance, paid 1,807 home visits in a mere eight months.[27] Similarly, the newly created Free Church of Scotland managed to establish some 150 mission stations between 1847 and 1850.[28] Each of the characteristics – emphases on the cross, the Bible, conversion, and activity – was in fact common to evangelicals on both sides of the Atlantic. The substance of the movement in Canada and Britain was identical.

Its development over time, furthermore, showed many parallels. Theological trends were broadly similar. At the opening of the nineteenth century nearly all evangelicals apart from Methodists and the eclectic New Lights of the Maritimes were Calvinists, albeit often very moderate ones. The Reformed tradition, however, as in Britain, steadily fell into decay. Robert Peden, for example, a minister of the Free Church of Scotland in Canada, adopted the Arminian ideas of the Scot James Morison and, like him, founded an Evangelical Union Church.[29] Holiness teaching, originally a Methodist distinctive, spread to other denominations, sometimes in the predominant British form propagated by the Keswick Convention.[30] The premillennialism that often became associated with the "higher life" holiness message was spread by the prophetic conferences at Niagara-on-the-Lake between 1882 and 1897.[31] While holiness and premillennialism pointed in a conservative direction, the growing acceptance of evolution and biblical criticism were contemporary liberal tendencies.[32] As in Britain, conservative and liberal figures co-existed in the same movement, even in the same institution, during the inter-war period. At Wycliffe College, the stoutly Protestant Dyson Hague who rejected the critical approach to the Old Testament was balanced by the broad-minded Benjamin Horan who understood scripture not as revelation but as the container of revelation.[33] All the movements of opinion were recognizable to British observers as expressions of the theological diversity they knew at home.

The prevailing attitudes of the Canadian movement were equally familiar. Anti-Catholicism, a potent force in the nineteenth century, loomed large among them. Although this stance had theological roots, it embraced a wide range of other social, political, and psychological dimensions.³⁴ Provoked by the strength of French-speaking Catholicism, it also was nourished by the large number of Protestants of Irish descent in Canada, especially among the Anglicans of Montreal and the diocese of Huron.³⁵ It enjoyed a long life. During the Second World War the Protestant Truth Society of Canada (affiliated with its equivalent in London) still claimed to distribute "dependable information on the diabolical strategy of Rome (political and religious) as she seeks to enslave individuals, communities and countries in her determination to dominate the whole world."³⁶ An offshoot of militant Protestantism, set up in 1869 to combat ritualism in the Anglican Church, was from 1873 called the Church Association, exactly like its English counterpart.³⁷ A wider body of evangelicals shared in sabbatarianism. In 1884 an English visitor discovered that the sabbath was kept as strictly in Toronto as in any other city he knew.³⁸ The temperance cause also made progress among evangelicals, leading in Toronto, for example, to the setting up in 1881 of a Coffee House Association modelled on English examples.³⁹ Temperance was one of the issues feeding into the social gospel, which, as in Britain, sprang largely from evangelical roots and contributed to the progressive political atmosphere of the Edwardian period.⁴⁰ All these views formed as much a part of Protestant culture in Canada as in Great Britain.

The remarkable similarity of the two national brands of evangelicalism can be explained in some measure by contacts made from the Canadian side. Quite a number of ministers originating in Canada served in Britain. The greatest Methodist theologian of the nineteenth century, W.B. Pope, was born in Nova Scotia and maintained links with his relations on Prince Edward Island during his English ministry.⁴¹ Donald Fraser, who served with distinction at the Free High Church in Inverness and afterwards at Marylebone Presbyterian Church in London, had grown up in Montreal.⁴² Bishop Ingham, who after responsibility for the diocese of Sierra Leone had become home secretary of the CMS, was a grandson of the first bishop of Huron and had attended school at Lennoxville, Quebec.⁴³ When, in 1946, the principal of Wycliffe College visited England, he managed to see as many as twenty-four of the institution's graduates, and he believed there were eleven more in the country.⁴⁴ The Methodists maintained a regular transatlantic exchange of personnel and official correspondence between their conferences, so that in many years between 1847 and the First World War, two or more Canadian ministers travelled to Britain.⁴⁵ Other evangelical leaders crossed the ocean to raise funds, to attract staff, or simply to enjoy an extended holiday.⁴⁶ Others, again, exerted an influence independent of visits to Britain. Oswald J. Smith, for instance, the twentieth-century pastor of Peoples Church, Toronto, was widely read by evangelicals across the Atlantic.[47] The Canadian input to the British movement was probably greater in the twentieth than in the nineteenth century. The greatest impact was undoubtedly made in 1994 with the Toronto Blessing, a brand of charismatic experience pioneered in the Vineyard Fellowship near the airport of that city. Gusts of laughter, varied by other uninhibited sounds and people falling to the floor, amazed the secular press and created a huge stir in the British evangelical world and beyond it.[48]

Canada did exert a formative role in British evangelicalism. There was, however, a much stronger flow of influence in the opposite direction. The tide of emigration regularly brought thousands of Christians over the Atlantic. Between 1815 and 1855 almost one million emigrants left Britain for British North America and although some moved on to the United States, most remained to practise whatever religion they had professed in the homeland.[49] By 1911 the General Assemblies of the United Free and Free Churches of Scotland were complaining that emigration was so large scale as to constitute a menace to the nation, the Free Church explaining that it imperilled the future of Protestantism.[50] When, seven years earlier, the evangelical dean of Peterborough toured Canada, he stayed with two of his former pupils from the CMS college, one of them now a bishop, and he just missed another who was also a bishop; he met a clergyman formerly in his Islington deanery who was spending the summer with his family in British Columbia; he visited Huron College, where the principal was the son of his old friend the former principal of St John's Hall, Highbury, in London; and his daughter called on the principal of Havergal College for Girls, Toronto, who was the sister of the bishop of Manchester.[51] Through such channels was evangelical influence from the motherland disseminated in the Anglican Church of Canada.

It was the same in other denominations. Over a hundred Baptists moved from Britain to pulpits or teaching positions in Canada during the nineteenth century.[52] All the professors at Knox College, Toronto, during the separate existence of the Free Church were born and educated in Scotland.[53] In the twentieth century the Anglicans actually secured a future archbishop of Canterbury as a teacher at Wycliffe College: Donald Coggan served from 1937 to 1944, his personal reserve being excused by his English origins.[54] The chief reason for the similarities between the expressions of evangelicalism in the two countries was the presence in the newer land of so many *emigrés* from the old one.

There were also supplementary reasons. Literature carried ideas westwards across the Atlantic. During the 1830s and 1840s more than half the material in *The Christian Messenger*, issued by Nova Scotia Baptists, came from Britain.[55] In 1864 the Eastern British America Methodist

Conference appealed for cheap editions of British Wesleyan works.[56] When in the early twentieth century the English Baptist minister F.B. Meyer visited western Canada, he was constantly greeted by people who had read his books.[57] The prestige enjoyed by things British was another factor. A desire to imitate the old country was responsible for the emergence of close reproductions of British models in Canada. Thus in 1864 the Canadian Methodist Conference reported the opening of the Wesleyan Female College, Hamilton, on the same principles as the Wesleyan College, Sheffield.[58] A similar motive led to the naming of places after spots rich in Christian associations in the homeland: thus a successful merchant in St Andrew's, New Brunswick, called the Presbyterian church he erected "Greenock" after his native town, and a CMS missionary renamed an Indian settlement in the Fort Alexander district Islington after the scene of the annual evangelical Anglican gatherings in that London suburb.[59] In part such gestures were merely sentimental; in part, however, they were an acknowledgment that Canadian religious ventures were heavily reliant on the power of the British purse. Canadian fellow-Christians, declared the Free Church of Scotland Colonial Committee in 1850, "are our children – a term which marks at once their weakness and dependence, and the love and care which they should receive at our hands."[60] But such a relationship could not outlast the steady growth of Canadian wealth and power over subsequent decades. The windows of Wycliffe College tell their own story: the earlier ones, installed in the early 1940s, represent events in the history of the English Bible; the later ones, put in subsequently, depict scenes from the church history of Canada.[61]

Even during the epoch of British ascendancy the degree of attention given to Canadian affairs was not constant. There were two periods when the prospects of the gospel in the new land particularly excited British Christians: the second quarter of the nineteenth century and the years immediately before the First World War. Both corresponded to times when the volume of emigration to Canada nearly equalled or even overtook the flow of people to the United States.[62] In the earliest years of British North America the influence of the metropolitan power was slight in ecclesiastical as in other ways. Of forty-four identified clergy in Upper Canada in 1812, only eight came from Britain.[63] In 1825, however, a Glasgow Colonial Society was established by evangelicals in the Church of Scotland to advance the faith in the Canadas and the Maritimes, sending out fifty active clergy over the next fifteen years.[64] For the Church of England, the CMS despatched its first missionary to the North-West in 1822, the second in 1825; and the Newfoundland School Society, launched in 1823 to provide instruction in accordance with the Bible, soon extended its operations to the mainland and united with the Colonial Church Society, whose interests had been primarily Australian, to form the Colonial Church and School Society in 1851.[65] British Wesleyan Methodism sustained a policy of control in British North America during these years, so that, for example, most of the superintendent ministers in New Brunswick came from England.[66] The Congregationalists and Baptists both commissioned deputations to the New World whose reports led to the creation of a Colonial Missionary Society (1836) for the Congregationalists[67] and a Baptist Canadian Missionary Society (1837) which widened into the Baptist Colonial Missionary Society two years later. "Is not," asked the Baptist delegates to the New World, "a colony our second country?"[68] An awakening sense of imperial responsibility produced an upsurge of support for Canadian church growth in the decades before mid-century.

After that point, however, Canada was relegated as a priority until, in the Edwardian period, the opening of the Prairies compelled attention to evangelistic opportunities in the West. Between 1900 and 1914 Canada was the single most important destination for British settlers.[69] What is more, central Europeans were also flocking in. "These newcomers," reported James Robertson, the superintendent of the Western Section of the Canadian Presbyterians' Home Mission, to the Free Church of Scotland, "differ from us not only in language, but in manners and customs, in ethical and religious views. The schoolmaster and missionary must do their perfect work if political, social, and religious troubles are to be escaped in the future ... Should not the parent churches help us to evangelize and assimilate them?" Already several Free Church and Church of Scotland congregations were contributing £50 a year towards this work.[70] From 1904 the Baptists launched a more elaborate scheme for namesake causes to be founded in the West with financial support from particular British churches. So a Ferme Park Church, a Regent's Park Church, a Westbourne Park Church and many other unfamiliar names studded the Prairies.[71] The Anglicans probably made the biggest effort. In 1906 G.E. Lloyd, later an energetic bishop, prodded the Colonial and Continental Church Society in England into backing a plan to raise the "Saskatchewan 60," five clergy and fifty-five catechists who would each be equipped for itinerant work with a ground sheet, two blankets, a porridge pot, a tea-billey, a pony, and a Mexican saddle. Three years later Lloyd persuaded the archbishops of Canterbury and York to issue their own appeal for the North-West.[72] In 1912 a party of clergy was commissioned by Archbishop Davidson in Westminster Abbey to be a Mission of Hope to western Canada, "a reminder in a newer land that the faith that had unified and enriched and blessed the centre would alone meet the needs of the circumference."[73] The crisis of the First World War, however, together with the subsequent economic malaise, quenched most of the British ardour for pioneering in the West. The CMS finally withdrew from Canada in 1921.[74] Although there were still to be outposts of British influence, most notably Regent College, Vancouver, in the late twentieth century, the Edwardian period was the last time when popular enthusiasm among British evangelicals helped shape the destiny of the Canadian movement.

What was the nature of the British impact? It is clear, first of all, that in the field of worship, the connection with Britain, as has so often been suggested, tended to shore up tradition and dignity. A Canadian Anglican associated with the Mission of Hope declared that "the Old Mother Church" stood for "a regular ministry, for a quiet, orderly form of worship, for a Prayer-Book service."[75] Bishop Ingham, a member of the Mission team, noticed with surprise that in Montreal Cathedral, which retained the evangelical shibboleths of the north-end position for the celebration of communion and not turning east for the creed, women sang in the choir wearing surplices and college caps. He commented darkly that they would "look better in the cap if their hair was under more restraint."[76] The English love of propriety was undoubtedly transplanted to Canadian soil. "I love the Church of England," remarked an aboriginal convert in the diocese of Saskatchewan in the early 1880s, "her services, her teaching, her Prayer Book."[77] Presbyterians from Scotland usually upheld a similar sense of decorum, deploring the "wild hubbub" of the camp and protracted meetings held by the Methodists. A Free Church minister witnessed one in 1845 when thirty people were praying together at the highest pitch of their voices. "I was forcibly reminded," he reported to Scotland, "of the text, 'God is not the author of confusion, but of peace.'"[78] But Methodists from Britain, where revivalism was stringently contained by the Wesleyan Conference, could be critical of camp meetings too. Morley Punshon, for example, feared that they might be "occasions of extravagance and mischief."[79] Likewise Frederick Bosworth, a Baptist originally from England, deplored in 1850 the "craving after excitement rather than instruction" among his Canadian co-religionists which produced "a style of preaching abounding in anecdotes and in harrowing appeals to the feelings, in a word, for sound rather than sense."[80] The influence which he had exerted as classical tutor in the Baptist college in Montreal (his asperity was no doubt a result of its recent closure) must have been heavily weighted in favour of a disciplined intellect. Although the greater proportion of the evidence illustrating British sympathies for restraint in religious services derives from the Anglicans and Presbyterians, some leading Methodists and Baptists shared the same inhibitions. In the field of public worship, the British factor tended to militate against free expression.

The British sense of possessing a civilizing mission had a parallel effect on the tone of evangelicalism in Canada. It was most evident in the attitude to the aboriginal peoples. An 1835 account of the CMS Red River Mission headlined the lamentable obstacles presented by the "Improvidence, Selfishness, and Obstinacy of the Native Character."[81] But settlers were also imagined to be, as Congregationalist visitors put it, "almost degenerating into a state of barbarism."[82] Early nineteenth-century evangelicals, like their forbears of the previous century, believed their task was to spread sound reason, good manners, and discriminating taste to the mass of the people.[83] They targeted remoter parts of Britain such as the Highlands of Scotland but also, especially from the years around 1830, the colonies. Apart from providing church buildings and effective ministers, they saw a particular need for schools for the children because of "the vast importance," as another Church of Scotland minister in Upper Canada put it in 1834, "of laying hold on and grappling with their minds ere they have passed the season of youth."[84] That is why the Anglican efforts for colonists began with schools.[85] As late as 1902 a Congregationalist agent of the Colonial Missionary Society in Newfoundland added to his normal duties a lesson in applied civilization – a set of lectures on hygiene, at which one appreciative hearer proudly announced that he always took a bath each year in June.[86]

The whole thrust of British policy was to promote the respectability that growing prosperity made possible. Punshon's most notable achievement in Canada was the erection of the grand and hugely expensive Metropolitan Methodist Church in Toronto.[87] Well into the twentieth century G.E. Lloyd created a Fellowship of the Maple Leaf to attract English public schoolboys to teach on the prairies.[88] The result of all these efforts was to temper evangelical religion with the ideals of good society. The British aim was to make not just Christians but gentlemen.

A particular dimension of the civilizing project was the advancement of theological education. At the first Presbyterian ordination on Canadian soil in 1770 the participants were apologetic about it sometimes being essential to approve a candidate "who had not a Liberal Education, or even the knowledge of the Latin tongue."[89] Their conception of a learned ministry made Presbyterians particularly preoccupied with theological instruction. Well-trained ministers, according to William Proudfoot, a United Secession pioneer in Upper Canada, in 1832, should "give a tone to the public mind and thus by the goodness of the article beat out of the field all half-bred adventurers." He may have had in mind the American Presbyterian Daniel Eastman whom he privately accused of ignoring "Grammar, taste, logic."[90] The Free Church followed the Church of Scotland in establishing a college in Upper Canada because, as a report to the latter body stated in 1866, it was desirable to train "a native ministry."[91] By that was meant ministers who were not educated in Scotland; but equally it indicated men who had not gone to college in the United States. For political as well as cultural reasons, a professional training across the border was suspect. Those who went south, furthermore, often never returned. It was with an eye to staunching the flow of candidates for the ministry into the United States that the Baptists created a college at Montreal in 1838 and the evangelical Anglicans one for the diocese of Huron in 1863.[92] For the Baptists, theological education was the area of greatest British involvement in Canadian denominational life.[93] For the Anglicans, the Colonial and Continental Church Society continued grants to one institution, Emmanuel College, Saskatoon, right down to 1954.[94] Often the staff of the colleges was drawn from the United Kingdom. If the theology was taught by men from the motherland, future ministers were being socialized directly into British attitudes. If theology, with financial help from Britain, was being taught at all, the moulders of Canadian evangelical life were imbibing the value of theory and reflection in religion as against experience and spontaneity.

The theology brought over the Atlantic, furthermore, often had a broadening effect. While remaining evangelical, it could be more progressive than received opinion in Canada or else more flexible than what emanated from the United States. This was not necessarily so: W.H. Griffith Thomas, for example, an Englishman who served at Wycliffe from 1910 to 1919, was a founding father of organized fundamentalism in North America.[95] Among the Baptists, however, perhaps the chief ongoing nineteenth-century theological debate in the Canadian denomination was between the traditional policy, largely retained in the United States, of closing communion to all but believers baptized by immersion and the stance which had come to prevail in England of opening the service to any Christians. Closed communion gained several victories in Canada in the mid-nineteenth century, but gradually the tide turned in favour of the more generous English position.[96] Among the Presbyterians, George Grant, principal of Queen's College, Kingston, from 1877 to 1902, exercised a moderating influence over the theology of his denomination. Grant's intellectual affinities were with Scotland, where he had been educated, rather than with more rigid orthodoxies propagated by the Princeton school in the United States, and through his recommendation of Scottish works younger Presbyterians learned to appreciate reverent criticism of the Bible.[97]

Two early twentieth-century controversies over biblical criticism illustrate the same tendency of the British connection to promote a more open version of evangelicalism. George Jackson, an English Methodist who acted as minister of Sherbourne Street Church, Toronto, from 1906 and professor of English Bible at Victoria University from 1909, provoked a furious debate in the Canadian denomination by frankly accepting the principle of higher criticism.[98] In 1925 Lawrence Marshall, a quiet scholarly Englishman who once missed a funeral he was supposed to conduct because he was browsing in a bookshop, found himself at the eye of a similar storm when he was appointed to the staff of the Baptist McMaster University. His denunciation as a modernist by T.T. Shields was the issue that precipitated a long-term schism among Canadian Baptists.[99] Neither man, in British terms, had stepped beyond acceptable limits of opinion in his evangelical denominations,[100] but each was considered too theologically advanced by substantial bodies of Canadians. The transatlantic influence, insofar as it was accepted, encouraged an accommodation between evangelical traditions and newer theological approaches. It was another way in which Britain was a force for moderation.

Yet despite all the evidence substantiating the claim that propriety and staidness were British ingredients in Canadian evangelicalism, there is another side to the issue. It was not only in the United States that religion was democratized around the start of the nineteenth century: Britain experienced the same dynamic impulse that swept obscure figures into prominent positions on a tidal wave of spiritual enthusiasm. Revival, associated with the disintegration of the religious establishments, unleashed a host of unlearned preachers who raised congregations and disturbed the authorities. Sects sprang up with strange heretical beliefs: Southcottians, Swedenborgians, and Freethinking Christians. Within the evangelical movement, there were groups such as the Peculiar People of Essex, founded by a farm labourer, who specialized in divine healing, and the Cokelers on the Surrey/Sussex border who regarded celibacy as the normal rule for Christians and so, in spite of their evangelism, tended to die out.[101] There were the Magic Methodists of Cheshire who held forest meetings where attenders would fall down "under the influence," remaining unconscious or seeing visions, and the exuberant Primitive Methodists whose camp meetings with all the paraphernalia usual in North America helped them grow rapidly into the second largest Methodist organization.[102] Although these enthusiastic bodies never supplanted the more sober denominations, their very existence points to the diversity of British evangelicalism. Even the more traditional churches contained effervescent elements. When the leading Canadian Methodist Egerton Ryerson visited England in 1833 he discovered in the Wesleyan services "no more decorum than in Canada, if as much."[103] The indecorous, the populist, and the religiously radical were to be found in Britain, and it is not surprising that they had an impact on Canada.

One of the chief exports from Britain was ecclesiastical fragmentation. Nearly all the denominations, whether traditional ones or the new populist groups, wished to be represented in British territory abroad. When in 1786 the Burgher Secessionist Presbyterian ministers, only three in number, created a presbytery in Nova Scotia, the Anti-Burgher Secessionist Presbyterian minister of Pictou refused to join. By 1815 the Burghers and Anti-Burghers in the province agreed to unite, but the merger was delayed for two years by new arrivals from Scotland who saw no reason to abandon their distinctive principles in the New World.[104] The recondite issue dividing them was whether or not a new freeman of a Scottish burgh should be allowed to take an oath to uphold the interests of the established Church of Scotland. By 1825 the united body, with some reason, declared that it did not "deem it requisite to perpetuate in the distant land in which it was planted, the accidental divisions of the mother country."[105] Nevertheless the representatives of the Church of Scotland, ignoring this protest, sent over from that year onwards a separate body of ministers, who, when in 1843 their church broke up in Scotland, duly had their own Disruption in Canada.[106] Methodism experienced similar institutional divisions so that during the 1840s there were six separate jurisdictions in Canada West alone.[107] A preference for reunion gathered pace more rapidly in Canada than in Britain, with the various branches of Presbyterianism and Methodism merging roughly half a century before their British equivalents. Observers in the homeland normally applauded the resulting Canadian freedom from "needless rivalries,"[108] but there is no doubt that most of the divisions had been British inventions in the first place. In this respect Britain was a source of disorder in the evangelical world.

It would be a mistake, furthermore, to underrate the religious vigour of the immigrants from Britain. Breadalbane Baptist Church in Glengarry County, Upper Canada, for instance, founded by Gaelic-speaking settlers from Perthshire in 1817, immediately set about evangelistic work, and more than doubled its membership to thirty by the following year. Its members were so keen on controversial theology that the church divided between 1821 and 1826 into two parties, one Calvinist, the other Arminian.[109] It seems to have been rare for ministers to initiate emigration,[110] but – a sign of the depth of their convictions – it was quite common for parties of settlers to invite a minister to join them once they had emigrated. This practice was easier among Dissenters, whose pastors had no manse and few prospects to tie them to their native land. So a significant number of zealous itinerant preachers, some of them founding fathers of the Congregationalist and Baptist movements in the Scottish Highlands, followed sections of their flocks to Canada.[111] The revivalistic enthusiasm of the Congregationalists from this source contrasted with the sobriety of their Yankee co-religionists arriving in Upper Canada, who tended to be absorbed into Presbyterianism.[112] Some of the Presbyterians themselves, however, especially those from the Highlands, could transplant to the New World an intense spirit of devotion. Emigrants from Ross and Sutherland who had settled around London, Canada West, held in 1845 an elaborate communion season, including a preliminary day for "solemn humiliation," a Friday experience meeting, and Saturday prayer meetings early and late together with a preparatory meeting in between, culminating in parallel sabbath communions in English and Gaelic and followed by Sunday and Monday evening services.[113]

Such searching occasions, which continued into the 1870s, could easily turn into local awakenings.[114] In the 1880s it was two newly settled recent converts from England rather than any official plan that launched the Salvation Army's first campaign in Canada. They appeared in Victoria Park, Toronto, wearing uniforms similar to those of English policemen with the addition, on their helmets, of the motto "Prepare to meet thy God!"[115] Immigrants of successive generations, bringing their deeply felt experience across the Atlantic, contributed some of the populism to Canadian religion.

Over and above the ordinary emigrants were the Christian pioneers who travelled to Canada with the specific object of spreading their version of the faith. They were few in number but made a disproportionate impact. Some became known for their polemics. In this category falls Clark Bentom, sent by the predominantly Congregationalist London Missionary Society to Quebec City in 1800. He argued vituperatively with the Catholic hierarchy about the right to perform baptisms and marriages and subsequently with the government, the result being a trial for libel, a short imprisonment, and an early return to England in 1805.[116] Over a century later, as Ian Rennie has recently pointed out, the early fundamentalist leaders of Canada, including T.T. Shields of Toronto, were mostly British in background.[117] Even in the middle years of the twentieth century there were still vibrant religious entrepreneurs coming from Britain. The smallest of the three British Pentecostal denominations, the Apostolic Church which believed in the perpetuity of the offices mentioned in the New Testament, despatched several pastors, prophets, and apostles, many of them Welsh, to preach the baptism in the Holy Spirit and the Apostolic Vision.[118] Canada long seemed a pristine mission field to some of the most ebullient British evangelical groups.

Their work was supplemented by visitors from Britain on the more radical wing of evangelicalism. Brief trips were rare in the early nineteenth century when the voyage was long and uncomfortable, but numbers increased later on as transport became much easier. Thus John Nelson Darby, the supreme British teacher of the more extreme party among the Brethren in England, travelled annually to speak at Guelph between 1862 and 1877, thereby injecting dispensationalism into the North American bloodstream.[119] The Scottish Brethren evangelist Alexander Marshall, after pioneering work in Canada during the 1880s, subsequently made a series of shorter visits and crossed the Atlantic altogether thirty-six times. His impact can be gauged by memories that he and his colleagues were met with cries of "Heresy! heresy!" and accused of being "breakers up of churches" and "sowers of division."[120] When the London undenominational evangelist Henry Varley took a mission at Brantford, Ontario, in 1875, crowds flocked to his meetings even though it was winter; enquirers were helped until after 2 A.M., drinking bars and billiard saloons were emptied, and 1,000 of the 12,000 inhabitants were said to have made a decision for Christ.[121] F.B. Meyer, conveying the message of the imminent second advent in the 1920s, found that there was less expectation of the Lord's coming in Canada than in Britain.[122] Once again, therefore, a British speaker was a stirrer of the waters. Even a bishop could play the same role. John Taylor Smith, a former evangelical bishop of Sierra Leone and subsequently chaplain-general to the forces, had a regiment paraded to hear him in St Paul's, Toronto, in 1935. "I thought we were going to hear something patriotic," remarked a soldier afterwards; "instead of that he gave us that old Methodist camp meeting stuff." Taylor Smith, who was famous for his directness, had told them they must be born again.[123] Thus strong-minded visitors from Britain often stiffened the backbone of Canadian evangelicalism. They were another medium through which British influence constituted a stimulant rather than an emollient.

What are the conclusions that may be drawn about the relationship of Canadian and British evangelicalism? A comparison, first of all, yields a high degree of similarity. There were contrasts arising from the land and its inhabitants, but the two movements were identical in essence and parallel in their evolution. The explanation for this strong affinity lies in the two-way process of personal and literary contacts and supremely in the impact of immigration. The input from the British side was greater, particularly at certain times, though by 1994 the Canadian influence was in the ascendant. Britain contributed, as has been pointed out, a preference for disciplined worship, civilized values, professional education, and broader theology. The British legacy, however, was by no means uniform. Britain also exported ecclesiastical fragmentation and, through emigrants, Christian pioneers, and visiting speakers, a great deal of the evangelical dynamic that is usually attributed exclusively to the United States. George Rawlyk has drawn attention to the radicalism of many evangelicals in British North America during the years following the American Revolution.[124] It deserves to be added that Britain subsequently played a part in sustaining enthusiasm, innovation, and extremism in the Canadian evangelical community. While decorum, restraint, and moderation were admittedly more characteristic contributions of the motherland, Britain also shared with the United States a religious populism that inevitably spilled over into her colonies. The energy of the common people was the motor of the evangelical movement across the whole English-speaking world. Hence it is a mistake to suppose that the United States was the single source of the livelier qualities of Canadian evangelicalism. The effects of the transatlantic connection did not always conflict with influences coming from south of the border. The British factor differed from the American not in its totality but in its balance. There was more of the customary in the religion of the Old World, but the effervescent was by no means entirely absent. Canadian evangelicalism readily absorbed the mixture of the traditional and the novel that the British movement fostered. "Oceans," the Methodist North American specialist Thomas Coke once remarked, "are nothing to God."[125]

4 "Who Whom?": Evangelicalism and Canadian Society

JOHN G. STACKHOUSE, JR

Vladimir Ilych Lenin was not, to my knowledge, either a Canadian or an evangelical. He did, however, tersely put the question to which I am attempting to respond. "Who whom?" Lenin once asked: *Who* in society shall be the subject of the sentence, *who* shall be the agent of influence, acting upon *whom* as object?[1] The matter compels me to ask both about the influence of evangelicals upon Canadian society and about the influence of that society upon evangelicals.

The inquiry and response to this pair of questions will propose research programs rather than provide authoritative answers. Scholarship on late nineteenth and twentieth century evangelicalism has progressed enough to offer promising clues and suggest intriguing lines for further investigation, but it has raised many more issues than it has settled. Several troubling matters of historical methodology need resolution before this research can be advanced successfully.

Incumbent upon everyone who discusses evangelicals and evangelicalism is the vexed assignment of defining just who and what it is that is under discussion.[2] For our present purposes, evangelicals are those Christian *groups* that trace their heritage back to the North Atlantic revivals of the eighteenth century and who have not since departed from the affirmations characteristic of these revivals. Or they are groups that since that time have formed links of fellowship with the original evangelical groups and have taken on those distinctive affirmations. Second, evangelicals are those Christian *individuals* who, regardless of their ecclesiastical affiliation, affirm those distinctive evangelical commitments.

What are these distinctive evangelical commitments? I understand them to be four-fold. First, evangelicals affirm the good news (the *evangel*) of God's salvation in Jesus Christ, both accomplished and symbolized primarily in his Cross and resurrection. Second, evangelicals believe this good news is expressed most authoritatively in the Bible. Thus evangelicals trust the Bible as their pre-eminent source for and ultimate standard of all God's revelation, and they emphasize it in preaching, small-group study, and individual devotional practice. Third, evangelicals understand this good news to require personal transformation. This transformation involves both a mystical and an ethical dimension. The faith must be experienced as a personal relationship with Jesus Christ and must be manifested in a disciplined life of increasing holiness.[3] Fourth, evangelicals are evangelists, people active in proclaiming this good news. To be sure, only a small minority are called as full-time evangelists. But Christian mission for evangelicals, while it has included a wide range of benevolent work in the world, typically has placed priority upon evangelism, and every evangelical believes it is his or her responsibility and privilege to introduce others to the gospel.

This definition can serve the present project in two ways. First, it can help us determine who are the evangelicals in Canadian society. It can help us avoid making mistakes such as assuming all Methodists or Baptists are evangelicals since, while the Methodist and Baptist traditions are obviously rooted in the eighteenth-century revivals, some Methodists and Baptists later departed from evangelical emphases. It can likewise keep us from believing the stereotype that evangelicalism is entirely restricted to small, sectarian groups when many Anglicans, Methodists, Presbyterians, and (after 1925) United Church people have been evangelicals. Second, it can help us answer our guiding question of influence as we explore whether, on the one hand, such Christians have been influenced by Canadian society, and whether, on the other hand, they have successfully impressed Christian convictions upon that society.

CANADIAN SOCIETY INFLUENCING EVANGELICALS

At the time of Confederation, anglophone Canadian society in both the Maritimes and Ontario seemed powerfully influenced by evangelical concerns. Since that time, however, and with accelerating speed in the latter half of the twentieth century, Canadian society has been less and less influenced by evangelicalism. In turn, though, Canadian society has influenced evangelicals in a number of ways.

To some extent the very victories in the social agenda of many nineteenth-century evangelicals – some of which were not realized until the early-twentieth – tempted them into social complacency.[4] While some heirs of the evangelical tradition grew increasingly concerned about the changing nature of Canadian society and so became active in the social gospel movement, the majority of evangelicals remained generally acquiescent through the first half of the twentieth century.[5] The continuing crusades for prohibition and sabbath observance are the most conspicuous exceptions to this rule. And occasionally a crisis provoked a reaction, as in the Canadian Protestant League led by Baptist fundamentalist T.T. Shields. The league involved a number of notable evangelicals (including Sudan Interior Mission founder R.V. Bingham) in its militant resistance to governmental support of Roman Catholics especially during the Second World War.[6]

In the tell-tale field of higher education, however, evangelicals tended either to ignore secular institutions or to complement them. The internationally recognized Prairie Bible Institute was typical of the dozens of Bible schools that sprang up in the 1920s and subsequent decades to educate pastors and lay people for Christian service. Such schools were alternatives to the secular universities that increasingly came to dominate higher education in Canada. But they were not simply reactionary alternatives, not Christian universities *per se*. Instead, they offered a different sort of education aimed at different goals: to produce pastors, missionaries, and trained lay people for denominations and independent churches that did not have seminaries or other means of higher education for such vocations.[7]

Furthermore, Bruce Guenther has shown that at least in the case of some prairie Mennonites, Bible schools could come into being to compensate for the refusal of provincial governments to allow Mennonites to form their own elementary and secondary schools. In this unusual sense, these Anabaptists, many of whom (notably the Mennonite Brethren and Evangelical Mennonite Conference) would increasingly identify with the transdenominational evangelical mainstream, were influenced by societal developments.[8]

Toronto Bible College (later Ontario Bible College) represents a different stance *vis-à-vis* Canadian society. It explicitly complemented the universities and denominational divinity colleges as it marked out its calling as a training centre for lay church workers. Indeed, Toronto Bible College prided itself on the university and divinity college training of its own faculty: no disjunction between society and evangelicalism was apparent.

If one briefly follows out the case of higher education into the second half of the century, striking changes become evident. The Bible schools which had happily worked outside the mainstream of Canadian education began to increase their formal educational standards for both faculty and students, and many schools sought closer ties and especially transfer-of-credit arrangements with the public universities.[9] For its part, Toronto Bible College reflected disenchantment with the mainline denominations among its constituency as it began to compete directly with the mainline divinity colleges. By the 1950s it was offering pastoral studies at the undergraduate level, and in 1976 it founded Ontario Theological Seminary, which soon became one of the largest seminaries in Canada. Other evangelicals began Christian universities, notably The King's University College in Edmonton, Redeemer College in Ancaster, Ontario, and the largest of the three, Trinity Western University in Langley, British Columbia.[10]

Dating back at least to the mid-1900s, evangelicals have been frustrated by many governments in the field of education. Ontario in particular has been a battleground at every level. The Christian Reformed denomination, a member of the Evangelical Fellowship of Canada, gave birth to two post-secondary institutions: the undergraduate Redeemer College in Ancaster and the postgraduate Institute for Christian Studies in Toronto. Upon perusing the academic qualifications of the faculty of both schools and the programs they offer, it is not readily apparent why such institutions have been stonewalled by government after government as they have sought a charter to offer the mainstream academic degrees of B.A., M.A., and Ph.D. Yet both schools have instead suffered on the margins of polite academic company with their alternative degrees.[11]

At the primary and secondary levels, evangelicals of various stripes, from fundamentalists through Pentecostals to Christian Reformed, increasingly have sought government assistance to run their versions of Christian schools. Appeals for such support on the basis of long-standing government funding of Roman Catholic schools and the obvious and increasingly official secularizing of what was once a Protestant public school system have met with little success. Similar campaigns have been launched in the 1980s and 1990s across the country. (Ironically, the unique arrangement in Newfoundland, in which certain denominations – including evangelical groups like the Pentecostals and Salvation Army – have run public school systems, is coming under sweeping review at the same time.) This key area of education, in which the circles of family, society, and values intersect, shows that evangelicals are responding to changes in Canadian culture that they find deeply troubling.

A growing number and variety of evangelical institutions have sprung up since the 1960s to reflect increasing evangelical unease over broader social changes in Canada. American sociologist Robert Wuthnow has suggested that the expanded reach of the United States government into the lives of its citizens has provoked a proliferation of such groups in that country.[12] Doubtless this is true in Canada as well. In an ironic twist on that thesis, however, evangelicals in Canada have organized partly because their governments also, as Pierre Trudeau would have it, have removed themselves from the bedrooms of the nation and accepted a variety of moral behaviours that evangelicals have wished they would not accept.

The Evangelical Fellowship of Canada has been the best known of these organizations since the mid-1980s, and its publications and briefs to provincial and federal governments all have made clear that evangelicals have been unhappy with many aspects of Canadian life, from decreasing Lord's Day observance to increasing rates of abortion.[13] The Citizens for Public Justice has joined in the public debate from its base among the Christian Reformed and has commented on a wide range of issues, from aboriginal land-claims to pornography.[14] The well-funded American organization Focus on the Family opened a Canadian office in the 1980s and has quickly established itself as an important voice for certain conservative evangelical interests. And in the mid-1990s, plans are being laid for an independent Christian think-tank in Ottawa, the Centre for Renewal of Public Policy, to be supported by evangelicals as well as other Christians, that would address a full range of public policy issues.[15]

Pro-life crisis pregnancy centres, food banks, and Christian counselling services also have supplemented more traditional evangelical social agencies like youth groups, Bible societies, and rescue missions as evangelicals increasingly respond to the range of needs that are not adequately – or, in evangelical eyes, properly – addressed by governments or other groups in society. As federal, provincial, and municipal governments across the country face massive debts and deficits, it seems likely that evangelicals will have to do still more to further their concerns and provide their distinctive forms of help to their fellow Canadians.

In both what Canadian society has done and has not done, therefore, evangelicalism has been affected. Evangelical commitments to Christ, the Bible, personal discipleship, and evangelism have not been compromised. But the emphasis upon evangelism in mission has been complemented by a broadening understanding of Christian vocation that, toward the end of the twentieth century, has recaptured something of the passionate nineteenth-century evangelical commitment to social action at various levels. Indeed, as Canadian society has become less and less importantly Christian, evangelicals have been provoked to rouse themselves to meet needs they previously had comfortably left in the hands of others.

EVANGELICALS INFLUENCING CANADIAN SOCIETY

Much more can and ought to be explored regarding the influence of Canadian society upon evangelicals since Confederation. What about particular pieces of legislation – like the revision of the Criminal Code in the 1960s or the federal policy of multiculturalism?[16] What about the cultural, political, and economic realignment of Canada with the United States after World War II? What about the rise of the status of women?[17] What about new technologies like the automobile, telephone, computer, and especially television?

A quite different question, however, is that pertaining to the opposite vector. Have evangelicals influenced Canadian society? We might begin with the category of religion itself. It appears that evangelicalism has not in fact significantly influenced other forms of Canadian religion. Roman Catholicism, long dominant in English- as well as French-speaking Canada, went through its own considerable internal changes, most obviously in its responses to the Second Vatican Council (1962–65) and the Quiet Revolution in Quebec during the same decade. But it is difficult to discern any "evangelicalizing" of Roman Catholics. To be sure, some greater interest in the Bible and in personal piety did become evident especially in the later 1960s and 1970s, but this was more obviously the result of two factors: the freedom opened up by Vatican II and the influence of the charismatic movement. It is true that the charismatic movement originated among Protestants in the previous couple of decades, but standard accounts attribute this to *American* Protestants like Oral Roberts and the Full Gospel Business Men's Fellowship.[18] Canadian evangelicals could claim little credit for the coincident interests of charismatic Catholics.[19]

The same could be said of Anglicanism. Evangelicalism historically had been represented in the Canadian church from colonial times, albeit as the party of a minority. Evangelicalism seemed to wax and wane in the twentieth century, with a recent flare-up of interest in the 1990s around the "Essentials Declaration" coming out of a national conference in Montreal in 1994.[20] Some dioceses, notably in Montreal, have been deeply influenced by evangelicalism, but most have been dominated by other kinds of Anglicans, and the evangelical wing has remained simply that. Perhaps most conspicuously, the so-called international Decade of Evangelism beginning in 1988, dear to the hearts of evangelicals, already looked moribund in Canada by 1995.

The United Church of Canada was founded in 1925 out of a welter of various (and not all harmonious) concerns. Many, like early moderator George Pidgeon, hoped such ecumenism would foster evangelicalism.

As the decades passed, however, the United Church tilted decidedly away from its evangelical heritage. It has had almost nothing to do with trans-denominational evangelicalism since the 1960s, a fact symbolized in the virtual absence of United Church people in the Evangelical Fellowship of Canada. By the later 1980s the United Church had scandalized evangelicals within and without its ranks by allowing sexually active homosexuals to be not only members in good standing but ordained to the pastorate.

For their part, both large denominations of Canadian Lutherans (the Evangelical Lutheran Church in Canada and the Lutheran Church – Canada) have remained remarkably isolated in their own styles and communities. There has been very little influence of Canadian evangelicalism upon these churches: indeed, there has been very little contact between any sort of evangelical (as we are defining the term) and these churches that saw themselves as maintaining the tradition of the "original" sixteenth-century "evangelicals."[21]

Thus, unlike the pattern in the nineteenth century as traced by historians such as John Webster Grant, Michael Gauvreau, and William Westfall, evangelicalism – even of the very broad sort described in these accounts – scarcely set the pace for Protestantism in Canada in the twentieth.[22] In the last quarter of the century, sociologists like Reginald Bibby and pollsters like the Angus Reid Group have shown that evangelicalism is a vital movement compared to the nominally large but rather anemic Roman Catholic, United, and Anglican denominations. But it is still the faith of a relatively small minority and has made very little impact on the religion of most Canadians.[23]

Bob Burkinshaw has pointed, however, to the work of evangelicals among youth as perhaps having more influence on other Christians than is readily apparent if one looks only at denominations and congregations.[24] It is clear that evangelicals have for at least two decades now had the most active organizations for young people – from summer Bible clubs and camps to winter organizations like Awana and Pioneer Clubs, and from congregational youth meetings to parachurch organizations like Campus Crusade for Christ, InterVarsity Christian Fellowship, the Navigators, and Youth for Christ. No one has yet attempted to measure the influence of all of these upon non-evangelicals in Canada. Furthermore, the effects on non-evangelicals of both religious broadcasting and the rapidly growing field of so-called contemporary Christian music – both of which are heavily dominated by evangelical views – have yet to be considered.

As we leave religion *per se* to turn to society at large, questions of historical method come to the fore. Where shall we look, what sources shall we interrogate, what criteria shall we use to determine the influence of evangelicalism on Canadian society, in the past and now? Three avenues seem to commend themselves.

First, we could ask the experts. *Beaver* magazine, a publication of the Hudson's Bay Company that offers Canadian history at a popular pitch, recently celebrated its seventy-fifth anniversary. To do so, it asked a handful of eminent Canadian historians to discuss that period under the following heads: politics, business, warfare, women, and society and culture. Religion was not important enough to deserve one of those heads. And only J.M. Bumsted gave religion any sustained attention.[25] Evangelicalism thus appeared briefly in this magazine's digest of recent Canadian history and only in social forms, like temperance societies, or in the persons of missionaries to Canadian Indians and Inuit, or in "fundamentalist Protestant sects."[26]

Recent standard histories of Canada reflect the same small-to-invisible stature of evangelicalism. In *The Illustrated History of Canada*, for instance, there is virtually no mention of religion in the twentieth century beyond temperance societies and the founding of the United Church. Bumsted's own two-volume history of *The Peoples of Canada* deals with religion *en passant* in its first volume that stops at Confederation, but the larger second volume deals with religion hardly at all, and evangelicalism simply does not appear.[27] The two-volume collaborative work of Robert Bothwell, Ian Drummond, and John English deals more regularly with religion in its treatment of twentieth-century Canadian history.[28] Even at that, though, it significantly tells the same tale as the other accounts: the Christian religion, and particularly Roman Catholicism and evangelical Protestantism, was strong at the turn of the century and remained so through World War I. Decline of cultural authority began after World War II and especially after the 1960s. The evangelical "sects" (as they are customarily called in such treatments) then began to flourish especially relative to "the big old denominations – Protestant, Anglican, Roman – all of which were stumbling erratically, and most of which had become far too polite to proselytize."[29] Whatever vigour such evangelicals enjoyed, however, was limited to the sphere of private life and popular culture – the sphere of sports and entertainment, hobbies and recreation, and other publicly unimportant diversions. When it came to politics and economics and high culture, it was assumed that evangelicalism either was unimportant or, in the case of Victorian hold-overs like prohibition, Lord's Day laws, and religious observances in public schools, it steadily lost ground.

What makes these historical treatments the more remarkable is that at least two of the historians involved, Bumsted and Ramsay Cook (who wrote the essay on Canada 1900–1945 for the *Illustrated History*), have themselves published monographs on Canadian religion –

indeed, on aspects of Canadian evangelicalism.[30] Other authors might well be disposed to ignore or deprecate evangelicalism.[31] Yet the very small presence of evangelicalism across the board here cannot be attributed solely to authorial prejudice.

Even a cursory reading of such survey texts shows, furthermore, how indebted these synthetic historians are to the analytical writers of monographs and articles. If Richard Allen will write a respectable book about the social gospel, the social gospel will appear in textbooks. If Ramsay Cook will write a respectable book about late Victorian Christian activism, "regenerators" will show up in at least some later narratives – if not his own![32] The perennial challenge and opportunity for historians of evangelicalism remains, therefore, to write the studies upon which later textbook authors can rely. The question is still open, at least at this level of consideration: do the textbooks say little about twentieth-century evangelicalism because evangelicalism was not important or simply because no one has yet delineated its importance?

A second way to determine the influence of evangelicalism upon Canadian society might be (to put the matter bluntly) to count noses. Are there lots of evangelicals in Canada, even a preponderance of them? A number of historians – if not from A to Z, then at least from (Phyllis) Airhart to (William) Westfall – have argued that in the early national period at least until the turn of the century the major Protestant denominations were generally evangelical – even the Church of England in Canada was strongly influenced by evangelicalism.[33] If this was so, then the allegiance of over half the population to the Methodist, Presbyterian, Anglican, or Baptist traditions as late as 1901 would indicate the presence of a large number of evangelicals in Canadian society.

However, no historian argues that the mainline Canadian denominations today are generally evangelical, or that they have been at least since the Second World War. Furthermore, as Reginald Bibby has shown, whatever Canadians' nominal allegiances may be, traditional Christian practices like church attendance have fallen increasingly to the wayside. This is true even among those he calls "Conservative Protestants," among whom less than half now attend church weekly.[34] The most generous estimates of evangelicals, those offered by the Angus Reid/George Rawlyk study, still placed evangelicals at only 15 per cent of the present Canadian population.[35]

To focus particularly upon certain key sectors of the Canadian population means to find no count at all, or few, of evangelicals. The sweeping generalization may well be true that at the turn of the century "all politicians professed faith" and that faith was almost invariably Christian of some variety.[36] But most Canadian politicians have been reticent about their religious commitments, and no scholar, to my knowledge, has ever attempted a detailed religious profile of even the federal Parliament through the years, let alone of provincial legislatures and municipal governments.

Certainly there have been notable politicians whose evangelical commitments were publicly known. Whatever one makes of the eccentric William Aberhart, for instance, his successor as premier of Alberta, Ernest Manning, enjoyed the esteem of evangelicals throughout his life, and Manning's son Preston is widely recognized as a professing evangelical. Sometime Social Credit national leader Robert Thompson wielded considerable influence both in federal politics in the Diefenbaker and Pearson years and in the evangelical subculture. British Columbia provincial cabinet minister "Flying Phil" Gagliardi was also an ordained minister of the church.[37] And the caucus of Brian Mulroney's Progressive Conservative federal government contained a number of identifiable evangelicals. Such instances could be multiplied here and there, but these particular biographies have yet to be researched thoroughly and assembled into a helpful composite portrait.

Turning to broader cultural affairs, one would like to know how many of Canada's leading writers have been evangelicals. How many Governor-General's award-winners, for instance? How many Nobel and Killam prize-winning scholars have been evangelicals? How many evangelicals have been named to the Order of Canada? How many Juno or Genie awards have been given to evangelicals?

Whatever the answer, a crucial question yet remains. It may be that this premier or that mayor, this scientist or that author, this industry leader or that entertainer professed and practised evangelical Christianity. Yet for evangelicalism to have had actual influence on Canadian society rather than simply presence in it, these evangelicals would have had to do their work demonstrably according to evangelical convictions. Their contribution to Canadian society at least would have had to be congruent with evangelical concerns and at times, one would hope, would have actually furthered those interests. Two forces, one internal to evangelicalism and one external, have militated against such self-consciously Christian work. First, evangelicals – who characteristically have been crystal-clear about the calling of evangelism – have often manifested both ambivalence and confusion regarding cultural involvement: ought evangelicals to pursue cultural leadership and, if so, how? Second, modernization's privatizing influence upon all traditional religion encourages traditional believers like evangelicals to keep religious convictions separate from public activity. Thus it may be that people who have undoubtedly been evangelicals in their private religious commitments have occupied positions of cultural influence but yet have not significantly influenced the culture along evangelical lines.

The third method of deciding about evangelical influence upon Canadian society would be to take the four-fold definition of evangelical convictions and examine how evident those convictions have been.[38] Has Canadian society been marked, first, by belief in and dependence upon the saving work of God in Christ? Are the Cross and resurrection of Jesus important, recurring symbols in our political life, in our literature, in our education?

The Cross continues to be important in Roman Catholic schools, while explicitly Christian symbolism of all sorts has been vanishing from public schools across Canada especially since the 1970s. In public the Cross is remarkable nowadays only as a vapid fashion motif.[39] Easter is still observed as a public holiday in Canada, but the main public symbols are of fertility: Easter eggs, rabbits, and the like. The pagan gods of spring have triumphed with the help of the gods of commerce. The very concept of "resurrection" probably is less well understood, let alone believed in, than reincarnation, with one-quarter of Canadians telling pollsters that they believe in the latter view of human destiny.[40] Jesus himself continues to appear occasionally in Canadian culture, particularly as a sort of "Jesus of Montreal" who haunts post–Quiet Revolution Quebec. And most Canadians continue the national tradition of saying that they believe that Jesus is the Son of God. But Canadian life generally continues without discernible influence from the Cross and resurrection, these two powerful symbols of sin and judgment and forgiveness and new life.

To speak of the second evangelical conviction regarding the authority of Scripture, it seems difficult to imagine a federal politician literally reading from the Bible in, say, a constitutional discussion. But this very thing occurred at the time of Confederation itself, as the name and motto of the new country, "The Dominion of Canada – *a mari usque ad mare* (from sea to sea)," was derived from Psalm 72:8: "He shall have dominion from sea to sea." Other Canadian politicians have from time to time and for whatever motives invoked Christian themes or vocabulary. Even Pierre Trudeau, not normally regarded as an evangelical Christian, supported the opening reference to God in the new Canadian Constitution of 1982. Biblical cadences and categories, though, have not been prominent in Canadian politics in any era. This absence deserves investigation. Today, in an officially multicultural Canada, it is understandable why individual evangelical politicians seem to take pains to avoid explicitly biblical language and logic. They must represent various constituents, they must speak in a pluralistic public conversation, and they must avoid being stereotyped as narrow-minded Christian bigots. But other explanations must be considered if it is true – as seems evidently to be the case – that Canadian political discourse *in general* of fifty or one hundred years ago also was mostly devoid of explicitly biblical themes. Were Christian convictions simply assumed to be held by the majority and so did not require explicit reference? Or was Canadian political life, even in the midst of Gauvreau's "evangelical century," separated off significantly from biblical concerns and categories, to the point that its guiding principles were secular, not sacred? And were evangelicals complicit – however unconsciously – in this compartmentalization?[41]

Canadian literature continues to include biblical motifs. The works of Robertson Davies, Margaret Atwood, and Margaret Laurence particularly come to mind. Again, however, these references are mostly allusions to the past and particularly to a lost faith and a lost world shaped by that faith. (Governor-General's award-winning poet Margaret Avison is a conspicuous counter-example in her lively evangelicalism.) In the field of popular music, Bruce Cockburn and Susan Aglukark are well recognized both for their individual talents and for the Christian content of their compositions, but they are exceptional in both respects.

Holy living, third, seems to have been something of which a Canadian could speak in public without irony until mid-century. Much of the prohibition debate, for example, turned on questions of Christian virtue as much as it did on health, public safety, and commercial interests. Many of Canada's colleges sought to foster Christian piety until well into the twentieth century.[42] Popular novelist C.W. Gordon commended Christian ideals to a wide reading public under the *nom de plume* Ralph Connor. It has been some time, however, since anyone outside church circles has taken such language seriously. Even the public debates over pornography and gambling centre on social and individual costs and benefits rather than explicitly Christian virtues. Today's most popular Canadian Christian novelist, Janette Oke, sells many books in both Canada and the United States via Christian retailers but is virtually unknown to the Canadian public at large. Canada has come so far, in fact, that when Christians across the country recently suggested abstinence as a serious policy to counteract teenage pregnancy and sexually transmitted disease, the proposal was widely judged to be utterly radical, even implausible.[43]

The fourth evangelical concern, for evangelism, seems diametrically contrary to the express policy of multiculturalism by which Canada has defined itself in the last two decades. Canada's remarkable heritage of sacrificially supporting Christian missions both at home and abroad has been undercut by the more recent pluralism of multicultural tolerance, a trend that powerfully exacerbates doubts about the ethics of proselytizing that reach back, actually, to earlier decades in this century.[44] Making converts nowadays, it seems, is perfectly appropriate for causes as diverse as anti-smoking, feminism, and, especially, the new orthodoxy of environmentalism, but it is un-Canadian to attempt to persuade another Canadian of the superior virtues of one's religious faith.

If we ask, then, whether English-speaking Canada has been deeply impressed by the four generic evangelical convictions, the answer begins with a highly ambivalent "yes" for the mid-nineteenth century and approaches closer and closer to "no" as the decades roll up to our time. Today it seems positively delusory to suggest that one will turn up positive and significant references to Jesus, the Bible, Christian discipleship, or evangelism by watching or listening to the CBC, reading award-winning literature, scanning *Maclean's* and *Saturday Night*, or perusing Hansard. For all of the vaunted vitality attributed to evangelicalism in Canada in the last quarter of the twentieth century, it is a vitality that seems privatized into a subculture with no discernible influence upon Canadian public life.

INFLUENCE AND VOCATION

Perhaps the most important development concerning the mutual influence of evangelicals and Canadian society has occurred since the 1960s especially and even more obviously in the last fifteen years. Evangelicals in the past have occupied both "outsider" and "insider" positions in Canadian culture. Originally evangelicals were eighteenth-century outsiders like Henry Alline's New Lights in Nova Scotia or the New York circuit-riding Methodists in Upper Canada, but some evangelicals became nineteenth-century pillars of Maritime and Ontarian society. Others, to be sure, like the Salvation Army, the Christian Brethren, the Mennonites, and the Pentecostals, stayed content on the sectish sidelines. As the twentieth century began to unfold, the sectish outsiders felt no responsibility to affect the culture. The churchish insiders, for their part, generally approved of the way things went in a society largely shaped by Christian principles. Yet the erosion of those principles was evident even early on in the fights over Prohibition, Lord's Day legislation, and other leading indicators of evangelical influence. By mid-century the tide had turned decisively, and the 1960s saw it recede with unmistakable quickness.

John Webster Grant has remarked that "Canadians emerged late from the Victorian era."[45] While this might be rued by some, evangelicals might be encouraged that the so-called delay could also be a way of speaking of the persistence of evangelical influence upon anglophone Canada until just a few decades ago. Whatever comfort evangelicals might draw from that history, however, is challenged by the rapid changes of subsequent years. That was then, and this is a very different now.

An impressive response among many evangelical leaders and institutions has been to abandon both the outsiders' outposts and the insiders' cocoons and to engage Canadian culture now as participants, even partners, in a pluralized Canada. Some evangelicals still call for a return to a Christian Canada. Others ignore a culture they see to be hopelessly corrupt and alien. But the pages of *Christian Week* and *Faith Today* as well as denominational magazines; the work of the Evangelical Fellowship of Canada, Citizens for Public Justice, and other lobbying groups; the public discourse of Christian politicians, scholars, and other leaders – all signal an attempt, however inconsistent and incipient it yet may be, to find this third way of exerting influence, of *exercising citizenship*, in a much-changed, multicultural Canada.[46]

One striking characteristic of this exercise, furthermore, is that so much of it is aimed at more generic Christian concerns of compassion, justice, and peace. The traditional evangelical concern for personal holiness in particular continues to be evident in lobbying regarding matters like pornography and abortion. Yet not only the Citizens for Public Justice (note: not "Citizens for Public Holiness") but also the Evangelical Fellowship of Canada itself have worked on behalf of economic fairness, political justice, social improvement, and other not-especially evangelical issues.

There is, by the way, an important complication to be recognized in any analysis of evangelical involvement with public policy. Some evangelicals – for example, the Evangelical Fellowship of Canada – evidently have engaged the culture from explicitly evangelical principles. But the question must be posed as to whether their particular recommendations regarding this or that matter of public policy really are generically evangelical or instead represent the views of just some evangelicals of particular viewpoints. It is not clear what would be "the" evangelical position, if there is any one position at all, on a wide range of issues that some evangelical spokespersons have nonetheless felt free to discuss in the name of evangelicalism in general.[47]

The wide-ranging intellectual task, then, already begun by organizations like the aforementioned, is to talk to the Canadian public about the public in public language that is yet thoroughly rooted in evangelical convictions. Some evangelicals, at least, are taking more seriously the possibility that influence can and ought to be wielded not only by activist evangelicals through energetic lobbying but also by intellectual evangelicals through effective thinking. Nonetheless, what American Mark Noll has observed about his own country, alas, is true also of ours.[48] Late twentieth-century evangelicals have little practice still in producing comprehensive and penetrating analyses of society and in offering judicious and winsome prescriptions for its ills. There is no significant journal of ideas for Canadian evangelicals. There are no evangelicals conspicuously participating in the existing national forums for intellectual exchange. There are no evangelical pundits who command attention from the leading media. Yet from the Constitution to the economy, from Inuit claims in the Arctic to Indian slums in the inner cities, from postmodernism to the information highway, from life-and-death ethics of abortion and euthanasia to quotidian matters of sales taxes and free trade – from sea to sea, Canadian society cries out for creative ideas that go beyond what seem to be the only alternatives in cultural discourse today: either "more for me and mine" or "deficit reduction above all."

To return to the second of our pair of central historiographical questions, then, it appears that some evangelicals today, as in the past, are attempting to influence Canadian society in these various respects without leaving marks of the four distinctly evangelical convictions. If such evangelicals are successful in their work, observers would therefore rightly conclude that evangelicals *authentically as evangelical Christians* influenced Canadian society, even if the peculiar set of emphases characteristic of *evangelicalism* did not. Determining how deeply a society is affected by such wide-ranging evangelical effort, therefore, would be much more than a matter of measuring the four typical evangelical concerns, a question instead of more generically Christian shaping. Still, a culture that bore *no* marks of concern for the Cross and resurrection of Christ, the authority of the Bible, the need for personal regeneration and discipleship, and the priority of evangelism could hardly be called an evangelical culture, even if it were a thoroughly Christian one.

For Vladimir Ilych Lenin, rejecting the status quo and exerting influence upon society was everything. For him, this world was all there is, and whatever is worthwhile in human existence must be found or made here. Political power was the only prize worth pursuing, and he and his Bolshevik comrades grasped it with utter commitment. For Christians who have themselves been grasped by God's saving power, however, utopia is neither an end already realized nor is it a goal to be coerced into existence. It is instead a gift hoped for as the Messiah-borne end of all earthly endeavour. Cultural influence for Christians, then, is a matter of vocation, not of salvation. Furthermore, in pursuing that vocation, they are to resist any baleful influence of culture, to refuse to become "conformed to this world" (Romans 12:3) even as they responsibly take their places in this or that role in this or that society.

Leninism now lies discredited, apparently crushed in the march of events and discarded on the ash-heap of history (although some of those ashes still smoulder). Canadian Christians may well pass by and shake their heads at this worldly folly, this short-sighted and misguided preoccupation with earthly power. They may also regard themselves as either safely quarantined from the stains of this evil age or, perhaps, comfortably incorporated into a still-Christian society. Yet Canadian evangelicals who recognize the call by their Master to be the very salt of the earth (Matt. 5:13) are wise to beware of any self-centred "outsider" separatism or of any smug "insider" complacency, either of which renders them *un*influential in their own society, and therefore makes them – as Jesus himself sternly warned – good for nothing but themselves to be thrown out and trampled underfoot.

PART TWO

Evangelical Impulse in the Methodist, Presbyterian, Anglican, and United Churches

5 "A March of Victory and Triumph in Praise of 'The Beauty of Holiness'": Laity and the Evangelical Impulse in Canadian Methodism, 1800–1884

MARGUERITE VAN DIE

To speak of the evangelical impulse in Canadian Methodism in the nineteenth century is to draw attention to a story of aggressive and apparently irrepressible growth, approvingly recorded and evaluated by contemporaries as "a constant exhibition of the glorious Gospel of Christ."[1] Where in 1792 Canadian work by the New York and Genesee Conferences of the Methodist Episcopal Church had counted only 165 members, by 1884, following a series of unions, the denomination could boast a total membership of 169,803.

Well served by contemporary clerical statisticians and historians in chronicling its "rise and progress," the denomination in Canada continues to receive considerable scholarly attention. Where Methodism in the United States stands out in the diverse landscape of nineteenth-century American religious history as a "puzzle," to use Nathan Hatch's term, in Canada, on the contrary, the denomination has been a rich source for students of religion.[2] From the earliest days in Newfoundland in the 1760s, its revivals have been documented and analysed, while its growth and development have been interpreted through such sociological models as the move from sect to church, or as part of a wider dialectical process between religions of experience and of order. Nor has Methodism's distinctive intellectual tradition been overlooked. While considerable scholarly disagreement exists about Methodism's place within the wider process of the secularization of Canadian society, there is little disagreement about the importance of the denomination's emphasis on social reform in nineteenth-century Canada.

And yet there are ways in which Methodism in Canada too remains an enigma. Although its institutional growth and its theological, intellectual, and revivalistic emphases have been amply documented, these have largely been viewed within a conceptual framework interpreting religious change as declension and accommodation.[3] Concerned to understand the process by which Canadian society has become secularized, historians have been less interested in unravelling the ways in which the sacred and secular were once intertwined at the level of everyday life. Moreover, with the exception of a handful of studies exploring the work of Methodist women, the main sources for historical understanding have been the writings of ministers and theologians. This is not surprising, given the "connexional" nature of Methodism, its reliance on an itinerant ministry to facilitate evangelical outreach, and the fact that its earliest histories and its statistical records were authored and shaped by male clergy. Nevertheless, as a recent study of the professions in nineteenth-century Ontario has persuasively argued, clergy perceptions were not unaffected by the vicissitudes of pressures on their own status.[4]

Thus, to explore the "evangelical impulse" in nineteenth-century Canadian Methodism, we do well also to examine the voices and experience of lay people. And by moving beyond intellectual and ecclesiastical history, we begin to cut at least a tentative trail into the field charted by Nathan Hatch's suggestion that through a study of Methodism, "We would more readily understand religion as experience and community rather than as abstract ideas."[5]

Two divergent accounts of lay piety, as experienced in that most intense expression of Methodist revivalism, the camp meeting, serve as a point of entry into understanding the central features of evangelical experience in the nineteenth century. This is followed by a more in-depth examination of lay piety, first in the pre-1850 period, and then at greater length, during the three decades before the 1884 union. Given the personal nature of religion and the need to integrate lay experience into the wider social context, the examination takes a layered approach. While individual stories and voices sketch out the landmarks of experience and active commitment, other more objective statistical and narrative sources are called on to set the broader framework.

Nowhere did the sound of salvation ring more joyfully for Methodist men and women than in the camp meeting. Here for several days as people gathered communally in the open air under the trees for a period of spiritual refreshment through preaching, prayer, and song, faith took on a new dimension. And yet the experience could also be widely divergent. The Methodist Episcopal itinerant Nathan Bangs, for example, describing the first mass camp meeting held in 1805 in central Canada, at Hay Bay on the Bay of Quinte,[6] gave an account of religious ecstasy on a communal scale: Here under fiery revivalistic preaching, men and women shouted, cried, and sang with such abandon that "It might be said of a truth, that the God of the Hebrews is come into the camp, for the noise was heard far off. The groans of the wounded, the shouts of the delivered, the prayers of the faithful, the Exhortations of the courageous penetrated the very heavens, and reverberated through the neighborhood."[7]

Contrast this description with that penned less than a century later of another camp meeting, Grimsby Park, seen as among the last "of the old-fashioned camp-meetings remaining in Canada." Organized in 1859 by a board of well-to-do Methodist laymen and ministers, in 1875 the Grimsby Park camp meeting had undergone far-reaching changes, as its earlier arrangement of rented tents was replaced by some seventy new gingerbread-trimmed cottages, built at private expense by families for whom the annual two-week camp meeting would form part of a longer season to escape the sweltering summer heat. In subsequent years the escalating needs of these families and short-term visitors would call for ever-greater improvements. First would come easy access by railway and boat, then a restaurant, grocery, and post office, platforms, and in time bathing and boat houses. Already in 1875, however, annual visitors could appreciatively note "an air of business and expansion about the whole place."[8] Written not by an enthusiastic revivalist but by Harriet Phelps Youmans, a well-bred matron whose childhood memories went warmly back to Grimsby Park's earliest days, this account breathed the gentility of family and kinship gatherings in an idyllic sylvan setting.

And here we face the enigma of nineteenth-century Methodism. Though a chasm seems to separate the enthusiastic piety of the 1805 Hay Bay camp meeting from the gentility of Grimsby Park Campground in 1875, in the eyes of their beholders each was seen as a true expression of Methodist spirituality. For participants like Youmans there had been no significant departure, and, although its material accommodation had changed, the Grimsby Park Campground of 1875 was considered to be in direct continuity with the "old-fashioned" camp meeting. Interlacing the domestic detail of this later camp meeting is Youmans's description of the steady fare of preaching when "an expectant hush fell upon the vast assembly," of spontaneous prayer meetings and communal singing long into the night, and of sabbaths whose sanctity called for campground gates be closed to all visitors.

Such manifestations of communal Methodist piety as the Grimsby Campground have been analysed as evidence of "the Domestication of American Methodism," or as a loss of innocence.[9] Canadian historians tend to concur, and have favourably contrasted the warm, ecstatic exuberance of the early camp meetings to a later evangelicalism that "put more stress on the religion of the head and less on the religion of the heart, and easily 'succumbed ... to the materialistic delights' of late-Victorian Canada."[10] While such readings are in keeping with a wider historiography correlating the acquisition of middle-class status with religious declension, they are, I would argue, posited on a dualism between the head and the heart, between mind and matter, which is at variance with the Judeo-Christian tradition. Instructive is the reminder by the Jewish theologian Abraham Joshua Heschel "that the good cannot exist without the holy for those whose piety is founded on the Scriptures," and thus, "the ultimate human dichotomy is not that of mind and matter but that of the sacred and profane."[11]

To early nineteenth-century Methodists, who in conversion had experienced deeply and intimately the divine Spirit within their own lives, the sacred could indeed transform the profane, God could come in the camp, believers could be united in community through the Spirit. Thus camp meetings with their rustic setting, their song, preaching, and prayer, and their leave-taking were occasions when profane time was able to take on a new and sacred dimension. For Harriet Phelps Youmans in a later era, the most treasured memory of the Grimsby Campground was the closing meeting, the one ceremony that at the time of her writing in 1900 still retained its original simple form. Singing "Shall We Gather at the River," the audience would form a circle to take leave of those who through their preaching, speaking, and organization had contributed to the meeting.

Historian Leigh Eric Schmidt reminds us that such gatherings formed part of a wider experience whereby North Atlantic evangelicals were knit together into "communities with a shared, even universal, sense of time and eternity."[12] Undergirding, therefore, what have come to be seen as the four central components of evangelical Christianity – the centrality of the Bible, repentance, salvation through the atonement, and a life of service – was a shared sense of time that knit believers into new forms of community. It was in a single moment of conversion that repentant believers casting themselves on God's mercy in the atonement experienced the presence of eternity, but it was a moment that led to lifelong change in which time took on a new, biblical ordering. This ordering shaped not only the sabbath and the times specifically set aside for collective gathering but also daily life in the home, workplace, and community.

The ordering, however, did not take place in "splendid isolation," but was in turn influenced by secular time and place. Historians such as E.P. Thompson and Deborah Valenze have explained how, as British society moved from an agricultural to an industrializing base, new rhythms of daily work were personally internalized and became expressed in changing patterns of community and worship.[13] Leigh Eric Schmidt has further drawn attention to the exuberant, open-ended, and lengthy patterns of devotion which so often characterized the worship of eighteenth-century evangelicals but which were in tension with their own ideals of improving time, and with more modern sensibilities of time reckoning.[14] Such insights are suggestive in helping to understand the ways whereby Methodists were able to assume a continuity with the piety of an earlier generation even when their own practice was visibly different.

The internalization of time varies with gender, age, place, and ethnicity. Therefore, in drawing on this concept as a means to explore further the evangelical impulse in the lives of nineteenth-century Methodist laypeople, I have limited myself primarily to those living in urban centres in mid-Victorian Canada, and who were, therefore, most influenced by the re-ordering of an agricultural rhythm of time to the structured discipline of a commercial and an industrializing society. Although Maritime Methodists have not been overlooked, and while the different branches of Methodism do receive an occasional nod, most attention here focuses on central Canada, the heartland of Methodism, and on its largest and wealthiest denomination, the Wesleyans.

The many thousands of Wesleyan, Bible Christian, New Connexion and Primitive Methodist immigrants who came to Canada from Britain in the decades following the Napoleonic Wars brought with them not only hopes for a better economic situation but also a deep need to draw on the familiar Methodist structuring of time in order to provide continuity between the old country, the overseas voyage, and their efforts to establish themselves in a demanding pioneer environment. Among the records of departure and adjustment are two separate diaries by William and Elizabeth Peters, Bible Christians from Cornwall, who in 1831 travelled with their three young sons in the company of a number of co-religionists to take up land in the township of Hope in central Ontario.

Written individually, their journals offer a unique prism into lay piety, and to the way it was shaped by concerns of gender and family. For William, drawing on his background as a lay preacher, continuity was offered by the opportunity to organize religious services on board ship, and once settled, to fill Sunday preaching appointments and conduct funerals in the absence of a regularly appointed preacher.[15] In the space of a year, in response to a recent revival, he and fellow Bible Christian settlers were already engaged in constructing near his new farm a chapel which he hoped would, along with a recently organized school for their children, act as an inducement for others to settle nearby.[16]

The journal entries of his wife, Elizabeth, for whom the ongoing need to provide for her family's material comforts offered less discontinuity with her earlier existence, reveal a much more implicit spirituality. While her husband expressed his faith primarily in the more visible and institutional forms of preaching, exhorting, and church building, she, during the long voyage, amidst a welter of domestic details, wrote of a deep sense of trust in providence, and a gratitude "to the All-Wise Disposer of Events that I have felt as happy on the sea as ever on land."[17]

Though grateful to have arrived safely in their new surroundings, invariably these early immigrants reflected with nostalgia on the communal religious life they had left behind. For George Pashley, a Wesleyan who in 1833 settled with his wife in nearby Colborne, Sunday was the day when memories of his native Yorkshire were most poignant, for as he ruefully noted, in his new home, "we had no Prayer Meeting at 6 oclock, morn. no Preaching to attend in the Afternoon, no Publick band meeting to go to in the Evening."[18] Great therefore was his rejoicing when, travelling in the countryside, he was able to link up with Methodists from the old country. "Here I was at home again, in the midst of my heavenly father's family, composed of English and Irishmen and Canadians ... Truly, O Lord thou hast spread a table for us in the wilderness," he exclaimed in his journal.[19]

More fortunate were those who settled in larger towns such as Toronto. Here by 1842, as recalled by one lay man, John Macdonald, George Street Wesleyan Methodist Church was already able to offer the following sabbath fare: a prayer meeting in the church at 6 A.M. in the summer (7 A.M. in winter), a 9 A.M. Sunday School, followed by a service at 11 A.M., Sunday School again at 2 P.M., and an evening service at 6 P.M., after which until about ten o'clock a band of workers called prayer-leaders in companies of three to four, ranged out over a wide area of the town, from Berkeley Street to the Asylum. This was supplemented during the week by a prayer-meeting on Monday, preaching on Thursday, and class meetings on Tuesday and Wednesday.[20]

For a young man like Macdonald, Presbyterian, single, and alone in the city, such a round of church activity offered both community and a way to fill his ample leisure time. Before eventually transferring his allegiance to the Methodists, he found himself, in addition to the two sabbath services in his own St Andrew's Presbyterian Church, attending five weekly Methodist services, omitting as a non-member only the class meeting. "There was," he later recalled, "a magnetism about the Methodist people which I failed to find among the Presbyterians; ... [They] grasped you by the hand and welcomed you as a stranger, asked you to their homes and bade you come again."[21] While Macdonald considered a natural Scottish reserve to be a contributing factor to this difference, he was also aware of the impact of the differing socio-economic status of the respective denominations. Thus where the membership at St Andrew's included a good number of professionals, merchants, and builders, the Methodists counted no professionals, and only a few modest businessmen, with the majority being artisans and tradesmen. Such independent trades, which linked the home with the workplace and allowed considerable flexibility in the use of time and opportunity for social interaction with customers, were able to retain the daily rhythm of an earlier rural life and resist the compartmentalization associated with industrial change and urbanization.[22]

A decade later, however, the comparatively humble socio-economic status of Methodists in Toronto, as well as in other urban centres, had changed sufficiently to include a number of professionals and well-to-do entrepreneurs.[23] Part of a more pervasive restructuring during the 1850s through railway building, demographic change, and rising farm output, the impact of social and economic change in Ontario has been well documented.[24] In the Maritimes, as well, where Methodists, though fewer in numbers, were long established, the 1850s were a time of economic optimism and growing political maturity. Although they had only recently begun to disengage themselves from their Anglican roots, New Brunswick's Methodists, the majority of them respectable tradesmen, were beginning to show their prosperity in their places of worship. In the last third of the nineteenth century the denomination would go on, one historian has noted, "to become the most rapidly growing element in the religious fabric of the province."[25] In Ontario, where between 1851 and 1871 the number of people living in places of 1,000 or more almost tripled, select samples of urban centres reveal Methodists dominant in the middle economic ranks, with a growing segment listing Canada as their country of birth.[26]

The effect of this changing socio-economic status upon religious life has not gone unnoticed. Historians have observed that the 1850s stand out as a time when Methodists and their preachers began to move from the fringes into the mainstream of respectable society. It has been noted that the combined effects of church disestablishment in 1854 and the prosperity of the membership laid the groundwork for a growing parity in clerical incomes between Wesleyan ministers and those of the Church of England and the Kirk.[27] Neil Semple and William Westfall have drawn attention to how the Wesleyan Methodists were able during the middle decades of the century to develop a more effective institutional structure which, along with a new interest in church architecture, moved the denomination into an increasingly recognizable ecclesiastical mode.[28] Indicative of its wealth and expansive mood in the three decades after 1851 is the further observation that, taking all groups together, Methodism became the province's most prolific builder of new churches, increasing their number by a factor of five.[29] In its many accounts of the large crowds gathered to celebrate these festive church openings, qualifying adjectives linking "respectable and devout" pepper the columns of the denominational newspaper, the *Christian Guardian*, as writers took pains to draw attention to the growing influence and prominence of Methodists.[30]

Given such indicators of gentility, it is not surprising that the 1850s in central Canada have been seen as a move away from the enthusiastic evangelism of the early Methodist itinerants towards what has been called a "tempering of revivalism."[31] Until the economic crash of the summer of 1857, the decade was indeed a period marked by economic prosperity for central Canada, a prosperity that did not fail to arouse the vigilance of the Methodist ministry in its annual pastoral address to the membership. "In the present age of worldly enterprise and speculation, you are exposed to more than ordinary temptations, so far [sic] to enter into the current of secular ambition as to be carried downwards by its overwhelming force," read the admonition of 1853.[32] Three years later saw the first of a series of unsuccessful attempts by lay people with select ministerial support to dismantle attendance at class meeting as a condition of membership. That year in addition to the habitual warnings against all "inordinate worldly influence," the membership was pointedly informed of the ministry's reaffirmation of the necessity of the class meeting as a means of grace, and one of "the ancient land-marks ... so distinctive of our church, and so promotive of our spirituality."[33]

It was Methodism's founder, John Wesley, who had offered the ominous warning that true religion would disappear within a generation should his followers ever become rich.[34] It would not be out of place, therefore, to surmise that the perceived "tempering of revivalism" of the 1850s represented the loss of the spiritual vitality so central in the accounts of ministerial efforts in the first half of the century, and which historians have taken as normative in assessing the evangelical pulse of Methodism in the later period. John Wesley, however, was not always systematically consistent in his pronouncements. In an oft-quoted sermon on the "Use of Money," he also admonished Methodists to "gain and save all you can." The latter exhortation, a recent biographer, Henry Rack, has suggested, "seems at least a practical concession to the acquisitive, market-oriented, capitalist society then developing."[35]

Where Wesley and his clerical brethren might give limited and reluctant concessions, devout laity, enmeshed in the daily demands of the market place, devised their own way to live out their calling. In urban centres such as in Halifax in the Maritimes, where Methodism had struck early roots, the practice of piety by middle-class members had been modelled well before the 1850s. There, as Allan Robertson has demonstrated, a number of prominent second and third generation Methodist businessmen and their wives had been engaged since the 1820s in establishing a strong presence in philanthropic and charitable activity. In so doing, they demonstrated "to the wider society in which they lived that mercantile capitalism and evangelical piety were not mutually inclusive."[36]

I would argue that this pattern, which extended to the heartland of Canadian Methodism in central Canada, did more than demonstrate that piety and capitalism could co-exist; it profoundly reshaped the evangelical impulse in Methodism. When viewed through the lens of lay piety rather than clerical anxiety, the enhanced social status of the membership in the 1850s revitalized the evangelical impulse rather than marked its deathknell. It would, moreover, give definitive shape to the Methodism of the 1884 union, a union entered into only upon the urgent advocacy of the laity.[37] The foundations of this impulse had already been laid in the communal pattern of sacred time, brought by immigrants, and re-established in Canada. Increased wealth, a large influx of new members, and a practical piety informed by the doctrine of holiness served to extend and deepen the evangelical impulse.

If numbers of converts are an indicator, the 1850s were in fact remarkably promising in Central Canada. Between 1849 to 1859 the membership of the Wesleyan Methodist church there more than doubled from 24,268 to 51,669, while that of the Methodist New Connexion rose from 3,389 to 5,708.[38] In the Maritimes, Wesleyan membership, which registered 11,750 in 1849, and in the next nine years grew by less than 2,000, in 1859 drew in 3,338 new members, largely through revivals in such major urban centres as Halifax, Saint John, and Charlottetown.[39] Although increases in givings for the local church are impossible to document in any general way, for the Wesleyan Methodists in central Canada, connexional funds (those over and above local building and salary costs but including church relief, contingent, educational, and superannuated ministry funds) more than doubled.[40]

Qualitatively different but equally significant in assessing the denominational pulse are the changed emphases in the methods of revival, as recounted by participating ministers in the *Christian Guardian*. While ministers continued to underscore their own role (be it in humility), they also took pains to note the absence of emotional manifestations in revivals, the disciplined involvement of the laity, and the practical expression of piety as the test of conversion.[41]

It was especially in the efforts of two American revivalists, James Caughey and Phoebe Palmer, that Methodist lay people in central Canada encountered the call to a more practical piety.[42] Appealing to middle-class sensibilities in their style and emphases in preaching, Caughey and Palmer were able to instill in lay people a new relevance to the Methodist doctrine of Christian perfection, also known as holiness or entire sanctification. References to holiness are never absent from ministerial accounts of the earlier period, but historians Peter Bush and Alden Aikens have noted a change in emphasis on the doctrine after 1851 in both the Wesleyan *Christian Guardian* and the Methodist Episcopal *Canada Christian Advocate*. The successful appropriation of this spiritual attainment by clergy and laity, as Bush has further pointed out, reflects the extent to which Caughey and Palmer were building on an existing revivalist tradition, which now in the 1850s acquired a new intensity.[43] Holiness emphasized for lay people heightened sense of the sacred, an abiding experience of God's love that went beyond the emotional moments of conversion to a daily structuring of time, which was practical and service oriented.

Thanks to an interest in lay biography dating from this period, a number of the most prominent converts have left behind a rich description of their experience. James Bain Morrow was raised in a devout Methodist family and employed as a sixteen-year-old clerk at the office of the Samuel Cunard steamship company in Halifax. After attending a series of revivals in his Sunday school at Argyle Street Methodist Church, he was able to write for the first time in his diary in the summer of 1851, "I find the service of Christ to be perfect freedom, and I have to rejoice in what I experience of the love of God."[44] And in Belleville, Ontario, during Caughey's revivalistic meetings in 1856, thirty-year old Jane Clement Jones, pregnant with her fifth child, experienced a new sense of consecration.[45]

Phoebe Palmer's own accounts of her work, such as that in Hamilton in 1857, emphasized the practical nature of revival and the role of organization and discipline among church membership in ensuring its success. She described an almost spontaneous welling up of piety and businesslike resourcefulness, when out of a group of between fifty and seventy-five who had assembled as usual for prayer meeting with her one evening in Hamilton, some thirty to forty had decided both to pledge to tithe as a sign of consecration to revival, and to bring along one person each to the next night's prayer meeting. The result had been eighteen days of meetings afternoon and evening, with the church reputedly continually filled to overflowing.[46]

Billed as a "Laity for the Times," Palmer's methods were congruent with the move towards lay ascendancy, when laity and ministers began more to resemble one another and when lay pressure was exerted for a better educated ministry.[47] By the 1850s the need for lay financial expertise to administer connexional funds began to bring together with ministerial members at the conference level some of the denomination's most prominent and active lay men, such as Richard Yates, Joseph Bloor, and John Macdonald of Toronto, and John Counter of Kingston.[48]

Prominent also at the local level, the denomination's well-to-do male members played a vital role as church trustees, members of building committees, fundraisers, and stewards. Here they were encouraged to assume positions of church leadership commensurate with their social status. In the town of Brantford, for example, which experienced a sustained period of union revival between 1856 and 1859, Methodists were able to count among their converts nine men who ranked in the highest 80–100 economic percentile, thereby doubling the congregation's well-to-do members, making it second only to the Anglicans.

Such an acquisition was significant, for although in the eyes of God all converts were equal, to keep a local church afloat financially, some converts were more equal than others. In a time of high transiency, the local church remained heavily dependent on the support of a small number of affluent donors. These prominent Methodists played a vital role not only in enhancing the church's local profile but also through good fiscal management in providing opportunities for church expansion and extension. Ministers might bewail the dangers of wealth, and later historians of evangelicalism such as Curtis Johnson (one of the few who has shown an interest in investigating its material base), have underscored its negative impact on evangelical values and on revivalism generally.[49] Contemporaries, on the other hand, assumed a positive connection between financial means and opportunities for evangelical expansion.[50] Enterprising, locally prominent class leaders not only attracted converts who shared their middle-class values but by virtue of such a membership could also count on the enthusiasm, financial resources, and potential church trustees needed to launch church extensions into more recently populated town wards. Such was the case, for example, in Brantford, where under the leadership of County Judge Stephen Jones and his wife, Margaret, in the aftermath of the revivals of the 1850s, the class drew, along with their wives, a number of prominent local citizens including a lawyer, secondary-school principal, contractor, carriage maker, merchant miller, dry-goods merchant, and mill owner.⁵¹ By 1870 the class was ready to launch a new church, Brant Avenue Methodist, to be situated in what was then largely a poor Irish ward but whose potential real estate value had not gone unnoticed.⁵²

The revivalism of the 1850s had been pivotal in the formation of such classes. These years, which saw Wesleyan membership double, and a new middle-class respectability noticeable among urban converts, had put great strain upon the traditional class meeting.⁵³ The most remarkable year, 1857, when over seven thousand converts flocked into membership, also happened to be followed by a dramatic decline in the three subsequent years.⁵⁴ Though much of the influx of members, as well as the subsequent rapid decline, was related to the devastating economic crash of the summer of 1857, poor class leadership was also cited as a reason for losing the recently converted. In a denomination where religion was seen to be the vital work of the Spirit, and where, in the absence of a settled ministry, much of the ongoing spiritual formation rested on the class leader, any appearance of cant, staleness, and formalism could only have a deterrent effect in attracting and retaining members. On the other hand, class leaders such as Stephen and Margaret Jones who were capable of addressing the spiritual concerns of new middle-class converts saw their groups expanding.

Given this situation, it is not surprising that articulate, devout converts were quickly asked to become class leaders. With their middle-class sense of time and purpose they injected a practical activism helpful in attracting young people as well as retaining older converts of their own social rank. In Halifax, James Morrow after his conversion assumed the leadership of a young boys' class and began a long career of active church work, which included lay preaching, leading a Saturday evening band meeting, assistance in church extension, leadership in the YMCA at the local and national levels, and being on the executive committee of the Book and Tract Society.⁵⁵ Jane Clement Jones for thirty-eight years was a tireless and highly conscientious class leader, first to young women, and after 1869 to a senior boys' class which over its fourteen-year existence counted a total of 707 young men. In addition she engaged in poor relief, conducted cottage prayer meetings in the homes of the poor, and played a major role in establishing Belleville's hospital, a Home for the Needy, and the Women's Christian Association. Her involvement in these activities, besides regular Methodist prayer and class meetings, love feasts, and Sunday worship, not to mention her role as wife and mother to eventually eight children, owed a good deal to a meticulous organizational ability and an overly developed conscience. "I would feel guilty if I did not go," she was approvingly remembered to have offered as grounds for her involvement in the church, her "second home."⁵⁶

In choosing to devote their energies as class leaders to the young, Jones and Morrow exemplified the concern of Methodist laity and clergy to extend the evangelical faith to the next generation. "Certainly the churches are becoming more earnest in behalf of children, and this is a great means of producing a deeper religion and a better type of character," the *Christian Guardian*'s opening editorial for 1864 solemnly intoned.[57]

The burden for bringing about the conversion of the young rested on the Sunday schools, which increasingly became an arena for revivalism among the children of the congregation and the town.[58] "Many children in connection with our Sabbath Schools during the past year, have been brought to God, become members of our Church, and regularly meet in class; and by their upright and uniform lives show the power of that truth which is also able to make the youthful mind wise unto salvation by faith which is in Christ," the Report of the Wesleyan Sabbath School Committee noted with pride in 1857. By that year, which registered an unusually high number of converts, the infrastructure to extend evangelical religion to the young was already firmly in place, consisting of an impressive 494 schools, 1,670 male and 1,344 female teachers, 9,048 male and 9,379 female scholars, and 83,045 library volumes.[59]

This was a field of activity that drew the town's most prominent men and women, many for extended periods of time, to sanctify their sabbath leisure time and extend the influence of evangelical religion. Sunday-school work was therefore not only pre-eminently lay work but it was also local, and relied on social networks for leadership and financial resources to pay for inducements to attendance, not least of which was the annual scholars' picnic or related outing. Thus while sabbath school teachers were divided relatively equally along gender lines, the superintendency was firmly in the hands of prominent local businessmen and professionals who brought to the task not only social rank but also the methodical habits of their work in the secular world. Such habits not infrequently managed to turn the superintendency into a form of entitlement, and thirty-year records such as that of William Pearson at Toronto's Richmond Street (and after 1871 at the Metropolitan Methodist Church) were by no means uncommon.[60]

Concern for the continuity of evangelical Christianity did not limit itself to Sunday-school work but expressed itself also in concentrated efforts among older youth. American scholars have analysed the attraction of nineteenth-century revivalism for women and charted female dominance in church membership.[61] Although a sustained analysis is still missing for Methodism in Canada, select data indicates no variance with this wider pattern.[62] Methodist church records in urban centres further indicate that by the 1860s large numbers of single young female converts were generally enrolled separately in large classes under the leadership of the minister or, less frequently, a gifted lay woman.[63]

There were no doubt quite practical reasons for this arrangement, but there were also points of affinity between ministers and the female membership. Both groups shared a sense of place and time which had been resistant to the reordering forces of a market-driven workplace. Noting such gender differences, Susan Juster and Clyde Griffen have drawn attention to the difficulties posed to men by evangelical piety because of its emphasis on the moral dimension of religion and its teaching that there could be no distinction between public and private morality.[64]

The conversion of young men was, therefore, considered to be of sufficient significance to receive specific mention in contemporary revival accounts.[65] For lay leaders this was an area that called for versatility and adaptability in finding ways to help this group integrate the private world of religious experience with the public workplace. The leaders of the 1850s, who had reshaped an earlier piety in ways more congruent with their own experience of time, continued to occupy positions of leadership in church life well after the 1870s, and thus were able to exert strong influence on the religious socialization of the next generation. In their efforts to draw young people into active religious commitment, they poured their energy into two areas, education and the use of leisure time, each of which was intended to combine secular life with a vision of the sacred.

In the same way that young women had been gathered into separate classes, the traditional class meeting became replaced by a young men's or boys' Bible class, instructed by respected lay people in business and the professions. These were supplemented with other opportunities for "mutual improvement," which over time evolved into more definedly social gatherings. Instructive here is the work of Jane Clement Jones in Belleville. Under her tutelage, a Bible class of eight young men, established in 1861, shortly thereafter chose to divide itself into ward committees in order to search the town for new members. Thanks to a combination of active recruitment and the incentive of generous teas and entertainment offered by Mrs Jones upon the attainment of specified numerical objectives, the total by 1878 had grown to 113, of whom 35 had been converted. By that date the class had hived off into two more groups, a Temperance Society and a more socially oriented gathering, open to both sexes, and simply called "Mrs Jones' Improvement Class."[66]

By the 1870s such a pattern of youth work had become common in urban centres. Segregated into Young Men's Bible Classes and Young Ladies' Classes for instruction in the faith, young Methodists managed to supplement their spiritual nurture with a variety of social and religious organizations. These included the more traditional "mutual improvement" and debating societies, and (after the opening of the Japan field in 1873), foreign missionary societies, as well as assistance in such specific tasks as parsonage cleaning and renovation, and fundraising for local congregational causes. Such activities played an indispensable role in the expansionist church building of the late 1860s and 1870s, and reflected what American historian Richard Bushman has termed "the refinement" of religion.[67] Young Canadian Methodists in urban centres applauded the move away from the old "barn-like" buildings characteristic of their denomination's earlier architecture and displayed their aspirations to taste and gentility in their fundraising and social activities. Lectures, especially by acclaimed British orators such as the Reverend Morley Punshon, president of the Canada Conference of the British Wesleyan Church from 1868 to 1872, were now a favoured means of raising funds.[68] Young women, as was the case with Toronto's projected Metropolitan Methodist Church in 1870, might offer a guided tour of their own works of art, to be auctioned thereafter in aid of the more traditional bazaar put on by the older women.[69]

Examples such as these, blending religious concerns with personal and collective refinement, abound in the records of urban Methodist churches and in the private correspondence of lay members. The spread of such refinement in religion was not without its contradictions, for it subtly incorporated middle-class gentility into traditional Christian values, and implicitly marginalized the poor.[70] In later years Canadian Methodists would seek to address this concern through such movements as the Social Gospel. In the 1870s and 1880s, however, annual reports of urban revivals, supplemented by membership data from select congregations, indicate that although some congregations had become largely middle class, converts were drawn from a wide spectrum of society.[71] Combining aggressive revivalism with a practical piety, Methodists advanced steadily in urban centres during the period 1851 to 1881, from 13.4 per cent to 18.9 per cent of the population in Toronto, for example, and from 16.3 per cent to 25.4 per cent in Brantford.[72]

In the course of these thirty years Methodist piety had changed significantly, and the distance that separated it from the radical evangelicalism of the early camp meetings was dramatic. A generation of urban lay leaders whose sense of time had been reshaped by the new ordering of a capitalist, industrializing society had tried to mould Methodist identity in ways congruent with their own experience. For religiously minded lay people, concerned to make a living in the daily marketplace, the dualism to be overcome had not been between mind and matter but between the sacred and the profane. By making a disciplined, consecrated use of time, establishing a wide range of voluntary associations, and exercising a special interest in the moral welfare of the young, they had tried to transform the secular world by integrating it inextricably with the sacred. In this way, to use the language of the old camp meetings, they had tried to ensure that "God was in the camp." And in devising useful institutions that combined devotion, discipline, and social concern, they were also, one might add, following an even earlier tradition – the example of their venerable founder, John Wesley.

Nineteenth-century Canada, however, was not the eighteenth-century England of John Wesley. The values and institutions that figured so prominently in the practical piety of the post-1850s have also been seen by some social and economic historians as integral to the formation of middle-class consciousness in the nineteenth century. An analysis of the socio-economic status of New Brunswick evangelicals, as well as local studies of urban centres in Ontario such as Hamilton, Toronto, and Brantford, have pointed to a correlation between evangelical piety and middle-class status.[73] Most recently, Gordon Darroch and Lee Soltow, drawing on a detailed examination of the relationship between religious affiliation and home ownership in the 1871 census in Ontario, have reinforced this conclusion and pointed out that "the groups with the strongest Protestant sectarian roots were most likely to foster middle-class standards of family life, social responsibility, and self-discipline."[74]

To unravel such an intricate interplay between evangelical piety and middle-class respectability is no small task. It calls on the historian to consider not only the form assumed by religion but also the complex array of material conditions of life that make a particular form possible. Where some later historians have perceived the changing material and social conditions of mid-Victorian Canada as a threat to evangelical Christianity, contemporaries instead saw opportunity. Methodist laity were able to maintain evangelical vitality precisely because they reshaped piety in ways congruent with the reordering of secular time which they encountered in the workplace. Thus the sacred and the secular did not become compartmentalized but on the contrary were integrated into a disciplined, activist form of religion, whose source lay in the holiness movement of the 1850s. As with secular time, so the sacred, when deeply experienced, could take on a new dimension in the experience of the middle class.

At the end of our analysis we return to the Grimsby Park Campground in 1875, newly refurbished in all its middle-class refinement. Here, as described in elaborate detail in the *Brantford Daily Expositor*, by late August there had arrived some sixty families whose duly printed names formed an impressive register of prominent Methodist families from nearby towns such as Hamilton, St Catharines, Waterdown, and

Brantford.⁷⁵ In a constant round of devotional activities (beginning with a daily 6:30 A.M. prayer meeting, and progressing through sessions of family worship, fellowship meetings, and sermons), the entire week was spent in a structured and highly profitable manner. Its culmination, however, came on the sabbath, the first in the re-organized campgrounds. Awaited with some trepidation in case divine blessing be withheld from this new venture, the day turned out to be an unforgettable experience. As the newspaper account exulted, it was indeed "a march of victory and triumph in which 'the beauty of holiness' was praised from morn till the second and third watch of the night. Many souls were enabled through the course of the day to testify to the power of Christ to forgive sins, and many others to witness the power of the blood of Christ to cleanse from all sin." But this was only the beginning, for on Monday morning there followed a sermon "that moved the congregation as one man to make a fuller consecration of their powers to the service of God, and helped their faith to a firmer hold on the Jesus of the Gospel ... Never has there been a camp-meeting held here where God was more manifestly present with His people," it was concluded.⁷⁶

Taking into consideration, as Stephen Cooley has recently pointed out, the formulaic nature of such camp meeting descriptions, it is nevertheless worth noting who it was who formed the subject and the intended audience of this account.⁷⁷ Here at Grimsby Park Campground, seventy years after Hay Bay, the assembled had become middle-class families, and as such, accustomed to highly structured time and to the amenities of urban existence. They nevertheless entered again into a familiar experience of biblical time and community, not in the ecstatic exuberance of radical evangelicalism but in a way congruent with their own experience in a world that had begun dramatically to change. Not unlike Bunyan's pilgrim, this generation of Methodists believed that the way to the heavenly city lay not through ecstatic rapture but through the mundane, everyday streets of the earthly city. The fact that a century later we know those streets were not as simple and straight as they expected should not blind us to the evangelical impulse that guided their journey.

6 Condensation and Heart Religion: Canadian Methodists as Evangelicals, 1884–1925

PHYLLIS D. AIRHART

In the fall of 1919 the Methodist Church joined with other major Canadian denominations in launching a national campaign for the Inter-Church Forward Movement. Methodism's ambitious goals included a 25 per cent increase in membership, the enlisting of 5,000 young people for "life service" as ministers or missionaries, and a financial target of $4,000,000 for its "connexional" activities coordinated at district, regional, national, and international levels. Each local congregation was urged to follow the carefully laid out week-by-week strategy beginning with attention to the campaign's spiritual aims, followed by a canvassing of every church member, and culminating in the collection of pledges on a designated Sunday in February 1920.

Advertisements and press releases prepared by a central executive committee to promote the campaign appeared in secular newspapers and in Methodism's own regional papers. "Where Will the 100,000 New Members Come From?" asked the headline of one of the earliest of those sent to the Methodist papers.[1] "Only a Revival in Every Congregation in the Nation Can Meet the Need of the Hour," a second headline responded, and the article continued: "This is a distinct and clarion call to every congregation to meet its own responsibility and carry on its own evangelistic effort ... We would see a revival which would tear down the sinner's barricades and hurl him on his face in cries for forgiveness, the Church aglow, the preacher on fire, the people at work for precious, undying souls, for whom Christ died and who are to face the Judgment and eternal destiny."

Canadian Methodist congregations did not heed this clarion call for a revival in every congregation and fell disappointingly short of its spiritual targets. However, the financial goals of the national campaign were easily reached and even exceeded. The difference in response to the spiritual and financial goals drew a thoughtful letter to the editor of the *Christian Guardian* which offered this analysis: "I think man is making religion a business today, following certain rules and forms ... [I]t has ceased to be a thing of the heart. It is hedged in and pressed down, until it is like the condensed foods of today, easily handled, but not of much flavour."[2]

The correspondent's claim is worth exploring in considering its relationship to the evangelical tradition. It is one way of characterizing the transition in Methodism as its members moved from the margins to the mainstream of Canadian Protestantism while, so it would seem, at the same time becoming minor rather than major players on the international evangelical scene in the twentieth century. Was the correspondent right in sensing that the basic assumptions of Methodism's emerging organizational culture were at odds with evangelical piety?

To answer this question it is important first to explore Methodism's role within Canadian evangelical Protestantism between the 1884 union of four major groups of Methodists and the 1925 union with Congregationalists and the majority of Presbyterians to form the United Church of Canada. Canadian Methodists went into both unions thinking of their faith as "evangelical." Yet there were significant changes in the presentation of their "heart religion" during those years which took shape at the time when an impulse toward incorporation was being widely felt in North American Protestant circles. Methodism was among the many denominations that in this period made structural changes which significantly altered their approach to both evangelism and social service. This reconfiguration of evangelical Protestantism involved not only the highlighting of commitment to service (alongside or instead of conversion) which we associate with the rise of the social gospel in this period but involved new ways of organizing for service as well. The old evangelical consensus, supported by the backbone of shared experience and belief and held together by a network of voluntary associations that criss-crossed denominational divisions, did not survive the transition. On the other side of the transition we discover new religious "cultures" coalescing to cooperate across denominational lines – each with new leadership, new networks, new institutional structures, occupying two worlds with seemingly little in common but a growing distaste for the other acquired as the boundaries between them became more firmly set.

No organization makes such a transition from old to new overnight, and the Methodist church was no exception. One organizational analyst has come up with the term "neutral zone" to describe the middle stage of the process. The characteristics which he finds in organizations moving through the neutral zone include disorientation, self-doubting, the re-emergence of old weaknesses thought to have been patched over, mixed signals, and a polarization between those who want to rush forward and those who want to go back to the old ways. Organizations going through the neutral zone are highly vulnerable: "Disorganized and tired, people respond slowly and halfheartedly to competitive threats. They may even sabotage organizational responses to outside attacks." But, he adds, the lack of clear systems and signals can be a source of creativity as well.[3] There are a number of indicators of such a transition in Canadian Methodism between 1884 and 1925 and evidence as well of a neutral zone transversing it.

An experiential piety rooted (especially in its early years) in a sometimes emotional conversion experience quickly became a distinguishing mark of Methodism as it made its way as a new movement. This "heart religion" manifested itself in the conversion experience to which its practitioners aspired, the guidelines for personal and public morality, the articulation of religious ideas, and the associational forms by which piety was cultivated. A dynamic and adaptable approach to the religious life moved with the geographical and social location of Methodists from frontier settlements to settled communities. By the 1850s, its members, particularly those whose religious sensibilities were influenced by middle-class assumptions about appropriate emotional response, were growing accustomed to lower levels of intensity accompanying conversion than were remembered by older Methodists. But even by the end of the nineteenth century the importance of a "definite" if not always dramatic experience was assumed by leading Methodists.[4] Social gospeller Salem Bland remembered the last three decades of the nineteenth century as "the golden age of evangelicalism" when a "mighty tide of life-changing influence" swept through the English-speaking world. Most Methodists in those days, he recalled, still entered the church as a result of conversion; the embers of this warm experience, though they might cool down, could always be fanned by revival into a blaze.[5]

Yet Methodism was never simply a "heart religion." From the outset its approach to the religious life was characterized by forms and rules, and even its name was reputed to have come from outsiders who derided Wesley's preoccupation with "methods." Its institutional style was systematic as well, and it owed a good part of its success in spreading the message of "heart religion" to effective organization of itinerant ministers and class members. Methodists were also among the organizers of numerous voluntary associations that flourished after the mid-nineteenth-century disestablishment of religion. Methodist men and women were admonished not only to be converted but to be "useful" Christians – they were "saved for service." The evangelical spirit of the late nineteenth century to which Bland referred and the concurrent flowering of voluntarism are thus likely more than mere coincidence. Voluntary societies for social reform and missionary work at home and overseas provided new opportunities and more visibility for lay leadership in Christian service which proved to be particularly significant for women.

Attention to organizational matters was clearly not a twentieth-century innovation. In fact Nathan Hatch has described Methodism as "the prototype of a religious organization taking on market form."[6] But by the twentieth century that "market" was changing and, not surprisingly, Methodism attempted to position itself to take advantage of the new conditions. Its church life came to mirror the organizational culture of the business world in a number of interesting respects. For example, a key feature of the business revolution which made its way throughout the western world around the turn of the twentieth century was its corporate character: in Canada, 275 individual firms were merged into 58 corporations between 1909 and 1911.[7] In their study of national denominational structures in the United States, Craig Dykstra and James Hudnut-Beumler have used the metaphor of the corporation as a way to describe the organizational pattern that superseded the non-bureaucratic "constitutional confederacy" that had characterized denominational life until the late nineteenth century.[8]

Prior to that time denominational agendas had focused on local and regional issues; for example, there were no boards to coordinate such activities as Christian education or home and foreign missions. Nineteenth-century voluntary societies, Dykstra and Hudnut-Beumler argue, were a step toward the corporation model but differed from it in important respects. They remained independent of local, regional, and national church bodies and reflected the deep tensions over many issues too sensitive to tackle by a denomination as a whole. But these voluntary associations posed a threat to denominational leadership since they were so successful in attracting the members and money that spelled influence in public affairs.[9]

Dykstra and Hudnut-Beumler note that as denominations took on a more corporate and bureaucratic cast, one of the first moves was to bring mission boards, publications, and even temperance work under central control. Controlling the foreign mission budget was a larger issue than efficiency and duplication of efforts (which tended to be sorted out on the mission field). Fundraising methods reflected this organizational shift: a unified giving campaign for *all* missionary activities replaced appeals made to each local congregation on behalf of *particular* activities. Denominational executives came to play a much larger role in conducting church affairs, preparing proposals to be ratified at national assemblies of local representatives who could do little beyond ratifying or rejecting them. Lay representatives, usually men from large and wealthy congregations, served as "corporate trustees" on denominational boards.[10] At least one Canadian denomination gravitated toward this model: building on its long-standing tradition of "connexional" links, Methodism quickly adopted the board structure, fundraising methods, and leadership style characteristic of a corporate denomination.[11]

But alongside this transfer of power from local/congregational to central/denominational control, Methodism and other denominations were affected by a transfer of people from rural to urban areas. Peter Drucker has analysed what he describes as "enormous transformations in all developed free-market countries" that accompanied the shrinking numbers of farmers and domestic servants and the rise to social prominence of a new class by 1900: the blue-collar workers in the manufacturing industry. Even though they were still a small minority (and not as exploited as domestic servants), they were highly visible and easy to organize. Drucker argues that "early twentieth-century society was obsessed with blue-collar workers." Those who referred to "the social question" had this new class in mind.[12] Thousands of those who in the nineteenth century would have become farmers or domestic workers instead looked for industrial employment which promised (and for the most part delivered) relatively better pay and a higher standard of living for work requiring little education and few new skills.[13]

It is the immigrant, often with non-Protestant and even socialist leanings, who usually comes to mind when we think of efforts to bring the working class into the churches. But the rural-born, perhaps in the Methodist case clinging tightly to a piety identified with the revivalistic traditions of the community left behind, are as important as the foreign-born in considering the growth of the new evangelical movements in urban areas. Methodism may have suffered a double loss from this transfer of people. Urban church members were discouraged by their failure to appeal to those who sought a different experience of religion from that found in the typical middle-class congregation or even labour churches. And of course the rural churches struggled to survive the loss of young adult members as they established homes and families elsewhere. Families, churches, and voluntary societies had generally combined to care for the social needs of the community in the nineteenth century; but changing family structures, fewer volunteers for service in rural areas, and the challenge of organizing volunteers in urban areas created a complicated situation. Drucker suggests it is understandable that we see people searching for new ways of handling social tasks, and government intervention finding widespread support as a solution.[14] For religious groups, this social mobility loosened the allegiance to *local* custom and tested assumptions about the congregational base of church operations.

The impact of this transfer of Methodist power and people in support of voluntary associations is illustrated by the handling of the temperance issue. A leading temperance newspaper reported in 1903 that the centre of reform had shifted: whereas special organizations had once accounted for most of the effective work, temperance societies were now declining in number and "in the churches of the land is the great working force and voting strength of the temperance cause."[15] The creation in a number of denominations of special moral reform departments gave the issue more prominence at the national level, lending it visibility and political credibility. But as the balance between voluntary societies and the denominational agencies shifted, one forty-year veteran of the movement was alarmed by the declining membership of temperance societies. He was disturbed to note the practice of relegating temperance work in local congregations to young people's societies.[16] One *Pioneer* editorial concluded that since denominations had taken up the temperance cause there was not the same need for separate temperance organizations – some had been little more than social gatherings at any rate. "The old societies, with their faithful membership, are still doing splendid work," the editorial writer commented, "but the country looks to-day to the Christian churches as the leaders in the warfare against the drink evil."[17] A year later, however, the *Pioneer* sounded a more uncertain note, speculating that there would be less bar-room drinking if the old temperance societies with their pledge-signing campaigns were as strong as in the past.[18]

Women were arguably the temperance workers most significantly affected by these political and denominational transitions. The shift to incorporate the work of social reform into denominational structures came at a time when most churches denied women voting privileges and representation in their courts. Women were less willing, or at least less able, to support and promote institution-building along such bureaucratic lines. Consequently they became nearly invisible in social reform work at the national denominational levels.[19] The Methodist Church was probably not untypical in its repeated failure to mention the temperance work of women. Some prominent denominational leaders were not above publicly making light of this work. One wonders how WCTU representatives at the meeting of the Quebec Branch of the Dominion Alliance felt upon hearing S.D. Chown's address. "Many developments are helping to roll our old chariot along," he remarked. "The zeal of our godly women always full of enthusiasm has been chastened by disappointment and corrected by experience so that it is now being applied with a wisdom, a certainty and force that it did not possess a few years ago. Their impetuosity has been curbed," he added.[20] Perhaps it is not surprising that the moral suasion aspect of temperance work, in which women were instrumental, began to suffer as the more staid bureaucratic strategies of the male denominational leadership took hold.

There are different angles from which to view the changing face of evangelical Protestantism as it encountered the new opportunities and challenges of the early twentieth century. Studies of piety, leading theologians, missions, and social reform have afforded important perspectives on a era during which many transcended old differences in order to cooperate for the "Christianization" of Canada, a vision shared by most Protestants at the turn of the century. Yet out of this widespread agreement over ends emerged two quite different cultures when it came to organizing the means to achieving them. Incorporation along denominational lines consolidated the mission and service activities of many but alienated others engaged in activities that had flourished in more local contexts. It is interesting to consider the impact of this impulse toward denominational incorporation in both setting and hardening the boundaries of these two cultures which came to characterize North American Protestantism for much of the rest of the century.

To put it another way, to what extent does twentieth-century evangelicalism consist, at least in part, of those who gravitated toward the leaders whose theological language expressed their dissatisfaction with the leaders and agencies (whether boards or colleges) of the emerging denominational bureaucracies that were supplanting the cooperative efforts of voluntary societies and other local initiatives? Even what we think of as the "social gospel movement" benefited from (and perhaps was in a sense even created by) the transfer of social issues from voluntary societies to national bureaucracies; most social gospel issues – concern for the poor, sabbath observance, temperance, and moral reform – were on the agenda of nineteenth-century evangelicalism as well. Often overlooked, given the attention to the close-to-home impact of the "social passion" – and perhaps more significant given the proportion of personnel and financial resources devoted to it – was the transfer of control of missions from local to national auspices. In the nineteenth century, social activism and cooperation in missions had been the driving force behind the evangelical voluntary societies; but as two religious cultures began to take shape, social reform and ecumenism became identified with "liberal" rather than "evangelical" Protestantism and derided as such.

Methodism's involvement in the Inter-Church Forward Movement in Canada (and in particular the response to the national campaign) illustrates the interplay of a number of these elements of transition. In the years between 1918 and 1924 Inter-Church committees involved Methodists in a network with few links to "evangelicalism" as it was being reshaped in the twentieth century. In the financial priorities and committee structure of the national campaign itself we find the agenda of leaders who, with their counterparts in the other major Protestant denominations, would comprise the ecumenical culture of which the newly created United Church of Canada became the most visible expression after 1925. As the report on the campaign to the Methodist General Conference noted in 1922, never before had "the five great communions, Anglican, Baptist, Congregationalist, Methodist and Presbyterian, co-operated in united programme and appeal to the nation for a great crusade." It was "a new era dawning."[21]

The network that had coalesced around the Inter-Church National Campaign expanded with the creation of the Inter-Church Advisory Council to which Methodists, Presbyterians, Congregationalists, Baptists, and (off and on) Anglicans sent representatives and financial support. The advisory council elected its last committee representatives in May 1924. At its 18 December 1924 meeting a special committee was set up to consider the council's "Future Policy" in a report to the May 1925 annual meeting. The archival files include no record of that meeting, but one wonders whether there was a tacit agreement that the creation of the United Church of Canada a month later would in effect reconstitute much of the network. The names of the denominational representatives of the advisory council are striking: those who guided the church union movement with their vision of liberal evangelicalism are visible primarily in honourary positions. Those who conducted the business of the council as officers and committee representatives of the council, on the other hand, bear a remarkable resemblance in both name and areas of responsibility to the first officers of the general council and the boards of the United Church of Canada.[22] In any event we find in the Inter-Church Forward Movement (and in particular the advisory council) a model of ecumenism that came to characterize mainstream Protestantism for much of the rest of the century: each of the largest denominations naming delegates, the number depending to some extent on size of its membership and financial contribution.[23]

The response of less prominent Methodists to this new organizational culture and its leadership is signalled in another set of documents related to the Inter-Church movement. The follow-up study of the Methodist Survey Commission, conducted at the conclusion of the national campaign, gives a glimpse of church life in 1920 from a perspective that differs in important respects from the national leaders. The records of the commission provide important information on rural Methodism, since four of the six visits made by commission representatives were organized as rural conferences for the areas surrounding Stratford, Woodstock, Belleville, and Chatham. The commission had hoped for a Canada-wide survey, but only one meeting (Montreal) was held outside Ontario. London, Ontario, was the other urban centre visited. In addition to the executive report of the survey commission, the archival records include a typed transcript of nearly 180 legal-size pages of field notes recording the comments made at these meetings. These two types of documentary sources invite comparison of the comments of those who participated in the regional meetings and the recommendations drawn from them by the commission executive.

Chaired by J.H. Gundy with Peter Bryce as secretary, the commission announced that its mandate was to gather advice on how the money raised during the national campaign might be distributed; it also hoped to contribute to "realizing more fully the spiritual results of the Campaign."[24] As the commission representatives met with local leaders, much of the discussion revolved around "the message of Methodism" which often led to consideration of changes in the results of evangelistic preaching which many had noticed in their lifetimes. The rural minister from Bay of Quinte who reported that he had never found it easier to win souls, with people almost inviting him to give them a chance to come to decision, was in a distinct minority.[25] The more common sentiment was discouragement with results when compared to the past. One minister ordained in the 1880s recalled that in first twelve years of ministry he never won less than 100 souls a year.[26]

There was no common explanation for the disappointing results. A layman who regretted that the Methodist church was not "gripping the constituency as it might" recalled the days when ministers preached of people fleeing from the wrath to come, of sin and salvation and a Saviour, and of a real devil. He now heard preaching about literature, science, culture, art, and the problems of everyday living.[27] Others countered by noting that the wage-earners had defected in response to the old preaching and there was still too much "talk about spiritual experience and too little about the carrying out of a real programme."[28] One person at the Bay of Quinte meeting defended the modern preaching style, arguing that they could not expect ministers to preach in the old way when they were not doing anything else in the old way: "The old-fashioned way was all right in its day, but I do not believe a man can get up and preach hell fire and brimstone as he could. There is a higher type of preaching today."[29] But some apparently disagreed for, one person noted, "many older men" were joining the Free Methodist church, seeing it as "nearer to the old type."[30]

One striking theme repeated at gathering after gathering, whether attended by ministers, lay men, or lay women in urban or rural areas, was the sense that the old evangelism was no longer effective because of changes in what was deemed as appropriate emotional expression. During an exchange at one of the women's meetings, participants commented that "people's minds are different"; they had been "taught to suppress" emotions. "We are not quite as natural people as we were," said one. "We have more to think of than previously." The class meeting's decline was connected to this different emotional make-up.[31] The commission's representative, Prof. Fred Langford, responded to the women's comments by observing that the fall revival at Victoria College had found little groups in bedrooms at Bible study. "There is a feeling," he added, "that we are not expressive in our emotional and religious life."[32]

A shift in emotional tone struck at the core of Methodist piety affecting not only such expressions of "heart religion" as the conversion experience but other distinctive Methodist features as well. At the Montreal meeting of the commission, Prof. W.A. Gifford described his class meeting experience as "the most permanent injury done to my life," where at the age of nine he "was urged to testify about experiences that I knew nothing about." He rejected the idea that the needs of the time would be met by the restoration of the past.[33] But Rev. Runnells defended the class and in particular the premium it had placed on experience. Raised in a Presbyterian home, he was attracted to Methodism because of the class meeting where members had no hesitancy in speaking about their religious experience. In his view, maintaining this emphasis was vital, for "when we get away from [the evangelistic note] we cannot compete with other churches in their ritual and their form of service."[34]

A shift in emphasis from an experience of conversion to ethics was how a number of participants described the transition.[35] "The religion dominating the world," claimed one London lay man, "is service to mankind." He considered that the church had squandered its opportunity to emphasize service, and other organizations such as the Rotary Club and the Chamber of Commerce were stepping in: "The Lord is springing up someone else to give the service. We know men who make the Rotary Club their religion. These societies are doing in themselves the Christian work for the Community ... We are serving ourselves and letting the church go."[36] Some ministers were concerned about the impact this "new religion" of service was having on the congregation. When asked why there were fewer conversions than in the past, one rural minister insisted that the preaching was as good as ever but the laity were not attending prayer meetings and other church services: "They are so engrossed in secular work that they do not help the minister to 'catch the fish' as they might."[37] Commenting on the disappearance of the class meeting and the difficulty of getting testimonies, a Bay of Quinte minister remarked, "We are rather serving than witnessing as a church."[38]

The most persistent concern expressed in the Survey Commission's meetings was for Methodist youth, and there were many calls for greater financial support of church activities for them. Both young and old described a wave of frivolity and pleasure-seeking which had become particularly pronounced after the war. Young people were more mobile with automobiles to take even those in rural areas to moving pictures, pool rooms, and dances in nearby towns. Not even the YMCA was considered a safe place to protect their morals.[39] The situation was serious enough for some to make a highly controversial proposal: that the church provide entertainment – even card playing and dancing – in order to keep the young people in the country. The dilemma for many congregations was how to compete with suspect secular organizations that specialized in attracting youth. Participants described feeling helpless since other churches, especially the Presbyterians, approved of dancing. Rural Methodist parents were particularly distressed with Victoria College which reportedly held dances right in Annesley Hall and hired professors who smoked.[40]

The criticism of Victoria went further, extending in a few cases to concerns about theological education. Some wondered whether questions raised at theological college created doubt in the pews.[41] However, theological education was more apt to be criticized by these particular groups for what it failed to teach (the special needs of the rural church being often cited as an example) and for holding up city positions as superior to rural ones. Complaints about Higher Criticism were surprisingly rare, although one minister linked the end of revivals with the loss of confidence in the authority of the Word of God.[42] Evidence of a debate over theological innovation was most pronounced at one of the Montreal meetings after Gifford charged that in the Protestant churches there was no "clearly conceived message that can be called an evangel in the church today." He maintained that in order to discover the message of Jesus for this generation ministers would have to let go of obsolete views of Scripture. St Paul had assumed the place where Jesus ought to be; the right idea of Scripture would restore Jesus to his place.[43]

Those who attended these gathering were not only worried that Methodism was no longer enjoying the successes of the past; they were concerned that its future was at risk with the declining number of candidates for the ministry. The reasons given acquired a familiar ring as they were repeated from place to place: many of those who might have gone into the ministry had not returned from the war; salaries were not high enough; parents were not encouraging their children to be ministers; the itinerant system of stationing ministers was autocratic; the ministry was no longer respected. There was no agreement on whether this crisis was the result of a presentation of religion that was too old-fashioned or too modern.

Methodism's way of linking religion and service was credited with expanding the sense of Christian responsibility and blamed for undermining the call to ministry. The chair of the commission, J.H. Gundy, was cited as an example of one who had responded to the church's insistence that "a man should make as good a contribution to life in business as in the ministry ... Our young fellows are seeing ways in which they can play their part as Christians in the other walks of life."[44] But this ran counter to an older sense of a call to ministry as the highest form of service. "There surely are men to give their lives to service, but they think they can serve just as well in other lines," commented one lay man.[45] A Montreal lay man recalled a time "when the church was the only means of a man expressing his religious and moral convictions, but today there are 101 institutions and organizations which are doing good work ... I do not come to the weekly mid-week meeting because I go to other places where I am helping my fellow-men."[46]

There were economic and demographic as well as theological factors affecting the ministry, in particular new employment opportunities. "It was continually said by my father, 'Get a good education and get off the farm,'" reported one man, and many responded to this advice in the past by going into the ministry.[47] Smaller family size, which made it more difficult to "dedicate one to the ministry," was a demographic change that might have reduced the number headed for ministry.[48] But coupled with a shrinking rural population was a growing manufacturing sector which offered well-paid jobs in the city requiring little or no educational preparation.

The education expectations for the ministry, on the other hand, were on the rise with the growing professionalization of the ministry. Educational costs made some think twice about their sense of call; as the young people in London pointed out, a young person would "sooner go into a factory and be a full fledged man in a month's time and know a little and earn a lot." To become a minister one had to spend as much to go to college as a doctor, added another, and doctors made more money than a minister.[49] Perhaps the unkindest cut of all was reported by a rural minister whose wife had told him that she could make more money herself than his salary.[50] These economic realities made lay involvement in the church, while engaged in a more lucrative form of "service," or choosing ministry in a denomination with lower educational requirements attractive alternatives to becoming a Methodist minister.

The Survey Commission completed its work by preparing a report of its findings. In contrast to the meetings themselves, it contained only muted references to the difficulties of squaring present reality with Methodism's evangelical past. It described ministers as "genuinely anxious and distressed about the lack of apparent success in their pulpit ministrations"; but as to whether the response to their pulpit message should be judged by the standards of the past it replied: "Has the time come when a new standard of success should be adopted? It is believed that we are in the transition stage, from the old to the new, in theology, in methods and form of public worship, in religious education, in our conceptions of evangelism and in our conceptions of social righteousness."[51] But no specific suggestions were made on how to move toward those standards, or even how they might be identified. The only other related reference came in the concluding summary which stated that it was evident that ministers and the laity generally were concerned with "the apparent lack of definite Conversion from the preaching of the word. They are far from satisfied in this regard, rather are they deeply distressed and they refuse to be comforted with other successful aspects of the Ministry."[52]

On the other hand, consolidation of smaller churches in the name of efficiency featured prominently in the final report of Methodist Survey Commission, far out of proportion to references recorded in the field notes.[53] Not surprisingly, closing down the community church was considered a last resort from a local perspective. It was, observed one minister, analogous to the situation of rural schools: it required "some Dominion body who could do this just in the same way as the [Dominion Ministerial Support Committee] helped to pull up all our salaries. The consolidated schools are only possible through the Provincial action."[54]

A clash of values – attachment to local community versus centralized efficiency – loomed on the horizon.[55] In Methodism's response to a campaign billed as an opportunity for spiritual education and fundraising we find evidence of a denomination whose leaders were defining its mission in terms of its "connexional" work. But this consolidation threatened to interfere with support for local expressions of outreach, mission, and service such as local evangelistic campaigns and voluntary societies for missions and social reform.⁵⁶ As one London layman observed, "I found that in soliciting funds for the campaign, the officials in Toronto seemed to be most interested in their departmental work than in our local churches."⁵⁷

And little wonder – over $4,000,000 was raised for and distributed entirely through "connexional" boards rather than local congregations. This apparently eliminated even support for the Women's Missionary Society (WMS) which had cooperated with (but retained its autonomy from) the male-controlled Missionary Society. When the pledge tally indicated that the goal had been exceeded, members of the WMS executive requested that some of surplus be used to support their missionaries.⁵⁸ Even though they claimed that their own local fundraising had been hampered by fear of appearing to be in opposition to the national campaign, the executive of the national campaign took no action to support their request: if a surplus materialized it was to be divided between the Missionary Society and the Superannuation Fund for pensions – recipients of the largest disbursement of funds to begin with!⁵⁹

Compared with these two draws on the funds raised by the national campaign, even other "connexional" concerns received a relatively small amount of money. The Missionary Society and Superannuation Fund each received approximately $1,500,000 and the Educational Society approximately $750,000. Funds for the other two boards were drawn from a $250,000 "Special Fund for Current Revenue." The specific amounts were not made public, but an indication can be inferred from the 20 January 1920 balance sheet (which indicates that over half the money had been raised and disbursed before the designated Sunday in February 1920): the debits included nearly $1.2 million to the Missionary Society; nearly $1 million to the Superannuation Fund; and almost $530,000 to the Educational Society. By comparison, disbursements to the remaining two boards seem rather meagre: $48,193.22 for evangelism and social service and $5,526.77 for Sunday school and the Young People's Society.⁶⁰

By 1925 the word "evangelical" was coming to symbolize different things for Methodists, depending in part on where one stood. For rural churches, for example, it was associated with an expansion and success that they were no longer experiencing. Those who could not see the proposed consolidation ahead as hopeful were left longing to go back to the place they had left behind. Emotion was accepted and even expected – Methodism remained for them a religion of the heart. But among those who saw Methodism as an organization with a mission that was national in scope, evangelism received little attention as a *connexional* priority, perhaps because of its more "local" character. From the margins this denominational incorporation might well have appeared "condensed," not only because of a more restrained emotional style but in the sense of "sameness" that resulted from its efforts to coordinate and consolidate the diffuse activities that had grown up around evangelical Protestantism.

The liberal evangelicals of the progressive period seemed most adept in articulating Methodism's seemingly contradictory impulses. It was they who with Presbyterians and Congregationalists of like spirit created a basis for church union and garnered support for its founding vision. But how effective were they as leaders outside and beyond the neutral zone? In the report of the executive committee of the Survey Commission and the Inter-Church Advisory Council we can detect the coalescing of a network of a new generation of leaders who would set the agenda of mainstream Canadian Protestantism after 1925 and manage its considerable financial resources. This is a group different in both composition and assumptions from the liberal evangelicals who had created and promoted the Basis of Union earlier in the century. These new leaders had their feet firmly planted on the other side of the neutral zone but were not always sure how to deal with those who were more slow to cross it.

The emerging model of ecumenism espoused by these new leaders of mainstream Protestantism seemed to have a corrosive effect on the old evangelical consensus. For example, the Evangelical Alliance in which the early supporters of church union had been prominent began to wane after 1903, overshadowed by union negotiations.[61] The last meeting of its executive was held in July 1918 – the year in which the Inter-Church movement began to take shape. Organized evangelicalism in Canada in the twentieth century has since been characterized by a non-denominational – at times even an anti-denominational – character. It has spurned the "ecumenical" movement while in practice exhibiting as much (perhaps even more) cooperation across denominational lines in missionary, educational, and reform ventures as mainstream Protestantism. Perhaps the networks associated with the two organizational cultures which emerged in this period tell part of that story. At any rate, it is interesting to note that membership in the new "evangelical alliance," the Evangelical Fellowship of Canada, can be taken out not only by a denomination (along the lines of early mainstream ecumenism) but by individual persons or congregations as well.

The decades between the unions of 1884 and 1925 were thus complex ones for Canadian Methodists, made all the more challenging because of the broader reorganizing process within Protestantism. At times Methodists probably sympathized with Alice and her adventures through uncharted territory as they considered that past: "'Who are you?' said the Caterpillar ... 'I hardly know, Sir, just at present,' Alice replied rather shyly, 'at least I know who I *was* when I got up this morning, but I think I must have been changed several times since then.'"

7 "We Will Evangelize with a Whole Gospel or None": Evangelicalism and the United Church of Canada

DAVID PLAXTON

In January 1983, even as national newspapers and magazines were wondering about the rise of "conservative evangelicals" in North America, a United Church presbytery in North Bay, Ontario, fired a well-known minister, apparently as a result of his evangelical style. Through a series of ecclesiastical and civil court cases that lasted almost a decade, the Rev. Ronald McCaw argued that he had been released not because of some obvious deficiency in his pastoral role, as the presbytery had claimed, but rather because "he was the victim of an anti-evangelical sentiment in the United Church of Canada."[1] McCaw was not, of course, the only member of the United Church to feel that evangelical Protestantism was unwelcome in his denomination. For years before his dismissal, McCaw and others had argued that the United Church had abandoned its evangelical roots – a creed of traditions, theology, and activity that had, they argued, been carried over from the eighteenth and nineteenth centuries and was established as United Church doctrine in the "Basis of Union." After his final court victory, McCaw summed up his feelings by pointing out that "we have been claiming for years that the church has been straying from the Basis of Union."[2] In his search for an evangelical past, McCaw was looking nostalgically to an older, purer United Church tradition – a tradition that more conservative members unashamedly identified as evangelical and to which they believed the church must return. This quest for evangelical renewal (by the 1990s a process many United Church people felt was necessary and overdue) did not begin, as some might expect, with a return to John Wesley or Thomas Chalmers or Jonathan Edwards. Rather, for many conservatives in the United Church, the evangelicalism they sought was to be found in the early history of the denomination, in the years of orthodoxy they believed preceded and followed the consummation of union in June 1925.

Some historians of Canadian religion, not to mention many Canadian Christians both in and out of the United Church, might find this search for an evangelical past in the denomination's early history puzzling. That the United Church was constructed on non- or post-evangelical foundations has become the accepted interpretation of both conservative and liberal historians of contemporary Canadian Protestantism.[3] Like John Stackhouse, many assume that the "United Church of Canada never was well represented among Canadian evangelicals" and, following the logic of this argument, they separate the United Church from traditionally evangelical ideas like the concern for orthodoxy, piety, mission, and personal evangelism.[4]

This assumption is based on the widely held truism that by the time of the formation of the United Church in 1925 there were very few traditional evangelicals left in any of the mainline denominations. Based on what Michael Gauvreau has astutely described as the well-travelled historiographical "journey from religious 'orthodoxy' through theological 'liberalism' to the eventual 'irrelevance' of Protestantism,"[5] many historians argue that by the 1920s, evangelicalism, if not already dead, was clearly withering in Canada's Protestant mainstream. Such conclusions tend to rest, however, on studies of those who self-consciously separated themselves from popular social and theological currents. As William Hutchison has argued, our understanding of the religious past is based too much on the actions and words of "dissenters and other outsiders" and not enough on "the more massive mainline religion they rejected, or from which they were excluded." His conclusion that denominational "history has not ranked high among our priorities" is at least as true in Canada as it is in the United States.[6]

The reality of mainline Protestantism in the first decades of this century cannot be encapsulated by exclusive, often misleading labels like "social gospel" or "theological liberalism." Though several excellent studies have established that some who fit these narrow categories were active and influential in the late nineteenth and early twentieth centuries, the Protestant mainstream cannot be reduced to the actions of a Salem Bland or a J.S. Woodsworth any more than it can be defined by a T.T. Shields. Unlike the fairly straightforward radicalism of these leaders, the majority faith of this period was a complex mix of traditional evangelicalism, rational modernism, and accommodating liberalism. For some, this often confusing mix of old and new was alienating, and they found refuge from its complexities in the safe enclosures of its fundamentalist and modernist margins. But for the majority the fringes were more unattractive than the middle, and most accepted the essentially moderate, liberal evangelical option that came to define the greater part of Canadian Protestantism in the early part of the twentieth century. It is in this moderate evangelical mainstream that we find the foundations of the United Church of Canada.

Though the United Church was formed from three denominations, it was, as John Webster Grant has argued, the natural result of a theological climate based on some broadly shared evangelical ideas. In the years leading up to the formation of the United Church, mainstream members of the large denominations were keen to make their theological position obvious, and the content of their publications and personal correspondence indicates that most accepted neither the extreme social gospel nor the reactionary individualist positions of the modernists and fundamentalists inside and out of their denominations. Instead, a majority of clergy and lay leadership embraced a theological position that integrated both the traditional evangelical emphasis on converting individuals and the well-established evangelical passion for creating a purer and more just society. In their common drive to establish a post-millennial Kingdom of God on earth, many mainline Protestants at the turn of the century agreed that the Kingdom could only be created by the conversion of individual sinners and the creation of a Christ-like society through practical Christian action. By concentrating on the words and actions of those on the margins of Canadian Protestantism, the interpretation of this pre-union period has tended to emphasize a dichotomy between those Protestants who sought social improvement and those who concentrated on the salvation of individuals – to distinguish, in other words, so-called liberals from so-called evangelicals. For the majority, however, this distinction made little sense, for it was unwilling to separate the need to redeem individuals from the duty of regenerating the society. For them, like the "liberal evangelicals" that David Bebbington has identified in Britain, "a combination of social concern and evangelistic zeal came naturally."[7]

During the first decades of the twentieth century, the era in which social Christian concerns are supposed by many to have replaced individual ones, many mainline Protestants maintained a belief in the necessity of a New Birth experience. Though some mainline thinkers were beginning to reject the evangelical emphasis on conversion, many, including those who were instrumental in the creation of the United Church, continued to employ a traditional though nuanced conversionist perspective. George Pidgeon, who was to become one of the most important actors in the drama of Church Union, was among those clearly committed to an evangelical understanding of salvation. The subject of the New Birth was a common theme in Pidgeon's sermons, a theme he maintained throughout his long preaching career. His early thought on the subject of the New Birth is contained in a sermon by that name that he preached on several occasions between 1900 and 1905. Concerned that some evangelical principles that he cherished were not receiving the attention they once had in the mainline denominations, Pidgeon warned about the dangers of neglecting these evangelical essentials and argued that the spiritual change of the New Birth must "be wrought in the soul of every individual." He worried, however, that the idea that salvation could be attained through living a good life was replacing the need not only to be converted but to seek to convert others. And all of this was due, he argued, to a lack of conviction about the force of the "Saviour's words" and a lack of effort "individually and collectively to rescue men from their danger and lead them to Christ & salvation." Christians needed, he said, to be aroused "to a sense of the danger of the unsaved & of the need of more earnest effort ... for conversion of sinners, both individually and as a congregation." His solution to this problem was not to make his message of faith more current or to substitute practical Christian action for conversion. His solution was the simple, traditional formula of evangelical Protestantism. The Bible, he insisted, taught the reality of the risen Christ – a Christ crucified and glorified who renews the souls of men. After reminding his listeners of this formula, he asked them to "apply these tests. Has God manifest power in you? Has His word become a force in your soul? Is the risen Christ more than a name?" If so, he suggested, all is well. But if the answers were not affirmative, "no matter what [his] virtues," Pidgeon claimed that the sinner remained outside the Kingdom.[8]

From 1900 when this sermon was first preached to the end of Pidgeon's ministerial career in the 1950s, this same concern for the conversion of sinners, and especially the centrality of the cross in the process of New Birth, remained paramount in his faith.[9] Although he was well known as a preacher "deeply committed to social reform" and is remembered as an effective social and moral reformer, he often took time in his sermons to separate himself from more liberal social Christians in the Presbyterian and Methodist denominations, those who believed that societies, not individuals, should be redeemed.[10] Pidgeon believed strongly in the necessity of individual conversion. In a sermon preached in 1924, for example, he argued that "Paul's entire emphasis is on the spiritual. He never fell into the mistake of thinking that he could change the spirit of human relationships by changing the system under which people lived."[11] Unlike some contemporaries who saw individual religion as selfish and ultimately unchristian, Pidgeon held that it was impossible to separate social and moral reformation from the biblical necessity of a New Birth.

This central emphasis on the salvation of individual sinners, combined with an obvious concern for social action and service (a liberal evangelicalism shared by many Presbyterians, Methodists and Congregationalists) formed much of the theological and bureaucratic foundations of the United Church of Canada. In a sermon preached in the months just following Union, Pidgeon emphasized the importance of what he called "The Spiritual and the Practical in the Church's Life." He opened the sermon by noting the first United Church General Council's statement, which called for the "re-consecration of spiritual life, revisualisation of the task of the Church, the re-dedication of the entire membership to God, and the extension of the Kingdom of God by definite evangelistic effort."[12] He noted further that the wording of this statement had led to some disagreement between those who felt that either the spiritual or the practical should be highlighted. Continuing arguments that he had maintained for years, Pidgeon stated that "Really the two are one. Spiritual revival is always the source of missionary activity; missionary enterprise is the necessary expression of spiritual renewal."[13] And, speaking as the moderator of the new Church, he summed up what the implications of this theological basis were. "In the United Church," he said, "we are laying stress on the central doctrine of the faith. Previously we emphasized secondary matters. But our differences are on points of minor importance and we made this the ground of separation from our brethren. There is a body of truth known as the Doctrines of Grace by the preaching of which men are saved. These are at the heart of our Statement of Doctrine. The emphasis which our Union places on this entitles us to expect new measures of the wonderful grace of God."[14] Pidgeon concluded this sermon by arguing that the new denomination was grounded in the desire to convert and save, and, more importantly, that it was in this central evangelical belief that the uniting denominations had found the common ground they needed to become one in the United Church of Canada.

By emphasizing the primacy of evangelical spiritual concerns, Pidgeon was not neglecting what he called the practical work of the church. The widespread acceptance of social concern and action by Canadian evangelicals in the nineteenth and twentieth centuries has been well documented.[15] The United Church was the heir to much of this social Christianity and was the spiritual home for a wide variety of social activists and to a number of social gospellers. The mainstream of the church, although well disposed to social Christianity, was, like Pidgeon, not willing to concede that evangelism and social service were incompatible. Indeed, this majority opinion concerning the proper relationship between saving souls and cleansing society was institutionalized by the creation of what would become the United Church's most powerful division, the Board of Evangelism and Social Service. Like its predecessors in the Presbyterian and Methodist Churches, the United Church board was established to continue the work of seeking conversions as well as cleansing the moral and social environment in which the church served. The inseparability of these two concerns was stated early by the first secretary of the general council, and later moderator of the church, T. Albert Moore. In the first number of the official United Church newspaper, the *New Outlook*, Moore discussed the proper mix of the twin concerns. In "The Mission of the Church in Personal Evangelism and Social Service," he boldly challenged both those in the new church who would have social service excluded from the denomination's agenda and others who would have the church become a mere social service agency. He asserted that the two were necessary if the church was to "avoid both an evangelism lacking in moral vigour, [and] a programme of social service divorced from deep religious incentive."[16] Moore, like Pidgeon, believed that evangelism without a social component, like social service without a profession of faith, was not true, evangelical Christianity.

The United Church's encounter with the Depression and World War II had a profound impact on this developing liberal evangelical foundation. During what John Webster Grant has described as the Canadian Protestant churches' "Years of Crisis,"[17] this United Church vision would be moulded equally by its confrontation with contemporary exigencies and its powerful evangelical inheritance. In 1931, during the depths of the Depression, Hugh Wesley Dobson, the western field secretary of the Board of Evangelism and Social Service, wrote to the secretary of the board describing the impact of the Depression in the West. Dobson, who was originally a Methodist and a dedicated social Christian, saw this time of crisis as an opportunity for advance. Though one historian has recently labelled him a "progressive social gospeller," Dobson's awareness of the nature of suffering and the possibilities that this suffering afforded the church indicates that his perspective was much more complex than the label "social gospel" allows.[18] Indeed, in this letter to his superior, Dobson suggested forcefully that "there is a recognition of the supreme opportunity that we have now for Christian evangelism. People are eager for any good news that we can give to them, and if the Christian message is, indeed, good news, we ought to be able to demonstrate it today."[19] He recognized that because of the

Depression there was increasing awareness of social problems; however, he was more aware of rising spiritual expectations. Indeed, throughout the Depression years he was enthusiastic about the growing demand for spiritual as well as social aid. As early as his 1930 annual report to the Board of Evangelism and Social Service, he described a new spiritual mood in the West: "Preaching regularly, and addressing congregations as well as small groups, I have found a growing favour toward evangelical Christianity. People hunger for help, and know their help cometh only from God. The year has been a very strenuous one, but one is encouraged by the recognition of more sober thought and a clearer sense of dependence upon God for forgiveness and help and for the enrichment of life."[20] This "favour toward evangelical Christianity" was, Dobson believed, a direct result of the Depression, and though he was disturbed by the material consequences of the economic crisis, he was sure that it would lead not only to important social reconstruction but, more importantly, to a return to evangelical Christianity.

By 1932 Dobson was convinced that a new spiritual season had begun in Canada. His letters and reports from that year are filled with an excitement about spiritual possibilities. He noted a distinct turning away from material concerns and a vital interest in spiritual ones. The trend he had identified in 1930 was continuing and was, he said in 1932, "revealed by a turning to an evangelical experience as the beginning of a new way of life ... Redemption is becoming a vital experience with many people and as a result Church work has an added zest and new meaning."[21] Contrary to the claim that United Church clergy were faced with the question "Why no revival?" throughout the 1930s, in 1932 Dobson wrote "that everywhere there is in actual fact a revival – of a purer and more undefiled religious life in our churches. So we are singing a song even in the night. The Christian movement always did thrive on pain. It became the way to salvation and progress."[22] For Dobson, then, revival was not a disappointing dream but an exhilarating and powerful fact, a fact that he related intimately to the spiritual longings and demands of those suffering under crippling social and economic hardship.

The evangelical possibilities of the Depression years were not lost on other sections of the United Church. As David Marshall has noted, throughout the thirties the leadership of the church pursued a program of aggressive evangelism, with the intent of both deepening the commitment of those affiliated with the church and bringing new members to the denomination through a profession of faith. Marshall interprets this enthusiasm for evangelical work as a conservative reaction to the religious Depression that the process of secularization was creating in Canada's Protestant community. Moreover, he argues that "the fact that an increasing proportion of the church's effort was concentrated on trying to create or organize a revival of evangelical religion was testimony to how desperate things were becoming."²³ Marshall's understanding of the widespread call for revivalistic campaigns presumes that the evangelical mood of the 1930s represented a break with the earlier United Church history and that United Church-led revivals were imposed on an uninterested and unreceptive populace. Nonetheless, if the many calls for evangelism are interpreted outside the "secularization" thesis and seen as a continuation of, not a break from denominational and social trends, a very different picture of the United Church's evangelistic activity in this period appears.

For architects of union like George Pidgeon, the bases of the United Church of Canada were distinctly evangelical, as his many sermons and publications from the Union period attest. It is not surprising, perhaps, that a conservative Presbyterian like Pidgeon should understand the new denomination in evangelical and evangelistic terms. Yet the belief that Union would be a period of spiritual advancement and an evangelical event was also widespread among those who were obviously more liberal than Pidgeon. Hugh Dobson, though he worried that the confusion caused by Union might impede Christian social work, was sure that the coming together of the three churches would be an "evangelical movement."²⁴ In the years before the consummation of Union, Dobson believed "that when the energy of these churches now taken up by their competitive rivalry is cooperatively devoted to Christian evangelism and high forms of service we will see at least the dawn of a new day of spiritual progress."²⁵ Clearly, Dobson saw the process of forming a United Church as an opportunity for furthering both the work of evangelism and of social service. From the time of Union, then, the desire to convert and advance was considered an important part of the passion for establishing the Kingdom of God. The reality for most leaders of the United Church was that true evangelical revival required evangelistic *and* social emphases, though the priority of the one over the other might fluctuate in different circumstances. Continued emphasis on these two traditional concerns, much more than the desire to "stem the tide of secularization," lay at the root of the United Church's evangelistic enthusiasm in the 1930s.

Seen from the perspective of continuity, then, revivals led or sponsored by the United Church in the 1930s fitted well with the understanding of the denomination in this period as in many ways an evangelical one. One of the most intriguing evangelistic efforts associated with the church in the thirties is the Oxford Group Movement. The Oxford Group Movement's emphasis on the need for an experience of conversion, its call for witnessing and sharing, and its dedication to moral reform were very attractive to men like George Pidgeon who shared these same emphases. Though much in the Movement's theological perspective was simple and of questionable social utility in an age of economic need, the evangelical basis of much of its program struck a chord not only with some United Church leaders but also with many Canadians. As the Oxford Group made its way across the country in 1933, it attracted larger and larger crowds, culminating in a meeting in Vancouver that attracted over 8,000 people. This popularity can be attributed partly to simple curiosity. It is clear, however, that the essentially evangelical basis of the movement, and particularly its emphasis on the requirement of a changed life through the experience of conversion, played well into the continuing mainstream belief that such an experience was, as Dobson had argued, "the beginning of a new way of life." Though it has been argued that the Oxford Group's simplistic answers to complicated social problems provided weary Canadians with a watered-down, easily swallowed Christianity,[26] it is perhaps more useful to view the movement as an expression of the evangelical beliefs of Canada's Protestant mainstream. For many who were searching for spiritual answers for present problems, the Oxford Group Movement was for a short period the most accessible manifestation of the "revival" that Hugh Dobson had identified in 1932.[27] The methods and theological bases of the movement may have had questionable evangelical credentials, especially in later manifestations, but the traditional chords it struck in the early thirties were matched well with the searching evangelicalism of the mainstream.

The direct influence of the Oxford Group Movement began to fade by 1934, the result of a change in public opinion that accompanied a shift in the Movement's emphasis from individually centred "life-changing" to a more collective and controversial "world-changing" perspective.[28] But the revivalistic mood it had both represented and encouraged continued on in the active life of the United Church. Aware that they were in the midst of a new spiritual season, the United Church's fifth General Council had requested in 1932 that the Board of Evangelism and Social Service prepare a statement on evangelism. The resulting *Statement*, which was presented to the sixth General Council in 1934, established firmly and in great detail the official United Church position on the question of evangelism and its place in the denomination. The document began with a definition of the term that made clear the United Church's interest in conversionism. "Evangelism," the *Statement* asserted, "means a powerful interest in human redemption as this is seen in the crisis of personal experience."[29] Though some of the document was clearly a response to the controversy caused by the United Church's involvement with the Oxford Group Movement,[30] the framers of the *Statement* were most interested in preparing a document that the denomination could use to continue and increase the revivalistic mood that was becoming a hallmark of Canadian Protestant life during the Depression.

Among the *Statement*'s many conclusions was the call for preaching missions, personal interviews, and personal testimonies intended to solicit "decisive responses."[31] This call and the reality of a continuing interest in evangelistic activity resulted in the United Church's involvement in a nation-wide campaign, which was to lead to the "evangelization of Canadian life." Writings from both Pidgeon and Dobson from 1936, the first year of this campaign, indicate that even through the harshest years of the Depression, and in the face of a worsening international situation, the evangelical presuppositions they had maintained at the time of Union were still very much alive. For both men, the evangelistic campaign was to be the first step in the process of Christianizing the nation. "The social idealism and passion of the Church in our time is truly of God," said Pidgeon, "and our first need now is to bring the Divine Spirit, who inspires it, into more complete control of the lives through whom it is to be carried into effect."[32] Though the close connection between the need first to convert and then to make socially active was threatened by debates in the thirties, many leaders stuck to their liberal evangelical perspective. The evangelical enthusiasm of the United Church had maintained, even when confronted with horrifying social suffering, that without individual salvation there could be no Christianization.

Near the end of the 1930s, however, Hugh Dobson was beginning to sense that some in the United Church, and certainly more than he had recognized previously, were questioning, or in some cases ignoring the necessary connection between conversion and Christian social action. For many years one of Dobson's favourite projects had been the efficient and effective maintenance of Redemptive Homes for Women. In 1938, in his interviews to fill a vacant superintendent's position at a home in British Columbia, Dobson was "surprised at the lack of accent on the thought of Christian redemption." In a troubled letter to J.R. Mutchmor, then secretary of the Board of Evangelism and Social Service, Dobson worried that the candidates he was interviewing "seem alien to the thought of changed lives through Christ," and stated that "I am sure our church must face more steadily the necessity of winning persons and families to Christ and redeeming them through God's Grace." Dobson was seeing a subtle but important shift in the United Church's perspective. Where previously he had been able to assume that those involved in Christian social service would recognize the need for individual redemption, he was now seeing that some no longer considered the one necessary for the other. His solution to this problem was simple, and, based on his theological presuppositions, not at all surprising. If the emphasis on winning persons was to be maintained, he argued, "A vast change must take place in 'the use of the Bible.' The old expository method is fading and the new sense of value of the Bible is not fortified by a clear enough knowledge on the part of many to break *the word* to the people through the use of the Bible ... We must keep on suggesting *the purpose* of Christian missions and the necessity of *preaching for a verdict*. Upon our Christian leaders must be laid what we used to call *'the burden of souls.'* New ways will be found for action but we need 'expectancy.'"[33] Though some have argued that the conversionist emphasis in Canadian mainline Protestantism was all but lost by the turn of the century, at the end of the 1930s Hugh Dobson was just beginning to become aware of what to him was a dangerous development.[34] Mainline clergy had, of course, worried for some time about the decrease in evangelistic emphases in their churches, but Dobson's awareness at the end of the thirties was particularly acute. He was obviously shaken by a degree of disinterest in redemption that he had not previously witnessed. For Dobson and most others who had helped found the United Church, to work for the Kingdom without concern for individual salvation was a theological impossibility. The succeeding years would show, however, that what Dobson was seeing was the beginning of a foundational shift in the theological identity of the United Church.

The activities of the United Church during the thirties were not limited, of course, to evangelistic pursuits. The minority of social gospellers in the denomination during the Depression were fighting for more radical solutions than those proposed by the supporters of evangelistic effort. In the early years of the decade, some of the more radical members of the United Church leadership and professoriate began to call for a total dismantling of the corrupt capitalist system which they felt lay at the root of the existing economic crisis. The demands from the church's left wing were effective in raising some limited denominational support for their almost purely social-service, though biblically based, agenda.[35] A more significant result of their limited success was, however, the institutionalization – among a minority – of a denominational theology based almost entirely on social activism, and divorced from the need to evangelize. As John Webster Grant has pointed out, even the limited success of groups like the Fellowship for a Christian Social Order allowed for the creation of a "dichotomy between evangelism and social action" and created a situation where the "advocates of the two were competing for attention."[36] The effects of this competition were that, at least in the minds of some, social service and evangelism became separated and the eventual victory of one over the other became, for the first time, a possibility.

The declaration of war in September 1939 heralded the end of a particularly vital period of evangelism in the United Church's history. Although Hugh Dobson had argued in 1940 that "every need for Evangelism in normal times is tenfold greater in war times and times when nations are in distress,"[37] the majority of the church's effort from 1940 to 1944 was aimed at confronting directly the social problems that the Depression and the coming of war had made obvious. The most conspicuous example of this "practical" work was the report of the Commission on Church, Nation and World Order, which was intended to provide leadership in the reconstruction of Canadian society in the aftermath of war. The document was presented to the eleventh General Council in 1944 under the title *Church, Nation and World Order*. The report was divided into several sections, each of which made specific recommendations about governmental and economic policy, and very few of which had any specific spiritual or Christian context. Though the document was billed as a "Christian Charter,"[38] at least one astute editorialist noted that the report was filled with recommendations "that have no exclusive application on their face to church organization," and concluded therefore that it represented a "paternalism which trespasses on the field of social service." The most significant aspect of the report was that after two years, numerous drafts, and countless presentations, *Church, Nation and World Order* was all but ignored. Though many of its recommendations eventually became central to the Canadian welfare state, the legislation establishing national pensions and family allowances had little to do with direct ecclesiastical influence. The report and its reception revealed that the effort to create a more just and equitable society, once the preserve of those who wished to Christianize the nation, had been taken over by secular agencies. Moreover, as the editorialist from Quebec made clear, many Canadians had come to see social service as the proper sphere of secular, governmental agencies and dissociated it from the true "spiritual" work of the church.[39]

In the years immediately following the end of the Second World War, the church's activism was guided by essentially the same theological concerns that had informed its evangelistic activities in the thirties. In its desire to maintain a peaceful society and to help the nation adjust to life after war, the United Church felt compelled to continue the work of "the building up of the Kingdom of God."[40] Near the conclusion of the war effort in Europe, the United Church initiated a program of aggressive evangelism that was intended, as in previous campaigns, to elevate the faith of the church's members and preach the gospel to the unchurched as well as "to help to rehabilitate our country and its people in home, in church, in community, in health, in work, and in security."[41] The "Crusade For Christ and His Kingdom" was met with a great deal of enthusiasm and expectancy by both the leadership of the church and the laity it was intended to reach. The opening of the crusade in Vancouver in September 1945 attracted some 10,000 people to a "colorful pageant" that featured "an 800-voice mixed choir ... set against a backdrop depicting the crucifixion and resurrection of Christ."[42] The continuing evangelical impulse of the church was obvious in the symbolism and the goals of the crusade and its aggressive style played well into the general post-war religious upswing. The crusade would be, however, one of the United Church's last attempts to affect widespread social change through direct, large-scale evangelistic appeal. In the years following the end of the crusade in 1947, the combined effects of a changing nation and the church's shifting view of itself and its role in the society brought the original United Church desire to "evangelize with a whole Gospel" into question.

The pageantry of the "Crusade for Christ" and the church's emphasis in the decade after the war on an aggressive and diversified evangelism were in keeping with a religious mood that permeated much of North American Protestantism throughout the 1950s. For over a decade after the end of the Second World War, the United Church of Canada was part of a general North American trend towards theological consensus, and throughout much of the 1950s the United Church maintained with a sense of theological certainty its consciously mediating evangelical position.[43] The continuing emphasis on the necessary links between conversionism and social action are perhaps best demonstrated by the confident words of the chairman of the Board of Evangelism and Social Service, George Birtch. In the board's *Annual Report* from 1959, he stated:

God's great goal (so the evangelist makes us understand) is to save your soul, and if He achieves that He must surely feel that the price of atonement has been satisfied. But Jesus came preaching not the soul's salvation but the Kingdom of God. He spoke not of crown wearing but of cross bearing and of urgent Kingdom work ... Evangelism that focuses attention on personal salvation as an end in itself rather than as a step on the way to glorious liberty of sharing with God freely in His Kingdom work is guilty of betraying the end for which Christ died. The chief end of God is not to save man's soul. God redeems man so that the chief end of man might be realized – to glorify God and enjoy Him forever.[44]

Although some in the United Church were actively continuing the liberal evangelical perspective upon which the denomination was founded, significantly, Birtch's remarks also hint at the stresses both within and without that were weakening this once solid theological foundation.

The twin concerns of evangelism and social service had always been held in a healthy tension in the United Church of Canada. The more conservative theological mood of the post-war years shifted the debate away from battles over the predominance of one over the other and towards discussions of the most appropriate means of evangelism and, more significantly, the goals of the denomination's evangelistic efforts. The 1950s were a period of heightened interest in evangelism – a reality that is demonstrated not only by the United Church's emphasis on national movements like the "Crusade for Christ," but also by the rise in popularity of a new breed of itinerant evangelists like the American Billy Graham and Canadian Charles Templeton.[45] Many in the church supported the work of these evangelists and some of their Canadian crusades were either endorsed by or conducted under the auspices of the United Church of Canada. Starting in the Maritimes in 1950, Charles Templeton led missions for the Board of Evangelism and Social Service and continued, as the secretary, J.R. Mutchmor, recalled, "on a coast to coast pattern, autumn after autumn."[46] Before he left the ministry and ended his evangelistic career in 1957, Templeton's missions were well attended and favourably received by many United Church leaders and members.[47] Billy Graham and his Canadian missions were not, however, so universally popular.

Though Billy Graham was only loosely associated with the United Church's evangelistic work in the fifties, opinion about him within the denomination was divided.[48] As George Birtch's 1959 defence of liberal evangelicalism indicates, some church leaders were reacting against evangelistic methods that saw the conversion of the individual as "an end in itself," a theological error that some in the denomination felt Billy Graham propagated. Though powerful men like Mutchmor and the theologian R.C. Chalmers supported Graham and considered him a "humble Christian gentleman," younger leaders, including many who were disposed to evangelism, were less likely to endorse the Graham crusades. Dr William Berry, once described by Mutchmor as "a colorful and able evangelistic leader," believed that Graham propagated a brand of evangelism with which the United Church had no connection – an evangelism that made conversion of the individual an end in itself and not a step towards practical Christian action. By the early sixties, this view of Graham and his particular evangelistic emphases had become officially if not generally accepted in the United Church. In 1963 when Graham returned to Canada to conduct missions in the Maritimes, the official United Church position was "not to endorse the Graham campaign."[49] Though there was widespread support for Graham in the

United Church, especially among the laity, the Board of Evangelism and Social Service chose to contradict some of its ministers in the Maritimes and not allow the denomination to be affiliated with the evangelist.[50] In the months following the board's decision, a series of letters to the United Church's official paper, *The Observer*, indicated that many in the church could not understand why the board had refused to support the Graham crusade. While one letter from a minister noted that Graham's mass evangelism was irrelevant in a time of racial tension, the others, all apparently from lay people, supported both Graham and his evangelistic methods.[51] By the early 1960s it was clear that evangelism and the United Church's attachment to it were becoming increasingly divisive issues.

The changing perspective on the United Church's relationship to evangelism was due in large part to a new generation of leadership. Until the 1950s most of the denominational leadership was composed of men who had begun their ministerial careers near the beginning of the century. These leaders, many of whom had fought for Union and helped to establish the church's theological foundations, generally held to a theology that made evangelism the basis of all other church work. This was a theological position that Pidgeon and Dobson maintained throughout their long careers and Mutchmor continued in 1965 when he argued that "Evangelism is the biggest subject in the church. It is top priority, the major concern."[52] For church leaders who had been raised in and vigorously supported the Protestant dream of establishing the Kingdom of God in Canada, the conversion of individual sinners was always a paramount concern. For the leaders who followed this first generation, however, establishing the reign of the spirit of Christ on earth was an increasingly untenable goal. Though many of the clergy in the fifties maintained the need for decision and sought conversions as a first step in the improvement of society, by the mid-1960s, it was becoming increasingly difficult to find leaders who supported the original liberal evangelical vision of men like Pidgeon and Dobson. Even Mutchmor, the moderator of the church until 1965, was by the end of his term already becoming something of an anachronism.

Throughout the 1960s many of the church's clergy and leadership began conspicuously to separate the denomination's work for social improvement from the previously primary evangelistic imperative. The combined influence of an urge to distinguish the denomination from a form of belief that many identified as American, the rise to power of a new generation of leadership that subscribed to neither the postmillennial hopes of its predecessors nor their passion for evangelism, and an identifiable rejection of denominational precedent in decision-making culminated in a newly aligned United Church of Canada.[53] The formation of the unmistakably evangelical United Church Renewal Fellowship in 1965 demonstrated conclusively that evangelicalism, liberal or otherwise, had been pushed to the periphery of the United Church.[54]

The separation of the conversionist impulse from the church's practical Christian work was institutionalized in 1971 when the Board of Evangelism and Social Service was dissolved, and its various activities were distributed among a number of new divisions. Though the end of the board was probably more a bureaucratic than a theological decision, the separation of evangelism and social service into distinct divisions of the church's work demonstrated that a new orthodoxy had been established in the United Church. Where it would have been almost inconceivable for many of the first generation of leadership to think of Christian social work apart from evangelistic effort, by the 1970s many in the church had abandoned the earlier conversionist commitment. This shift was not limited to the leadership but was part of a general suspicion of evangelism and evangelicals – a suspicion that was, by the early seventies, evident at all denominational levels. The last secretary of the Board of Evangelism and Social Service, W. Clarke MacDonald, noted that "evangelism" had become "a Word in the Shadows," and lamented that even to mention it was likely to "turn people off."[55] Nonetheless, he argued that evangelism was central to the mission of the United Church and concluded by noting the evangelical basis of this mission and suggesting,

[The] trouble is we've tried to be reconcilers with smooth words, suave manners and the latest psychological gadgetry, but *we ought to know, if we've read the New Testament, that to be a reconciler in the name of Christ requires a Cross.* We'll use every method, music – dance, celebration – group relationships – electronic media and whatever God puts into our hands – but *if we are involved in Total Evangelism we'll not use it as a substitute for the message of the Cross but as a communicator of it. Because that's where total evangelism has its roots.*[56]

Though by this time a minority position, MacDonald's argument for "Total Evangelism" in 1971 demonstrated that the evangelical impulse was still alive and active in some parts of the United Church of Canada.

In the last quarter century this evangelical impulse has not disappeared. Though many in the denomination would not now recognize the conversionist, activist, biblical, and crucicentric emphases shared by many of an earlier generation, public-opinion surveys conducted in 1993 indicate that a notable segment of the church's membership continues to subscribe to these traditionally evangelical ideas. Sixty-four per cent of those polled agreed with the crucicentric belief that "through the life, death and resurrection of Jesus, God provided a way for the forgiveness of *my* sins."[57] Though the experience of personal conversion has become less meaningful than previously, it remains important to 12 per cent of the membership.[58] And 25 per cent agreed that it is "very important to encourage non-Christians to become Christians," indicating that the desire to evangelize continues to influence a significant minority.[59] Finally, and perhaps most notably in a denomination that never was well known for a literalist biblical perspective, some 30 per cent of the general membership agreed at least moderately with the statement "I feel that the Bible is God's Word, and is to be taken literally word for word."[60] Evangelical thought, though not well represented in the official positions of the denomination during the last thirty-five years, demonstrably retains some influence among the membership of the United Church.

These numbers do not indicate, of course, that the United Church of Canada is an evangelical denomination, for it clearly is not. Nonetheless, they do suggest that the widespread assumption that the church "never was well represented among Canadian evangelicals" is not nuanced sufficiently to help us understand its complexities. The residue of evangelicalism in the United Church today is what remains of the theology of many of the denomination's founders – an evangelical inheritance that was neither as pristine as the one to which some conservatives in the church would like to return nor so disconnected from traditional influences that it can be ignored by those who would interpret the United Church, both past and present. Understanding this evangelical impulse is central to an understanding of the United Church of Canada.

8 "Crackling Sounds from the Burning Bush": The Evangelical Impulse in Canadian Presbyterianism before 1875

DUFF CRERAR

Canadian Presbyterians of 1875 chose as their emblem the ancient symbol of the burning bush, and the motto *nec tamen consumebatur*, rendered in English as "not however being consumed." In academic battles over concepts such as Canadianization and secularization, most historians of Presbyterianism have been drawn either to the light of theology or the heat generated by battles over Clergy Reserves, education, missions, or the installation of organs in church.[1] Recent scholars have demonstrated that a distinctive, accommodating evangelicalism emerged from the colonial era and played a central role in creating the mind and policy that characterized Canadian Presbyterianism until 1925. The focus of these studies has been on the clerical leadership of Presbyterians, and leads to the conclusion that the heart of the Presbyterian churches was their clerical and professorial elite. It is important, however, to point out that another historical aspect of the burning bush in Canada has been left virtually unexamined. What of private Presbyterianism: the world of piety, morality, and nurture, seen best not through the prisms of presbytery or pulpit but of pew, parish, and parlour? Tracing and decoding the fainter crackling noises from the lower branches of the burning bush may also help us understand better the conflagrations that almost consumed the Presbyterian Church in Canada in later decades.

Presbyterians take great pride in their clergy and with justification point to the leading role they played in producing influential thinkers to guide Canadians through the stormy seas of ideological, scientific, and social change. Studies of Presbyterian thought have illuminated their defence of what Goldwin French termed "the Evangelical Creed" in Victorian Canada.² Scholars note that Canadian Protestant thought by the time of the First World War was remarkably vigorous (though later years revealed that the war with modernity was far from won) and give a generous portion of the credit to Presbyterian preachers and professors who first skirmished with progress before 1875.³

Michael Gauvreau suggests that the beginning of this Canadian evangelical pilgrimage goes back to the Pictou Academy of Presbyterian Seceder Thomas McCulloch. Gauvreau's study of William Caven, William Maclaren, Donald MacVicar, Robert Burns, and George M. Grant argues that Presbyterian thinkers bested the challenges of Darwinism and German historicism by developing a "reverent criticism": reconciling conflicts between reason and revelation by making evangelical faith the higher authority. Buttressing faith with Baconian thought and methods of biblical criticism that drew the teeth of German and British theological speculation, these teachers developed a Presbyterian faith that was Bible-centred, conversionist (and open to revivalism), populist, democratic, and activist: a creed that energized the believer to be a self-conscious agent in the salvation of individuals *and* society. By taming the scientific pretensions of historical study, Gauvreau argues that Canadian divines built a unique popular theology, which blended evangelicalism and selected aspects of Scottish Common Sense, reverent Baconianism and a providentialist, post-millennial view of sacred history. This reconciliation made Canadian Protestantism both a unique transfer point and a viable middle way between European and American controversial theologies of the late nineteenth century.

To Gauvreau, Canadian Presbyterian thinkers both moderated and modernized the old Calvinist orthodoxy by bringing it into the evangelical form which Lowland Scottish Secessionists taught in places such as Pictou and which they soon found echoed in Canadian divinity halls of Knox, Queen's, and Presbyterian College in Halifax. This old gospel with new horizons enabled Canadians to avoid the pitfalls of old-school American Presbyterianism and to welcome both the apologetic writings of a Henry Drummond and the fervent piety of the Moody revivals, so laying the foundations of the optimistic liberal-evangelical mind.⁴

This view has been challenged, however, by those who argue that such theological and ideological triumphs were in fact disasters for religion because they undermined its staying power from the inside.⁵ David Marshall contends that Canadian preachers, by modernizing the evangelical creed, actually assisted the process of secularization by making faith subject to reason instead of revelation and by sacrificing the miraculous for the subjectivism of modern philosophy, history, and comparative religion. He sees the period before the 1870s as a difficult time when more and more Presbyterian clergymen abandoned the certainties of evangelical Calvinism. Presbyterian ministers, he argues, sought ways to save faith from the setbacks to religion dealt by pluralism, disestablishment, voluntarism, public schools, and the growing comfort of modern life. To Marshall, revivalism, social reform, theistic evolution, melodramatic preaching, and modern hymn tunes all were symptoms of a diseased consumerist Protestantism, which did not regenerate Presbyterians but hastened their drift away from the Kingdom of God towards Vanity Fair and the Secular City.[6]

One of the central figures of this debate has been George M. Grant. Raised in the Pictou enclave, the "lion" of Halifax (as his congregation dubbed him) stands for either what was best or worst in the Presbyterian mind between 1875 and World War I. Scholars have tried to explain, for example, Grant's controversial defence of the "heretic" D.J. Macdonnell (a position that exposed sharp divisions between Presbyterian arch-conservatives and liberal evangelicals) as the outcome of his pre-1875 religious formation.[7] Barry Mack's quest for the historical Grant has opened up important windows into both the evangelical impulse and the pre-1875 Presbyterian folk-mind of the Maritimes (and perhaps colonial Canada) and shows that both Gauvreau and Marshall painted their portraits with overly broad brushes.[8] As Mack traces Grant's development from the Westminster Confession Calvinism of Pictou (which Mack argues did not yet admit an open atonement) through Scottish seminary training, he shows that Grant's mature theology exhibited the balance of paradoxes and propositions, intellectual modernity, and prophetic evangelicalism characteristic of David Bebbington's "Romantic Evangelical."[9]

Grant's broad churchmanship denied neither his Pictou Calvinist and Common Sense Seceder roots nor the zeal of Highland piety, because it found expression in the widening scope of Scottish evangelical Presbyterianism. As a student of the Auld Kirk's Norman McLeod, and drinking deeply from the fountains of Thomas Carlyle and Luther, Grant found the ideal formulation of his faith in Glasgow and helped shape the faith of many in his home church by bringing together the best of the old Calvinist orthodoxy with the new emphasis on an open atonement and a historical view of both the Westminster Confession and the Scriptures.[10] This led to his re-discovery of the Old Testament prophets' denunciations of injustice which, along with Carlyle's critique of modernity, opened the way for him to understand his Highland neighbours' suspicion of both progress and Seceders. This created in Grant and his Canadian admirers a vision of broad churchmanship and the Godly

Commonweal which would harmonize, not polarize, Presbyterian factions in the 1870s, and which he and other preachers of his ilk readily applied to a developing Canada.

Therefore it is no surprise for Mack, as it might be for Marshall, to find Grant defending the Ulster, Lewis, and Greenock revivals against Canadian critics, assisting the 1875 Nova Scotia revival, and mingling affectionately with the McDonaldites of Prince Edward Island.[11] When Grant took his first pulpit in Halifax, his critique of scholastic Calvinism was welcomed by lay and clergymen of the Nova Scotia Synod. Grant seemed especially gifted in his ability to emphasize the open atonement and internal witness of the spirit with traditional Calvinist terms and thus was able to ease doubts and transcend the squabbles of Kirk and Anti-Burgher men. To Canadian hearers wearying of the tensions between Highland revivalism, Puritan introspection, or evangelical Westminster scholasticism, it seemed indeed that he had closed a broken circle.[12]

Theology aside, Mack paints vividly the turmoil at the heart of Maritime Presbyterianism. Pictou was a microcosm of transplanted Scots piety and prejudice, where Gaelic-speaking, Church of Scotland Highlanders distrusted English-speaking, Secessionist Lowlander missionaries such as McCulloch or the Gael James McGregor. Fortunately for Grant (and in Mack's view, colonial Canada) the Seceder missionaries had the evangelical confidence in religious experience that protected them from Old World Moderatism and New World latitudinarianism. At the same time, they were progressives who sneered at Highland tribalism: when the Glasgow Colonial Society decided to send evangelical Auld Kirk missionaries to the Maritimes, cultural, spiritual, and political war in the Pictou enclave was inevitable. Grant grew up in the midst of a debate over whether or not the deferential, Tory, Gaelic, and non-voluntarist Church of Scotland or the liberal, democratic, progressivist, English-speaking way was to triumph. Grant could thus understand similar Scots Presbyterian conflicts anywhere else in colonial Canada and could help bring harmony in the years before 1875. And Mack makes it clear that many Canadian Presbyterians were as tired of heresy-hunting as Grant and that the elders of Halifax and other Maritime congregations supported and furthered Grant's efforts before 1875.[13]

What, then, shall we make of the evangelical impulse and the colonial Presbyterian mind? Marshall's assumptions and definitions of religion, secularization, and orthodoxy have stirred up challenges across the spectrum of religious scholarship. Gauvreau's trail is too broad to distinguish the ways in which Grant, and perhaps other thinking Presbyterians, were perceived by parishioners. Both scholars examined popular preachers or preaching scholars: we have thus stimulating pictures of an urban male intellectual elite.[14] But were the religious experiences and ideas of lay men or women ever as clear or well defined? Not every Presbyterian in the throes of doubt joined the Methodists or abandoned evangelical piety: some, such as the restless young A.B. Simpson, blazed an entirely new trail. As Darrel Reid has shown, the Calvinist-Puritan introspection of this Secession-Free Church youth evoked a Presbyterian evangelical impulse so potent it produced a new denomination, rather than a withered evangelical cinder.[15] Perhaps we are some distance yet from any firm conclusions about all the links between high intellectual history and the evangelical impulse in the Presbyterian flock.

What of the evangelical impulse in the organization and worship life of the Presbyterian churches? The picture emerging today has come a long way from the stereotypical cold, moralistic kirkman preaching to a cold but none-too-moral congregation. John Moir, Laurie Stanley-Blackwell, and Richard Vaudry have created new profiles of colonial Presbyterian movements. Moir, with Elizabeth McDougall, traces the progress of the Glasgow Colonial Society's missionaries in British North America. This work, along with Moir's studies of Secessionists, Church of Scotland evangelicals, and the Disruption, makes it plain that by far the great majority of clerics coming to Canada in this period were evangelicals, whatever their Presbyterian denomination. The pre-Disruption Canadian Church of Scotland was so stocked with evangelicals that the ratio of Auld Kirk men to Free Kirk men in Canada soon reversed that of Scotland, with Free Churchman dominating in Canada.[16] Thanks to them, scholars may argue that evangelicalism, in both positive and negative ways, set the public agenda for Canadian Presbyterianism long before 1875.

The evangelical Free Church in Canada has received more attention than that of any other Presbyterian denomination. Richard Vaudry has outlined its remarkable growth, from a tiny sprout of twenty-three congregations to the fourth largest denomination (embracing one tenth of the population) in Canada West by 1861. To Vaudry, the very formation of the Free Church was a form of revivalism, progressing from union with the United Presbyterians in 1861 to the 1875 general Presbyterian union when, as Moir points out, Canadian Presbyterians, boasting over 1,000 congregations, formed the largest Protestant denomination in Canada.[17] Focusing on institutions, Vaudry describes the acts of the Calvinist evangelicals who launched some of the most prominent reform enterprises in Canadian history, ranging from foreign missions, temperance, sabbath-keeping, and anti-Roman Catholicism to the abolition of slavery and assistance of blacks in Canada.[18] Moir and Vaudry also link Princeton Old School Presbyterianism with many

Canadian Free Churchmen, subsequently producing Canadian ultra-conservatives who challenged Grant's generation of teachers and preachers after Presbyterian Union – with schismatic consequences by 1925.

On the other hand, Vaudry's characterization of regions and groups of Canadian Presbyterians does not always stand up to close scrutiny, perhaps because he and many other historians treat the Church of Scotland as almost uniformly anti-evangelical and identify Presbyterian evangelicals as almost entirely Free Church.[19] Although he does point to the work of leading lay men such as the Toronto Browns and Montreal's John Redpath and describes the official expectations authorities had of a functioning eldership, Vaudry has not probed the concerns and activities of less-prominent Presbyterians through their journals and letters. Assessing Canadian elders by class, occupation, wealth, and ethnicity and relating them to deliberations and General Assembly voting (as has been done for the critical years leading up the Disruption back in the Church of Scotland) remain to be done.[20]

In the last decade historians have assessed the character of Presbyterian piety, with special attention being paid to the "Long Communion" or "Holy Fair." Laurie Stanley-Blackwell, John Webster Grant, and George Rawlyk have vividly described the large, open-air, five-day Communion Seasons.[21] Grant has also identified many oft-overlooked Presbyterian revivals. Though the first wave seems to have been limited to the American Presbyterian congregations of Upper Canada before 1837 (where Bible classes, prayer concerts, and preaching were used to "get up" awakenings), a small but steady flicker of revivals characterized Presbyterian Canada, especially the Highlander parishes of both the Free Church and the Church of Scotland. Particularly impressive were the revivals beginning in the late 1850s and recurring into the 1870s in non-Gaelic parishes, characterized by the new wine of American-style techniques, and both giving and getting more public female involvement than had been noted in earlier awakenings.

Augmented by the insights of Leigh Eric Schmidt's study of Holy Fairs in Britain and the United States, Rawlyk and Grant have explored Long Communions through the categories of both social history and religion, noting that open-air communions were expressions of ethnicity as well as sacred commemorations, often heralding the beginning or climax of a deep spiritual awakening.[22] They also were empowering seasons for lay evangelists or catechists (not always elders) who, in the tradition of the oft-anticlerical "Men" of old Sutherland and Ross-shire, took over the Friday-night prayer and instruction meetings.[23] Along with Stanley-Blackwell, Grant and Rawlyk have identified Glengarry, the rural, Gaelic-speaking, and later, Free Church parishes throughout the Canadas, Pictou, and Cape Breton as locations where, though they might even have damned the excesses of New Light antinomians or American Methodists, Presbyterian parishioners were far from spiritually cold.

Both Grant and Stanley-Blackwell have noticed the decline of Long Communions by the 1870s. Ministers complained of spiritual deadness and worldliness of dress and behaviour. They became more and more critical of lay leadership outside their control and resented the old-country criticisms by the laity. Communions occurred more and more often indoors, and clerical intervention turned into domination. Probably the waning of Gaelic language and culture also contributed to the decline of this characteristically Highland expression of spiritual intensity.[24] The urban revivals of the 1870s, however, still had a long history ahead of them.

The theme of Presbyterian indigenization continues to attract attention from scholars, revealing the dynamics between clergy and laity shaped by ethnicity and Old-World traditions. Harry Bridgman's biographical study of William Morris, Isaac Buchanan, and Robert Burns has illustrated little-known aspects of Presbyterian lay experience. In his examination of both Morris (who was anything but evangelical) and Buchanan (one of the most prestigious and mercurial evangelicals in Upper Canada), Bridgman detects equally high levels of anticlericalism. Both had serious clashes with their own clergy and left church work convinced that ministers were impractical, lazy, incompetent, and grasping for dominance. Both tried to limit the power of the clergy in higher church government and were embittered when they failed. One wonders if other Presbyterians ever grew disenchanted with their ministers, especially after contending with the likes of the belligerent Robert Burns?[25]

Bridgman also illuminates some of the personal problems of evangelical Presbyterianism lay men in his accounts of Isaac Buchanan's conversions. The first, in the 1840s, exhibits many of the marks of classic evangelical Calvinism, yet Buchanan's Puritan-like obsession with marks of election failed him when business collapsed. A clear impression of how much the Presbyterian evangelical perspective is broadening by the 1860s, however, is clear from Buchanan's 1866 second conversion, when evangelicalism and the oscillations of the balance sheet were separated by inner assurance, mediated by a northern New York State Presbyterian's sermon. While Bridgman may portray Buchanan too much in terms of the Protestant work ethic, his isolation of this inner experience demonstrates how scholars need to examine carefully the personal papers of other lay Presbyterians.

Stewart Gill's study of William Proudfoot, whose career laid the groundwork for the Secessionist United Presbytery in the Canadas, reminds students that the light and heat generated by the Disruption can distract from other less-spectacular Presbyterian groups. Though Gill is concerned with indigenization, his study of Proudfoot opens a window into the entire western Upper Canadian Presbyterian experience. The ambitious, progressive Proudfoot exhibited the Lowlander-Seceder contempt for the Gaelic ways of the Highlander, almost blinding him to their mission potentiality. Yet even as he gritted his teeth when dealing with them (to Proudfoot, Highlanders were always looking for a Gaelic kirkman whose congregation they could desert to), it was Proudfoot who encouraged Gaelic-speaking Pictou Academy men to come to the Canadas. However limited his gifts of appeal were, Proudfoot wanted to carry the gospel to sinners of every race, creed, and stage in Canadian life.

Nevertheless, Gill's study proves that separatism, not union-building, dominated the first years of missionary effort in the Canadas. Proudfoot's contempt for American Presbyterian revivalism indicates the extremely narrow, ethnic, and cultural nature of his evangelicalism and shows how far the United Presbytery had to evolve before it could unite with the Free Church. Even more extreme was his contempt for ministers who drifted from voluntarism: Proudfoot denounced William Bell (a Secessionist on government salary to the Perth Military Settlement) as a "tax eater" and refused to cooperate with any of that ilk, however evangelical their preaching. On the other hand, his realistic portrait of a frontier mission reminds scholars that evangelical Presbyterianism was anything but a monolith before 1875. Often ministers of each group carried on in great isolation from each other, trying to maintain communication (and communion) between parishes as widely separated as Perth and London, York and the Huron Tract.[26]

One of Gill's most important findings is Proudfoot's observation that many Presbyterians immigrated to the Canadas to escape the confines of their homeland and so kicked over the kirk's traces during their homesteading years, until family and missionary brought them back to pew and communion table. Later, respectability would triumph in the evangelical kirks, and elites would pack the sessions of urban parishes, but for Proudfoot, William Bell, and William Jenkins of Richmond Hill, the first challenge was creating a viable parish, gathering the flock and disciplining it, sheep by contrary sheep. In fact, for all his attempts to Canadianize his kirk, Proudfoot is clearly depicted as holding to his Lowland Secessionist principles, as if he was still in Scotland. Thus the modest success of Proudfoot's Secessionist work, for all his forward-sounding sentiments, reveals the many factors that self-limited its evangelical impulse. Bridgman's work on the Scottish nationalism of his subjects also confirms the impression that the Canadianization of Presbyterianism was oft-delayed until just before 1875.

Whatever impression scholars have created of the public light and heat of evangelical Presbyterianism, their neglect of parish studies shows how little scholars still know of what that the flame was doing among the twigs. While the work of parish and presbytery chroniclers yields vital evidence, it has yet to be gathered for comparative analysis and connected with diaries, census records, and family studies – even judicial records.[27] A distinctive mark of the Reformed tradition has been the ruling elder. Thanks to Robert Burns and Sir Walter Scott, the elder has been generally condemned for hunting down the transgressions of the weak but failing to censure the hidden sins of the mighty. Popular accounts of Canadian Presbyterianism usually perpetuate the quaint image of Ralph Connor's *The Man From Glengarry*, ("All had the look of elders ... hoary, massive, venerable"), though Donald MacMillan's *The Kirk in Glengarry* takes the elders and kirk sessions more seriously.[28]

The kirk session exercised a religious discipline that is still the least-understood aspect of Canadian Presbyterianism, for session minutes are closed documents: they are the property of the local church, and both church law and tradition ban non-elders from reading them. Animosities from Church Union in 1925 (when many session clerks claimed old minutes as their personal property, rather than surrender them to the United Church) deepened the mystery surrounding the session court. Add to this log-cabin fires, long-buried (but not forgotten) church feuds, and family scandals (plus many, many misplaced cardboard boxes), and one can see that there are grave impediments to the study of Presbyterian parish governance. Nevertheless, the location of a significant body of session records, and the recent interest shown by scholars in family and personal piety in Canadian life, have prompted the following brief inquiry into Upper Canadian (later Ontario) Presbyterianism between 1816 and 1875.[29] From the session minutes of twenty-two Secession, Church of Scotland, and Free Churches, a profile of Presbyterian parishes can be sketched which seems to come from a somewhat different world than that discussed by most scholars.

In Upper Canada the majority of Scots and Irish settlers arrived after 1816, and many transplanted from their homeland a vigorous tradition of session discipline and Calvinist piety, resurrected in the revival fires that swept Great Britain. Soon numerous "Scotch Blocs" and other ethnically cohesive rural Ulsterman settlements arose, each characterized by the Lowland accents or Gaelic dialects of the settlers' origins. Most of the first Presbyterian congregations that emerged from this period, given the chronic shortage of ministers, depended upon elders, who read sermons, gave scripture lessons, led devotions on sabbaths, and, when they had time, petitioned their mother churches relentlessly for "godly" ministers. For inspiration and guidance, most elders drew on the practice and precept of their home parishes, but there were some who based their work on new manuals recently brought from Scotland and Ireland.[30] Many elders or elders-to-be were aware of the debate over parish leadership that evangelicals such as the Canada-destined Robert Burns of Paisley had started in the General Assembly of the Scottish Kirk, calling for more "working" or "active" elders to be appointed to ruling office (and, of course, vote with the evangelical ministers in the General Assembly).[31]

In Upper Canada the sessions soon exercised vigilance over a wide field of moral and spiritual offences, trying to recreate in the new parishes the same or even purer versions of godliness than they had left in their Clydeside, Ulster, or Highland ones. Canadian elders summoned members for offences today considered more appropriate to a civil magistrate. Though church records from the earliest days are exceptionally rare, it is clear that in the first Secessionist churches, discipline began early. In the Perth Military Settlement, beginning in 1818, elders of William Bell's First Presbyterian kirk session cited members for cases ranging from fornication to business fraud.[32] Duelling remained a concern in Perth, as some hotheads appealed to the trial of honour. An alert session cited any member rumoured to have issued a challenge, but in 1833, an undetected affair of the heart led to the famous fatal wounding of Robert Lyon by the banks of the Tay, and it was William Bell's Secessionist session that suspended from communion the penitent survivor, John Wilson, for manslaughter.[33]

Such zeal was denounced by Perth dissidents (among them Alexander Morris), who called a minister, reputedly more moderate on moral and spiritual issues, to found a rival Church of Scotland kirk. (Bell claimed that most of the Morris faction had been under one censure or another from his own session.) Ironically, and to Bell's delight, Rev. T.C. Wilson proved to be an even more zealous evangelical than he, and the new St Andrew's session waxed vigilant against drinking and shady business dealings as well as the other sins of the flesh. The founding fathers of the new kirk, already bemused by Wilson's excessive use of the strange phrase "born again," wondered what manner of minister the Glasgow Society had provided. Between 1830 and 1848 St Andrew's kirk session dealt with 103 cases involving drunkenness, sexual offenses, and absenteeism, as well as charges ranging from shoplifting, dancing, fraud, attempted murder, and exposure of newborns, and setting a man's dog on his mother-in-law. The nearby hamlets of Beckwith and Ramsay (later Almonte) also developed a strong and vibrant session government. Here moral offences provoked elder summonses for fornication, which usually ended in private confession to session and private admonition, followed usually by baptism of the child and reconciliation to membership for parents. Surprisingly, given the reputation that writers such as Peter Ward give sessions for chauvinistic severity, the Beckwith and Franktown sessions (among others) usually took great pains to spare the feelings of the women involved. Husbands who beat their wives were forced by session to confess and repent.[34]

But it was not always the Seceders or Free Churchmen who were the most zealous in discipline. In Perth, Bytown, and Smith's Falls, Church of Scotland elders policed a wide range of crimes, many characteristic of their urban and commercial environments. Alcohol offences occupied half of their case load, while others ranged from business infractions to petty larceny. Running the Rideau Canal locks and Royal mails on the sabbath brought the lock-master before session. Perth remained a moral battlefield where all Presbyterian churches, whatever their official differences, waged a combined offensive on sin. Judging by their session minutes, sexual crimes ranked a poor fourth: evidently sessions believed that drink, land, and money created more trouble than sex. Nor did they demand more from a penitent than flesh and blood (or pocket) could bear: Presbyterian tavern-keepers along Pike Lake were told to sell off their stock at the end of the current logging season rather than close immediately with unpaid debts! And the elders' reach was long: members charged with immoral conduct who moved from Perth to Ramsay or Smith's Falls soon found that the sessions of both parishes were in communication, forcing members to return to the session in whose jurisdiction the alleged sin took place. Although the quarter-session records for Bathurst district have not survived, clearly in other areas session minutes and judicial records might fruitfully be compared by social and legal as well as church historians.

The implication of some elders in moral, land, and property disputes created some of the most unedifying spectacles in the parishes. Elders enjoyed the deference of most of the flock, but this obedience could be swiftly withdrawn when one compromised his integrity. When elders harvested trees off others' back lots, committed forgery or perjury, shoplifted, or harassed poorer members for unpaid debts, appeals often brought Presbytery visitations. Several elders were severely disciplined in this period, which makes it hard to see sessions as closed oligarchies that could not be unseated by surly congregations.[35] To whom much was entrusted, much was expected. Nor was a moderator himself above discipline or even dismissal, as the Osgoode Free Church session minutes from 1856 to 1860 reveal. There a bitter and prolonged kirk fight pitted elders against not outright sinners but those who considered themselves the godly of the flock.[36] The resulting struggles allowed many elders to make martyrs of themselves, while the ministers of a few churches were convinced they faced hotbeds of anticlerical contumacy. This pious but proud disunity in some Presbyterian parishes left vivid and lasting community memories of elders who ruled not wisely but too much.

Although in most Church of Scotland parishes disciplinary zeal moderated after the 1850s, in most Free Churches the practice continued into the 1860s. After Presbyterian union in 1875, however, kirk-session discipline tailed off, just as the Long Communions declined. Yet this decay occurred in the very decade when both clerical and session anxiety about the decline in parish religion peaked, and revivals broke out in widely spread congregations across Upper Canada. With the exception of Zorra, however, where revival meetings almost led to a congregational schism, most session minutes examined were strangely quiet about revivals, even those reportedly taking place in their own parishes. Churches experiencing revivals also seem to have had little or no change in the number or nature of discipline cases. Had kirk-session discipline only caught the obviously incorrigible who were untouched by revival fires? Did disciplinary zeal and parish revivalism have no necessary connection? Were elders losing their grip, becoming irrelevant in the broadening church of the 1870s?

Perhaps an answer lies in revisiting a Canadian literary classic that describes the Glengarry Great Revival of the 1860s. An eye-witness of the event, C.W. Gordon recaptures vividly in his novels *The Man from Glengarry* and *Torches through the Bush* aspects of the Indian Lands Free Church and its revival. Gordon introduces us to the session of the church: old-fashioned, austere, learned, and stern Calvinists who sat on a separate bench in worship, exuding authority. Their piety and probity were beyond question, and yet the parish was stagnant spiritually. The elders were out of touch with the youth. At a wake they argued over whether or not the deceased was saved; and Calvinist orthodoxy, with its doubts over election, was bested by a warm open-atonement piety (significantly, held by the youngest elder and a Yankee Methodist neighbour).[37] Gordon makes it clear that the Rev. Murray, for all his zeal, had too wooden a personality to generate revival.

Nevertheless, the true heroine of the Glengarry parish, Mrs Murray, had planted at great personal cost the seeds of revival, with her Bible class, modern hymns, and maternal nurture of the young men of the kirk. The young men learned more of faith from her than from the elders, though they held them in great respect. The revival that ensued, while the men claimed credit for it, clearly owed its origins to the woman behind the minister in front of the session.[38] Whether or not Gordon's difficulties with his father and idealization of his mother skewed his perspective on the Great Glengarry Revival, in the light of recent studies of Presbyterian and Congregational family and female piety, these may be telling passages and show how much more needs to be done to explore the role of gender and family nurture in the Presbyterian chronicle.[39] If the old-style eldership and its Westminster austerity had outlived their influence by the 1860s, what does this say for the future of the elder after 1875 Presbyterian Union?

Session minutes also give insight into the turmoil evangelical zealots might stir up. William Bell had one Cameronian elder try to split his church, though when the session held firm, the zealot left to found his own work. In the sizeable Ramsay parish, members and session clashed over the choice of minister, as elders protested the induction of an "Auld Kirk" minister, believing him not to be an evangelical. This resulted in a disastrous four-year pulpit vacancy, as prominent elders boycotted the services. Then, through the moderating influence of the rump session, the congregation joined the Free Church, under which circumstances the rebel faction claimed victory and returned. In both rural Zorra and urban Bytown (later Ottawa), the Plymouth Brethren lured elders out of the kirks after traumatic session debates in the 1870s, a phenomenon testifying both to the appeal of millenarianism and revivalism to Presbyterians and the existence of serious Presbyterian lay-leakage into evangelical sects.[40] Perhaps by the end of the nineteenth century parishes were exporting their most sectarian leaders to other folds.

Canadian Presbyterian studies have undergone a major expansion, and thanks to the efforts of a wide number of scholars over the last few years, we know now a great deal more about the development of evangelical Presbyterian thought and about the organization and work of the Free Church. We know that during the three decades between the Disruption and Presbyterian Union, there grew among Canadian Presbyterians a sense of confidence, mission, millennial hope, and militant idealism. And yet we still do not know very much about the religious experience of evangelical Presbyterians and their parishes before 1875. We just do not know enough about their local leadership – both in its religious experience and community impact.

In eastern Upper Canada few minsters were as well known as William Bell. A pioneer who began in the Perth Settlement in 1816, he presided over Presbyterianism in the Rideau back-country until his death in 1857. Usually characterized as austere, dour, and sour, his journals reveal a wry sense of humour. One Sunday in 1825, after the congregation was dismissed, he noticed a man "sitting in a pensive mood in the corner of a back seat. He was so fast asleep that he had to be shaken before we woke him up. You may judge of his surprise on seeing him surrounded by the Session. He offered no apology but made a quick retreat."[41] The lesson is clear: let no Presbyterian historian today be caught napping by the enigmatic men of the kirk session!

9 From Preaching to Propaganda to Marginalization: The Lost Centre of Twentieth-Century Presbyterianism

BARRY MACK

In 1893 at the International Christian Conference held in Chicago in conjunction with the Congress of Religions, George Monro Grant, principal of Queen's University, presented the report on the condition of Protestantism in Canada. On the surface, things looked satisfactory from a Presbyterian perspective. Unlike in many parts of Europe, Grant judged "church-going habits" to still be "universal": "The Lord's day is reverently observed in every part of the land. The ministry of the gospel is held in high esteem."[1] He pointed to an abundance of candidates for the ministry and broad support for foreign missions as further encouraging signs. Canada, he observed with pride, was still rooted in its British past and had little "connection with the political and ecclesiastical life of the United States." It had only experienced the beginnings of the grave social problems that were such a conspicuous feature of the American landscape. "There is faith in the heart of young Canada," he concluded.

One hundred years later Grant's characteristically hopeful assessment seems naive. Did he not sense the tide of secularity about to wash over Canada in the last century of the millennium? Surely a more astute observer would have been filled with foreboding, some presentiment of the extent of the disaster that lay ahead? Perhaps he ought to have been more aware of the dangers of John Watson's influence at Queen's. But what he could not have been expected to foresee was how quickly the full-orbed evangelicalism, which still provided a generous theological centre for the Presbyterian Church in the 1890s, would give way in the early years of the twentieth century, first to a moralistic obsession with national regeneration and then, after the debacle of Church Union in 1925, to a reactionary narrowing of the evangelical tradition.

Shortly after Grant's death in 1902 the Presbyterian Church underwent a theological sea change. An older generation of church leaders who had grown up in pioneer Canada and owed their positions of leadership in large part to their ability to preach compellingly of God's grace and love was replaced by a band of crusaders who wanted to use the church as an instrument for moral improvement. Charismatic leadership exercised through the General Assembly was replaced by a Toronto-based bureaucracy that promoted propaganda for a variety of moral causes: pacifism, prohibition, the suppression of the "social vice," racetrack betting, and "scrofulous" French novels. And when the First World War was declared, Presbyterian pulpits were turned into recruiting stations for what was unambiguously declared to be a sacred cause.

This younger generation of Presbyterian leaders were curiously schizophrenic in their attitude towards modernity. On the one hand, their rhetoric was full of talk about progress and efficiency and the application of modern business methods to the church. They were proud that they were modern men with up-to-date attitudes about the world and an up-to-date theology. They were apparently confident that the universe was evolving as it should. Nevertheless, their attitudes on a whole range of subjects betrayed considerable anxiety about Canada's future. They lived in the continuous apprehension of some perceived threat to Canada's national existence, be it militarism, foreign immigrants, moral vice, the liquor interests, immoral literature, racetrack betting, or German militarism. This sense of an abiding threat to the middle-class norms of "anglo conformity" easily gave rise to belligerent assertions about what it was that stood in the way of the Kingdom of God being established on earth and spawned a willingness to use coercive measures to achieve what they deemed worthy ends. The apocalyptic language to which they were drawn often seemed to be born less of hope than fear, a sense of the waning prestige of the gospel's power to make people new.[2]

In any case, the irenic wisdom that characterized the leadership of the Presbyterian Church in the first generation of its existence disappeared in the second. When the new leaders pressed hard for the cause of Church Union, the effect was to alienate a significant part of the Presbyterian laity – some of whom turned in reaction towards American fundamentalism. The tragic failure of Church Union resulted in the polarization of the denomination into an activist wing that entered the United Church – only to have to combat the reduction of the gospel to a form of socialism – and the continuing Presbyterians who were themselves largely polarized between the advocates of a form of biblical and creedal fundamentalism and those attached to a more liberal view. Between 1900 and 1925 the Presbyterian Church in Canada lost its centre. Instead of the personal and the political, faith and works, worship and social activism, prophesy and mysticism being held together in church and pulpit – as they were during the years when Grant was principal of Queen's University – the twentieth century has witnessed a blind and destructive clash of fragments. Church Union represented the defeat of a moderate mediating evangelical centre that might have helped the Presbyterian Church to better withstand the secular wasteland of twentieth-century Canada.

As principal of Queen's from 1877 to 1902, Grant was as aware as anyone of the decay of traditional belief and the menacing signs of faithlessness in the culture around him. He had to look no further than his own family. His wife expressed a concern that "the whole tendency of things nowadays is that all people who think about things at all" were becoming "divorced from the church": "Even I who am almost like a snail in a shell can't help noticing it. Even in our small immediate college circle and in every newspaper and periodical one sees except the 'religious press' a sort of rationalism is in the air."[3]

Charles Macdonald, whose Chair in Mathematics at Dalhousie College Grant had helped raise money to endow, predicted gloomily that "Physics and Metaphysics will pulverise Theology, and whatever residue is left will be rejected as indigestible."[4] Allan Pollock, professor of Church History and Practical Theology and later principal of Presbyterian College, Halifax, the minister who had spotted Grant's promise as a teenager and had arranged for his education in Scotland, complained in 1895 on a visit to the home country that the pulpits were "full of negations" and "philosophy" – "A cold air blows over them and the people are neither convinced nor fed."[5]

By the 1890s fear for the future of the Presbyterian Church was fairly widespread. It was certainly all around Grant. Undoubtedly it was one of the reasons some young Presbyterians like Adam Shortt and Mackenzie King, who struggled as undergraduates with the call to ministry, opted instead for professional careers in disciplines more closely aligned with the scientific climate of the age. Grant feared that Canada was joining in the age of godless materialism already evident in other parts of the world. Nevertheless, he held on to the hope that the evangelical centre in which he lived would find powerful, new theological expression. But while he waited, he drew comfort from the fact that the widespread defection of the wealthy and the working class from the church had not yet occurred. Canada was still a predominantly rural society, and churches and schools still constituted the nodal points in most communities.

Grant was also encouraged by the fact that Canadian Presbyterianism had avoided the theological polarization that afflicted its American sister. After the Macdonnell heresy trial of 1875-77, Canadian Presbyterians had arrived at a *modus vivendi*. The Westminster Confession was accepted as the theological standard of the church, without being pressed in every detail or used as a club against those who doubted that it represented an ultimate reading of Scripture in every respect. It was accepted as the "high-water mark" of Puritanism and was, therefore, to be respected as that from where the church was coming – even while many in the denomination looked forward to the day when the church would confess its faith in a new and fresh way. Grant's strategy, while he continued to await a new theological synthesis, was to hold both to the old orthodoxy and the new biblical criticism, as it was filtered through Scotland.

In 1906 William MacLaren, principal of Knox College and staunch defender of confessional orthodoxy, came to a similarly favourable estimation of the condition of the church. He pointed with pride to the statistical growth of Canadian Presbyterianism since the Union of 1875 and to its enthusiastic support for missions: "In 1875 there were 682 ministers and in 1906 over 1500. In 1875 there was one Presbytery with eight ministers west of the great Lakes, in 1906 there are Four Synods, twenty-two Presbyteries and congregations and preaching stations almost numberless. At the time of the union in 1875, there were sixteen missionaries in the foreign field, now there are 198. At the earlier date there were 150 home missionaries, last year there were reported 655."[6] Communicant membership had tripled to 253,392. Total contributions had increased almost three and a half times. And whereas in 1871, 14.8 per cent of the Canadian population was Presbyterian, forty years later in 1911 that percentage had risen to 15.5 – making it the largest Canadian Protestant denomination.

MacLaren implied that these signs of divine favour were not unrelated to the "distinctly evangelical" teaching that had characterized Knox College in the sixty years since its founding. Throughout its history, he boasted, Knox had "held fast to the Reformed type of doctrine and neither its professors nor its students have felt that they needed to apologize for so doing."[7]

MacLaren judged that the great work of the Presbyterian Church had been the practical one of establishing Christian faith and institutions in a new land. And he ventured to think that this concentration on "the salvation of souls and the upbuilding of the Kingdom of Jesus Christ" was one of the safeguards that had kept "theology pure and wholesome." There had been no "substantial change in the system of theology held by the Church" – no wandering "from the fundamental verities of the Christian system." Such an assessment represented a vote of confidence in the new faculty members at Knox, like the Old Testament professor John Edgar MacFadgen, who represented the Scottish school of biblical criticism. Even a conservative like MacLaren, who spent a lifetime expounding and defending the Westminster Standards, was open to the possibility of reformulating the faith. He accepted, for example, the "Basis of Union" of the proposed new United Church as a suitable statement of evangelical faith – until he discovered that there would be no effective subscription to it required by clergy.[8] The only sign of disquiet in MacLaren's 1906 address was a warning about the influence of "Pantheistic philosophy" that led to the rejection of the supernatural.

One of the reasons that the Presbyterian Church in Canada was in relatively good shape at the beginning of the twentieth century and poised to become one of the stronger Reformed churches in the world was that it had enjoyed a generation of excellent leadership. The men who had brought the various strands of Presbyterianism into the Union of 1875 did much to shape its success in the quarter century that followed. The possibilities of 1875 had been realized because Presbyterians of different stripes had worked together. Moderation and "forbearance," even a certain respect for theological pluralism, characterized the Canadian Presbyterian Church.

The cautious receptiveness to "reverent" biblical criticism and the relationship of trust and respect between old and new are reflected in a 1901 letter from George Adam Smith to John Mark King, principal of Manitoba College. King, whose teaching and writings reflected the warm evangelicalism of Freidrich Tholuck and Julius Muller, managed to secure Smith to lecture at the college during the summer session. When Smith left Winnipeg, he wrote back, "I am fully aware that ... the somewhat bungling attempts of us younger men to obtain fresh conceptions of God's truth must seem crude and raw to the larger experience of our elders. But if there is anything that will keep us sober and cautious it is the sympathy and confidence of older men like yourself."[9]

King did not sense danger in the way Smith handled the Old Testament. What he worried about was a growing tendency to substitute "moralizing discourse" for evangelical preaching, which centred on the atonement and the themes of forgiveness, grace, and redemption. Even if moralizing avoided the obvious traps of hypocrisy and self-righteousness and led to a genuinely paternalistic concern for others, it could not be expected to nourish a faith of any depth or earnestness.

Besides King, Grant, and MacLaren, the acknowledged giants of the church included James Robertson, the Mission Superintendent (who single-handedly organized the spectacular growth of the church in the West that MacLaren pointed to with such pride), William Caven at Knox, and Donald Harvey MacVicar at Presbyterian College, Montreal. Although geographically spread out along the forty-ninth parallel and reflecting different strands of Presbyterianism, they worked well together, and the church prospered under their direction. Differences of opinion on political issues like prohibition, Sunday streetcars, or the extent to which a perceived Roman Catholic hegemony was a threat to be resisted did not impede cooperation on other matters.

Grant was, it may be argued, the acknowledged prophet of Canadian Presbyterianism. From his arrival at Queen's in 1877 until his death in 1902 he used his position as principal as a pulpit from which to address the nation. In clear and incisive prose he urged the country he had helped bring into being to do its duty and live up to what it still professed to believe. On a whole range of public issues – legislation to eliminate oriental immigration, treatment of native peoples, French-Canadian suspicion of imperialism, Separate schools in Manitoba – Grant preached on the side of the angels.

In Grant's case, preaching on matters of public morality, like the treatment of native peoples or other minority groups, was not an alternative to the gospel but rather an application of principles implied in the gospel. He pointed out that the chances of missionaries getting a decent hearing on Indian reservations or in China would be greatly diminished by glaring injustices perpetrated by a nation still presuming to call itself Christian. Cultural contempt, sometimes expressed in government legislation, was not the way to win hearts.

Evangelical witness in the Presbyterian Church in the 1890s included an openness and willingness to discuss social and political issues that accompanied industrialization. It is in this context that the famous Theological Alumni conferences inaugurated at Queen's by Grant in 1893 need to be understood. Rather than Adam Shortt's lectures on political economy being viewed as the beginning of the social gospel in Canada, they ought to be seen as part of an evangelical response to the social challenges of an industrializing Canada.

Social criticism was not a substitute for orthodox evangelical conviction. Evangelical preaching, which often included an activist concern to reform society, continued to be centred on the Cross and to stress the need for personal conversion. However, there was room in the Presbyterian Church at the beginning of the twentieth century for open and honest discussion of social and theological topics. At the same time, one senses a careful attempt by both liberal and conservative evangelicals to maintain a balance between tradition and innovation and to avoid both obscurantism and provocative theological radicalism.

Despite troublesome signs of secularity within the larger culture, it should be stressed that the Presbyterian Church still had a broad evangelical centre. The personal and the political, faith and reason, worship and social concern, prophesy and mysticism had not yet been sundered.

Within the space of a few years, however, the old guard that had provided wise leadership for the first quarter century of the church's existence passed on. John Mark King died in 1899, Grant, James Robertson, and Leslie Mackay, pioneer missionary to Formosa, in 1902, and Caven and MacVicar in 1904. Keith Clifford has suggested that the effect of the rapid disappearance of the old guard was to create a leadership vacuum, into which William Patrick, King's successor at Manitoba College, moved with his proposal for Church Union.[10] By 1907 a new leadership elite had emerged – the "Presbyterian Progressives." They included C.W. Gordon (better known as Ralph Connor), John Shearer, who had been active in the campaign for the Lord's Day Act, J.A. Macdonald, editor of the *Globe*, George Pidgeon, minister of Bloor Street Presbyterian Church where most of the "Progressives" attended, T.B. Kilpatrick, who had replaced William MacLaren as professor of Systematic Theology at Knox College, and Robert Falconer, president of the University of Toronto and brother-in-law of Alfred Gandier, who became principal of Knox College in 1908.

However, most of the new leadership lacked pastoral credibility. Falconer had no experience in the active ministry. J.A. Macdonald's real interest lay in journalism rather than curing souls. Gordon spent many years as minister of St Stephen's, Winnipeg, but it is not clear that he was a great success as a pastor. (A significant section of his congregation, rather than following him enthusiastically into Church Union, became part of the theologically conservative Elim Chapel.) John Shearer served in Erskine Church, Hamilton, but became involved almost immediately in the work of the Lord's Day Alliance coalition of which he became full-time secretary in 1900. The rest of his career was spent in the more congenial task of organizing moral crusades. Though Gordon became moderator of the General Assembly in 1921, Gandier in 1923, and Pidgeon in 1925, the second-generation Presbyterian elites apparently lacked the authority and respect that the leaders of the earlier generation had commanded within the church at large.

As well, the new leadership elite was much more geographically centralized than the one it replaced. Except for Gordon, they all lived in Toronto (and Gordon spent a lot of time on the train). They exerted their influence not by any charismatic authority or the respect that former students naturally accorded them on the floor of General Assembly but by effectively controlling the newly formed bureaucracy housed in the Confederation Life Building. As the denomination grew and shifted its centre from Montreal to Toronto, the older Boards of Home and Foreign Missions were augmented with secretaries, editors, and support staff who produced Sunday school resources and kept the presses humming with the voluminous literature of the Board of Moral and Social Reform, of which they were all members.

The new leadership loved "moralizing discourse," and produced it in staggering quantities. In books, tracts, pamphlets, church magazines like *The Presbyterian* and *The Westminster*, newspapers like the *Globe*, and long reports to the General Assembly, Canadians were incessantly warned about the evils of opium, the necessity for prohibition, the shame of sabbath desecration, the corruption of municipal politics that turned a blind eye to "the social evil," and a variety of similar topics. Such moralizing was not entirely new in Presbyterian circles – the Presbyterian Progressives faithfully reflected one strand of the Free Church tradition reflected in Caven and MacVicar. What had changed was the bureaucratization and institutionalization of such concern. Unlike J.S. Woodsworth, who actually worked with the immigrant poor in North End Winnipeg, Presbyterian Progressives urged other people to take up such "settlement" work. Their mission consisted of having pamphlets translated into Ruthenian, German, French, and Yiddish, and distributed free "with the view to Canadianizing, as well as evangelizing these newcomers."[11] And they spent time writing letters to various politicians so that vice could be suppressed by law. Looking at the careers of some of these men, it is hard to repress the cynical thought that voyeurism and moral indignation made good copy for the middle-class audience who attended church, subscribed to church periodicals, and read the *Globe*. There was something very satisfying in contemplating and then getting vexed about the sins of others.

The influence of these Presbyterian Progressives soon expanded beyond their particular responsibility for informing the church on moral and social issues, however. They also took an active hand in reshaping theological education at the colleges. The main purpose of theological education, in Charles Gordon's judgment, was to fit the majority of theological students for "practical efficiency." This meant new courses in "sociology." Students needed to study "local regions, social and industrial conditions ... the relief of poverty, the prevention of crime, and other forms of social service."[12] Brian Fraser notes that the initiative in setting policy, once clearly in the hands of the church, increasingly shifted, so that "By 1912 ... a new strategy of legislating first, then educating people in the process of implementing the policies, emerged."[13]

The educational process worked in only one direction. Taking for granted the achievements of the earlier generation in building up the church, the newer generation turned their attention to the more glamorous task of reforming the country. The basic strategy of the "Social Uplifters" was propaganda. Public opinion needed to be shaped so that governments could be pressured into passing legislation deemed desirable for keeping Canada pure. In their hands the broader evangelicalism of the first generation was reduced to a moralistic middle-class ethic of sobriety, probity, and thrift, to be imposed by coercion if necessary.

Brian Fraser is pleased to call these Presbyterian Progressives "evangelical liberals" and attributes considerable ideological conformity to them as a group. He points especially to the influence of an idealist interpretation of Christianity propounded by John and Edward Caird in Glasgow, and the Scottish evangelist, Henry Drummond. His conclusion is that, unlike John Watson, these men used an Idealist framework as a conservative apologetic for the evangelical faith of their childhoods.[14] But it can fairly be asked what exactly qualifies them as "evangelical" other than the fact that they sometimes used the language of their youth for rhetorical effect.

Addressing Canada's Missionary Congress in 1909, J.A. Macdonald urged that "Men who themselves are thrilled by the Christ-life and inspired by the Christ-spirit and constrained by the Christ-motive must go into the social life and into the business life and into the political life, and into all other avenues of thought and life, and there live out the Christ-idea."[15] This was hardly the language of the apostles. And if this is how Presbyterian Progressives defined evangelism, it is scant wonder that a real evangelist like Jonathan Goforth got a cold reception during his 1909–1910 furlough from China.[16]

The question of how much of the evangelical tradition was retained by the Presbyterian Progressives is more complicated than Fraser implies. Charles Gordon, for example, had spent his time at Knox College trying to play football and singing in the glee club rather than reading philosophy. The writer who had influenced him was Henry Drummond, but the main impact of Drummond's *Natural Law in the Spiritual World* (1882) and the *Ascent of Man* (1884) had been to shift the centre of Gordon's "theology" from the atonement to an immanent expectation of the Kingdom of God breaking into history.[17] The net result can hardly be categorized as "liberal evangelicalism" – of the sort that one associates with New College Edinburgh in the 1890s – but something considerably more heterodox. Gordon would eventually dismiss the Atonement as a "semi-heathen Jewish doctrine antagonistic to the character of infinite love God sustains to Man ... [Christ] offered no sacrifice on Jewish Altars or otherwise to His God, no Blood of Atonement. He gave his life as a sacrifice to the principles he proclaimed ... The doctrine that God and man were one in the person of the infant

Christ, or the Man of Sorrows as he expires on the cross, is the imagination of a superstitious, benighted mind, and an idolatrous belief out of harmony with this enlightened age."[18]

Perhaps it is unfair to lay all of Charles Gordon's heterodoxy at the feet of Henry Drummond, but Drummond was responsible for at least one major confusion – namely the possibility of Christian theology being "scientific." Instead of being content with drawing analogies between the natural and the spiritual world, long a stock in trade of natural theology, Drummond assured his readers that there were "spiritual laws" which could be empirically established. The practical consequence of this on Gordon's thinking was to subordinate Christian faith to whatever was deemed in the modern world to be "scientific."

In 1880 Grant had railed in the *Canadian Monthly* against the pretensions of positivism: "Blind to all but physical facts, the new dogmatism to be feared" was that which "assures us that what cannot be brought under the cognizance of the five senses is really non-existent."[19] He had warned Agnes Maule Machar, who was dabbling in mesmerism and spiritualism, that Christian faith had its own basis of authority in history and the self-authenticating testimony of the Holy Spirit, which were quite independent of the scientific method.[20]

But the younger generation was not so sure. They reflected a new willingness to regard scientists, the interpreters of natural law, as the arbiters of spiritual truth. They at least flirted with the idea that faith required empirical justification. The notion of a faith that could be "scientific" lay behind the curriculum revision desire to establish a Chair of Sociology at Knox College in 1920.[21]

Robert Falconer does not seem to fit the label "liberal evangelical" very well either. His biographer notes the influence of Harnack's theologically simplified ethical interpretation of the gospel and speaks of "Falconer's vision of a morally rejuvenated society inspired by a reunited Protestant Church." Falconer was a Presbyterian minister who refused all invitations to preach.[22] As a student he may have been impressed by Drummond, but rather than encouraging Falconer to engage in any "urban evangelism," the main consequence seems to have been an enthusiasm for sociology, first as principal of Presbyterian College, Halifax, and then as president of the University of Toronto.[23]

Not all were comfortable with such theological interpretation. At the pre-Assembly Congress in 1913 Charles Gordon introduced a note of fear in his presentation on "The Canadian Situation." He noted that the population of Canada had increased by 34 per cent between the 1901 and the 1911 census. During the decade Presbyterians had overtaken Methodists as the largest Protestant denomination – but the figure that caught his attention was that while the Presbyterians had not quite kept pace with population growth (32.5 per cent) and the Methodists had fallen significantly behind it (17.6 per cent), the Anglicans had more than doubled their membership (53 per cent).[24] Some attributed this to heavy immigration from England during those years, but theological confusion in the Presbyterian pulpits may also have had something to do with it.

It was not just the laity who were confused. Adam Shortt, who had been a favourite student of Watson's and was in a better position to assess his influence on Presbyterian pulpits than most, noted in his diary for 1907 that he had been to hear a certain Dr Rose preach:

By attempting to demonstrate that there was no need to worry in this life as everything was working out the will of God and would all be right in the end he was, so far as successful, proving the futility of churches, preachers, and all other efforts and institutions for human reformation as well as demonstrating the non-existence of wickedness and worthlessness of all moral judgements. However, like so many of us, preachers and otherwise, he was blandly unconscious of the logical application of his sermon.[25]

Perhaps it was because of sermons like this that Shortt soon left the church in which he had been born and had once intended to become minister, to become an Anglican. One wonders how many other Presbyterians in the pews were getting restless. There are grounds to suspect that the synthesis between British Idealism and evangelicalism among Presbyterian Progressives was a good deal less stable and less orthodox than Fraser believes.

Whether from theological confusion or some other motive, it is clear that the Social Uplifters turned away from the traditional evangelical concerns of sin, grace, and redemption and invested their real energies in matters of moral and social reform. The balance between the personal and the political was broken.

Moral crusading had obvious pitfalls and the Social Uplifters fell into most of them. In a 1911 publication on *Social Service*, O.D. Skelton had echoed Grant's caution against "committing the Church to hard and fast endorsation ... of policies on which there is a wide difference of opinion among honest men."[26] But there was something about the new leaders of the Presbyterian Church that drew them into such perils. One senses that a theological vacuum at the centre of their ministry and theological disorientation led to a passion for moral and political reform. Ministers had to preach *something* on Sunday morning; moralizing on selective topics is what came easily.

In 1914 Gordon found a new cause in the war, which he saw as an apocalyptic battle of the forces of good against the forces of evil. He proved to be a very able recruiter, especially among the men of his own congregation. One hundred and sixty of them joined the 43rd Cameron Highlanders and "Ralph Connor" became Canada's most famous chaplain. When more than half of the 43rd were killed at the Somme, Gordon left the front to become an effective propagandist for the Allied cause in the neutral United States. His addresses from those years demonstrate rhetorical talent, but they also belie his lack of theological depth. He would later change his mind on this subject as well and repudiate his role in the war. But these doubts did not interfere with his effectiveness as a propagandist at the time, and by the time of his second conversion, he had found new causes in Church Union and the League of Nations.[27]

Robert Falconer was no more balanced or sophisticated in his view of the war than Gordon. The war was "a clash of two views of life; the one or the other must go. It was a fight to the finish between 'Prussianism' and all those who boasted civilized values. As such it was the greatest of moral struggles."[28] The same qualities that made Gordon, Falconer, and other Presbyterians such effective propagandists for the Allied cause during the war, however, made them poor leaders in the already polarized Church Union debate that was tabled during the war. Keith Clifford in *The Resistance to Church Union* notes the millennial thinking that transformed a rational debate about the relative merits of organic versus federal union into an apocalyptic struggle between the forces of good and evil, light and darkness. The irenic wisdom of an earlier generation had given way to a new style of leadership. At the 1923 General Assembly in Port Arthur, W.D. Reid, up to that point a moderate supporter of union, decided that the time had come to "include me out." His plea of a gradualist approach was met by Charles Gordon's diplomacy: "We will force you rebels in by an Act of Parliament, whether you like it or not."[29]

The reaction to such leadership was inarticulate resistance to Church Union, mostly by lay people who had proven themselves so indifferent to attempts to organize them into a moral lobby in the generation leading up to 1925. Obviously resentments and distrust had been building for some time, but the proposal for Church Union focused the discontent. When the smoke of battle cleared, the continuing Presbyterians, filled with anti-clericalism and a sense of betrayal, found themselves short of ministers. Many turned to American fundamentalism for new leadership. In 1925 the continuing Presbyterian Church passed a "unanimous motion of thanks to J. Gresham Machen, of Princeton Theological Seminary in securing men for our congregations and minority groups, and for his substantial and continued interest in our cause."³⁰ Apparently Machen saw in the "no" to organic church union a sign of his own opposition to all forms of ecumenical cooperation.

Another indication of the fiercely conservative reaction was that Thomas Eakin was only appointed principal of Knox College in 1926 after his personal acceptance, "without any evasion, equivocation, or mental reservations," of the Westminster Standards.³¹ The issue that had apparently been settled in 1877 with the Macdonnell heresy trial re-emerged as the key question in 1925. In *"Church Union" and the Presbyterian Church in Canada* (1928), Ephraim Scott declared that the continuing church needed "no other theology or creed than the wondrous love for sinners, and the wondrous redemption from sin, of which [the Westminster Confession and Catechisms] tell in their peerless human summary of the teaching of Scripture."³² Union produced a considerable theological narrowing in the continuing church.

Creedal conformity to the Westminster Confession "without any evasion, equivocation, or mental reservation" became the central theological issue against which Walter Bryden, who soon emerged as the key figure at Knox College, had to contend. His campaign against "rational" or "scholastic" or the "propositional orthodoxy" of double predestination and limited atonement was a significant force in keeping the continuing Presbyterians out of the fundamentalist camp as a denomination. His neo-orthodox critique and charismatic presence in the classroom gave students at Knox College a sense of identity *vis-à-vis* the United Church without slipping into theological reaction. With the intensity of an Old Testament prophet, he pointed students to the existential reality of the Judging-Saving Word of God and the central task of evangelical preaching in the practice of ministry. In his own person he showed the way to an evangelical witness that was not fundamentalist.

Bryden's critique of the theological liberalism that underpinned the Church Union movement was radical. In his 1934 book, *Why I Am a Presbyterian*, he mocked the moralizing middle-class domestication of the gospel that had characterized Presbyterian (and Methodist) Progressivism. He noted, for example, the "Christian education campaigns designed to make 'young people worthy Canadian citizens or splendid idealists' but which 'had not been radical enough to create *Christian* experience, or induce in them a desire for genuine Christian service ... The whole effort, although not without certain commendable features, has been largely built upon the false supposition that a form of entertainment is more interesting to young people than genuine religion.'"³³ Bryden protested eloquently against the proliferating power of bureaucratic and administrative complexes and middle-class attempts to reduce the gospel to an ideology of Rotarian good citizenship.

The problem with the Basis of Union of the United Church, in his judgment, was its "uninspired prosy correctness ... There is no compelling vision of God in it."[34] Real confessions, for which men and women were prepared to die, were not generally the product of the committee room. They arose out of the dust and sweat of the arena and reflected the struggle of arduous engagement with the Word of God in a fallen world. "Creeds were not made," Bryden told his students, "they were always born, often born in blood."[35] Bryden's model was the confessing church in Germany, and the theologian he pointed his students to was Karl Barth. He saw the Canadian church, no less than its German sister in Nazi Germany, as engaged in a great *Kulturkamff* against the miasmas of theological liberalism. True ministers needed to be confessing theologians, preachers who had "been apprehended by the Truth itself, having had living witness borne to it in faith and by the Holy Spirit," and who were "thus under constraint to affirm that Jesus is Lord" and to bear witness to that fact.[36]

In Bryden the continuing Presbyterian Church found an evangelical prophet. His influence on theological students at Knox was by all accounts enormous.[37] His theology can fairly be categorized as biblical, crucicentric, and stressing the need for conversion. It was evangelical. In dialectic and paradox and in his talent for unmasking human pretension, he communicated to his students a powerful vision of God. Yet while Bryden helped steer the church away from creedal and biblical fundamentalism, he too represented a narrower version of evangelicalism than that which had prevailed in the nineteenth century. There is some justice in the charge of irrational "fideism" levelled at this work.[38] The relationship between faith and reason, nature and grace, the personal and the political was far from clear. It seems fair to say that Bryden sounded the "No" of judgment more convincingly than the "Yes" of redemption; his program was critical rather than constructive; more world denying rather than world affirming. One wonders about the ultimate impact of this teaching on the preaching of his students. He certainly did not offer them a clear and simple-minded theology designed for popular impact on a complacent, middle-class society.

Bryden himself had little direct clout at the General Assembly. His subversive influence was confined to the classroom; the denomination as a whole slipped into political reaction after 1925. During the 1930s the continuing Presbyterians had virtually nothing to say about the Depression. The official response was to encourage individual congregations to take up relief work. (But the national church failed to support even such large-scale efforts as Morris Zeidman's Scott Mission in Toronto, which fed up to a thousand people a day.) Whereas the United Church mounted a broad campaign to send freight cars of clothing and supplies to relieve suffering in the Prairies, Presbyterians worried that efforts in this direction might tempt the church into becoming "a glorified Social-Service Commission."[39] In 1936 the Committee on Evangelism and Church Life and Work proclaimed "the fundamental, social and economic need of today is the protection and proper use of the Lord's Day."[40] Opportunities for evangelical preaching – which surely entails a social dimension – were squandered when Presbyterians were still in a position to exert some influence.

By the time of Bryden's death in 1952 the Presbyterian Church as a whole had become committed to a socially conservative neo-orthodoxy. All of the staff at Knox College, with the exception of David Hay, and most of the staff at Presbyterian College were Bryden's students. This orthodoxy was enshrined in the adoption of the *Statement on Church and Nation* (1954) as a subordinate standard in 1970 and reflected in the wide use of *Living Faith* (1984) in the pews. G.M. Grant had lived in the hope that the evangelical centre out of which he had come would find powerful new theological expression in the twentieth century.[41] *Living Faith* cannot claim to be a creed born in blood, but it does reflect the evangelical centre towards which Grant was trying to steer the church a hundred years earlier.

Since the 1970s the neo-orthodox consensus in the church has been eroded. The theological colleges, in particular, now reflect considerable theological pluralism: process, liberation, feminism. But it is hard to estimate what effect this has had on the church as a whole. There is good reason to believe that the church is considerably more theologically conservative than either the colleges or church office. This is part of the explanation for the acrimonious gulf that has opened up between church and college after the spate of new appointments made at Knox College in the mid-1970s.[42] A more positive development since the 1960s is that the Presbyterian church has regained a willingness to speak on social issues and, more rarely, to do something about them. There has been a rediscovery of the social dimension of faith and an acknowledgment that the gospel entails more than individual piety.

This represents a recovery of the activist dimension of evangelical faith that disappeared in 1925. Pronouncements from the General Assembly on various issues of social justice – unemployment, divorce, abortion, corporate responsibility, native peoples, nuclear war, racism and apartheid in South Africa, opposition to the death penalty, and many other topics have become common.[43] The 1960s also saw the General Assembly accept the ordination of women as elders and ministers – despite the opposition of members of the conservative Renewal Fellowship, many of whom continued to point to the Westminster Standards as the key to church renewal. But it is also clear that the

Presbyterian Church remains considerably more conservative, theologically and politically, than the United Church. The 1994 Report on Human Sexuality reaffirmed that homosexual acts are contrary to biblical norms; this appears to close the door to ordination of avowed and practising homosexuals.

The 1990s finds the Presbyterian Church in Canada thinking hard about its future. It may have rediscovered its evangelical centre but its witness has now been pushed to the margins of Canadian society. In 1926 its membership was 160,000; seventy years later its aging congregations number less than that. In 1991 only 2.4 per cent of all Canadians claimed Presbyterian affiliation. Canadian Presbyterianism has, obviously, not done well in a consumer society, and it has been particularly unsuccessful in attracting and holding young people. However continuing Presbyterians understood themselves in 1925, they are now a small minority group in a religiously pluralistic society. Moreover, the denomination seems to lack the strong leadership that characterized it a hundred years ago.

Questions about direction, especially at the theological colleges, are sharpened by a sense of institutional crisis. Fund-raising schemes and membership drives mounted by the national church have not been very successful in recent years. The Second Century Advance raised only a third of its targeted $3,000,000 goal when it was abandoned in 1985. The Committee on Church Growth to Double in the Eighties admitted defeat the following year. More recently the "Live the Vision" campaign, despite its large budget and flashy, expensive American style, reported to the 1994 Assembly that it would end with only 60 per cent of its $10 million dollar objective. The 1995 General Assembly passed a budget that will significantly reduce staff at Church Office.

In 1891 a joint committee of the Knights of Labour, the Single Tax Association, the Trades and Labour Council, the Women's Enfranchisement Association, the Eight Hours League, and the Nationalist Association approached the Presbyterian Church to affirm its solidarity with the poor against the oppression by the rich. It is hard to imagine a similar coalition approaching the church today. Presbyterian support is not worth much politically any more. The days of influence in the corridors of power are gone, and the statements issued by General Assembly rarely get newspaper coverage. But numbers are not everything. George Grant concluded *Ocean to Ocean* with a rhetorical flourish: "We come of race that never counted the number of its foes, nor the number of its friends, when freedom, loyalty, or God was concerned."[44]

Such phrases roll off the lips more easily when numbers are not a problem than when they are. The twentieth century has not been an easy one for Canadian Presbyterians. But a central biblical paradox is that weakness can be transformed, by God's grace, into strength. Walter Bryden's hope for the Presbyterian Church in 1925 was that "through a new dependence upon God because of its difficulties and weakness, [it] might return to a simpler, stronger and more evangelical preaching."[45] Now that it is freed from the possibilities and temptations of political power, if true preaching again calls the church into faithful living, who can say what the results of its witness will be in the next century?

10 Evangelical Anglicans and the Atlantic World: Politics, Ideology, and the British North American Connection

RICHARD W. VAUDRY

In 1861 and 1862 Isaac Hellmuth, the newly appointed archdeacon of Huron, made two trips to England to canvass his evangelical friends for "funds for the establishment of a sound Evangelical College from which men may be sent forth to proclaim the Gospel of Jesus Christ in all godly simplicity and fullness."[1] From a financial point of view Hellmuth's trips were a resounding success. He raised some £23,000 for the proposed college, as well as a further endowment of £5,000 for the principalship and a divinity chair from Rev. Alfred Peache.[2] The trips, however, were not without controversy. In January 1862 Hellmuth addressed the Islington Clerical Meeting on the state of the Church of England in British North America. The speech became the focus of an attack by Bishop of Montreal Francis Fulford on both Hellmuth's integrity and honesty and on the evangelicalism he represented.

This episode provides a convenient window into the nature of mid-Victorian evangelical Anglicanism in the British North American colonies. It reminds us that British North American Anglicanism existed within the cultural matrix of the Atlantic world. J.D. Bollen's comments that "the English Churches not only perpetuated themselves abroad; they reinforced the cultural ties of mother country and colonies" and that colonial missions "were part of the phenomenon of empire"[3] was as true in British North America as it was in New South Wales. Moreover, as D.H. Akenson has argued, "the Anglican Church has been grossly misunderstood in Canadian historical writing, at least as it operated on the parish level, and the misunderstanding has its roots in a failure of historians to study its transatlantic background."[4] The Fulford-Hellmuth clash in Quebec also reveals much about the divided state of colonial Anglicanism. It is but one instance of the hostility displayed between evangelicals and high churchmen in the Victorian church, whether in England, Australia, or British North America. It thus points to the fruitfulness of viewing Victorian Anglicanism through the prism of politics, of treating the institutions and structures of the Anglican church, in British historian John Brewer's phrase, as an "alternative structure of politics."[5] Although a growing body of literature in Britain and the United States is examining the relationship of religion to contemporary politics, few historians seem to have studied the church as a political institution. Treating the church as a political structure brings into clearer focus the ideological clash between evangelicals and high churchmen and their fight for supremacy within the structures of the church. To make such assertions, however, is to fly in the face of a number of entrenched Canadian historiographical traditions.

EVANGELICAL ANGLICANISM AND CANADIAN HISTORIOGRAPHICAL TRADITIONS

Evangelical Anglicans have not been well served by historians in this country. It has been increasingly recognized that the writing of Canadian religious history has followed the main contours of Canadian historical writing. What is true of religion in general is true of Anglicans in particular. From the late nineteenth century until the 1960s, historians of Anglicanism in Canada such as J. Lantry, William Bertal Heeney, T.R. Millman, T.C.B. Boon, and Philip Carrington have shared a preoccupation with national church-building as the religious expression of nation building. Philip Carrington, for example, saw as one of the principal themes of *The Anglican Church in Canada* the way in which "local traditions have grown together into a national Church, with a character of its own and a contribution which it can make to the national life of our great country and to the development of the Anglican Communion as a whole."[6] This preoccupation with church-building tended to produce a consensus view of Anglican history. Theological, ethnic, and political cracks in the church's edifice, which seemed so evident to Victorian contemporaries, were papered over, giving a false impression of the state of the church. T.R. Millman's study of synodical government, for example, was so concerned with constitutional ends and with the church's coming of age that he glossed over the intense conflicts such issues engendered.[7] Accordingly, conflicts between evangelicals and high churchmen, though not entirely ignored, were downplayed. More recent historiography, though it has jettisoned some of the consensus paradigm and is more willing to recognize the divided nature of Anglicanism, has still tended to misrepresent evangelicals as "low churchmen." At the very least, this accepts at face value the mid-nineteenth-century high church polemic against them.[8]

If emphasizing ideological and political conflict runs counter to such consensus views of Anglican history, writing within a framework that stresses the importance of the Atlantic world seldom finds a receptive audience among most Canadian historians. Phillip Buckner's 1993 presidential address to the Canadian Historical Association mounted a trenchant critique of such insularity. He argued that "Canadian historians have locked themselves into a teleological framework which is obsessed with the evolution of Canadian autonomy" and in so doing have excised the Canadian experience from that of the larger Atlantic world.[9] Yet as Buckner and others have argued, it was precisely this Atlantic and imperial context that gave shape and direction to events in British North America. Indeed, the Atlantic was not an impenetrable barrier to communication but a conduit that transmitted people, news, ideas, and money back and forth between Britain and British North America. Emigration was not a terminal point in this process; it was but one link in an entire chain of ongoing cultural diffusion and communication. People in the Atlantic world, moreover, spoke a common language of political and religious discourse and operated within a shared framework of ideas. When in 1849, for example, Armine Mountain, son of the third bishop of Quebec, wrote to his sister Harriet, wife of Principal Jasper Hume Nicolls of Bishop's College, "I am afraid Nicolls will not escape the charge of Puseyism if he has permitted chanting the service," he was writing in language of common religious discourse and controversy which made as much sense in Lennoxville as it did in Oxford.[10] In short, Britons on both sides of the Atlantic were linked by a series of formal and informal ideas and networks that continued throughout the nineteenth century.

BRITISH NORTH AMERICAN ANGLICAN EVANGELICALISM

In the course of his remarks at Islington in 1862 Hellmuth made two sweeping claims about Anglicanism in British North America. First, he suggested that there were very few evangelicals within colonial Anglicanism, and second, he asserted that "several of the Canadian dioceses are deeply tainted with the leaven of Tractarianism; and that the local Colleges, at which the Canadian clergy receive their training, are almost wholly under this baneful influence."[11] The *Record*, the London mouthpiece of the ultra-Protestant Calvinistic wing of the evangelical party in the Church of England, commenting on Hellmuth's speech, called on English evangelicals to support the work in British North America; but it suggested that any money given go either to the newly proposed Huron College, or to the Colonial Church and School Society (CCSS), which the paper considered the only sound channels into the colonies.[12] The work of both these institutions was intertwined with the career of Isaac Hellmuth. When the reports of Hellmuth's speech reached North America, they were greeted with derision in some quarters. The most vitriolic came from the bishop of Montreal,[13] who had crossed swords with Hellmuth on a number of previous occasions, not least concerning the former's recent elevation as Metropolitan. Although he spent a considerable amount of time and energy attacking Hellmuth's integrity, of more interest to our present purposes are Bishop Fulford's comments about evangelicalism and Tractarianism in Canada. He denied that Tractarianism was rampant in Canada: "Knowing as I do, what has passed for Tractarianism in England," he remarked, "I really believe it would be far more agreeable with truth to say, that any single Diocese in that country would exhibit more evidence of such tendencies than the whole of Canada put together." As far as evangelicals were concerned, he commented, "passing from these topics to the complaint of the 'great want of evangelical men in these colonies,' and the discouragement they are supposed to meet with here, I would ask whether the Archdeacon is himself the type of what is to be considered as an Evangelical man? If he is, I believe, and certainly hope he is right in stating, that they are not numerous; I confess men of such stamp have never had any encouragement from me."[14]

Fulford went on to suggest that evangelicals were not as scarce as Hellmuth claimed. According to him they occupied the cathedral at Toronto, all the churches of Kingston, three of the churches in Montreal, one in Quebec City, one in Hamilton, and the church at London. Indeed, in the third of his pastoral letters on the subject of Hellmuth, Fulford went so far as to suggest that "in my own diocese, the clergy as a body are faithfully Evangelical ... but not acting as members of a party; and that, not marked out by any adherence to party-action, on one side or the other, such as he might wish to encourage, it would not be easy for any one to class the clergy of this diocese generally under distinctive heads, or otherwise than as 'hard-working clergy'; 'godly, good men' to use his own expressions, with whom any sincere churchman might gladly co-operate."[15]

When Hellmuth made his remarks at Islington he had been associated with the Diocese of Huron for less than a year. Prior to that he had spent almost his entire British North American time in Lower Canada (excepting a brief time at the Cobourg theological institute before he grew so dissatisfied with A.N. Bethune that he "transferred" to Bishop's College),[16] first as a student, then as professor of Hebrew and Rabbinical Literature at Bishop's College, and then as secretary of the Colonial Church and School Society.[17] Hellmuth's upbringing and career, though unique in several respects, does serve to illustrate the interconnectedness of Anglican evangelicalism in the Atlantic world. Hellmuth was a Polish Jew who was converted to Christianity under a missionary from the London Society for Promoting Christianity amongst the Jews. He became an Anglican in Liverpool where he was influenced greatly by Hugh McNeile,[18] the fiery Irish evangelical Anglican constroversialist who helped turn Liverpool into what Ian Rennie has called the most evangelical city in England.[19] Whether Liverpool was the most evangelical city or not, it was certainly the most Irish city in England and a natural place for the growth of one of the most virulent strains of anti-Catholicism, of which McNeile was the chief proponent. While Hellmuth may not have shared the same degree of anti-Catholicism, it is certainly not surprising that he would eventually find a congenial home among the Irish evangelical contingent in Huron Diocese which gathered around Bishop Benjamin Cronyn. Hugh McNeile's formative influence on Hellmuth is a reminder that a "Recordite" tradition existed within British North American Anglicanism. The English Recordites (after their London newspaper the *Record*) emerged as an influential group in the 1820s, effectively challenging the older Clapham Sect tradition for leadership within evangelical Anglicanism. Rather than the Claphamite emphasis on what Don Lewis has called "a 'moderate and cultured' evangelicalism, which would accommodate itself to the surrounding culture,"[20] the Recordites were belligerently confrontational, seeing their ideal of "the United Kingdom as a Protestant Christian Nation in the form of traditional Christendom" in danger, both from within (Tractarianism) and without (Roman Catholicism and rationalism).[21] To what extent evangelical Anglicans in British North America replicated this Recordite tradition has yet to be determined. It seems clear, however, that there was such a tradition within colonial Anglicanism.

The Hellmuth-Fulford exchange also points to the intractable problems surrounding definitions of "evangelical" and "high church," especially in the mid-Victorian period. Peter Toon has suggested that "to distinguish an Evangelical High Churchman from an Evangelical with a high doctrine of the visible, episcopally governed, national Church is not easy and between about 1833 and 1848 perhaps impossible in some cases."[22] Still, Toon's definition of evangelical Anglicans is a useful place to begin:

An Evangelical Anglican has a strong attachment to the Protestantism of the national Church with its Articles of Religion and Prayer Book. He believes that the Bible is authoritative in matters of faith and conduct and is to be read individually and in the home as well as in church. He emphasises the doctrine of justification by faith but with good works and a specific (holy) life-style as the proof of true faith. He claims to enjoy a personal relationship with God through Christ, the origins of which are usually traced not to sacramental grace but to a conversion experience. And he sees the primary task of the Church in terms of evangelism or missions and so emphasises preaching at home and abroad.[23]

While in the mid-nineteenth-century context it may sometimes be difficult to distinguish evangelicals from high churchmen, it should be laid to rest, once and for all, that all evangelicals were low churchmen; the two should not be confused or, as most historians of the Canadian church do, be considered interchangeable. A very brief glance at the origins and continuing use of these terms in seventeenth- and eighteenth-century England should help clarify matters. Both the terms "high" and "low" derive from the politico-religious debates surrounding the Revolution Settlement of 1688–89. High churchmen (ironically the bulk of the "lower" clergy) were lukewarm in their enthusiasm for the new sovereigns, William and Mary, though their consciences did not force them out of the Establishment like their nonjuring brethren. They zealously defended the traditional rights of the established church and were implacably hostile to "dissent" and "nonconformity." They dubbed their opponents in the Church of England "low churchman" because of their rather anemic defence of the Establishment and their willingness to offer concessions to the Nonconformists to secure their allegiance to the church. Although these were thus largely political designations, they came to connote theological divisions as well. While a strict reading of the history of the Church of England would have to distinguish between low churchmen and Latitudinarians, in practice by the eighteenth century the two were virtually indistinguishable. Both Latitudinarians and low churchmen exhibited the tolerant, undogmatic spirit of the age of the Enlightenment and seemed prepared to soften the more unpalatable features of theological orthodoxy as contrary to reason and good taste. By contrast high churchmen, while firmly set against the Latitudinarians, had worked out their theology and churchmanship in response to Puritanism. Thus they attempted to steer the Church of England through a middle course between Puritanism and Rome. While remaining firmly within the Protestant camp, they softened many of the characteristically Reformed theological positions and, in terms of church order and worship, were prepared to embrace or at least accommodate many of the "Catholic" elements the Puritans had rejected. They stressed episcopacy as the divinely ordained order for the church and maintained that the ministry of the church derived its authority from its lineal descent from Christ's apostles. The Puritan minister became the high church priest, celebrating the sacrificial eucharist in which Christ was present in a real (though not transsubstantiary) sense. The Restoration theologians who formed the bedrock of the eighteenth- and early-nineteenth-century high church tradition had regarded the apparent antinomianism of the Civil War sectaries as one of the chief threats to true religion, and they thus "attempted to frame their doctrine of justification in language which allowed more to the necessity of good works and human endeavour than had been common among Protestant divines."[24] Accordingly high churchmen were suspicious of evangelical churchmanship and theology. The latter's emphasis on justification by faith alone might well lead at the very least to a complacency about "the necessity of good works" and in the extreme to antinomianism. Evangelicals' conversionist theology diminished or was even antithetical to a high church understanding of sacramental grace and was far too individualistic. Moreover, to high churchmen, evangelicals were also soft in their churchmanship. They did not place sufficient emphasis on the doctrine of apostolic succession, and they were prepared to cooperate with dissent in a wide range of evangelistic and philanthropic activities. Despite the tendency of British North American high church bishops like George Mountain of Quebec to tar their evangelical opponents with the low church brush, this should not be taken at face value.[25] Evangelicals represented an entirely different tradition within Anglicanism from that of the low churchmen. With this in mind it is necessary to attempt some assessment of the varieties and relative strengths of evangelical Anglicans in British North America.

Of the first twenty-two bishops in British North America, probably only four were prepared to identify with the evangelical cause. The first two bishops of Rupert's Land, David Anderson and Robert Machray, worked under the auspices of the evangelical Church Missionary Society. The other two, Benjamin Cronyn and Isaac Hellmuth, were successively bishops of Huron from Cronyn's election to the newly created see in 1857, down to Hellmuth's resignation in 1883, when he became suffragan to Bishop Robert Bickersteth of Ripon.[26] Cronyn was at the centre of a strong Irish evangelical contingent in the western part of Upper Canada and had important family connections to the Blakes in the Diocese of Toronto.[27] Indeed, the Cronyn/Blake family connection was probably the most important evangelical network among Ontario Anglicans. Hellmuth joined Cronyn there in 1861, became the first principal of Huron College when it opened in 1863, succeeded Cronyn as bishop in 1871, and was the driving force behind the establishment of Western University (later the University of Western Ontario).[28]

In addition to these four there were two others in particular who would probably be called evangelicals but who avoided controversy, tried to remain aloof from strictly party warfare, and who seemed to work easily with both evangelicals and high churchmen. The first was Charles James Stewart, second bishop of Quebec (1826–1837), a man who, while refusing to be identified with any one party in the church, had close associations with the evangelicals.[29] The third son of the seventh earl of Galloway, Stewart was born at London and educated at Corpus Christi College, Oxford. Stewart had some interesting connections to English evangelicals. Before he went up to Oxford his tutor had been Rev. Eliezer Williams, whose father had been converted under George Whitefield. Stewart's sister, Lady Catherine Graham (wife of Sir James Graham), has been identified as a friend of Wilberforce and "a disciple of" Isaac Milner. Stewart's biographer, T.R. Millman, refers to his "simple evangelical religion" having "caused him, while in England, to be suspected of Methodism. Word of this, oddly enough, had even come to the ears of the King, who took occasion to warn Bishop [Jacob] Mountain about Stewart, much to the Bishop's consternation."[30] Though his aristocratic origins would have placed Stewart far above any other clergyman or bishop in the Canadian church, he remained a man of simplicity and piety. He is probably best remembered as a missionary and as one of the substantial builders of the old Diocese of Quebec. Whereas Cronyn and Hellmuth represent a brand of evangelical Anglicanism that operated within an Irish cultural matrix and was implacably anti-Roman, anti-Tractarian, and belligerently confrontational, Stewart, if he can be classed as an evangelical, breathed the cultured, irenic air of the Clapham Saints. In noting these differences, however, we must not lose sight of the fact that timing was important in determining such attitudes. When Stewart became bishop of Quebec in 1826, he had already spent almost two decades as a travelling missionary under the auspices of the Society for the Propagation of the Gospel in Foreign Parts (SPG); as bishop, he continued to be concerned above all else with the planting and sustaining of churches. His ministry also predated the theological and ecclesiastical ferment of the late 1830s and 1840s. Cronyn and Hellmuth, on the other hand, both emigrated to British North America in those critical decades and emerged as persons of considerable influence in the 1850s and 1860s, when the more settled nature of the institutions of colonial Anglicanism allowed for a greater measure of ecclesiastical controversy.

The second central-Canadian bishop with evangelical sympathies was Ashton Oxenden, bishop of Montreal and Metropolitan from 1869 to 1878. He might be termed an evangelical with some high church (but no ritualistic) sympathies. In his autobiography he had the following comments to make about the evangelicals:

> The *Church System* however had little or no place in their creed. Christ, and His glorious sacrifice; the work of the Holy Spirit in individual hearts; conversion from sin and the world to a godly and Christian life; the efficacy of prayer, and the devout study of God's word – on all these points I was heart and soul with them. But the view of the Church as a corporate Body called into existence by our Lord Himself, and employed by him as the appointed Agency to carry on His work, was scarcely recognized; and I felt this to be a serious deficiency which I could not pass over. Indeed I verily believe that the great "Oxford Movement," which has issued in the High Churchism of the present day, was the natural outcome of the previous deficiency of definite Church teaching.[31]

While thus appreciating certain aspects of the Oxford Movement, Oxenden expressed his dislike for the "cold orthodoxy" of the old high churchmen, and some aspects of Tractarianism and ritualism. "I have always entertained," he wrote, "a rooted objection to the childish displays, the studied postures and movements, the unauthorized gorgeousness of vestments, and the subtle phraseology unknown in the Church's formularies." These and "sundry other dilutions of Romish teaching and practice" he found quite objectionable, even while acknowledging that some men who are regarded as very high church can preach the gospel as effectively as their evangelical brethren.[32] Still, Oxenden found himself compelled to side with the evangelicals rather than the ritualists: "That whereas the prominent teaching of the one was that of Apostolical Succession as regards the authoritative powers of the Ministry, and the efficacy of the Sacraments as the sole channel of salvation; the teaching of the other was simple faith in Christ as the Great atoner, and an entire submission to the inspired word of God. My heart therefore has ever responded to the latter system rather than to the former."[33] Oxenden had come to Canada with something of a reputation as a tract-writer.[34] While curate of Barham in the Diocese of Rochester, he had published a series called "The Barham Tracts" and found himself frequently in opposition to the Tractarian Archdeacon Denison.[35] As J.I. Cooper pointed out, they "were written by a believer for believer. They did not defend, they clarified. The authority of the Holy Scriptures was basic to all Oxenden's writings. So equally were the Sacraments of the Church."[36]

As for the other bishops who occupied central and eastern British North American dioceses, they can arguably be classified as follows: the old high church school, including Charles Inglis, Jacob Mountain, Robert Stanser, John Inglis; the high churchmen of the Tractarian period who were influenced in varying degrees by the Oxford Movement, including those intimately involved with Tractarianism, like John Medley of Fredericton and Edward Feild of Newfoundland; and those who were influenced by and sympathetic to some aspects of the Oxford revival, like Francis Fulford of Montreal, John Strachan and Alexander Neil Bethune of Toronto, George Mountain of Quebec, and John Travers Lewis of Ontario.[37] While the differences among these bishops should not be glossed over, it is quite apparent that all were on the high church side of the ecclesiastical controversies of the mid-nineteenth century, though they reacted in varying degrees of sympathy to the Oxford Movement and were generally cautious when it came to matters of ritual. It would be fair to say that most of the bishops moved between two poles on a spectrum of belief and practice. At the one end was the failure of the Canadian bishops to condemn as unsound the teachings of Provost Whitaker of Trinity College in Toronto and to uphold Bishop Cronyn's protest against the same.[38] At the other pole was the decision of the Provincial Synod of 1868 to condemn a series of ritualistic practices including the elevation of the elements during Holy Communion, the use of wafer bread, incense, candles on the altar, and the wearing of medieval vestments.[39] Two observations clearly stand out. In the first place, evangelicals worked in an environment shaped by a preponderance of high church bishops with relative degrees of sympathy for evangelicals. Being almost always in a minority influenced evangelicals' actions. Second, most of the bishops were by and large moderates in their attitudes to Tractarianism and ritualism, especially after Newman's defection to Rome in 1845.

If we turn from the bishops to the clergy, we find a similar pattern. The diocese that had the largest concentration of evangelical clergy was, not surprisingly, Huron. But even here, at least at its inception, evangelicals did not constitute a vast majority. If we take the clerical votes for Benjamin Cronyn in the Episcopal election of 1857 as indicating relative numbers, we find that twenty-two clergy voted for Cronyn and twenty voted for A.N. Bethune.[40] At the same time the situation did not remain static in Huron, with one historian claiming that "Cronyn turned the new diocese into an almost exclusively Irish Low Church preserve, directly in opposition to much of the churchmanship of Strachan and Bethune."[41] The next strongest contingent of evangelical clergy appears to have been in Montreal. Indeed, J.I.Cooper and Philip Carrington pointed out that there were strong evangelical and Irish links between Huron and Montreal. William Bennett Bond of St George's, with first Edward Sullivan and then J. Carmichael as assistants, and M.S. Baldwin at St Luke's constituted the clerical heart of Montreal evangelicals in the 1860s.[42] In Quebec, particularly after its division from Montreal in 1850, one could count the number of evangelical clergy on one hand – E.W. Sewell at Trinity, Quebec City; Isaac Hellmuth at Bishop's College and St Peter's, Sherbrooke; Thompson, a CCSS missionary at Stanstead; and Gilbert Percy at the cathedral in Quebec City. In the Diocese of Ontario, centred on Kingston and created in 1862, though there were pockets of evangelical strength, particularly in Kingston, the general clerical tone of the diocese was high church. As in Quebec, there were a number of graduates of the Tractarian St Augustine's College, Canterbury, in the parish. Though his connections with Ireland and Trinity College, Dublin, probably helped get him elected bishop in 1863, John Travers Lewis's attitude towards evangelicals in his diocese might well be described as hostile. It was reported in 1895 that Lewis would not ordain graduates of Wycliffe College, because to his mind they had a defective and deficient view of episcopacy.[43]

While not wishing to minimize completely the role of either evangelical bishops or clergy, it is probably safe to say that the evangelical laity constituted the real strength of the movement in British North America. From William Henry Draper to the Blakes and to President Daniel Wilson of the University of Toronto, the Anglican evangelical laity of Toronto, for example, were a very prominent and powerful group – politically, economically, and socially. H.E. Turner is surely correct in his observation that the membership for the evangelical Church Association "reads like the Anglican contingent at the tip of Ontario's pyramidical class structure."[44] Many were very confrontational and played a role in a number of controversies with the high church faction in the Diocese of Toronto.[45] An examination of the evangelical laity in Quebec City at mid-century reveals some similarities, but should also caution us against thinking that all socially and economically powerful Anglicans were evangelicals.

During the synodical controversy of 1857–59, a group of evangelical laity calling itself the Lay Association of the Church of England emerged and took the lead in opposing the constitution proposed for the Diocese of Quebec, and in particular its provision for a bishop's veto. The evangelicals associated with the Lay Association, though including some prominent members of the Quebec City business and legal establishment like Jeffrey Hale, George Hall, Andrew Stuart, and Richard Pope, did not constitute in any sense the dominant group. Indeed, the laity who opposed the Lay Association during the synodical controversy probably contained the more prominent Anglican members of the Quebec legal, business, and political establishment – men like James Bell Forsyth, Frederick Andrews, and George Okill Stuart. This, of course, tells us only some things about those laity involved in public controversy, and thus very little about those men and women whose conduct and demeanor were quiet and unobtrusive, and whose influence rarely extended beyond the boundaries of their parishes.

Though evangelical Anglican bishops, clergy, and laity joined forces within the church to do battle with their high church and Tractarian opponents, they also showed common cause with evangelicals from other denominations in a wide variety of missionary and philanthropic endeavours. In all this they exhibited the activism which Bebbington has seen as a hallmark of evangelicalism. Their participation in these activities, however, deserves comment. British North American high church Anglicans were implacably opposed to cooperation in any enterprise with "dissent." Upper Canada's high church mouthpiece, *The Church*, frequently warned in the 1840s against churchmen participating in and promoting societies not under strict Church of England control. "Our decided and strong opinion," it declared in 1842, was "that the Church in this Province is never in so great danger, as when shaking hands and fraternizing with Dissent."[46] As well, George Mountain was unwilling to lend official Anglican support to the transdenominational French Canadian Missionary Society while a number of prominent Anglican evangelicals from the Montreal region were active in its promotion.[47] Participation in such pan-evangelical societies became a hallmark of British North American Anglican evangelicals as it had in Ireland in the 1820s, and this at a time when evangelicals in England, particularly in the 1830s, and representing both the Clapham Sect inheritance and the Recordite tradition, had increasingly distanced themselves from Nonconformist evangelicals.[48] It seems clear that British North American Anglican evangelicals cooperated earlier and with greater enthusiasm than did their English counterparts. Though the evidence is certainly not conclusive, perhaps this greater sense of interdenominational cooperation is indicative that much of evangelical Anglicanism in British North America flowed in Irish rather than English channels.

THE CHURCH AS A POLITICAL INSTITUTION

What the foregoing survey seems to indicate is that in almost every diocese British North American evangelical Anglicans were a minority who stood little chance of ever gaining control of the structures of power. Clearly, as far as Anglicans were concerned, the first two-thirds of the nineteenth century was manifestly not the evangelical century. Yet the failure to dominate and control did not lead (as it led mid-nineteenth-century Presbyterians, for example) to the creation of new denominations. For the most part, evangelical Anglicans remained within the Anglican communion. They survived by establishing alternative structures and institutions that would best serve their needs. Thus those who did not like Trinity College, Toronto, set up Huron and later Wycliffe Colleges; those who did not like Trinity College School or Bishop Strachan School established Ridley and Havergal; those who could not get their copy published in the *Dominion Churchman* established the *Evangelical Churchman*.[49] And in the earlier decades of the nineteenth century, evangelical Anglicans who found the pages of the *Church* too uncongenial established in succession two relatively short-lived evangelical alternatives: *The Berean* (Quebec City) and *The Echo and Protestant Episcopal Recorder* (Port Hope).[50] Indeed, it might even be argued that the creation of the Diocese of Huron could be seen in this light. The re-establishment of all of these institutions reflects the intense hostility and suspicion that existed between high churchmen and evangelicals within British North American Anglicanism.

These political fights were played out with considerable intensity in the Diocese of Quebec in the 1850s over the intertwined issues of Tractarianism, the role of evangelical voluntary societies, and the nature of synodical government. Evangelical Anglicans in Lower Canada had to operate within two concentric circles of religious culture: The closest circle to them was the immediate Anglican, dominated by a high church group centred on the Mountain-Nicolls family connection.[51] Albeit, if the third bishop, George Jehoshaphat Mountain, is anything to go by, this high churchmanship was moderate, reasonably irenic, suspicious of Tractarian excesses, but also suspicious that evangelicals were not quite sound enough in their churchmanship. The larger cultural context was obviously shaped by the majority Roman Catholic population and by the resurgence of Catholic ultramontanism under the leadership of bishops Bourget and Lartigue and the ultramontane paper, *Les Melanges Religieuses*.[52] This latter context gave a greater sense of urgency and alarm to the political fights occurring within the former.

The first of these political fights involved a clash of personalities and principles between Rev. Gilbert Percy and Rev. Henry Roe over alleged Tractarian teaching in the diocese. The second was a dispute between Mountain and the Colonial Church and School Society, which goes some distance towards illustrating the differing attitudes to voluntary church societies; and the third was an intense political dispute over the introduction of synodical government in the diocese.

In the first dispute, Percy, a graduate of Trinity College, Dublin, and thus part of a strong Irish evangelical contingent in British North America, in an open letter to Bishop Mountain on 24 April 1858, charged "that Tractarian tendencies are stealthily, but steadily, developing themselves in our midst."[53] This alleged Tractarianism Percy traced to the parish of Henry Roe, one of Mountain's close associates and a later Harold Professor of Divinity in Bishop's College. Percy's charge seems to represent an increasing anxiety among evangelicals in the 1840s and 1850s that the Church of England was being undermined, and that this was all the more insidious because it was being undermined from within. By the time Percy's letter was published, the effects of the Oxford Movement had been felt for upwards of twenty-five years. What had seemingly begun as the cry of a few Oxford academics against an Erastian state's proposal to reform the Church of Ireland soon turned into the most thoroughgoing theological and ideological revolution the Church of England had seen since the Reformation.[54] Thus when Percy raised the spectre of Tractarian teaching within the diocese, he not only assured himself of a ready audience but could capitalize on many of the anti–Roman Catholic fears of the Protestant community. Percy's fears, in short, were not different in kind to those raised by Benjamin Cronyn against the views of Provost Whitaker of Trinity College, Toronto.

The Percy/Roe clash was also related to a conflict between Bishop Mountain and the Colonial Church and School Society. The CCSS owed its immediate origins to an 1851 merger between the Colonial Church Society and the Newfoundland and British North American School Society.[55] Both had been founded by English evangelical Anglicans and must be seen as part of that great wave of voluntary societies, domestic and foreign, that were established in the late-eighteenth and early-nineteenth centuries as one of the singular manifestations of the evangelical revival in Britain. In 1851 this newly formed CCSS had two principal aims, one strictly missionary and the other educational: namely, the spread of evangelical Christianity by means of clergy, catechists, and Sunday schools; and the establishment and maintenance of other schools.[56] By 1851 the CCSS employed over seventy missionaries and agents throughout the British North American colonies, including a French mission at Sabrevois in the Richelieu Valley of Lower Canada and a mission to the "Free Coloured Population" in western Upper Canada, the latter being supported by Benjamin Cronyn and the congregation of St Paul's, London, Canada West.[57]

The controversy that erupted between Bishop Mountain and the CCSS in 1858–59 was not entirely new; it was part of a long-standing uneasiness which his brother bishops of Montreal (Francis Fulford) and Toronto (John Strachan) felt towards the society regarding the CCSS as both a rival to the Society for the Propagation of the Gospel and as subversive of "ecclesiastical order and discipline." The bishops called upon the archbishop to withdraw his support. The heart of Mountain's objections was that the CCSS was partisanly evangelical and that it undermined episcopal authority within the diocese. "I could not ... overcome certain misgivings," he wrote in 1859, "as to its claim to be regarded as a thorough and genuine Church of England society, free from any marked party character." This he contrasted with the "noble and ancient" SPG, which in his eyes was entirely free of the CCSS's party spirit.[58] Moreover, it was Mountain's assertion that the CCSS undermined episcopal authority by its practice (also followed by the Church Missionary Society [CMS] and similar societies) of vesting in its central committee the power to appoint, relocate, or remove its missionaries.

The Percy allegations about creeping Tractarianism and Mountain's misgivings about the CCSS can thus be seen to be related. This smouldering controversy between evangelicals and high churchmen reached its culmination in the synodical controversy of 1858–59, which exposed to public view all the latent theological and ecclesiastical fissures in the diocese. For two years it dominated both public and private discussions. It was, moreover, a political fight *par excellence*: competing parties were established and mobilized; positions were staked out, attacked, and defended in a lively pamphlet war; the daily press, particularly the *Quebec Mercury* and the *Quebec Gazette*, took sides on the issues and attacked each other's coverage; bills were introduced into the Legislative Assembly and Council, and its members were lobbied by both sides; and the election of delegates to the first meeting of the synod was hotly contested in some parishes. It engaged the attention of both the clergy of the diocese and its most prominent laity.

The heart of the matter, in short, turned on the question of whether the bishop would have a veto over synodical legislation, and whether or not such a power was inherent to episcopacy. When Mountain attempted to present such a constitution to the diocese in the spring of 1858, he encountered serious and unexpected opposition, not only from the evangelical clergy of the diocese but from the group of prominent laity calling themselves the Church of England Lay Association, led by Jeffrey Hale, a man of some standing in the Quebec City community and a leading evangelical. In place of Mountain's constitution the Lay Association put forth their own proposal for a constitution that would have placed significant powers in the hands of the laity.[59] The formation of this association prompted the formation of an opposing group of laity led by, among others, George Okill Stuart, a prominent Quebec City lawyer and MPP, and a man whose family had had long and deep associations with the Church of England in Quebec. The formation of these two opposing lay groups and the pamphlet war in the winter and spring of 1859 had a clearly defined political goal – the influencing of lay opinion in anticipation of the election of delegates to the forthcoming Synod of 1859. Throughout the spring of 1859, then, a battle for the hearts and minds of the laity of the diocese was in full force.

Both sides used whatever resources and influence they possessed in an attempt to influence the election. The battles were particularly intense on election day in the Quebec City parishes. For example, on 26 April 1859 in its lead news item, the *Quebec Mercury's* headline screamed "SYNODICAL ACTION – DISGRACEFUL RIOTS IN THE ESTABLISHED CHURCHES – MINISTERS VIOLENTLY ASSAULTED!!" The news report was of a meeting held in the National School Room the previous day, for the purpose of electing three delegates to synod from the cathedral, and recounted the use of physical force and intimidation by the leaders of the Lay Association. The article further related a riot that had apparently lasted for some six hours and had resulted in the elections being "abruptly closed."[60] The reports in the *Quebec Gazette* were far more sanguine about these events. A consistent supporter of the Lay Association, the *Gazette* commented that "there was violence, but it was provoked, and therefore, not surprising. Men will not humbly submit to be tricked out of their rights, either by the clergy or by a set of men who desire to overshadow their fellows by an assumed and false respectability."[61] Despite the best efforts of rioters and pamphleteers and their tactics of coercion, intimidation, and persuasion, the Lay Association and its clerical supporters failed to capture the synod politically, and thus George Mountain and his "High Church party" emerged victorious.

Bishop George Mountain regarded the synodical controversy of 1858–59 as "a great crisis in which [the Church of England's] ... distinctive principles are deeply involved."[62] It also serves as a useful lens through which to view colonial Anglicanism. Though its Canadian setting gave shape and direction to the controversy, it was the broader imperial framework that established the political and ideological parameters for these disputes. The principal evangelical actors, Gilbert Percy, from Trinity College, Dublin, and Jeffrey Hale, from an important English imperial family, remind us of the cultural make-up of colonial Anglicanism, with its convergence of English and Irish traditions. Moreover, it was the ongoing legacy of the Oxford Movement that posed a significant threat to the evangelicals' political and theological culture. Although William Westfall has argued that the ideological impact of the Oxford Movement on British North American Anglicanism was minimal, it would appear that its political impact was far more significant.[63] Whether fully justified or not, there were suspicions in the minds of some Quebec evangelicals that Tractarianism was making headway in the diocese and that this needed to be resisted firmly. Bishop Mountain's reluctance to support the Colonial Church and School Society was taken as further proof that the diocese was not as congenial a place as evangelicals might have hoped for. The diocese thus clearly illustrates the divided nature of the Church of England in the mid-nineteenth century. Although the high church party had long dominated its structures and institutions, it was also home to a significant minority of evangelicals. Never powerful enough (unlike their counterparts in Huron, Toronto or Montreal) either to dominate the diocese or to establish enduring alternative structures which they could control, this group was vocal and confrontational. Given the nature of the diocese and the sorts of issues at stake, it is not surprising that it could quickly degenerate into warring camps. Both parties in the church used every available means – press, pamphlets, pressure, electioneering, even the occasional riot – in an attempt to seize power and effect change. The introduction of synodical government, and with it, the drafting of a constitution that would set the tone in the diocese for the foreseeable future, was one such occasion. From this perspective the Lay Association's assault on the structures of the church can be seen as a failed *coup d'etat*. Stripping away the veneer of peace, unity, and respectability thus reveals a church profoundly divided by competing ideological visions, and containing groups prepared to use all the political savvy they could muster in pursuit of those ends.

11 Redefining Evangelicalism in the Canadian Anglican Church: Wycliffe College and the Evangelical Party, 1867–1995

WILLIAM H. KATERBERG

We must be prepared to ask ourselves if the Church really does have a continuing role to serve in our culture. Do we really have anything to say that affects people's lives? Is it worth the effort to keep the doors open and struggle on? Are we really an anchor for people's lives, or perhaps just an antique, something highly valued by some but stored on a shelf to be dusted off on special occasions?

Rev. William Hockin, St Paul's Church
(Bloor Street), Toronto, March 1994[1]

In June 1994 in Montreal a diverse gathering of people met to discuss the future of the Anglican Church in Canada. One of the speakers, the Rev. Harry Robinson of Vancouver, described the situation confronting his church today. "The gospel is at a crossroads," he claimed. "Anglicanism has served a purpose in history and probably will continue to do so. But it's the gospel in a post-Christian Canada that really is important." The groups represented at the conference – evangelicals, charismatics, and Prayer Book Anglicans – had their own agendas, but they all affirmed Robinson's statement. The Anglican Church had to renew its commitment to the gospel of Jesus Christ. To accomplish this goal, delegates re-articulated in the "Montreal Declaration" the essential tenets of the Christian faith and addressed some of the major social issues confronting their church in the 1990s.[2]

The conference produced notes of triumph and sadness, opportunity and regret. United by the event, the participants praised "God for his saving grace and for the fellowship" they had enjoyed with God and with each other. Despite this declaration, Harry Robinson confessed that as an evangelical he had always felt like an alien in the Anglican Church.[3] His testimony reflected the bitter-sweet feelings of many people at the conference. After all, only an obvious crisis in the life of the Anglican Church in Canada had produced the slim opportunity for renewal that might exist in the 1990s. J.I. Packer, a prominent English clergyman now at Regent College in Vancouver, echoed these mixed feelings, wondering whether there would be a place for him in the Anglican Church in the future. "Survival," he said, "has become a critical issue."[4]

The Essentials '94 Conference in Montreal raises crucial questions about the place of evangelicalism in the Anglican Church in Canada. How is it that evangelicals could feel so out of place in their own church? They have never been dominant, but they have always been a significant minority, winning a grudgingly respected place during the early twentieth century as a dynamic, growing wing. And how is it that evangelicals can cooperate today with high church defenders of the Prayer Book? Historically these groups were mortal enemies. Even charismatics and evangelicals generally have looked on each other with suspicion as much as friendship. In short, what continuities and changes have shaped evangelicalism in the Anglican Church in Canada from the 1860s to the 1990s?

During the 1860s, evangelical Anglicans could be found in most parts of the Dominion, but large numbers existed in only a few areas. In the dioceses of Montreal, Huron, and Toronto, evangelicals had reached enough of a critical mass to contest church "party" politics effectively. For example, in the Diocese of Huron, evangelicals had elected Benjamin Cronyn as bishop during the 1850s. A few years later they organized Huron College in London. And in the North-West and Arctic, English evangelicals with the Church Missionary Society ran most of the parishes and missions. These dioceses had several evangelical bishops, usually appointed from England by the CMS. In the early 1870s Toronto became the most vibrant centre of evangelicalism with the development of several key institutions.[5]

The Toronto evangelicals began to organize effectively in 1869 with the formation of the Church of England Evangelical Association. This association merged with the Church Association of the Diocese of Toronto in 1873. Both organizations championed evangelical Protestantism and endured harsh criticism from the high church clergy, the church press, and Bishop A.N. Bethune for acting outside of the control of the diocese. Despite this opposition, leaders in the Church Association worked quickly, and in 1874 began efforts to establish a periodical and a divinity school. In response, Bishop Bethune moved to impeach several clergy for disparaging the government of the church. But after more than 2,000 lay men signed a petition in protest, the accused clergy were cleared of all charges.

Two years later the Church Association's efforts bore fruit. In 1876 the *Evangelical Churchman* began publishing with the primary goals of maintaining the Protestant character of the Church and encouraging missions. In 1877 the same evangelicals founded the Protestant Episcopal Divinity School (PEDS, later Wycliffe College). Within a few months they had hired the Rev. James Paterson Sheraton of Pictou, Nova Scotia, as principal and accepted several students for the 1877–78 school year. Students at the school in its first two pioneering decades included most of the leaders of the evangelical party during its heyday in the first two decades of the twentieth century.[6]

From the start, Bishop Bethune opposed the brash new institution, calling it "unnecessary." He argued (not incorrectly) that the PEDS would incite conflict and divisions and vowed not to ordain its students. His death in February 1879 removed this obstacle and also presented the evangelicals with an opportunity to gain a stronger foothold in their diocese. They took it. Sheraton proved to be a capable leader and the PEDS drew on local clergy and laymen for its teachers and administrators. For example, the irascible, dynamic S.H. Blake, a prominent Toronto lawyer, served on the school's executive committee and supported it financially until his death in 1914.

More immediately, both the evangelical and high church parties mobilized their forces to contest the Diocese of Toronto election to replace Bethune. After a series of deadlocks, with the clergy supporting high church candidates and the laity favouring evangelicals, the two sides reached a compromise. The evangelicals would dissolve the Church Association, though not the *Evangelical Churchman* or the PEDS, and the high church party would support Archdeacon Arthur Sweatman, a moderate evangelical from the Diocese of Huron. With this arrangement the two sides reached a tense, short-lived truce. As for Sweatman, he took charge of a growing diocese fractured by church parties, each of which considered him an ally and expected his favour.

Sweatman turned out to be a capable diplomat who generally refused to choose sides during his thirty-year tenure as bishop of Toronto. Nevertheless, he met the evangelicals' immediate expectations in his inaugural address. "I have laid claim to the further character of being an Evangelical Churchman," he said. "It is much to be regretted that so unexceptional a definition should have been narrowed down to the designation of a party. I hold that the chief glory, the very *raison d'être* of the Reformed Church of England is that she is an Evangelical Church. The very purpose of her purgation from Romish traditions was that she might be the depository and dispenser of the pure, unadulterated Gospel of Christ." With Sweatman's election, the well-organized Toronto evangelicals had concluded a series of modest but meaningful victories.[7]

This success gave the evangelicals confidence, and their new school proclaimed its principles proudly. Unlike Sweatman, the PEDS played church politics eagerly. In 1881 its managing board criticized the church for neglecting gospel preaching: "We are firmly persuaded that the pressing want of our church today is the preaching of a simple, definite, and free Gospel as the great means appointed by God of bringing men to Christ ... Nothing else can awaken, and nothing else can satisfy the awakened, and build up earnest, living Christians ... We are convinced that only a ministry loyal to our Protestant and Reformed Church and thoroughly imbued with the principles of the Evangelical truth, can be in thorough sympathy with our people, and build up the temporal interests of our Church in this land."[8] Typical of evangelical Anglicanism at that time, the declaration rang with both enthusiasm and defensiveness.

A more detailed sense of the character of evangelicalism in the Anglican Church during the 1880s and 1890s can be gleaned from the PEDS statement of principles, which indicates that although rationalism (liberal-modernist theology) was a concern, ritualism was considered the more immediate danger. The principles combined denunciations of high church-ritualist error with statements of evangelical belief. The Bible was described as "the sole rule of faith" in opposition to the "error" that made it and tradition "the *joint* rule of faith." It also stated that salvation comes through "justification by faith in Christ," not through the "sacramentarian system" and concluded with the blunt declaration that "Upon these *Fundamental Truths* Evangelical Churchmen and the Sacerdotalists are now at issue." Simply put, there could be no compromise.[9]

Only a few evangelicals questioned these rigid assumptions. In 1895 Frederick J. Steen, a PEDS graduate serving a parish in Berlin, Ontario (who later taught at the Montreal Diocesan College, where he was accused of teaching liberal theology), complained about the bias of the *Evangelical Churchman*. He told editor Henry John Cody that many evangelicals did not respect the paper, though Steen did not blame Cody personally. "[It] seems that you too are bound down by your environment," he wrote, "and in taking up the paper have been obliged to take up its past spirit and traditions which certainly are not congenial to you." Steen specifically protested the one-sided reporting and short-sighted attitudes of the newspaper. "If it's a matter of attacking High Churchmen, say almost anything," he complained. "They are already opposed to the paper – they haven't a dollar's worth of interest in it and can't hurt it, but if your remarks concern foibles of low churchmen go very gently, it's not Christian-like to hurt their feelings ... I am beginning to wonder whether it's only evangelicals that have such."[10] Steen wanted evangelicals to abandon the party rancour that constrained and clouded the gospel they preached.

The evangelicals continued to grow in numbers and influence in the Canadian church during the 1880s and 1890s. By the end of the century there were a half-dozen or more evangelical bishops. The PEDS was renamed Wycliffe College in the 1880s and federated with the University of Toronto. It was also recognized by the church as an official institution and was on its way to becoming the largest Anglican divinity school in Canada. Finally, the Canadian North-West continued to be an evangelical preserve, as the missionaries appointed there tended to be evangelicals. Wycliffe College contributed to this pattern by living up to its missionary mandate and supplying the West with numerous summer students, priests, and bishops. Wycliffe graduates had begun to prove themselves. Clearly, the evangelical star was rising.[11]

From the turn of the century until the First World War the evangelical party probably achieved its greatest growth and widest influence. Evidence of remarkable growth comes from the number of divinity students enrolled at Wycliffe College and other evangelical schools. St John's College in Winnipeg was governed by the evangelical archbishop of Rupert's Land, S.P. Matheson. In Saskatchewan, Rev. George E. Lloyd, a Wycliffe graduate from England and a future bishop, led Emmanuel College. In 1910, evangelical Anglicans formed Latimer College in Vancouver. Its first principal was W.H. Vance, a Wycliffe graduate.[12] And at Huron College in London and the Diocesan College in Montreal, evangelicals continued to be influential.

Despite this competition, Wycliffe College grew spectacularly after 1900. By 1910 it had over one hundred students, including several from England, numbers which it maintained until the war. Because of this growth, and to establish Wycliffe as a place of serious scholarship, Thomas R. O'Meara, who took over as principal in 1906, expanded the faculty to meet the college's teaching needs. In 1910 he hired W.H. Griffith Thomas, the widely respected principal of Wycliffe Hall, the evangelical Anglican college at Oxford. The college also hired C.V. Pilcher and H.K. Mowll from England, who became bishops in the Australia church during the 1920s and 1930s.[13] Wycliffe's success reflected the surge in numbers of evangelicals in the Canadian church and the evolution of the institutional base of the evangelical party. Its growing corps of graduates spread the influence of evangelicalism in the Anglican Church throughout Canada, in the North-West and Ontario especially, but also in the Maritimes and eastern Quebec.

This success was not lost on Principal O'Meara. In a memorandum to Wycliffe's council in 1909, he emphasized the need for the college to take advantage of its historical opportunity to influence the church and the nation.[14] In response to this need, and to pay for the new faculty members, O'Meara stepped up efforts to solicit financial support and inspire interest in Canada and England. Together with N.W. Hoyles, Wycliffe's president, he often travelled to England during summer months, raising funds among wealthy evangelicals.

The embattled evangelicals thus secured a respected place in the Anglican Church as a whole during the first two decades of the twentieth century. The *Canadian Churchman*, which had been patronizing and hostile to evangelicals and Wycliffe College in the 1890s, took a milder tone during the early 1900s. After the evangelicals bought the paper in 1912, and chose Griffith Thomas as editor, their influence within the church rose even higher. That the evangelicals had threatened the high church majority's dominance was reflected in efforts during the 1910s by Trinity College in Toronto to unite with Wycliffe.[15] The evangelicals assumed, probably correctly, that amalgamation was designed to undercut their influence. Moreover, Wycliffe's obvious success meant that it did not need Trinity as much as Trinity needed it. After World War I, however, Trinity and Wycliffe would on occasion share faculty to deal with shortages and illnesses.

The growing influence of evangelicals in the Anglican Church in Canada and their increasingly respected place in it affected the evangelicals in return. During the early years of the twentieth century, evangelicals generally became more moderate on matters of churchmanship. These developments were reflected in the role played by such strident leaders as Dyson Hague, an acknowledged expert on liturgy, during the revision of the Canadian version of the Book of Common Prayer and the hymn book. The Canadian revision of the prayer book (completed in 1921) adapted it to Dominion politics and changed the church calender somewhat but, despite pressure, did not involve liberal doctrinal changes or ritualist "innovations." Hague was part of this project from the start, and the Canadian revision was, in his judgment, a model of "conservative yet progressive adaption."[16] Similarly, Hague encouraged greater use of holiness songs and revival hymns during worship. As a member of the committee that revised the Canadian Church's hymn book (1905-1908), he fought to include more contemporary hymns, contending that old, plain songs and Gregorian chants did not appeal to modern ears.[17]

Not all the evangelicals were happy with the revised Hymn Book. Indeed, a few considered it a betrayal of the evangelical cause. In 1909, William Armitage, rector of St Paul's Church in Halifax, complained to

H.J. Cody that too many ritualist hymns had been included in the new hymn book. "My mind is quite made up concerning the Hymn Book," he declared angrily. "Its acceptance means the death of the Evangelical cause in Canada. I do not hesitate to say that the men who surrendered to the Sacerdotal element on the Compilation Committee, betrayed us. And they have made it exceedingly difficult for others to defend our position, for they are quoted everywhere as representative men on our side." Armitage especially blamed Hague as an "acknowledged leader" and "champion of Protestantism."[18]

That Armitage judged Hague suspect (some evangelicals said a "loose cannon") because of his work on the hymn book indicated how rigid evangelical views could be. That he complained to Cody, who was much more moderate than Hague, was perhaps strange, but it reflected Cody's position as the unofficial leader of the Canadian evangelicals (or in S.P. Matheson's words in 1911, the "High Priest and Apostle of evangelicalism" in Canada[19]).

World War I interrupted the evolution of the evangelical party. Many students left Wycliffe College to serve as soldiers and chaplains, and the college itself reluctantly housed army training units. Although the college kept on going with drastically reduced numbers, the war years left it ravaged. W.H. Griffith Thomas, the celebrated English import, developed a poor relationship with the administration. He complained about his workload, the house Wycliffe rented for him, and his salary. In turn, Wycliffe criticized him for spending more time in interdenominational activities (at the Toronto Bible College, for example) than at the college and in the Anglican Church. Several times Thomas offered to leave to allow the college to meet its budget more easily. With vastly reduced numbers of students, Wycliffe no longer needed or wanted him, he felt. By 1919 Thomas had left for Philadelphia, freed of institutional duties and hoping to spread his influence more widely in the fundamentalist movement. Wycliffe kept his departure quiet, but rumours of mutual animosity and vague reports that Thomas considered Wycliffe doctrinally lax spread among alumni. Some of the college's supporters even threatened to withhold money if it did not offer a satisfactory explanation for the episode.[20]

Thomas's departure symbolized the stalled momentum of the war years and exemplified the unsettled reaction many evangelicals had to changes in their party and church. In 1919, for example, William Armitage wrote to Principal O'Meara to comment on the recent synod. He noted the ritualist threat in the on-going prayer book revision and argued that the Montreal Diocesan College had lost its evangelical character. Wycliffe College also troubled him: "Even at Wycliffe we need a more definite Evangelical note. Forneret said to me the other day, 'Why

[Dean] Owen preaches a far more Evangelical sermon than [Robert] Renison ever does.' This he gave as a reason for a rapprochement with Trinity [College]. Of this, I say nothing here, but I do think that we must have from all our men a truly Evangelical message. That after all is the important thing in which to ground men who are coming on."[21] Though still strong, the evangelicals entered the 1920s with distinct sense of uneasiness. Hope remained that they could inflame the church with the gospel, but the reality of change caused deep concern.

It is difficult to characterize the evangelical party during the 1920s and 1930s, but the interwar years probably were a time of consolidation rather than decline. On the one hand, when Wycliffe College celebrated its sixtieth anniversary in 1937, fourteen evangelical bishops attended, including the primate. A few may have been missionary bishops from Asia, but this figure suggests that about one-third of Canada's Anglican bishops during the 1930s were evangelicals.[22] On the other hand, although the number of students at Wycliffe reached 75 in 1925 (including 12 from overseas) and 84 a few years later, the college never again achieved its pre-war level of students.[23] The situation for Wycliffe and the church worsened in the 1930s, as the harsh impact of the Depression on church finances meant that many dioceses, despite their needs, were not hiring new priests or summer students. Student aid also felt the impact. By the mid-1930s, the college's student body had fallen to less than fifty.

More important than numbers, the religiosity of students at schools like Wycliffe changed. W.E. Taylor, the acting principal in 1930, noted an "unsettlement" in the thinking of some students, who did not want simply to accept the traditions being handed down to them. They wanted to think their own way through modern intellectual problems. Taylor attributed this tendency to the effect of university life and teaching, but it is more likely that students came to university with questions. Serious students usually got through their times of doubt stronger and better for them, Taylor believed, but these developments still troubled him.[24]

Student "unsettlement" reflected changes in the mood of the Anglican Church as a whole. In the minds of many evangelicals, rationalism, relativism, and biblical criticism had become more serious threats than in years past. Wycliffe thus added declarations about the historical and doctrinal truth of the Trinity, incarnation, atonement, resurrection and ascension, and Person of the Holy Spirit to its list of principles. The new list also described missions as an essential part of the church's work, "implied in Christian discipleship, and involving world-wide witness to the Gospel of Jesus Christ."[25]

Not surprisingly, in 1930 Wycliffe College chose its new principal for his unshakable evangelical credentials. The Rev. Robert McElheran of Winnipeg did his best to lead Wycliffe on the narrow path of evangelical orthodoxy at a time of profound social turmoil. "I try to remind myself constantly of the fact that, as Principal, I am not free," he said in 1931. "It is not mine to do as I like. I have a heritage to guard and a great and wonderful institution to guide." His goals as principal were simple: protect the evangelical Protestant character of the college, train men for the ministry and missions, and ensure the loyalty of students to the Bible, prayer book, and church.[26]

One of the first problems McElheran had to deal with was the growth of ritualist practices among evangelical clergy. This problem illustrates the ways in which the evangelical party was diversifying, even fragmenting, during the 1930s. In a 1932 report to Wycliffe's council on his trip to the Maritimes to visit graduates, McElheran noted the opposition Wycliffe men faced in many dioceses. He praised those who held firm: "I cannot speak too highly of the devotion and loyalty of men who carry on their work with any degree of loyalty to their principles, in the face of such persistent opposition." He was concerned, however, because some evangelicals had accepted ritualist practices, such as the eastward position during communion, which he considered "a significant thing."

In response to the renewed threat of ritualism, McElheran stressed that Wycliffe needed to support the isolated evangelicals of the Maritimes. The college also needed to keep its own house in order. "I am more convinced than ever, after such an experience as this," he said, "that everything must be done in the College to train the men on sound lines." His fear was simple: "If [students] leave Wycliffe with their ideas hazy and their principles not well grounded and well established, it is not to be supposed that they will go into dioceses where everything is against them and suddenly become convinced Evangelicals. We must see to it that when men leave here they know the principles of Wycliffe College with respect to the Church, the ministry and the sacraments."[27] Dyson Hague, similarly, argued that Wycliffe should stick to its principles, or it was not worth preserving. Like McElheran, he grew somewhat defensive and became more convinced than ever of the need for a dependable evangelical college in the Canadian church.[28]

McElheran's response to the liberal theological climate of the day was as unequivocal as his attitude towards ritualism. In the mid-1930s he began restating the college's principles at annual trustee meetings to remind Wycliffe supporters of their roots and duty. In his 1937 report he touted Wycliffe as a rock in a time of change and upheaval: "[It] has been a year of great anxiety throughout the world. International unrest, national fears, social and industrial disturbances and great and grave personal problems. It is a happy thing ... that, in the midst of all the changes and chances of this mortal life, the institution committed to our care is one that stands for those eternal principles and that unchanging truth, which is the only security."[29] Only the gospel could save an "erring world."

Not surprisingly, at the same time that some evangelicals worked to shore up orthodoxy, others explored more liberal paths. In 1937 C.V. Pilcher, a former Wycliffe professor who had become co-adjutor bishop of Sydney, Australia, wrote to H.J. Cody. Cody had been rector at St Paul's Church in Toronto for three decades but had left a few years before to become president of the University of Toronto. Pilcher described the theological climate in his Australian diocese to Cody. He depicted its conservatism, noting that anyone there who denied the extremely conservative doctrine of the verbal inspiration of the scriptures was considered a modernist. In response, many liberal evangelicals found themselves allied with Anglo-Catholics against the conservatives.[30]

Pilcher's letter does not mean that a cabal of liberals lurked covertly in the Canadian church. It simply indicates that some evangelicals had chosen to explore the liberal limits of evangelicalism. For example, Professor B.W. Horan at Wycliffe taught an irenic, somewhat liberal theology. Similarly, H.J. Cody participated in the England-based Liberal Evangelical Group Movement and encouraged the growth of similar groups in Canada and the United States.[31] His successor at St Paul's, former Bishop of Athabasca Robert Renison, got into hot water with some members of his parish over his vague conclusions in a sermon on the Virgin Birth.[32] Clergy like Horan, Cody, and Renison broke from the more rigid orthodoxy being promoted by McElheran and Hague. Their faith can perhaps best be described as a "mediating" evangelicalism.[33] They probably did not reject the essentials of orthodoxy, contained in Wycliffe's principles, but their existence is evidence of the diversification of the evangelical party in Canada during the interwar years.

By the end of the 1930s the evangelical party thus had begun to come apart at the edges. Some clergy were exploring liberal theology and accepting ritualist practices. Wycliffe generally continued the conservative evangelical tradition, but students and faculty there no longer accepted the old verities without question. In addition, the growth of colleges in the West had undercut Wycliffe's influence. And Toronto, once the centre of the evangelical party, no longer dominated it nationally. Though still influential in key regions, the evangelicals had lost their momentum and begun to fragment.

During the 1940s and 1950s evangelicals in the Anglican Church faced both familiar problems and new ones. In his 1940 trip to the Maritimes, Professor F.D. Coggan (later Archbishop of Canterbury) reported that "Wycliffe men are sometimes ostracized because they are Wycliffe men. This results in a fear ... of not being moved, a thing as bad for the work as for the men and their families." He advised the new principal, Ramsay Armitage (William's son), to watch the Maritimes carefully lest Wycliffe men be squeezed out. This would be unfortunate, he wrote, for "The East greatly needs men who, by sheer force of a positive message and a spiritual life, will win their way."[34] Ritualism and Wycliffe's policy towards it also remained an issue. During the 1950s Wycliffe went through an official re-evaluation of its basic principles. In the process the evangelicals fundamentally questioned and debated the nature of evangelicalism.[35]

Despite these concerns, Wycliffe College continued to be a vibrant place. During the late 1930s and early 1940s professors ran summer preaching schools in various regions to keep in touch with graduates and spread the evangelical gospel. Principal Armitage's estimate of the college's influence on the Canadian church reflected this vibrancy. He believed that Wycliffe, more than any other institution, had kept the Anglican Church Protestant and "reasonably" free of extreme ritualism. Nevertheless, he was concerned about complacency. "The spiritual tone of our student life must continually be developed, not only through the Morning and Evening Chapel Service but by the students own prayer groups and Christian associations," he stated. "There is always in a Theological College the danger and tendency of taking spiritual values for granted."[36]

After the war, when church leaders expressed concern over the lack of new clergy for the church, Wycliffe dedicated itself to meeting the need. Armitage emphasized this with conviction: "It is my hope that as Wycliffe gave the lead in its earlier history to the emphasis on the Missionary side of the Church's life Ministry, so now at this second critical juncture it will again give the lead in providing for the more efficient training of its students before, and its graduates after ordination at least for the critical period of early ministry."[37] By the late 1940s the number of students at Wycliffe had climbed from Depression and wartime lows to more than fifty.

During the early 1950s Canadian evangelicals also became concerned about promoting unity among themselves and other Anglicans. This concern probably was a reaction against both the theological conflicts of the 1920s and 1930s and the violence of World War II and the Cold War. In his 1951 report to the college's trustees, Armitage addressed the "grave danger" of division: "We in Wycliffe must stand for a comprehensive and unifying Evangelicalism. Here there must be room for the conservative and for the liberal evangelical, neither ruling the other out. Those who would lay claim to the great name of Evangelical may not insist on any one hard and fast undeviating pattern nor on any rigid measuring rule." Armitage thus challenged Wycliffe to "hold fast" to its reformational principles, avoid "hard literalism," and preach the "freedom of the gospel."[38] He held Wycliffe to this challenge by getting the college to appoint a committee of representatives from the council, faculty, and younger graduates to re-evaluate its basic principles.[39]

The committee reported to the college's trustees in 1953. It noted that with the growth of diocesan colleges, the field of students Wycliffe could recruit from had fallen and the college needed to strengthen its evangelical appeal. Thus, though it fully endorsed the college's principles, the committee suggested that a simplified statement be prepared. The committee was divided, however, in its attitude towards "churchmanship." A minority pressed for the college to retain its traditional anti-ritualist stance, but the majority also felt that the time was ripe for change. Many Wycliffe students came from parishes that used ritualist practices, and many graduates went to such parishes. The majority thus argued that "To try to define evangelicalism in terms of the north end or east side position of the Celebrant at the Holy Communion, appears to a good many graduates of the College to be contending over what is no longer an issue, and to exhibit a sense of unreality with regard to the living religious issues which face the Christian Church to-day."[40] Wycliffe should maintain its reformational principles and "Prayer Book churchmanship" without alienating people by insisting on non-essential low church practices.

The committee reported again in 1954, still divided. All agreed that a "statement of the essential evangelical insights" in contemporary terms was necessary, but only a majority believed that "recognition should be given to the fact that the expression and emphasis of Evangelicalism has changed and broadened in recent years." This majority argued that evangelicals should constantly guard against the "temptation to allow secondary things to assume a place of primary importance. Whatever was the importance of such things as a Cross, Candles, Stoles, Position at the Communion in earlier days – it may have been primary – we are convinced that their place is not primary now."[41]

At this time the college also made an effort to beautify its chapel, to use visible signs to communicate God's inward, spiritual grace. It is not clear what happened to the report, but during the 1960s Wycliffe pruned its statement of principles to the bare evangelical essentials, taking out the anti-ritualist and anti-modernist statements that had been part of it. These changes sanctioned ritualist practices that had been going on among some evangelicals since the 1930s. They also represented the new bonds developing between high church and evangelical Anglicans and probably were an attempt to bridge the gap growing between liberal and conservative evangelicals.

All of these changes did not mean that the evangelicals had abandoned their roots. When Billy Graham came to Toronto in 1955 and visited the college, Wycliffe threw its support behind him without reserve. Principal Armitage praised Graham's work and noted that his crusade had generated excitement throughout Toronto, reminding him of revivals from the turn of the century. Revivals on a smaller, more intimate scale occurred among Anglicans in Montreal during the 1950s. Leaders like Ross Prendergast of the Church Army used small group meetings and weekend retreats to encourage conversions. Anglican evangelicals also frequently attended McGill Inter-Varsity Christian Fellowship during the 1950s and 1960s.[42] Although they had abandoned strict adherence to low church views, evangelicals continued to support revival and interdenominational cooperation.

The 1940s and 1950s, despite being times of change, thus were reassuring for evangelicals in the Canadian Anglican Church. Reflecting the conservatism of these decades, the churches grew along with the general population. After the traumas of theological liberalism, the Depression, and world war, like other Christians, evangelical Anglicans regained a sense of hopefulness about the future. And though the evangelical movement did not experience the momentum and rapid growth it had once enjoyed, things seemed better than in preceding decades. Evangelicals had secured a comfortable place in the Anglican Church. Old low church–high church lines had blurred considerably and the rancour of the past – over liberalism and ritualism – had evolved into more irenic attitudes by the 1940s. That the growth of the 1940s and 1950s did not keep up with that of the general population – and thus was not necessarily a sign of health – was not recognized at the time. In retrospect, what seemed like a time of success for the Canadian churches hid complacency and stagnation.

During the 1960s, evangelicalism began to decline in the Canadian Anglican Church. Rather than sudden, headlong decline, both evangelicals and the Anglican Church suffered gradual, almost imperceptible decay, like death from a nagging bleeder rather than a major hemorrhage. From a high of 1,358,000 members in 1961, the ACC dropped gradually to 720,000 in 1994.[43] More importantly, the church had become theologically stagnant. In *The Comfortable Pew*, a controversial study commissioned by the church for Lent in 1965, Pierre Berton argued that "If large masses of people are bored with the Church, it is surely because the Church has failed to excite their imaginations or their consciences. And it has failed to do this ... because it has had very little to say to them in terms of the twentieth century world in which they live. Christianity has, in the past, always been at its most vigorous when it has been in a state of tension with the society around it."[44] Spiritual complacency, Berton concluded, had left the church irrelevant to many Canadians.

Some evangelicals recognized the truth of Berton's criticisms and argued that these problems needed to be addressed quickly. Desmond Hunt, rector of St James' Church in Kingston, started a book study on *The Comfortable Pew*.[45] At a November 1968 Wycliffe College council meeting R.H. Soward, the chairman, reported that the problems facing the church and college required "the greatest amount of judgement and imaginative thinking" in their history. This did not mean giving up essential truths or principles, he cautioned, but it did require rethinking the college's role in light of the immense changes happening in the church and society at that time.[46]

In 1970 Principal Leslie Hunt described these changes as a "crisis of faith" in the church. "There is a dire need today," he stated, "for a convincing voice and a strong lead to help people back to a reasonable basis of faith where the focus is on the person of Jesus Christ – his revelation of God the Father and man's eternal dimension. This will never be done by clergy who are not quite sure what they believe, why they are in the ministry, or what hope there is for a limping church with its back to the wall." Citing the college's "great responsibility" to be relevant in this situation, Hunt spoke the hip language of the day. "We are planning faculty-student seminars," he said, "to make our students aware that they are going out with the Gospel into a changed, radical and far-out world where the majority do not want to listen to the Gospel anyway and where there are a thousand competing voices to be heard."[47]

The incomplete evidence available suggests that while the number of evangelicals shrank along with the church, pockets of success continued. English evangelicals still predominated in the Arctic, and across the country scattered evangelical parishes continued to uphold and spread the gospel. At St James' in Kingston, Desmond Hunt carried on the evangelical tradition during the 1960s, promoting the gospel using up-to-date methods and attracting students from nearby Queen's University. On a larger scale the Diocese of Montreal experienced a revival of evangelicalism beginning in the mid-1950s. Similar stories suggest that while the church was suffering nationally, strong leaders in key parishes and dioceses and interdenominational connections kept the evangelical tradition alive.[48] But, as in the past, many evangelicals likely began to feel as much at home in interdenominational organizations as in their own church.

Anglican decline and evangelical alienation continued into the late 1980s and early 1990s, when the steady decline in numbers, poor morale, and a financial crisis forced the Canadian church to recognize that it was on the edge of dissolution. Canada had become a post-Christian society. Adolescents, single adults, and families with young children had all but disappeared from all of the mainline churches; the vast majority of their churchgoers had become middle-aged and elderly. In this unhealthy demographic situation, characteristic evangelical concerns that the simple gospel and personal faith were not being encouraged in the mainline churches won a wider hearing. In addition, churches that did show growth tended to be conservative ones that offered a clear, orthodox Christian message.[49]

Evangelicals in the Anglican Church thus began to sound prophetic. And they had evidence to prove the power of their message.[50] Evangelicals in the Church of England experienced modest growth and renewal from the 1950s into the 1990s. In Canada during the 1980s evangelical institutions like Wycliffe College in Toronto and Regent College in Vancouver became lively places attracting large numbers of Anglican and non-Anglican students. This evangelical success has been recognized in the church lately. Of the approximately three dozen Anglican bishops in Canada today, one-third can be described as evangelical.[51] Finally, the charismatic movement in the Canadian church has affected about thirty per cent of parishes and twenty per cent of clergy and bishops.[52]

In addition to their own success, Anglican evangelicals also began to find unexpected allies. Old lines between high and low church Anglicans had broken down in years past. Now new lines which had been developing for some time crystallized, pitting conservative-orthodox Anglicans against liberal-modernist ones. Conservative ritualists, charismatics, and evangelicals began to find that they had their orthodoxy in common, and old conflicts over style of worship and minor points of theology became relatively unimportant.[53] The Essentials '94 Conference in Montreal was one of the results of this coming together. The conference was a sign that evangelical Anglicans have, in a sense, self-consciously "returned" to their church to help bring renewal. Interdenominational connections nurtured them over the past three decades; now they are trying to regain influence in their own church. One example of this resolve has been the work of Tom Robinson and Barnabas Anglican Ministries, an organization dedicated to bringing evangelical renewal to parishes and dioceses across the country. The 1990s thus signal a turn inward by evangelical Anglicans in Canada, as their church is perhaps ready to listen to their message. It is not clear, however, what percentage of Canada's 720,000 Anglicans support this movement. A large minority probably passively favours a return to orthodoxy, while a smaller group promotes it actively.[54]

These developments raise intriguing questions about the character of evangelicalism in the Anglican Church and elsewhere. It likely is impossible for historians to define the evangelical "impulse" itself. That is a task for saints (and maybe theologians). Nevertheless, in the past decade or so historians have come to define the major *observable* components of evangelicalism as a diverse "family resemblance." Evangelicals, they say, find their unity in four main principles: conversion, the unique authority of the Bible, the centrality of the Cross and resurrection, and missions and activism.[55] One of these principles, typically, is emphasized more than the others, such as in fundamentalists stressing the inerrant authority of the Bible or Henry Alline's followers devoting themselves to the experience of radical conversion. It thus is helpful to see the principles as movable fences, with the evangelical "impulse" somewhere inside. Scholars can easily shift them, like snow fences, to deal with particular groups and movements or adjust them to changes over time.

Whatever the combination or configuration, the four-part definition of evangelicalism does raise fences. It is low church Protestant in its emphasis on *sola scriptura* and its suspicion of ritual and tradition,[56] and during the nineteenth century evangelical Anglicans were stridently low church. During the twentieth century, however, the evolution of the evangelical party in the Anglican Church belies these assumptions. Many evangelicals have accepted ritualist practices, and in the past two decades have participated in Anglican-Roman Catholic talks about reunion. From the other side, small communities of high church charismatics who practise a ritualist-ecstatic form of Christianity have flourished in Canada, the United States, and England. Perhaps most importantly, at the Essentials '94 Conference, evangelicals, charismatics, and prayer book Anglicans united to defend orthodoxy and tradition.

Other historical and contemporary examples also support disentangling the implicit connection scholars generally make between low church views and the evangelical impulse. Nineteenth-century Roman Catholic parish revivals and revivalist orders, the Roman Catholic record in foreign missions, charismatic Roman Catholics in the twentieth century, evangelistic missions run by Anglican ritualists in England's inner cities during the 1870s and 1880s, and the biographical connections between evangelical Anglicanism and the Oxford movement – all of these cases indicate that the rigid lines usually drawn between evangelicals and "catholics" should be blurred.[57] Furthermore, in the 1990s a traditionalist pope has released an evangelical tract for the times,

Crossing the Threshold of Hope (1994). And conservative evangelicals and Roman Catholics have worked to build informal ties and draft declarations of common purpose and basic unity, especially on the defence of orthodoxy and social issues.[58]

Arguably, therefore, historians interested in the evangelical impulse need to allow for a broader paradigm of family resemblances. They should avoid the implicit connection usually made between low church style and evangelical piety and should question whether the Protestant doctrine of scripture *alone* is essential to evangelicalism. Some historians have taken these steps. For example, as a result of his survey of evangelicalism in Canada reported in *Maclean's* in 1993, George Rawlyk has argued that a large minority of Roman Catholics can be considered evangelicals. Other historians disagree. John Stackhouse has argued vehemently that because Roman Catholics recognize tradition as authoritative together with scripture, they cannot be considered evangelicals.[59]

The common use of the term "evangelicalism" today reflects its recent lineage. The "demand for the label *evangelical*," as Donald Dayton argued in 1991, has its roots "in the power politics of the neo-evangelicals after World War II."[60] The neo-evangelicals wanted to move beyond fundamentalism, and, in part, they began to write the history of American evangelicalism to give a sense of tradition, respectability, and sophistication to a marginalized religious community. Not surprisingly and not inappropriately, they defined evangelicalism in their own image. Certainly not all historians of evangelicalism are part of this community, but many are. More importantly, the evangelical school in Anglo-American historiography has largely been defined by the neo-evangelical historians.[61] If, however, the history of evangelicalism in the Anglican Church is an indication, a model of "family resemblances" that can include people from high church traditions should be developed.[62] John R. Sperry, retired bishop of the Arctic, made a similar point recently. "My own view," he said, "is that the term 'evangelical' must rightly be separated from dress, terminology, ritual practice and anything else that does not affect the foundational commitment to the Faith as revealed in Holy Scripture. Even in England, belonging to either of the main parties, or even to the liberal centre, never was a special mark of spirituality."[63]

Perhaps a model of "family resemblances" could be explored on an orthodox-evangelical basis. Although a few historians have already complained that the term evangelical has become unwieldy and overburdened, and though adding high church Anglicans, Roman Catholics, and Orthodox Christians would exacerbate the problem, it is artificial to analyse these groups in isolation from each other. Scholars have published a wealth of insightful work examining evangelical Protestantism, but the next logical step is to explore the similarities and differences between self-identified evangelical Protestants and other Christians. This project might lead to new questions and new insights into the history of Christianity in the modern and postmodern world. It might uncover trends and turning points that historians have missed and might encourage new perspectives on old questions. Useful points of comparison include the populist use of print and electronic media, responses to modernism, the impact of cultural movements (such as romanticism and consumerism), changing roles of women, missions, and membership growth in the nineteenth century, and secularization in the twentieth. At worst, historians would suffer from a wealth of new data and insights.[64]

This project probably would not help to define the evangelical "impulse" itself. Spirituality and piety are impossible to define with certainty. Scholars can get to their manifestations, but not to their heart and soul. By exploring new models of "family resemblances," historians would gain a more complete understanding of manifestations of spirituality and piety during the past 250 years. And they would better understand the place of Christianity, of evangelicals, and other Christians, in the modern and postmodern world.

PART THREE

Baptists, Mennonites, and Lutherans

12 "The Footprints of Zion's King": Baptists in Canada to 1880

DANIEL C. GOODWIN

In 1880 I.E. Bill, the aging Baptist revivalist, pastor, and historian, wrote that nowhere "in this wide world are the foot-prints of Zion's King more distinctly seen than in the rise and progress of a vital Christianity, as associated with the origin and multiplication of Baptist Ministers and Churches in these Maritime Provinces."[1] The triumphalist language reflected Bill's satisfaction at almost eighty years of unprecedented growth and influence of Baptists especially in Nova Scotia and New Brunswick. The grass-roots evangelical impulse of the late eighteenth century had profoundly infused Maritime Baptists with the capacity to win converts and help shape the emerging colonial culture.

In contrast the Baptist churches in Ontario and Quebec to 1880 played a strikingly less important role in the development of culture and society. Plagued by an ethnic, linguistic, and theological diversity spread throughout a wide geographical area, central Canadian Baptists became largely preoccupied with solving internal denominational problems while the growing Methodist and Presbyterian denominations began to exercise hegemonic influence on colonial Protestant evangelical life. In spite of their evangelical orientation, Baptists in central Canada were unable to engage their culture effectively and therefore remained a minor religious force in the region.

The statistical evidence from the census figures for 1881 reflects the "regional factor" in Canadian Baptist history. For example, nationwide, Baptists accounted for 6.9 per cent of the total population. In Ontario, Baptists were 1.6 per cent under the national average at 5.3 per cent, while those in Roman Catholic-dominated Quebec were the smallest, holding the allegiance of only 0.6 per cent of the population. In that same year the percentage of Baptists on Prince Edward Island was close to that of Ontario at 5.7 per cent. The remarkable strength of Canadian Baptists in 1881 was to be found in Nova Scotia and New Brunswick with 19.0 per cent and 25.2 per cent respectively. This made Baptists the largest Protestant denominational grouping in New Brunswick and the second strongest in Nova Scotia. These percentages underscore the regional realities of Canadian Baptists.[2]

Perhaps the most important difference between the Baptists of the Canadas and the Maritimes was that there was a radical evangelical tradition in the eastern provinces, especially Nova Scotia and New Brunswick, in which the Baptists of the region were soundly rooted. However, in the Canadas no such common foundational ethos emerged among the Baptists, which left them divided and without a gospel that could effectively penetrate the culture.

The religious culture in which Maritime Baptists emerged was one forged during the First Great Awakening (1776–1784) in Nova Scotia. This religious stir, characterized by mass revival with ecstatic conversions, was fuelled by the emotionally charged preaching of Henry Alline and other New Light preachers. The result of this religious movement was the disintegration of the prevailing Congregational church establishment and the creation of a loosely connected association of Allinite New Light churches which regarded externals in religion, such as the sacraments, as "non-essential." Thus, both infant sprinkling and believers' baptism by immersion were accepted as valid in these churches.[3]

The freedom granted to the New Lights, because of Allinite ambiguity over the externals of religion, led in the 1790s to an extreme form of antinomianism that became known as the New Dispensation. This radical Gnostic expression of New Lightism led to incidents of breaking of traditional Christian morality and, in one case, a religiously motivated murder. Not surprisingly, many New Light preachers and lay people sought to distance themselves from the excesses of the New Dispensation and stressed instead religious respectability.[4]

Until recently, the accepted interpretations of the Maritime radical evangelical shift to order have been cast in the New Light to Baptist paradigm. Historians have underscored the powerful desire among most Allinite preachers by 1796 to achieve a level of respectability within mainline colonial society that would give them a similar status to that held by the Methodists and Presbyterians. However, what is not usually noted is that the longing for order and an acknowledgment of the sacraments as important, if not crucial, suggests that the New England Congregationalist background of the New Lights was not altogether destroyed during the Great Awakening. Respectability, church discipline, and the solemn observation of the sacraments under the supervision of formally ordained and recognized clergy, which had been the norm of Congregational church life in New England, reappeared in 1799 with the formation of the Baptist and Congregational Association. The following year only churches that baptized believers by immersion were accepted into the association, and by 1809 only churches that permitted immersed believers to the communion table were extended membership.[5]

Although the fears of excesses unleashed by antinomianism pushed many New Light leaders and churches toward a Regular Calvinist Baptist position, it is not altogether clear why believers' baptism by immersion became the unifying and identifying ritual for these former New Lights. It has recently been argued that "the Baptist patriarchs became more or less ardent Baptists largely because they were compelled to do so in order to survive as ministers, when faced with the remarkable popular movement that swept through the Yankee heartland of Nova Scotia and the Saint John River Valley in the late eighteenth century and the early years of the nineteenth." This "rage for dipping," so described by Anglican Bishop Charles Inglis of Nova Scotia, was a populist grassroots movement, motivated, in part, by certain millennial expectations that the world would soon end with the return of Jesus Christ who would gather unto himself those "born of water and the Spirit." This populist "rage for dipping" easily identified being "born of water" with believers' baptism by immersion.[6]

Although baptism may have been a religious practice that was energized from the bottom up by eschatological speculations, the reason for its permanent place in nineteenth-century Maritime Baptist life must be found in the dynamic of the ritual itself. Had there not been a firm continuity with the religious practices and experiences of the First Great Awakening, it is doubtful whether former New Lights would have been so content to remain within the Baptist tradition. In fact it might be argued that the New Light to Baptist transition was possible because Allinite spirituality – characterized by rapturous conversions and intense ecstatic religious expression – was recast into a distinct framework centred around the evangelical ritual of believers' baptism by immersion. The marriage of Allinite religious experience and immersionist baptism created, for many, an almost irresistible baptismal spirituality.

It is clear that both the Regular Baptists and the Free Christian Baptists – both strongly connected to the region's Allinite heritage – made effective evangelistic use of this ritual. It is not overstating the case to say that the use of outdoor baptismal services gave Maritime Baptists not only their identity but their most effective tool for proselytizing the great "unwashed." By establishing their ritual within the religious culture early in the nineteenth century, the Baptists effectively dominated the populist evangelical impulse which left the evangelical rituals of the Methodist camp meeting and the Presbyterian long communion relatively impotent in presenting the "visible gospel" to the residents of Nova Scotia and New Brunswick. Since the baptismal service was a hybrid of grass-roots Allinite spirituality and immersionist baptism, the Baptists became the religious tradition most solidly rooted in the emerging colonial religious culture.

If the outdoor baptismal ritual was energized from the bottom up, it was also controlled from the top down. In their search for respectability and stability, many of the so-called Maritime Regular Baptist patriarchs not only accepted the central ritual of "dipping" but controlled it in such a way as to exercise church discipline over behaviour and beliefs. Receiving the ritual publicly was a proclamation to the effect that the candidate was to be accepted into membership of the local Baptist church. Maintaining such a membership required that the member adhere to Christian morality and a basic level of biblical orthodoxy. A breach of these expectations often led to church discipline.[7]

That a less radical and more conservative Maritime evangelicalism emerged in the early decades of the nineteenth century was not exclusively the result of disillusioned Allinite preachers seeking a better way. Indeed, as Nancy Christie has persuasively argued, the War of 1812 abruptly curtailed the spectacular expansion of radical evangelicalism in the Maritimes and introduced a revival of conservatism by linking anti-republicanism and anti-Americanism. Since evangelical denominations such as the Baptists theoretically granted each member an equal voice, it was believed that such freedom might contribute to civil unrest. Thus, Baptist leaders who had tried to temper the more disorderly components of radical evangelicalism progressively allied themselves with the more conservative impulse within colonial society. According to Christie, "the respectable majority was all too effectively co-opted by Toryism, leaving the radical fringe at the margins of early Victorian culture."[8] This conservative shift within Maritime culture served the Baptist leaders' quest for respectability.

If the desire to achieve respectability had been firmly established in the Maritime Baptist psyche in the early years of the nineteenth century, the means to accomplish this goal was substantially strengthened in 1827 with the founding of the Granville Street Baptist Church in Halifax. Comprised almost exclusively of former members of St Paul's Anglican Church, this newly formed Regular Baptist church contained a number of well-educated and socially prominent men such as brothers James and Lewis Johnstone, a lawyer and a physician respectively. J.W.

Nutting, also a lawyer, was a graduate of King's College and prothonotary of the Supreme Court. E.A. Crawley, another graduate of King's and a lawyer by profession, had just begun his practice in the city. As an influential importer and merchant, John Ferguson was one of the first Baptists to represent the emerging Maritime business elite. John Pryor, who had recently graduated from King's, would along with Crawley eventually become a key leader in Baptist higher education.[9]

All of these men had willingly renounced their Anglican past and had publicly received believers' baptism by immersion. These urban professional leaders shared a pilgrimage similar to other less sophisticated Baptists, for most had forsaken their pedobaptist heritage, be it Anglican, Congregational, Methodist, or Presbyterian, to join the immersionists. However, the common heritage between the former Anglican elite and other grass-roots Baptists ended at the baptismal waterside. These men represented a new branch grafted onto the Maritime Baptist family tree. Far from their modestly educated farmer and fisherman cousins, these men represented a powerful political and economic clique within colonial society. That their Anglican past persisted beyond their immersion is clear in that these men began to seek a respectability for their new-found denomination which was similar to that which they had enjoyed in the established church. Baptist higher education with public funding and formally trained clergy became issues of grave importance for the Halifax clique as they had been for many of the founding fathers of the denomination. But whereas the founding fathers – most of them former disciples of Henry Alline – were in a position only to dream of the trappings of respectability, the Granville Street Baptists were in a position to help make the dream a reality.

Possessing a relatively homogeneous spirituality fused with immersionist baptism, New Brunswick and Nova Scotia Baptists of both the Calvinist and Free Will varieties were poised for growth during the first half of the nineteenth century. However, a very different Baptist story was unfolding on Prince Edward Island. In fact, the socio-cultural conditions of the island province paralleled those of Upper Canada much more than the neighbouring Maritime colonies. Unlike Baptists in Nova Scotia and New Brunswick, Island Baptists were not an indigenous movement born in the aftermath of the Great Awakening. Rather, the few Baptists who did settle on Prince Edward Island were primarily Scottish Baptists who had been influenced greatly by the revivals of Robert and James Haldane in Scotland. The first Scots Baptist preacher in the colony was Alexander Crawford. A native of Argyleshire, he came to Yarmouth, Nova Scotia, in 1810 and at once began to teach and preach. Although he held to the tenets of evangelical Christianity, his rational and systematic Scottish Baptist mind could not tolerate the radical New Light Baptist evangelicalism he encountered in Yarmouth. Writing to Edward Manning, the Regular Baptist patriarch, he reported:

the first of that denomination I conversed with in Yarmouth could give me no reason of the hope that was in them, (after varying the question every way I was capable of) but dreams, and visions, and feelings of the mind: they had a scheme of salvation totally independent of Christ's person and work. Indeed they seemed to have no idea of either, after I had explained it to them as well as I could, except the view they had of his person in their dreams and visions, and the knowledge they suppose they had of his work in their own souls.[10]

Crawford was unable in good conscience to enter into fellowship with the indigenous Nova Scotia Regular Baptists because of their radical evangelicalism. Therefore, he relocated to Prince Edward Island in 1815 and laid the foundations of Baptist churches at East Point, Tryon, and Bedeque.

His preaching was well received by a small, struggling group of Island Baptists because his more rational and less emotional brand of evangelicalism struck a responsive chord among the Scots settlers. The radical evangelical Baptist ethos of Nova Scotia and New Brunswick would never be well received on Prince Edward Island in the nineteenth century. Only when the erudite Charles Tupper, an atypical Baptist preacher from Nova Scotia, became a settled pastor on the island would these Scottish Baptist churches begin to affiliate with sister churches on the mainland; even then, the Baptist growth and influence on the Island colony was limited. The immersionists had failed to establish in the cultural matrix of the island colony the crucial ritual of believers' baptism by immersion early in the years of settlement. Furthermore, in this religious culture shaped by Scottish forces, the radical evangelical impulse of the region could only find acceptance in the ecstatic form of Presbyterianism promulgated by the McDonaldites.[11]

A radical, populist evangelical impulse emerged in early nineteenth century Upper Canada which was not unlike the New Light stir in late eighteenth-century Nova Scotia and New Brunswick. However, the proponents of ecstatic conversions, visions, and emotionally charged preaching came not from the tiny Baptist presence in the colony but from the Methodists who "grew at an even more dizzying rate in Upper Canada than ... in the United States."[12] By 1805 preachers such as William Case, Henry Ryan, and Nathan Bangs had firmly established the evangelical Methodist ritual of the camp meeting in the religious culture of the colony. This ritual became one of the key evangelistic tools for Upper Canadian Methodism – just as the baptismal service had been for Baptists in Nova Scotia and New Brunswick – and goes a long way to explain the denomination's phenomenal growth and religious hegemony in the colony. In 1881 Methodists in Ontario boasted 30.7 per cent of the population's allegiance, which contrasted sharply with the Baptists' 5.5 per cent. Unlike their co-religionists in Nova Scotia and New Brunswick, most of the original Baptists in Upper and Lower Canada came from Scotland and England and the United States. Each of these immigrant Baptist groups brought a distinct religious and cultural heritage which had been developing for over two centuries; given their different backgrounds, each tended to operate in isolation under the common name of Baptist. The diversity of these groups inevitably gave rise to recurring patterns of tension that hindered any cooperative plans for evangelistic growth.[13]

In 1816 the first British Baptists settled in Breadalbane in the Ottawa River valley. Gaelic-speaking immigrants from Perthshire, Scotland, they established a church based on the principles of James and Robert Haldane. Fiercely independent in church polity, these Baptist congregations held to a low view of ordained, professional ministry and appointed elders to administer the ordinances and preach the gospel. Furthermore, they held to the open communion position, allowing all Christian believers, regardless of affiliation, to receive the Lord's Supper.

In 1819 the Reverend John Edwards, from Portsmouth, England, arrived in Kingston and three years later settled in Clarence in Upper Canada. Although influenced by the Haldane revivals, Edwards had also been affected by the English Baptist appreciation for an educated ministry, the interdependence of local churches, and open communion. Other English Baptist clergy included men such as William Fraser, who became the first ordained pastor of the Breadalbane church, and John Gilmour, who responded to the call of a small group in Montreal and founded the St Helen Street Church there in 1831. Although the Scottish and English Baptists tended to hold to somewhat different views of ministry and congregational autonomy, they were both committed to the open communion position.

Regular Baptist missionaries from the United States established a string of churches along the southern border of Upper Canada and the Eastern Townships of Lower Canada. By 1800 there were eight Baptist churches in the Canadas: Caldwell's Manor, Sutton Flats, Stanstead-Hatley, and Abbott's Corner in the east, and Hallowell, Thurlow, and Cramahe-Haldimand in the centre, and Clinton/Beamsville in the west. These strict Calvinistic Baptists, who came to the Canadas in the aftermath of the American Revolution, were, in contrast to the British Regular Baptists and the Scottish Baptists, strongly committed to the principles of closed communion and the interdependence of local churches.[14]

Even greater diversity was imported from the United States when Free Communion and Free Will Baptists established their presence in the Oxford and London areas respectively. Since both groups were Arminian, they sought official organic union, which was accomplished in 1841. Never achieving numerical significance, the denomination fell apart in the 1860s. Given their theological differences with the Regular Baptist majority, these Arminian Baptists were marginalized even further from the evangelical mainstream than their Calvinistic co-religionists. Furthermore, the effective use of the Arminian gospel by the Methodists ensured that the Free Communion and Free Will Baptists would not be able to provide a sufficiently unique presentation of evangelical Christianity.[15]

Although the cultural and theological diversity of Baptists in the Canadas tended to hinder unity, there were attempts at cooperation in education and mission to the French Roman Catholics of Lower Canada. In 1838, after almost a decade of discussion, the Regular Baptists of Canada founded Canada Baptist College. This had been preceded by the formation of a triad of societies which had worked together, though not always in harmony, to make the venture possible: the Upper Canada Baptist Missionary Society, the Canadian Baptist Missionary Society in Canada East, and the Baptist Canadian Missionary Society of London, England. Although the suggested site for the college had initially been the centrally located settlement of Brockville, "the combination of available property, the presence of Newton Bosworth [an able preacher and teacher], and strong support from well to do Baptists in Montreal had decided the immediate location of the College. Although no official records explain the choice in site, the location became permanent."[16]

The first principal of Canada Baptist College was Dr Benjamin Davies (1838–1843) whose salary was paid by the Baptist Canadian Missionary Society in Britain. Holding a Ph.D. in oriental languages from the University of Leipzig, he instructed the young men under his care in Greek, Latin, Hebrew, Syriac, and Chaldee. Not surprisingly, most of the churches in central Canada did not see the relevance of such education for preachers. As Theo T. Gibson puts it, for them "the unlettered outpourings of an overflowing heart meant more than a polished sermon, however orthodox."[17]

During Davies's tenure as principal, he influenced well over twenty young men preparing for ministry, developed the institution's library holdings, and expanded the curriculum to include the classics. In 1843 he left his post to assume the position of theological tutor and president of Stepney College in England. The following year John Mockett

Cramp became the new principal of Canada Baptist College. Under his leadership the curriculum was expanded to include a secondary classics department for younger men and more practical courses to prepare students for the pastorate, and a new facility for the college was erected. In 1849, in the face of mounting debt and imminent closure, Cramp resigned as college principal and two years later became the president of the struggling Acadia College in Wolfville, Nova Scotia.[18]

The factors that led to the closing of Canada Baptist College reflect the divisions among Regular Baptists in the Canadas. T.A. Higgins, in his biography on Cramp, suggests that one reason for the failure of the institution was that the college was too far from the centre of Baptist population.[19] Since the majority of Baptists lived in Canada West, they did not enthusiastically support the distant school in Montreal. Furthermore, the Scottish and English Baptist influence at the college meant that open communion views were regularly promulgated, which outraged many preachers and churches influenced by the American closed communionists. In the minds of many Baptists, higher education became associated with the open communion stance itself.

In an attempt to calm the issue the Canadian Baptist Missionary Society refused to establish a policy on the communion question. This refusal had led Baptists in Canada West to criticize the society for supporting the Grand Ligne Mission which, in its earlier days, had not practised believers' baptism by immersion or closed communion. The mission to French Roman Catholics had been founded in 1836 by Henrietta Feller, a Swiss Protestant converted in a Haldane revival in her native land. Holding to open communion and open membership, the mission was nevertheless supported by Baptists in the Canadas and across the border. However, the baptism by immersion of Feller and evangelist Louis Roussy in 1847 and the linking of the mission to the Canada Baptist Mission Society in 1849 ushered in yet one more Baptist group in the Canadas.

All of these factors tended to hinder support from Canada West for the college. Furthermore, when financial assistance from England was withdrawn in the midst of an economic depression in the Canadas in the late 1840s, the collapse of the institution was inevitable.

If the short history of the Canada Baptist College quite specifically points to the divisions among the Baptists in the Canadas, the failed attempts at creating denominational structures beyond the association level illustrate in a general way the widespread inability of the Baptists to cooperate meaningfully. Although early Baptist churches, usually of the Calvinistic stripe, created local associations of like-minded churches, there were virtually no attempts to form larger unions for collective action until 1833. In that year the Eastern, Western, and Haldimand Associations formed the Baptist Missionary Convention of Upper Canada, which became extinct as quickly as it was formed "for want of concert and energy."[20] In 1837 the strictly closed-communion Eastern and Western Associations met with the less strict London churches in the hope of bringing them into the Upper Canada Baptist Missionary Society, but the squabbling over the communion question plagued any attempt at cooperative ministry.

Six years later in 1844 the Canada Baptist Union was organized in order to address the Church of England's attempt to claim the status of established church and the related problems of the clergy reserves and the founding of a provincial university. Recognizing that associations had failed in the past to manage an alliance, the union sought general support from open and closed communionists and every Baptist minister. Although led by prominent Baptists in Upper Canada, the union failed to generate enough support to speak with any authority for the constituency. By 1848 it is clear that the "Union" was virtually ignored by most Baptists in Canada West. The same year this disappointment led to yet another attempt to create a wider denominational organization. The western associations of Haldimand, Eastern, Western, Grand River, and Johnstown created the Regular Baptist Missionary Union of Canada. Aspiring to support home and overseas missions, Sunday schools, and a denominational newspaper, this union sought to defend religious liberty and the voluntary principle in religion. However, the fiercely independent spirit of most of these churches weakened support for this initiative as tensions over open and closed communion and independence versus interdependence of the local church continued to take centre stage.[21]

From the 1850s onward Baptists in the Canadas would undergo a metamorphosis that was directly linked to what William Westfall refers to as "the new culture of Protestant Ontario in the Victorian period."[22] Westfall identifies a dialectical process whereby the religion of order, represented by Anglicanism, and the religion of experience, represented by revivalistic Methodism, merged to form a Protestant consensus in the second half of the nineteenth century. Although never part of the Protestant mainstream in the Canadas, the Baptists, especially in Ontario, were given an opportunity to achieve respectability in spite of their numerical insignificance.

By 1858 the Regular Baptist Missionary Convention of Canada West and the Regular Baptist Missionary Convention East had been formed to assist struggling churches, educate the laity, provide a Baptist voice in provincial affairs, and employ evangelists to plant churches. Although the eastern convention included both open and closed communionists, there was a willingness to work together for common goals.

Scholars have not explored why this new spirit of cooperation emerged at mid-century. It seems possible that a number of influential Baptist ministers and wealthy businessmen sought respectability for their denomination within the Protestant consensus. To accomplish this goal it became necessary for Baptist churches to cooperate with one another under the leadership of well-trained ministers. This general shift among those in leadership is perhaps best seen in the person of Robert Alexander Fyfe. Educated at the Canada Baptist College during the tenure of Principal Davies, Fyfe was cautious about the emotional excesses of evangelicalism and sought to forge a denomination that would adhere to the balance of order and religious experience so often associated with Victorian respectability. After successfully serving major pulpits in Montreal and Toronto, in 1860 he became the first principal of the Canadian Literary Institute in Woodstock, Ontario. Although committed to the theological education of pastors, Fyfe believed that those preparing for ministry "could develop more naturally and more prolifically from a much larger nucleus of intellectually and spiritually disciplined young people."[23] Higher education became a means whereby Baptists in Ontario and Quebec could increase their influence in society beyond their members. In an 1868 address on Baptists and education, Fyfe remarked: "Everyone knows that ... well educated people have the most influence in the community. Here if parents wish their children to succeed in the race of life, ... they *must* educate their children ... Our work, then is to arouse [parents] ... to the importance of giving to their sons and daughters all the education which they can possibly afford; and then ... meet the demand which we have created."[24] Only with a properly educated laity and clergy would Baptists be guaranteed a powerful voice within society.

Fyfe's view of his denomination in the second half of the nineteenth century was one that shunned the excesses of revivalistic experiential Christianity. If Baptists were to be an important force, they would have to resist the "measures of questionable propriety [in order] to awaken" people to the gospel message. Baptists would have to create a future based on religious restraint, educational excellence, a rational gospel, and respectability within the Protestant consensus.[25]

If Fyfe reflected a desire among better-educated clergy for denominational respectability, high-profile lay leaders such as the Honourable Alexander Mackenzie, Canada's first Liberal prime minister, and Senator William McMaster represented the longing of many upwardly mobile central Canadian Baptists for acceptability among a growing entrepreneurial and political elite. According to George Rawlyk, McMaster, like "many other leading Canadian Baptists in the latter part of the nineteenth century ... was obsessed with the desperate search for denominational respectability. One important way to achieve this end, it was felt, was to build a respectable Baptist university. Another way was to construct a 'Baptist cathedral,' the new Jarvis Street Baptist Church."[26]

The growing Baptist business elite produced a challenge to local Regular Baptist churches which had traditionally mediated disputes about "business or trading transactions." In 1866 the ever-diplomatic and ambitious Fyfe counselled his constituency to permit its members to solve their business conflicts outside of church meetings: the "church was designed for the mutual spiritual benefit of its members, and not to settle intricate business difficulties."[27] If Baptists were to play a role in the new order, the emerging business elite would have to be free from local church discipline in matters relating to commerce. This price for respectability was one that leaders such as Fyfe were willing to pay.

By 1880 Regular Baptists in Ontario and Quebec had achieved denominational unity after almost eighty years of failed attempts at cooperation. As denominational distinctives tended to be eroded within the Protestant consensus, it became clear that the small differences which had been so divisive among Baptists in previous generations no longer seemed as important. As an emerging religious and business elite assumed leadership of the Baptist constituency, the necessity of religious respectability precluded any major debate of the communion question that raged in the 1840s and 1850s, However, it would be a respectability that did little to extend Baptist growth and influence in Ontario and Quebec.

If the Baptists of Ontario and Quebec remained on the periphery of provincial religious life even after achieving a level of respectability, the same cannot be said for their co-religionists in the Maritimes. As the Baptists of Nova Scotia and New Brunswick experienced phenomenal numerical growth during the first four decades of the nineteenth century, they challenged the pedobaptistic denominations, especially the Presbyterians, Methodists, and Anglicans. As outdoor baptismal services became the identifying ritual of the Baptists, the ordinance formed a focal point of controversy from 1811 to 1848. Through these years an extensive literary debate erupted, producing no fewer than twenty-three published polemical tracts and full-length studies of theology, along with scores of newspaper articles.

The crucial years of this controversy coincide with what historian D.C. Harvey has called the "intellectual awakening of Nova Scotia" from

1812 to 1835.[28] This period was marked by an increased integration of ethnically based communities and churches, and the emergence of newspapers, magazines, schools, and libraries, all of which contributed to the making of a collective identity in the Nova Scotia population. It was a time when residents of the province began to articulate a perspective all their own. For Harvey the emergence of a distinctive literature by such notable authors as T.C. Haliburton, and the popular demand for more responsible government, as promoted by Joseph Howe, served as indicators that an indigenous culture was coming into existence.

A glaring omission in Harvey's discussion of this cultural revival is the central role played by religious debate, prompted by the Baptist growth in the region. Numerical and geographical expansion of the Baptists motivated pedobaptists to defend their views of baptism and to attack the immersionists. The ensuing "literary" exchange not only motivated the Regular Baptists to defend their most important evangelical ritual but created a demand for indigenous Regular Baptist authors to engage the sophisticated theological arguments and biblical word studies by better educated Anglicans and Presbyterians. From 1823 to 1848, the Baptists contributed ten published tracts and full-length books to the controversy. William Elder was the first immersionist to enter the debate. Since he was modestly educated, the effort tended to be somewhat superficial when compared to the Presbyterian literature of the 1820s. However, by the mid-1830s, the Regular Baptists were producing carefully crafted theological treatises such as E.A. Crawley's *A Treatise on Baptism*; and studies firmly grounded in the original biblical languages were published by Charles Tupper in the late 1840s. While this much-neglected polemical debate shaped the religious contours of the intellectual awakening in Nova Scotia, it was also a means for Regular Baptists in the Maritimes to achieve acceptability. At the close of the baptismal controversy, in 1848, it was evident to the reading public that the Regular Baptists could produce an academically sound defence of their central rite of passage. With the support of Acadia College, the Anglican-turned-Baptist elite in Halifax, and a number of brilliant and educated preachers in the constituency, the Regular Baptists of the Maritimes proved they could be as theologically nuanced as any other denomination in the region. Respectability had come to touch even the radical evangelical ritual of believers' baptism by immersion. By the end of the nineteenth century many Maritime Baptist churches, especially in the towns and cities, had dismantled the outdoor baptismal community service in favour of a privatized, sterile baptismal tank inside the meeting house.[29]

If Maritime Regular Baptists were ardent promoters and defenders of their central ritual, they were not narrowly sectarian in their vision for

Christian higher education. To compete with Anglicans and Presbyterians, the Baptists established institutions of higher learning which did not require religious tests of students and faculty as long as they were professing Christians. In 1828 Horton Academy was founded in Horton, Nova Scotia, followed by Acadia College ten years later. In 1836 Baptists also founded the Baptist Seminary in Fredericton. The emergence of the three educational institutions suggests that the stereotypes of Baptists being unintellectual or even anti-intellectual were not true for Maritime Regular Baptists, even during the first half of the nineteenth century. Barry Moody has persuasively argued that the philosophy of Christian higher education at Acadia in the nineteenth century represented a remarkable "breadth of vision and breadth of mind." "It was in the Christian character of the professors and the Christian character of the institution itself, not in the content of the courses or the selection of the curriculum, that these Baptists placed their reliance."[30] Consequently, Acadia confidently engaged the major intellectual currents of the century such as Darwinism and German idealism. It was believed that warm evangelical piety and the radical evangelical New Birth experience would sustain Acadia in face of any of the modern ideologies. In fact, for the rest of the century the ultimate success of Acadia College would be measured not in the Latin memorized or the literature analysed but in the souls won for Christ. Even Acadia's British Baptist president J.M. Cramp, who was never completely at home with the radical revivalist tradition, wrote in 1863, "We greatly need the baptism of the Spirit here. In other respects our prospects were never more favourable. But oh that God would come, in the might and majesty of his grace, to call the dead to life."[31] The sporadic revivals that swept through the college throughout most of the nineteenth century assured many Maritime Regular Baptists that their mission in Christian higher education was being fulfilled.

While there were always those in the Regular Baptist constituency who remained suspicious of any higher education, Acadia symbolized the joining together of the radical evangelical impulse and the deep desire among the Baptist elite to achieve respectability by engaging colonial culture. Throughout the century Baptist students who became leading professionals and academics received not only their postsecondary education at Acadia but also a revived evangelical faith that often had a lasting impact on their lives.

If the radical evangelical impulse and the commitment to achieving respectability were meshed at Acadia, they can also be seen in the union of the Baptist Association of Nova Scotia and Prince Edward Island and the Baptist Association of New Brunswick in 1846.[32] Although both of these associations had "maintained a friendly interest in the progress of the other," they had remained "two bands" until a growing commitment to foreign and domestic mission and education prompted them to create a convention. In 1845 the Regular Baptists of the Maritimes sent out their first foreign missionary under their own auspices. The Reverend Richard Burpee and his wife set out for Burma from Boston on 20 April 1845. The Burpees were the first missionaries to be independently supported and commissioned exclusively by any denomination in British North America. This achievement alone pointed to the necessity of creating a more carefully defined and cooperative denominational structure.[33] The Baptist Convention of Nova Scotia, New Brunswick, and Prince Edward Island also promoted Sunday school work, temperance, Bible distribution, and church planting. No longer could a leading denominational family such as the Regular Baptists be perceived as being narrowly sectarian and unwilling to cooperate, organizationally, with like-minded believers. Far from denying the primitivist impulse so evident in the first generation of Maritime Regular Baptists, denominational leaders at mid-century remained convinced that their restoration of mere Christianity would be served by organic union and wider cooperation among Calvinistic Baptists. Six years after the creation of the Baptist convention, J.M. Cramp wrote in his pamphlet *The Future of the Baptists and Their Duty to Prepare for It*:

that if we would assume and maintain, as a denomination, the position to which we are entitled, we must, in the first place cultivate with growing earnestness, intelligent and warm-hearted piety. – we must adopt measures for the exposition and diffusion of our sentiments on those points in which we differ from other religious persuasions; – we must seek to extend our christian influence by home missionary efforts, conducted on a liberal scale; – we must foster rising talent, and give to all the Lord's servants opportunities of being employed in his cause, according to their respective gifts; – we must cherish an enthusiastic zeal for education; – we must effectually engage the sympathies of the young; we must be ever ready to promote social improvements and to forward philanthropic designs; and we must exemplify, in the whole unbroken union, devotedness to the Saviour, and believing reliance on divine aid.[34]

While one might be tempted to argue that the shift from "sect to church" among the Regular Baptists significantly undermined the radical evangelical impulse inherited from eighteenth-century New Lightism, in reality the evangelical ethos was merely recast into a denominational organization, which through believers' baptism, higher education, home and foreign missions, philanthropy, and Sunday schools sought to pass on the new birth experience to the second and third generations. In fact, while more research must be done, it is reasonable to argue that the essence of the evangelical impulse among the Calvinistic Baptists did not fundamentally change although its means of expression multiplied as they sought to engage colonial culture.

It should be pointed out that from 1830 to 1875 the Free Christian Baptists of New Brunswick also experienced a "steady transition from an Allinite 'sectarian' [perspective] to an evangelical 'church' outlook" – a transition that significantly altered its evangelical ethos. Under the leadership of Ezekiel McLeod, the denomination initiated the practice of settled pastoral leadership that replaced the traditional Allinite office of evangelist, published the *Religious Intelligencer*, and started to embrace the fashionable architectural style of the Gothic revival for its large congregations by the end of the century. In short, the formerly Allinite denomination had become a member of the evangelical Protestant consensus by 1880, sponsoring Bible societies, Sunday schools, the temperance movement, and home and foreign missions. According to David Bell, McLeod down-played traditional Free Christian Baptist doctrines to prepare the way for unity with the Regular Baptists. This was achieved in 1905–06 when "Free Baptists were at last respectable. But they had succeeded in detaching themselves from this unserviceable past only at the cost of jettisoning the very thing which made them distinctive and justified continued separate existence. Respectability in the eyes of the world had been achieved, but only through the entire negation, suppression and abandonment of the tradition of Henry Alline."[35]

As one compares the Regular Baptists to the Free Christian Baptists, it seems possible that both groups, while controlling the excesses of their common radical evangelical heritage, effectively reshaped their late eighteenth-century Allinite tradition to fit the realities of British North America in the latter two-thirds of the nineteenth century. Quite simply, while respectability and denomination-building certainly eroded radical religious behaviour that was often unacceptable to Victorian sensibilities, the evangelical ethos remained constant. Old wine had indeed been poured into new wineskins.

In conclusion, an examination of Baptists in Canada to 1880 reveals an evangelicalism as varied and complex as the regions of the nation. The Baptists in Ontario and Quebec represent what might be called a formal evangelicalism, which was preoccupied with competing notions of correct order and polity. This focus prevented them from entering the popular evangelical ethos which was forming at the beginning of the nineteenth century. While thousands thronged to camp meetings and revival services to experience the radical evangelical gospel message, the Baptists remained divided and numerically small as they debated the finer points of the "communion" question. By the 1860s a new generation of Baptist preachers sought to lead their denomination into a new era of respectability and prestige through higher education and the powerful influence of a Baptist business elite, and by becoming a participating member in the emerging nineteenth-century Protestant consensus. While this strategy was moderately successful, it did little to realize the grandiose vision of the central Canadian Baptist leaders for their denomination. In 1880 the formal evangelicalism of the Baptists in Ontario and Quebec was so similar to the moderate prevailing evangelical consensus that they had little to offer central Canadian society that was distinctive.

Baptists in the Maritimes, on the other hand, were among the principal architects and inheritors of the region's religious culture. Their roots in the ecstatic evangelicalism of the First Great Awakening combined with the formal evangelicalism of the respectability-seeking Regular and Free Christian Baptist patriarchs and with the powerful Anglican-turned-Baptist group in Halifax to create a gospel that penetrated the hearts and minds of countless Maritimers. The radical revivalist tradition had been recast into a variety of forms including education, religious debate, home and foreign missions, and convention structures. Far from jettisoning their religious origins, Maritime Baptists took the gospel into arenas where the types of evangelicalism represented by Henry Alline and E.A. Crawley could never have gone alone. This hybrid of ecstatic and formal forms of evangelicalism continued to resonate with many Maritimers throughout most of the nineteenth century.[36]

13 "Shelter from the Storm": The Enduring Evangelical Impulse of Baptists in Canada, 1880s to 1990s

P. LORRAINE COOPS

In 1880 I.E. Bill, a prominent Maritime Baptist, remarked that there was "a future for Baptists" in Canada, as they had "a past that has laid foundations broad and deep upon which to build."[1] This over-optimistic view reflected the Baptists' steady growth during their first hundred years in what is now Canada; it was a growth energized by a flexible and evolving evangelicalism in which lay men and women occupied a nearly equal footing in the church. A firm commitment to their own brand of evangelical religion gave Canadian Baptists, they were certain, the spiritual strength to withstand the nineteenth-century challenges of science, liberalism, and modern thought, and it has provided an ethos, some would argue, that has given Canadian Baptists shelter from the storms of twentieth-century marginalization and fragmentation and an increasingly secular society. Despite external events and internal controversies, over two hundred years after the first Canadian Baptist churches were planted, the Baptist faith survives as a largely experiential religion – a religion of the heart which embraces differing ethnic, cultural, and doctrinal tenets.

While Canadian Baptists can be fitted into the standard mould that encompasses all evangelicals – conversionism, combined with an equal stress on biblicism, crucicentrism, and activism[2] – their strongest focus is on conversionism and activism. For Canadian Baptists the internal experience of conversion combined with an outward expression of their faith through activism are the means by which their eighteenth-century beginnings are linked to their nineteenth-century growth and twentieth-century continued survival. Indeed, it is the contention of Canadian

Baptists that living the Christian life is inseparable from conversionism. The ongoing emphasis on adult conversion and baptism as well as activism and fellowship – an experiential faith that requires active involvement, be it through proselytizing, preaching, missions, education, or good works – remains the key to understanding and tracing the evangelical ethos of the Canadian Baptist world view during the 1880 to 1990 period.

CANADIAN BAPTISTS, 1880–1900

The 1881 census reported that Baptists made up 6.9 per cent of Canada's population.[3] The membership was divided principally between the Maritimes, where Baptists were one of the dominant Protestant denominations, and Ontario, where Baptists were numerically well behind the Methodists, Presbyterians, and Anglicans. The strongest concentrations were in Nova Scotia's Annapolis Valley and throughout New Brunswick, where in both areas Baptists outnumbered all other Protestant denominations. It must be remembered, however, that although the majority of members in most regions at the end of the nineteenth century were mainline Baptists, a significant number held to Free Baptist doctrines and practices.[4] This was especially true in New Brunswick, where the various Free Baptist groups made up perhaps 40 per cent or more of the total Baptist membership by the turn of the century. By the 1880s, two of the original points of contention between the two Maritime groups, Calvinistic views and associationalism, had become largely non-issues, and the remaining point of contention, close versus open communion, was nearing resolution. Eventually this final obstacle was dealt with through a statement in the Basis of Union that allowed each denomination to grant membership on its own terms. Thus, even by the 1880s, some twenty years before most Maritime Free and mainline Baptists united under one convention, nearly all groups held similar views on conversion and activism, and each could rightfully claim the name Baptist.

Canadian Baptists, unlike other mainline Protestant denominations, held to the necessity of adult baptism and individual church autonomy but nonetheless still fell well within the nineteenth-century evangelical mainstream. Links between the evangelical Protestant denominations created what has been called an "evangelical consensus." A by-product of this bond was that "the evangelicalism of the outsiders became more and more the evangelicalism of the insiders. Rather than denouncing and prophesying to the culture from its margins, now evangelicals enjoyed status in the culture as they attempted to improve it."[5] As well, the vitriolic condemnation that denominations hurled at each other during the late eighteenth and early nineteenth centuries had been tempered by a sense of "His Dominion" – a Christian Canada based upon evangelical tenets and principles.

Most Baptists believed that they had a role to play in the creation of this "Christian Canada," and, like other Protestant groups, set about to spread the Word from sea to sea. With stable bases in the Maritimes and Ontario, Baptists looked elsewhere in Canada to plant their brand of Protestantism. Commissioned by Baptists in Ontario, Alexander MacDonald initiated in 1873 the first organized Baptist venture into western Canada. He is reported to have said upon his arrival in Winnipeg to discover only one other Baptist in the city, "I did not come to find Baptists, I have come to make Baptists."[6] MacDonald organized the first Baptist church in western Canada, consisting of seven members, in Winnipeg in 1875.[7] By 1884, churches had been planted in what would become Saskatchewan and Alberta, and the Baptist Convention of Manitoba and the Northwest Territories had been organized. Through the combined efforts of the Baptist Convention of Oregon and Washington and lay people in British Columbia, Alexander Clyde established the First Baptist Church in Vancouver in 1887; ten years later the Convention of Baptist Churches in British Columbia was formed.[8]

These home mission ventures were not the only area that showed promise; the major foreign missionary endeavour also proceeded apace. Like many other Protestant denominations, Canadian Baptists became increasingly involved in this key feature of nineteenth-century North American evangelicalism. Foreign missions captured the minds, hearts, and pocketbooks of thousands of Canadians, and every major Protestant denomination sponsored missionary work in Asia, South America, and Africa. Women in particular vigorously answered the call to help "spread the word" in foreign lands, seizing the opportunity to achieve both spiritual and personal fulfilment. Through an intricate network of "sending societies" such as the various Foreign Mission Boards and Women's Missionary Unions, money was raised, missionaries were recruited, trained, and sent overseas, educational and medical materials supplied, mission schools and compounds built, and reports, newspapers, and inspirational and promotional literature published. These highly organized sending societies, supported by individuals and churches across Canada, hoped to establish a "Christianized" world, a vision that Canadian Baptists shared.

The first independent Canadian foreign missionaries were the Maritime Baptists Richard E. and Laleah Johnstone Burpee, who sailed for Burma in 1845. By 1865 the Foreign Mission Board of the Maritimes had been incorporated, and in 1873 the missionary pioneers known as the "Serving Seven" were sent to Burma to spread the gospel among the Karens.⁹ Meanwhile, Ontario Baptists opted for foreign mission involvement at their 1866 Convention, and sent out their first missionaries, Americus Vespucius and Jane Bates Timpany, under the auspices of the American board the following year. By 1874 Ontario Baptists were supporting an independent mission at Cocanada, India. And by 1875, although not without some dissention, the Maritime Foreign Mission Board accepted an offer to set up an independent Maritime mission station at Bimilipatam, India, just to the north of the Ontario field. The two mission groups worked side by side for many years, but despite repeated calls from the missionaries in the field for amalgamation, it was not until 1912 that the two foreign mission boards joined forces.

While India attracted most of the foreign mission attention, in 1898 Archibald B. Reekie went to establish a mission in Bolivia, following a call to spread the gospel among the indigenous people who had been influenced by Roman Catholic missionaries since the early eighteenth century. Activism took on a different dimension in Bolivia, where the missionaries participated in "political" actions such as land reform. However, the main focus of the Canadian Baptist missionary enterprise remained rooted in their evangelical heritage and their original mission fields in India.

The primary activity for all Canadian Baptist foreign missionaries was to tell the "old, old story" in hopes that the seeds they planted would bear fruit in the form of conversions. Thus, while education and medical services were key components of the foreign missions, they were always subordinate to the overriding goal of "winning souls for Christ." The insistence upon this goal – at the expense of the social gospel objectives of looking after the physical as well as the spiritual well-being of those ministered to – may be seen in the attempts to recruit a male physician for the India fields.

In April 1909 Walter V. Higgins, a missionary and at the time Home Secretary of the Maritime Board, announced that the board had been approached by Dr Reginald Morse of Lawrencetown, Nova Scotia, who wished to go to a foreign mission field. Morse had also been in touch with the American Baptist Missionary Union (ABMU), and Higgins feared that unless additional funds could be raised to sponsor a medical missionary, Morse would be lost to the American Baptists: "It would seem altogether too bad if we lose him from our field ... It is a rare chance we now have and it may be a long time before we get another like it ... and [I] feel that the Lord has been grieved and hindered in his purposes of grace for the Telegus [sic]."¹⁰

In the 12 May 1909 edition of the *Maritime Baptist*, Higgins announced that "as the treasurer had reported quite a change for the better in finances, the board voted unanimously to offer the appointment to Dr. Morse." The board anxiously awaited Morse's decision as "he had already felt unable to wait ... and had turned to the A.B.M.U. in Boston for appointment." Morse's response was recorded in the 2 June 1909 edition of the *Maritime Baptist*: "The board has received word from Dr. Morse to the effect that he feels compelled to decline our offer of appointment to India." Higgins elaborated on why Morse decided not to go to the Telugu fields: "He has come to feel that a possible opening in China would be better suited to his tastes and capabilities. It seems that he would prefer to enter a fully equipped hospital and begin full medical work at once without the necessity of having to acquire the native languages. Moreover he has come to feel that he would prefer to make medical work his entire business and to leave others to evangelize."

Higgins's analysis of Morse's "change of heart" was not surprising given the Maritime Baptists' sense of the missionary enterprise: "From the first we have made it clear that what we need in our mission is a man who would devote himself at first almost exclusively to the work of mastering the native tongue, build up a medical plant from the foundations, and in all his work make the evangelistic aim paramount. Doubtless Dr. Morse has under the circumstances decided wisely."[11]

As Canadian Baptist interests strengthened at home and abroad over the course of the nineteenth century, the denomination's leaders looked to solidify the gains already made and, at the same time, to enhance the Baptist reputation within Canadian society and ensure a stable foundation for future church members. To achieve these ends the leadership embarked upon what would become a cornerstone of the Baptist experience in Canada – the education of its ministers and laity within a Baptist environment. In the realm of higher learning, evangelical activism took on the roles of teacher, scholar, and institutional founder. Acadia University in Wolfville, Nova Scotia, was founded in 1838 to serve the needs of Maritime Baptists; and McMaster University (now in Hamilton, Ontario) was founded in Toronto in 1887 – as an outgrowth of the theology department of the Canadian Literary Institute (Woodstock) – to serve the educational needs of central and western Canadian Baptists.

These universities were designed with men in mind, but, as Barry Moody notes, in the case of Maritime Baptists, women eventually gained entrance despite early "mixed feelings about providing a formal education for females." By 1836 the Baptist New Brunswick Seminary in Fredericton was opened to both male and female students, and by the 1850s the debate was no longer over whether women should be educated but rather about what methods to use in teaching female students and the level to which this education should go. As Moody suggests, "establishing a female seminary was one thing; admitting women to the full college was obviously quite another." However, "few Baptists seemed willing openly to doubt the wisdom of providing as much education for a female as she was capable of handling." By 1880 women began to take liberal arts courses at Acadia, with the board of governors recommending that "the privileges of the college ... be open to the sons and daughters ... on the same conditions."[12] In 1884 Clara Belle Marshall became "the first woman to take a bachelor degree at Acadia University," nine years after Grace Annie Lockhart of Mount Allison College had become "the first woman to earn a Canadian degree."[13]

The founding of McMaster illustrates the Baptist leadership's desire to do "everything humanly possible to improve the educational standards of [the] denomination's ministers as well as its lay people. Like many other leading Canadian Baptists in the latter part of the nineteenth century, [Senator] McMaster was obsessed with the desperate search for denominational respectability. One important way to achieve this end, it was felt, was to build a respectable Baptist university."[14] Although McMaster offered arts degrees, its charter also clearly expressed the founder's goal to establish "a Christian school of learning":

the study of the Bible, or sacred scriptures, shall form a part of the course of study ... And no person shall be eligible to the position of chancellor, principal, professor, tutor, or master, who is not a member in good standing of an Evangelical Christian Church; and no person shall be eligible for the position of principal, professor, tutor, or master in the faculty of theology who is not a member in good standing of a Regular Baptist Church, and the said Board of Governors shall have the right to require such further or other tests as to religious belief, as a qualification for any position in the faculty of theology.[15]

With the establishment of Baptist conventions on the Prairies and in British Columbia, the western leadership sought to create their own institution of higher learning. Thus, Brandon College opened in 1899 to provide theological and arts education to western Baptists. However, as Walter Ellis suggests, devising an institution for western Baptists proved a challenging task: "Sub-themes from the Brandon College story include the issue of provincial rivalries among Baptists [and] the vexatious difficulties posed as congregationalists struggled to devise a polity appropriate to the twentieth century." Moreover, Ellis notes, "Brandon's ambivalent relationship to McMaster merits further study as the school attempted to adjust to the needs of the indigenous west fettered by academic rigidities and agendas set elsewhere."[16] Nonetheless, Brandon shared with McMaster and Acadia the underlying premise of a Christian education – "the development of right character" to be achieved by "surrounding the student during the period of college life with positive Christian influences and ideals." And, as Ellis concludes, "On the basis of this criteria, Brandon College was an unqualified success because her legacy was and is in her graduates."[17]

As the nineteenth century drew to a close, Canadian Baptists could look back on an impressive list of accomplishments. They entered the twentieth century with their evangelical heritage intact, with institutions designed not only to educate their clergy and lay members but also to foster Baptist ideals, and with a missionary focus at home and aboard. However, this sense of achievement and potential was merely the calm before the storm of the twentieth century.

SCIENCE AND MODERNISM

In order to survive, all groups, no matter how strong their legacy and how dedicated their membership, must have within them the ability to adapt to changes over which they have little or no control. Canadian Baptists faced such threats to their survival, or at least to their continued growth and development, as a result of the twentieth-century rise of science, liberalism, and fundamentalism. Just how Baptists reacted to these challenges shows a great deal about their strengths and weaknesses. Maritime Baptists, for example, saw little threat from the new field of science. As the prominent New Brunswick Baptist minister and educator Wilfred Currier Keirstead suggested in a turn-of-the-century sermon, science posed not a threat, but an opportunity:

It would be well for the leaders and teachers of religion if they would learn something of the love of truth that characterizes the man of science ... The cry then today against the advance of science into the realm of the religious life is a false alarm. We have nothing to fear from science but everything to hope. We need to fear ... the spirit that is in our churches today only too manifest when there is some advance in truth that strikes against some cherished custom.[18]

Such views help to explain why Maritime Baptists, unlike Baptists in central Canada and in the West, were able to weather the storms of scientific investigation, higher criticism, and evolutionary thought. Studies by George Rawlyk and Barry Moody suggest that Maritime Baptists were "surprisingly open to a variety of theologies and ideological perspectives largely because their approach to religion was not only largely experiential rather than doctrinal but also because it was accommodationist rather than being narrowly rigid."[19] In his discussion of Acadia University, Moody suggests that "In their approach to the challenges of science ... Acadia and the Baptists revealed a breadth of vision and a breadth of mind remarkably free of fear or narrow prejudice, sectarian or otherwise ... What one does see is a quite astonishing willingness to at least consider the various alternatives, to explore where perhaps some others were afraid to do so."[20] Rawlyk and Moody also suggest that some key Baptists could "calmly" debate Darwin and thus managed to reconcile science and religion.

The same sense of "accommodation" can not be said to have existed within the central Canadian Baptist fold. For example, a series of "controversies" in the first decade of the twentieth century over appointments to McMaster University highlight the ways in which Baptist mainline evangelicalism could be stretched, sometimes to the breaking point.

What came to be known as the "Matthews Controversy" centred around the issue of the orthodoxy and the theological stance of Professor I.G. Matthews, a University of Chicago–trained Old Testament scholar. As a result of criticism of Matthews's apparent modernist views by such influential denominational leaders as Elmore Harris, McMaster's chancellor, A.C. McKay, set up a committee to study Matthews's belief system. In a report submitted to McMaster's Senate on 29 May 1909, the committee found that while Matthews accepted "many of the 'results of critical scholarship' he nevertheless 'held firmly to the inspiration and supernatural character of the Old and New Testaments.'"[21] The Senate concluded its investigation with a statement regarding the University's position on higher education:

McMaster stands for freedom, for progress, for investigation. It must welcome truth from whatever quarter, and never be guilty of binding the spirit of free enquiry. As a Christian school of learning under Baptist auspices, it stands for the fullest and freest investigation, not only in the scientific realm but also in the realm of Biblical scholarship. Holding fast their historic position on the personal freedom and responsibility of the individual, refusing to bind or be bound by any human creed, rejecting the authority of tradition and taking their stand on the word of God alone as the supreme and all-sufficient rule of faith and practice, the Baptists have ever been ready to accord to all students of the Sacred Scriptures the largest possible measure of freedom consistent with loyalty to the fundamentals of the Christian faith.[22]

Following the Senate's report, the issue was put before the entire Ontario/Quebec Convention in 1910, where signs of strain began to appear between the hardline and mainline camps. Harris continued to pursue his charges against Matthews despite the findings of the Senate investigating committee. In what would prove to be an ironic twist of fate, T.T. Shields, pastor of the influential Jarvis Street Church in Toronto, was asked to sponsor a motion from the floor that would cut off the increasingly acrimonious debate. (This is, of course, the same hardline T.T. Shields who would create, in the 1920s and 1930s, a schism within the denomination over issues such as the liberalism and modernism he envisioned in every corner of McMaster.) As McMaster himself had been a member of the Jarvis Street Church and thus the doctrinal statements of the church and the university were similar, it is quite likely that Shields agreed to the request in order to placate his congregation and the leadership of the convention, and to accommodate the more mainline stance of the convention. This, however, would be the last time Shields would be accommodating or mediating. In the meantime, McMaster and the Ontario/Quebec Convention were able to recall their evangelical heritage and, at least for a time, accommodate to changing societal values. As George Rawlyk concludes in his discussion of McMaster University,

The Senate response to the "Matthews Controversy" is important in at least two ways with respect to Baptists and Christian higher education in central Canada. First, McMaster's Senate and also the Convention explicitly endorsed the key role of higher education in bringing about human "progress" – bourgeois progress and consumerism. Second, it was emphatically agreed that accommodation was indeed possible between the evangelical consensus and the new scholarship. And, moreover, it was contended that McMaster University had a special role in bringing about this accommodation which, for some, was merely the articulation of the liberal evangelical point of view.[23]

Immigration to Canada during the late nineteenth and early twentieth centuries also posed a challenge for Baptists – one that was slightly different than for other denominations. Certainly the goal for most Protestant churches was to Christianize and Canadianize the growing number of non-Anglo-Celt, non-Protestant immigrants, many of whom settled in western Canada. To achieve this end various programs were initiated, including inner city missions, Sunday school programs, and rescue homes and shelters; meeting immigrants at the docks and train stations; setting up rural churches/missions and spreading the gospel through education, language classes, and activities aimed specifically at children. Due to their limited presence in western Canada, Canadian Baptists focused their efforts mainly on ethnic Baptist immigrants, most of whom came from Germany and Scandinavia[24] and arrived with a faith, culture, language, and church structure already in place. As they did not have to be converted to Christianity, nor to the Baptist faith, much of the church's effort went into forming fellowship and community links with these immigrant groups, and activism took the form of evangelistic outreach. These ethnic groups initially maintained ties with Canadian Baptist conventions and associations; but in 1920 German Baptists cut their ties with western Baptists to join other churches in Canada and the United States that shared a common German heritage and intense interest in missions. Swedish Baptists relinquished their Canadian affiliation in 1948 to join the Baptist General Conference of the United States.

Despite the growth of ethnic Baptist groups and the westward spread of Baptist churches, by the early twentieth century Baptists as a denomination were moving towards the margins numerically. For example, in 1881 Baptists had made up 6.9 per cent of the population in Canada and 14.3 per cent of the population in Manitoba. By 1911 these percentages had fallen to 5.3 per cent and 3.1 per cent respectively.[25] As the general evangelical culture shifted towards the Social Gospel, Baptists, especially in Ontario, found themselves even more marginalized.

THE TURBULENT TWENTIES

Although the twentieth century would continue to challenge the Baptists' evangelical heritage and world view, the 1920s and 1930s were the decades that were the most decisive. At the heart of the controversies and schisms was the ministry of Reverend T.T. Shields. Almost single-handedly he managed to fragment the Canadian Baptist evangelical ethos into two "armed camps" – the hardline versus the mainline. The debates between the two factions were acrimonious and eventually led to the splintering of the Ontario/Quebec, British Columbia, and Western Baptist Conventions.

While "liberalism" provoked some dissent among the Baptists during the first two decades of the century, it took someone of Shields's stature to bring the issue to a crisis. As John Stackhouse suggests, "historians may debate definitions of fundamentalism, but standing squarely in the middle of anyone's definition is Canada's best known and most influential fundamentalist, Thomas Todhunter Shields."[26] The military cant of his language, the vehemence of his rhetoric, and his uncompromising stance represent several of the key defining elements of fundamentalism as a movement rather than a doctrine: "As far as I am concerned, I will have no compromise with the enemy. I have declared again and again that I have resigned from the diplomatic corps; I am a soldier in the field, and as God gives me strength, everywhere, as long as I live, in the name of the Lord, I will smite [modernism], and I will make it as hard as I possibly can for any liberal professor to hold his position; it will not be my fault if he does not get out of a job."[27]

Shields had been "accommodating" at the 1910 Ontario/Quebec Convention during the "Matthew Controversy," but by 1919 he was taking a far more confrontational stance. Just prior to the 1919 Convention the *Canadian Baptist* published two editorials which Shields viewed as "liberal." The convention leadership tried to counter Shields's attacks with an amendment "that set out a typical Baptist response to such a call for the delineation of orthodoxy: it affirmed the Bible was the Word of God; the right of the individual to private interpretation; and the evil of controversy arising from doctrinal precision."[28] Shields, ever the eloquent speaker, gained enough support after an hour and a half speech that the motion was shouted down from the floor, and the editors of the *Canadian Baptist* were chastised for their "liberal" leanings.

Shields's victory marked the beginning of his all-out campaign against what he perceived as modernist thought within the denomination. Not surprisingly, McMaster University was the focus of Shields's attacks. And when the university granted an honourary degree to the "liberal" American theologian W.H.P. Faunce, Shields brought the matter before the 1924 Convention. Again the convention followed Shields's lead, and the McMaster board members were officially reprimanded. The situation came to a head in 1926 when Shields set up the Regular Baptist Mission and Education Society to channel funds away from what he referred to as the "bastion of liberalism," McMaster. No longer able to reconcile Shields's hardline stance with the convention's accommodating evangelicalism, the leadership forced him to leave the convention. Shields and his supporters within the Ontario/Quebec Convention then established the Union of Regular Baptist Churches of Ontario and the Toronto Bible Seminary.[29]

Meanwhile in the Canadian West a similar fundamentalist campaign against Brandon College beginning in 1912 resulted in a subsequent defection from the General Baptist body.[30] When considering the events that led to the schisms in central and western Canada, it must be remembered that the diverse cultural and ethnic backgrounds of the Baptists in these regions had led to squabbles for over a hundred years prior to hardline evangelicals' decision to leave the fold. This was in stark contrast to the situation in the Maritimes, where a unity of spirit and culture among the Maritime Baptists meant that in times of conflict cooler heads could prevail.

Although during the late 1920s Baptist unity was increasingly threatened by the rising tide of fundamentalism, the United Baptist Convention of the Maritimes did not suffer from the same schisms as their western counterparts. The fundamentalist position in the Maritimes was promoted by John James Sidey, a self-proclaimed leader of the Maritime Baptist critics of liberalism, who shared a similar background and world view to T.T. Shields. Sidey, however, did not possess the presence or influence within the Maritime Convention which had enabled Shields to command such a strong following within the Ontario/Quebec Convention. By the fall of 1931, Sidey and his compatriot, Reverend J.B. Daggett of Prince Edward Island, had created the framework for a parallel Baptist convention. Sidey's group had its own educational institution, the Kingston Bible College, and held a yearly convention preoccupied with premillennial and fundamentalist themes. Encouraged by Shields, Sidey withdrew from the United Baptist Convention of the Maritimes in 1934 but refused to leave his Kingston, Nova Scotia, parsonage. As a result the Baptist leadership found itself in the uncomfortable position of turning to the courts to settle a denominational dispute. The Kingston Baptist Parsonage Case went before the Nova Scotia Supreme Court 21–25 May 1935. As has been argued, the case was supposed to be over ownership of church property but ended up being "a remarkable confrontation between two groups of Baptists, two ideologies, and two ways of life. It was essentially a battle between fundamentalism and a more accommodating spirit."[31] In a manner reminiscent of the Scopes controversy, Christian beliefs were put on trial. In the end, the accommodating spirit won out and only a few churches followed Sidey out of the convention.

The outcome of the Kingston Parsonage Case does not mean that mainline Maritime Baptists were more "liberal" or "modernist" than their counterparts in central and western Canada. Rather, it suggests that theological and doctrinal extremes were truly marginal in the Maritimes, and that the vast majority of Maritime Baptists felt comfortable with their irenic evangelical orthodoxy. Eschatology was not of central importance to Maritime Baptists, and they had little inclination for hardline evangelical anti-cultural and anti-societal views, as George Rawlyk has noted: "The conservative evangelicals were not as alienated from societal norms as were the fundamentalists ... [and] tried to balance evangelical spirituality and liberal learning; theirs was a religion of the head and the heart. They refused to abandon the revivalists traditions ... but they also refused to close their eyes and ears to modern scholarship."[32]

THE CONTINUING EVANGELICAL HERITAGE

Harry Renfree has recently contended that in order for Canadian Baptists to keep their vision alive, they must retain a strong sense of their evangelical heritage.[33] As they have done in the past, Canadian Baptists must recall the core beliefs in a personal, experiential faith and a commitment to activism. Their strength has always depended on individuals, and it will be committed and active individuals who will ensure the survival envisioned by I.E. Bill over one hundred years ago.

Such individuals will have to be strong in their faith, for Canadian Baptists face challenges not only from outside their own denomination but, perhaps even more importantly, from within. These internal challenges are, as John Stackhouse suggests, the result of a new evangelical consensus forged during the twentieth century. This revitalized evangelical culture has raised new questions for evangelical Christians, one of which concerns "gender roles in church and family." For in the past "the vast majority of evangelicals ... espoused the principle of male leadership in both spheres."[34] In time, however, gender roles became blurred because during periods of "revival and missionary enthusiasm," evangelicals "expected lay people to serve with vigour in 'religious' work at home and in the 'foreign fields' of missions. This meant that women often performed in leadership roles ... normally denied them in other churches and indeed in their own cultures."[35]

Certainly for the churches within the Canadian Baptist Federation, the concept of an experiential faith has always enabled women to express their spirituality in a variety of ways within the church, the community, and society. From Hannah Maria Norris's single-handed creation of the United Baptist Women's Missionary Union during the summer of 1870 through to the present, Baptist women have played a prominent role within the missionary enterprise.[36] As Carrie Hammond recalled of her arrival in India, "The first single lady to our Telugu mission ... stepped into the ranks without making much of a stir. But a few years later the whole question of a single lady's position in the mission came up for consideration and adjustment, and it is so satisfactorily arranged that it has never required attention since."[37]

The controversy Hammond alluded to arose during the last two decades of the nineteenth century and centred around to what extent women missionaries in the field should have a say in the running of the mission. Always more numerous than their male counterparts, the women often found themselves alone either at the mission compound or out touring among the villages. Under such circumstances it was often the women themselves who knew best how to distribute the funds donated by the members back home. However, the Foreign Mission Board could not bring itself to relinquish male authority – even despite the male missionaries' staunch support for greater control by the women. In the end, while the board insisted on the continuation of male stewardship, the reality on the field was that the male missionaries often simply put their stamp of approval on decisions made by their female cohorts.

What is interesting when considering the foreign mission endeavour is the remarkably single-minded and unified belief in the goals of the mission that was shared by both male and female missionaries throughout the entire span of Canadian administration of the India mission.[38] Without exception, the female and male missionaries agreed that the primary goal of the mission was to bring the gospel message to the Telugu of India. All services they rendered, be these medical or educational, were entirely designed to facilitate the acceptance of and conversion to Baptist evangelical ideals. Male-female contention was virtually absent in the field as the missionaries went about their business. Each had a role to play, and each did so in a spirit of gratitude that they had been called to do just that. In the process of carrying out their missionary duties, the women developed strong and distinctive religious voices that enabled them to participate in, rather than simply assist the mission enterprise.

Although the Canadian Baptist evangelical impulse granted an activist role to women in the missionary enterprise beginning in the late nineteenth century, the question of the ordination of women was not so easily resolved. Even after the ordination in 1954 of Canadian-born Josephine Kinley Moore – the first Canadian Baptist woman to be ordained[39] – debate continued among Canadian Baptists as to the doctrinal and biblical "legitimacy" of a female ministry. At the Atlantic Baptist Convention in 1986, for example, it was moved that "the coming council be directed in keeping the Biblical principles, no longer to examine women for ordination to pastoral ministry."[40] The convention decided to delay voting on the motion until the following year, but battle lines were drawn between the opposing sides. The issue was so important that Michael Lippe, editor of the *Atlantic Baptist* and a strong advocate for women's ministry, devoted the April 1987 edition of the *Atlantic Baptist* to the "Role of Women in Ministry."

Individuals on both sides used the Baptist evangelical heritage, creed, and doctrine to argue their case, and both camps cited the passage from Galatians 3:28 – "there is neither Jew nor Greek, there is neither slave nor free person, there is neither male or female, for you are all one in Christ" – as supporting evidence for their respective positions. On 20 August 1987 a secret ballot was taken on the motion. The results were 149 in favour of withdrawing ordination from women, 570 against and 7 abstainers.[41] Despite this outcome and despite the case that Acadia Divinity College now encourages husband and wife pastoral teams, it is telling that in the late 1980s almost one-quarter of those attending the convention were not comfortable with the concept of a female ministry. There clearly remain within what George Rawlyk has termed the "accommodating spirit" of the Maritime Baptist experience links to a more conservative and less accommodating past. It should also be pointed out that most Canadian non-Convention Baptists vociferously oppose the ordination of women or even women deacons.

An examination of the conservative element within the Canadian Baptist experience which took a stand against the ordination of women provides insights into the denomination's future survival and its current evangelical impulse. For although conservative, evangelical, non-Baptist groups – such as the Pentecostals – are the most dynamic in terms of membership growth and vitality, the more fundamentalist or conservative Baptist churches are at least holding their ground and in some cases growing in the number of their adherents. And while most Baptist churches in Canada remain affiliated with the mainline Canadian Baptist Federation, this organization continues to lose members.[42]

The growth of fundamentalist/conservative Baptist groups over the course of the twentieth century has been enhanced both by consolidation of existing groups and by the establishment of new ones. For example, the Fellowship of Evangelical Baptist Churches in Canada, created in 1953 by the merger of the Union of Regular Baptists Churches of Ontario/Quebec (1927) and the Fellowship of Independent Baptist Churches of Canada (1933),[43] was further strengthened in 1965 with the inclusion of the Convention of Regular Baptists of British Columbia (1927) and the Prairie Regular Baptist Missionary Fellowship (1930).[44] Fellowship Baptists support several educational institutions and work closely with other fundamentalist groups in various transdenominational evangelical organizations, fellowships, and networks. As well, a new player on the Canadian Baptist field is the Canadian Convention of Southern Baptists, which was created in 1985 and during its short existence has seen significant growth in its membership.[45]

In contrast to the early twentieth century when the "fundamentalist fringe" within the Baptist Convention was constantly on the defensive against both modernism and the so-called liberal Baptists, it is now the accommodating Convention Baptists who find themselves increasingly marginalized. For during the past two decades, the Convention Baptists have become more conservative in their evangelicalism, in many respects more like the Fellowship Baptists, their former adversaries. If this trend continues, it may be that a common conservative evangelicalism may bring these two groups together. Miracles are still possible, some would say. Perhaps, then, the future for Baptists in Canada lies not with the accommodating mainline but with the those who are firmly a part of what Stackhouse calls the new twentieth-century evangelical consensus.[46] Thus, while the evangelical heritage of Canadian Baptists seems certain to endure into the twenty-first century, it remains to be seen which interpretation will attract most of those Canadians who call themselves Baptist.

14 Living with the Virus: The Enigma of Evangelicalism among Mennonites in Canada

BRUCE L. GUENTHER

The term "Mennonite" conjures up many images. Some associate it with those who eschew modern technology by travelling in horse-drawn buggies. Older Canadians may remember press coverage of obstinate German-speaking settlers who allegedly refused to bear arms during the two world wars. Other impressions have been formed by authors like Rudy Wiebe whose fiction depicts Prairie Mennonites. And some point towards humanitarian organizations like the Mennonite Central Committee as the quintessential portrait. A multitude of images could be added to this collage to portray the range of experiences, traditions, and beliefs that make up the history and identity of the approximately 200,000 Mennonites in Canada.

Mennonites first arrived in Canada in 1786 when a group of Swiss-German Mennonites from the United States settled in Upper Canada. But it was not until a large migration beginning in 1874 of Dutch-German Mennonites (known as the *Kanadier*) from Russia that the group became a sizeable component of Canada's ethnic melange. This was followed by an influx of 20,000 Russian Mennonites (identified as *Russländer*) during the 1920s which dramatically altered Mennonitism in Canada. During the 1940s some Mennonites experienced a transformation which moved them into the mainstream of social, cultural, intellectual, religious, and artistic life.

While certain doctrines of the sixteenth-century Anabaptists remain as central aspects of faith, twentieth-century Mennonites are a house divided. Far from being one monolithic, homogenous association, the approximately thirty Mennonite groups that have existed in Canada create a complex mosaic of customs, lifestyles, and theological beliefs. Although with such diversity it is difficult to generalize, no one denies the significant, but varying, influence that evangelicalism from both continental and North American sources has had and continues to have on Mennonites. Conversely, Mennonites have, particularly during the twentieth-century, played an important role in the development of transdenominational evangelicalism in Canada. Nonetheless, evangelicalism, at least in its North American form, remains an enigma for many Mennonites, and considerable polarization characterizes the Mennonite response towards evangelicalism.

On the one hand there is a litany of complaints against evangelicalism. Some decry the "awful and terrible destruction" that it has presumably caused,[1] or see it as an alien force that has "created considerable ideological and theological confusion."[2] According to others, its inadequate soteriology left Mennonite groups with a weakened ecclesiology: the individualistic accent on personal salvation minimized the more corporate, communitarian ideals of Anabaptism and its emphasis on *nachfolge* (discipleship).[3] Yet others are uneasy about a movement tainted by "individualism, militarism, lack of concern for peace and reconciliation, narrow orthodoxy, child evangelism and capitalist, competitive economics."[4] "In becoming evangelical," laments Delbert Wiens, "we are exchanging our Mennonite birthright for a mess of pottage."[5] Those representing this polarity zealously guard Mennonitism from further infestations of the so-called evangelical virus.

On the other hand, there are Mennonites who actively nurture a strong sense of kinship with evangelical Protestants. Evangelicalism liberates them from the spiritual sterility caused by over-emphasizing the maintenance of cultural and ecclesiastical traditions. Many testify that "the assurance of salvation" offers spiritual and psychological relief from the anxiety of merely "hoping" that one might obtain salvation. Evangelicalism is considered to be the essence of biblical Christianity that lifts Mennonites above the artificial boundaries created by ethnicity or the prioritization of "non-essential" doctrines like non-resistance. Some hail it as the biblical foundation on which the Mennonite church was founded, and those who give a less-than-whole-hearted endorsement of contemporary evangelicalism are accused of being defectors corrupted by "liberalism."[6] Others claim that the Mennonite ethnic and theological perimeters hinder church planting efforts in non-Mennonite communities. Mennonite denominations (and individuals) are not always fully aligned on one side or the other. Some groups manifest considerable ambivalence towards evangelicalism because of the presence of both emotionally charged extremes under one denominational roof.

Among other observations about the relationship between evangelicalism and Canadian Mennonites, major themes emerge: (1) that evangelicalism's biblicism, relationship to pietism, and incentive for mission created a natural compatibility with certain Mennonite groups; (2) that evangelicalism facilitated and accelerated the pace of Canadianization among Mennonite immigrants, thus weakening the ability of some Mennonite denominations to retain their unique distinctives; (3) that evangelicalism attracted members from traditional Mennonite groups by simultaneously offering a spiritual and cultural emancipation and by retaining a certain suspicion and reticence towards "the world": it served both as an emancipating (and modernizing) influence and as a conservative force; and (4) that the influence of evangelicalism mediated and even legitimated certain North American cultural values that mitigated against Anabaptist communitarian emphases.

One of the difficulties is deciding where to draw the line between Mennonites and evangelicals. In this essay, "evangelical" will refer broadly to Protestant groups that fit inside the elastic descriptive creedal quadrilateral provided by David Bebbington.[7] Although many – but not all – Mennonites fit within the evangelical tradition, they are not *just* evangelical.[8] While there is considerable variation, Mennonites attach less importance to doctrinal statements and creeds, and generally understand conversion to be part of an overall transformation that is verified in a life of discipleship as a voluntary member within a believing community and not simply as an isolated, climactic, one-time transaction between an individual and God. In addition, Mennonites believe in adult baptism, the separation of church and state, and non-resistance. Although Mennonite churches comprise a worldwide multicultural network, in Canada the term refers to more than a theological orientation and remains closely linked to particular Dutch-German-Russo or Swiss-German ethnicities.

THE SWISS MENNONITES

The Swiss Mennonites were the first Mennonites to settle in Canada, and the first to develop strong links with evangelical Protestants. Early in the nineteenth century certain Methodist practices appealed to the Swiss Mennonites who were emerging from their ethnic enclaves. Increasingly forced to compete with other religious movements for the loyalty of their members, and without the geographical isolation that later helped their co-religionists in western Canada preserve a distinctive way of life, many Swiss Mennonites concluded that efforts to prolong a strategy of cultural isolation were no longer practical. As a result they began emulating the revivalistic Methodists by experimenting with

Sunday schools, English preaching, and extra meetings for prayer and evangelism. The varying responses to such novelties divided the Swiss Mennonites into three streams during the 1870s. Eschewing "modern" innovations were leaders like Abraham Martin who convinced many that the incursion of evangelical ideas was a compromise; these coalesced to form various Old Order Mennonite groups.

A second stream, led by Solomon Eby, was the group that most thoroughly absorbed a range of evangelical emphases and practices. This became the Mennonite Brethren in Christ (MBC). From the outset the MBC emphasized the need for emotional, climactic personal conversions, and aggressive evangelistic and missionary endeavours. They quickly abandoned Mennonite organizational, doctrinal, and cultural traditions for the sake of missionary outreach and therefore represent one of the most rapidly assimilated Mennonite groups in Canada.

The Mennonite Brethren in Christ became a unique conglomeration on account of an eclectic selection of theological emphases. From the Pentecostals they borrowed "a stronger emphasis on the Holy Spirit, though never sufficiently to satisfy those who were really Pentecostal at heart; from the Calvinists, elements of predestination; and from the Darbyites, pre-millennialism."[9] But they borrowed most heavily from the Methodists, accepting their ideas regarding a second work of grace, doctrines of holiness and complete sanctification, new forms of church government, and evangelistic techniques. Many Swiss Mennonites found the Brethren attractive because they represented a familiar but more "socially respectable" form of religion. By the 1920s they were equal in numerical strength to the Mennonite Conference of Ontario (MCO).

The Brethren in Christ's aggressive evangelism quickly took them beyond the Mennonite theological and cultural boundaries. Use of the English language was accepted during the late nineteenth century. Members of Brethren churches frequently assumed leadership positions in business, education, and civic affairs. More than half of their young men entered the armed forces during World War I without fear of censure. The Brethren were one of the first Mennonite denominations to organize women's missionary societies. From the time of its inauguration in 1921 the faculty at the Brethren Bible school in Didsbury, Alberta (Mountain View Bible College) was interdenominational, and the language of instruction was English.

By the 1930s the Mennonite Brethren in Christ was hardly recognizable as a Mennonite church. Ministers rarely, if ever, spoke on the subject of non-resistance. Many considered the denomination's historic association with Mennonitism to be a serious handicap for effective missionary outreach. Pressure mounted, particularly in western Canada where the public image of Mennonites was associated with Hutterites and Doukhobors, for the church to "lay aside every weight" and change its name.[10] In 1947 it became known as the United Missionary Church, and later simply as the Missionary Church. The complete abandonment of distinctive Anabaptist doctrines followed shortly after; all links with Mennonite conferences were eventually severed.

The majority of Swiss Mennonites, the third stream, adopted evangelical theological ideas and practices more slowly and formed the Mennonite Conference of Ontario – and its counterpart in the West, the Alberta-Saskatchewan Mennonite Conference. Although it meant surrendering time-honoured customs, evangelical Protestant practices were utilized as the means by which to preserve and even propagate Mennonitism. Despite their involvement in the formation of key evangelical institutions in Canada, they did not, unlike the Mennonite Brethren in Christ, relinquish their commitment to non-resistance, nonconformity, and a disciplined church.

The influence of the Sunday school movement served as the window through which other evangelical Protestant practices and concerns entered. The Mennonite Conference of Ontario Church polity was revolutionized when non-ordained people became involved in the work of the church. Further, "it helped hold the young people's interest, increased Bible knowledge, elevated spiritual life, promoted the missionary movement, and generally enriched church activity and expression."[11] By 1900 the MCO was pulsating with enthusiasm for revival and missions. This found institutional expression during the early twentieth century through annual week-long revival meetings in local congregations, which led to the organization of congregational Bible conferences. Their success, in turn, led to the inauguration of the Ontario Mennonite Bible School in 1907 (renamed the Ontario Mennonite Bible School and Institute in 1951) at Berlin (later Kitchener), Ontario. As the first Mennonite Bible school in Canada, it became by far the most important institution among Swiss Mennonites in Canada until its closure in 1969.

Particularly influential in the Mennonite Conference of Ontario during the first half of the twentieth century were the "big four" who, through their respective positions as ministers and evangelists and as administrators and teachers at the Bible school, directed the MCO towards an integration of evangelicalism and Mennonitism. The four were Samuel F. Coffman (son of evangelist John S. Coffman), Clayton Derstine, Oscar Burkholder, and Jessie Martin. With the exception of Martin, all either attended or developed close ties to the Moody Bible Institute, which reinforced their commitment to evangelism and missions and confirmed their outspoken approval of premillennialism. All emphasized that salvation was experiential, emotional, and based on a conscious commitment. Coffman and Derstine had experience in publishing, and maintained a broad international network of evangelical friends. As one of the founders of the Bible School and Institute, Coffman was a mediating influence between different theological approaches and eschatological points of view. Although he was a premillennialist, he recognized how potentially divisive the dogmaticism of some dispensationalists might be within the Mennonite Conference of Ontario. Coffman simultaneously maintained amiable relations with American fundamentalists R.A. Torrey and W.B. Riley, and American Mennonites J. Horsch, H.S. Bender, and J.C. Wenger.

The energetic Derstine moved to Canada in 1924. During his 52-year ministry he travelled over a million miles, preaching more than 24,000 times. He actively maintained strong links to transdenominational evangelicalism: he was, for example, involved as one of the six founders of InterVarsity Christian Fellowship, serving on the board of directors and assisting in drafting its Basis of Faith.[12] He was a frequent speaker at Youth for Christ rallies, at Christian Business Men International meetings, and at various non-Mennonite churches. He was hardly a stereotypical provincial, belligerent fundamentalist.

Despite their support for and participation in transdenominational evangelicalism, the "big four" were aware that it posed a potential threat to the Mennonite identity of the Mennonite Conference of Ontario. And although evangelical emphases were integrated by the conference, not all Mennonite traditions and emphases were suddenly forgotten. The "big four" stressed the "extra fundamentals" of nonconformity and nonresistance. They taught that the true church must be separate from "the world" and be visible as a nonconforming community. The Mennonite tradition of nonconformity was similar to the evangelical desire that Christians live "holy" lives. Although taboos governing the behaviour of members among Mennonites and evangelical Protestants often reflected an unfortunate juxtaposition of culture and faith, and they often degenerated into a judgmental legalism in both movements, the mutual interest in preserving the purity of the church created a natural compatibility.

The "big four" also actively promoted peace theology. During World War I, Coffman and Martin participated in various inter-Mennonite peace committees and helped negotiate exemption from military service for Mennonite men. Coffman served as the designated spokesperson before the Canadian government on behalf of the Ontario Peace Churches. There is considerable irony in the fact that dispensationalism, which has frequently been denounced by Mennonite scholars as part of a dogmatic and militaristic theological system incompatible with and foreign to orthodox Mennonite theology and practice, helped to strengthen rather than to destroy adherence to non-resistance by reinforcing Mennonite separatism and quietism. Dispensationalism helped Martin make a distinction between "worldly pacifism" as a political option and "evangelical New Testament non-resistance." Assuming the inevitability of "wars and rumours of wars," political pacifism was perceived as a "Satanic delusion, a mighty and deceptive force intended to deceive the church and lead her headlong into the clutches of modernistic and liberalistic leaders."[13]

As the "big four" neared the end of their careers, the Mennonite Conference of Ontario, along with other Mennonites groups, began to feel the impact of those influenced by H.S. Bender's plea for the rediscovery of an Anabaptist vision.[14] Following World War II many Conference men who had served in alternative service camps into which they had been rudely forced recognized their need for theological training at more advanced theological institutions. Consequently some attended Toronto Bible College, but larger numbers attended Goshen College and Seminary and Eastern Mennonite College in the United States. At Ontario Mennonite Bible School and Institute, older faculty were gradually replaced by seminary-educated teachers who were more often than not trained at Mennonite seminaries. Beginning with John Garber during the 1950s, faculty gradually made the transition from premillennialism to amillennialism.[15] During the second half of the twentieth century the Mennonite Conference of Ontario has become more involved in inter-Mennonite ventures. These associations, along with the establishment of Conrad Grebel College on the campus of the University of Waterloo in 1963, reinforced a more distinctly Anabaptist world view and identity among members of the conference and created a greater distance from evangelical Protestants.

CANADIAN CONFERENCE OF THE MENNONITE BRETHREN CHURCH

The Mennonite Brethren (or *Mennoniten-Brüdergemeinde*) trace their origins to Russia in 1860. The Brethren's openness to a variety of non-Mennonite influences contributed substantially towards facilitating a renewal of spiritual vitality, but has also left an ongoing "legacy of ambivalence with regard to their identity as a faith community and their place within the larger Mennonite world."[16] The prioritization of evangelical emphases like conversion and missions has perpetuated this ambivalence to the present and has submerged somewhat the consciousness of their historic identity. This explains why the Mennonite Brethren have been particularly susceptible to diverse religious and theological influences in the North American context. The historical uncertainty concerning their Anabaptist roots and their natural compatibility with the emphases and priorities of North American evangelicalism contributed towards their acculturation and the steady pressure for the dissipation of their ethnic and Anabaptist distinctives. The Mennonite Brethren have, of all Mennonite groups in Canada, been the most active supporters of transdenominational evangelicalism. In fact, some contemporary observers suggest that they are virtually indistinguishable from, and on the verge of being subsumed under, a generic kind of North American evangelicalism.

The first Mennonite Brethren arrived in North America as a small part of the *Kanadier* migration that settled in the United States during the 1870s. From the outset they acquired a reputation as a "mission-minded" group. Although this impulse facilitated the numerical growth of the group, it also militated against the maintenance of a distinct Mennonite identity, accelerated the process of acculturation, and contributed towards its ambivalence towards evangelicalism.

During the late nineteenth century and early part of the twentieth, cultural and linguistic boundaries restricted the Mennonite Brethren outreach efforts to other German-speaking Mennonite groups. Evangelistic tasks were performed largely by commissioned *Reiseprediger* (itinerant ministers). Like frontier preachers of other denominations, their message was simple and anecdotal with a strong emphasis on conversion. Consistent with the Anabaptist emphasis on discipleship, they inculcated the conviction that *Lehre* (doctrine) and *Leben* (life) should be coordinated. Reflecting their sojourn in the United States, many of these early preachers greatly admired D.L. Moody and had been influenced by Moody Bible Institute, Northwestern Bible Institute, and the Bible Institute of Los Angeles where the missionary impulse, the biblicism, and the emphasis on conversion reinforced the Mennonite Brethren priorities.

The ongoing influence from transdenominational evangelicalism gradually expanded the missionary vision of the Mennonite Brethren beyond their linguistic and cultural boundaries, thereby furthering the process of acculturation. Playing a vital role in this transition were their Bible schools. As early as 1910 Canadian Mennonite Brethren began discussing the possibility of establishing a Bible school. These plans came to fruition through John F. Harms, a prominent Bible teacher who formed Herbert Bible School in 1913. The purpose of the school was to equip students for Sunday school work, evangelism, and work as German language teachers in elementary schools. The example of the Herbert Bible School illustrates several early trends among Mennonite Brethren *Kanadier*: "While desiring to retain their German heritage, they were also open to the larger world of English evangelicalism and were prepared to use English language in outreach and ministry."[17] In 1918 Harms moved back to the United States, and the school closed.

It was reopened in 1921 by William J. Bestvater, a Winnipeg city missionary and a popular Bible conference speaker. He gave the school its particular image, which was used repeatedly as a model for other Bible schools (e.g., Bethany Bible Institute in Hepburn, Saskatchewan, which started in 1927 in part through the influence of George Harms, a graduate of Moody Bible Institute). By writing several German textbooks for use in Mennonite Brethren Bible schools and editing a modest periodical entitled *Das Zeugnis der Schrift*, Bestvater disseminated dispensationalist eschatology among the Brethren.

Although retention of the German language remained a priority among *Kanadier* Mennonite Brethren, by the beginning of the twentieth century a transition towards English was well under way among North American Brethren. The Canadian process, however, was interrupted during the 1920s as the *Kanadier* Brethren were almost overwhelmed by a wave of 20,000 German-speaking *Russländer* Mennonites fleeing the aftermath of the Bolshevik revolution. This influx changed dramatically the complexion of the Mennonite Brethren in Canada. Because of their numbers, leadership skills, and education, the *Russländers* soon dominated the denomination. In general they were much more willing to take vigorous action to preserve their heritage of *Deutsch und Religion* than were those with *Kanadier* roots. Vitally concerned about transferring their particular blend of culture and faith to successive generations, the new immigrants invested considerable energy in pursuing strategies and developing institutions that would achieve these objectives. They recommended that all congregations establish German "Saturday" schools; they encouraged members to assume district school-board positions to further the instruction of German and religion in the time allotted by the government within public schools; they provided considerable impetus for more Bible schools; they placed enormous pressure on parents to demonstrate their faithfulness by ensuring that their children obtained facility with the German language. Driving this campaign was the fear that without ethnic solidarity safeguarded by pervasive loyalty to the German language they might not be able to sustain an authentic Mennonite faith in a new environment. As the use of English became more prevalent, the rhetoric on the part of some became more extreme. The preoccupation with the language issue narrowed the *Russländer* understanding of missions: pre-eminent was the *innerste Mission* (inner mission) which focused on a concern for the spiritual life of those within the Mennonite Brethren stronghold, particularly the youth; and secondary was home missions, i.e., reaching out to the scattered Mennonites and other German-speaking people. Outreach activity beyond these linguistic boundaries was not readily endorsed or encouraged.

As noted, the influx of *Russländers* gave the Mennonite Brethren Bible school movement an enormous boost. Almost immediately upon their arrival in 1925, the Winkler Bible Institute was started by A.H. Unruh, a former teacher at the Tschograw Bible School in the Crimea. From the late 1920s continuing throughout the 1930s the Mennonite Brethren started at least twenty additional schools in western Canada. A primary objective in each was to ensure that *Deutsch und Religion* were imparted to the younger generation. However, the use of Bible schools as a means to secure the preservation of the German language among younger Brethren was largely a failure. During the 1930s, differences concerning language and missions resulted in a growing divergence between Mennonite Brethren in Saskatchewan where the *Kanadier* were more numerous, and those in the rest of Canada. While they shared with their fellow *Russländers* Mennonite Brethren a vital concern for the Mennonite people, the *Kanadier* Brethren had come to understand missions – at least since the early twentieth century – in more universal terms. Disputes concerning the two issues were related: as the Mennonite Brethren became more bilingual, the broader view of missions prevailed.

The use of the Bible schools to preserve the German language came into conflict with the desire on the part of young, enthusiastic students to obtain training to minister in non-German, non-Mennonite settings that demanded an ability to use the English language. Pressure from the students was unrelenting, and their aspirations had to be taken seriously: student enrolment figures at Prairie Bible Institute and Briercrest Bible Institute indicate that from the late 1930s onwards Mennonite students (not all Mennonite Brethren) consistently made up 25–35 per cent of the student body. Ongoing losses to "English Bible schools" were persuasive: by 1940 the change-over to English at Bethany Bible Institute was essentially complete, and other Mennonite Brethren Bible schools soon followed suit.

The desire to engage in missionary activity was not, of course, the only reason the younger generation wanted to learn English. Nevertheless, it was more than just a convenient rationalization for language transition. A significant number of Mennonite Brethren students were regularly involved in summer ministries that targeted non-Mennonite communities. From the late 1920s until well into the 1940s, about 30 per cent of the personnel recruited by the Canadian Sunday School Mission (CSSM) came from Mennonite denominations (a significant proportion were Mennonite Brethren).[18] Many others participated both as students and as staff members in organizations like InterVarsity Christian Fellowship and Campus Crusade for Christ. These early associations contributed considerably towards forging permanent links between the MBs and transdenominational evangelicalism.

Not all Mennonite Brethren were happy about the relationships between evangelical schools and mission societies and their young people. Leaders complimented the "vitality" which these organizations inspired but complained about the drain of personnel and monies. In response, a concerted effort was made to establish Mennonite Brethren mission agencies. These included the Bethany Prayer League Children's Mission – organized in 1932 and renamed the Western Children's Mission in 1937 – the West Coast Children's Mission formed in British Columbia in 1939, and a new "higher Bible school" (Mennonite Brethren Bible College) in Winnipeg to train teachers, missionaries, and church workers, who would "in our spirit and under our supervision" fill positions of leadership in Bible schools, churches, and mission agencies.[19] The development of denominational institutions and infrastructure during the 1940s and 1950s can be seen, in part, as a reaction against transdenominational evangelicalism.

The Mennonite Brethren's natural compatibility with, and their long history of involvement in, transdenominational evangelicalism in Canada, has, however, created an ongoing affinity. The Brethren were members in the Evangelical Fellowship of Canada (EFC) since its inauguration in 1964 – the only Mennonite denomination involved at the time. In addition, a number of Brethren have served as leaders within EFC (e.g., Harold Jantz, F.C. Peters, and John H. Redekop). Others who developed ties with evangelicalism include David E. Redekop, who was converted through the camp ministry of Canadian Sunday School Mission, served as the camp director at Camp Arnes, has been the national moderator of the Mennonite Brethren, and in 1977 became the chairman of the international Committee of the Christian Business Men's Committee; and Harold Jantz, formerly the editor of the *Mennonite Brethren Herald*, and the founding editor of *Christian Week*, a bi-weekly tabloid that has become a valuable window on Canadian evangelicalism.

This affinity with evangelicalism is not unrelated to the Mennonite Brethren's ongoing struggle concerning the nature of their Mennonite identity, a subject that has preoccupied conference discussions and countless editorials and books. Many have been alarmed by reports that only half of Canadian Brethren currently uphold the historic peace position.[20] During the last decade a growing chorus of voices have been heard calling Brethren back to Anabaptism.[21] Despite such initiatives, the ambivalence towards evangelicalism that characterized the Mennonite Brethren from the outset is likely to continue for a long time to come.

EVANGELICALISM AMONG TRADITIONAL MENNONITES

In contrast to most other Mennonite groups, the more traditional Old Colony and Sommerfelder Mennonite churches kept the influence of evangelicalism at bay. Both were part of the larger *Kanadier* migration that settled on two land reserves in southern Manitoba during the 1870s (some later re-settled in the other western provinces). Varying responses towards the municipal system of land division and government public schools created several factions during the 1890s: both the Old Colony and Sommerfelder Mennonite emerged as large groups intent on preserving traditional ways of life – by maintaining an extreme form of separation from the world that minimized contact with all outside influences.

The beliefs and practices of both groups are very similar. Like most Mennonite groups, both tried to give their children basic skills in reading, writing, and arithmetic (usually only up to grade six), but education beyond an elementary level was deemed unnecessary and even undesirable. As a result, until the late 1960s very few received more than a grade-eight education. Although neither group has a uniform dress code, like the Hutterites, they prefer dark colours. Jewellery (including wedding bands) and neckties are considered ostentatious. While the dress codes have relaxed somewhat in recent decades, "modern" fashions are still rigorously eschewed.

Central to Old Colony and Sommerfelder Mennonite community life is the church – a plain building, until recently, unpainted (this served as a sign of humility). Men and women use separate entrances and are seated apart on long wooden benches which were, until the 1960s, without backs. Worship services generally last two or more hours and consist of a combination of singing, silent prayers, an "introduction" to the sermon, and a lengthy sermon. Although theoretically all members of the two communities are considered equal, in reality, ministers are given a considerable degree of respect and power as the spokespersons for God.[22] Formal training for clergy is considered unnecessary. Any male member of the congregation is eligible to be chosen as a minister – a position held for life without financial remuneration. Sermons are read: eye contact with the congregation and expressive motions with hands or shoulders are avoided while preaching. Most of the sermons have been hand-copied and handed down through successive generations. The bishop, who is elected from among the ministers by the "brotherhood" (all male members), is the undisputed leader of the church. He alone administers the rites of communion and baptism.

Church membership is attained by baptism after a period of catechetical instruction. In theory, members join the church voluntarily; in practice it is a matter of social necessity as a prerequisite for marriage. Neither church has a written constitution: the catechism is the full extent of formal explications of doctrine. Rules are unwritten and interpreted by leaders based upon their understanding of tradition. Despite ambiguity and differing opinions over the years concerning the definition of worldliness, leaders agree that the church ought to be separate from "the world." Conformity is enforced by the threat of excommunication and social ostracism.

In contrast to their collective display of conformity, there has always been a persistent tradition of dissent. Despite the bitter rifts created within families, a steady trickle of dissenters have left these two churches to join other Mennonite denominations or evangelical Protestant churches. Seldom have these individual voices of dissent organized for the purpose of expediting change. There are, however, notable exceptions, and in each instance evangelical ideas and influences played a key role. The first such attempt resulted in a schism within the Sommerfelder Mennonite Church in Manitoba in 1936 which led to the formation of the Rudnerweider Mennonite Church (renamed the Evangelical Mennonite Mission Church [EMMC] in 1959). The second was an exodus out of the Old Colony in Saskatchewan in 1974 that resulted in the formation of Osler Mission Chapel, which has functioned largely as an autonomous congregation. The most important difference between the two is that the Rudnerweider schism occurred sooner, and the dynamics took longer to evolve, but the denomination as a whole experienced the same transitions that took place much more rapidly in Osler Mission Chapel. In addition, the Evangelical Mennonite Mission Church, like the Mennonite Conference in Ontario, managed to incorporate various evangelical emphases without negating entirely certain historic Anabaptist distinctives like non-resistance. The desire to remain identified as a Mennonite group has created some ambivalence concerning the evangelical influences that shaped their ethos in earlier decades.

The Evangelical Mennonite Mission Church came into being following the eviction of four ministers who zealously pressed for reforms within the Sommerfelder Mennonite church. The church constantly found itself caught between those who wanted to incorporate practices observed in neighbouring Mennonite churches (e.g., Sunday schools, choirs, *Jugendvereine* [Christian Endeavour] programs, missionary reports, evening Bible-teaching and evangelistic services), and those who rigorously opposed any changes.

Approximately 3,000 Sommerfelder Mennonite people joined the four excommunicated ministers to form the Rudnerweider Mennonite Church. The new group initially retained many practices from the old church – for example, use of the catechism for the instruction of baptismal candidates, the three-tiered organizational structure, and baptism by pouring. But immediately apparent was a new emphasis on the necessity of a personal conversion experience and participation in evangelism and missions. Although the four leaders were initially overwhelmed by the task of organizing a new *gemeinde*, they gradually inaugurated changes: worship services began including audible prayers, choirs were started, regular *Jugendvereine* programs were initiated, and hymnals with musical notation replaced the traditional *Gesangbuch*.

From the outset, evangelistic outreach at home and abroad was a stated priority and has remained an integral part of the denomination's identity. Cultural and linguistic boundaries initially circumscribed outreach activity to families, friends, and strangers "in the home context," i.e., persons of similar German background. Later on, regular evangelistic preaching tours to Old Colony areas in Saskatchewan by Evangelical Mennonite Mission Church ministers resulted in the formation of several congregations during the 1940s.

Involvement in foreign missions took longer to develop, but when it did begin it served as the conduit for an influx of new ideas and cultural changes. Despite the suspicions concerning certain doctrines propagated by transdenominational Bible schools, dozens of EMMC young people attended schools like Millar Memorial Bible Institute, Briercrest Bible Institute, and Winnipeg Bible Institute.[23] Many of these graduates volunteered for missionary service, and by the end of the 1950s EMMC missionaries were serving under seven different missions, six of which were transdenominational evangelical organizations. Although leaders liked the enthusiasm for missions that contact with transdenominational schools and organizations promoted among their people, they became increasingly disillusioned with the independence that tended to characterize these organizations and their missionaries who often viewed "themselves as individual crusaders for Christ with relatively little regard for the established church."[24]

Transdenominational evangelical schools and mission agencies also served as an important conduit for popularizing dispensational premillennialism. Efforts to reintroduce the more traditional amillennial views were rejected, at least until recently, as evidence of liberalism. Although the theme of the "second coming" has waned during the last decade, the fact that many ministers, particularly in Saskatchewan, continue to be recruited from transdenominational Bible colleges has kept dispensationalism alive.

The 1940s and 1950s were tumultuous years for the Evangelical Mennonite Mission Church. Unlike the Mennonite Brethren in Christ, they maintained their adherence to the doctrine of non-resistance. Members who enlisted during World War II were summarily excommunicated. Considerable pressure came from the younger generation to use more English within the church. Attendance at public schools, the pursuit of employment opportunities in cities, attendance in transdenominational Bible schools, and participation in evangelistic outreach put the evangelical Mennonites in closer contact with Canadian society. By the late 1950s, services were becoming increasingly bilingual, and by the mid-1960s most were unilingually English.

In 1959 the Rudnerweider opted to change their name to the more anglicized Evangelical Mennonite Mission Conference. This was accompanied by a change from the bishop system to a more localized conference system of administrative leadership which permitted more lay participation. It reflected the group's growing desire to forge its own unique evangelical-Mennonite identity. Towards this end the church made a concerted effort to develop its own mission program, which led to expansion into Ontario. By 1979 the amount of financial support missionaries serving with "faith missions" could receive from the denomination had been severely restricted.

At present the ambivalence among some Evangelical Mennonite Mission Conference people towards the evangelical institutions on which they relied to bring new vitality to the traditional Sommerfelder Mennonite forms and to facilitate their own process of cultural accommodation is split along geographical lines. In Saskatchewan most ministers are recruited from transdenominational Bible colleges; in Manitoba, many evangelical Mennonite students attend Steinbach Bible College, an inter-Mennonite school that emphasizes Anabaptist theology. Reflecting the diversity within their constituency, denominational leaders seem content to continue struggling towards an identity that represents a synthesis of evangelical and Anabaptist beliefs and practices.

The story of Osler Mission Chapel provides more clues to why denominations with strong evangelical emphases almost invariably became the preferred option among those dissatisfied with the religious experience within the Old Colony and Sommerfelder Mennonite traditions.[25] Evangelicalism simultaneously offered what was perceived as both a spiritual and cultural emancipation while leaving important aspects of their traditional world view intact.

The birth of Osler Mission Chapel in 1974 centred around a young Old Colony minister named Jake Wiebe. Although he had received a box of frequently used sermons from the bishop, Wiebe opted instead to use his Bible and preach extemporaneously. His disregard for tradition was made worse by an evangelical emphasis on the necessity of a individual conversion experience and on the doctrine of assurance of salvation which contrasted with the Old Colony understanding of salvation as the acceptance by God of a faithful community.

Despite his departures from tradition, Wiebe was supported by many in the pews. The bishop, along with the other ministers, greatly disapproved of Wiebe's innovations; they saw his popularity as a threat to their own authority, and for this he was suspended from his duties as a minister. In response, Wiebe's family and a dozen other families started a new congregation in Osler, Saskatchewan. The structure adopted for Sunday morning worship services marked a decisive departure from previous practices: segregated seating was abrogated, and services became bilingual with English as the primary language. Plans were made to inaugurate a regular Bible study for adults, a church library, and a program for teens. A standard pattern quickly became evident: aspects of previously disallowed cultural and church practices were integrated, creating an immediate sense of emancipation and "progress." At the same time a certain reticence, an innate Old Colony fear and suspicion of worldliness, kept other common practices within Protestant evangelical churches from being fully accepted. However, many of these practices have gradually been permitted as the desire – and in some cases the pressure – from the younger generation for a greater degree of acculturation intensified. Eventually choirs and musical instruments were permitted; young people were encouraged to consider post-secondary education (at first this only meant attending certain acceptable Bible schools, but more recently this has included public universities); participation by lay people increased; wedding ceremonies became more elaborate; members began to travel more widely and participate in municipal politics; contemporary fashions became more acceptable; and incremental changes in the church's administrative structure signalled a move towards a professionalized ministry.

The influence of evangelicalism played an integral part in this transformation. First, the strong biblicism of evangelicalism was particularly appealing after years of struggle to reform a religious system that refused to permit the open study of the Bible for fear of how it might threaten both traditional practices and the personal authority of the bishop. Second, the conviction that participation in missions is an integral aspect of Christian faithfulness drew them towards evangelicalism. More than half of Osler Mission Chapel's annual budget has consistently been used for supporting missionaries. In addition to being an outlet for evangelistic zeal, the emphasis on missions served as a catalyst that legitimized and accelerated change.[26] Contact with transdenominational mission organizations led them beyond their ethnic boundaries.

Third, the Old Colony emphasis on nonconformity, and their preference for geographical isolation that allowed them to preserve their distinct language, faith, and ethnic identity, nurtured a "static dualistic nature of reality": there is a kingdom of God and a kingdom of this world, and there is no point in encouraging any kind of intercourse or communication between these worlds.[27] The group's historic success in maintaining a bifurcated existence gave them a special affinity for a similar ambivalence towards culture found within certain corners of evangelicalism. The Anabaptist emphasis on nonconformity was comparable to the evangelical motif of "being in the world" but not "of the world." Evangelicalism provided a theological framework and a religious environment in which certain aspects of Canadian culture could be accepted, yet it also simultaneously allowed the people of Osler Mission Chapel to retain intact the suspicion of "the world" that had served as the integrative principle within Old Colony theology and culture. This evangelical motif was appropriated as the "biblical" foundation for drawing new cultural and moral boundaries in the unfamiliar territory of Canadian culture. It helped Osler Mission Chapel leaders to control and guide the pace of acculturation by simultaneously permitting an increased level of integration into Canadian culture and serving as the mechanism for controlling or restricting the process by reinforcing their previous Mennonite separatism when changes threatened to move them beyond their comfort zone.[28]

The use of evangelical motifs to facilitate the process of acculturation brought some unintended consequences: as changes were accepted within the church, members also, often uncritically, increasingly sought the accoutrements of middle-class Canadian life. Rearguard battles over what could be permitted within the church kept Osler Mission Chapel leaders from developing a more proactive response to the way relatively benign changes were unwittingly legitimizing consumeristic and individualistic lifestyles.

In conclusion, three points should be understood about the symbiotic relationship linking Canadian evangelicalism and the Mennonites. First, both movements need to become more conscious of the relationship between culture and faith. Evangelicalism rightly confronted Mennonites about ethnic distinctives which sometimes became intertwined and coterminous with matters of faith. However, evangelicals have erred by assuming that, or at least acting as if, their own expression of faith is somehow culturally neutral or non-ethnic.[29] Since World War II, the term "evangelical" has come to denote (among other things) a particular community with identifiable schools, presses, heroes, and authorities – it has developed its own unique subculture.[30] Mennonites are often frustrated by the way evangelical Protestants seem oblivious to, or at least uncritical of, the way certain theological emphases unwittingly propagate cultural values (e.g., individualism, consumerism, nationalism). Mennonites resent the denigration of their theological distinctives as "non-essential" – usually implicitly translated to mean "unimportant" – as well as the homogenizing impulse within evangelicalism that accompanies the emphasis on nurturing a transcending spiritual unity among all Christians. If taken seriously, such critical response from Mennonites could serve as a valuable mirror by which "mainstream" evangelicals in Canada might see the cultural components of their faith.

Second, some Mennonites correctly observe that evangelical Protestantism has sanctioned individualism and consumerism, but err in blaming manifestations of these values within their communities entirely upon evangelicalism. Mennonite scholars often unfairly caricature evangelicalism, using it as a scapegoat, and neglect to provide more complex nuanced explanations for the historic diversity and current transitions within evangelicalism. As a result certain prejudices concerning evangelicals have taken on mythic proportions. For example, John E. Toews's observation that "many [Mennonite Brethren] have bought into values so prevalent in contemporary evangelicalism: subjectivity, personal feelings, self-improvement, pragmatism, materialism, and rampant individualism" is accurate enough as a statement of comparison, but the inference that evangelicalism served as *the* only conduit – it has indeed been *a* conduit – for such maladies is blame misplaced.[31] Mennonites have amply demonstrated that they are quite capable of becoming materialistic without help from evangelicalism.

Third, Mennonites tend to define themselves against more established traditions. The need to exaggerate differences to make themselves distinguishable from Protestant groups with whom they have much in common has led some Mennonites to overreact against evangelicalism. As a result, Rodney Sawatsky warns, the desire among Mennonite educators to inoculate students against the evangelical "virus," and their desire to liberate students from "right-wing, nationalistic communities" may, ironically, be producing "secularists." There needs to be an appreciation for evangelicalism as a dynamic movement that embraces a variety of theological, cultural, and ethical orientations which cannot simply be equated with fundamentalism, militarism, or civil religion. "Mennonites could do much worse," continues Sawatsky, "than to participate actively, even if selectively, in the current revitalization of evangelicalism. Here we will find allies in a common agenda. Such ecumenism will serve [us] better than to define ourselves 'over against' these fellow Christians."[32] Such ecumenism will not be possible unless evangelicalism is perceived as "the story of many different people with their own distinguishing traditions, history, and language" in which each group is encouraged "to recognize the strength of their particularity and nurture it to make a distinctive contribution."[33] In addition to assisting "mainstream" evangelicals in recognizing their ethnicity, it would permit Mennonites to feel comfortable as part of the kaleidoscope that makes up evangelicalism in Canada.

15 Lutheranism and Evangelicalism: Travelling in the Same Circle of Influence

BRYAN V. HILLIS

Lutherans have a special and prior claim to the term "evangelical," even if Canadian Lutherans have an aversion to being identified with the evangelical movement. Although historical connections are scarce,[1] Lutherans and evangelicals share some ideologies and perspectives. Furthermore, when Canadian Lutheran theologians have written about evangelicalism, they have displayed a certain naïveté regarding evangelicalism and how Lutheran theology may be related to it. This paper will establish those historic theological connections and show what Lutheranism and evangelicalism share and do not share, at least in the Canadian context.

THE TERM "EVANGELICAL" IN LUTHERAN HISTORY

Lutherans, even Canadian Lutherans, are loathe to relinquish their claim on the term "evangelical." This is obvious from the beginning of the merger discussions that culminated in 1985 in the Evangelical Lutheran Church in Canada; it was assumed "evangelical" would be included in the title of the new church. It is no accident either that of the five Canadian Lutheran denominations listed in the *Yearbook of American & Canadian Churches 1995*, three – The Estonian Evangelical Lutheran Church, The Latvian Evangelical Lutheran Church in America and the Evangelical Lutheran Church in Canada – have "evangelical" in their title. What is ironic about this situation is that the two

Canadian Lutheran denominations not using the term are often identified with what is commonly called the evangelical movement. Those two are the Lutheran Church – Canada (an offshoot of the Lutheran Church – Missouri Synod [MS])[2] and the Church of the Lutheran Brethren, an even more theologically conservative denomination which does not attract much attention because of its small numbers.[3]

Yet the Lutherans of North America have not exactly embraced the term "evangelical" and what it signifies in the evangelical movement. E. Clifford Nelson, one of Lutheranism's foremost historians, states that historically Lutherans "loved the word 'evangelical' [but] became restive and nervous about being classified simply as evangelicals."[4] Mark Ellingsen, an American Lutheran scholar of evangelicalism, asserts that while many Lutherans in Europe and elsewhere explicitly identify themselves as part of the evangelical movement, in North America "the number of Lutherans who do in fact identify themselves as evangelical is infinitesimally small."[5] Not even the denomination most often identified by outsiders as belonging to the evangelical movement, the Lutheran Church (MS),[6] has ever claimed membership in the National Association of Evangelicals.[7] More recently, when Kenn Ward wrote his popular book describing the largest Canadian Lutheran denomination, the Evangelical Lutheran Church in Canada, he thought it necessary in his opening pages to remark, "Some of us are a bit uncomfortable with that word 'evangelical' in our name."[8] What is it about the term that prompts Lutherans to embrace it as a title but not in the context of the evangelical movement as commonly understood?

To answer that question, a quick review of some European Lutheran history is necessary. Soon after Luther's departure from the Roman Catholic church, he made the oft-quoted disclaimer, "I pray you leave my name alone, and do not call yourselves Lutherans but evangelicals."[9] Luther's focus was on the gospel or "evangel" orientation of the protest movement as distinguished from the perceived emphasis on tradition and authority in the Roman church. Those confessions that Luther's followers used to proclaim their distinctiveness from the Catholic and other new-born traditions actually shunned the name "Lutheran," preferring instead "evangelical" or "churches of the Augsburg Confession." "Lutheran" was in fact a *schimpfname* or term of jest or insult that Catholics used to refer to the evangelicals of sixteenth-century Germany. The use of "Lutheran" accelerated after the Peace of Augsburg (1555) when the principle of *cuius region eius religion* (religion of the sovereign is the religion of the people) was recognized as law. Still "evangelical" was used primarily in reference to the followers of Luther, and Lutheran and evangelical became practically synonymous.[10]

In 1648 the decisive Treaty (or Peace) of Westphalia not only resolved the major religious conflicts among the Germans but also recognized Lutherans *and* Calvinists as imperially legitimated representatives of the non-Roman "evangelical churches." Hence after 1648 "evangelical" was no longer equated solely with Lutheran interests because the Reformed church also was recognized as a legitimate non-Catholic entity. In fact, "evangelical" was used even to refer to some aspects of the "left wing" or Radical Reformation, since all of these groups claimed to have been "liberated from Rome by the Gospel."[11] Their religious lives now governed by the *evangel* and not the traditional church, they all maintained that *they* were remaining most true to the *evangel*: "The result [of the Peace of Westphalia and the controversies with Reformed groups thereafter] for the Lutherans [particularly] was a genuine distaste for being lumped into an undifferentiated ecclesiastical mass known simply as 'evangelicals.' They therefore insisted, 'We are indeed evangelicals, but we are *Lutheran evangelicals.*'"[12]

Fears that the term increasingly connoted a sense of pan-Protestant inclusiveness between 1600 and 1800 seemed corroborated in 1817. The Prussian King Frederick William III (1797–1840), wanting to achieve religious unity in order to present a stronger, more united face to his chief political rivals, the Catholic Hapsburgs of Austria, enacted a royal decree bringing about the union of Lutherans and Calvinists in what was called the "Evangelical Christian Church," known more popularly as the "Prussian Union Church." With this edict Lutherans and Reformed were placed under the authority of one department of the state, and the two churches were to be "de-confessionalized" in the sense that pastors were to subscribe to their particular confessions *only insofar* as they agreed with other approved Reformation confessions. Calvinists were not happy with this arrangement, for they felt that Lutherans had not gone far enough in rejecting Roman liturgical forms; Lutherans, more attached to their confessions than ever, were even more opposed. Article VII of the Lutheran Augsburg Confession insisted that the gospel be preached in its "purity" and the sacraments administered according to the *evangel* or gospel.[13] For Lutherans such evangelical content as articulated in the Lutheran Confessions simply could not be glossed over by an act of state, and they increasingly relied on their confessions through the nineteenth century.[14]

As a result, by the nineteenth century the term "evangelical," despite its history, lacked authenticity for Lutherans. It was no longer perceived as directly tied to the gospel as found in their Lutheran Confessions; rather it had become a term that glossed over the differences between Lutherans and other non-Catholic reformers whose proclamation of the gospel was suspect in the Lutheran view. Lutherans came to use the term "confessional" because they believed that in the distinctive Lutheran Confessions, as contained in the Formula of Concord, the gospel was most clearly proclaimed and preserved.[15]

Such an account explains why most Lutherans have this strange attraction to a term which they otherwise avoid as it is applied in the evangelical movement. The term is part of their history and indicates for them their *raison d'être*, an opportunity to witness to the content of the gospel. But this is obviously not the same "evangelical" of the evangelical movement, and the distinctiveness of Canadian Lutheran history indicates why there is an aversion to something as North American as the evangelical movement.

HISTORICAL DISTINCTIVENESS OF LUTHERANISM IN CANADA

Evangelicals and Lutherans in Canada have distinct histories. While it may be impossible to date the first evangelical service on Canadian soil (if for no other reason than it is doubtful that agreement could be reached on who the first evangelicals were), Canadian Lutherans do not have the same problem. According to Carl Raymond Cronmiller, Christian IV of Denmark and Norway commissioned the Danish Lutheran sea captain Jens Munck to establish the northwest passage for the commercial interests of his realm. On 7 September 1619 Munck and his crew of sixty-five Lutheran men arrived at Port Churchill. Since Rev. Rasmus Jensen, a Lutheran clergyman, was one of the crew, Christmas was celebrated that year with a service that included Holy Communion. Unfortunately neither the clergyman nor the expedition survived disease and the cold Canadian winter.[16]

In some ways this first Lutheran worship service is paradigmatic of the development of Lutheranism in Canada, and thereby helps explain its relationship with evangelicalism. Lutheranism arrived as part of an established church on an official voyage. Its first service was held for its own among its own by its own; it was very ethnic in origin. The service included a sermon and the Lord's Supper, typical of the Lutheran confessionalist emphasis on preaching of the Word and practice of the sacraments. Lutheranism arrived in an insular way and left quietly; no contact was made with others and its survival was contingent upon the arrival of more Lutherans. And Lutheranism remained an ethnic religion that kept to itself and looked after its own.

The same could be said for Lutheranism in the United States. As Mark Noll has noted, there was a certain Calvinist-Lutheran disengagement in sixteenth-century Europe, but this was not the basis for the stand-off between modern Lutherans and the evangelical movement. Noll looks to five defining moments for evangelicalism since the mid-eighteenth century: 1) affirmation of the American Revolution; 2) appropriation of a form of Christian enlightenment as found in Scottish common-sense realism; 3) commitment to revivalism; 4) experience of cultural domination; and 5) resistance to modernism.[17] In these moments American evangelicalism seized the opportunity to act and thereby defined itself as a separate entity. Such was not the case for Lutheranism, and as Noll argues, this accounts at least in part for the distance between Lutherans and evangelicals in the United States.

If Lutherans in the United States did not have those defining events, neither did they have them in Canada. Norman Threinen, probably Canada's foremost Lutheran historian, outlines what he considers three "pivotal points" in Canadian Lutheran Church history: 1) the mid-eighteenth century, when the first Canadian Lutheran congregation in Lunenberg, Nova Scotia, struggled to retain its identity as a Lutheran community; 2) Confederation, when Lutheran churches, quite independent of the political process, struggled with the question of how Canadian they should be relative to the American Lutheran churches; and 3) World War II, when Lutheran chaplains were grouped with "other Protestant" minority groups. Threinen detects a trend here in that Canadian Lutheranism gradually, and certainly since the Second World War when it tried so hard to show it was not German, became more ecumenical.[18] In so doing, it also became more mainstream and acculturated even while it became more socially active. Lutheranism's identity was to be preserved by something other than the historical choices it made.

In contrast with the development of evangelicalism in Canada, Lutheranism's ethnic origins maintained its status as an "outsider" denomination until at least the Second World War. The first Lutheran congregation was established by a struggling German-speaking group in Lunenberg, Nova Scotia, in 1749 as part of the British effort to colonize the area with loyal settlers.[19] Repeated waves of Lutherans from continental Europe and Scandinavia only strengthened the impression that this was an immigrant religion from countries where Lutheranism was the state religion, whose members had to acquire English once they came to Canada.[20] Ethnic diversity did not enhance a unified Lutheran presence. Nor did the hard life of pioneering and the chronic lack of pastors make it any easier for Lutheranism to act as a religious force in Canadian life. Lutheranism's very survival as an outsider group dictated a more severe confessionalism that strengthened the cohesion of the flock but allowed little opportunity for contact with other denominations. Furthermore, Ellingsen notes that Lutheranism's elitist Kantian foundations were simply not appreciated in the popular North American context.[21] In summary, Canadian Lutheranism had neither the resources nor the inclination to be any more than it has become, a small and late member of the mainstream of the Canadian religious culture.[22]

HISTORICAL CONNECTIONS BETWEEN LUTHERANISM AND EVANGELICALISM

There are some links, at least theologically speaking, between evangelicalism and Lutheranism, notably in the history of pietism. Reflecting this is the fact that the Evangelical Lutheran Church of America, the parallel to Canada's largest Lutheran denomination, the Evangelical Lutheran Church in Canada, has made some first attempts at ecumenical dialogue with evangelical representatives and found that the pietistic heritage showed promise for future discussions.[23] Moreover, Harold Brown had argued that Lutheranism's most important gift to evangelicalism was pietism, "a chiefly Lutheran phenomenon."[24]

Historical connections between Lutheran pietism and evangelicalism are relatively easy to establish. Significantly, it was the "pietist circles in Europe that responded most quickly and generously to appeals for help from America."[25] Herman Francke was largely responsible for the propagation of the pietist ideology when he set up his orphanage and seminary at Halle whence many a seminary graduate bound for North America emerged.[26] Among these were C.F.W. Walther, one of the principal leaders and founders of the Evangelical Lutheran Synod of Missouri, Ohio and Other States,[27] the synod that was later named the Lutheran Church–Missouri Synod; and Nicholas von Zinzendorf, a graduate of Halle, who sponsored the Moravian Brethren.[28] The high point of Lutheran pietism came in American colonial times when pietists like Henry Melchior Muhlenberg, a participant in the Great Awakening with Jonathan Edwards,[29] had to defend their form of Lutheranism in an increasingly confessionalist atmosphere.[30] It was also one of North American Lutheranism's most prominent leaders and avowed pietists, Samuel Schmucker, who helped forge the Evangelical Alliance in 1846.

Contemporary links between pietism and Lutheranism are evident in the use of evangelical methods. For instance, in the late 1980s more clergy from the Lutheran Church–Missouri Synod and the Lutheran Church–Canada were entering the Doctor of Ministry program at Fuller Theological Seminary than the combined programs of their own denominational seminaries. Both John Pless and Carter Lindberg have written penetrating analyses of how these evangelical methods have their roots in the German Lutheran pietistic movement of the eighteenth century.[31]

Lutheran pietistic origins are usually traced to Philip Jacob Spener (1635–1705), a German who had gained a thorough and appreciative knowledge of Luther from his teacher Johann Dannhauer. Pietists like Spener considered themselves simply enacting what had been established by Luther in theory; they liked to think of themselves as the second reformation necessitated by the rather stale orthodox confessionalism that had become characteristic of seventeenth-century German Lutheranism. Christians needed to act upon, not just believe in, the principles of reform Luther had initiated.[32] To articulate those concerns Spener wrote an introduction to the postils of Johann Arndt, which was reissued separately a year later under the title *Pia Desideria: or Heartfelt Desires for a God-pleasing Improvement of the True Protestant Church*.[33] Spener's focus was the subjective aspect of salvation – an idea that his enemies ridiculed as "pietistic" because too much individual effort seemed required for one's own justification. Spener's pietism included:

the need for, and the possibility of, an authentic and vitally significant experience of God on the part of individual Christians; the religious life as a life of love for God and man, which is marked by social sensitivity and ethical concern; utter confidence, with respect to the issues of both life and death, in the experientially verifiable authenticity of God's revelation in Christ, as found in the biblical witness; the church as a community of God's people, which must ever be renewed through the transformation of individuals, and which necessarily transcends all organizationally required boundaries; the need for the implementation of the Reformation understanding of the priesthood of all believers through responsible lay participation in the varied concerns of the Christian enterprise; a ministry which is sensitized, trained and oriented to respond to the needs and problems of a given age; and finally, the continual adaptation of ecclesiastical structures, practices, and verbal definitions to the mission of the church.[34]

Historian Harold Brown characterizes American evangelicalism as having a series of features resembling those found in Spener's *Pia Desideria*. They include:

1) emphasis on straightforward, simple Bible preaching with a strong didactic content; 2) formation of innumerable fellowship groups within and without existing churches; 3) emphasis on life rather than doctrine, in practice, despite a heavy dose of doctrine in much evangelical preaching; 4) stress on the importance of individual conversion, not necessarily but often including a highly emotional conversion experience; 5) emphasis on the Scripture as the "only perfect rule," with a comparative disregard for other "externals," such as creeds, doctrine,

church regulations and the sacraments; 6) inclusivistic tendencies of a particular kind; few or no distinctions are made among "brothers and sister in Christ."[35]

Though Brown was writing especially of American evangelicalism, these characteristics seem to apply to Canadian evangelicalism as well. Walter Freitag, church historian at Lutheran Theological Seminary in Saskatoon, identified the pietist movement as one of three types of Lutheran churchmanship in Canada.[36] Freitag strengthens the argument for the relationship between Canadian evangelicalism and Lutheranism when he shows how the traditional evangelical emphases on conversion, personal testimonies, awakenings, foreign missions, non-liturgical worship, strict codes of moral behaviour, and a congregational polity stressing a high degree of lay involvement were features of Lutheran pietism also.[37]

Lutheran pietism reached Canada by way of nineteenth-century Norwegian immigrants. The most obvious legacies of this Norwegian pietism are the Canadian Lutheran Bible Institutes,[38] although the Lutheran Evangelistic Movement (limited to confessing Lutherans) and the World Mission Prayer League remain active as well. Pietism also survived, albeit in muted form, alongside confessional orthodoxy in the various Norwegian synods of North America.

There are a few other indirect connections between evangelicals and Lutherans. During the 1930s and 1940s, Dr Ole Hallesby (1879–1961), a Norwegian Lutheran professor at the Independent Theological Seminary in Oslo, wrote eight books pertaining to Christian faith development, which were translated into English and published by Augsburg Publishing House of Minneapolis. These books were widely read by members of the InterVarsity Christian Fellowship and other evangelicals.[39] As well, although there are no established organizational ties, Canadian Lutherans have not hidden their admiration for the work of Billy Graham; however, the absence of a sacramental and social dimension prevented any "whole-hearted approbation."[40] Mark Noll describes how after World War II Carl Henry involved Lutheran scholars in his version of evangelicalism by having Lutherans author ten of eighty-five books promoting evangelical convictions; however, that Lutheran influence quickly faded as there is only one Lutheran in ninety-nine authors involved in the more recent *Word Bible Commentary* and *Expositor's Bible Commentary* series.[41] Eugene Rudolph Bertermann, an ordained Lutheran Church–Missouri Synod clergyman who was heavily involved in evangelical parachurch organizations and president of the National Religious Broadcasters, was also actively involved in the Lutheran Church (MS) Lutheran Hour Broadcast,[42] itself a series having many affinities with other forms of evangelical broadcasting. In addition, Dr

Oswald Hoffman, renowned speaker for the Lutheran Hour, and Richard Jensen, Lutheran theologian, are known to have addressed evangelical gatherings.[43] Lutherans also participated in the KEY 73 campaign, an evangelical initiative. More recently, Lutheran pastors of both the Missouri Synod and Canada variety have "embraced enthusiastically" the Church Growth Movement, a program for increasing church membership usually associated with the evangelical movement and Fuller Theological Seminary. This program has become so popular that a Missouri Synod pastor wrote in the *Concordia Theological Quarterly* that the Church Growth Movement "is becoming a tidal wave in our synod at the present time."[44] There is also little question that the Missouri Synod and Lutheran Church–Canada, the most confessional and theologically conservative of the Lutheran synods, is adopting evangelical techniques, as a book published by the denomination's official publishing house clearly indicates.[45]

THE LUTHERAN "EVANGEL" OF EVANGELICALISM

Various scholars have already indicated that evangelicalism has its roots in the theology of the Reformation.[46] But those roots have usually been regarded as more immediately connected with various Reformed traditions. Is there a Lutheran perspective on evangelicalism and its theology? Obviously such a question is fraught with problems, not the least of which is that both Lutheranism and evangelicalism are movements of such diversity that generalities can become mere caricatures.[47] Nevertheless there is something commonly called an "evangelical movement," and there is a "Lutheranism," both of which bring to mind certain concepts.

The "evangelicalism" of the contemporary evangelical movement has received its most clear characterization by David Bebbington.[48] Most contemporary evangelicals and church historians agree with Bebbington's "quadrilateral" description – conversionism, biblicism, activism, and crucicentrism – which makes his typology even more trustworthy.

How does a Lutheran (and particularly a Canadian Lutheran) perspective compare with such evangelical theology? Lutheran theology continues to be distinguished by its emphasis on the state of justification the undeserved find themselves in as a result of God's grace; this constitutes the well-known "justification by grace through faith" slogan of Lutheranism. The trusting relationship that God has established through His grace was revealed most fully in the incarnation, suffering, and resurrection of Christ. Luther's *theology of the Cross* is especially central to Lutheran theology as the Cross is evidence of the hidden nature of God which is revealed only through the grotesque death instrument of an ancient culture. Although this may sound very close to Bebbington's characterization of evangelical "crucicentrism," Lutherans would also argue that it is impossible to be sure of the precise mechanism of salvation;[49] Gustaf Aulen's *Christus Victor* is a good example of Lutheran ambivalence regarding how "God was in Christ reconciling the world to himself."[50] The reason for such ambivalence is that Lutherans are convinced justification has its origins in God's grace and that grace manifests itself in a faith which must trust *that*, not *how*, God has saved his redeemed. As a theological textbook used in a Lutheran seminary states, the "death and resurrection of Jesus cannot thus be assimilated to an immanent rational scheme."[51]

Like evangelicals, Lutherans hold the Bible to be central to their faith. As the most explicit revelation of God's will, both in demonstrating our guilt under the law and proclaiming our righteousness as a result of Christ's work, the Scriptures stand above all other literature.[52] Also like evangelicals, Lutherans have had their share of disputes regarding how literally inspired, inerrant, or infallible the Scriptures are, even though (or perhaps because) the Lutheran Confessions do not specify a theory of scriptural interpretation.[53] But where Lutherans may differ from evangelicals is in their subordination of the writings of the Bible to the gospel message of justification. For Lutherans the Word is not merely the Bible; the Word is Christ. The Scriptures *witness* to the true Word of God, but they are not to be *identified* with the central message of the evangel, namely that Christ was and is God incarnate.[54] As such, the Scriptures remain the most important means of God's grace, but they are not the sum total of God's Word and therefore are not to be interpreted in a literalist manner. The historical and continuing action of Christ, especially as found in both Word and Sacrament, truly constitutes God's Word of grace to the world.[55]

Dr Erwin Buck, professor of New Testament at Lutheran Theological Seminary in Saskatoon, distinguishes Lutheran hermeneutics from those of the evangelical or, as he calls it, the neo-conservative movement. His main criticism is that the evangelical biblical scholars are far too worried about demonstrating the inspiration and even the inerrancy of Scripture, thereby tending to "harmonize" the biblical witness. He argues that most evangelical scholarship tends to treat critical biblical scholarship with distrust and suspicion, though he also acknowledges that some evangelical biblical scholars are embracing tools like historical criticism. On the other hand, Lutherans are not afraid to embrace critical methods of interpretation because they recognize that the Word of God is not the Bible itself but what the Bible is indicating, namely Christ. He applauds the "neo-conservatives" for exerting a steady influence "in a windy theological climate" but warns his readers about the evangelical excesses of arrogance and presuppositions that do not take the text seriously.[56] What is interesting about Buck's criticism of the "neo-conservatives" is that it seems directed as much against the biblical scholarship emanating from Lutheran Church–Missouri Synod and Lutheran Church–Canada schools as that from evangelical schools.[57]

Conversionism and activism definitely are not typical Lutheran emphases. Lutherans are simply too comfortable with the historic ecclesiastical tradition of infant baptism to emphasize a datable event or process of conversion. If one is to take justification by grace through faith seriously, God is able to redeem a baby as easily as an adult.[58] Though Lutherans agree with evangelicals that the imputation of righteousness should involve living a life of gratitude to the Creator, they are also very mindful of Luther's little Latin phrase *simul iustus et peccator* ("simultaneously righteous and a sinner").[59] As justified by grace as one may be, sinful human nature will all too often obscure one's reconciled state. Hence a justified person must trust the established means of God's grace as given in the sacraments of baptism and the Lord's Supper.[60]

In the same way, while the Lutheran mission effort has never been entirely absent, Lutheran confidence in justification by faith has led to a certain fatalistic apathy regarding the salvation of others.[61] Most Lutherans believe they are to propagate God's message of salvation where they can out of concern for their fellow humans, but both failures and successes in leading others to a knowledge of God's work are tempered by the foundational doctrine of justification by grace alone. As Lutherans cannot save themselves, so they cannot save others but must trust in God's good work to bring their neighbour to the same state of salvation.[62]

Confessional Lutheranism has always been reluctant to be "activistic" in the social or political sphere.[63] One of the few Canadian Lutheran voices to recognize that need is William Hordern, past president of the Lutheran Theological Seminary in Saskatoon. Hordern has argued persuasively that social activism is an intrinsic part of being a Lutheran justified by grace;[64] he has also recognized that evangelical groups are not monolithic in being politically conservative and that there are many who are very progressive in their political strategies.[65]

CONTEMPORARY CANADIAN CRITIQUES OF EVANGELICALISM

There are Canadian Lutheran scholars who disagree that there are many affinities between Canadian Lutheranism and evangelicalism. Walter

Freitag, the Evangelical Lutheran Church in Canada professor at Lutheran Theological Seminary in Saskatoon, makes no distinction between fundamentalism and evangelicalism, calling the latter simply a new name for the former.[66] Freitag states that there are no historical incidents of cooperation, although there was a "friendly disposition towards fundamentalism" by Canadian Lutherans which manifested itself in the Lutheran Bible Schools, various pronouncements by American Lutheran bodies (e.g. "Minneapolis Theses," "A Brief Statement," "United Testimony of Faith and Life") which applied also to Canada, and some efforts to keep doctrine "pure," which Freitag calls "repristination" theology.[67] Freitag also notes the connection between "fundamentalism" and the Lutheran pietistic movement. Despite his tirade against the "fundamentalistic" nature of evangelicalism, he admits that there are "Lutheran evangelicals." He carefully notes that such Lutheran evangelicals who insist on the comfort of "what the Bible says" and remain separate from Christian ecumenism are not really true to the truly Lutheran spirit of "evangelical Lutherans." Conversely, evangelical Lutherans acknowledge that what is important is the gospel of Christ and, as Freitag writes, "let the gospel of Christ be the hermeneutic of the Bible."[68] If Freitag is representative of a Lutheran constituency, some Lutherans are comfortable with "evangelical" as an adjective when applied to themselves (i.e. "evangelical Lutherans") but not as a noun (i.e. "Lutheran evangelicals") because the noun usage identifies Lutherans too closely with "the evangelical movement" with which they feel uncomfortable.

Freitag also indicates another extreme of Lutheranism that acts suspiciously like the evangelical movement, namely Lutheran confessionalism. Lutheran confessionalists are those who, in their reliance on the *Book of Concord* and its contents, have become hermeneutical literalists of these non-biblical texts. The confessionalists' emphasis on the purity of doctrine as established in the sixteenth century misses the Christological emphasis of the Lutheran hermeneutic, Freitag argues. The result is an exclusivistic, non-ecumenical position that does not encompass the nature of evangelical Lutheranism.[69] Without doubt, one of Freitag's targets here is the Lutheran Church–Missouri Synod and Lutheran Church–Canada. It is interesting that this denomination, usually regarded as most "evangelical" by non-Lutherans, is one that Freitag and other Lutherans characterize as confessional rather than evangelical. The reason the Missouri Synod and Canadian Church are mistaken as evangelical by non-Lutherans is its conservative theological stance which is a result of its confessionalism, not its evangelicalism.[70]

Walter Koehler, a professor at the Saskatoon seminary, takes a more nuanced approach in describing evangelicals, citing three main groups within the movement – fundamentalists, charismatics, and neo-evangelicals. This last group, of which he obviously does not consider himself a member, is the focus of his analysis. He argues that the orthodoxy of the neo-evangelical movement is very close to that of the Protestant Reformation, where "*sola Scriptura, sola gratia, sola fides and solus Christus*" were dominant. His "simple description of neo-evangelicalism would include that group in Christendom whose dedication to the gospel expresses itself in a personal faith in Jesus Christ as Saviour and Lord and whose understanding of the gospel is normed solely by the Scriptures as the written Word of God."[71]

Koehler regards neo-evangelicals as trying to fill the void created when liberal Christianity moved even further to the left and fundamentalism became separatistic in its movement to the right. He also emphasizes the bibliocentrism of evangelicalism, noting that evangelicalism will use higher criticism except "where it militates against the authority of Scripture." Although he does not state it in exactly the same terms as Bebbington, Koehler does describe evangelicalism's centrality of Christ and his atonement, its activism in mission work and social concerns, and its high standards of morality or "distinctly Christian lifestyle."[72] Koehler concludes his analysis with a clarion call to fellow Lutherans:

Many Lutherans presently seem to be in a straddle position. They have one foot planted in evangelical theology, strengthened by their view of the means of grace and sacramental theology, and one foot in the stream of mainline Protestantism.

One of the positive things about neo-evangelicalism is that it can encourage us to reconsider some of our heritage. Lutherans can benefit from a reminder of what it means to affirm Scriptural authority and to live under that authority. We need to regain an emphasis on evangelism – because we too are guilty, to a degree, of stressing social action at the expense of evangelism. We need to eschew some of the radical thinking regarding the Trinity and the person of Jesus Christ, and see the theological limits and dead-ends as well as the benefits in certain of the liberation theologies. We need to see that Christian experiences must be grounded in the Word.[73]

Koehler only briefly mentions sacraments, but this is part of a matrix of issues that distinguishes Lutherans from evangelicals. Mark Noll refers to this matrix as the distinctive history that Lutherans possess,[74] while Lutherans like David Scaer and William Lazareth refer to the Lutheran confessions that inform Lutheran theologizing.[75] Another part of the equation is the Lutheran emphasis on "Word *and sacrament*" where sacraments emphasize the dispensing of God's grace.[76] Much of this sacramental emphasis is due to the distinctive emphasis of Lutheranism on justification by grace.[77] However, much of this matrix of history, sacrament, and confessions is also related to the middle ground that Lutheranism occupies between Catholicism and other descendants of the Reformation movement. Lutherans, like their founder, have always considered themselves part of the tradition of the universal church. As a reforming movement, Lutheranism has indicated its sacraments and confessions are critical in defining Lutheran identity. Even Lutheran pietists, as close as they may be to the evangelical heritage, affirm this tradition while emphasizing the need to live, not just intellectually assert, the reforming ethic.

Unfortunately the historic connections between Lutheranism and evangelicalism are difficult to trace; however, the theological connections are plain and the circle of influence obvious. Canadian Lutherans have a connection with evangelicals through pietism and other theological emphases such as the centrality of Christ and the Bible. Obviously, there has always been an evangelical impulse within Canadian Lutheranism – never a majority, yet a significant minority. The fact that pietism did not become the dominant stream in Canadian Lutheranism, overshadowed as it was by confessionalism, however,[78] is a key indication that Lutheranism and evangelicalism are travelling in the same sphere of influence, even if their orbits are not identical. Canadian Lutheranism is not characterized by the activism of evangelicalism, though there is nothing in Lutheran theology that precludes it; in fact, the very existence of the Lutheran pietist movement indicates that the lack of activism in Lutheranism is due more to a moral laziness than a lack of agreement with the concept. Conversely, evangelical emphasis on conversionism does stand in sharp contrast to Lutheran justification by grace alone through faith. Yet both evangelicals and Lutherans by virtue of their history and function share the need to be reforming and prophetic. As Walter Koehler described the function of the evangelical movement, "They [evangelicals] are indicating to us today the value of upholding the great principles of the Reformation. Thanks be to God."[79]

PART FOUR

Holiness, Christian and Missionary Alliance, and Pentecostalism

16 Sailing for the Shore: The Canadian Holiness Tradition

MARILYN FÄRDIG WHITELEY

On 22 November 1903 Albert Mills wrote in his diary about a sermon he had just heard. Brother Armstrong, he said, first spoke about Secret Societies. "He then goes to the church question and shows how people have but the form of godliness and deny the power and so on. He says some people would rather stay with the sinking ship and pump water than get into the lifeboat and sail for the shore."[1]

Mills was a member of a small band that a little more than a year before had organized a church called the Holiness Gospel Workers, later incorporated as the Gospel Workers Church in Canada. It was one of a number of holiness groups formed in Canada in the late nineteenth or early twentieth century. There had been controversy as to whether it was right for these groups to organize as separate societies – hence "the church question." For Armstrong, the "sinking ship" was Canadian evangelicalism, particularly as embodied in the Methodist Church, for that was the home of most of these holiness people. The lifeboat was, of course, the Gospel Workers Church. Mills added his own comment: "Bless God for a lifeboat in this part of the country."

The earliest of the holiness groups formed in Canada is commonly known as the Canada Holiness Association.[2] Nelson Burns was its first president. It was active in the area stretching from Toronto to London and south into the Niagara peninsula. Second was the Holiness Movement Church, founded by Ralph Horner. Its congregations were mainly from the Ottawa Valley south into New York State, and also, before long, on the Prairies. The Gospel Workers Church was closely related to it. Frank Goff, who had been converted by Holiness Movement evangelists, founded this small group, located mainly in Grey County, Ontario. Then in the second decade of the twentieth century, there was a split within the Holiness Movement Church. Some stayed in that church, while others, including Horner himself, formed the Standard Church of America.

The holiness tradition in Canada is not limited to these groups. There are also ones that came to this country from outside its borders: from Britain, the Salvation Army; and from the United States several organizations, most notably the Free Methodist Church and the Church of the Nazarene. The holiness tradition also includes the Keswick movement and various holiness associations, and such small groups as the Christian Workers.[3] All these have significant Wesleyan roots. The Reformed or Holiness Baptists in the Maritimes represent another tradition. Ultimately all these stories must be studied together. Yet the groups that were rooted in the Methodist church and originated in Canada around the turn of the century form an important unit, and the examination of this part of the holiness tradition may illuminate the strains developing within the Canadian evangelicalism of the time.

In common with other evangelicals, holiness people expected a specific experience of conversion. What distinguished them was their emphasis on a further work of grace that went by many names, among them holiness, the second blessing, Christian perfection, baptism of the Holy Ghost, and entire sanctification. Methodists cited the views of John Wesley when they asserted their belief in the necessity of holiness. Wesley, however, had said various things about holiness, and his statements were not easily reconciled.

In the years following Wesley's death both the emphasis placed on this belief and its precise definition continued to vary, but holiness remained an important part of the Wesleyan heritage. In the mid-nineteenth century a distinctive formulation of the tradition was spread by Phoebe Palmer through both her evangelistic work and her writings. Later, Methodists lamented that the experience of sanctification was no longer frequently preached or sought, but they retained the ideal of holiness in their tradition. Those who came to be identified with the holiness movement went beyond the mainstream Methodists in emphasizing the importance of sanctification as an essential part of the Christian life, and in expecting it to be an instantaneous work of grace.

Each of the Canadian holiness groups originated as the result of conflict – three out of conflict within the Methodist Church, and the fourth, the Standard Church of America, out of conflict within the Holiness Movement Church. The events surrounding these crises have received most of the scholarly attention given to the holiness movement.[4] The public grounds of contention are important, but these were not just conflicts at the denominational level. Members of Methodist congregations made supporters of some holiness beliefs feel unwelcome. In turn, these holiness people found the mainstream church seriously wanting and felt better nourished in groups that emphasized sanctification. The conflicts regarding holiness signalled a crisis in Methodism and evangelicalism in Canada. To understand it, we must not focus only on charges and judgments – we must try to hear the voice of those who took to the boats, as well as that of those who stayed on board the larger vessel.[5]

The histories of each of the holiness groups in Canada present an opportunity to examine briefly some larger themes. Burns and another member of the Canada Holiness Association, Albert Truax, were removed from the Methodist ministry because of their doctrinal views, but the formation of the association raised issues about Methodist attitudes toward "excessive emotionalism" and "sectarianism." Although Horner was deposed from the Methodist ministry on disciplinary grounds, his ministry challenged acceptable practice in Methodist worship. Goff was a lay evangelist when he organized the Gospel Workers. He was not forced out of the Methodist Church but chose to organize a new group. This raises the question of come-outism: why did a separate organization seem necessary? Finally, a study of the Standard Church of America suggests problems concerning leadership, for leadership was the basic issue in that rift. Yet such difficulties were not confined to that denominational split, for there were problems in the leadership of all three founders, Horner, Goff, and the earliest of these men, Burns.

Nelson Burns was born 22 March 1834 in Niagara and was ordained in 1866. He spent only a brief time on the circuit lists of the church and soon returned to teaching. In 1878 he was granted his request for supernumerary status. As a boy of about fourteen, Burns had read Phoebe Palmer and secured the "blessing of holiness."[6] In the "unfavourable conditions" of his congregation he had failed to retain the blessing, but as a young preacher he again obtained sanctification. He became known as a holiness preacher, and also as a "circuit smasher" because of the disruption provoked by his emphasis on holiness.[7]

Burns and others formed an association that held its founding meeting on 30 December 1879.[8] Almost immediately, John Carroll wrote a letter to the *Christian Guardian* expressing concern, an opinion that was to be echoed by many others. He affirmed Methodist commitment to the aim of John Wesley "to spread Scriptural holiness over the earth," but it should be part of the everyday life of all sincere Christians. Carroll warned against those who "make a specialty of it" and "talk by the hour to a very small coterie of *illuminati* who pique themselves on a terminology peculiar to themselves."[9] He continued, "If we turn attention to the special, let us not forget the ordinary."

This was a general anxiety about the holiness specialty. Soon, however, Burns elicited a more specific concern. He developed a strong theory of divine guidance – a form of Gnosticism – asserting that a Christian accepting God's absolute guidance could make no regrettable mistakes. Following the 1889 appearance of his book *Divine Guidance or The Holy Guest*, criticism of Burns's theories increased. The concerns became charges, and at the 1894 meeting of the Guelph Conference, Burns was deposed from the ministry.[10]

He continued to lead the Canada Holiness Association and to edit its paper, the *Expositor of Holiness*. The association's membership was largely from a Methodist background, but those of other denominations attended the conventions and camp meetings that it organized.[11] The meetings emphasized personal testimony as opposed to preaching. As Burns's associate Albert Truax expressed it, "It were far better to empty all the pulpits than to close the mouths of the witnesses in the pews." Truax also observed, "another peculiarity of the Association is its absolute indifference to membership ... All that is wanted is just enough members to elect officers to barely hold the organization together. Beyond that the less machinery the better."[12] No doubt principle was involved, but perhaps Truax also made virtue out of necessity. At first Burns had a cordial relationship with holiness advocates in the United States, but as he developed extreme views on divine guidance, their favour turned to strong disapproval. The Canada Holiness Association had felt affinity with the Salvation Army and the Christian Alliance, but Burns became increasingly opposed to these and to all other forms of what he regarded as legalistic Christianity. As alienation from former allies increased, there was a change in the platform that appeared on the back cover of the *Expositor*: by February of 1893, the phrase "Avoiding Needless Controversy which Engenders Strife" had disappeared.

Those who remained members through the "sifting times" of the trials of Burns and Truax[13] continued to hold meetings and conventions. Burns died in 1904, and Truax became president. The following year the First Church of the Christian Association opened in Toronto, and later minutes of the Association noted that members in Grand Prairie were planning to build a church.[14] A convention in 1921 is the last meeting recorded in the minute book. There the organization decided to "investigate the question of obtaining the right of marrying."[15]

What began as a group of people interested in "upholding the doctrine and the extension of the experience of Entire Sanctification"[16] had become a religious body seeking institutional authority. In 1892 Burns had observed that "this movement could not take the form of a denomination after the pattern of other sects without ceasing altogether to be the spiritual movement it now is."[17] Although the group moved toward denominational identity, perhaps its awareness of being a "spiritual movement" helped to prevent it from making a complete, successful transition to that state. Yet, cut off in 1894 from the Methodist Church, it could no longer bring the holiness specialty to most Methodists, and so it failed to develop a clearly defined role.

Nelson Burns wrote of his "constitutional diffidence."[18] This was a phrase that no one would apply to Ralph Horner, and the movement associated with Horner's name is very different from the Canada Holiness Association. Horner was born in 1854 near Shawville, Quebec, and was converted in 1872. About two months later, at a camp meeting, he learned that a second work of grace was possible. He wrote, "It was not more than five minutes from the time that I heard of my privilege until I was entirely sanctified." He was "melted, molded, refined, and enflamed with holy, consuming love."[19] Very soon after his conversion, Horner began to conduct services and lead prayer meetings, and in 1882 he was received on trial for the Methodist ministry. After studying at Victoria College and at a school of oratory in Philadelphia, he was at last ready for ordination.

There was a problem, however. Horner maintained that God had called him to evangelism and that he had always been clear about this in his dealings with the Methodist Church. But that body had no special form of ordination for evangelism, and the Montreal Conference expected him to submit to its jurisdiction. He finally agreed to "reverently obey" his chief ministers after he felt assured that the conference would give him evangelistic work even though it could not ordain him for it. And so, on 29 May 1887, he was ordained.

Horner spent the next three years in evangelism, and in 1890 when he was assigned to a circuit, he arranged for the work there to be done while he continued to conduct revivals. In 1891 he was once more designated for evangelistic work, but controversy continued, and in 1894 the "Horner case" came before Montreal Conference. After much discussion, he was placed in the hands of the stationing committee, which once more assigned him to a circuit. He refused to go, was suspended, and the following year was deposed from the Methodist ministry.

Unlike Burns, Horner was not condemned for doctrinal irregularities. His was clearly a breach of church discipline as he defied ecclesiastical authority. Yet behind this concern for the maintenance of discipline lay something more. Reports of Horner's revival activity had disturbed many Methodists. This was not simply revivalism with a holiness specialty: this was holiness revivalism at which physical "manifestations" were frequently present. Horner himself had long experienced prostration from time to time during his private devotions,[20] and in the "cyclones of power" that often occurred during the revival services he led, others also experienced prostration and other phenomena.[21]

In his autobiography, Horner was the star. He made only a passing reference to a few weeks he spent "drilling a class of evangelists,"[22] but there were others, women and men, who came to be associated with this holiness evangelism. Horner was under the jurisdiction of conference although he might defy its authority, but these lay evangelists were not subject to such control, and the church expressed its concern to "guard the Church from being injured by unqualified persons or those whose views or methods are likely to be the cause of injury to our work."[23] Thus, as a cautionary measure, the Montreal Conference decided in 1893 to grant licences to evangelists.

To obtain licences, applicants had to answer a number of questions. They were asked about their theology and their loyalty to the church and its ministry. These questions reflect the church's general concern, but the remaining ones indicate a more specific interest. Evangelists had to state their views on prostration, on "permitting several persons to pray or speak at the same time," and on "professedly uncontrollable laughter." The surviving correspondence indicates how determined the Methodists in power were to protect the church from such disorder.[24]

A number of letters and editorials in the *Christian Guardian* also expressed this concern. In August of the following year, 1894, an editorial appeared under the title "Noisy disorder in worship is no evidence of holiness," and it was followed two months later by another, "Disorder in Religious Services."[25] In the second of these the editor stated that it was possible to have "full consecration ... without physical demonstration; and ... noisy display without religious principle." He acknowledged that there had been "remarkable physical prostrations in the past in connection with great revivals" but argued that such events were no guarantee of divine activity.

This is how the Methodists in power saw the threat of Horner and his pupils. There was no room in their respectable church for such "disorderly performances."[26] And so the Methodist church was unwilling to accommodate the desire of Ralph Horner for a special status as evangelist. He, of course, was equally unwilling to accommodate to the demands of his denomination, and so his name was removed from the list of Methodist ministers.

By the time he was no longer a Methodist minister, Horner had followers. One complaint raised against him at the 1895 Montreal Conference was that he had "form[ed] another Society, and sent out laborers into the fields occupied by our Ministers, who solicited members to leave the Methodist Church, and unite with his organization."[27] What he now needed was ministerial status, and this he obtained through the Wesleyan Methodist Connection in New York.[28]

Horner opened a Bible college and edited a newspaper, *The Holiness Era*, which reported the progress of the group that was forming. In 1896 he and his supporters attempted to incorporate as the Wesleyan Methodist Connection of Canada. But opposition by the Methodist Church to the "Horner Bill" was strong and effective, and the Hornerites selected another name, the Holiness Movement Church in Canada.[29] Its incorporation was approved in 1902.

At its first general conference in 1899, the church built on its work at earlier special meetings to lay out procedures and regulations. It gave consideration to sabbath schools, rules for singing, the licensing of local preachers, the receiving of plate collections, and the proper dress of preachers; clearly its members had learned from the Methodist Church how to organize.[30]

Concern with plain dress was characteristic of the holiness movement. Earlier, Nelson Burns had resisted pressure in the Canada Holiness Association for such a requirement; for him it was a legalistic denial of the Spirit's guidance. The Holiness Movement Church's records include, however, regulations concerning the apparel of preachers and lady evangelists, and discussions of appropriate dress for members. Their discipline required "wearing no gold, feathers, flowers, lace, costly or showy silks, or showy colors, regulating and not following the fashions."[31] The "stripping room" where people removed their gold and ornaments was one of the features of Horner's revivals. Holiness Movement regulations also prohibited alcoholic drinks and tobacco, worldly amusements, membership in secret societies, and the purchase of life insurance; members were expected to tithe. Those earnestly seeking after holiness, and those who had received it, were expected to demonstrate holiness in their daily lives.

Hornerites held another distinctive belief. Horner wrote that he had received a "baptism of the Holy Ghost and fire" which was an "extra gift for soul winning."[32] Although this belief was shared with some radical groups in the United States,[33] it was not common in the Methodist holiness tradition. To the Holiness Movement Church, however, this third gift was an empowering experience. The workers held an annual Feast of Pentecost and testified to "the flaming crown of fire" and the power to preach which they received.[34]

Another characteristic of the church was its foreign mission emphasis. Particularly active was the Egyptian work which began in 1899. The church that developed there became one of the conferences of the Holiness Movement Church, along with the Manitoba Conference, and the

Ottawa Conference which had most of its membership in eastern Ontario but also a small amount in Quebec and in New York State.

It is within this eastern Ontario area, near Gananoque, that Frank Goff was born in 1873. As a young man he experienced sanctification under the ministry of two lady evangelists associated with Horner, and then he undertook evangelistic work. In 1898 he felt called to the Meaford area of Grey County. There he gathered a group of converts, some of whom received the further experiences of sanctification and baptism of the Holy Spirit. Goff followed Horner in preaching three works of grace, and, also like Horner, he did not discourage manifestations during revivals.

Although Goff's workers were predominantly of Methodist background, a varied group might attend their services. In July 1902 Albert Mills, one of Goff's followers, wrote in his diary, "The people were almost equally divided as to denomination, Baptist, Methodist and Presbyterian, most of whom came in with us, which we hope will bring about more of a oneness amongst all."[35] Mills saw this work as a renewal, quickening people in the existing churches.

Yet two months later Goff and his workers decided to form a separate organization with its own congregations. Goff was not a Methodist minister, and hence, unlike Horner and Burns before him, could not be removed from the ministry. Apparently he did not even cause a stir in the official circles of the Methodist Church, although there was tension at the local level.[36] Unlike the Holiness Movement Church, the Gospel Workers Church was not formed out of necessity but by choice. Thus it is instructive to look for indications of why they chose to become a denomination.

Mills lamented "the coldness and formality that had crept into the church."[37] He also decried its worldliness, which indicated that it had fallen away from its true calling. After attending a "magic-lantern" lecture given by a Methodist minister, he wrote, "Does the Lord allow his servants whom he has called to preach the Gospel to perishing souls to go about the country with such fandangoes?"[38] He rejoiced at the way his associates paid off debts: "No church fairs, fowl suppers or other ungodly fundraisers," and early in 1904 he referred to "the barrenness and rottenness of the Methodist church."[39] Methodists might believe that they were upholding the Wesleyan tradition of scriptural holiness; these advocates of holiness considered this a false claim.

Goff and his colleagues were concerned for the care of their converts. On the eve of the meeting at which the workers decided to organize, Mills wrote, "Many are beginning to see the need of uniting so that they may receive proper teaching and instruction. This must take place in the near future." The day after the meeting he observed that they had only acted under necessity: "It has been proven over and over again that when people though they may have been well blest go into the ordinary churches, the deadly leaven of coldness and spiritual lukewarmness eats like a canker into the tender heart of the newly converted souls and ere long the whole lump is leavened."[40]

And so in September of 1902 the Gospel Workers organized. They ordained first Goff and then other men to their ministry. The group developed a discipline based on that of the Holiness Movement Church. Gradually they acquired other signs of denominational status, publishing a paper, the *Holiness Worker*, and obtaining a campground. Although they were too small an organization to develop a Bible college, they instituted a course of study for their workers.

In personal conduct they were similar to the Holiness Movement Church, opposing life insurance, for example, and adopting plain dress. "I change my watch case with a gold deer on the back," Mills wrote, "for a plain nickel case and get a fountain pen on balance."[41] In addition, they actively opposed the liquor traffic, and, with the rise of the pentecostal movement, Goff, unlike Horner, took a clear stand against speaking in tongues.

The group was not large enough to support its own mission program. Only in 1949 did it send a woman worker to Japan. Until then, it encouraged contributions which it passed on, principally to the Holiness Movement's Egyptian mission. After its early brief period of expansion, the Gospel Workers Church did not increase further in size. Up until the 1950s, it survived as a regional embodiment of the Canadian holiness movement.

Meanwhile, change had come to the Holiness Movement Church. The independence of spirit that had brought Horner into conflict with the Methodist Church continued to exert itself and gave rise to a split. The formation of the Standard Church of America has received little attention, probably because it lacked a substantive issue of theology or practice like those that had caused the earlier divisions.[42] It is impossible now to draw a full picture of the schism; the relevant minutes survive, but parts of the discussion were expunged, and the remainder leaves many questions unanswered. Nevertheless, the general outlines are discernable.

As early as 1913 all was not well, for at the May 1914 meeting of the General Conference Special Committee, Horner resigned to protest an occurrence the year before. He was then permitted to "withdraw his withdrawal," with the understanding that the next General Conference would consider making him life honorary bishop, and ordain a younger man as bishop.[43] At that next meeting in December 1914, the General Conference opened intending "to bring about a state of peace amongst us."⁴⁴ This turned out to be no easy matter. Horner remained bishop, with A.T. Warren appointed as his assistant.

The 1915 meeting of Ottawa Conference was filled with conflict, although it too attempted to "discuss ways and means of promoting and bringing unity in the work of God." The proposed method was to divide the territory, so that "certain territories in the Ottawa Conference not in favor of the administration of the present Bishop be set apart to be presided over by presiding officers acceptable to the Districts over which they are placed."⁴⁵ This proposal was defeated.

When the Ottawa Conference met the following year, there was a definite indication that it was not simply business as usual. There were an extraordinary number of questions and conflicts in what were normally routine matters, namely the examination of ministerial characters and preparation of the conference roll for the following year. This was followed by appeals which were acted on at the General Conference later in that year. When it came time at the General Conference to examine the character of the bishop, Horner left, and a list of objections was considered in his absence. On 22 December 1916 the group discussed a lengthy motion which ultimately declared that "the said Rev. R.C. Horner by such improper conduct has forfeited his right to retain among us the office of Bishop and that he be hereby declared to be no longer a Bishop or Leader in the Holiness Movement Church and that he henceforth cease to exercise the functions of such office."⁴⁶ The motion was carried with 33 yeas and 20 nays.

But the matter was not ended. In May 1917 the General Conference Special Committee convened in Ottawa and attempted to negotiate with Horner. He had not handed over various properties of the church, and by now he was publishing a rival paper, the *Christian Standard*, in which he had called a meeting of the Ottawa Conference Special Committee and Annual Meeting to begin the following week in Stittsville. Negotiators went back and forth attempting to heal the rift, though at the same time the General Conference committee sought the advice of a lawyer. Horner's group declared the actions of the previous General Conference illegal, and no settlement was effected.

The Ottawa Conference minute book bears mute testimony to the conflict. It includes the minutes of the Stittsville meeting, and of an Ottawa Conference meeting called by Horner and held in Kingston that November. In the eyes of those attending them, these were meetings of the Holiness Movement Church. Then the book was returned to the other branch of that body. In 1918 the Ottawa Conference declared "the roll formed by the Journal secretary for the conference of 1917 irregular and wrong" and ordered a new roll formed based on the names of the 1916 conference. That roll noted many names "withdrawn," "irregularly withdrawn," or "dropped," but it also listed some new names.[47] Its body was irrevocably divided, but the Holiness Movement Church would continue.

Horner, of course, had already weathered many storms, and even in old age he would not be defeated. And so the *Christian Standard* reported, "The first session of the Kingston Annual Conference of the Standard Church of America met at Stittsville, Ont., Aug. 26th, 1918 ... The Conference opened with our dearly beloved Bishop R.C. Horner in the chair ... There were thirty-nine who had their characters passed and their names enrolled as Conference members. A number also passed examination and received work under official authority. Melting waves of Divine Glory came over our souls as we listened to the Brethren and Sisters give their Christian experiences."[48]

The new denomination already had a periodical. It opened a Bible college and a book room in the fall of 1918, and that December it dedicated its first new church. In 1919 the Standard Church of America was incorporated in New York State, where it had some work, and in 1920 it received its Canadian charter. Even before its first annual conference the group had held its first camp meeting in Alberta.[49] Eventually the church comprised four conferences: Western, Kingston, New York, and Egyptian.

Ralph Horner died in September 1921. His church continued to hold camp meetings and holiness conventions to lead people into the experience of sanctification, and, like the Holiness Movement Church, it supported a strong mission program. It sent its first missionary to Egypt in 1919 and soon had work in China as well. Although in North America it remained a small denomination, its missionary activity gave the Standard Church of America a distinct identity.

Horner's role in the division of the holiness movement is not only evidence of his own autocratic leadership style. It is an example of the problems of leadership that plagued each branch of the movement. The Gospel Workers minutes for a special session of conference two weeks after the annual meeting of 1926 record an incident that differed only in degree from several others. Frank Goff complained of criticism and lack of appreciation, and the group responded by passing "a hearty vote of thanks for his efforts and sacrificing labors."[50] Nelson Burns stated that at first he prayed requesting "the privilege of utterly refusing any office in the Association," but he, too, appeared possessive about his leadership, and acutely conscious of when it was in jeopardy.[51] It took a stubborn strength for each of these leaders to persist in the face of the hostility which they saw in the world around them. Perhaps the reverse side of this necessary characteristic was an excessive need for the loyalty and expressed support of those whom they considered friends and allies.

The history of the holiness movement in Canada had to this point been filled with conflict and division, but that is not the end of the story. In 1920 a motion was made at the Ottawa Conference of the Holiness Movement Church that delegates be appointed to an interdenominational holiness meeting. But when it met with opposition, the mover withdrew the motion because he wished to avoid the impression that might be made by its defeat.[52] Two years later, however, after the death of Horner, the Holiness Movement Church was attempting to "bring about a better relationship" between themselves and the Standard Church, and in 1924 they invited the Gospel Workers to send a delegation.[53] And late in 1925, the General Conference appointed a Fraternal Relations Committee "to meet a like committee of other holiness churches ... with a view of considering a closer and better relationship among the holiness churches."[54] The Gospel Workers showed a similar interest. The *Holiness Worker* carried reports of interdenominational holiness conventions, and in December 1925 the workers appointed a committee "to meet the committee of the Holiness Movement Church or other bodies to discuss a closer relationship or any other subject necessary to be considered."[55] Apparently interest ebbed, but the 1950s saw a renewal of activity. Talk of church union was in the air at home and abroad. In Canada the Free Methodist Church and the Wesleyan Methodists were holding conversations. And the Gospel Workers and Holiness Movement churches recognized that something needed to be done.

In the Holiness Movement Church, W.J. Stonehouse had been elected superintendent of the Ottawa Conference, and he noticed the statistics of the church: in Canada it had just over 800 members. As Stonehouse later remarked in an interview, "That just hit me like a brick."[56] He saw in that one figure the explanation for the group's problems supporting its mission program, its publication, and its Bible college, and so he encouraged merger.

Stonehouse felt that the Holiness Movement Church had most in common with the Free Methodists. The church leaders were not unanimous, however. At a meeting of the Ottawa Conference in 1953, ballots were cast to express preference, with fourteen for the Free Methodists, four each for the Standard Church and the Wesleyan Methodists, and one for the Nazarenes.[57] For several years there was an exchange of fraternal delegates among denominations. There was also informal contact as members of the several holiness groups participated together in meetings of the Canadian Holiness Federation which, according to one speaker there, "promoted more love toward those of other holiness denominations" so that they "no longer judge the denomination by the idiosyncrasies of some eccentric member of the group."[58]

A ballot at the 1957 Holiness Movement General Conference showed the Free Methodists again the clear preference with twenty-three votes, while the Standard Church gained eleven, the Nazarenes two, and the Wesleyan Methodists none. The negotiating committee continued its work, and on 1 January 1959 the merger of the Holiness Movement Church with the Free Methodist Church was accomplished, although a small number of the congregations chose to remain as "Independent" churches.

The Gospel Workers were a smaller group to begin with, and they suffered a more noteworthy decline. As their first-generation leaders left the ministry, the group was not able to replace them from within its own ranks. At one point it asked the Holiness Movement Church for help; later it received Nazarene ministers.[59] Early in the 1950s, the Workers considered amalgamation with the Free Methodist Church, and a small number of congregations did join that group, but ultimately the church of choice was the Nazarenes. It was a remnant of the small denomination that finally entered the union: at its last meeting there were five members of conference who were ministers (three men and two women), seven lay delegates, and five ministers from other denominations who were serving Gospel Workers charges.

Only the Standard Church of America remained – with a few hundred members and adherents. The other denominations that had originated in conflict with the Methodist Church of Canada had merged with holiness groups that by the 1950s were well established in Canada but had their roots in the United States.

There were changes of other kinds. In an article on the holiness movement Malcolm Greenshields described a 1989 visit to a Free Methodist campground.[60] Although there was holiness preaching, Greenshields suspected that many of those in attendance would have been bewildered by questions about sanctification. No longer was this a people of plain, modest dress and simple possessions; their bathing attire and motor homes were indistinguishable from those in other holiday settings. Camp meetings had become "retreats for the regenerate ... Bourgeoisification had set in."[61]

To the people of the holiness tradition a century earlier, it seemed that the Methodist Church had betrayed its heritage. They saw evidence of this in the worldliness of the church and in its rejection of the full activity of the Spirit. For the Canada Holiness Association, this rejection was seen in the dismissal of the guidance of the Holy Ghost and in the resulting legalism; for others, it appeared in formalism in worship with concomitant fear of emotion and physical manifestations. The holiness people wanted to reform Methodism, to make it true to their understanding of its Wesleyan origin. For all, this entailed a strong holiness "specialty." For those in the tradition of Horner, it meant living according to regulations that separated the holiness people from the worldly. But in the process of their revolt, they became associations, congregations, and denominations. The early excitement was replaced by institutional preoccupations, and their lively commitment to be a holy people proved difficult to maintain.

Albert Mills finally became president of the small denomination he had served so long. When he addressed the tiny group in 1954, he was no longer a young man condemning "the barrenness and rottenness of the Methodist church" and rejoicing in the Gospel Workers' mission as a lifeboat. He was an old man, painfully aware of his denomination's failures. He lamented, "Had *we* [ministers and laity] walked in God's full light things would be very different to-day."[62] The words suggest that his holiness church, like many individuals who had been reached by holiness preaching over the years, had "failed to retain the blessing."

17 Towards a Fourfold Gospel: A.B. Simpson, John Salmon, and the Christian and Missionary Alliance in Canada

DARREL R. REID

Except for those touched in some way by A.B. Simpson's writings or by the mission of the Christian and Missionary Alliance (CMA), few Americans or Canadians in the late twentieth century have either heard of or recognize their contributions to evangelical Christianity at all. Yet Simpson and the Alliance were prominent players in the world of late nineteenth-century revivalist evangelicalism. For those in the United States and Canada who joined the movement, the Alliance was a gathering of believers from all and no denominations to proclaim and celebrate Jesus Christ as "Saviour, Sanctifier, Healer and Coming King." Despite its relatively small size, the CMA has a continuing presence in the evangelical world, both through its energetic missionary program and through the influence it has had upon other religious traditions.[1]

A.B. SIMPSON AND THE CMA

Albert Benjamin Simpson was born on 15 December 1843, the fourth child of James and Janet Simpson, in Bayview, Prince Edward Island, where his father was in charge of the timbering and shipbuilding component in a network of family enterprises. When an Empire-wide depression struck the colony in 1847, his father sold the business and relocated the family to Chatham in Canada West (present-day Ontario).

His parents were devout United (Secessionist) Presbyterians and, according to Simpson's autobiographical account, the young man's spiritual formation was carefully regulated by his father, a disciplinarian and strict sabbatarian. Simpson was also exposed to the broader manifestations of evangelical culture sweeping the transatlantic world, the most significant of which was the impulse to foreign missions. For Albert's family there was a personal stake in missions; for several years they had sat under the ministry of Rev. James Geddie, later Canada's missionary pioneer to the New Hebrides Islands, and had caught his vision for reaching "the world for Christ."[2] At the age of nine Albert was deeply moved by reading a biography of the Rev. John Williams, martyr missionary of Erromanga, and by fourteen he had decided that God was calling him to be a minister.

By all accounts Simpson possessed a nature keenly aware of the Almighty and of God's requirements of fallen humanity, both of which were magnified by his vivid imagination. Deeply preoccupied with his acceptability to God, the intense young man's spiritual journey was tortuous and marked by emotional turmoil, a nervous breakdown, and a fervent but ultimately successful search for the New Birth. This process was precipitated by a series of events early in the fall of 1858 when, as a boarding student at Chatham Grammar School, he narrowly escaped drowning in an incident along the Thames River. Simpson found himself on the edge of eternity without assurance of his salvation. Hardly had he recovered from this experience when its effect was magnified by his exposure to the fiery revivalistic preaching of the Englishman Henry Grattan Guinness, who was passing through Chatham.[3]

Guinness brought a message unlike anything the young Simpson had ever heard. His words pierced deeply into Albert's conscience, and he was cast into a state of deep conviction. He returned to his boarding house in a state of near-emotional collapse. Later that night, according to Simpson's account, "there came a fearful crash, in which it seemed to me the very heavens were falling. After retiring to my bed I suddenly seemed to see a strange light blazing before my eyes and then my nerves gave way and I sprang from my bed, trembling and almost fainting, and immediately fell into a congestive chill of great violence that almost took my life."[4]

This shattering experience forced Simpson to leave school the next day and return home to his family's farm. His physician diagnosed his condition as a total collapse of the nervous system and ordered him to stay away from books for a year. This traumatic psychological collapse coincided with a ten-month period of mental and physical agony during which Albert dreaded dying in an unregenerate state. At length his despair was relieved. After reading Walter Marshall's *The Gospel Mystery of Sanctification*, he at last understood that Christ's gospel was for him personally. Falling upon his knees and looking up to heaven, he was able to declare "Abba Father, Thou are mine, and I am Thine."[5]

After a year of recuperation Simpson entered Knox College, Toronto, to study for the ministry of the Canada Presbyterian Church (CPC). He arrived at a particularly significant time, for by the fall of 1861 Knox was poised at the threshold of what has been termed the golden age of religious education in Canada.[6] During his studies Simpson encountered in distilled form the committed, confident, outward-looking evangelicalism of Canadian Secessionist-Free Church Presbyterianism.

In college he proved to be an exceptional scholar.[7] As well, through the heavy supply preaching expected of Knox theological students, he earned a reputation as a gifted orator. This reputation was confirmed upon his graduation in 1865 at the age of twenty-one when he accepted a call to be pastor of Knox's Church, Hamilton, one of the larger and more influential churches in the Canada Presbyterian Church.[8]

Between 1865 and 1873 Simpson made a considerable mark on the life of Knox's Church, in the process greatly enhancing his ministerial reputation. He was, without question, widely perceived as a minister of exceptional talents, and a churchman with a broad vision for evangelism and social activism centred upon the ministry of the local church. In Knox's Church he had found a congregation eager to follow him. The ambitious young minister also began to make a name for himself within the courts of the Canada Presbyterian Church.[9]

Despite his apparent success, however, he was becoming increasingly restless in his own life and ministry. This was due both to family turmoil and what has been described as an "expectational gap" between the idealism and the more prosaic reality of actual ministry. In response, he became increasingly involved in new interdenominational evangelical organizations, particularly the YMCA and Evangelical Alliance.

Simpson's attendance at the Evangelical Alliance's 1873 New York conference was a turning point in his life and ministry. Certainly the Alliance's ideal of worldwide evangelical cooperation touched him deeply, as it did many other of his Presbyterian contemporaries. But for Simpson it had the additional effect of redirecting his hopes for the renovation of the institutional church towards worldwide evangelical ecumenism. Surely, he contended, the cooperation of the world's Protestant churches would usher in a new spirit of evangelism, activism, and service. His attendance at the conference also changed his life in a more practical way. While in New York, he preached at the prestigious Thirteenth Street Presbyterian Church, where he impressed a visiting delegation from Louisville, Kentucky, who happened to be seeking a minister. Their ensuing call to him proved successful, and he left Canada for the United States in December 1873.

During his six-year pastorate at Chestnut Street Presbyterian Church (1874–1879), Simpson presided over a period of significant growth and evangelistic outreach – but also of revivalistic upheaval and political turmoil. His Louisville ministry saw a radical transition in his own life and ministry as well, for it was during these years that he encountered many of the "forward movements" of late-nineteenth-century evangelicalism. Soon after his arrival in Louisville in 1874, according to his account, his restless personal search for holiness ended when he experienced the "second conversion" of sanctification. The catalyst for this was William Boardman's *The Higher Christian Life*, which appealed to Simpson's prophetic expectancy and idealism, and connected the sanctification experience with the broader movement of the Holy Spirit in the last days – the "Latter Rains" of the Holy Spirit.

A second powerful influence was a revival conducted by D.W. Whittle and P.P. Bliss in 1874,[10] in which Simpson played a major role. It would be hard to overestimate the impact of the revival upon Louisville. During the campaign, meetings were jammed with thousands of people from all and no denominational backgrounds, and for nearly eight weeks Louisville virtually ground to a halt. Thousands of conversions were reported. If, as leading holiness advocate Robert Pearsall Smith asserted at one Louisville meeting, the revival was evidence of "a great tidal wave of religion sweeping over all parts of the country and accomplishing wonders,"[11] then Simpson was determined to ride it. For him this increasingly meant moving towards non-denominational evangelistic ministries typified by Moody, Whittle, and Bliss which, in turn, were energized by growing holiness, restorationist, and premillennial thought.

The revival's success convinced Simpson that bold and innovative means were needed if the Christian church was to meet the challenges of the late nineteenth century. What he envisioned was a new form of ministry that combined the outreach of urban evangelism with the spiritual nurture and community of the institutional church. Over the next four years he launched a number of bold evangelistic crusades and built a new church structure – the Broadway Tabernacle Presbyterian Church – that was meant to anchor a new movement "born of the Holy Ghost" with aggressive evangelism as its central aim. Simpson's dramatic spiritual journey, however, was followed only from afar by the leadership of his church; his innovations, rather than revolutionizing the Christian church, brought him instead increased strife with his session, and another nervous breakdown during the summer and fall of 1877. After three years of rising tensions and political turmoil in Chestnut Street Presbyterian Church, Simpson concluded that his hopes would not be accomplished in Louisville.

In 1879, feeling drawn towards new conceptions of ministry, he resigned to assume the pastorate of Thirteenth Street Presbyterian Church, New York. There, in addition to caring for his large flock, he produced *The Gospel in All Lands*, a highly regarded illustrated missionary periodical that promoted interdenominational cooperation in the cause of foreign missions, which he saw as crucial to the church's mandate in the Last Days. Despite his frenetic activities, however, Simpson was growing increasingly dissatisfied with the ministries of a large denominational church. And despite some significant successes, his personal and spiritual life was in turmoil. His decision to leave Louisville, apparently taken without consulting his wife, prompted a period of bitter family strife which extended over the next three years and only abated well after he had left the Presbyterian Church in 1881.

It was during this period of emotional and physical anguish that Simpson encountered and embraced the concept of divine healing. Attending a conference at Old Orchard Beach, Maine, he heard a great number of people testify that they had been healed "by simply trusting the Word of Christ, just as they would for their salvation." These testimonies drove him to undertake an intense personal search of the Scriptures on the subject, during which he satisfied himself that divine healing was part of Christ's "glorious gospel" for him. Convinced of this, one Friday afternoon he went to a pine woods, knelt, and pledged his belief in the doctrine of divine healing and his willingness to use it for God's glory. When he arose he "knew that something was done. Every fibre of my soul was tingling with a sense of God's presence. I do not know whether my body felt better or not – I did not care to feel it – it was so glorious to believe it simply, and to know that henceforth He had it in hand."[12] While this experience was followed by numerous tests of his faith, Simpson saw that day as the beginning of his life as a divinely healed person. From then on, according to his testimony, he felt supernaturally enabled to carry on the tremendous responsibilities which before had nearly crushed him.

Later in 1881 Simpson became convinced that baptism by immersion was the only scriptural mode and, choosing to follow his convictions, was himself baptized by the pastor of a small Italian Baptist congregation. This event precipitated his departure from the Presbyterian Church. No longer willing to perform infant baptisms, Simpson decided to resign from the pastorate of Thirteenth Street Presbyterian Church and begin an independent ministry, his heart having been "drawn to a wider field of mission work among the masses of non-church people than he as pastor of a particular church could perform."[13] He had become completely convinced that his vision for urban evangelism and foreign missions could not be accommodated within the walls of a single church.

In 1882 Simpson began a small fellowship which rapidly grew into a thriving, evangelistically minded church called the Gospel Tabernacle, a

"Free Gospel Church" based upon the "Scriptural and voluntary principles [of] evangelistic and missionary work among the neglected and non-church-going population."[14] Taking this needy urban group as its parish, the fellowship spread rapidly into numerous areas of evangelistic and social outreach among the poor of New York.

Underscoring Simpson's ministry was his distinctive doctrinal formulation known as "the Four-Fold Gospel": Jesus as Saviour, Sanctifier, Healer, and Coming King. Little was new or distinctive about the first and last of these "folds." Along with most of his evangelical contemporaries, he believed that all who repented and believed through the atonement of Christ and the work of the Holy Spirit would be saved. Reflecting his new-found premillennialism, he saw Christ's premillennial coming as the great hope of the church and the goal of all its Christian work.[15] The inner two "folds" – Sanctifier and Healer – were of special significance to Simpson, however. He held that sanctification was not a slow, gradual process but a second work of grace, received by faith, in which Christ himself was implanted instantaneously in the believer, enabling him or her to rise to a new and higher plane of spiritual power and effectiveness. Simpson's view of sanctification was semi-mystical, in that Jesus immersed the believer in the Holy Spirit. Above all, Simpson emphasized the in-dwelling Christ in the believer as the motive power for life, peace, and power in ministry. But the most distinctive and controversial of his teachings was his doctrine of divine healing, which he maintained was one of the benefits of Christ's atonement for humanity. It was Simpson's preaching and practice of divine healing that gave him and his movement fame and notoriety during the 1880s.

In 1883 Simpson's congregation founded the Missionary Union for the Evangelization of the World and established the Missionary Training Institute – among the first of a wave of North American Bible institutes – to train workers for foreign missions. Simpson had a flair for publicity and advanced his movement with a series of conventions which were attended by thousands, and which featured high-profile speakers from different denominations.[16] From then until the present conventions have played an essential part in Alliance worship, missions, fundraising, and expansion.

Four years later in 1887, encouraged by the great enthusiasm of his followers, Simpson oversaw the birth of two new organizations: the Christian Alliance (CA), a non-denominational revival fellowship dedicated to promulgating such "present truths" as complete sanctification in Christ, divine healing, and the premillennial return of Christ; and the Evangelical Missionary Alliance (EMA), an association within the Christian Alliance designed to advance the cause of world missions.[17] Although as originally conceived the EMA was meant to function under the umbrella of the Christian Alliance, over the next ten years foreign missions moved to the forefront and overshadowed the holiness and social activist impulses in Simpson's ministry. A crucial development occurred between 1891 and 1893 when 300 Alliance missionaries were sent to foreign countries under the auspices of the EMA. By 1893, after six years of operation, the Alliance had missionaries working on forty stations in twelve mission fields: Belgian Congo, Sudan, India, China (central, southern and northern), Japan, Bulgaria, Palestine, Alaska, Haiti, and the Dominican Republic.[18] Foreign missions quickly overwhelmed the earlier holiness emphasis within the Alliance organizations. This new reality was recognized in 1897 when the two fellowships were merged to become the Christian and Missionary Alliance. The development would have a significant effect upon the Alliance in Canada, where Canadians were drawn primarily to the Alliance's holiness and healing emphases and less to foreign missions.

The first decade of the twentieth century brought new challenges and trials for Simpson and the CMA. With its rapid growth came doctrinal controversy, which the Alliance, with its fraternal outlook and inclusive doctrinal standards, was particularly ill-equipped to handle. The most significant challenge, from the nascent Pentecostal movement, was particularly painful for Simpson, who had seen himself and his movement as being on the leading edge of the "forward movements" of the End Days. Now, however, the Alliance were being accused of obstructing a new work of the Spirit. The conflict sent shock waves throughout the Alliance, amid charges that the Pentecostal testimony was being stifled by Alliance leadership (including Simpson), a number of prominent leaders and Alliance branches left the organization to join the Pentecostals.[19] In response, the Alliance leadership took steps to "clarify" its doctrinal stance and to gain control of properties belonging to affiliated churches. This direction was confirmed at the General Council of 1912, which ratified a new constitution that put the Alliance decisively on the road to denominationalism.

The reorganization also effectively removed a beleaguered Simpson from the front rank of Alliance leadership. Battered and weary, he withdrew from the day-to-day operations of the CMA, retiring to his beloved Missionary Training Institute, where he continued a full schedule of preaching, teaching, and writing until 1918, when health difficulties forced him to withdraw from active ministry. In 1919, after fifty-four years of ministry, Simpson died in Nyack, New York, at the age of seventy-six. At his death he left behind a diverse and expanding movement that had spread across the continent and around the world. Yet it was a very different movement than he had envisioned at the beginning of his independent ministry. Conceiving the Alliance as a fraternal and non-denominational holiness and missions society, he eschewed all trappings of contemporary denominational life: rigorous doctrinal formulation, ecclesiastical machinery, and a competitive "us-them" mentality. He had hoped to avoid these through a spirit of revival and evangelical ecumenism, but three tensions at the heart of the Alliance combined to redefine his organization in ways he was powerless to prevent.

First was the tension between his vision of an interdenominational fraternal fellowship and ongoing denominationalizing tendencies that grew over time and through circumstances. Second, although he originally conceived of the Alliance as a holiness society with a missions outreach, the latter quickly overwhelmed the former and rapidly reoriented the priorities of the entire organization. And finally, although he conceived of it as a flexible fellowship leading the "forward movements" in the Last Days, the Alliance's very successes – particularly in the area of foreign missions – forced upon it much of the machinery necessary for any organization to maintain any institutional existence. This institutional inertia, in turn, limited the Alliance's ability to respond to and absorb new movements such as the Pentecostals. In the years following Simpson's death, a new generation of Alliance leaders resolved these tensions, opting for denominationalism over ecumenism, foreign missions over holiness, and fundamentalism rather than "forward movements." The CMA was on its way to becoming what it is today, for most intents and purposes: a generic evangelical denomination with an emphasis upon foreign missions.

JOHN SALMON AND THE ORIGIN OF THE CMA IN CANADA

Although its roots are sunk deeply into the same pool of holiness thought, the Christian and Missionary Alliance in Canada did not originate with Simpson's organization. The origins of the CMA in Canada can be traced to Rev. John Salmon (1831–1918), who, like Simpson, was a visionary leader, a social activist ministering to the neglected of society, an eager anticipant of the imminent second return of Christ, and a firm believer in the holiness doctrines of sanctification and divine healing. He was also a prickly individualist never completely comfortable within the confines of mainstream Canadian denominational life.

His path to the Fourfold Gospel followed a rather different spiritual trajectory. Born in 1831 and orphaned at age five, he was reared by a devout Presbyterian grandmother. At age fourteen he ran away to sea where he learned the dissolute ways of the sailor. Converted after reading a gospel tract, he left the sea and identified with the Methodist community in Montreal which, seeing promise in the earnest young man, supported his education for the ministry at Victoria College, Cobourg, between 1856 and 1862. Upon graduation Salmon joined the Methodist ministry, serving briefly on the Wilton-Odessa circuit near Kingston before being appointed to the Coaticook-Barnston circuit near Sherbrooke in the Eastern Townships of Quebec. Here he came into contact with the Adventists and their doctrines of premillennialism and believer's baptism by immersion. Intending to refute Adventist doctrines, Salmon earnestly searched the Scriptures but ultimately became convinced that his earlier convictions were unscriptural and the Adventist ones right. Determined to act upon his new-found conviction, he was baptized in 1866 by immersion, after which he tendered his resignation from the Methodist ministry and identified himself with the Adventists. Demonized by the former, he became a "triumph of grace" to the latter.[20] Thereafter followed a stormy two-year Adventist sojourn. In 1868 Salmon broke his association on doctrinal grounds and affiliated himself with the Congregational Union of Ontario and Quebec. In the late 1860s and 1870s he served as a congregational minister in western Ontario where he was also influenced by visiting Plymouth Brethren evangelists. His relationship with Congregationalism was broken for a short while because of a dispute with his Embro congregation over church indebtedness; he resigned on 3 October 1880, and from the Congregational Union three days later.

What prompted this action? Certainly Salmon's tempestuous personality and firmly held convictions played a role. But his move also coincided, as had been the case with Simpson, with his growing attraction to the aggressive urban evangelism of the YMCA. Although Salmon's early contacts remain unclear, it is known that he attended an interprovincial conference of the YMCA at Ingersoll, Ontario, in October 1880, where he heard presentations by Alfred Sandham, secretary of the Toronto YMCA, and William Howland, a future mayor of Toronto. What is clear is that this conference had a profound influence upon him and changed the direction of his ministry. He was quickly drawn into the orbit of a broad, Toronto-centred interdenominational fellowship characterized by urban evangelism, social outreach, and premillennialism.[21]

By 1882 Salmon had returned to the Congregational Church, which he served for the next five years among Toronto's "neglected classes." Yet increasingly, his interests took him along non-denominational paths. A key development in this regard was his involvement in the 1884 founding of the Toronto Mission Union, to "extend the knowledge of the Gospel of our Lord Jesus Christ among the inhabitants of Toronto and its vicinity and especially the poor and neglected classes, without any reference to denominational distinctions or peculiarities of church government."[22] Salmon also became more and more committed to the principle and practice of divine healing. Aware of the controversy his new-found belief in divine healing would spark, he at first muted his teachings on the subject. This changed in 1885 when, afflicted with a disease of the kidneys, he attended one of A.B. Simpson's first healing conventions in Buffalo and met Simpson for the first time. According to Salmon's account, "When the invitation was given to any who desired to be prayed with, I at once took my place with those who went forward. God met me right there while suffering a great deal during the service. I was healed while a number of friends were praying for me, having been anointed with oil, and having the hands of the brethren laid on my head."[23] Rejoicing, he immediately arose and joined the team of Simpson workers, and later gave his testimony to the assembly.

This began a close association with Simpson which lasted the remainder of Salmon's life. Shortly thereafter he left Yorkville Congregational Church and began an independent fellowship, which became the nucleus for the CMA in Canada. Although he had followed a different route, Salmon had found his own way to the Fourfold Gospel: he had a Methodist's commitment to sanctification, an Adventist's belief in the premillennial return of Christ and believer's baptism, a Congregationalist's belief in the autonomy of the local congregation and rejection of ecclesiastical coercion, and a belief in divine healing confirmed in his mind by his own experience.

While Salmon's espousal of divine healing pushed him to the fringe of mainstream religious discourse in Canada, it also placed him at the forefront of the "Deeper Life" movement in Toronto. As with Simpson in New York, Salmon's doctrinal reorientation and his departure from denominational affiliation coincided with an upsurge in his social and evangelistic activity in Toronto. The focus for this activity was Bethany Church, an outgrowth of the faith meetings, which served both as the centre for a broad range of social and evangelistic activity in Toronto and as the spiritual heart of the Alliance in Canada. The most distinctive aspects of Bethany Church were its doctrines of divine healing and the premillennial return of Christ, both to be guarded by the strict independence of the local church.[24] For three decades following its establishment, the activities of Bethany Church grew aggressively, branching into ministries wherever there was a recognized need and someone to fill it. One of Salmon's most significant – though short-lived – initiatives was his establishment in 1893 of the Toronto Missionary Training School (MTS) "to train young people, male and female, for missionary and evangelistic work."[25] Among the earliest of such institutions in North America, the training school was innovative and egalitarian. Non-denominational and charging no tuition fees, it offered students a one-year program of Scripture-based studies. Although the school was well attended in its first year, in the fall of 1894 it faced tough competition from a well-financed competitor, the Toronto Bible School (now Ontario Bible College and Seminary). With deep financial backing and support, the Toronto Bible School quickly drew off most of Missionary Training School students, and the school ceased operations one year later.

Salmon was an enthusiastic supporter of Simpson's ministry, and had been so from his first meeting with Simpson in 1885. Their relationship was formalized in 1887 when Salmon attended the founding conventions of the Christian Alliance and Evangelical Missionary Alliance at Old Orchard, Maine. Salmon was elected a founding vice-president of the Christian Alliance, a position he held until his death thirty-one years later. Salmon and those from his growing healing network were particularly drawn to the Christian Alliance, with its concern to spread the cause of the "Deeper Christian Life" among Christians of all denominations. In 1889 the Dominion Auxiliary of the Christian Alliance was established, a largely self-governing organization which was responsible, among other things, for the dispersion of Canadian funds and resources. The terms of membership were broad enough to be acceptable to many Canadian believers: a declaration in Christ as Saviour, Sanctifier, and Healer. Belief in the premillennial second advent of Christ and baptism by immersion was not considered essential. The establishment of the Dominion Auxiliary was followed in rapid succession by the establishment of local branches in Hamilton, Toronto, and Peterborough.[26]

Although it bore many similarities to its American counterpart, there was much about the Dominion Auxiliary that was self-consciously Canadian – or at any rate non-American. First, as proclaimed prominently in its literature and conventions, the Alliance did not seek to interfere in the work of the denominations. That this message was largely accepted – or at least not actively opposed – by the mainstream Protestant denominations seems proven by their cooperation in providing venues for Canadian Alliance conventions.[27] Second, it seemed propelled by the winds of the spirit at the end of the age. People were drawn by what appeared to be new revelations of the spirit through the "rediscovery" of healing and premillennial truths. It is significant that divine healing proved to be *the* major defining factor of the Canadian Alliance during the early years. In addition to its autonomy, as Alliance historian Lindsay Reynolds has argued persuasively, Canadians who joined the Alliance were drawn to its messages of holiness and healing and believed the Alliance would not compete with other denominations. Foreign missions also received less emphasis in the Canadian Alliance. This, Reynolds argues, was because Canadian Alliance members were confident that this cause had been taken up effectively by their denominations.

During the latter years of the nineteenth century the Canadian Alliance rode a wave of public fascination with divine healing, which for a time became the focal point for the movement in Canada. Among the movement's most prominent personalities were evangelist Maggie Scott, a founding vice-president of the Canadian Auxiliary; John Salmon, whose healing meetings were broadly publicized throughout central Canada; and Mrs Ellen Hatch, a prominent healing advocate and social issues activist.

Doubtless, from the point of view of its members and supporters at the turn of the century, the Christian Alliance in Canada had limitless potential. By the outbreak of World War I, however, the Canadian Alliance was on the verge of disappearing altogether. Its precipitous decline can be attributed to three main factors. First, changing organizational emphases within the larger Alliance organization increasingly undercut the themes that attracted Canadians. This was dramatically illustrated by the 1897 merging of the Christian Alliance and Evangelical Missionary Alliance into the Christian and Missionary Alliance, which signalled the dominance of foreign missions and the eclipse of the holiness stream within the Alliance. As part of the restructuring, the Dominion Auxiliary was absorbed into the new organization and lost its self-governing status. This action caused great alienation within the Canadian Alliance in general and among its leadership in particular. The result, according to Reynolds, was that "the wonderful lay enthusiasm, which had characterized the early Canadian movement, gave way to apathy. A cloud of uncertainty which would not be lifted for several decades hung over the Canadian segment of the Alliance."[28]

Second, to an extent greater than that of their American colleagues, Canadian Alliance members were concerned about denominationalizing tendencies within the Alliance. Its non-denominational status had been one of its principal attractions to Canadians, and evidence to the contrary – ordaining its own ministers, for example – drove members and leaders from the organization. Third, by the outbreak of the First World War, the divine healing movement was in eclipse. This was due primarily to rising public scepticism about the movement's claims, which was driven by media reports of false claims and deaths caused by lack of medical attention.[29] This scepticism was echoed increasingly by church leaders, including several prominent evangelicals. This rising chorus of criticism coincided with a de-emphasis of diving healing teaching within the Alliance in general.

Despite the many indicators of its imminent demise, however, the Christian and Missionary Alliance in Canada did not die. Rather, over the past half century it has established itself as one of Canada's fastest-growing denominations.[30] A major factor in its rebirth has been a reorientation in the denomination's doctrinal and organizational emphases. Throughout its growth phase, the Alliance in Canada has been characterized by its enthusiasm for foreign missions, by innovative ministries and by a pragmatic, non-dogmatic approach to ministry. This transition can be seen in two vignettes that capture the essence of the present-day CMA in Canada.

URBAN TABERNACLE EVANGELISM (1920-30)

During the 1920s a second wave of religious enthusiasm boosted the fortunes of the CMA in Canada. This was accomplished by the large-scale conference, which had been the lifeblood of the CMA from the beginning, and at which it excelled. In Canada during the 1920s, however, conferences held under Alliance auspices took on a new vitality and purpose which, in turn, changed the nature and focus of Alliance. The impetus came from an energetic young preacher named Oswald J. Smith, whose Toronto ministry had a major and defining effect upon the form and pattern of Alliance ministries for years to come. Although Smith's views never really were in accord with traditional Alliance holiness distinctives,[31] he became available at a time when the fortunes of Parkdale Tabernacle – the troubled successor of Salmon's Bethany Church – were at their lowest ebb. In a triumph of expediency over dogma, Smith was appointed by acclamation to lead the Parkdale Tabernacle in 1921. Later that year he and the Parkdale Tabernacle proposed an evangelistic campaign to be held in Toronto conducted by Alliance evangelists F.F. and B.B. Bosworth, who had just conducted a highly successful campaign in Detroit and who preached on the "traditional" Alliance topics of sanctification and divine healing. Despite initial misgivings by the District of Canada committee about the Bosworths' doctrines, the Alliance decided to bring the evangelists in for a series of meetings from mid-April to late May 1921.

The Toronto Bosworth campaign proved to be one of the most significant religious events ever held in the city. Beginning in Parkdale Tabernacle (capacity 900), the meetings were quickly moved to Massey Hall (capacity 3,400) to contain the crowds eager to attend. Although in their preaching the Bosworths were careful to subordinate divine healing to salvation, sanctification, and the life of the Spirit of Christ within the believer, press reports inevitably focused upon instances of healing.[32] For their part, the Bosworths did little to play down either the expectations of their audience or the press: "The man who says the days of miracles are over is just ignorant of history ... God, through the atonement, offers you just as freely the healing of your body as the forgiveness of your sins."[33]

For four weeks crowds poured daily into Massey Hall. Although the meetings generated controversy within religious circles, this only heightened interest.[34] The Bosworth campaign prompted an unprecedented outpouring of religious devotion and was a huge evangelistic success. And no organizations benefited more than the CMA and the Parkdale Tabernacle. Oswald Smith and the CMA saw in the excitement a tremendous opportunity to expand and launched into an aggressive tabernacle-building program to capitalize upon the convention successes. Their efforts resulted in the Christie Street Tabernacle (capacity 2,700), a utilitarian structure which for the remainder of Smith's Alliance ministry became the centre for evangelistic ministry in Toronto.

Smith's successes in church-building and evangelism influenced the pattern of Alliance ministries in Canada. Where once the Alliance had been a holiness and healing society, now it became primarily an evangelistic soul-saving organization; where it had once been intended to complement the work of the denominations, now it rang with the sounds of Smith's dispensational and fundamentalist rhetoric. Such themes, in large part absent from Alliance ministries in Canada previously, coincided with a general shift in the CMA away from the evangelical ecumenism of its founder. They, in turn, further estranged the Alliance from its denominational counterparts and hastened its move to denominationalism. This approach to church growth and evangelism was confirmed when the Bosworths returned to Ottawa in 1924. The campaign energized the Alliance in the Ottawa area, and had, if possible, an even greater effect upon that city than their earlier campaign had upon Toronto. During the meetings, donations were sought for the building of an Alliance Tabernacle, and in 1925 a large structure known thereafter as the Ottawa Gospel Tabernacle was opened on Bank Street.

For a time the Bosworth campaigns thrust the CMA to the forefront of revivalist religion in central Canada. Capitalizing on the publicity, the Alliance pushed ahead with a number of aggressive ministries centred in large urban areas. Invariably run by dynamic and assertive leaders, these new ministries took the Canadian Alliance in the same direction the American organization had already moved – decisively away from the fraternal holiness society envisioned by its founder and towards becoming a fundamentalist denomination. There is a certain irony here, however, for the message that did so much to propel the Alliance upon its new fundamentalist track was none other than Simpson's original Fourfold Gospel. During the 1920s the Bosworth campaigns functioned much as Simpson and Salmon had intended: as a meeting place where holiness-minded Christians of all denominations could celebrate God's new works preliminary to his return.

THE CALL OF THE WEST

Even as Alliance ministries were being reshaped and revitalized in central Canada, developments in the West exerted an even more profound influence upon the CMA in Canada. The story of the Alliance's early days in the West is largely one of a tiny organization seeking to expand under conditions of the utmost stringency. Like their counterparts in other Canadian churches, Alliance leaders in the 1920s were drawn to the West, which presented a huge challenge and new religious frontiers to explore. The CMA faced the same problems as the other Protestant churches – but had virtually no resources with which to solve them. The situation was compounded by Alliance headquarters in New York, which judged all requests for assistance by whether or not they generated financial support for overseas missions. Working under such constraints, Alliance leaders were forced to innovate and experiment. Centred in Edmonton, where a small church had been established in 1922, the Alliance began its efforts to evangelize the West.

Among its earliest initiatives was the Great West Mission, launched in the spring of 1922 under the direction of Rev. John H. Woodward. As evangelistic campaigns go, this one operated on a shoestring. Run only during the summers, it was staffed by student volunteers from the Missionary Training Institute in Nyack, New York. The young missionaries were given only enough money to buy a horse, harness, and blanket before going out to evangelize an assigned area. Accommodations and food were to be found *en route*.[35] While returning missionaries brought back inspiring tales and were moderately successful, it quickly became apparent that more innovative means were needed if the West was to be reached with the gospel. One of these was the Alliance Gospel Car. Although the concept of using automobiles for ministry did not originate with the Alliance – they had already been used as mobile chapels by Anglicans and the Salvation Army – it was the first to use them extensively for evangelization and ministry. Under Woodward's direction a car was bought and outfitted in 1924, staffed with two young missionaries, and sent out on what was to be an extensive tour of the West. The mobile mission station made it no further than its first stop at Gwynne, Alberta, where the missionaries' preaching prompted a major revival which lasted six weeks.[36] Although the Gospel Car brought limited successes, it was apparent to the Alliance officials that such methods, inspiring as they were, would not leave a lasting witness.

During the mid-1920s Woodward hit upon the ideal medium: radio. While historians have noted William Aberhart's effective use of the medium during the 1920s and 1930s, the Alliance did as much to pioneer religious broadcasting in Canada. Given the CMA's history, radio was a natural fit; it blended the excitement of conferences with the potential to reach a vast audience at relatively little cost. Convinced that radio was the key to Alliance success in the West, Woodward established Canada's first religious broadcasting station, under the call letters CHMA, with a power of 125 watts. The station carried the Alliance message to a huge audience across the prairies for years. According to W.E. Mann, "The growth of the Alliance [especially in the West] in the period 1930–46 was closely linked to the policy of continuous radio broadcasting ... Other sectarian leaders became alert to the success of Aberhart and the Alliance, and rushed to get air time."[37]

Virtually from the beginning of its expansion to the West, leaders such as Woodward recognized that the Alliance's success would require support by educational institutions offering a practical Bible education for western workers. Although an Alliance Bible school opened in Toronto in 1924, western leaders remained convinced that success in the West depended upon western educational facilities. Despite clear instructions to the contrary, Woodward opened the Great West Bible Institute in Edmonton a short time later. New York CMA headquarters closed both Canadian schools in 1929 due to shrinking income, but this setback was reversed with the establishment of the Canadian Bible Institute in Regina in 1941. This school, now supplemented by the Canadian Theological Seminary, remains the sole CMA educational institution in Canada.

Since the first Alliance initiatives in the 1920s, the West has come to exert a dominant role in the Canadian CMA, with the number of western churches in 1937 surpassing those in central Canada. The gap has continued to grow ever since. Today there are two churches in the West for every one east of the Ontario border; and when inclusive members are considered, the ratio grows to three to one.[38] Along with that growth have come developments that define the Canadian Alliance today: a major revival in western Canada under the Alliance evangelist twins, the Suteras, during 1971 and 1972; the impulse towards autonomy from the American church in 1980; and the growth of a number "super church" ministries across the West. As the Alliance centre of gravity has shifted west, so too the denomination has virtually completed the transformation from that of a non-denominational fraternal holiness society to that of a generic evangelical denomination characterized by an inclusive evangelical doctrinal stance and a vigorous foreign-missions emphasis. That shift, more than anything else, has been the key to the CMA's impressive numerical successes in Canada. Drawing members from numerous denominational backgrounds, especially from the Mennonites, the Alliance has steered clear of traditional doctrinal controversies while offering its adherents emphases consistent with mainstream evangelical values.

A QUESTION OF IDENTITY

Until relatively recently the CMA has seen little need for historical introspection. Buoyed by significant postwar growth and with its origins and history safely stowed, Alliance looked to the past with thanksgiving and to the future with hope.[39] For its part, the Canadian CMA has shown impressive numerical growth in all categories for virtually all its post-independence existence.[40] Since early in the 1980s, however, there has been an unprecedented re-examination of the denomination's origins and the direction of its development.[41] This re-examination, to a large degree, has been conducted by Canadians. A significant contribution to the debate was *The Birth of a Vision: Essays on the Ministry and Thought of Albert B. Simpson*, which called for a scholarly re-examination of the origins of the Alliance.[42] Building on his work in that volume, Charles Nienkirchen went on to challenge earlier denominational histories by locating the founder and his movement within proto-Pentecostal circles and charging that the Alliance's development in that direction was arrested by a new generation of Alliance leaders, especially historical revisionists like A.W. Tozer.[43]

The Canadian Alliance has not been exempted from searching analysis. Leading the debate has been the denominational historian Lindsay Reynolds, who decries what he sees as the Alliance's drift away from its founding doctrinal distinctives. He has since been joined by Arnold Cook, the current president of the CMA in Canada, who sees the denomination as being threatened by what he terms "historical drift," a process by which once-dynamic church movements become overwhelmed by affluence and complacency. According to Cook, members of the CMA "are at a very, very vulnerable point in our history."[44] Portraying the history of churches on a curve of birth, maturity, and decline, Cook locates the Alliance at the verge of the latter. And only revival can extend, or actually reverse, this trend: "With God-inspired vision, and lives set apart in holiness, this is a point where actually a new and higher curve can begin. Truly this crisis is a moment of opportunity if we will seek God for revival."[45]

What has caused this crisis of confidence despite such seeming success? Since its founding as a separate denomination in 1980, the Canadian Alliance has committed itself to supporting and sending abroad every missionary candidate qualified to go. Over the past two years, however, missionary giving has not kept pace with the numbers of available candidates. The result has been a shortfall in 1994 of $840,000 in its Global Advance Fund despite revenues of nearly $8 million.[46] This situation has led to increasing calls for re-evaluation, repentance, and revival within the Alliance, and to a message reminiscent of the early A.B. Simpson: "Our first calling as Christians is not to evangelize or to support missions, or even be diligent workers in the Church. It's to be holy."[47]

Coming as they do after a century of ceaseless change, such calls for a rediscovery of the essence of Alliance spirituality and purpose are poignant. For change itself has been the one constant of the CMA. Growing out of the vast tide of holiness at the turn of the century, the restless spiritual movement was focused for a brief moment by A.B. Simpson and held in momentary equilibrium by his doctrinal formulation of the Fourfold Gospel. Even as it came into organizational existence in 1887, however, this equilibrium fell under attack. Within a decade it had been shattered, some would argue, never to return. Yet it has been in the very call for revival and "holiness unto the Lord" that the Alliance has found its meaning and validation. Whether it calls, and whether it receives, it seems fair to say that the Christian and Missionary Alliance in Canada will continue on its voyage of spiritual discovery well into the new millennium.

18 Canadian Pentecostalism and the Evangelical Impulse

RONALD A.N. KYDD

In 1994 Mark A. Noll argued in *The Scandal of the Evangelical Mind* that Pentecostalism has been one of three forces that have undermined evangelical intellectual life. In the same year Ralph Winter, the founder and president of the U.S. Center for World Missions, made the statement that "God is pentecostalizing the Church."[1] These contrasting opinions draw attention to the place Pentecostalism occupies in the wider Christian community. An exploration of the relationship between Pentecostalism and Canadian evangelicalism illustrates the seriously convoluted experience of Canadian Pentecostalism within the evangelical community at large.

A BRIEF HISTORY OF CANADIAN PENTECOSTALISM

Pentecostalism as a religious tradition arose in the United States in the first decade of the twentieth century. Its primary emphases were the baptism in the Holy Spirit, speaking in tongues, evangelism, and eschatology. The movement reached Canada in 1906, becoming established first in Toronto at a mission operated by James and Ellen Hebden. In 1907 it took root in Winnipeg, and in the same year made its way to the West Coast. Alice Wood carried the news of Pentecost to Swift Current, Saskatchewan, in 1908, and it broke on the east coast in 1911 through the efforts of Alice Garrigus.

The American nature of Canadian sectarianism has been noted often,[2] and Pentecostalism illustrates this clearly. Although some of the thirteen Pentecostal denominations now active in Canada did not grow out of immediate contact with groups in the United States – for example, the

Independent Assemblies of God International of Canada and Global Missions/Sharon[3] – for most, American influence was definitive.

One of the Canadian Pentecostal groups that traced their origins to American evangelistic efforts was the Church of God (Cleveland, Tennessee). The exact circumstances of this group's appearance in Canada remain unclear, but the first foothold was temporarily secured at Scotland Farm, Manitoba, in 1920.[4] After this nothing more is known of this fellowship until it was established in both Saskatchewan and Ontario in the 1930s through the work of resident American evangelists and pastors.[5] The foundings of the Pentecostal Assemblies of Newfoundland and Italian Pentecostal Church of Canada followed somewhat similar patterns.[6]

Americans were also key players in the formation of the Pentecostal Assemblies of Canada (PAOC), which came into existence through the labyrinthine organizational meanderings of the Assemblies of God (USA).[7] Over the next decade the PAOC incorporated (1919), the two groups joined, and finally negotiated a separation (arising from doctrinal[8] and structural[9] differences).

American influence of a different kind impacted on the experience of the Apostolic Church of Pentecost, which arose out of doctrinal controversy revolving around the uniquely Pentecostal doctrine known as "Jesus Only." As articulated by Andrew Urshan, it taught that "'the lord Jesus Christ,' is the ONE PROPER NAME of God for this dispensation; because in Him, Jesus Christ, Our Lord, all the Fullness of the Godhead dwelt; and to Him, all power in Heaven and earth, was given; that repentance and remission of sins should be preached in Jesus' Name ONLY."[10]

This doctrine came into Pentecostalism at a camp meeting in California in 1913 and reached Canada the same year. Franklin Small, in Winnipeg, embraced the teaching, and after a series of bitter events, his loyalty to it led to the formation of the Apostolic Church of Pentecost, separate from the parent body, the PAOC.[11] Over the last four decades the denomination's doctrinal statement has been modified to accommodate both trinitarian and oneness beliefs,[12] but the point here is that this was a theological position articulated first in the United States and subsequently exported to Canada.

It is clear from the preceding examples that American influence was very important in establishing the Pentecostal movement in Canada. And this influence continues to be felt to a greater or lesser degree by most Canadian Pentecostals. Indeed, some Canadian groups are still part of organized districts of American-based denominations, including the United Pentecostals, which have their headquarters in Hazelwood, Missouri, and the Church of God, whose central office is in Cleveland,

Tennessee. On the other hand, over the last several decades there have been moves to autonomy by some Canadian Pentecostal bodies.[13]

Having taken root in Canada, Pentecostalism followed an interesting growth pattern.[14] As table 1 illustrates, Pentecostalism expanded most rapidly between 1971 and 1981. In 1991 Ontario had the largest number of Pentecostals with 167,175. In terms of proportionate strength, Newfoundland led with 70.6 Pentecostals for every 1,000 Newfoundlanders, which compares with 16.2 Pentecostals in every 1,000 people in Canada as a whole.

Table 1
Pentecostal Growth Rate, 1901–1991[15]

Year	Total number of Pentecostals	Pentecostals per 1,000 population
1991	436,435	16.2
1981	338,790	13.9
1971	220,390	10.2
1961	143,877	7.9
1951	95,131	6.8
1941	57,646	5.0
1931	26,301	2.5
1921	3,355	.38
1911	513	.07
1901	–	–

The steady, gradual increase in the number of Canadian Pentecostals over the course of the twentieth century has been accompanied by an extremely varied development of the individual Pentecostal groups. For example, one of the primary features of the Apostolic Church of Pentecost experience was an amalgamation. After years of difficulty establishing itself in eastern and central Canada, in 1949 this denomination began to take steps to merge with the Evangelical Churches of Pentecost. Finding common ground not only in their general Pentecostal doctrines and experiences but also in their insistence that once people come to faith in Christ they can never "fall from grace," the two groups forged a union in 1953.[16]

In contrast, the PAOC has been racked by divisions. The first resulted in the establishment of the Apostolic Church of Pentecost. And the second, which involved many issues including organization and doctrinal precision, spun off the Global Missions/Sharon group of North Battleford.

Development took yet another form in the experiences of the Church of God and the Church of God of Prophecy. These two groups evolved in similar ways, and for each, immigration since 1960 from the Caribbean (where these two denominations have had major missionary programs) has been a critical factor in contributing to their rapid growth in urban areas. Reflecting this development, in August 1994 both denominations for the first time appointed people from the Caribbean to chief leadership positions.

The development of these four groups hint at the complexities of Pentecostal experience in Canada. And this diversity was also obvious at an unprecedented meeting of leaders of Canadian Pentecostal denominations held on 24 October 1994, at which it became clear that a strong consciousness of change had arisen in many areas of Pentecostal life, from personal morality to prayer services at altars. The ready acceptance of change was brought into question, however, in a paper submitted by the Rev. Barry Buzza of the Foursquare Gospel Church of Canada. Buzza's probing demonstrated the importance of finding ways to reflect on the complex nature of the shifting Canadian Pentecostal experience.

A SOCIO-RELIGIOUS ANALYSIS OF CANADIAN PENTECOSTALISM

Two models are directly applicable to any analysis of the Pentecostal tradition in Canada. The first is the theorizing done in connection with church and sect. Max Weber and Ernst Troeltsch[17] developed the fundamental ideas for this model, which have received carefully nuanced acceptance[18] along with some criticism.[19] While scholarly opinion varies widely, there is some consensus on the importance of societal tension as a means of identifying a group as a church or a sect.[20] Benton Johnson put it succinctly: "A church is a religious group that accepts the social environment in which it exists. A sect is a religious group that rejects the social environment in which it exists."[21]

An important feature of the church-sect model is the idea of institutionalization. This concept was introduced by Weber, who called it "routinization," and was refined by H. Richard Niebuhr. Since then it has been modified and applied by many other scholars.[22] In 1942 Walter Muelder applied the idea of institutionalization to the Pentecostals in the Central Valley of California.[23] In fact, both Muelder's concept and the whole church-sect typology apply well to Pentecostals not only in California but around the world, and specifically in Canada. Of course, when looking at Canadian Pentecostalism through this particular lens, one must be careful not to oversimplify. Groups experience institutionalization differently, and the process most certainly does not move in only one direction.

Bryan R. Wilson, a British sociologist, advanced the discussion considerably when he argued that were at least seven different types of sects and that they do not all experience institutionalization. In fact, he emphasized that the group of sects most likely to undergo the process is the group that he calls "conversionist,"[24] that is, the group of sects that goes into the world and attempts to bring about conversions.

All of the Canadian Pentecostal groups at one time or another have fitted Wilson's description of conversionist sects perfectly.[25] All have urged separation from the world, referring explicitly to personal morality, politics, and military service.[26] This "separation" established their sectarian character, but, like all conversionist groups, they have also been driven by a passion for evangelism.[27] And like other conversionists, they have experienced institutionalization.

The development of organizational structures within Pentecostalism, however, came about only with considerable angst within the movement. Pentecostals were initially strongly against any kind of organization. The Hebdens had spoken for most when they stated, "Not only is the free leading of the Spirit against man-made organizations, but the unity of the Spirit demands its abolition."[28] Against this background, the 1930s saw an exchange of correspondence between a concerned official who thought that structure was beginning to stifle the "moving of the Spirit" and the general secretary of the PAOC, A.G. Ward, who observed, "We must not fail to recognize that as a Movement grows numerically and new departments are opened up, of necessity it must be carried on in the most efficient business-like way. We have certainly outgrown some of our former policies and methods of conducting affairs, and now we must either make the necessary changes and improvements or be forced into retrogression."[29] Not impressed, the official to whom Ward wrote left the denomination five months later. At approximately the same time the general superintendent of the PAOC was basing his arguments for organization upon the predictability and order that one could see in God's creation.[30]

The move towards organization was accompanied around the middle of the century by the PAOC's discovery of its social responsibility. In 1957, for example, E.N.O. Kulbeck, editor of the denomination's paper, made a passionate call for Christians to become involved in government,[31] and about this time Pentecostal politicians began to appear. They were not many, and they represented various parties, but some served in cabinets and one became a high-profile labour leader.[32] Along with organization and social responsibility came other features of institutionalization. Pentecostals became involved in philanthropy, operating nursing homes and a hospital, and the PAOC provided financial counselling for its people. Thus by mid-century the PAOC was well on its way to denominational status, having emerged as a significant religious force in Canadian society.

While the church-sect model helps illuminate some aspects of Canadian Pentecostalism, a second analytical model, provided by Bruce Reed of London, England, offers another way to look at the development of this group. Reed based a theory of human behaviour on feelings of dependence and on an oscillation which he felt people go through between two modes of experience. He argued that when people individually or corporately are in one mode, they see themselves as dependent on objects or persons outside themselves for shelter, affirmation, and encouragement.[33] Feelings of weakness and disorientation are parts of this experience, which Reed called a "regression to extra-dependence."

The second mode of experiencing being is quite different. Once people have found sustaining relationships, they begin to feel "reordered." Confidence grows, and they start to think that their futures and their general well-being are in their own hands. Reed named this "intra-dependence," wherein resources necessary for effective living are found in themselves. These two modes of experience can be thought of as "periods of autonomous activity [the first] and periods of physical or symbolic contact with sources of renewal [the second]." Reed theorized that the normal flow of life involves repeated oscillation between these two modes of experience or types of dependence.[34]

The application of this model to the PAOC yields some interesting results. In the case of the PAOC, and perhaps some of the other, older Pentecostal groups such as the Apostolic Church of Pentecost, the early part of the twentieth century was an "extra-dependency" phase, during which people sought God out of a deep sense of need. By mid-century, the PAOC, at least, had reached an "intra-dependency" phase. With a sense of vitality, it was reaching out to the wider society in a variety of ways.

The PAOC's self-assurance was challenged in the 1960s and 1970s with the beginning of the charismatic renewal. People from settings as far removed from each other as mainline denominations and the drug culture were having profound encounters with God. Many of these people made their ways into Pentecostal churches, and the impact was dramatic. They came with boundless enthusiasm and with new modes of music flowing out of the vividness of their life-reorienting religious experiences. The Pentecostals rejoiced to have these people, because they swelled their numbers and because they reminded them of what they thought Pentecostalism used to be. Prompted by a sense of relief at experiences rediscovered and by guilt due to apparent inhibition, many Pentecostals eagerly joined their new brothers and sisters in their exuberant celebrations of their experiences with God.

However, in the process, aspects of the Pentecostals' institutionalization were aborted and the development of a true intra-dependent phase in which people would reach into society with responsibility and confidence was significantly compromised. In reaction, many Pentecostals reverted to an earlier stage of corporate experience in which religious experience was privatized and internalized.

As a result, many Pentecostal churches have become rather confusing places, characterized by several strata of attendees. The deepest stratum is composed of the children and grandchildren of the original Pentecostals, who tend to be less demonstrative and less enthusiastic. This group provides most of the leadership, service, and financial resources to the congregations in which they are found. The next stratum is made up of members whose roots are in "Pentecost," and who are trying to recapture the dynamism of the "old days" which they are too young to have experienced. The third stratum is formed of non-Pentecostals and non-charismatics, who ally themselves with Pentecostal churches because they like the contemporary music, the refreshing worship, and the vitality of programs offered, such as youth ministries.

The charismatics constitute the last stratum. They joined because they heard that Pentecostals appreciated the kinds of experiences – glossolalia, for example – which they had been having, and because they preferred a lively and demonstrative form of worship. Some have moved into leadership and service, but most have not. Loyalty to the congregation is often not a deep concern among them, and they are prepared to leave more readily if their worship needs are not met.[35]

All of these developments have made it very difficult for many Pentecostal churches to retain or achieve any sense of identity. This in turn has placed obstacles in the way of rediscovering an "intra-dependent" phase in which Pentecostal churches reach into the communities around them in concrete ways.

CANADIAN PENTECOSTALS AND THE EVANGELICAL IMPULSE

When considering the place Pentecostals occupy among Canadian evangelicals, one basic comment should be made – they embraced "the quadrilateral of evangelical ideology"[36] virtually from their inception. A statement from a 1911 issue of *The Good Report* illustrates this: "THIS MOVEMENT has no great man at the head of it, but recognizes the HOLY GHOST, honors JESUS, magnifies the BLOOD. It has nothing to join; no law but love, no creed but Christ, and no text-book but the Bible. Our motto is, a whole GOSPEL for a whole man, and to the whole WORLD. Jesus is our Saviour, sanctifier, healer, baptizer, 'Glorious Lord and coming King.' 'Everything in Jesus, and Jesus everything.'"[37]

Such views clearly indicate that Canadian Pentecostals have qualified as evangelicals from the outset. And this ought not to be surprising, given the backgrounds of some of the people who came into the movement during its first decades. Among these were the PAOC's first general superintendent, G.A. Chambers, who had been with the Mennonite Brethren in Christ;[38] A.G. Ward, who became general secretary-treasurer in the 1930s, and who had ministered among both the Methodists and the Christian and Missionary Alliance;[39] and R.L. Dutaud, who pastored in Quebec, and who had been a Baptist.[40] It would appear that the Pentecostals had harvested quite effectively among those whom John Stackhouse called the "sectish" evangelicals.[41] In fact, R.E. McAlister, the first general secretary-treasurer of the PAOC, boasted that the Pentecostal movement "had taken the very cream from every denomination."[42]

However, Canadian Pentecostalism also proved attractive to evangelicals from mainline denominations. Henry Charles Sweet, who became deeply involved with the Pentecostals, provides a detailed example of this. Sweet was ordained among the Baptists in 1897, and studied at Crozer Theological Seminary, where he earned a B.D., and at the University of Manitoba, where he graduated with a B.A. He joined the Presbyterians in 1904, graduated with the Th.D. from Evangelical Theological Seminary (now Dallas Theological Seminary) in 1928, joined the faculty of Winnipeg Bible Training School (now Providence College) the same year, and became its principal in 1929. The applications he submitted to various places contain statements of faith which, when added to the above material, help us to determine that Sweet was a person whose evangelical credentials were beyond question.[43]

Sweet appears to have first encountered Pentecostals while ministering in Conquest, Saskatchewan, in 1914. By 1916 he was active within this group in Winnipeg, even baptizing in water a son of A.H. Argue, one of the movement's early leaders. Surprisingly, he was one of the signatories on the Apostolic Church of Pentecost's application for a federal charter in 1921.[44] His decision to leave Winnipeg Bible Training School (WBTS) on 5 January 1931 rested on his refusal to deny the validity of speaking in tongues. Once he had severed connections with the WBTS, he became the principal of a new Pentecostal Bible school that opened in Winnipeg in 1931. With interruption, he taught there until it closed in 1950. However, even throughout this period, he continued to preach at the nondenominational Elim Chapel in Winnipeg.

Sweet was only one among several mainline evangelicals who identified with Pentecostalism in the second and third decades of the century.[45] J.E. Purdie, an Anglican priest throughout his life, was another. Purdie was called by the PAOC to open a Bible school in Winnipeg in 1925. He accepted and modelled the school after his Alma Mater, Wycliffe College in Toronto. By 1930 the enrolment had grown to more than 120 students. Other mainline evangelicals who turned to Pentecostalism were

D.N. Buntain, a Methodist, and T.T. Latto and J.W. McKillop, who came from Presbyterian backgrounds. Such individuals shared the Pentecostals' spirituality and passion for Christ and made strong contributions to the young movement in education and administration. They also contributed significantly to the movement's growing institutionalization, which is perhaps not surprising considering their former mainline affiliations.

While Pentecostals attracted a number of important leaders from mainline evangelical groups, relations between the two groups were often acrimonious. This was the case even though, with the exception of the practice of speaking in tongues, Canadian Pentecostalism was thoroughly evangelical throughout the early decades of the twentieth century. The experience of H.C. Sweet is illustrative. In 1930 the board of Winnipeg Bible Training School took action with regard to the Pentecostalism which was appearing within its student body. It affirmed that the school was not Pentecostal, that it was not in sympathy with Pentecostalism, that it would not permit Pentecostal demonstrations on its premises, that in the future Pentecostal students would not be accepted, and that every board and faculty member would have to subscribe to and support the position outlined. With reference to Sweet, Edward Hildebrandt declared: "Dr Sweet, who if not Pentecostal himself, was at least sympathetic towards Pentecostalism, immediately tendered a verbal resignation since he felt that he could not accept the last clause."[46] There can be no question but that at times feelings ran very high indeed. Of course, this should not be surprising given the Pentecostals' doctrinal stance, the emotionalism the evangelicals saw among them, and the depredation they occasionally inflicted upon evangelical ranks.

These conditions of identification and tension existed into the 1960s. Pentecostals consistently identified themselves as fundamentalists or evangelicals,[47] but they did not attempt to develop relationships with other Canadian evangelicals. They were not welcome; they were smarting from rejection, and they viewed evangelicals as lacking spiritual power.[48] However, signs of a thaw among the Pentecostals had begun to appear in the 1940s, when *The Pentecostal Testimony*, the official magazine of the PAOC, began to report on the activities of the American National Association of Evangelicals (NAE)[49] and other evangelical groups. The flow of evangelical-related news items increased in the 1950s, when E.N.O. Kulbeck became editor of the magazine.

By the 1950s some Pentecostals were establishing relationships in the wider evangelical community. During this period the Rev. C.H. Stiller in Saskatchewan became a close friend of Justice Emmett Hall, and the Rev. A.C. Schindel was well received by InterVarsity Christian Fellowship

(IVCF) on the campus of the University of Saskatchewan. It has been noted that to younger Pentecostals, Schindel was a voice calling "to a thoughtful Pentecostalism and not to sectarianism," and that other Pentecostals were encouraging young people to consider studies at universities and seminaries.[50] For some Pentecostals during the 1940s and 1950s, Youth For Christ, which was seen as a dynamic, up-tempo organization well suited to the evangelistic ministries of "charismatic" Pentecostals in Winnipeg and Saskatoon, provided an entry into evangelicalism.

The 1960s witnessed significant developments in the relationship between Canadian Pentecostals and evangelicals, with the instrumental figure being Dr J. Harry Faught. Faught, born near Eganville, Ontario, graduated in 1953 with a Th.D. from Dallas Theological Seminary, where he twice experienced difficulty due to his involvement with the PAOC and the Assemblies of God (USA).[51] In 1954 he was installed as pastor of Danforth Gospel Temple, a PAOC church in Toronto. In the years that followed, he established a reputation in Toronto as an articulate spokesperson not only for the Pentecostals but also for evangelicalism,[52] commenting on current religious, social, and political events.

During the 1950s and early 1960s Faught called a series of more or less formal meetings in an attempt to bring evangelicals in Toronto into contact with each other. These resulted in the organizational meeting of the Evangelical Fellowship of Canada (EFC), on 16 February 1965, which was presided over by Faught.[53] Faught was elected executive chairman and in 1966 became the EFC's second president. In addition to chairing meetings and recruiting members, he carried out specific plans. Acting on behalf of the EFC, he invited Dr Carl Henry to conduct a lecture tour across Canada in the spring of 1967. Faught accompanied Henry on the tour and was actively involved in the discussions following the lectures. In 1973 Faught, who had moved to Calgary in 1968, was invited to become full-time executive secretary of the EFC but declined.

One of the more interesting measures Faught implemented during his early involvement with the EFC had to do with membership. He had observed that the National Association of Evangelicals' policy of building membership around evangelical denominations had excluded evangelical individuals from mainline churches. He insisted that membership initially be limited to individuals so that evangelicals from all Canadian denominations could join.[54] This policy opened the way for three of the first six presidents of the EFC to be Presbyterians, and it has contributed to Canadian evangelicalism's avoiding a strong tinge of fundamentalism.[55]

All of this was not achieved without difficulty. Pentecostals worried that Faught was compromising on the principle of baptism in the Holy

Spirit, and they attacked him from the right. On the other hand, some evangelicals feared his Pentecostalism and harassed him, also from the right. Twice in 1965–66, promotional meetings in the Maritimes for the EFC were not able to be held because evangelicals would not attend a meeting at which Faught, a Pentecostal, would be speaking.[56]

Since the 1960s, Pentecostal involvement in the EFC has increased. Currently, at least six Pentecostal denominations have membership in the EFC. This increased involvement is also evident in the leadership ranks. For example, from 1977 to 1983 the Rev. Charles Yates, then general secretary of the Pentecostal Assemblies of Canada, served as president of the EFC, and Dr Kenneth Birch, executive director of Canadian Ministries for the PAOC, was recently elected to fill that office. As well, in 1983 Brian Stiller, an ordained minister with the PAOC, was appointed executive director.[57]

In considering the leadership that Canadian evangelicalism has found in Pentecostalism, it is important to note that these individuals have come from one particular sector of the movement – from the PAOC. This is not all that surprising, given the size of the PAOC and the large leadership pool from which it has to draw, as well as its institutionalization and geographical dispersion. Harking back to the earlier discussion of theoretical models, these factors have created a diversity which allows the denomination to appear sectarian at one time and church-like at another, depending on which subgroup one looks at and in what circumstances. This two-toned appearance of the denomination is also evident in its leadership, which has tended to come from among those who, while holding to fundamental doctrines, are at the same time successful at interacting with the wider culture. It is with this group of Canadian Pentecostals that evangelicalism has felt most comfortable. But as Faught's experience demonstrates, evangelicals have not been completely at ease with the relationship, realizing that the cultured few do not necessarily represent the many.

Despite increased interaction between Pentecostals and evangelicals, Brian Stiller, executive director of the EFC, finds that very few Pentecostals are on boards or staffs of national evangelical organizations. He feels that this is partly because during the time of mutual exclusion, Pentecostals built programs internally to care for their own needs. Now such Pentecostals neither want to lose control of these programs through mergers nor have them weakened through the allocation of funds to parachurch agencies.[58]

However, Stiller also observes that when he visits churches, he sees little difference between Pentecostal assemblies and other evangelical congregations. Many evangelicals, for example, have adopted what is considered to be a Pentecostal style of worship. Indeed, it might be in this area that Pentecostals will have their most lasting impact on Canadian evangelicalism. For despite periodic increased interaction and perhaps a similarity in style, most Pentecostals and evangelicals have failed, thus far, to achieve any deep or completely trustworthy relationship.

That Canadian Pentecostals today are still in the process of defining who they are and how they should relate to evangelicals is not surprising. The movement is after all a relatively recent phenomenon, and while its growth has been dramatic, its development, like that of other religious movements, has been marked by diversity and struggle. In trying to understand the Pentecostal experience in Canada, the concept of institutionalization is helpful, but this process, summed up as "tension reduction," has unfolded differently among the various Pentecostal groups and subgroups within the larger denominations. Perhaps Bruce Reed's idea of oscillation between "intra" and "extra-dependence" provides the clearest explanation for the various shifts within Pentecostal history and for Pentecostalism's present-day tentative bond with evangelical groups.

Whether or not one accepts the application of Reed's analysis to Canadian Pentecostalism, it is clear that Canadian Pentecostals have been firmly in the evangelical camp from their inception. However, it is also apparent that the relationship between the two groups has not always been harmonious, and this tension has frequently been palpable as evangelicals have decried Pentecostalism's emotional excesses, while Pentecostals have scorned a lack of real power in evangelicalism. Nonetheless, at the moment many barriers are breaking down, largely because many other evangelical groups are being "pentecostalized" – as the charismatic movement becomes a more and more significant force.

PART FIVE

Evangelical Networks, Leaders, and Revivals

19 The Winnipeg Fundamentalist Network, 1910–1940: The Roots of Transdenominational Evangelicalism in Manitoba and Saskatchewan

D. BRUCE HINDMARSH

Not long ago a pastor was reported to have warned his flock against falling away from the faith and getting involved in "sex, drugs, and fundamentalist sects."[1] Whether or not one regards a "fundamentalist sect" as something as morally corrosive as free sex and illegal drugs, the terminology for the religious historian is certainly hazardous, or at least problematic. The dominance of the church-sect thesis in Canadian religious historiography, for example, has been challenged by John Stackhouse and replaced with a more nuanced portrait of evangelicalism. Stackhouse has also sought to direct attention away from fundamentalists like T.T. Shields and William Aberhart (regarding them as exceptional) and has rejected the term "fundamentalist" as generally inappropriate in the case of mainline Canadian evangelicalism and its transdenominational institutions.[2] So it seems that neither "fundamentalist" nor "sect" is of much use in describing Canadian evangelicals.

However, while aware that the term "fundamentalism" has certain negative connotations, I have chosen to retain the word here to describe the conservative evangelicals in Winnipeg and the Prairie West in the first half of the twentieth century, because, "fundamentalist" is what they called themselves, and more importantly, because the Winnipeg fundamentalist network was closely linked with Protestant fundamentalists in the United States and elsewhere. There were points of discontinuity, but the overwhelming continuity of the Winnipeg network with American fundamentalism must not be obscured. Moreover, a convincing case has been made that within American fundamentalism there was a moderate, centrist tradition which was defined less by militancy than by its focus upon evangelization, world missions, and personal holiness.[3] This precisely describes the character of the Winnipeg fundamentalist network,[4] an important regional movement within Canadian evangelicalism that has been largely overlooked.

In the secondary literature on Canadian fundamentalism, it has been Aberhart in Calgary and L.E. Maxwell at Three Hills who have tended to dominate the picture on the Prairies. But it is a mistake to see evangelicalism on the Prairies only through the prism of Alberta. My purpose here is to identify and describe the character of a distinct fundamentalist network in Manitoba and Saskatchewan. This regional network originated in Winnipeg with the founding of the Ellice Avenue Mission (Elim Chapel) in 1910 and enlarged to include Winnipeg Bible Institute in 1924, the Canadian Sunday School Mission in 1927, and numerous other organizations. From this beginning an overlapping constituency of individuals and institutions developed which embraced the expanding Prairie hinterland to the west as a mission field. This network became dominated by premillennial dispensationalism, but its preoccupation with home and foreign missions remained more central and urgent than the familiar fundamentalist agenda aimed at defending Christian civilization against the onslaught of theological modernism, evolution, and communism. By 1940 this network was well established and provided the basis for a regional and even international sense of evangelical identity which transcended denominational and ethnic loyalty. Increasingly, however, the sense of the Prairies as an economic frontier and a religious mission field gave way to the reality of the Prairies as a local neighbourhood in the global village, and fundamentalist institutions became less preoccupied with the rural mission and more concerned with institution-building and professionalization.

THE ORIGINS OF ELIM CHAPEL, C. 1910

In 1910 Winnipeg was the third largest city in Canada. There the myth of the Canadian West which had fired the imaginations of generations of central Canadians came to a point. Even a Chicago newspaper in 1911 could carry the enthusiastic report,

> All roads lead to Winnipeg. It is the focal point of the three transcontinental lines of Canada, and nobody, neither manufacturer, capitalist, farmer, mechanic, lawyer, doctor, merchant, priest, nor labourer, can pass from one part of Canada to another without going through Winnipeg. It is a gateway through which all the commerce of the east and west, and the north and south, must flow. No city, in America at least, has such absolute and complete command over the wholesale trade of so vast an area. It is destined to become one of the greatest

distributing commercial centres of the continent as well as a manufacturing community of great importance.[5]

This ebullient report from south of the border reflected the unprecedented boom in Winnipeg's population and economy from the turn of the century until about 1913.[6]

Westminster Presbyterian church, established in 1892 just north of Portage Avenue in central Winnipeg, grew quickly during this period.[7] At the same time Sidney T. Smith (1878–1947) and John Bellingham (1880–1937) were active lay workers in the church. Bellingham was an elder on Session, and he and Smith were both popular teachers of a Sunday-afternoon Bible class. In the summer of 1910 these men were joined by two other families from the church, and together they opened the Ellice Avenue Mission in west-central Winnipeg as a nondenominational outreach to the community. Early the next year Bellingham submitted his resignation to Session because of the time and attention he was devoting to "other work."[8]

That "other work" would become one of the most important centres for nondenominational conservative evangelicalism in western Canada. Although independent of Westminster, the Ellice Avenue Mission was not chiefly a "come-outer" movement of theological protest. (The famous fundamentalist–modernist battles in the denominations, north and south of the border, were still more than a decade away.) It was rather a lay-sponsored initiative in urban evangelism, at a time when traditional churches barely kept pace with the city's growth. While J.S. Woodsworth was expounding his social gospel and establishing the All People's Mission north of the tracks, the wives of Smith and Bellingham went up and down the streets on the south side of the tracks, inviting boys and girls to come to Sunday school to hear the message of personal salvation. Adults were invited to attend a Bible class while the children were in Sunday school, and an evening service was conducted by Smith and Bellingham or supplied by visiting preachers. Initially a local community outreach run on the British mission-hall pattern, the work grew quickly, and within three years the congregation moved into larger quarters nearby and called themselves variously the Winnipeg United City Mission or Elim Chapel.[9]

Over the next decade the church gained a reputation as a key evangelical centre in the city. The undenominational character of the mission was emphasized in a newspaper article in 1914 which described it as "a voluntary association of Christians who desire to come together for mutual help and fellowship in spiritual matters and to do a definite Christian service in the city."[10] In addition to regular week-night lectures, the old Walker theatre and other large venues were rented on

Sunday afternoons for mass meetings that featured well-known Bible lecturers.[11] One church member recalled that the crowds were so great that those wishing to attend were given theatre-style admission tickets to guarantee a seat.[12] During the war special meetings were also held for servicemen, and as many as a thousand were sometimes addressed at one time.[13] A contemporary newspaper article gave the enthusiastic report that "in no city on the continent is there a place which, in proportion to its opportunities, has contributed more during recent years to the carrying on of a definite Gospel and Bible work in all its varied forms."[14]

In the two decades from the end of the First World War until Bellingham's death in 1937, Elim Chapel continued to grow, and rose from its position as Winnipeg's united evangelical mission to become an internationally known pulpit closely allied with Protestant fundamentalism in the United States and elsewhere. From its beginnings Elim did not have a traditional pastor but was run by competent lay leadership with the help of a full-time superintendent. Bellingham himself retired from business in 1923 to give the work his full attention as superintendent.[15] A pattern developed whereby internationally renowned evangelical speakers would be invited to preach for a month at Elim Chapel and hold a week of special meetings. Many were attracted to Elim Chapel by this arrangement.

When the work had grown to the point where a new building was needed, Sidney Smith, by this time a prominent and wealthy grain merchant, bought a vacant Presbyterian church on Portage Avenue in 1927 as a new downtown venue for the mission. Church polity under Smith was unique. With a select board of directors and another board of managers, both under the general chairmanship of Smith (who also held the title to the building and paid for its upkeep), it would be an understatement to say that Elim Chapel was run like a business: effectively, Sidney Smith was president and John Bellingham was the CEO.[16] There could be few better examples of the entrepreneurial ethos of fundamentalism generally and of Winnipeg and the Prairie West in particular during this period.

Its setting makes Elim Chapel a distinctive case study in North American fundamentalism, since Winnipeg was an almost "instant" city in the same period that Elim Chapel was founded. In terms of the kind of developments taking place at Elim Chapel, Winnipeg was a city without a significant identity-giving past. The pedigree of American fundamentalism was noticeably absent there. The history of the late nineteenth-century conservative coalitions of Princetonian theologians, urban revivalists associated with D.L. Moody, holiness advocates, and premillennial dispensationalists – all of whom came together in Bible conferences and institutes – did not exist in Winnipeg, except insofar as newcomers to the city had had such experience elsewhere.[17] Moreover, because Elim Chapel was already an independent evangelical enterprise in 1910, Winnipeg fundamentalism would not be the scene of a fundamentalist-modernist denominational battle in the more polarized theological climate of the later interwar period. There would be no separatistic fundamentalism in the style of T.T. Shields, since the matrix for fundamentalism was already independent and undenominational. On the other hand, neither would there be a strong tradition of mediating or liberal evangelicalism to moderate Elim Chapel's fundamentalism, since Elim was removed from that tradition, disseminated as it was chiefly from the mainline seminaries of the period.[18]

What happened in Winnipeg instead was that two lines of history came together at a specific point in time: the line of Elim Chapel's development from a local community mission to a prominent city-wide ministry, and the line of American fundamentalism's progression from a loose conservative coalition to a more self-conscious movement prepared to defend Christian civilization. These lines intersected in Winnipeg in about 1917 when Sidney Smith began regularly bringing famous fundamentalist preachers to the city, many of whom stressed eschatological and dispensationalist themes. Within a few years fundamentalism was planted in Winnipeg, and the city became one more neighbourhood in the international fundamentalist community. Elim made its position within this community clear in 1918 when it established a statement of faith that included conservative positions typical of the Bible and prophecy conference movement, and the later fundamentalist coalition. These included the verbal and plenary inspiration of the scriptures, substitutionary atonement, the final apostasy of the church, and the personal and premillennial advent of Christ.[19]

It would not be over-arguing the point to say that Sidney Smith was the single conduit for all of this.[20] Born in London, Ontario, in 1878, Smith went to Winnipeg in 1902 and soon became a multi-millionaire as president of the Reliance Grain Company. Director of several American and international corporations and involved in oil and gas speculation, he was twice president of the Winnipeg Grain Exchange. It is a testimony to his prominence in the business community that when he died in 1947, trading halted on the floor of the Exchange and members observed two minutes silence. But this international stature in the business world was only a mirror of his stature within the evangelical world. Smith was not a typical or an uncontroversial fundamentalist, since drinking, smoking, and dancing were reputedly familiar practices in his home, and his own moral probity was doubted by some.[21] Nonetheless, Ian Rennie has commented on his stunning rise in American fundamentalism in the 1920s, noting his presence on the boards of the Moody Bible Institute and Dallas Seminary, his work organizing Bible conferences in American cities, and his tenure as president of the World's Christian Fundamentalist Association in 1925.[22] One member of Elim Chapel at this period recalled that Smith's wide business and religious contacts made it possible to bring many of the evangelical "giants" of the English-speaking world to Winnipeg.[23] While some speakers came from Britain (Graham Scroggie and G. Campbell Morgan), Australia (Dr L. Sale-Harrison) and Toronto (A.B. Winchester from Knox Presbyterian), the greatest number came from the United States, including such renowned fundamentalists as A.C. Gaebelein from New York and W.B. Riley from Minneapolis. The dispensationalists William Evans and Lewis Sperry Chafer featured prominently, as did Harry Ironside and a long list of speakers associated with Moody Bible Institute and Wheaton College. Equally renowned invitees included the directors of international foreign mission agencies such as R.V. Bingham of the Sudan Interior Mission or Robert H. Glover of the China Inland Mission.[24] Through the influence of Sidney Smith, Elim Chapel became, in modern parlance, extremely well networked.

However, Elim Chapel was not wholly preoccupied during the 1920s and 1930s with the militant defence of Christian civilization against its ideological enemies. And while these themes were sometimes present in advertising and pulpit discourse, Winnipeg and the Prairie West were viewed not chiefly as a liberal establishment to be opposed but as a mission field to be reached. "Being missionary in spirit," one enthusiastic newspaper article noted, Elim Chapel "is gaining an intimate knowledge of the needs of the great western provinces" and beginning a definite program of Bible instruction and evangelism.[25] With these emphases Elim Chapel soon became an important matrix for the development of a broader fundamentalist constituency in Winnipeg and throughout the Prairie West. Consequently, by 1930 A.C. Gaebelein could speak of the far-reaching impact of Elim Chapel's work and claim that it extended over the entire Canadian North-West as well as into Minnesota and North Dakota.[26]

WINNIPEG BIBLE INSTITUTE (1925) AND THE CANADIAN SUNDAY SCHOOL MISSION (1927)

If Elim Chapel represented the urban mission in Winnipeg during the interwar period, then Winnipeg Bible Institute (WBI) represented the educational mission, and the Canadian Sunday School Mission (CSSM) the rural mission. These organizations were at the centre of the

Winnipeg fundamentalist network, and while not formally affiliated in any way, their memberships overlapped and their goals were similar. As can happen with organizations so closely united in objectives and personnel, there were jealousies and tensions at times, but these ought not to obscure the fundamental solidarity of the movement. As Henry Hildebrand, who was involved in all three organizations as a young man, put it: "CSSM, Elim Chapel, and Winnipeg Bible Institute were pretty well handmaids in those days."[27]

The priority of Elim Chapel in this network is apparent when one examines the origins of Winnipeg Bible Institute and the Canadian Sunday School Mission in the 1920s. In both cases prominent members of Elim Chapel gave significant leadership to these organizations in their formative periods.

The Winnipeg Bible Training School, as it was first called, began in 1925 under the leadership of Harry L. Turner, a former Christian and Missionary Alliance missionary who was concerned to train women and men for Christian work in the fast-growing Prairie West.[28] Turner was assisted from the beginning by Muriel Taylor, a member of Elim Chapel. His leadership did not last long, however, and over the next several years the school saw a succession of principals and school locations, and experienced serious financial difficulties. By 1929 the school was seriously considering closing its doors. It was at this juncture that A. Clarke Hunt, president of Mid-West Paper Sales and former treasurer at Elim Chapel, was asked to take over as chairman. Like a businessman performing the "hostile" takeover of a failing company, Hunt turned the school around and gave effective leadership to Winnipeg Bible Institute (as it was soon to be called) for the next two decades. His influence was enormous, though he is only the most prominent of many examples of the overlapping constituency that developed between Elim Chapel and Winnipeg Bible Institute during these years.[29]

The story is much the same with the Canadian Sunday School Mission. About the same time Winnipeg Bible Institute was being established, J. Lloyd Hunter (1890–1943), an energetic missionary with the American Sunday School Union in Montana, North Dakota, and Minnesota, was considering coming to Manitoba to begin similar work in rural Canada. W.B. Riley of Minneapolis, a trusted friend and advisor, gave Hunter the name of John Bellingham at Elim Chapel as a contact. In 1926 and 1927 Hunter met with Bellingham and a group of Christian businessmen including Clarke Hunt and several other members of Elim Chapel and board members of Winnipeg Bible Institute. Organizing themselves as the Canadian Sunday School Mission, this group dedicated themselves to supporting Hunter in rural evangelism in Manitoba. The work of the CSSM under Hunter recalls the vigour and dedication of the early Methodist circuit-riding preachers. After Hunter's first summer, for example, he reported that he had spent sixty-four days in the field, travelled 2,500 miles, preached eighty-two sermons, and started seven Sunday schools. The primary aim of the mission was soon stated as being to carry the gospel to "otherwise unreached" areas of the Prairie West, and clearly defined territorial districts were established to which a missionary would be sent to begin and supervise a circuit of nondenominational Sunday schools.[30]

Winnipeg Bible Institute's aims dovetailed nicely with those of the Canadian Sunday School Mission, since they supplied each other with personnel: Bible institute students staffed many of the Sunday schools, and promising young converts from the Sunday schools were encouraged to go on for further training at the Bible institute. It is no surprise then that Lloyd Hunter actually served on Winnipeg Bible Institute's board for a period. Conversely, Muriel Taylor of Elim Chapel, an instructor at Winnipeg Bible Institute, was also involved in the Sunday school work from its beginning, and became general secretary from 1929 to 1951. Clearly, there was a small cast of actors in Winnipeg who played multiple parts in the unfolding evangelical drama on the Prairies. Perhaps the best example of this was C.L. Johnston, who was not only a long-serving member of all three boards but at the same time directed an outreach from Elim Chapel of children's services at dozens of locations around the city, involving individuals from each of these organizations.[31]

The Sunday School Mission spread quickly throughout Manitoba and Saskatchewan. It later assimilated other provincial Sunday school associations and became a truly national organization by 1950. In the particular case of Manitoba and Saskatchewan, its work in rural evangelism, and that of Winnipeg Bible Institute in education, may be credited directly with extending the Winnipeg fundamentalist network throughout the Prairie region. The patterns of extension during the late 1920s and the 1930s may be illustrated through the overlapping stories of a few key individuals.

SIMON FORSBERG IN SASKATCHEWAN AND WINNIPEG

The first, and one of the most influential, was Simon E. Forsberg (1899–1979) from Tacoma, Washington. Forsberg was in Canada for only five years, but he was an important channel of dispensational premillennialism and lastingly marked the people and institutions he touched with a concern for correct doctrine – which, for Forsberg, included the rejection of Pentecostalism. Forsberg had been pastor of an independent gospel church in Chicago for several years and had attended evening classes at Moody Bible Institute. In 1926 he entered the Evangelical Theological College (later Dallas Theological Seminary). As a student he developed a keen desire to pioneer home-missionary work in Canada, and in the autumn of 1929, after graduation, he moved to Moose Jaw to serve as the preacher at the Gospel Tabernacle and a teacher at W.J. Millar's Moose Jaw Bible Institute, then in only its second year of operation. Millar was an erstwhile associate of T.T. Shields but was a strong dispensationalist, and Forsberg was well suited to work with him.[32] Forsberg had earlier been in contact with the Canadian Sunday School Mission, and once settled in Moose Jaw, he wrote to ask them to extend their work into Saskatchewan. With seemingly boundless energy, he travelled incessantly during the summer, often on behalf of the CSSM, speaking as an evangelist and Bible conference speaker in Canada and the United States.[33] Within a few years Forsberg would move on to Winnipeg to take over as principal of Winnipeg Bible Institute, but while still in Moose Jaw he had already significantly influenced a few key Saskatchewan leaders.

For example, during the summer of 1930 Forsberg and his old friend John Mitchell (1892–1990) from Washington toured the western provinces.[34] They were invited to speak at the Trossachs Mission church south of Regina by D.R. Aikenhead, a fellow member with Forsberg of the local CSSM committee. Trossachs and the surrounding area had long been the scene of spectacular revivalist activity, and an annual tent meeting a half-mile north of the village attracted thousands of people throughout the 1920s and 1930s. Aikenhead managed the campground from 1919 to 1930 but was growing restive about its charismatic emphases. When Forsberg arrived, he gave Aikenhead a crash catechism in dispensational spirituality and persuaded him to abandon his Pentecostalism once and for all. Aikenhead then moved to Saskatoon in 1931 where he founded the Gospel Chapel, taught in the Saskatoon Bible Institute, and continued his involvement with the CSSM, becoming provincial superintendent in 1932. Here again in Saskatoon, as earlier in Moose Jaw, we observe the Winnipeg "multiple player" pattern of independent Gospel church, Bible institute, and Sunday school work. Through these and other contacts, Aikenhead became firmly linked to the Winnipeg fundamentalist network by the early 1930s. In fact, in 1938 Aikenhead moved to Winnipeg to replace Hunter as the national director of the CSSM.[35]

The Saskatoon Bible Institute at which Aikenhead taught had other significant connections to Forsberg, and key personnel such as the principal, Richard Nixon, and another teacher, R. Wesley Affleck, owed much to him. Nixon, for example, had trained under Forsberg in

Moose Jaw, and upon graduation in 1931, he became a CSSM missionary in Saskatchewan. He then established a Bible school near Melfort, moving it later to Saskatoon, where it continued until 1939. Affleck, like Aikenhead, was a preacher at the Gospel Chapel as well as a teacher in the school, and, also like Aikenhead, he would eventually follow the well-worn path to Winnipeg.

In the summer of 1931 Forsberg applied for and was awarded the vacant post of principal at Winnipeg Bible Institute. His move to Winnipeg established important links between fundamentalist organizations in Moose Jaw, Saskatoon, and Winnipeg.

Forsberg's career in Winnipeg illustrates the evolving character of this overlapping network. Just before Forsberg's arrival, Winnipeg Bible Institute had experienced a significant controversy over the expression of Pentecostal gifts under the principalship of H.C. Sweet.[36] In the spring and summer of 1930, while drafting a statement of faith, the board and Sweet recognized that they disagreed over "certain teaching points" and, consequently, Sweet officially resigned, though he continued to act as interim principal for a period. In the autumn about fifteen Pentecostal students became very demonstrative in the school's chapel worship.[37] Sweet supported these students, one of whom, Henry Hildebrand, recalled being invited to Sweet's home, where he took part in a prayer meeting in the attic with Sweet and others, during which he was surrounded and pushed down in the midst of loud cries, in a frenzied attempt to have him experience spiritual empowerment.[38] Aware of public criticism over such episodes, the board, led by Clarke Hunt, stepped in halfway through the school year and drafted a strong anti-Pentecostal statement, prohibiting any further manifestations by students on or off the school premises, requiring concurrence of the full board and faculty, and setting out an admissions policy that would screen out Pentecostals. Hunt, who had drafted the statement, committed the funds to cover an immediate severance payment to ensure Sweet's prompt dismissal. Within two weeks ten students withdrew from the institute. Sweet and many of the students went on to form their own Pentecostal school, Western Bible College.[39]

Evidently, then, Hunt shared the same non-Pentecostal convictions as Forsberg, and when Forsberg came to Winnipeg in the aftermath of this crisis, he "cleaned house." He brought a new "no-nonsense" emphasis upon discipline and theological rectitude. The school shifted decidedly from an accent upon "holiness" and the higher life to a stress upon "rightly dividing the word of truth" along dispensational lines. Forsberg arrived in 1931 with a statement of faith in hand, and he demanded and enforced total compliance, without reservation, on the part of board and faculty. Whereas the 1930 statement had had only eight brief points, Forsberg's had twelve longer ones, including an anti-evolution article affirming a literal creation, and an eschatological statement about the Rapture and the millennium.[40] A definite theological shift had taken place at the school.

This shift was reflected likewise in the classroom, where Forsberg expanded the course offerings in theology and added a course on "Dispensational Truth." For this he mimeographed his own notes, a condensation of Chafer's theology, and passed them out to the class. (These same notes would later be mimeographed and passed out to students at Briercrest Bible Institute in their theology classes.) The new emphasis upon doctrine and discipline was also apparent in the school calendar. Whereas it had earlier stressed simply the united non-denominational training of workers for the task of world evangelization, Forsberg introduced defensive themes, lamenting the spread of false doctrine and worldliness, and the prevailing ignorance of biblical teaching. The school motto echoed these concerns: "Holding Fast to the Faithful Word."[41] And in student life, Forsberg introduced a more organized and energetic approach to practical student work in mission and evangelism. The board regularly received detailed statistical reports on the activities and results of the students labours.[42] In sum, Forsberg brought a stress upon detailed Bible exposition, disciplined dispensationalist teaching, and activism in mission. Thus, in official doctrine, classroom teaching, public discourse, and practical service, Winnipeg Bible Institute had become under Forsberg the Dallas Theological Seminary of the Canadian Prairies.

Hildebrand claimed that Forsberg gave the school very strong theological direction, though as a person he was inclined to be "a bit dogmatic." The truth is that Forsberg could be downright irascible.[43] Despite this, he was extremely popular and well loved by students, and exerted a significant influence upon the thinking of many pioneer missionaries in Manitoba and Saskatchewan. Under Forsberg, the Winnipeg fundamentalist network was marked enduringly by a stress upon doctrinal rectitude and a disavowal of Pentecostalism.

HENRY HILDEBRAND IN MANITOBA AND SASKATCHEWAN

If Forsberg was a key figure shaping the character of the expanding network at several points in different locales, Henry Hildebrand (b. 1911) is a good example of someone who was himself shaped by that network and who reproduced its central emphases and structures elsewhere. Moreover, Hildebrand's career helps to illustrate not only the extension of the network into Saskatchewan but also the process of ethnic assimilation which frequently occurred as a secondary by-product of the undenominational concern for missions characteristic of the Winnipeg fundamentalist milieu.

A *Russländer* Mennonite, Hildebrand was a teenager when he emigrated with his parents to southern Manitoba in 1925.[44] In the spring of 1929 he learned 500 verses for the Bible memorization contest of the Canadian Sunday School Mission, and thereby earned a free week at summer camp on Lake Winnipeg. It was there that he experienced an evangelical conversion. The camp was staffed chiefly by Winnipeg Bible Institute graduates, and Grace Furness, who was one of those who counselled Hildebrand at the camp about his spiritual state, was a member of Elim Chapel. Fired by his experience at camp, Hildebrand first thought to go to the Mennonite Brethren Bible school in Winkler, but when Lloyd Hunter arranged a job for him in Winnipeg, he enrolled at Winnipeg Bible Institute instead. There he was inspired by the teaching of Forsberg, whom he later considered one of the most important influences on his life. He went to a Mennonite Brethren church during his first year but later on attended Elim Chapel because of its proximity and the famous preachers who came to speak there. His summers were devoted to working with the Canadian Sunday School Mission in rural Manitoba and Saskatchewan as a "circuit riding preacher." Fully assimilated to the fundamentalist ethos through these connections, Hildebrand was well prepared for the call in 1935 from the members of a small nondenominational gospel assembly in southern Saskatchewan to be their pastor and to start a Bible school.[45] Significantly, the call came from a businessman named Sinclair Whittaker (1888–1974),[46] who had been himself converted by Lloyd Hunter of the CSSM.

The school Hildebrand and Whittaker established in 1935 was the Briercrest Bible Institute, in many ways modelled on Winnipeg Bible Institute, with numbers of the early students and teachers having taken at least some of their education there.[47] Hildebrand kept up his links with the CSSM, and soon the pattern of students doing Sunday school work and Sunday school converts going to Bible school was duplicated at Briercrest. In 1937 Hildebrand took over from Aikenhead as the provincial superintendent of the Sunday School Mission.[48] If with Forsberg we observed the gradual linking up of fundamentalist clusters with Winnipeg, with Hildebrand and Briercrest, Winnipeg fundamentalism appears virtually to have planted a "branch office" in southern Saskatchewan.

There were, of course, many denominational and nondenominational Bible schools begun on the Prairies during these years. And the pattern, already observed, of independent Gospel Chapel, local undenominational

Bible school, and energetic Sunday school work in the surrounding area, was repeated time after time in towns across the West. On a small scale, this pattern reflected the relationship between Moody Church, Moody Bible Institute, and the American Sunday School Union in the American Midwest. These American institutions exerted an enormous influence upon the Canadian Prairies, and Smith, Hunter, Forsberg, Aikenhead, Annie Hillson of Briercrest, and many others had connections with one or more of them.[49] In Manitoba and Saskatchewan, however, the chief fundamentalist clusters owed their local origins to or later became significantly influenced by the Winnipeg milieu.[50]

While we have observed this with Moose Jaw, Saskatoon, and Briercrest, the situation was somewhat different in southern Manitoba, where Mennonites predominated. Here, Steinbach's Gospel Tabernacle and Bible School, Mennonite Brethren by origin, were effectively taken over by Ben D. Reimer (1909-1994) after he graduated from Winnipeg Bible Institute in 1940, and these institutions were transformed significantly in the direction of Winnipeg fundamentalism during his twenty year term as principal.[51]

Further cases could be illustrated, but it is clear that by the beginning of the Second World War the Winnipeg fundamentalist network had expanded to embrace a significant regional constituency in Manitoba and Saskatchewan. About the time of the war it may be argued that a process of institutional routinization, which paralleled the wider cultural process of modernization, had taken place within the fundamentalist network as the period of the pioneers passed. At Elim Chapel this was reflected in the passing of legal title to the church property from Sidney Smith to a self-governing congregation, and in the appointment of a full-time, regular pastor in 1939. From then on Elim Chapel would take on increasingly the character of one downtown church among many with a conventional pastoral ministry serving a traditional congregation. In the Bible institutes this routinization was reflected in growing concern after the war for accreditation, through the granting of degrees, the advanced training of faculty, and the certification of the schools by accrediting agencies. In the work of the Canadian Sunday School Mission, many local Sunday schools developed into regular church congregations, and the summer camp work was institutionalized through the extensive development of permanent facilities. But the central preoccupation of the overlapping constituency defined by these organizations continued to be the evangelization of the unreached and the fostering of personal holiness. The network also continued to manifest Forsberg's concerns – to be predominantly dispensational and to be marked by a concern for correct doctrine and by non-Pentecostal worship.

THE CHARACTER OF WINNIPEG FUNDAMENTALISM

What else may be said, in conclusion, of the character of this constituency as a whole? The first and most distinctive trait of Winnipeg fundamentalism was the consciousness of everyone involved that the Prairie West, urban and rural, constituted a vast field for evangelical missionary endeavour.[52] The religiously under-serviced rural and urban settlers were seen by the fundamentalists as a people to be reached with the gospel. John Mitchell, for example, commented in the diary of his tour of the Prairies in 1930 that in Manitoba there was "very little gospel testimony. Very little teaching of the Word," and that Manitoba's direst need was for "Preaching and teaching of the Word. Self-sacrificing Bible evangelists and pastors. A compassion for the thousands."[53] The fundamentalist mentality in this context, however, is better described as one of frontier entrepreneurship than of dissent from a religious establishment.[54]

Moreover, the fundamentalist constituency in Manitoba and Saskatchewan (in the phrase of David Elliot) "knew no borders." Americans such as Forsberg and Hunter figured largely in the pioneering of the North-West in both the United States and Canada, but equally Sidney Smith's influence was enormous throughout the United States and especially in Minnesota, where he had a summer home at Detroit Lakes and set up a miniature of Elim Chapel. A figure like John Mitchell defies categorization, since he was born in Yorkshire, migrated with his parents to the American Midwest, but then soon afterward moved to the Canadian Prairies for several years. Educated at Brandon College but also at Dallas Seminary, he married a Saskatchewan woman but served chiefly various charges in the American North-West. Although one of the founders and a long-term faculty member of Multnomah College of the Bible in Portland, Oregon, he was frequently back on the Canadian Prairies as a conference speaker for several weeks. He was, clearly, equally at home on both sides of the border.

All of this defines fundamentalism on the Canadian Prairies as neither distinctively British nor distinctively American. It was distinctive chiefly of the Prairie West in Canada itself, since the fundamentalist constituency did not differ markedly from the patterns of immigration and ethnicity which predominated in the West generally: this was a region open to European, central Canadian, and American settlers and to pioneers, economic or religious, of all sorts. This religious movement, more than the traditional denominations which had their historic roots elsewhere, uniquely expressed the character of the Prairies. In missiology terms, the movement grew more along indigenous than exogenous lines.

It should be plain by now that the label "sectarian" is of very limited use in the description of Winnipeg fundamentalism. The centre of the movement was not rural but urban, in one of the largest cities in Canada, and the principal fundamentalist satellites beyond Winnipeg originated in some of the largest cities in the region. And although ethnicity was not a central preoccupation of the Winnipeg fundamentalists, the dominant ethnic group was British-Canadian, the same group that predominated on the Prairies generally. Moreover, the leadership in Winnipeg was drawn from highly successful urban elites, not promising material out of which to make a religious culture which perceives itself in "outsider" terms. And finally, these fundamentalists made the point repeatedly that they were undenominational. As if to vex future church-sect theorists, the first sentence of Winnipeg Bible Institute's first calendar proclaimed its fellowship to be emphatically "non-sectarian."[55] Clearly, the Winnipeg fundamentalist network calls into question the whole picture of evangelicalism on the Prairies as a sectarian movement. While the fundamentalists saw society divided into the unregenerate and the regenerate, the worldly and the unworldly, they did not see themselves as particularly alienated. On the contrary, they saw themselves very much in the forward current of life.

Even within the range of contemporary evangelicalism in Canada, the Winnipeg fundamentalists cannot be characterized as particularly narrow or exclusive in their mentality. In the interwar period the Canadian Sunday School Mission and Winnipeg Bible Institute each had several board members and supporters from mainline churches, such as the Anglican and United churches. One of the Winnipeg Bible Institute's principals in the late 1930s, for example, was a graduate of the broadly interdenominational Toronto Bible College.[56] Moreover, young people from Elim Chapel went on to study not only in local Bible institutes but also at Knox College and Wycliffe College in Toronto, at Toronto Bible College, and at Princeton Seminary. From this fundamentalist network, missionaries were recruited from all the major foreign missions agencies. And the Bible institutes and the CSSM advertised or were frequently written up in the *Evangelical Christian* and the major American evangelical periodicals. Even that organization which John Stackhouse sees as the bellwether of a national, united evangelical fellowship in Canada, InterVarsity, found some of its greatest support from Elim Chapel from its earliest days when organized by Howard Guiness in Winnipeg in 1929.[57] The Winnipeg fundamentalist network perhaps offers a mid-point, in both ideological and geographic terms, between the extreme poles of evangelicalism which Stackhouse identifies in this period with the "churchish" Toronto Bible College and the "sectish" Prairie Bible Institute.[58]

Likewise, the rural mission needs to be seen in terms of shifting cultural perceptions during this period. Gerald Friesen has demonstrated how the Canadian Prairies at the beginning of the century were the subject of the last great romantic celebration of rural life, associated with images of purity and productivity. The farm was seen in Virgilian terms as the foundation of the economy, and the guarantor of moral goodness. The conventional wisdom was that "the country that grows wheat can grow men." During the 1920s, however, there was a gradual shift in sensibilities toward urban standards, technologies, and cultural works. Whereas farmers "had once been in the van of economic progress, the admired pioneers of empire and nation," writes Friesen, "now they were perceived to be slow-witted, eternally bitching 'sons of the soil.'"[59] This far-reaching shift in sensibilities, hastened by the Great Depression, has much to do with how fundamentalism on the Prairies has come to be perceived in retrospect. "Rural" has become synonymous with backwardness, anti-intellectualism, and obscurantism. This is not, however, a correct picture of Winnipeg fundamentalists in the Prairie West from 1910 to 1940.

Throughout this period the Winnipeg fundamentalists demonstrated a keen sense of contemporaneity, whether in running a church or a mission board like an up-to-date business, allowing a large scope for women in teaching and missionary roles, renting a downtown theatre for mass meetings, or exploring all the possibilities of print media, advertising, and, above all, the use of radio in the 1930s and 1940s.

Finally, it must be stressed that the Winnipeg fundamentalist network calls into question typologies of Canadian evangelicalism which would locate the key centre of the movement on the Prairies chiefly in Alberta. For example, between Winnipeg fundamentalism and the Prairie Bible Institute, established by L.E. Maxwell (1895–1984) at Three Hills, Alberta, in 1922, there were far fewer and less close ties than with the other institutions examined thus far in Manitoba and Saskatchewan. This was in part a function of social and economic geography: the distances were far, and the arid region that straddled the southern Alberta–Saskatchewan border was some of the least densely populated territory in the West. But there was also a difference in ethos, which related to Maxwell's quietist spirituality with its pronounced emphasis upon the renunciation of the self, his mistrust of dispensational or systematic theology, and the commune-style economic life of the institution. Of course, the shared emphasis upon home and foreign missions drew Maxwell and Prairie Bible Institute partially into the orbit of Winnipeg fundamentalism, but while the two constituencies overlapped in mission concerns, they remained in other ways two evangelical solitudes. For all that Prairie Bible Institute has exerted a significant influence in Alberta and throughout a large American constituency, it should not be taken as typical of evangelicalism as a whole on the Prairies. The roots of transdenominational evangelicalism in Manitoba and Saskatchewan, at least, may be found rather in the Sunday school begun in central Winnipeg by John Bellingham and Sidney Smith in 1910.

20 "The Heavenly Railroad": An Introduction to Crossley-Hunter Revivalism

KEVIN KEE

> As great as ... Moodie and Sankey, or Torrey and Alexander and some old-timers declare even greater.
> *Toronto Daily Mail and Empire,* 1934

Early in the winter of 1888 the thoughts of many Canadians turned to events unfolding in Ottawa's Dominion Methodist Church. On 8 January the Methodist evangelistic team of Hugh T. Crossley and John E. Hunter – probably, in terms of converts made, the most successful Canadian evangelists ever – had opened six weeks of services in the building, an event that had been attended by the nation's lapsed "Episcopalian" prime minister, Sir John A. Macdonald. Frequenting regularly with "Governors, Senators, and members of Parliament," Macdonald even celebrated his seventy-third birthday by appearing at the revival meeting.[1]

At the end of the evangelists' scheduled stay, when the host minister requested that they remain for one more week of services, the prime minister rose and asked the privilege of seconding the motion. That same night a remarkable event occurred in the life of the man who often scoffed at religion. Macdonald had once jested that Canadians had shown in the election of 1878 that they preferred John A. drunk to his opponent, the dour Scots Baptist, Alexander Mackenzie, sober. However, on this evening, the *Toronto World* reported: "When, in answer to an appeal by Mr Hunter, that all who wished to become Christians and desired the prayers of the audience would stand up, the premier of the Dominion, whose name has so long been the synonym of iniquity to many worthy grit minds, arose with his wife."[2] According to the Methodist *Christian Guardian,* "When the well-known form of the Honourable Premier arose in the centre of the church many strong men bowed their heads and wept for joy. The Right honorable gentleman himself was deeply affected."[3] After dining at Ernscliffe, Hunter attested that "Sir John is a changed man."[4] Major newspapers heralded his conversion and highlighted the sacrifices the hard-drinking politician was willing to make for his new-found faith. "Sir John and his estimable wife," one noted, "have banished wine and everything of that kind from their house for the past two weeks, and by the help of Almighty God. So says Sir John, 'banished it shall be as long as he lives.'"[5]

Mr M. Leeson, president of the East Elgin Conservative Association, probably echoed the sentiments of many other Canadians in a letter he penned to the prime minister: "I have been greatly delighted to here of you taking the stand you have of late in coming out manfully on the Lord's side ... I have prayed for you many times and I know God does here and answer Prayer. May the Lord help you to live verry near to him day by day fully trusting in His Promises."[6] Mr Leeson believed that God had answered his petitions, Canada's leader was now on "the Lord's side," and the land had moved one step closer to becoming "God's Dominion." And it had all been accomplished through the efforts of the famous evangelistic team of Crossley and Hunter.

Crossley and Hunter preached an open, accommodating Christianity that appealed to Canadians from all walks of life. Listeners were encouraged to commit their lives to Christ, to turn from their sinful ways, and to help make Canada a sanctified nation. This was their promised land, and the vehicle that would carry them to it was the six-week revival. Balancing the Methodist fervour of the past with a late-nineteenth-century desire for respectability, the evangelists co-opted the techniques of the theatre, making their services entertainment events and turning themselves into celebrities. Through the use of homespun metaphors and sentimental stories like "The Heavenly Railroad," they preached a message of simple faith and victorious living that persuaded converts to avoid "social sins" like dancing. As far as Crossley and Hunter were concerned, God wanted the best for his people, and that meant happiness in both this life and the next. It was a formula that proved remarkably effective – many were eager to ride the evangelists' revival train. Their popularity attests to the vitality of revivalism at the end of the nineteenth century; it also offers clues as to how revivalism had been compromised to ensure its appeal.

Despite the immense success of Crossley and Hunter in Ottawa and many other North American cities and towns, their story has eluded serious historical examination. It is important therefore to assess briefly the lives of the evangelists as a first step toward reviving a quickly fading folk memory.

Hugh Thomas Crossley was born in 1850 and John Edwin Hunter in 1856. Both were raised in nominally Christian homes in the backwoods of Canada West and were converts of camp meetings in their youth. While studying together at Victoria College in Cobourg, Ontario, they began conducting revivals for the benefit of students and townsfolk alike. Following ordination, they spent ten years ministering to various congregations. Then in 1884, the year of Canadian Methodist union and D.L. Moody's revival in Toronto, Crossley and Hunter banded together to form the most successful revival team of late-nineteenth-century Canada.

The story of their union would be repeated in almost every town and city they visited in North America. It was their belief, noted a reporter in Detroit, "that their present co-partnership resulted from nothing short of a Providential coincidence." Despite their previous experience as co-evangelists and their frequent visits together since college days, "it had not once occurred to them that the qualifications of one would supplement the nature of the other ... But one night this same thought came to both. Each sat down at once to write the other, and the letters proposing a union of forces passed on the route."[7] It was no burning bush; nevertheless the evangelists viewed it as a significant sign – a call out of the wilderness of rural Ontario, to lead God's people to the promised land – a sanctified Canada.

After obtaining the consent of their respective conferences, they met at Hunter's home in Essex Centre and opened their work there.[8] Success came swiftly. At the height of their popularity, engagements for their services were booked three years in advance. When Crossley died in 1934, one obituary claimed that "over 200,000 publicly accepted Christ following their numerous campaigns."[9] The *Toronto Daily Mail and Empire* declared that "their fame was as great as that of Sankey and Moodie, or Torrey and Alexander and some old-timers declare even greater." "The late Mr Crossley," the article continued, "brought more converts to the penitent form than any other single individual of his generation."[10]

In an age when the parson was considered, in the words of one historian, "the person par excellence,"[11] many contemporaries viewed these travelling evangelists as the greatest practitioners of their day. They noted that the evangelists' success was not limited by the size of the community, its wealth, or the age of its adherents. Crossley and Hunter found converts in large cities and tiny villages, and in audiences of all classes and ages.

Following D.L. Moody, they orchestrated a flexible program that kept their audiences busy and involved. However, they surpassed the predictable Moody by easily altering their methods to meet the anticipations of the crowd. On occasions when they were expected to adhere to the regular Sunday code of conduct, they conducted services that were praised for "keeping with the name and house of God."[12] But in other communities, amongst congregations which appreciated a more fervent approach, the evangelists delivered with excessive emotional appeals.

This penchant for accommodation reflected the two men's contrasting personalities. For a church and a society in transition, Crossley and Hunter were the perfect combination. Lending an aura of righteous respectability to the service was Crossley's role. He was a calm, happy evangelist, described by one reporter as "affable and pleasant, as near bordering on the phlegmatic as a revivalist well can be, and seldom loses the pleasing smile with which he cushions his hardest knocks."[13] His straightforward preaching style was frequently noted. "His sermons are plain, pointed, logical, persuasive, and powerful," a reporter commented. "His language is that of the home, the shop, the world, but perfectly free from slang. He puts the matter plainly before the people ... [showing] vigorous thought and careful preparation."[14]

This approach, while adding an air of respectability, was not enough to attract thousands of North Americans. Hunter seemed to provide the missing ingredient. Juxtaposed to his urban, scientific, courteous, respectable partner, Hunter was rural, emotional, confrontational, and flamboyant. Throwing off any pretention to learning, he represented the determined circuit-rider of the early nineteenth century, reminding his older listeners of a bygone era in the Methodist Church. Hunter's "magnetism" and "nervous fire" were nostalgic symbols of the fervour of the past, slightly tempered to meet the new demands for respectability.

In the words of one reporter, Hunter "was a hotbed of enthusiasm, active on his feet and ready with his tongue, a restless spirit who does two hours work in one."[15] While his partner's face beamed, "on the contrary, Rev. Mr Hunter seldom or never smiles, and then but in an apologetic manner. He is nervous and forceful in delivery, using free, frequent and vivid gestures. Occasionally he drops into the Yankeeism of slurring his words, as for instance in the sentence, 'We haf t' take diffunt ways t' catch diffunt men.'"[16] Evidence suggests that Hunter's slur and strange accent were largely contrived.

Hunter also adopted a staccato approach to oratory, wasting no time with words in his hurry to usher souls into the kingdom. His comments covered a variety of topics in minimal time. The discourse was often disjointed and more than a little confusing. As an observer in Chicago noted, Hunter "followed no set line of argument, but talked rapidly and impressively, paying no particular attention to commas, while his periods were riveted with a recommendation to 'Pray now; God is here with you.'"[17]

To modern-day observers, Hunter's idiosyncratic style would be distracting, but to his contemporaries it represented something of the exotic. The frequent gesticulations, contrived accent, rapid-fire delivery, and habit of pacing back and forth across the platform or running up and down the aisles, combined to create a persona that aroused curiosity, encouraged comment, and generated further interest. Yet Hunter was more than an eccentric orator: at heart he was a born actor.

As his son Ernest Crossley Hunter put it, "My father was more emotional in his preaching than Crossley ... he had graceful movements of body and hands, something of the quality of an actor."[18] Hunter's melodramatic displays, as much intuitive as contrived, seemed geared to startle and completely overwhelm his listeners. One evening in Detroit, "Mr Hunter spoke of the child's first prayer, then dropping on his knees repeated very feelingly, 'Now I lay me down to sleep,' and told how that prayer followed men and women through life."[19] This was not unusual. As a reporter in Chicago observed, Hunter was "apt to drop to his knees at any point during the discourse."[20]

Hunter's forte was the delivery of dramatic Bible expositions. Here his extemporaneous preaching and theatrical instincts were on display. With an actor's sense of informed improvisation, he drew on his surroundings to enliven and enrich his message. Ernest Crossley Hunter recalled "one meeting when a train could be heard rushing past the church shrieking its whistles. Father stopped in his message and asked the congregation to pray for the engineer, the fireman, and all the passengers on that train."[21]

Borrowing directly from the theatre, Hunter masqueraded a variety of popular roles. He had a fondness for playing the comedian, a role no doubt appreciated by the good-humoured prime minister. A tract Hunter published on tithing offers a glance at what one observer described as his "racy"[22] style of exposition: "A hoarder of gold is a fool twice told. Gathering riches is like gathering nuts – you scratch your hands getting them and break your teeth in cracking them. Money is like manure – it is no good until it is spread out."[23]

Hunter also drew on a varied repertoire of emotions. An audience in Belleville in 1888 caught a glimpse of how confrontational the evangelist could be. After only four days in "The Bay City," Hunter declared that "he never saw a greater lot of cowards than the people of Belleville."[24] On other occasions he was capable of speaking in the most sorrowful of tones, as he and his audience mourned over lost chances at salvation. The story entitled "The Heavenly Railroad," which was included in one of Hunter's tracts, was read at least once in every city. Purported to be true, it related an incident on an American train headed west:

A "little girl ... scarce four years old" boarded a train alone. Soon the conductor arrived to collect tickets and fares. The young lady innocently informed him that she had no ticket, that she was bound for heaven to visit her dead mother who had sung to her of the heavenly railroad. "Mister, do you sing to your little girl about the railroad that goes to heaven?" she questioned. The conductor confessed tearfully, "No ... I have no little girl now. I had one once, but she died some time ago, and went to heaven." The child again asked, "Did she go over this railroad, and are you going to see her now?"

"By this time," Hunter continued, "all in the carriage were upon their feet, and most of them were weeping." As the sentimental parable ended, the child queried, "What shall I tell your little girl when I see her? Shall I say to her that I saw her pa on Jesus' railroad? Shall I?"[25] Geared to break through the apparently hard hearts of the fathers in the audience, the tale inevitably brought men and women to tears.

Hunter conducted a gospel train of his own, carrying his audience from heights of joy to depths of grief. The mood of the audience was dictated by its engineer, and Hunter's skills of manipulation were noted wherever he travelled. One journalist commented after attending a revival service, "It would be a difficult thing to find a person with better tact and skill in manipulating a crowd of people, or more thoroughly efficient and powerful in exhortation or appeal than Brother Hunter."[26] Sir John A. Macdonald, one of the few who might have rivalled Hunter's oratorical skills, undoubtedly would have been impressed.

If nothing else, the prime minister was entertained. According to Hunter's son, "People who liked music went to church. People who liked dramatic entertainment went to church. A good sermon was regarded as a good night out."[27] In cities and towns that boasted relatively few amusements, and less that could be sanctioned by the church, the services were a welcome distraction from the daily grind of urban life. As an added bonus, this entertainment was "approved" by clerics and citizens alike. Each evening for a six-week run Crossley and Hunter would stage the biggest show around. Contemporaries marvelled at their success. One newspaper article opened with the observation that "a stranger would have been lead to ask the question last night, what is going on ... in the city. Are Booth & Barret here?"[28]

Keen observers of the time might have been struck by the similarities of the evangelistic meetings in their local Methodist church and the shows in the nearby opera house or theatre. After entering a Crossley-Hunter revival service and jostling their way to the best available seats, they might try to attract the attention of one of the ushers selling souvenir hymn-books, the evangelists' own *Songs of Salvation*. (If they chose to save the expense, they would be unable to join their Christian brothers and sisters in song.) After a few hearty laughs (or tears) at Hunter's routine, and some sentimentalism supplied by Crossley's sermon and songs, they would exit the sanctuary and on their way home perhaps pass the local stores where they could purchase souvenir cabinet photos of the esteemed revivalists.[29] At their workplace the next day, they would share the previous evening's events with the other employees and perchance encourage them to go and view the show for themselves.

Crossley and Hunter's reputation for staging exciting, soul-saving revival shows guaranteed capacity crowds in every sanctuary they graced. It also brought them unrivalled fame. In the late nineteenth century, no single actor dominated Canadian theatres, and partisan dailies presented either hagiographical or acrimonious depictions of the country's political leaders. Few could compete with the near-universal respect accorded to God's spokesmen by newspapers. The evangelists were celebrities and bore all the trappings of their position.

Crossley and Hunter were the "talk of the town" wherever they travelled. After their departure from Sault St Marie, a reporter observed, "In almost every house which I have entered, I have heard their names mentioned with delight. Their portraits are to be seen in many parlours."[30] In the homes of Roman Catholics, the Pope might watch over the house from a hallowed section of the wall; their Protestant neighbours reserved the same space for Crossley and Hunter.

Like present-day celebrities, they were flooded with mail and gifts from appreciative admirers. The people of Ottawa in 1888 were especially beneficent – they could not forget the prime minister's conversion. In Canada's capital city the evangelists were "recipients of many tokens of friendship; among others may be mentioned a handsome fur lined overcoat and cap presented to Mr Hunter by a Presbyterian lady; also another costly fur lined coat, gauntlets, and cap presented to Mr Crossley by a half dozen of gentlemen who have been greatly blessed by his faithful preaching. The overcoats and accompaniments must have cost between $200 and $300."[31]

Three years later, in South Dorchester, the archbishops of God's revival church were the recipients of the most highly prized of gifts. In the summer of 1891 newspapers announced the opening of the Crossley Hunter Methodist Church, South Dorchester.[32] The building stood as a symbol of their contribution to church growth at the apex of Methodist power in Canada, until it closed in 1964.

Recognition of the evangelists' status came from many sectors of society. Perhaps most important was the attention granted by those in political power. Often they were converts, like Belleville's mayor, who according to one report, "had attended the meetings out of curiosity and had gone forward and was now happy in the love of God."[33] And when the politicians failed to go to Crossley and Hunter, the evangelists went to them. They routinely made guest appearances at institutions of distinction, often publicizing the event themselves.

The defining moment in their development as evangelist-celebrities came with the apparent conversion of Prime Minister Macdonald. The story of the development of the statesman's relationship with Crossley and Hunter and his spiritual rebirth was heralded across the land that spring of 1888 and retold by the evangelists in every city that later hosted a Crossley-Hunter revival. No detail was spared in outlining the special bond between the revivalists and their eminent convert, and Hunter never failed to provide particulars of the event during interviews. According to Hunter, he and his partner were more than just the vehicles for the conversion of the prime minister: "When he came to bid us good-bye there were tears in his eyes and ours, and we felt very much drawn to him and that he felt a fatherly interest in us. The last thing he did was to turn as he was going down the stairs from the vestry and kiss his hand to us, which he seemed to do as tenderly as a mother would throw a kiss to her child. This was the last time I saw him."[34] The story was filled with pathos and solemnity, and at the centre stood Crossley and Hunter. Like the characters in Hunter's "Heavenly Railroad" and Crossley's poignant ballad, "Papa, What Would You Take for Me," the evangelists were children who had become the means of conversion for their parent.

Hunter's claim to sonship was enhanced by a calculated adjustment to his countenance. In the same interview, the reporter noted that "there is a striking resemblance between Mr Hunter's physiognomy, since he has divested himself of his mustache and that of portraits of Sir John taken when he was a young man ... There is the curly hair, the prominent nose and the pleasant countenance of the deceased statesman. And by the way the evangelist communicated the fact that he was first known as 'John A.', although he is now known as 'John E.', the second name not being given him at baptism, but the first 'John A.'"[35] Hunter knew good publicity when he saw it, and he spared no opportunity in highlighting the strange coincidence. Whether or not Hunter manufactured the tale of his name change is irrelevant. Significant was the zeal with which he "communicated" that story to the public.

He was equally willing to divulge other details of his personal life; and the public was eager to know them. Interviews frequently focused on the evangelists' salubrious eating and exercise habits.[36] Crossley's bachelorhood was another subject of frequent discussion. His eligibility evidently made him the interest of many young women across the continent. An interview for the *Winnipeg Sun* revealed that "A wife is picked out for Crossley in almost every place they go – so says

Mr. Hunter – but he escapes from the net."³⁷ Nets seemed to be set wherever Crossley trod. Instead of discouraging the trappers, Crossley informed those who were unaware. In a letter published in the *Winnipeg Free Press* he announced: "Lest any person should say as one did, 'I don't think Mr Crossley thinks of his wife, for I never heard him speak of her,' I might say that I am still enjoying single blessedness."³⁸ He would enjoy it to his death.

Recognizing themselves as objects of sexual attraction, the evangelists used those emotions to ensure the attendance of vast audiences. Not surprisingly, the majority of those in the pews were women. Occasionally their presence was overpowering. When, for instance, Crossley and Hunter tried to restrict women to the galleries of Brantford's Wellington Methodist church (in an attempt to make room for the men), chaos resulted. A report published in the local newspaper chronicled the event. When the balcony was filled, the women "held an impromptu overflow assembly around the doors leading to the body of the church [where] they stood and hustled one another." At eight o'clock Hunter finally "gave the word that the ladies might be admitted ... in an instant the crowd rushed in pell mell and the edifice was filled to its utmost capacity."³⁹

Hunter probably enjoyed the spectacle. Regardless, he recognized the correlation between audience numbers and his persona. What one observer referred to as his "unbounded egotism"⁴⁰ was manifested in Kingston, where "the Rev. ... said that the excuses made for not coming to the meetings were peculiar and sometimes ridiculous. Some would not come because they did not like him; he was sure the ladies would not make that excuse."⁴¹

Hunter was not exceptionally handsome, but he did place a special emphasis on his appearance. Contemporaries took notice. According to a reporter in Hamilton, "he doesn't look one bit like a minister. His face is smooth shaven except for a diminutive black moustache. His black suit was the perfection of cut and fit and his boots were exquisitely made. His hair is black and when seen on the street in ordinary attire the suspicion would be apt to arise that he was the ADVANCE AGENT OF A THEATRICAL TROUPE."⁴²

The writer undoubtedly relished the irony of his description. As far as Hunter was concerned, the theatre was the gateway to ruin and eternal damnation. It was also his main competition. As a substitute to the bawdy shows in local playhouses, Hunter offered his own form of Christian entertainment. More often than not, the evangelists won the contest. As theatres closed for lack of business, churches hosting revival meetings filled to overflowing. The theatre was not alone as it withered under the evangelists' attacks. Alcohol, card-playing, and especially dancing were damned with the same frequency. But why were Crossley and Hunter so emphatic in their denunciations of these "carnal" pleasures, and why were these sins singled out for attack while others were ignored?

The evangelists effectively mirrored the concerns of a denomination rooted in perfectionist theology. Since the mid-nineteenth century, Methodist literature, class meetings, sabbath sermons, and revivals had emphasized perfection and articulated strict guidelines for personal behaviour. So strong was this conviction that delegates to the 1886 General Conference took it upon themselves to pass a "Footnote" proscribing drinking alcohol, playing cards, attending the circus or theatre, and dancing. The emphasis on individual reform included society, and Canadians in all denominations were soon working to create a country devoted to the principles of the Protestant Reformation. This "crusading evangelical Protestantism" was perhaps best articulated amongst Methodists by E.H. Dewart, the editor of the influential *Christian Guardian* from 1869 to 1894. For Dewart, it was the church's responsibility both to rebuke sin and reform the individual. As far as he was concerned, "the churches ... have much more to do with the reformation of society than has science or legislation."[43]

Many viewed revivalism as a natural vehicle for this reformation. It was only fitting that Crossley and Hunter reserved time in their sermons to expose the sins that poisoned individual souls and society in general. They were unflinching in their support of the 1886 Conference Footnote and proved to be useful instruments in its implementation until Methodists abandoned it in 1910. In Belleville in 1908 the *Daily Intelligencer* reported that "Drink, the dance, racing, theatre, cards, and cheap shows were condemned as 'the tropical hatcheries of the death-dealing evils of our times.'"[44]

In his book *Practical Talks on Important Themes*, published in 1895, Crossley devoted one chapter each to "The Theatre," "The Cards," "The Weed," "The Licensed Liquor Traffic," and "The Parlour Dance." For Crossley, dancing (and its motivator, sexual desire) was a direct competitor of Christian chastity. After all, it was conceived in the theatre. "The waltz," for instance, "was born December 20th, 1787 – first seen in a Vienna theatre, the progeny of a licentious stage and its consort, the ballet. This amorous, gyratory hugging was, for a time, thought to be too shockingly indecent to be tolerated anywhere else."[45] As Crossley's examination continued, dancing and sexual immorality became almost synonymous. "One has said: 'As alcohol is the spirit of beverages, so sex is the spirit of the dance; take it away, and let the sexes dance separately, and dancing would go out of fashion very soon and become nil.'"[46]

Failure to adhere to the approved code of conduct brought obvious disaster. "The chief of police of New York," Crossley warned, "testifies that 'three-fourths of the abandoned girls of that city say that they were led to ruin by dancing.'"[47] Choosing to dance could not only destroy your life on earth, it could damn your soul for eternity. Crossley implored, "Beloved, you know ... that heaven and hell are realities, and that voices divine and human warn and invite you. Will you ... bid defiance to God and eternal disaster, as you go on with the dance and other carnal pleasures, while you neglect to seek the salvation of yourself and others till ... you are lost eternally?"[48]

Hunter echoed Crossley's sentiments with stronger words. Rather than begging listeners not to indulge in the dance, he confronted and humiliated the men who taught it. In contrast to the evangelists, who were "real" men in control of their passions and thus free of sin, dancing teachers were portrayed as effeminate sops. Hunter usually summed up his attack on their manhood in a few words. "Dancing masters are poor stuff," he told the people of Detroit, "spider-legged, eye-glass wearing dudes."[49] On another occasion, he noted in his inimitable way: "I would as soon see the arms of an orangoutang around my wife's or sister's waist as the arms of one of these lecherous dancing masters."[50]

Comments like this drew crowds. But they also drew opposition, from Christians with sturdy thighs and clear vision who had little in common with the ape world. Some audience members in Hamilton in 1889 (to cite just one example), who saw nothing wrong with these liberties, were affronted by the evangelist's choice of image and demanded an apology.[51] But Hunter did not budge, and his partner supported him. Crossley consistently argued that while an action might not be immoral, that did not necessarily make it acceptable. The slightest appearance of evil should make the questionable activity anathema. Simply put, if the Bible did not sanction it, if Jesus would not do it, how could one of his followers? The evangelist made his maxim clear: "Never compromise, but always and everywhere set an example worthy of imitation; so shall your life before the world, like Daniel's, be unimpeachable."[52]

Just as Daniel and his comrades distinguished themselves in the Babylonian court by their abstemious conduct, so new converts were to distinguish themselves through self-discipline. In a Crossley and Hunter revival, a conversion to Christ carried a conversion to a whole new way of living. In this manner Christians provided a visible sign of their commitment to Christ, separating themselves from the sinful behaviour that had characterized their "former life." Safe within the boundaries of propriety, they enjoyed a sense of belonging. Circumspect behaviour became a badge of distinction, testifying to the convert's new relationship with God and his church.

However, there was a danger that some might take too seriously Crossley's call to a new life free of sin. Striving toward sinless living (culminating in the experience of "sanctification") had been a central tenet of Methodism since the 1850s, when the revivals of James Caughey and Phoebe and Walter Palmer popularized the notion of a distinct "second blessing." Forty years later, the preoccupation with holiness resurged to the point that it became a concern for Protestants of all denominational stripes.[53] This time, however, holiness was viewed as an experience that paralleled or even replaced conversion. Seekers also manifested a hunger for spectacular "special blessings" that the more established, conventional churches apparently refused to offer.[54] This widespread longing for sanctification led many frustrated Methodists out of their staid churches and into radical movements led by the likes of Ralph Horner. Although Horner's movement failed to achieve spectacular growth, it was a cause for concern to Methodist special evangelists. Crossley had to make sense out of the confusion, while preaching an alternative message that would keep inquisitive Methodists in their churches, where they belonged. In this regard, he was largely successful.

Crossley's standard sanctification sermon opened with the reassurance that there was little, in fact, to be anxious about. "Many think of and trouble about the witness of the Spirit," he remarked. "Let God attend to His own work – which he ever does – as we do our part ... So shall the witness of the Spirit be given, received, and retained more or less clearly."[55] God did not want to make it difficult, Crossley told his readers: "God wills to us, by promise and command, the Beulah land of perfect love."[56] At the same time he empathized with those who felt anxious. For several months after his conversion, he had agonized over the experience of sanctification. But at a meeting led by Walter Palmer, he learned that Christian perfection was simply loving God with all of his heart. In a few moments the mists of confusion cleared, and Crossley "by faith received Him to fill my heart with His love; *yea, with Himself*, for 'God is love.'"[57]

This was the message he passed on to his listeners. Drawing on the familiar "altar theology" of the past, he reinterpreted Palmer's "shorter way" to perfection to meet present and future anxieties. And from 1884 to 1910 his sermon, titled "Perfect Love," provided the answers that penitents required. According to a report in the *Belleville Daily Intelligencer* in 1908, he told the people of the Bay City:

Justification and sanctification took place at the same time, and that all justified people had the Holy Ghost. The matter of entire sanctification and the fullness of the spirit remained, and to his mind perfect love covered the terms that we used, and the one perfected in love enjoys both. There being degrees of love every one should seek to have his love perfected, and it was not to be attained but obtained. When obtained it changed the life and made the possessor more amiable, easier to get along with and of more service in the cause of God.[58]

Recognizing that many would appreciate a step-by-step plan outlining how this gift from above was "obtained," Crossley included one in *Practical Talks*: "(1) We believe and meditate upon the love of God in Christ; (2) His love inspires our love; (3) a desire for His love to fill our hearts springs up; (4) we believe Christ is able and willing to satisfy this desire; (5) we trust Him to do it *now*, and (6) the great work is done."[59] It was that easy. By a simple act of the mind, the great work was done. But most Christians probably recognized that staying in "Perfect Love" would take much more effort.

To reassure those anxious about falling out of "perfect love," Crossley promised victory. His message would be an antecedent to the powerful "Victorious Life" movement that transformed North American Christianity beginning in the early 1900s. It was a far cry from the "sorrow for sin" that had characterized Methodist revival conversions in the early nineteenth century, and which continued into the twentieth century under Ralph Horner. For Horner, conversion and sanctification required being dead to the world but alive to Christ. For Crossley and Hunter, the two acts demanded minimal sacrifice and guaranteed happiness.

In a chapter in *Practical Talks*, titled "Questions about Temptations," Crossley asked, "Why do Christians in general not live a higher, better, happier, more exemplary and victorious life?" They could, he pointed out, "by the grace of Christ, be more than conquerors. God can, according to His word, destroy the body of sin, that 'henceforth we should not serve sin.' (Rom. vi. 6)."[60] Others were frightened to commit all to Christ for fear of offending him with their personal imperfection. On this point Crossley was also clear: they should not worry. They had very little to do – Christ did all the work. "Trust yourself," he urged, "with all your weaknesses, idiosyncrasies, faults, failings, cares and sorrow, to Jesus. Yea, trust your unmanageable self into the hands of Him Who is able to manage you."[61] It took little effort to live a God-pleasing life. "Christ dwelling in the heart makes a life of trust and obedience easy," Crossley promised.[62]

But Christians could gain more than an easy life. They could be energized and empowered. This promise of power was obviously appealing. "The secret of a vigorous and victorious Christian life," Crossley stated, "is the constant indwelling of the Spirit of Jesus Christ in us. He, abiding in us, so dominates our minds and controls our lives as to *energize our activities, give power over self and sin*, as also power to witness for Him and influence others for the Saviour."[63]

Enjoying personal power did not require a life of self-denial: instead, it was a prelude to happiness. To the people of Ottawa Crossley declared: "Coming to Christ will take away none of your pleasures."[64] Several weeks later, he told the citizens of Belleville that "Those who were not christians denied themselves more pleasure than did christians."[65] To the readers of *Practical Talks*, he contended, "Faith is the life of domestic happiness, of financial prosperity, and of social harmony."[66]

Doubters in the crowd would have noticed that God had indeed blessed with "financial prosperity" others in the sanctuary. Especially in Ottawa, Crossley's claims would have appeared self-evident. The participation and financial benevolence of the wealthy were not unusual at the time.[67] When funds were required to maintain or expand the work of the church and its evangelists, many among the upper classes made substantial contributions. They were obviously an integral factor in the Christianization of society.

The organizational skills and financial aid of the upper classes were required if the nation was to be transformed, if Canada was to become "God's Dominion." In town after town, observers noted the conversions taking place. After a revival in Kingston in 1889, the *Daily British Whig* recognized a "toning up [of] the morality of hundreds of citizens."[68] According to a writer in Brantford, "one piece of news that will be a source of great joy to mothers, sisters, and probably sweethearts, is the fact that about every young fellow that is met on the streets has given up drinking. To use the ordinary vernacular, the boys say, 'I am on a rock,' which, being translated means, 'I am not drinking.'"[69] A report from Calgary boasted: "Many non-church-goers have been brought in; a prize fighter, and at least one saloon-keeper being among the number."[70]

Sometimes, however, "toning up the morality" of a town to please the local elites seemed to take precedence over converting its citizens' hearts. Hunter often challenged his listeners to "right their wrongs" and pay their debts during his lesson devoted to Bible exposition. In Peterborough the local daily contained a summary of how "he spoke of Jacob making restitution and said there would have to be a good deal of restitution in Peterborough ... If they had taken a dishonest dollar, they might bury it under the years of a life time but on the judgment day it would come to the top. 'Go,' he said, 'and pay your doctor bill and your grocery bill; pay them all but your whiskey bill.'"[71] In Winnipeg a journalist reported, "One thought particularly dwelt upon" during Hunter's discourse "was the duty of making restitution. Several examples were mentioned, showing that seekers of the Divine favor must be willing to restore what they may have wrongfully taken from others."[72] On other occasions Hunter was more direct: "Pay your debts or you will go to hell,"[73] he told the people of Belleville.

He obviously had the approval of the creditors of Canada. A newspaper in Montreal, for instance, headlined a report of a revival service with "Pay Your Doctor's Bills And Grocery Accounts."[74] The newspaper barons in Belleville took another approach, commenting after the evangelists had left that "If there are not a lot of debts squared up as a result of these meetings it will not be the fault of the evangelists, who have talked pretty plainly on this question. Last night Mr Hunter said that the first thing a man does when soundly converted is to pay up his old debts."[75] Assuming that the plebeians' memory was short, the newspaper did its duty and reminded them of the particulars of their saving faith. It was all well and good to rejoice with the angels over the new converts to the kingdom, the creditors ruminated, but back on earth there was business to be settled.

There were others besides the doctors, grocers, and creditors who stood to gain from the evangelists' message. Railroad owners – the richest of the rich in late-nineteenth-century Canada – hoped the evangelists' influence would ensure sober and safer employees running the lines. During their sojourn in Winnipeg, Crossley and Hunter were invited to "the gents' department of the CPR waiting-room," where "several conductors, engineers, brakemen, firemen and general railway hands connected with the more practical work of a railroad" had been assembled. To this hard-drinking, church-scoffing crowd, Hunter expanded upon a tract he had published expressly for railwaymen. The local newspaper reported how

He described the route of the "Lightning Express on the Black Valley Railroad" as follows: Leave Tippleton at 6 A.M. (applying to the man who must get a drink before breakfast); Topersville at 7 A.M., Drunkard's Curve at 9 A.M., Rowdywood at 10 A.M., Quarrelville at noon (when the drunkard comes home and fights with his wife), Prisonburg at 2 P.M., Beggarstown at 4 P.M., Deliriumville at 6 P.M., Demon's Land at 10 P.M., Black Valley at 11 P.M., Dead River at 11:59 P.M., and Destruction and Damnation at midnight. Tickets for sale in all bar-rooms. Agent A.L. Cohol; T.O. Bacco, assistant.[76]

Hunter concluded by reading the touching story of "a conductor and a little girl" (the "Heavenly Railroad" related above); the newspaper evidently did not consider this salvation message useful enough to print.

Crossley then followed by preaching on the "two great railroad lines leading to the other world, the broad gauge, of which Satan is the general superintendent; and the narrow gauge, where the general superintendent is Christ." He went on to list the Christian railwaymen in

Winnipeg and other cities, then pointed out that "Unlike the devil's railroad, the narrow gauge trains were all running all the same way, and there was no danger of a collision or smash up." The men in the audience would have taken this both figuratively and literally. Christ's way, marked by sobriety and self-discipline, kept them safe on the rails to heaven, and on the rails spanning the country. Just in case they missed the point, Crossley followed by urging "railway men to abstain from strong drink."[77] In this message the story of salvation was almost incidental. Ending alcoholism was the first priority for Crossley and Hunter. It was also the first priority of the railroad owners. To them, Crossley and Hunter were useful tools: their gospel, if taken to heart, ensured earthly profits.[78]

The manipulation of divine means for temporal ends was even more blatant in Oakville. Here the local newspaper made no attempt to dissemble – the gospel of Crossley and Hunter was good because it was useful. As the reporter put it,

However one may differ with the means and methods employed by these two gentlemen *to persuade people to give up bad habits and evil associations and then lead better lives*, we believe them to be sincere, *and it is because the masses believe this also* ... is the reason that they are listened to by such crowds, and so attentively ... We advise all our readers to go and hear them, you certainly can receive no harm and it may result in doing you much good. *Believing as we do that the better a man is both morally and spiritually, the better neighbor and citizen he will be, we hope that their services will be crowned with the same success as last year even more abundantly.*[79]

The journalist obviously had little use for the "means and methods" of the evangelists, but the "masses" enjoyed them, and they made local ruffians better citizens. He wished the revivalists success.

Thanks to Crossley and Hunter, quiet and order prevailed in cities and towns across the Dominion. Souls were saved, bar rooms emptied; wives, mothers, and daughters rejoiced. And many of the local elites were happy too. After all, they reaped the benefits of a quiet town populated by more orderly workers.

A strange thing had happened to the revivals of these evangelists. The message of conversion to a new life pleasing to Christ had become, at least for some, a message of conversion to bourgeois norms pleasing to Canada's elites. Crossley and Hunter's vision, and the vision of many in the Methodist Church, was for a Christianized Canada, a land that could truly call itself God's Dominion. The support of railroad barons and political leaders was central to realizing that goal, not only because their presence provided an air of respectability, and generated the interest of many others but also because they had the power to help sanctify Canada.

For this reason, the conversion of mayors, members of parliament, and especially the prime minister was of the utmost importance. But in order to appeal to them, and to the influential "middling classes," Crossley and Hunter had to compromise their method and message. They conducted entertaining services, reassuring penitents that if they avoided societal ills like dancing, they would reap the benefits of a sanctified, victorious, happy life and a treasure-filled mansion in heaven. And in the case of Sir John A. Macdonald, simply standing proved sufficient.

The conversion of the prime minister of the Dominion attests to revivalism's vitality at the end of the nineteenth century. But the event also offers clues to the decline of the movement in the twentieth century. "Societal norms" are subject to change, and when the circumspect, bourgeois behaviour triumphed by Crossley and Hunter lost its appeal – best symbolized by the dropping of the "Footnote" by Methodists in 1910 – the evangelists' message no longer appeared relevant. Sir John A. Macdonald was no Moses, and his conversion did not turn Canada into the new Israel. At the dawn of the new century many leaders of the Methodist Church turned to a different vision for reform: the social gospel. They hoped that this vehicle might finally bring Canadians to the promised land.

21 "The World of the Common Man Is Filled with Religious Fervour"[1]: The Labouring People of Winnipeg and the Persistence of Revivalism, 1914–1925

MICHAEL GAUVREAU AND
NANCY CHRISTIE

At the height of the Winnipeg General Strike, Rev. A.E. Smith, later a self-proclaimed communist, judged that the effectiveness of the gospel must come "from the people" and that it was the religion "of the multitude – the common people" which ultimately sustained the "Soul and Spirit of the Methodist Church."[2] This characterization of the intense spirituality of the Canadian working class compels historians to re-evaluate the now almost standard assertion that Canadian workers abjured Christianity in favour of the theology of socialism and labour activism.[3] Even non-Marxist historians of the Winnipeg General Strike have contended that the tenets of social Christianity – what they term the "social gospel" – constituted the central ideological vehicle for the radicalization of labouring people.

This perception of the way in which Protestantism intersected with labour activism in the period surrounding the events of 1919 has been derived wholly from the views of the trade-union leadership and a select few Christian Socialists, namely J.S. Woodsworth and William Ivens.[4] This undue prominence accorded the labour leadership has arisen because of the adamantine desire of labour historians to uncover the roots of the politicization of Canadian workers in the twentieth century and, as such, has rested upon an unproven ideological convergence between ordinary workers and their "radical" leaders.

It is therefore important to consider the oft-ignored but no less important tradition of working-class revivalism. The majority of workers were not incipient Christian humanists as David Bercuson, Richard Allen, and Ramsay Cook have suggested; rather, the core of working-class religious culture in Winnipeg revolved around the old-time gospel verities of the atonement, personal conversion, and the divinity of Christ. It may be argued that in Winnipeg there existed a definite and enduring disjuncture between social Christianity, which functioned essentially to cement the reformist ideals of the middle class with the aspirations of the labour leadership, and the religious experience of the majority of the workers who remained attached to the more conservative and traditional culture of evangelicalism.

This religious traditionalism of Winnipeg workers has, in turn, wider implications for interpreting the periodization of revivalism in Canada. Why did revivalism endure well into the 1930s as the mainstream of the Protestant experience? Perhaps it flourished because of its broad appeal among ordinary Canadians. This was especially so following the events of 1919 when the middle-class Christian leadership of Winnipeg felt particularly constrained to address the reality of labour protest and hence actively sought to incorporate working-class forms of piety into the institutional church.

The divisions between middle-class and working-class experiences of religion were manifested in the heated debates in the pages of the *Winnipeg Free Press* just before the outbreak of the First World War over the question of tendering an invitation to the popular American revivalist Billy Sunday. At the behest of Rev. Salem Bland, the Ministerial Association invited Sunday to Winnipeg in the spring of 1914[5] in the full recognition that Sunday's sermons, which they compared with those of the great evangelist of the First Great Awakening, George Whitefield, were "specially adapted to the class from which his audience was drawn,"[6] namely the working people of North America. His supporters stressed how Sunday's non-theological, simple, and "manly" talks, although often coloured by some "eccentricities of expression" and Anglo-Saxon slang, were nevertheless powerful and dramatic in their execution and thus enormously effective in converting the "submerged class, the down and outs," even those who lay beyond the reach of the Salvation Army.[7] With choice phrases such as "You big stiffs, come back to God" and "Wash that streak of yellow off your back and confess Jesus," Sunday's exhortations caused both men and women to fall to their knees in the circus-tent sawdust, tears streaming down their cheeks as they openly declared themselves for God. Of particular attraction to poor, urban dwellers, this intense and overwhelming sense of enthralment by the power of the gospel tended to make them "forget themselves completely, forget their surroundings, forget their station in society."[8] Many of Sunday's middle-class detractors condemned his tawdry and sensationalist techniques. The Unitarian Horace Westwood, for example, chided Sunday for his lack of "Christian culture, dignity, and reverence."[9]

C.W. Gordon, whose later religious novels were intended to appeal to a wide popular audience, reproached detractors of Sunday like Westwood: "I decline to accept the judgement passed on any evangelist by a man who does not believe in Jesus Christ as the son of God, who has no place for the atonement and for the cross of Christ in his theology."[10] To offset the middle-class criticism that Sunday was a vulgar buffoon, Gordon hailed him as a master of homiletics and an evangelist of vivid expression and "utter simplicity." He drew particular attention to the fact that Sunday's tent meetings drew tens of thousands of people, largely the unchurched from the "industrial" world.[11]

Prior to the First World War, religious belief and denominational affiliation were outstandingly high in Winnipeg.[12] However, many middle-class Protestant constituencies remained troubled over what they perceived as the low rate of church membership among the working classes. By appealing to temperance sentiment among middle-class Christian reformers, W.J. McIvor of Knox Church in Cartwright, Manitoba, attempted to obviate this opposition to Sunday, recounting how in a single night in Pittsburgh the American evangelist, through his unvarnished denunciation of sin, induced 35,000 working men to pledge themselves to destroy the liquor traffic.[13] Moreover, for those middle-class Protestants who feared the attractions of radical labour activism among male workers, numerous newspaper columns emphasized the indispensability of traditional evangelicalism in enlisting men into Christian service and exalted the achievements of the American revivalist Charles Stelzle and various members of the fundamentalist Moody Bible Institute among the railway shopworkers of Winnipeg.[14]

By the early twentieth century the majority of Winnipeg's middle-class Protestants had become thoroughly imbued with what they viewed as the more modern tenets of social Christianity and were repelled not only by Sunday's low-brow manner but by his emphasis upon personal sin and public conversion and by his fundamentalist theology. Not only did middle-class Protestants prefer a more learned style of preaching[15] but those who continued to encourage revivalism did so only because it might stimulate the application of Christian ethics to society. Hence, middle-class churches endorsed the revival campaigns of the thoroughly genteel British evangelist Dr Joshua Stansfield, largely because his ultimate message was that personal salvation would naturally lead to social redemption.[16] Similarly Mrs Catherine Booth-Clibborn, a noted British evangelist and temperance advocate, enjoyed an immense following among middle-class women because she preached that social Christianity was effective in combating socialism and anarchism on the war front.[17] If revivals were to remain central to the Protestant experience, they must, in the estimation of many middle-class church-goers, shift their emphasis away from the "hypnotic and emotional suggestions acted on by men in masses" to the firmament of economic and social reform.[18]

What is apparent is that, among the middle-class Protestants of Winnipeg, older forms of piety, including revivalism with its attendant emphasis upon the sacrificial atonement and public conversion, had become eclipsed by what was deemed a more respectable and modern emphasis upon Christian nurture.[19] By 1915 the tenets of social Christianity had captured the allegiance of the Protestant congregations of Winnipeg's respectable South-End neighbourhoods. Sermons by prominent social activists such as Rev. J.W. Macmillan, professor of social ethics at Manitoba College, the cartoonist J.W. Bengough, and the women's suffrage leader Nellie McClung, along with labour sympathizers Revs. Salem Bland and A.E. Smith, endorsed welfare reform, the right to strike, and the ideal of a living wage.[20] Thus social Christianity served to reinforce the alliance between middle-class progressivism and labour reformism. Prior to the 1919 General Strike, which irrevocably disrupted this labour-progressive coalition, it had become commonplace for Protestant clergymen such as Rev. David Christie of Westminster Presbyterian to eschew the old-fashioned "mumbling of prayers" in favour of an insistence upon righteous living as the "true form of worship." He and other reformist clergymen who envisioned God's Kingdom as primarily a "social entity" spoke on themes such as "The Doomed Social Order and the Approaching Triumph of Christ and Labor" and "The Question of the Churches' Relation to Unemployment and the Present Social and Individual Order."[21] Protestant clergymen and labour activists such as F.J. Dixon often met under the auspices of Church Brotherhoods, which were exclusively male organizations, for the purposes of discussing political economy themes such as the single tax, protectionism, and the curbing of monopolies through forms of Christian "socialism." In 1915 a "Friendly Debate on Socialism" was held in Broadway Methodist church where numerous clergymen and labour leaders joined hands to discuss the ways in which the common collectivist ideals shared by Christian and socialist concepts of "service" could become incorporated into greater state involvement in managing the social order.[22]

Thus, in Winnipeg, the *de facto* centre of Richard Allen's "radical" social gospel, the popularity of social Christianity was confined almost exclusively to middle-class Anglo-Saxon congregations. In turn, it was essentially these middle-class congregations that decisively rejected old-style revivalism, with its antiquated emphasis upon conversion, in favour of what Wesley College professor W.F. Osborne referred to as the mature reflections of ethical and social considerations:

> The emphasis on effective religious appeal today has almost completely shifted from the effort to secure hasty decisions under overheated conditions to the attempt to compass mature reflection under the influence of ethical considerations. The itinerant evangelist resorts not unnaturally to a counting of heads and a tabulation of results and frequently to the employment of trivial devices which, however gratifying for the moment, have been proven to be productive of consequences reverse of lasting. The preaching that permanently influences the modern man must be marked by a certain substantiality.[23]

At fashionable churches such as Augustine Presbyterian, prominent clergymen such as Leslie Pidgeon addressed contemporary concerns in sermons entitled "Social Responsibilities," while working-class people regularly attended mass meetings at the Dominion Theatre where revivalists like Dr S.J. Reid inveighed against liberal theology and its "moral influence theory" and relied instead upon the old-style doctrine of the atonement as the veritable course to Christian devotion.[24]

That there existed a yawning gulf between the ways in which the middle- and working-class congregations of Winnipeg conceived the Christian experience is clearly demonstrated in the following juxtapositions between the churches located south of Portage Avenue and those that lay immediately north and west of this central civic axis[25] which divided the English-speaking middle and working classes. For example, in March of 1915 the Bethel Mission, situated in Winnipeg's notorious North End, advertised "A warm welcome to common folks where plain gospel sermons are preached and favourite hymns are sung," an evocation of the old-time Methodist evangelism which contrasted volubly with the evening sermon offered at Broadway Methodist, "The Romance of the City of Constantinople." On 17 February 1917, while Rev. T.G. Bethell preached in the solidly working-class Wesley Church on the premillennialist theme of "Revelation and the City of the Golden Crown," in the city's wealthy Young Methodist Church the Rev. Whiting preached against the supernatural elements in Christianity, including the divinity of Christ and the centrality of the atonement.[26] Once again, at Young Church, on 12 January 1918, the principles of practical Christianity were driven home in a thoroughly contemporary sermon on "The Adjustment of Christianity to Modern Problems," while those clergymen ministering to the working people of Knox Presbyterian and the Calvary Evangelical Church reaffirmed the old verities of conversion and atonement in two evangelistic sermons – "God's Challenge to Man" and "My Belief in the Divinity of Christ."[27]

The special appeal of traditional evangelical preaching to the working class was strongly evoked by A.E. Smith in his semi-autobiographical novel, *The Passing Shadow*. In it Smith told the story of Roger Bilson, a young apprentice printer who, prior to his conversion beneath "the spell of emotional religious eloquence and passion" personified in the preaching of that "ideal revivalist," Rev. Charles Johnson, had lived the life of a sinner who "sobbed in penitential fears." Even though Rev. Johnson ministered to a working-class congregation and was interested in improving the material circumstances of their lives, he did not rely upon the liberal strains of ethical Christianity but rather strongly proclaimed "the theology of Salvation from Hell." Johnson's services were characterized by exhortation, song, and earnest prayer, where many wept as they sought that "inward sense of Joy" that came from the spiritual awakening of conversion. In this church, as Smith attested, the working people were in complete harmony with the sentiments of their minister. "The glad people sang and prayed themselves into a condition of emotional fervency that everyone seemed to enjoy." That the congregation remained in "deep sympathy" with their minister was a direct consequence of the fact that Rev. Johnson knew little theology except for his "instinct" for God's love. While being "saved" was no longer accepted in wealthier congregations, according to Smith, for working people "the emotional orthodox religion was sufficient."[28]

A.E. Smith's ideal of the "religious traditionalist" found its real-life fulfilment in the person of Rev. John Maclean, Smith's dear friend and the pastor of the Bethel Mission. This church was located in the North End of Winnipeg, in a neighbourhood populated by marginally employed unskilled workers and the skilled tradesmen who worked for the Canadian Pacific Railway. That there existed two streams by which religion intersected with the lives of the working classes of Winnipeg was confirmed by Maclean himself. As he wrote in a letter to Rev. Dr J.W. Saunby, a Methodist missionary in Tokyo, the one route to incorporating workers within Protestantism was manifested in the liberal theology of Ivens, Bland, and Woodsworth. However, Maclean preferred the tradition with which he himself was most closely identified. As he wrote, "the great doctrines of the Christian faith" – that is, the old orthodoxies of personal sin and atonement – paralleled a real sympathy "toward all real movements tending to help the working man."[29]

Maclean's observations about the way in which Protestantism functioned among the working people of Winnipeg well demonstrate that a liberal theology that placed priority on social ethics was not necessarily the intellectual corollary of practical Christian endeavour.[30] Both A.E. Smith and Maclean associated what they called "a more aggressive policy for work among the common people" – namely community work[31] – not with a theology of social redemption but with the old-time gospel of personal evangelism. Even though Maclean subscribed to *The Voice* and *The Western Labor News*,[32] and his eight years at the mission were largely spent in locating 5,000 jobs for the unemployed, dispensing Patriotic Fund relief to the wives and children of soldiers, and sending money to those in imminent danger of dispossession by the bailiff, he nevertheless continued to see his central goal as the bringing of souls to Christ. After a typical day in which he secured rail fare for two unemployed men at the Industrial Bureau, found a job for Robert Ramsay, a sixteen-year-old Belfast lad, and visited the homes of those people "who are in very sad circumstances," Maclean remained adamantly wedded to the priority of evangelism as the key to "winning the minds and hearts of the people."[33]

Historians might query Maclean's claim that evangelism enjoyed immense popularity among Winnipeg's workers and that old-style prayer meetings,[34] though largely defunct in middle-class congregations, were instrumental in securing hundreds of conversions. However, to dismiss the spread of evangelicalism as nothing more than the imposition of middle-class religious values upon an unwilling working class is belied by the flood of letters and testimonials to Maclean from actual common folk. A typical example of the many mill-workers, printers, and railwaymen who wrote of their conversions[35] was the case of Fred Franklin, a crippled worker who wrote to Maclean after the 1919 strike thanking him in a "sweet & tender" letter for his years of spiritual help. Writing from his residence on William Street in Winnipeg's far North End, Franklin thanked Maclean for sending him his book:

I cannot understand how you can trust me with this and expect this from me, a wise winner of souls, for I am unworthy and am fighting temptation, doubt and fear all the time, and sometimes cry out to God in my soul why do you allow me to suffer so, then comes the thought perhaps my Father is allowing me to be buffetted so that I may know how to help another with similar temptations. This act of yours in giving this little book to me has made me think very hard these last few days and count the cost. With my Saviour working through me I am willing to be used and will take more time in reading the Word that He may have something to work upon through me.[36]

The most compelling evidence of the equation between working-class piety and the older Wesleyan traditions of revivalistic religion was provided by W. Prince, a millworker who recounted a spiritual journey identical to that of the young A.E. Smith:

> I joined the Method Church and go to Church every sunday and I felt a drifend lad all to gether & tuck the lord super on sunday and I put a third of my money for the Lord they are trying to get enuf of money to send a missionary to chinar to disprace [disperse] the Bible and I think that will take a lot of money But we dont think nothin of that as long as the poor peple get the book of God I was a bad lad once but science I come to the Mission I think It maid a good lad of me and I follow it up and I think of you ever sunday when I go to Church and I go to Bible Class on Sunday aftnoon so I tink I am on the right parth. What do you think of it and I say my prayers every night and moring and I think God hear them I wish I could see you so we could have a good talk together. I will try and send a money order to help you little Mission, if you tell me if it is all right to send you I had a god talk with the minster on weday aftnoon and was to his house to supor and went to prayer meating and injoied it very much I was telling him how I firs come to God and he was intrested to hear my story ... dear frend I would like to have one of you picturs to show the minster and I would like it my self so I can say you was the man that got me i for I like the way you speak and I come to hear you and I felt my self coming to God. I try to get my frend to come to Church but I cant get it in his head but I am trying to get him very hard and he is coming near all the time.[37]

On 12 February 1916 Rev. John Maclean delivered a sermon entitled "The Wrath to Come," which, as the *Winnipeg Free Press* reported, insistently sounded the old gospel themes: "The tragedy of modern times is that men have lost the sense of sin, and have little or no fear of its consequences, and while the future holds the penalties of transgression, and the present makes scars in the soul, there is great need for arousing earnest thought on the subject, which will ensure deep and thorough conviction."[38] Certainly Maclean's Bethel Mission in the extreme North End was wholly infused with evangelistic piety, but what is significant is that the success of this form of spirituality among ordinary folk was replicated in all the Anglo-Saxon working-class churches of north-west Winnipeg. Other missions such as Maple Street and St Giles Presbyterian were known as particularly popular among the working man and found spiritual favour among hundreds who populated the poorest quarters of the city.[39] Evangelistic services formed the mainstay of the religious practice of these churches. At St Giles the Rev. Dr Charles Stewart took the Book of Revelation with its premillennialist message as the text of his sermon in August 1915, while in 1918 the Winnipeg Central Mission filled the capacious Liberal Hall on Notre Dame and Princess with a "Popular Gospel Service for Everybody."[40]

Interest in the series of "real, vital, popular gospel services" flowered at Nassau Street Baptist Church, while the downtown church, Broadway Methodist, successfully drew upon a working-class constituency by advertising that it was "a real Home Church ... The messages from the pulpit are spiritual and helpful, and Christ and the Gospel are kept to the front." Most importantly, it did not take up a collection, and it emphasized community help for the unemployed and the urban poor.[41]

As early as 1915 Zion Methodist initiated the practice of making evangelicalism more accessible to the working people of Winnipeg by conducting its services in popular venues such as the Starland Theatre at the corner of Logan and Main, in the heart of the working-class district of the North End. This strategy was accordingly adopted by the Elim Chapel at the corner of Sherbrook and Ellice, which well into the 1920s remained one of the most vibrant centres of gospel work and revivalism in Winnipeg. While in 1915 such middle-class garrisons as Young Methodist were consigning the conversion experience to obsolescence in sermons such as "Is Conversion a Reality?" and "Do We Have Any Such Happenings Now?"[42] working-class Protestants were most emphatically drawn to revivalist practices, especially to Elim Chapel, whose "aggressive gospel work" and Bible study could reach an audience of 600 at each week-night sitting. There workers listened to sermons such as "Instantaneous Conversion," "Why I Believe the Bible to Be the Inspired Word of God," "Satanic Plans Which Failed," and "Three-fold Repentance."[43] Touted as "thoroughly orthodox in doctrine and belief," Elim Chapel held nightly lectures and an extremely popular Sunday mass meeting, where, by all accounts, "great spiritual results were derived."[44]

Elim was thus a natural forum for evangelical campaigns like those of the Irish evangelist Rev. S.J. Reid. In the fall of 1915 Reid commenced a highly successful series of revivals, in which he used the old familiar hymns and the rousing music of the Army and Navy Veteran's band to strike home his gospel attack upon the vague moralism of liberal theology. Indeed, he struck at the heart of social evangelism by holding one of his "eloquent appeal[s]" in the YMCA where "quite a number of the audience" expressed their "trust and faith in the Savior." Between September and December of 1915 Reid's evangelistic campaign grew in its power,[45] and on 5 December he began to wind up his tour with a "Popular Service for the People" in the Dominion Theatre where he urged a conversion experience upon his audience with "Why I am a Christian."[46]

Not only did personal evangelism and the doctrines of the old "orthodox" gospel flourish throughout the working-class neighbourhoods of Winnipeg's north-west but premillennialism made a powerful impression upon these congregations. In 1915 M.A. Howlett spoke to the Associated Bible Students of Winnipeg on "What is the Anti-Christ?" while at the West End Gospel Hall W.J. McClure spoke on "The Second Coming of Christ: Personal, Premillennial, and Imminent," a theme made even more popular in its appeal to Winnipeg's workers by stressing that it would be delivered in "a sound, scriptural, orthodox way."[47] By 1916 the transformation of premillennialism from a fringe movement in small gospel halls to the mainstream of Protestantism was signalled by its relocation to downtown Winnipeg's large and popular Dominion Theatre. There on 5 February the prominent American fundamentalist Dr Arno Gaebelein gave the Sunday morning service on "The Second Coming of Christ" and a series of weekday lectures on the book of Revelation, all accompanied by the strains of the City Mission Orchestra.[48] The Methodist Rev. John Maclean visited one of these premillennialist evangelistic services in 1916 and was immensely impressed with it, largely because it reminded him – and perhaps many other Methodists – of "an old time Methodist revival service with singing and prayer."[49]

Despite the social crisis engendered by the Winnipeg General Strike, premillennialism grew apace, even dislodging the Methodists from Wesley Church, which occupied the heart of Anglo-Saxon and working-class north-west Winnipeg in 1919. In explaining the apparent failure of Methodism in this neighbourhood, Maclean declared that Pentecostalism, with its direct appeal to the emotions, had attracted people from all classes and parts of the city but that it had had a particular resonance among working-class people.[50] There was no clearer example of the alienation of Winnipeg working folk from both Christian social reform and labour radicalism than their complete rejection of the Rev. William Ivens of McDougall Methodist. Historians have not only assumed that there was a convergence between Ivens's support for radical labour protest and the views of his congregation but they have misread the ousting of Ivens from his church as clear testimony of the hidebound repression of unionism by a small clique of middle-class reactionaries.[51] In point of fact, Ivens left McDougall Methodist because his working-class parishioners disagreed with his sermons on the One Big Union. Indeed, the decision of McDougall Methodist's working-class congregation to force the resignation of Ivens in 1919 affirmed Rev. J.E. Hughson's observation that "humble working Christians" wanted no truck with the intricacies of such reform palliatives as the single tax and socialism.[52] Significantly, Ivens was replaced with Rev. G.O. Irvine, "a pronounced Premillenarian."[53]

Because of the dramatic adherence of the city's north-end communities to traditional evangelicalism, revivalism enjoyed a significant presence on the Winnipeg religious scene well into the 1920s. In 1916 a series of successful three-week revival services were held at Maclean's Bethel Mission and in the United City Mission, where "the abiding truths of the gospel for sinners" were presented in sermons such as "Rivers of Living Water" and "O Earth Hear the World of the Lord," which brought out many seeking redeeming grace to the Dominion Theatre.[54] Some churches, such as Old Knox Church in the market district of Winnipeg, held continuous revival meetings, but in 1918 its attendance flourished when the "Travelling Railroad Evangelist," W.R. Greenman, spoke with particular intensity and directness to the unionized core of Winnipeg labour, the railway shopworkers.[55] Broadway Baptist also recognized that when the evangelical gospel was preached by fellow-tradesmen, its message found a particular resonance among Winnipeg's working men. Thus the former railway worker Britton Ross was invited to speak to "large and enthusiastic" audiences on the "Reality of Sin," where his personal and direct manner seemed to find favour with the "man in the street."[56] That same spring the Methodists joined with the Salvation Army for a two-week campaign at St John's Methodist and Fort Rouge Methodist which lay in the centre of the south-end railway shops.[57] However, the crowning moment of the revival season arrived when the conservative evangelist Dr French Oliver, known to Winnipegers as "the Billy Sunday of the West," opened a two-week revival mission in Zion Methodist Church. There three immense congregations were treated to old-time gospel sermons attacking modern social ethics and the principles of social Christianity that had come to permeate middle-class Protestant congregations. His traditional evangelism drew such large crowds that people stood in both the ante-rooms and the aisles, and many were turned away. According to the *Free Press*, "scores of men and women voluntarily [came] forward to testify their desire to lead a new life." So successful was this city-wide revival in increasing church membership to unprecedented levels, especially among the working classes, that during the civic strike of May 1918 arrangements were undertaken to organize a follow-up campaign of six to eight weeks to be held in the summer of that same year.[58]

It has become an article of faith among historians of Canadian labour and the left that the Winnipeg General Strike was the crystallizing event in the creation of a modern politicized labour movement and in forging a sense of coherence and unity among Canadian workers.[59] Moreover, it has become a truism regarding the events of 1919 that the Labor Churches, which had been created by the clergymen strike leaders such as William Ivens and J.S. Woodsworth, became the gravitational centres of working-class religious expression in the aftermath of the civic strike.⁶⁰ It is true that in 1919 the Labor Churches did strategically organize large brass-band parades⁶¹ in order to draw public attention to their strength, but these hearty demonstrations of worker unity belied the actual fractiousness then taking place within these religious bodies. In the working-class suburb of Elmwood, inhabited by railway workers and their families, the Labor Church was horribly split between those who wished to reject the divinity of Christ and those who upheld the sanctity of the Bible and the validity of conversion.⁶² Throughout the month of July 1919, in the immediate aftermath of the General Strike when labour unity was still at its apogee, these temples were instrumental in serving male workers and appeared to be particularly effective among foreign-born union members.⁶³

By 1924, however, the Labor Churches had become signal beacons of working-class lethargy, as A.E. Smith himself reluctantly admitted. Smith and his cohorts railed against the "old conservatism" of the railway workers who (led by William Ivens, one of those Labor Church leaders who remained committed to the divinity of Christ) failed to accept the idea of a national labour party.⁶⁴ Even though Smith's sermons at his Brandon People's Church remained Christian in character,⁶⁵ their message of a new social order founded upon Christian brotherhood and labour equality failed to attract workers. Ironically, it was the lectures on social redemption by Beatrice Brigden and Smith's assistant, Billie Hill, that consistently attracted middle-class adherents and actually served to alienate workers because their intellectual socialism was unintelligible to them.⁶⁶ The large presence of middle-class elements in these citadels of labour activism was likewise reported upon by John Maclean; his diary observed that A.E. Smith's first meeting of the Brandon Labor Church featured an address by James Marion, general secretary of the New South Wales Temperance Alliance,⁶⁷ and that Marion's anti-liquor theme found particular resonance with middle-class reformers. The moralizing, middle-class tenor of the Labor Churches was confirmed when Billie Hill, in a manner both patronizing and censorious of working-class values, criticized the workers who refused to financially support the People's Church for their "apathy" and their lack of thrift. As the disillusioned Hill caustically concluded: "If workers gave what they spend on tobacco there would be Labour Temples in every town."⁶⁸

For all the social ferment excited by the Winnipeg General Strike, this episode of class conflict seemed to have had very little effect upon the pattern of working-class religious culture in Winnipeg. At Broadway Methodist large audiences of workers continued to respond to the attractions of personal piety, which stressed individual consecration, the personal study of the Bible, prayer, faith, and work for Christ. As Rev. John Maclean's wife observed of one of these popular prayer meetings,

"It was an old time Methodist meeting."⁶⁹ And of Maryland Methodist, Maclean declared "that the old Gospel had lost none of its power and that whatever else happens that religion would abide."⁷⁰ Even in the heartland of labour radicalism, the North End, in the months following the eruptions of the strike, people continued to flock to the Old Gospel services preached by the Rev. F.W. Lee at the Maclean Mission.⁷¹

If working-class piety did change, it did so in the direction of premillennialism and fundamentalism. Maclean's reflection that following the war the people seemed peculiarly susceptible to all forms of religious teaching⁷² appears to have been borne out in Winnipeg, where in 1919 the perfectionist piety of the holiness movement had gained a foothold,⁷³ while the Hornerites had become active just outside the city.⁷⁴ Of this popular evangelicalism Maclean remarked: "This is really old time Methodism, such as I knew in the backwoods of Ontario nearly fifty years ago and many of the members come from some of the best Methodist homes in the city. They preach a spiritual Gospel, and seem to have no fads, as divine healing, though they believe in it, or the Second Coming. They are out and out for winning souls. That is what modern Methodism should be after all the time, and because we do not, we are failing in our work. We seem to be too polite to be real soul winners."⁷⁵ The most striking testimony to the enduring popularity of revivalism among Winnipegers was the highly successful city-wide revivals held by the British evangelist and ex-chaplain Gypsy Smith in the fall of 1919 and by the "Woman Billy Sunday," Aimee Semple McPherson, in the winter of 1920. During Smith's campaign, Winnipeg's largest auditorium with a seating capacity of 4,000 was filled to capacity for every night of his revival sojourn. It was reported that hundreds of people, most importantly working men and returned soldiers, the most volatile elements during the strike, stood up and professed their faith in Christ.⁷⁶ The final men's meeting was so overflowing that one observer ruefully commented that they would have needed a British football park to hold the vast crowd of earnest Christians.⁷⁷

The social class whose religious experience was most affected by the strike and its aftermath was the middle class, whose congregations lay largely south of Portage Avenue. Because our perceptions of how middle-class adherents responded to the strike have been almost wholly derived from the way in which Ivens and Smith were dismissed by a small ultra-conservative cadre within the Manitoba Methodist Conference, historians have all but ignored the effectiveness with which the strike focused middle-class attention on the labour question. Although most clergymen opposed the principle of a civic strike, they nevertheless responded favourably to the labour movement's goals of collective bargaining and the ideal of a living wage. Sermons such as Dr David

Christie's "The Spiritual Significance of the Strike," Rev. Hamilton's "An Attempt at Bolshevik Revolution Recorded in the Scriptures," and Rev. George Dick's "God's Call to the Working Man" were characteristic of the attitude to labour protest of ministers in middle-class congregations.[78]

Most importantly, the strike seemed to jolt middle-class congregations into recognizing the need to adapt their social Christianity to accommodate the more evangelistic tenor of working-class Protestantism. Following the strike, the common refrain of Methodist and Presbyterian ministers was that their churches must become more democratic and inclusive of the "masses of people."[79] Rev. Scott, who was sympathetic to the needs of the workers of Winnipeg, told his middle-class congregation at Augustine Presbyterian that "[a]ll our philosophy and speculation have failed to discover any other power that can uplift and renew humanity," and he exhorted them to rediscover the more traditional ideals of the atonement and of the Cross.[80] That working-class religious practices were beginning to influence middle-class religious sensibilities in Winnipeg after the strike was illustrated by the fact that Protestant laymen endorsed the need for revivals and conversions and began to reassert the predominance of individual over social regeneration. More telling still, the Methodist Ministerial Association in 1920 instituted plans to convert Grace Church with its large working-class constituency into a downtown evangelistic mission.[81] Stolidly middle-class churches such as Holy Trinity south of Portage Avenue became more hospitable to the renewed claims for personal piety, and in 1922 even welcomed the premillennial pastor Sidney T. Smith who spoke on "The Millenium" and "The Great Tribulation."[82] It is this middle-class recognition of both the plight and the rights of Winnipeg workers in the months following the turbulent events of May–June 1919 that is crucial to explaining why, during the 1920s, revivalism re-entered the mainstream of Canadian Protestantism and why personal piety rather than social regeneration formed the bedrock upon which the more modern principles of social service were constructed.[83]

Even Rev. William Ivens, that icon of labour radicalism, was compelled to recognize the tenacity of evangelical religion among the working classes. In his final letter slipped past J. Handel, the chief turnkey at Stony Mountain Prison, Ivens confided to A.E. Smith that if religion was not to be eclipsed by materialist ideologies, the heart of the labouring men would have to be kept loyal to the "*Real* religion" and the principles of Christ.[84]

22 The Transplanted Mission: The China Inland Mission and Canadian Evangelicalism

ALVYN J. AUSTIN

> It became clear to us, as time went on, that we could not look to the [China Inland] Mission in England for advice in the developing of our North American work. This was not because our English friends were lacking in wisdom, but because their experience had been insular while our need was continental.
> Henry Frost, *Memoirs*[1]

COMMON CHRISTIANITY

In 1888 Hudson Taylor (1832–1905) came to Toronto via the United States. Founder of the China Inland Mission (universally known as the CIM, now the Overseas Missionary Fellowship), Taylor was the most famous missionary of his day, a leader who exemplified the CIM nickname, "Constantly In Motion." "We did not know what God was leading us to America for," Taylor wrote, "though we felt we were following His leading." When D.L. Moody suggested that he set up an American branch of the CIM "that might work as a feeder of men and money," Taylor announced that it would be better for the Americans to start an independent mission modelled on the CIM, for "a transplanted mission, like a transplanted tree, would have difficulty in striking root in the new soil."[2]

As long as Taylor remained in the United States, he saw no reason to change his mind. As one of his entourage said, "There are big hearts and heavy purses in America, but like the old country, men are bound by preconceived notions."[3] Taylor's tours from Northfield to Chicago and as far west as Kansas sparked a variety of missionary movements, including the Student Volunteer Movement for Foreign Missions, and invigorated Moody's two-year-old Bible Institute, but did not lead to an American branch of the CIM.

As soon as Taylor crossed the border to speak at the prophetic conference in Niagara-on-the-Lake, Ontario, the difference was palpable: "Collegians at Northfield and parsons at Niagara."[4] He barely mentioned the CIM, and he spoke "as a little child might speak, as a prophet might speak, as one who sees a vision of a needy land and a dying people might speak. And when, after a hour, he finished, there was a great sigh from the listening throng, followed by a silence which was profound."[5] After Taylor left, the meeting broke into "organized pandemonium" as people became "intoxicated with the joy of giving," pledging $2,000, enough to support eight "North American workers" in China for a year. Led by what he saw as God's guidance, Hudson Taylor abruptly changed his mind and announced the formation of a Canadian branch of the CIM: "To have missionaries and no money would be no trouble to me, for the Lord is bound to take care of his own ... But to have money and no missionaries is very serious indeed. And I do not think it will be kind of you dear friends in America to put this burden upon us, and not to send from among yourselves to use the money. We have the dollars, but where are the people?"[6] The dollars were American, the people were Canadian: fifty-five of the sixty-three applications came from Canada, as did twelve of the fourteen single women in the "first North American party."

Toronto used to be one of the great evangelical cities of the world, and the China Inland Mission, one of the great evangelical agencies in England, struck deep roots into its fertile British soil. From the beginning the Toronto CIM was an autonomous branch, equal to London and Shanghai (and later Melbourne), and responsible for selecting and financing its own missionaries. As North American headquarters, Toronto became the centre of a continental enterprise, with applications coming from as far away as California, Nebraska, and Kentucky, and in Canada from Vancouver, Winnipeg, and Montreal.

In 1901 the North American director Henry W. Frost, an expatriate New Yorker who had created the Toronto CIM, made a precipitous "leap in the dark," and moved the North American headquarters to Philadelphia. As an American living in Toronto for twelve years, he wrote in his memoirs, he "never gave up looking for a new movement in the cloud, this time towards the States."[7] However, whereas in Toronto Frost was constantly in demand as a speaker, in Philadelphia the only people who dropped into the mission office were "cranks [who] had vagaries of faith and prophecy which they desired to set forth in detail." Frost was shocked that the "standard of doctrine and life in the States is much lower than that which prevails in Canada, and apostasy has increased so rapidly in these eastern parts that it is impossible to tell what one is going to meet with, even in the most apparently spiritual persons."[8] Frost concluded, "I never got the spiritual hold upon the Christians in the eastern States that I had had upon those in Canada," because "my expositional, devotional and premillennial presentation of

God's Word was not particularly welcomed by American Christians."[9] Those qualities – expositional, devotional, premillennial, and one other, irenic – were exactly the characteristics that did appeal in Canada; and they tell a great deal about Canadian evangelicalism at the turn of the century.

It is important to examine the thirteen years between 1888 and 1901 that Toronto was the North American headquarters of the China Inland Mission, and in particular its shift (which reflected a shift in the larger Canadian society) from being a colonial branch of the British evangelical family to a branch plant of American fundamentalism. The CIM was one of several British associations that established branches in Canada – the YMCA, the Brethren, and the Salvation Army, among others – as beachheads to the United States. And when Americans joined these associations, they did so as junior members to Canadians – a most unusual occurrence!

In England the CIM was a family – as the Quakers were a family – through intermarriage, shared piety, distinctive dress (in the case of the CIM, a Chinese gown and pigtail) and distinctive language. This resulted in "a largely homogeneous character, both in respect of doctrinal belief and the type of personal piety within it."[10] Like all families, it was broad enough to include many personalities. It included every kind of evangelical one can name: Quakers who sat like statues of marble listening to the silent Spirit; prayer-book Anglicans who established dioceses of episcopal rectitude; Salvation Army types who marched through Chinese villages with tambourines and blood-and-fire banners; German and Swedish holy women who specialized in praying for the sick and dying; jump-up revivalists from the American Midwest trying to recreate "burned-over districts" in China; some of the first Pentecostals of the world-wide movement of 1906–07; "liberals" who were "repelled" by the "extreme piety"[11] of their colleagues; and Canadians one generation removed from the farm who were constantly explaining the vagaries of British ways to over-enthusiastic Swedish Americans.

Hudson Taylor utilized existing transatlantic networks to transplant the CIM. In England the CIM had been present at the creation of some of the most important evangelical institutions. These included Dr Barnardo's Homes, the Keswick holiness movement, Moody's British revivals, the anti-opium crusade, dozens of small faith missions (e.g. the Regions Beyond, Sudan United Mission), and at least three Bible schools: Mildmay Conference, Guinness's East London Training Institute, and Spurgeon's Baptist College. In the twentieth century the CIM helped create InterVarsity Christian Fellowship.

In Canada and the United States the CIM utilized the continental networks of Moody and A.B. Simpson to repeat the same process. It helped establish, among others, Toronto Bible College, Vancouver Bible Training School, Moody Bible Institute, Philadelphia College of the Bible, Dallas Theological Seminary, and the Bible Institute of Los Angeles. In the United States the CIM became one of the key institutions of fundamentalism. Nevertheless, in the 1930s, long after the CIM had moved to Philadelphia, Toronto remained more important, as the publishing centre and receiving home for American applicants.

The CIM could become Canadian in Canada and American in the United States – as it was Chinese in China – because it was an interdenominational association. If one looks at Canadian evangelicalism through a denominational focus, one sees divisions and turf wars, as the major denominations – Methodist, Presbyterian, Church of England, and Baptists – grew to national institutions, each an empire unto itself. Canadian churches, though, stopped at the border.

If one examines an interdenominational associations like the CIM – or the YMCA, or Toronto Bible College, or InterVarsity – one is aware of the inclusiveness and flexibility of Canadian evangelicals. Perhaps this cooperative spirit was most apparent in the "common Christianity" of the Ontario public school system. Canadian religion, Sara Jeannette Duncan wrote, was "not beautiful, or dramatic, or self-immolating; it was reasonable."[12] It was in this soil that the CIM flourished, and like other Anglo-Canadian organizations, crossed the border and brought an "attraction and freshness" to American Christianity.[13]

THE TRANSATLANTIC CABLE

Hudson Taylor founded the China Inland Mission in 1865 as a "special agency" for less qualified, spirit-filled workers who came out of the transatlantic, transdenominational revival of 1859–60. "Where is the channel through which simple hearted labourers who, brought to Christ through those remarkable Revivals, and wished to devote themselves to missionary work in far lands, could reach their purpose?" Taylor asked. "But I could find no such channel."[14] The CIM would work in harmony with established societies; and indeed Taylor steered qualified candidates – ordained clergy and doctors – to more conventional missions. "There is ample scope for the highest talents that could be laid upon the altar of God," he wrote, yet "the proposed field is so extensive, and the need of labourers of every class so great, that 'the eye cannot say to the hand, I have no need of thee'; nor yet again the head to the feet, 'I have no need of you.' Therefore persons of moderate ability and limited attainments are not precluded from engaging in the work."[15]

During its first decade the CIM was one of the small "unnoticed religious movements"[16] on the sectarian fringe, attracting mainly Brethren

(George Muller, Dr Thomas Barnardo, and W.T. Berger, the "cofounder" of the CIM), Church of England (William Pennefather of Mildmay), and Quakers (the Howard family of Tottenham). As it became respectable in the 1880s, it cut across denominational and social barriers. Although most of its missionaries were still working-class people with a fair English education (as evidence, they could learn Chinese), it did recruit a few university graduates and members of the evangelical aristocracy. By this time, the CIM was "interdenominational": Christians "may belong to different regiments, but they all belong to one army": the Baptists were the Coldstream Guards, the Presbyterians the Highland Brigade, the Church of England the Royal Guards, and the Methodists "the Artillery, because they make a greater noise."[17]

Hudson Taylor's North American tour in 1888 was preceded by a wave of publicity surrounding the recruitment of the Cambridge Seven (1885), young aristocrats giving up stately homes to live on faith in the outback of China. Their story, published as *The Evangelization of the World*, was distributed free to every YMCA and YWCA in the British Empire and North America; Robert Speer, a founder of the Student Volunteer Movement, stated that, apart from the Bible and *The Personal Life of Livingstone*, no book influenced him more.[18]

Once Taylor decided to establish a Canadian branch, he approached Toronto as he would have London: he sat down with a railway timetable to chart "an itinerary, date by date and city by city, until Toronto might be reached at an appropriate time."[19] "My Father manages the trains," he said, "and I'll be there."[20] Whether he realized it or not, his passage through the provincial towns and cities – Niagara-on-the-Lake, Stratford, Belleville, Ottawa, Montreal, Hamilton, Brantford, London, Woodstock, Galt, and Guelph – followed a well-worn trail laid by British evangelists like John Nelson Darby and Grattan Guinness, the silver-tongued "herald" of the 1859 revival,[21] and in reverse, by American evangelists like James Caughey and Phoebe Palmer.

At each place Taylor connected with the colonial extended family of British evangelicalism. In Niagara-on-the-Lake a monument marks the spot where Taylor spoke at the Niagara Believers' conference in 1888 and again in 1889. Niagara was the "mother" of the prophetic conferences that proliferated throughout North America from the 1870s until the First World War. It was there that Americans came to learn British-Canadian spirituality in the teachings of Keswick holiness and premillennial dispensationalism, and also where the American millenarian movement took on the character of a "protodenominational fellowship."[22]

In Galt and Guelph Taylor connected with the Darbyite Brethren who had established a summer camp nearby. In Hamilton it was the YMCA.

This small Bible-study group, run by young English immigrants, provided at least thirteen CIM missionaries in the first years.[23] Taylor's most curious connections – at least to historians a century later – were in Stratford and Belleville. Here he met Annie MacPherson and her sister Mrs Merry, who ran the Marchmount Homes. These homes, like the Barnardo and Quarrier Homes, became so prominent as massive child-emigration schemes which brought some 80,000 orphans to Canada that it is easily overlooked that the leaders remained faithful to a premillennial vision of saving brands from the burning. Thomas Barnardo and Miss MacPherson had been supporters of the CIM since 1865, and some of their graduates had gone to China.[24]

At least two of Taylor's 1888 party were on the staff of the Marchmount Homes, and the Reverend Robert Wallace, chaplain of the Belleville home, became a key member of the Toronto council. Before the Toronto CIM became established, the Wallace home in Belleville was the receiving home for CIM candidates, where Wallace and his wife, Ellen Agnes Bilbrough, a woman of "limitless devotion" and "rare gifts," judged their aptitude for service. Wallace contributed "frequent and generous gifts" to the CIM and in 1896 was the first council member to visit China. After retiring from the Marchmount Homes in 1915, he joined the CIM staff as treasurer in Toronto and Philadelphia.[25]

When Taylor had passed through the smaller cities and reached Toronto, he stayed only long enough to appoint a grandly named "International Auxiliary," with two officers, Alfred Sandham, director of the Christian Institute, as secretary for Canada and Henry Frost for the United States. When Frost protested that he knew nothing about interviewing candidates or forwarding funds, Taylor replied, "Quite true, but the Lord will help you." This statement, Frost wrote, was "distressingly simple, characteristic of the man, but not exactly practical in its application."[26] With this enigmatic blessing, after a memorable torch-lit parade down Yonge Street to the train station, Taylor took his fourteen recruits and was gone, off to China.

TORONTO: THE CHURCHES

Hudson Taylor had planned to reach Toronto "at an appropriate time" – and the summer of 1888 was fortuitous. Three years before it had assumed the nickname of "Toronto the Good" for the moral campaign of Mayor William Howland, and by the 1890s it was a city run by and for evangelicals. As Ian Rennie described it:

Both men and women gave themselves to church planting. They started many home missions including Yonge Street Mission and Toronto City Mission. They led the work of the Upper Canada Bible Society, the Upper Canada Tract Society, and YMCA and YWCA, and the publishing firm known as the Willard Tract Depository. They manned the committees of the denominational missionary societies, as well as those of the recently founded faith missions, the two most prominent of which were the China Inland Mission ... and the Sudan Interior Mission, the last having its home base in Toronto ... They founded the Home for Incurables (now Queen Elizabeth Hospital), the Haven for Fallen Women, the Newsboys' Home, and had a major part in the formation of the Hospital for Sick Children.[27]

The China Inland Mission entered Toronto under the auspices of the Christian Institute, a short-lived slum mission that deserves to be rescued from historical obscurity, for in its brief life it was responsible for the establishment of the CIM, the Canadian branch of the Christian and Missionary Alliance and its associated Missionary Training School, and indirectly for the Sudan Interior Mission. It was the "Toronto Blessing" of a century ago, with the same manifestations and an emphasis on A.B. Simpson's gospel of divine healing. Located on Richmond Street West in lower St John's Ward, the Christian Institute was built by Howland and William Gooderham, the philanthropic member of a well-known brewery family, and run by Alfred Sandham, an eccentric numismatist and YMCA secretary who had started out a Methodist and ended up, as Frost wrote, "I know not what."[28]

When Frost arrived to take up residence in Toronto, "one thing was plain," he wrote, "namely, that we were in a strange land and facing strange experiences."[29] Nevertheless, he realized that the CIM would not succeed as long as it remained in the Christian Institute. Sandham was "not as much in sympathy with our Mission service as he had been ... and showed a disposition to criticize the methods with our candidates." Sandham wanted to turn the Christian Institute into a Bible training school that would "thoroughly equip our would-be-missionaries," and whose teaching would include healing. Frost was opposed because he felt the mission home should not be for "training," but for "testing," that is, how to live on faith.[30] Sandham resigned from the CIM, and the mission moved to a rented twelve-bedroom mansion at 632 Church Street, on the corner of Charles Street, "in the best residential portion of the city."[31] Henry Frost, his wife, Abbie, and their seven children moved next door.

Henry Weston Frost was a pragmatic Presbyterian. The descendent of post-Mayflower Pilgrims and a graduate in engineering from Princeton College, he was a well-to-do owner of mills and gas utilities in Attica, New York. He had flirted with politics, hoping that the Progressives could save the world. He had converted to premillennialism at the

1885 Niagara conference and applied to the CIM. Although Frost had travelled to London, he had been turned down by the council; nevertheless he had remained committed, and was Taylor's host during his 1888 visit. Only thirty, an energetic young man but subject to black depressions and anguished scriptural study, Frost established the CIM in Toronto.

The Canadian pattern was to take British models, simplify them, democratize them, and return to their common Christianity. With the zeal of a convert, Frost accepted the CIM's faith principles without reservation. He resolved as an individual and a mission not to go into debt, even to the fraction of a penny; his business background ensured divine bookkeeping. The mission would not sign a lease, for example, since "the Lord might not enable us to fulfil" the rent; the council members signed on its behalf.[32] Frost kept separate books for contributions designated "for China" and "for Home." This meant he was remitting thousands of dollars to Shanghai while thirty or more candidates living in the mission home had no food to put on the table. Then, as if miraculously, someone would appear at the door with a brace of partridge, a ton of coal, or a cheque in exactly the amount prayed for. "We lived from hand to mouth in those days," Frost recalled, "but it was God's hand and our mouth; and this is a distinction which makes a great difference ... Our episodes of scarcity were intended to be new revealings of God's love and power, if only we could be attentive to the inner meaning of things."[33]

In its choice of council members, the CIM was certainly attentive to the inner meaning of Toronto evangelicalism. Frost made the same tacit arrangement as the London CIM: support the churches, while maintaining a council of premillennial conservatives. Whereas London was top-heavy with Brethren, Toronto was predominantly Presbyterian (seven of the eleven who can be identified, of fourteen, on the 1889 Toronto council). In addition to Wallace, they included the Reverend Dr Henry Martyn Parsons of Knox Church, one of the warhorses of premillennialism (and contributor to the Scofield Bible), and William J. Erdman, director of the Niagara conference and Frost's spiritual mentor.[34] The appointment of Thomas Wardrope, secretary of the Foreign Missions Committee of the Presbyterian Church in Canada, cemented a semi-official relationship that continued well into the twentieth century under Wardrope's successor on both committees, R.P. MacKay.

The other semi-official relationship was with the Church of England. In Canada as in England, no interdenominational association, either liberal or conservative, could exist without the participation of Anglicans; otherwise it would be "sectarian." The Anglican church conferred an aura of legitimacy, dignity, and broad churchmanship. The ubiquitous layman, Samuel Hoyles Blake, was the linchpin of the interlocking directorates of Toronto evangelicals. He sat on the CIM council until his death in 1912, as well as on the boards of the Christian Institute, Toronto Bible Training School, Wycliffe College (which he founded), the Missionary Society of the Church in Canada and innumerable others. Another CIM councillor was T.C. DesBarres, minister at St Paul's, the CIM's neighbourhood church; among the first applicants in 1888 were two of his parishioners, spinster sisters aged forty-five and fifty, who had to be declined.

Relations with the Anglican church were cemented in 1910 when the principal of Wycliffe College, T.R. O'Meara, joined the council. O'Meara provided a peculiarly Anglican service for the CIM: identifying high-church candidates. One man, he warned, attended a church "of an advanced ritualistic type ... I myself cannot see how any thoroughgoing Protestant who knows experientially the gladness and liberty of the Gospel of Christ would be comfortable and at home in such surroundings."[35] Like many Anglican evangelicals, O'Meara was more comfortable with some non-Anglicans than many in his own church. Yet, as featured speaker at the 1915 Niagara Conference to celebrate the fiftieth anniversary of the CIM, he could not share communion with the rest of the council for fear of launching the college into "public controversy."[36]

Two other Wycliffe College faculty, whose careers indicate the place of Canada in the international CIM, should be mentioned. The first, Howard K. Mowll, educated at Cambridge and ordained in Manchester was teaching at Wycliffe when he was appointed assistant bishop of East Sichuan, the joint CIM-CMS diocese. He was later bishop of Sydney, Australia, where he became a prominent evangelical speaker. The other, W.H. Griffith Thomas, another distinguished English scholar, came to Canada with a Keswick delegation and remained as professor of Old Testament at Wycliffe. He became a prominent fundamentalist and helped found the Anglican seminary in Vancouver and Dallas Theological Seminary (which opened after his death in 1924).

Just because the CIM had good relations with the churches does not mean that there was no controversy. In China, the three Canadian missions, Presbyterian, Methodist, and Anglican, all collided with the CIM's territorial ambitions. The Presbyterian confrontation started when Taylor reached Toronto in 1888. A few weeks before, Jonathan Goforth – the controversial Presbyterian missionary – had set out, "in Abrahamic ignorance," for Henan, which the CIM claimed as its field. Taylor warned Wardrope against Goforth's "unwise impetuosity," for "the proposed incoming of a large body of inexperienced missionaries has alarmed the officials and greatly increased the difficulties."[37] The problem was resolved when Taylor met Goforth in Shanghai, and found him to be a kindred spirit. The CIM withdrew from North Henan – the way the CIM resolved questions of comity – and Goforth remained one of the CIM's closest friends.[38]

A more immediate concern to the churches was the CIM's fund-raising at home. The CIM claimed to be able to support a missionary for half what a conventional mission could, which put pressure on the mission boards to lower their salaries. "Mr. Frost tells me," R.P. MacKay wrote, "the 600 C.I.M. missionaries are satisfied – many of them – on $250, returning annually thank offerings of as much as 20%." Donald MacGillivray, a Henan pioneer, tried to live on $500, and when his experiment proved a failure, he charged that the CIM could live so cheaply because they "number few educated men. Their missionaries are mostly from the bench and forge in Sweden and Germany and the U.K. ... Libraries they have only heard of ... Their single men are constantly flying about and the equipment they use, not to say need, is very meagre."[39]

The Methodists, always wary of any movement that might divert money from "connexional" channels, was suspicious of the CIM because its friends among the "pretended non-sectarian teachers" (i.e. Brethren evangelists) were scouring the Ontario countryside.[40] Gooderham was the only Methodist on the CIM council, and he was not replaced when he died in 1889. Relations with the Methodist church became strained in the 1890s when a former CIM missionary named Isabella Crossthwaite started "operating" among the churches of southwestern Ontario. She had gone to China in 1889, where she lasted one year before she was fired for instability; two years later, she returned as an independent. By 1897 the Methodist Foreign Missionary Society warned Methodists to be "on their guard" against her.[41]

TORONTO: THE SECTARIANS

The China Inland Mission's relationship with the so-called sectarians was more ambiguous than with the churches. This can be seen in the controversy over divine healing. Healing in answer to prayer and anointing with oil – the so-called "third blessing" – was a contentious issue among late nineteenth-century evangelicals. "Christianity has won most of its triumphs without the aid of miracles," a Toronto Baptist thundered. "The men and women who have best exemplified the power of Christianity have never experienced nor expected miraculous interference."[42] Nevertheless, at the turn of the century, in reaction to the medicalization of society, there was a renewed interest in all forms of alternative medicine, including faith healing.

The first and most famous healer in the CIM was Maggie Scott, who joined with her sister Christina in 1890. Daughter of the Presbyterian manse in Maxville in eastern Ontario, Maggie had been paralysed and blind until she was cured by Dr Cullis of Boston who ordered her to "arise and walk." Within six months Maggie, aged nineteen, "stepped out on her own, travelling from town to town, holding evangelistic meetings and telling the story of her physical healing." She visited every place between Montreal and Guelph. When the Dominion Alliance (the Canadian branch of the Christian and Missionary Alliance) was founded in 1889, Maggie Scott was elected one of two women vice-presidents. She contracted consumption in China and returned home to die. Her passage from Shanghai to Maxville was transcendent, causing a "solemn hush" wherever she went. Sister Tina lived a year longer and died in China. After their deaths, brother Daniel, aged twenty, applied to take their place; he was turned down for poor health.[43]

A sadder case was Miss P.R. de Long, who sailed in 1903. A graduate of Gordon Baptist Training School in Boston, she developed a "serious mental condition" characterized by repeated attempts "to destroy herself ... that she might ... rise from the dead and so convince the world of God's infinite power." She arrived in Toronto in an "entirely hopeless" condition and had to be committed to an asylum; she finally threw herself in front of a train. Such cases caused the mission to re-examine why "prayer was offered for many years, and by saints who seldom knew what it was to have prayer remain unanswered; but full healing was never given."[44]

In 1904, after almost twenty years of controversy, the CIM considered "the vaccination question ... to be of such importance that it has been made compulsory."[45] Frost's own attitude to healing was more vexed. He had made several trips to China, and while there had witnessed – and experienced – divine healing. In later years he turned to a "somewhat peculiar mission which was quite apart from my work for the Mission." This was "the cure of souls ... to minister to those in need and especially to those in sorrow was my greatest joy."[46] In his book, *Miraculous Healing*, he differentiated it from "divine healing," because all healing was from God. Nevertheless, Frost concluded, Satan used the allure of healing to lead Christians "into unbalanced and extravagant positions ... it is to be remembered that the occupying of any super-scriptural position will eventually lead one, if he is honest, into discouragement and ... the darkness of despondency, amounting in some cases to despair."[47]

Frost's pilgrimage away from faith healing reflects a similar journey by Rowland V. Bingham, founder of the Sudan Interior Mission (SIM). In 1893, Bingham, a young English Salvation Army captain, was converted to healing theology by Pastor John Salmon, founder of the Dominion Alliance. Bingham founded the African Industrial Mission, forerunner of the SIM, based on the CIM with a touch of divine healing, to take the gospel to the Soudan, the swath across equatorial Africa ("land of the blacks," not to be confused with the present-day Sudan), known as the "White Man's Grave." Bingham's two companions died within a year, and he returned to Toronto "shaken to the very foundation." He had gone out "trusting in promises of healing that seemed plain, clear and explicit in the Bible, and yet I had buried in the [Soudan] two of the most faithful Christians whom I had ever met. Had the promises failed?"[48] Bingham and the SIM – like the Alliance itself – eventually repudiated the belief in healing. "To teach that healing is a part of the atonement and that all Christians have therefore the right to expect and experience it, is to cause heartbreak and disappointment."[49]

In the twentieth century, the China Inland Mission and the Sudan Interior Mission became intertwined, different voices of the same call. R.V. Bingham and E.A. Brownlee, Frost's successor as Canadian director, sat on each other's boards, shared the same platforms and attended the same missionary conferences. They were charter members of the Interdenominational Foreign Missions Committee, the separatist organization that replaced the liberal Association of Foreign Mission Societies in 1914.

THE NEW BEGINNING

In 1893 Henry Frost made his first trip to England to help reorganize the international CIM. As an American, Frost wrote, he hoped the "autocratic constitution" of the CIM could be "Americanized, that is, democratized." During this trip, he drafted the first constitution for the mission, and its first doctrinal statement. Hitherto the CIM had not needed a creed, but once written, it defined "membership" – a code word in the CIM. In conventional missions, the "members" were the people at home who contributed the funds, sat on the boards, and wrote the publications. They determined policy and theology by controlling the purse strings and the type of missionaries they sent out. The missionaries were their "agents," paid employees who could be fired or rewarded according to how the home church perceived their work. In the city, the "members" of the CIM were the missionaries in the field; the people at home its "agents." Frost defended the practice, because as an association, the CIM was "not a church, and, hence, not related to the instructions given in the Word in respect to church organization."[50]

Frost returned from England to launch a "new beginning." One evidence of this was the North American edition of *China's Millions*, the

CIM monthly. Another was the call that went out to the Bible schools that the CIM "could not do better than take the equipment provided by a Canadian or American Bible Institute as a standard of preparation," even though

> some men and women without such an equipment would be found acceptable; and we were convinced that Seminary-bred men were much to be desired ... We were convinced that we should seek for the friendship, not of doctrinally and spiritually loose Christians, but of those who were sound in the faith, prayerful in spirit, devoted in service, evangelistic in purpose and, generally but not exclusively premillennial in attitude. We felt that one person of this quality would be worth to the Mission and China a hundred persons of another sort, and we were ready, as far as needed, to throw our lot in with the socially humble and financially poor, if only we could maintain scriptural and spiritual integrity.[51]

"In view of our decision in respect to the Bible Institutes," Frost concluded, "we determined to foster contact with these as much as possible."

The effect was immediate and phenomenal. When Taylor visited Moody Bible Institute in 1894, the Toronto office received thirty-five applications from Moody's students in three months, twenty-nine men and six women – an unusual proportion; five men and two women were accepted. Altogether, 1894 proved a bumper year, with the largest number of applicants in its history: seventy-one men and forty-six women, of whom twelve men and thirteen women were accepted. Frost thought Toronto could do better than this sectarian effort.[52]

After the CIM had left the Christian Institute, Sandham and Salmon had started the Toronto Missionary Training Institute, the first permanent Bible school in Canada, and in 1893 the school was taken over as an Alliance work. To this point there had been no Baptists on the Toronto CIM, an unexpected oversight, since Baptists made up about one-third of the applicants. This was resolved when the Reverend Elmore Harris joined in 1893, another friendship that lasted twenty years. Harris was a dynamo in a city filled with them; Ronald Sawatsky calls him a "Canadian Baptist Extraordinaire." He was wealthy, a Harris of the Massey-Harris farm machinery company, and had already built two substantial churches, Bloor Street, which he pastored 1882–89, and Walmer Road, the largest Baptist edifice in Canada.

In May 1894 Harris gathered a biblical twelve men, most of them on the CIM council, to explain his "great design" for Toronto Bible Training School (TBTS) (now Ontario Bible College), to be housed in the Sunday school rooms. Henry Frost spoke "strongly in favour of such a school

& stated that out of 500 applicants of service for the C.I.M. many had been refused because of want of proper training."[53] The meeting was unanimous, and then made an unexpected motion: the Baptists voted themselves out of the majority by increasing the size of the board. The TBTS board was rigidly interdenominational, more so than the CIM, always containing at least one minister from each of the five main denominations, and well into the 1950s, a United Church representative. Nevertheless, TBTS kept its reputation as a Baptist institution.[54]

When Toronto Bible Training School opened its doors in September 1894, among its first students were several CIM candidates, including three women from Iowa who took a term of remedial Bible training while awaiting funds to take them to China.[55] By the turn of the century the majority of CIM candidates had some Bible school training, and if they did not, they enrolled at TBTS while in the CIM home. No Bible school, not even Moody Bible Institute, had a stronger influence on the CIM – and vice versa – than TBTS. The first instructors at the school included Henry Frost ("The Last Things"), H.M. Parsons ("Dispensational Truth"), T.C. DesBarres, W.J. Erdman, and four other members of the CIM council. By the twentieth century the councils of the two institutions were virtually identical; they overlapped so many organizations that the meetings were scheduled on the same day, so the councillors could move as a group from the CIM, to Toronto Bible College, to Yonge Street Mission, to the Sudan Interior Mission.

The influence of the second principal of TBTS, the Reverend John McNicol, was world-wide, since he sent a hundred missionaries to the CIM – and hundreds more to the farthest reaches of the regions beyond. He became principal in 1911 on the death of Elmore Harris, and remained principal, in effect, for forty-five years. McNicol had two teachings that had a profound impact on CIM spirituality. One was his Bible study called "Thinking through the Bible," which consisted in reading the English Bible in consecutive order. In the first class of the first year, he would start "in the beginning" with Genesis, and proceed verse by verse, book by book, until three years later he ended with the "Amen" of Revelation. His other innovation – perhaps the greatest expression of the irenic nature of Toronto evangelicals – was what he called "the Corporate Headship of the Holy Spirit." All decisions of the school – the students, the faculty and eventually the board – had to be unanimous. No theological controversy was allowed to break the spirit of the school; although the majority of teachers were "fundamental but not dispensational," hard-line teaching was never espoused. Consequently from the nineteenth century to the middle of the twentieth, Toronto Bible College (renamed in 1911) – and Canadian evangelicals – had a continuity that was not torn asunder by the religious wars of American anti-modernism.

THE CANDIDATES

Henry Frost was not wrong when he said that many applicants to the CIM were rejected because of lack of proper training. He meant this particularly in the spiritual realm, but also in the social realm. Nothing shows the complexity and diversity of the CIM better than the record of applications to the Toronto office: 742 individuals between 1887 and 1901.[56] Some applications came from across the street, from people who saw the sign and came to inquire; the next might be from Pueblo, Colorado, where Mary Brayton found the CIM blowing in the wind – literally a page of *China's Millions* on a park bench. She came to Toronto and remained there for thirty years, as the "faithful, loving and devoted" bookkeeper.[57]

The CIM selected about one in seven applicants. Many applicants were "not fitted in every way"[58]: a fifteen-year-old orphan at Alma Ladies College; a widow in her sixties with three daughters, asking to be considered as a group; superannuated ministers with grown children; divorced women; single parents; ex-Roman Catholic priests. The reasons for rejecting an applicant tended to be standardized: poor health, family objections, too young, too old, in debt. Few were rejected on theological grounds, although the common terms "scripturally unsound" and "needs training" covered a multitude of sins.

The overwhelming cause for rejection was peculiar to the China Inland Mission, and concerned marital status. CIM policy was to send only unmarried men and women to China – a reversal of conventional missions – so that the women would have two years of practical and language training before settling down to raise a family. Of the fifty married couples who applied, only seven were accepted. Edgar A. Brownlee, later Canadian director, was a rarity, an educated man (B.A. and B.D. from McMaster University) with a wife and child. Even those who were engaged (an "attachment") were questioned whether marriage or career had priority. Occasional remarks indicate broken engagements when one partner was accepted and the other turned down. When the man was accepted, he tended to stay home; when the reverse happened, she often went to China anyway.

Few applications list previous occupations, except to note soul-saving work among the "poor neglected ones" in Indian reservations and inner-city slums. But the CIM did attract the socially humble and financially poor. Of those applications that did list occupations, the ones for men included harness maker, farm-hand, mechanic, upholsterer, shop employee, grocer, bookkeeper, and factory worker. Many women had cared for their parents ("obligations," another reason for turning down an applicant), or worked as a teacher, dressmaker or tailor, housekeeper, servant, bookkeeper, stenographer, or nurse.

In terms of denominational affiliation, two distinct patterns emerge from the applications, on either side of the border. The vast majority of Canadians – 90 per cent – belonged to the five national denominations, Presbyterian, Baptist, Methodist, Anglican, and Congregational. In the United States, only 70 per cent belonged to these same denominations, and some of those were in separatist groups like the Cumberland Presbyterians. Seventeen per cent of Americans listed one church – the Moody Church in Chicago – as their only affiliation.

TRANSPLANTING THE TRANSPLANT

By 1901 the Toronto CIM was in an anomalous situation. Frost and J.S. Helmer, the treasurer, were Americans, "living on British soil. *China's Millions*, our monthly paper was printed in Toronto, but its chief circulation was in the States. Our Prayer Union was centralized in our Canadian centre, but the larger part of its membership was in America. And most interestingly, our greatest opportunity for witnessing to the needs of China was in the States, but almost all of our speakers were from Great Britain."[59]

Yet when Henry Frost moved the North American headquarters of the CIM to Philadelphia in 1901, he did it so quickly that he did not confer with the Toronto council: "It was too late to ask for their advice. The most I could do was to announce my intention of transferring our family residence and beginning the work of the Mission at the new centre."[60] The council felt "abandoned" and "deserted." "The consensus of thought," Frost recalled, was that "I had built up the work in Canada; that it had developed around my personality, that it should collapse if I should leave it ... I said that if it was the case ... then the sooner I left the better ... a true work of God did not hang on the life of any one man."[61]

Having two national centres presented unforeseen difficulties. Frost thought of himself as a supranationalist; now the "very prosperity for which we had prayed," Frost wrote, produced

> a feeling of discontent. Toronto fearing what an increase in America would mean to it, and Philadelphia gathering the idea that it was destined, as compared with Canada, to be easily the chief ... I never felt that I had fully succeeded in denationalizing our service, some of our Canadian friends remaining Canadians and some of our American friends remaining Americans, and each clinging to his national prejudices ... My prayer then was, and still is, may the good Lord mix us up more and more! It will be a happy day when each of us will be constrained to say, 'I am a citizen of no mean city,' meaning by this, the heavenly Jerusalem.[62]

The "climax of discontent" became so severe that responsibilities were formally allocated to the two centres: Toronto was responsible for all applicants from Canada and the midwestern United States, by far the largest part of the field, while Philadelphia became the receiving home for candidates from "the east." The two councils were "advertise[d] ... as one" North American council, which did meet a few times – in Niagara-on-the-Lake when the prophetic conferences were revived in the 1910s. The Toronto council met regularly with six or eight in attendance; Philadelphia could seldom gather a quorum. Toronto was the working office, with a large staff, processing most of the candidates, editing *China's Millions*, and providing deputation speakers. Philadelphia was head office.

Establishing one regional centre, Philadelphia, made it easier to open others. London, Ontario, opened in 1904, was to be a halfway point between Toronto and Chicago but failed to reach the American Midwest. The next was Vancouver, in 1914, which became an important centre during the First World War when many British CIMers were stranded there by the disruption of shipping. Robert Burkinshaw has shown the pivotal importance of the CIM in Vancouver, where it repeated its old pattern and helped establish Vancouver Bible Training School.[63] Two American centres were opened in Chicago (1924), connected with Moody Bible Institute and Wheaton College, and in Los Angeles (1925). At BIOLA, the first Canadian to join the CIM, Alexander Saunders, who joined in 1886 and was now blind and crippled, established the missionary department and taught there for several years.

With its Americanization both in Canada and in China, the China Inland Mission took on a harder fundamentalist edge. Confronted with what he perceived as the apostasy of the United States in the latter days, Frost took on a crusade to save the nation. He contributed to *The Fundamentals* ("What Missionary Motives Should Prevail?" in 1915), and *China's Millions* became a vehicle for dispensational teachings, with guest editorials by Charles Trumbull and A.T. Pierson. The CIM became one of the key institutions of American fundamentalism, one of those that validated the orthodoxy of the others: a fundamentalist school exerted a certain kind of authority, training the younger generation; a mission society had a different kind – whether to accept the graduates of those institutions.

Frost retired from active leadership of the CIM in 1930 at the age of seventy-three, after forty-two years as its director. Looking back on his life, he expressed amazement with God's leading. Evangelicals, he concluded, were "a peculiar people," in the biblical if not the modern sense.

We are evangelicals, and hence, liberalists are not attracted to us. We are evangelistic, and hence, educationalists prefer other organizations. We are, in personnel, largely premillennial, and hence those who do hold this view of truth are specially sympathetic to us. And what has been, in these particulars, is likely to be ... It is my earnest prayer, whatever separation from others our position may require, that we shall never allow to rise amongst us the critical and censorious spirit ... It has been the glory of the China Inland Mission, that, remaining preeminently true to God, it has sought to be to men, the poor as well as the rich, the false as well as the true, the bad as well as the good, their servants for Jesus' sake.[64]

Henry Frost remained, despite his supranationalism, an American, as his fundamentalism showed. But his irenic words also show that he had been affected by his thirteen-year sojourn among the Canadian evangelicals.

23 Evangelical Bible Colleges in Twentieth-Century Canada

ROBERT K. BURKINSHAW

In the virtual absence of seminaries and liberal arts colleges under conservative evangelical control until the 1960s, evangelicals in twentieth-century Canada were typically trained in Bible institutes and colleges. And despite the dramatic development of evangelical seminaries and liberal arts colleges in Canada over the past three decades, Bible schools consistently remained the choice of the great majority of students enrolling in evangelical post-secondary institutions. When considering these facts, three questions come to mind. First, is it possible to demonstrate something of the magnitude of the influence of the Bible school movement upon Canadian evangelicalism? Second, how can that influence be explained? And third, what is the significance of the dramatic changes, beginning in the 1950s and continuing into the 1990s, taking place within the Bible college movement?

Earlier studies have demonstrated the numerical significance of the Canadian Bible institute/college movement. Bruce Guenther noted that eighty-five Bible schools were founded in western Canada alone before 1952, and one-quarter of those, nearly all local Mennonite schools, began before 1930. Over half were founded during the Depression, and the remaining quarter between 1940 and 1952.[1] W.E. Mann's list, published in 1955, missed many Bible schools, including all the Mennonite ones, yet he drew attention to twenty-seven schools in the Prairies which enrolled 2,090 students in 1947.[2] In 1960 S.A. Witmer reported that 3,300 students were enrolled in forty-four reporting institutions.[3] And according to figures gathered by *Faith Alive*, total full-time equivalent enrolments peaked in the mid-1980s at 8,300 students in seventy-six schools.[4] By the early 1990s that figure had dipped to about 7,000 students, of which 5,000 were in schools in western Canada, 1,300 in Ontario and the remaining 700 split almost equally between Quebec and the Maritimes.[5]

The most startling, and perhaps significant, figure is provided by Bruce Guenther who states, "A conservative estimate indicates that at least 200,000 people have spent at least one academic term at a Canadian Bible school or college."[6] There are good reasons to accept his figure, for the lists of graduates (a reported cumulative over 60,000 from existing Bible colleges by the mid-1980s[7]) does not include students who studied for only one or two years and did not graduate. In addition, many schools founded prior to 1960 were no longer in existence by 1985 and did not contribute to the total.

These estimates, while inexact, indicate that a significant number of students at one time or another attended a Bible college/institute. What impact these schools and their students have had on Canadian evangelicalism is difficult to assess fully, but a few examples will help illustrate something of this influence on the growth, character, and shifts in theological orientation of several denominations.

The interdenominational Prairie Bible Institute (PBI) is perhaps best known for its enormous impact upon world missions through its training of several thousand missionaries.[8] Less well known is PBI's impact on numerous evangelical denominations. Many PBI graduates who did not go into foreign missions saw the vast, often isolated, regions of western Canada as an important home-missions field and became engaged in the planting of large numbers of churches, many of which eventually entered evangelical denominations. For example, PBI was probably the single most formative influence upon the Canadian Evangelical Free Church (EFC), which by the 1990s included about 10,000 people concentrated between western Saskatchewan and British Columbia.

Capitalizing on evangelistic radio broadcasting the EFC sponsored with PBI in the 1930s, EFC congregations in Alberta and western Saskatchewan (almost all led by PBI graduates) quadrupled between 1938 and 1945. In the process the denomination lost many of its original Scandinavian characteristics and became far more identified with North American evangelicalism than with ethnic distinctions.[9] PBI's influence on the growth of the EFC and on the weakening of its ethnic identity grew further by the merger of a group of PBI-related independent churches in Saskatchewan and Alberta in 1957.[10]

The 1950s also saw rapid expansion by the EFC in British Columbia. Most of the new churches were planted in isolated towns and villages of the province's interior regions, and a key factor in their establishment was the availability of PBI graduates to pioneer the work. They came imbued with the missionary fervour for which the school was famous, and sought out places where few or no evangelical churches existed. Most needed to be at least partially self-supporting through other employment, but they managed nonetheless to plant a string of congregations throughout the newly settled regions of the province.[11] PBI influence continued to be strong, and as late as 1966 thirty PBI graduates were serving as pastors of EFC churches in Canada.[12]

The Mennonite Brethren (MB) were also profoundly shaped by the Bible school movement, both by institutions within and outside the denomination. In 1963 a denominational publication gave prominence to MB educational leader A.H. Unruh's frequent reminders that "it would be difficult to conceive of the Mennonite Brethren Church without Bible Schools." That booklet provided ample evidence for his assertion by noting that 90 per cent of the Canadian MB missionaries abroad, 86 per cent of the missionaries at home, 67 per cent of the Sunday school workers, and 59 per cent of the ministers had some Bible school training. In addition, over 80 per cent of the membership of all the national MB committees and boards were alumni of Bible schools.[13]

The MB schools contributed to an evangelistic thrust that helped change the character of sections of the denomination.[14] Gerald Ediger argues that in the 1930s and 1940s "Saskatchewan Bible Schools were on the leading edge of Mennonite Brethren accommodation to the English language." Schools at Herbert and Hepburn incorporated English in instruction and encouraged outreach to the English-speaking people of the surrounding areas. In Manitoba, generally more conservative on the language issue, several MB Bible College students began an English-language radio broadcast in Winnipeg in 1947, and the next year the student-run Home Missions Committee took the radical step of reporting to the denominational conference in English.[15] In British Columbia, Bible school teachers at the South Abbotsford church advocated using English to remove the language barrier to outsiders, and in 1949 established British Columbia's first MB English-language congregation.[16]

Nondenominational Prairie Bible schools also helped bring about changes in the MB churches. Many Mennonite youths (including those from groups other than MB), after several years at one of the local MB schools, continued their studies at a larger school such as PBI or Briercrest Bible Institute.[17] Such sojourns only strengthened MB students' evangelistic, English-language orientation.[18] Briercrest's influence over the MB increased in the 1980s as more MB churches in the West selected Briercrest graduates, rather than graduates of their own denominational schools, as youth pastors.[19]

While the EFC and MB denominations serve as examples of the Bible school movement's impact in forging an identity that was more North

American evangelical than immigrant ethnic, evidence is available that other, largely Anglo-Saxon-based denominations were influenced by the Bible school movement in more conservative theological directions. A case in point is the Baptist Union of Western Canada (BUWC), which, even after the more militant conservative churches in British Columbia and Alberta departed in the late 1920s and early 1930s, still counted large numbers of theologically moderate conservatives among the more liberal members. By the 1970s the liberal minority had all but vanished, and the denomination became almost solidly conservative, but generally not militantly so.

The role of the Bible schools should be considered as one important factor in this shift. BUWC minister J.E. Harris, for example, principal in the late 1940s of Vancouver Bible Institute (which attracted numbers of BUWC students) viewed his position as giving him the opportunity to influence his denomination in a more conservative direction. He wrote in 1950, "the Bible school movement is a notable sign of the divine activity to counteract the deadening influence of Modernism in the Church's life ... Bible school teaching [has] been widely effective in bringing about that return to the Bible and its message that is essential to the revival."[20] While ministerial candidates with only Bible school training often were not acceptable in BUWC churches, especially in urban centres, many Bible school graduates nonetheless filled pulpits in the denomination, and some played important roles as home missions workers and lay leaders.[21] Many Bible school graduates also went on to further studies, often in evangelical Baptist seminaries in the United States, and numbers of these served in large urban congregations and positions of denominational leadership. Former BUWC area minister Mel Ralston noted that as late as 1991 fifty of the 269 ministers listed in the *Yearbook* had completed at least some of their studies in Bible schools. These people, he argued, often occupied significant positions and were of great influence in moving the denomination in a more conservative direction.[22]

On a more localized scale, Maritime Christian College of Charlottetown, Prince Edward Island, played a major role in reorienting the Churches of Christ/Christian Churches of the Maritime provinces in an evangelical direction. In 1960 at the time of the college's establishment by members of the conservative Christian Churches, the majority of Christian churches in the Maritimes were affiliated with the more liberal Disciples of Christ, and only six with the more conservative Churches of Christ. By the early 1990s, however, only five congregations remained affiliated primarily with the Disciples, while thirty-five, many of them strong and growing, shared the more evangelical orientation of the

Churches of Christ. Maritime Christian College was central to that change. It trained the majority of preachers and elders in the Maritimes. Its president of twenty-three years, Ken Norris, provided frequent pulpit supply in most of the congregations and preached regularly on radio for years. Its faculty and students assisted in the planting of new churches in all three provinces, and it sponsored annual, large-scale public lectureships and youth rallies. The school was never large, reaching approximately thirty full-time equivalent students several times in the 1980s and 1990s; but with a respected leadership and a constituency of about forty congregations, it was still a decisive, shaping force.[23]

How did these schools, often considered insignificant and academically unsophisticated, and almost always operating on shoestring budgets, become so influential in Canada? Why did they attract support and large numbers of students? W.E. Mann points out the very real populist appeal of the schools. His observations are weakened, however, by a crude application of the church/sect hypothesis in which these schools' popularity is seen primarily as a means of social mobility for opportunity-starved youth.[24]

A more useful approach is that of Roland Miller, who states that any attempt to understand Bible schools must be done in the context of their own distinct mission: "They are schools committed to the effective teaching of a specific syllabus and the development of lifestyles exemplifying their understanding of life and truth ... the Bible school system in [for example] Saskatchewan represents an impressive edifice dedicated to the learning and practice of religion, defined as the Christian faith."[25] Bible schools used somewhat similar language to define their purpose. Phrases such as "training ... in a thorough and practical knowledge of the Bible," "character development and spiritual maturity," and the sending forth of "workers with an extreme love of souls" are found throughout their records.[26]

The twin purposes of the Bible schools – teaching the Bible as truth rather than as an academic subject, and training for practical Christian living and ministry – are key to understanding their growth. The two emphases provided Bible schools with both considerable populist appeal – to a biblicist and activist evangelical constituency – and a far greater flexibility than that enjoyed by more traditional liberal arts or theological church-related colleges. Conservative biblical doctrines appealed to many Canadians, especially in the Prairies, and in a period when many evangelicals had lost confidence in, for example, the theological departments of Brandon, Acadia, and McMaster,[27] large numbers saw Bible schools as trustworthy in terms of traditional evangelical doctrines and emphases.

The Bible schools' practical, ministry-oriented approach was also well received,[28] as can be seen in the regular reports in institutional publications of the extent of students' activities in various ministries. These included detailed statistics of the number of evangelistic tracts distributed, of homes and hospital beds visited, of street sermons preached, and of Sunday school and mid-week Bible classes taught. The statistics most proudly presented by many schools, however, were those indicating the number of graduates entering some kind of full-time ministry, whether on the foreign mission field or at home. Clearly, the activist evangelical constituency appreciated schools in which students actually did ministry rather than merely focus upon theological studies.

Of equal importance to the schools' success was the very flexible approach they adopted in most aspects of their endeavours. The schools' practical, non-academic goals meant that the leadership felt few of the constraints that would have been placed upon them had they been governed by more conventional academic requirements and traditions. And this relative freedom provided them with the flexibility to adapt to local conditions and the needs of their constituents. Indeed, Bible schools in Canada provide an excellent example of the unusually adaptable nature of evangelicalism.[29]

One of the clearest and best-known examples of this flexibility is in the area of admissions requirements. Bible schools were open, at least until the 1960s, to students without high-school graduation. Entry standards thus were low, but they reflected the realities of the educational context in Canada. Simply put, in the first half of the twentieth century an insistence upon high-school graduation would have made the vast majority of Canadian youth ineligible for admission. That would have been an unacceptable and unthinkable limitation, given the purposes of the schools. During the 1920s and 1930s only about 15 per cent of Canadian students graduated from high school. This figure did not rise above 25 per cent until several years after the end of Second World War and just reached 50 per cent by 1960.[30] H.H. Hildebrand estimates that in the 1930s, before the completion of a provincial system of high schools in Saskatchewan, only 10 per cent of the constituency of Briercrest Bible Institute had gained graduation diplomas.[31] The Bible schools' reflection of educational trends among the general population continued as opportunities to complete grade twelve became more widespread, so that in 1960, when half of Canadian high-school students were graduating, Bible schools too reported that just over half of their students were high-school graduates.[32]

Bible schools also displayed a great deal of flexibility by accepting students not usually admitted into theological colleges. While many schools encouraged students to consider entering full-time ministry, such a vocational goal was not a criterion of admission, and thousands of individuals planning on lay vocations enrolled. Indeed, for many decades Toronto Bible College did not seek to train pastors, believing that to be the prerogative of the seminaries, but it did strongly urge its students to consider mission work.[33] The MB school in Winkler, Manitoba, typified many other schools, stating as its goals to provide both a "general" training for laity – "such people who desire to enter into a deeper spiritual life and who seek to understand the Word of God, for private as well as for general use" – and a "special" training for people "who desire a preparation for public service, that is, as ministers, evangelists, missionaries."[34]

The inclusion of laity provided an opening for women, who were welcomed and often formed the majority of the student body in Bible schools at a time when they were barred from seminaries.[35] Although most evangelical groups, apart from some holiness and Pentecostal churches, did not generally approve of women in formal pastoral roles, their pragmatic approach to evangelism did not prevent single or married women from playing active roles in home and foreign missions.[36] For thousands of such women, Bible-school training provided a degree of knowledge and skills that was otherwise inaccessible. Women were active as faculty members in most schools but usually taught the more "appropriate" subjects of music, English, missions, and Christian education. However, in a surprising number of Bible schools, including PBI, Eastern Pentecostal, Canadian, and Moose Jaw (later Aldersgate), women also taught Bible courses.

Bible schools were accessible to a wide range of students because of very low or, in some cases, non-existent tuition fees. Unlike most liberal arts or theological colleges for which tradition often demanded expensive buildings, high-cost urban locations and regularly paid faculty and staff, Bible schools operated far more flexibly and cheaply. While Toronto, Vancouver, and most major Prairie cities were each the site of at least one Bible school by the 1930s, most schools were located in lower-cost small-town and rural locations. Such schools kept expenses down by raising much of their food on their own farms until the 1980s, or by receiving donations from nearby rural supporters. As well, most schools, whether rural or urban, began operations in unpretentious facilities such as rented or loaned houses or church buildings. Peace River Bible Institute, for example, operated in a different town in each of its first three years, occupying a total of four loaned and one rented house in its first two years.[37] Winnipeg Bible Institute (later Winnipeg Bible College and then Providence College) occupied thirteen premises, most of them rented, in its first forty-five years.[38]

A major factor, of course, in holding down costs, and thus tuition, was the availability of faculty willing to work for very low stipends.

This usually precluded those with advanced training, and thus the majority of Bible school teaching staff were not highly educated – with some notable exceptions, such as J.E. Purdie of the Pentecostals' school in Winnipeg, Walter Ellis of the Vancouver Bible school, and the degreed faculty of Toronto Bible College. Experience and success in evangelism and Bible teaching were deemed more important than academic degrees for those teaching young people to be Christian workers. Such teachers displayed great flexibility in carrying out a large number of responsibilities which, in addition to teaching, usually included administration, preaching, fund-raising, student recruitment, dorm parenting, and maintenance work. They often lowered costs further by supporting themselves through itinerant and supply preaching during the spring and summer months when classes were not in session. In some settings local pastors or missionaries on furlough helped with part-time lecturing, for which they received little or no remuneration.

Accessibility for students was also enhanced by their location in areas of demand, which explains why so many schools sprang up in centres such as Pambrun and Briercrest in Saskatchewan, Three Hills and Sexsmith in Alberta, or Victoria Corners, New Brunswick. At issue here was the cost of transportation. During the Depression, for example, the cost of a ticket to a city hundreds of miles away was a sufficient impediment to prevent many potential students from going to Bible school. Thus residents in a great variety of locales issued requests to begin schools in their own districts.

One of the most significant differences between Bible schools and traditional theological colleges, and a major factor in providing the former with the flexibility needed to adapt to the realities of their particular constituencies, was a general lack of control from denominational boards and bureaucracies. Independent schools such as PBI, Briercrest, Peace River, Millar Memorial, Winnipeg, Toronto, and Vancouver were subject to the least outside controls, but a surprising number of denominational schools resulted more from local initiative and entrepreneurship than might otherwise be expected. For example, Northwest Bible College in Edmonton, now a regional school of the Alberta Conference of the Pentecostal Assemblies, experienced a maverick start in 1946 under the leadership D.N. Buntain, pastor of the city's Central Tabernacle. Buntain's vision for a regional college, which would train lay leadership and clergy to focus on expanding Pentecostalism within Alberta, faced denominational opposition both from within and outside the province. Yet Buntain persisted, beginning the school in his church's basement, and, as it grew and its graduates proved effective in ministry, the Alberta District gradually came to support it.[39] Similarly, in 1941, twelve years after central authorities of the

Christian and Missionary Alliance had ordered the closure of fledgling Bible school ventures in Edmonton and Toronto, members of the Alliance in Regina launched the Canadian Bible Institute. The school was founded in defiance of the continuing wishes of Alliance authorities in eastern Canada and the United States, who were not fully convinced of the need for *any* Alliance school in Canada, let alone in *western* Canada. Official recognition was not granted for nearly five years, by which time the school was a thriving institution with an enrolment of over 150 students and ownership of a renovated three-story hotel in the city's downtown core.[40]

The results of this general pattern of entrepreneurial rather than bureaucratic origins included a great deal of innovation in the development of strong, mutually supportive relationships between the schools and their supporters. This was most clearly evident where strong and trusted leaders such as L.E. Maxwell or H.H. Hildebrand were at the helm, but it was not limited to those cases. Unhindered by traditional denominational restrictions and taking advantage of an evangelical sort of ecumenism that viewed most denominational differences as secondary, school leaders built strong, denominationally mixed constituencies. Because regional churches were crucial to gaining funding and students, schools regularly and eagerly sent speakers, musical teams, and literature to them as part of their public relations activity. Various schools also experimented with innovative new forms of communications such as radio, often with considerable success in bringing in revenue and new students. And many schools annually hosted huge missions rallies attracting hundreds and sometimes thousands to their campuses.

For their part, churches and home missions organizations came to rely on what the Bible schools had to offer, including the training of workers and ministers, supply preaching, musical talent, wider fellowship through missions conferences, and youthful energy for children's camp and home missions work. Many nondenominational Bible schools offered more resources and support than did churches' own denominational structures, and consequently they exercised great influence beyond that exerted directly on students. Denominationally and ethnically diverse constituencies often felt more loyalty to Bible schools than they did to any denominational structures. Indeed, Joel Carpenter's observation that Bible schools often functioned as "regional coordinating centres"[41] for conservatives is apt for a variety of settings in Canada – both urban and rural – as the schools built strong constituencies that were key to their success.

Faced with a rapid increase in educational levels and expectations in the general population in the 1950s and 1960s, Bible schools initiated a number of significant changes. By the late 1960s the rate of entrants with high-school graduation stood at 70 per cent, approximately triple its level in the immediate postwar period and five times the level of the 1930s.[42] At the same time a major expansion made university education somewhat less elitist than it had formerly been in Canada. A number of the older schools responded to these increasing levels of education by becoming degree-granting Bible colleges rather than diploma-granting Bible institutes. In 1948 the Winnipeg Bible Institute gained a provincial charter to grant a four-year Bachelor of Theology degree and was renamed the Winnipeg Bible Institute and College of Theology. Most of its students, however, remained in the Bible institute program.[43] In 1956 Toronto Bible College more successfully launched its first degree program, the Bachelor of Theology.[44]

Accreditation with the Accrediting Association of Bible Colleges (AABC) became a common goal for degree-granting Canadian schools. In the absence in Canada of national or regional accrediting agencies as existed in the United States, the AABC became the only option for the Bible colleges.[45] Accreditation required fairly stringent standards in the areas of faculty qualifications, library holdings, length of academic year, admission requirements, liberal arts (or "general education") course offerings, and various other aspects of college operations. The usually lengthy process of accreditation is illustrated by the case of the Canadian Bible College, the Alliance school in Regina, which became a fully accredited member of the AABC in 1961, one of the first Canadian schools to achieve this status. The process was initiated by the recommendation of the denomination's General Council in 1953, and the school quickly responded by lengthening its academic year from the typical seven months to nine months and by releasing several of its faculty from summer assignments to allow them to work on attaining Masters degrees. In 1953 only one faculty member held an M.A., but by 1959 nearly all full-time faculty possessed that degree or were working towards it. The library collection doubled from 4,000 to 8,000 volumes, and entrance requirements were raised to high-school graduation, with exceptions made for a limited number of mature students. The school's promotional material also reflected the changes, as the stress shifted from a nearly exclusively spiritual and practical focus to include an emphasis on the importance of developing the intellect. The efforts paid off, and the AABC granted associate status in 1960 and full accreditation in 1961.[46]

A new development took place in Winnipeg in the 1960s during which time the Canadian Mennonite Bible College became an approved teaching centre of the University of Manitoba. Under the terms of the arrangement the Bible college offered a number of courses in the arts and humanities, including religious studies, for university credit, subject to approval by the relevant university departments.[47] In the early 1970s Canadian Nazarene College made a similar arrangement, and the Salvation Army's Catherine Booth College followed in the early 1990s.[48]

Critics of the rising academic standards were not lacking, but they were answered in a number of ways. H.H. Hildebrand's response to criticism at Briercrest was that the new generation of students, most of them high-school graduates, were asking far different questions and demanding a different level of response than were those when he began the school in the 1930s.[49] Other leaders pointed out that some foreign countries were not accepting missionaries without recognized degrees.[50] Alvin Martin, president of Canadian Bible College, also cited the changing socio-economic status of evangelicals. He sought to explain that some of the changes at his institution were a response not only to the growing educational expectations among Canadians in general but to the fact that the Christian and Missionary Alliance had "some of the largest evangelical churches in the cities of Western Canada."[51] While most Bible college leaders did not mention such factors, it is clear that by the 1960s many evangelical denominations had moved from their accustomed place on the margins of society[52] and were not adverse to upgrading their institutions to reflect their new status.

While twentieth-century Canada has not proved a fertile field for autonomous Christian liberal arts colleges,[53] a significant process began in the 1960s that saw five new evangelical liberal arts colleges formed by the 1980s. The first of these, now Trinity Western University, was established as a junior college by the Evangelical Free Church in British Columbia's Fraser Valley in 1962. In 1979, in a reversal of a century-long process of the secularization of liberal arts education in Canada, it was granted autonomous degree-granting powers by the province. It grew quickly and remained the largest of the new breed of evangelical schools, and by the mid-1990s was enrolling approximately 1,500 full-time equivalent students.[54] At the opposite end of the country, the United Baptist Bible Training School in Moncton became Atlantic Baptist College in 1970, a two-year liberal arts college. In 1983 it was empowered to grant baccalaureate degrees and in the early 1990s was enrolling over 200 students and planning for a large new campus.[55] Also in New Brunswick, St Stephen's University opened its doors as a nondenominational school in 1975. In the two decades since it has remained unique in offering a classic liberal arts education from a strong faculty to a tiny student body not numbering above two dozen.[56] Two colleges with a Reformed heritage and commitment to the integration of the Christian faith within a solid liberal arts program opened in

Alberta and Ontario: King's College (since University College) opened in Edmonton in 1979 and gained degree-granting powers in 1983, and Redeemer College opened in the Hamilton area in 1982.[57]

From the late 1960s through the 1980s the concern to upgrade the educational qualifications of evangelical pastors led to a flurry of activity in establishing seminaries under explicitly evangelical control. The majority of evangelical seminaries were established as graduate divisions of the larger Bible colleges, but the first developments occurred on university campuses. By the late 1960s Acadia Divinity College, Nova Scotia, became a conservative evangelical Baptist institution.[58] Regent College began in 1969 at the University of British Columbia with the twin purposes of training full-time Christian workers and lay men and women, and it quickly grew to become one of the largest seminaries in Canada.[59] At about the same time that Regent College was being founded, the Alliance was developing Canadian Theological College (later Seminary) on the campus of Canadian Bible College in Regina.[60] Winnipeg Bible College began a seminary division in 1972, and the following year the North American Baptist Divinity School began offering graduate courses on the North American Baptist College campus in Edmonton.[61] In 1976 at the site of Ontario Bible College, one of the largest seminaries in Canada, Ontario Theological Seminary came into being, and PBI began a graduate program in 1988.[62]

Two unique evangelical seminaries were initiated in the 1980s. Briercrest Bible College began offering seminary courses on a modular concept, and short courses, none longer than two weeks, were offered on a full or part-time basis throughout the year by the early 1990s.[63] Then in 1988 the seminaries of three denominations – Evangelical Free, Fellowship Baptist, and Baptist General Conference – began a consortium known as Associated Canadian Theological Schools (ACTS) at Trinity Western University. None of the three were large enough to mount a strong program on their own, but by pooling their resources they established a program that attracted 160 full-time equivalent students within five years.[64]

A majority of post-secondary evangelical students still favoured the Bible colleges in the mid-1990s, but both of the new options made impressive gains while Bible college enrolment faltered and then declined. In the mid-1980s, Bible college enrolments peaked at about 8,300 students while the five evangelical liberal arts colleges together enrolled just over 1,000, and the seminaries considerably less.[65] By 1991 the gap had narrowed considerably as Bible college enrolment had dipped to about 7,000 while the five liberal arts colleges had more than doubled to 2,300 full-time equivalent students and the evangelical seminaries passed the 1,000 mark.[66]

Bible colleges faced a squeeze from two directions as the seminaries assumed much of their role in training pastors and missionaries, and as high-school graduates increasingly sought out evangelical schools that granted liberal arts degrees. Bible colleges responded in a variety of ways, generating a great deal of controversy in the process. A number of schools sought to broaden their offerings to include liberal arts courses that were transferable to provincial universities – courses not traditionally associated with Christian ministry, and courses providing training in a widening range of "parachurch" and support ministries. Leaders of colleges moving in this direction identified with the term "progressive Bible Colleges" that Kenneth Gangel brought into usage in the mid-1970s. Gangel contrasted "progressive" colleges with "traditional" schools which he described as having "an exclusive commitment to vocational Christian ministry; a single and simple curriculum; an emphasis on terminal training; and complete separation from secular training." On the other hand, "progressive" colleges were marked by a broader definition of ministry that included an emphasis on preparatory rather than terminal training and a willingness to pursue relationships with public education.[67]

The larger Bible colleges had already added a significant number of liberal arts courses in the 1960s and 1970s as part of the AABC accreditation process. In the 1980s and 1990s they added more and sought to improve the quality of those they offered in an attempt to attract students who might otherwise proceed directly into university or Christian liberal arts studies after high-school graduation. Ontario Bible College's charter was amended in the late 1980s to allow for increased liberal arts offerings so that up to two years of credit could be transferred to universities.[68] Winnipeg Bible College changed its name to Providence College in 1991 in order to reflect the breadth of its offering in "music, education, humanities and social sciences."[69] In several provinces, particularly in the Prairies, hard-won transfer agreements with the provincial universities were obtained and advertised widely.[70] And several colleges including Providence, Briercrest, and Prairie designed Associate of Arts programs for university transfer students.

Vocational programs in early childhood education, teaching English as a second language, secretarial training, business administration, accounting, computer studies, aviation, and institutional cooking began appearing in Canadian Bible colleges especially in the 1980s and 1990s. In addition, some schools, such as Swift Current Bible Institute, entered into agreements with community and regional colleges which allowed students to combine biblical and vocational studies.[71] The new vocational programs were explained to school supporters on the basis that ministry must be defined much more broadly than it had been previously.

PBI (where, significantly, the undergraduate school was renamed Prairie Bible College in 1986) argued in a new program rationale that "'serving God' is defined inclusively so as to challenge students to strengthen the church and to evangelize and make disciples in all places; the market place and the church and the mission field."[72] Other schools argued that they needed to train "bi-vocational" or "tent-making" pastors and missionaries who could support themselves and their ministry by another vocation.[73]

Many of the new vocational skills were of great use in the burgeoning evangelical churches and institutions as well as in the larger society. Some new and expanded programs specifically sought to fill the need for the growing number of multi-staffed evangelical churches, Christian social service organizations, and parachurch ministries. Youth, Christian education, children's and camping ministries, and music programs were strengthened, and more specialized programs such as sports ministries and community support services were added in the 1990s. Indeed, Walter Unger of Columbia Bible College believes that the future of Bible colleges lies in their ability to train program staff for churches and parachurch ministries and a growing number of Christian social service organizations.[74]

As Bible schools changed and adapted from the 1960s onwards, a question that increasingly demanded an answer focused on what those changes really signified. Was the upgrading of academic requirements a healthy continuation of the flexibility and adaptability that had allowed Bible schools to gain such a foothold in Canada in the first place? Did the broadening of the definition of ministry, the focus on service ministries and vocations, represent something of a return to the practical, lay-oriented roots of the Bible school movement? Supporters of the new directions have pointed to studies that indicate that Bible college students are motivated by more altruistic values and are less materialistic than their secular contemporaries. Progressive Bible colleges, it has been claimed, are providing such students with practical ministry and service training and a better understanding of culture through liberal arts training while continuing to provide a strong biblical foundation.[75] Furthermore, many students have seemed to be attracted by the new emphases, and some of the schools following the progressive model, such as Providence, Briercrest, and Columbia Bible College, enjoyed stable and even growing enrolments during the early 1990s, a very difficult period for many other Bible colleges. Northwest Baptist Theological College, which affiliated with Trinity Western University in the late 1980s, enjoyed remarkable growth after affiliation, indicating that students desired both Bible college distinctives along with assured university transfer credits.

Others, however, have seen in the new directions a compromise with trends in society and an unhealthy catering to the upwardly mobile evangelical "market." In so doing, it has been argued, schools lose not only their original flexibility in admissions standards but they also abandon their mission to provide biblical training for a wide range of students. Brian Stiller, executive director of the Evangelical Fellowship of Canada, was not entirely critical of the new trends, yet he sounded this warning in 1984: "But as seminaries grow and colleges require higher entrance standards, who will train those who simply want to learn the Bible and who have no designs on professional ministry?" Stiller wondered as well about motives: "Is the commitment of our schools to gain academic credibility a new form of worldliness?"[76] John Stackhouse has also raised concerns about the "universitizing" of the Bible colleges and cautions parents and students against being overly concerned with gaining marketable skills before spending significant time in "life training."[77]

In contrast, at least some students were apparently not attracted by the increasingly formalized training offered by the larger Bible colleges and chose instead the older versions of the Bible schools. From the late 1970s into the 1990s, hundreds of Canadian students each year travelled to various Torchbearer Capenwray Bible schools in England, Germany, New Zealand, Australia, and British Columbia where the major focus was on expositional-style Bible teaching.[78] Peter Reid, a Capenwray instructor based in British Columbia, expressed an important characteristic of the Capenwray orientation when he recently argued that "the pursuit of *academic excellence and degrees* has hindered the training of disciples of the Lord and the development of spiritual leaders."[79] During the same period, hundreds of Canadian students travelled each year to Youth with a Mission's Discipleship Training Schools in Canada and elsewhere for a five- or six-month Bible training and outreach experience.[80] A number of others studied at newer, informal Bible schools, many of them associated with independent charismatic churches. In the mid-1980s the Baptist Union of Ontario and Quebec established the Baptist Leadership Training Centre, a one-year Bible school focusing on lay training, paralleling somewhat the work of the Baptist Leadership Training School in Calgary. Mount Carmel, a similar school in Edmonton run by Christian (Plymouth) Brethren, after low enrolments in the 1980s grew to near capacity in the mid-1990s.[81] Some of the older, smaller Bible schools, such as Millar College of the Bible, Full Gospel Bible Institute, Nipawin Bible Institute, and New Brunswick Bible Institute, which had resisted the trend towards degreed status and continued to offer a more traditionally oriented practical and biblical school curriculum, noticed some modest improvement in enrolments in the early 1990s after declines in the 1980s. Finally, some of the larger, more progressive Bible colleges, recognizing that demand had not disappeared for the type of focus that had originally contributed to the strength and influence of the Bible school movement, recently added or strengthened first-year programs that focused on the Bible, "spiritual formation," and outreach.

The debate cannot be settled easily, but some observations are in order. It is noteworthy that diversity was a key component in the first half-century of the development of the Bible schools in Canada. Settings such as Toronto called for different emphases than did rural Saskatchewan or New Brunswick. The need for such diversity has not disappeared among Canadian evangelicals in the 1990s – indeed, it has become greater, even though geographical factors may not play as large a role as they once did. On the one hand, the need for evangelicals to gain university education in order to positively serve and influence Canadian society in a variety of capacities has been recognized by many. The relatively few Bible colleges that can afford to mount academically credible programs with good credit transfer records may play an important bridging role into the university world for many young people. Some Bible colleges also seem well positioned to meet the need for training the staff required by specialized ministries for church, parachurch, and social service agencies.

At the same time it needs to be recognized that 83 per cent of Canadian youth between the ages of 18 and 24 were not enrolled in university in 1991, presumably because of a lack of ability, interest, or opportunity. Furthermore, high-school drop-out rates were still at 24 per cent in the same year.[82] One must wonder whether some Bible schools have forgotten their populist origins by appearing to prevent the participation of many through high admission standards and rising costs of university-style programs. Presumably, thousands of evangelical youth are not suitable candidates for university but would benefit from the type of Bible and life training that Bible schools have traditionally offered. As only a few Bible colleges are large enough to be able to offer the wide range of programs appropriate to the great diversity of needs present, it thus appears that rather than homogenization, increasing diversification among the Bible schools is warranted.[83] Modern Bible colleges, like their predecessors, must wisely adapt their schools to some of the changing social realities while at the same time keeping in mind the historic emphases that have enabled the Bible schools to make a unique contribution in Canada.

PART SIX

Women, Spirituality, and the Evangelical Impulse

24 "Canada's Gift to the Sawdust Trail": The Canadian Face of Aimee Semple McPherson

EDITH L. BLUMHOFER

In Mount Forest, Ontario, in the summer of 1915, Aimee Semple McPherson quietly launched her evangelistic career. The occasion was an invitation to preach at the nondescript Victory Mission just off Main Street, a place so small that she laughingly dubbed it a "dolls' church." Ten years later, McPherson reigned supreme in the field. Her meteoric rise is generally understood as both mirror and product of southern California popular culture in the post–World War I era. Her contemporaries represented her as the "prima donna" of revivalism, a superb actress who easily provided the best show in show-obsessed southern California.[1] In 1933 *Vanity Fair* called her "the only living woman whose first name alone is sufficient to carry a headline on the front page of any North American newspaper."[2] California and Hollywood, then, frame an interpretation of McPherson's colourful life that focuses on the 1920s (especially on public, controversial moments). In this rendering McPherson's background and her religious claims become incidental to the apparent "real" story – a story brimming with power, money, sex, and intrigue.

A generation ago Brown University historian William McLoughlin noted that history had done Aimee Semple McPherson a double injustice: it perpetuated Menckenesque evaluations taken from sophisticated liberal journals on the one hand and kept alive the distorted exhibitionist images of the tabloid press on the other.[3] McLoughlin judged that neither medium took McPherson seriously and mused about the difference it might make if one started her story at the beginning instead of in the 1920s.

Starting at the beginning leads to Canada, for Aimee Semple McPherson was born Aimee Elizabeth Kennedy on a family farm west of the southern Ontario village of Salford on 9 October 1890. The daughter of a Methodist farmer, James Kennedy, and his second wife, Minnie Pearce Kennedy, a Salvationist, Aimee was reared in a close-knit, staunchly Protestant community where the rhythms of life revolved around the land, the churches, and the community. It is to this southern Ontario culture, deeply conscious of its British heritage, that one must turn to explore the cultural and religious impulses that shaped Aimee Semple McPherson. Her name and her style may be inextricably linked in the public imagination with Los Angeles, but she spent her formative years in Canada. She travelled widely, but in important ways she never strayed far from southern Ontario.

McPherson acknowledged her Canadian roots in small and large ways. Perhaps most significantly, she told and retold the story of her life until her rendering of it became part of the ritual life of her immense following. An attentive listener could hardly fail to notice that most of what she said was about Canada. Wherever she preached around the world, she stood before each audience at least once as a Canadian farm girl who had made good. "From Milkpail to Pulpit: The Story of My Life" was her most popular and disarming sermon, crafted to establish and vindicate her calling. It offered a glimpse into a world view that resonated with the deepest intuitions of millions and the populism that made her "everybody's sister."

Two aspects of McPherson's story offer revealing glimpses into the world of Canadian popular evangelicalism: first, the Salvation Army in southern Ontario and second, early Canadian Pentecostalism. McPherson found enduring models and inspiration in her experience of the early Canadian Salvation Army. She discovered an arena in which to develop them in the overlapping and layered networks that sustained early Canadian Pentecostalism. Both contexts influenced the choices that precipitated her stunning rise from oblivion to fame and moved her from southern Ontario to southern California.

THE SALVATION ARMY

The first Salvationists to "open fire" in Canada came in advance of regular troops. In February 1882 a group of immigrant English Salvationists began unofficially holding meetings on the streets of Toronto. Another commenced an unrelated assault on London in May. By early summer both requested official recognition from the Army's headquarters in London, England. General William Booth promptly delegated Major Thomas Moore, Commander of the United States Territory, to appoint officers and start a Canadian corps. By the fall of 1882 the Salvation War on Canada was rapidly gaining momentum. Within a year soldiers established Army corps in twelve Canadian cities including two directly related to McPherson's story – Lindsay and Ingersoll.[4]

On Friday, 27 July 1883, Lindsay's weekly newspaper informed the city's upright citizens that the Salvation Army "intend[ed] to commence the contest against all sin and error in this town on Sunday, July 29th."[5] Rumour had it that atheism was rampant in Lindsay, and Captain Charles Wass let it be known that he "invited and expected" all friends of Christianity to assist the prosecution of the war "against the giant foes of Christianity."[6] The first service on Sunday competed with those of the city's established churches but nonetheless drew "a fair number" for a program that included "strange features" that "differed altogether from the routine of the usual form of religious service."[7] In place of the ordinary fare, Army officers (including one woman) led the audience in songs set to popular tunes, prayers and testimonies, all of which were interspersed with brief exhortations. The Army had come to "get right hold of the hearts of the people," its officers announced, and they apparently succeeded. By Sunday evening (just two services and eight hours after the initial onslaught) the opera house was crammed with curious citizens. The next week the Army engaged a local music hall for six weeks of nightly meetings. Area pastors commended a visible increase in attention to religion and applauded the Army.

Tensions simmered just beneath the surface, but they only underscored the Army's appeal. Army "march outs" brought loud singing and boisterous drumming into the streets, and the business community worried about runaway horses. The city's chief constable grumbled that the Army's popularity greatly increased his duties since it always attracted crowds. But most citizens commended the Army's progress. When the one-month-old Lindsay corps "deployed into line" in a "grand parade" in Toronto early in August, the *Post* commended it for winning well over 120 local converts and urged it to prosecute the gospel war until Lindsay's remaining 3,400 unchurched citizens had succumbed to its regenerating influence.[8]

New converts did not constitute all of the Army's fruits. An undetermined number of church members also found their hearts warmed and their emotions stirred by the fervour, the colour, and the personal warmth of the soldiers. Among these in Lindsay were two members of the Methodist church, Mary Pearce and her daughter, Minnie. Mary Pearce's death late in 1884 did not deter her daughter, who by then – thanks to the Army – was proficient on the trombone, tambourine, and drum. Barely 15 years old, Minnie Pearce left home for the rugged but fascinating life of a soldier. Her days were filled with street meetings, parades, illustrated sermons, dramas, entertainments, and religious emotion expressed in shouts of joy and tears of agony as she knelt on the hard floors of southern Ontario's first citadels. In 1886 health problems contributed to her decision to trade itinerancy for employment on a farm near Ingersoll. The fact that Ingersoll had an energetic Salvationist corps eased the transition.[9]

The Ingersoll corps had enjoyed even more immediate success than Lindsay's Salvationists. The Army launched its Ingersoll offensive in July 1883. Within six months Salvationists from around Ontario converged on Ingersoll to dedicate a new barracks with a seating capacity of some 700. A "battle song" celebrated the occasion:

The Army here in Ingersoll has gone down, down, down
Down where the vilest of the vile could be found;
We wage a war on rum,
The devil hates our drum,
But we shall hear the Saviour say "well done."[10]

The Ingersoll corps had been established by three female officers – Captain Annie O'Leary (known as the "devil teaser") and Lieutenants Mattie Calhoun and Mercy Little. Over the next twenty-five years numerous other strong women provided Ingersoll corps leadership. Minnie Pearce joined a corps that offered ample opportunity to cultivate her gifts and expend her energies.

In the summer of 1886 Minnie Pearce married James Kennedy, an established farmer some forty years her senior and father of three grown children. Every day Minnie made the five-mile trip from their farm near Salford to the Ingersoll barracks. In recognition of her dedication, she was named sergeant major of the Ingersoll corps, an honourary distinction intended to dignify the unpredictable, unglamorous work of keeping things running smoothly. She also took on the job of corps correspondent, submitting regular reports to the Army's Toronto headquarters detailing the situation at the Ingersoll battlefront.

This, then, was the Army ethos into which Aimee Kennedy was born in 1890. The Army faithful lived by simple rules that valued self-discipline, hard work, and total consecration to the cause.[11] The troops assembled under the Army's blood and fire flag, wore uniforms or identifying sashes, and took their message out of the barracks to the people. The Army encouraged dramatizations of the gospel, experimented with new technology (like magic lanterns, gramophones, and stereopticons), offered popular entertainments, promoted women in positions of responsibility, and tackled social problems (especially "demon rum") with a will. It was also significant – especially in the light of Aimee Kennedy's future career – that this was a singing Army. For the first few years each issue of the Canadian *War Cry* carried columns of testimony songs – words set to popular tunes – submitted by converts. The poetry was often mediocre and the theology unsophisticated, but the vibrancy of the experiences described was undeniable. In contrast to church music, Army singing was accompanied by amateur pianists and anyone who played a portable instrument. Tambourines and brass and percussion instruments seemed better suited than organs to the rousing, toe-tapping music, "glory dances," and other evident "tokens of blessing" Salvationists favoured. The music was participatory and joyous. It was emphatically the people's music. Her tambourine was one of Aimee Semple McPherson's lifelong trademarks – and a legacy from her Army childhood.

Some deemed all of this sensationalist. In fact the Army's sensational character probably had more to do with style than with content. Its message was standard Wesleyan fare on sin, holiness, and free grace, aptly summarized by Herbert Booth, son of Army founders William and Catherine Booth:

Grace there is, my every debt to pay;
Blood to wash my every sin away;
Power to keep me sinless day by day,
For me! For me!

Canadian Army enthusiasts cheerfully agreed with critics who complained that there was no religion in many Army tactics. Rather, religion was the overriding intention of noisy, attention-getting pageantry and entertainment. It was the result, not the substance. From the bass drums that read JESUS SAVES to the testimony shirts and sashes embroidered on one side with the new names such as "Hallelujah Jim" and "Glory Tom" that some converts assumed (Aimee Kennedy's read "God's Little Child") and on the other with testimonies like "Washed in the blood of the Lamb"; from the setting of religious lyrics to show tunes to parades with banners and brass bands; from the red, blue, and gold flags emblazoned with the words "Blood and Fire" to the soldiers' demurely proper dress uniforms, everything about the Army was calculated to attract notice and arouse curiosity.

All of this fired Aimee Kennedy's imagination: one could try anything as a means for communicating the gospel, and religion should be joyous. The Canadian Army in its early phase offered infinite scope for adaptation, experiment, and creativity.

In Ingersoll the churches quickly came to terms with the Salvationists. Army entertainments and special events drew the members of the region's conventional churches, who regarded the Army as less than a church but much more than a social agency. Most commended its ability to reach people the churches failed to hold and applauded its devotion to the temperance cause. With the churches, the Army received a share of Ingersoll's Christmas donations for the poor. Army bands played for civic and religious functions. The Army used Ingersoll's largest building, King Street Methodist church, for programs that overflowed its own auditorium. On the other hand, the Sunday pulpit exchanges that characterized Ingersoll's older Protestant churches did not follow. If Salvation Army zeal was commendable, Salvation Army worship style was not quite respectable – at least not for Sunday mornings – and respectability was a hallmark of the region's churches.

Ingersoll's acceptance of the Army was culturally rooted as well in a wider fascination with the Booths. The secular Canadian and American press reported regularly on the worldwide travels of the imposing General William Booth and his family. Everywhere heads of state, royalty, and titled nobility received the Booths and socially prominent people honoured them. Such recognition conferred status and made Salvationists in Ontario's scattered outposts proud to be part of a vital global spiritual and social renewal.

General Booth was famous, dignified, and very much in charge, but it was his daughter Evangeline who left a lasting impression on the Canadian Army in its formative years.[12] From 1896 until 1904 Evangeline Booth ran the Canadian Army with efficiency and flourish. She loved costume and pageantry and gained renown for her illustrated sermons. Her first, "Miss Booth in Rags," filled Massey Hall, the Dominion's largest auditorium, just a few weeks after her arrival and established her as a Canadian celebrity. She became the darling of respectable middle-class Protestants who flocked to her wherever she went. It is likely that Evangeline Booth's "Miss Booth in Rags" was the model that Aimee Kennedy later adapted and made famous in her illustrated sermons.

The early Canadian Salvation Army, then, illuminates the origins of Aimee Semple McPherson's religious style. More specifically, the Army in Ontario during Evangeline Booth's tenure provides helpful clues, for the larger southern Ontario context was important too. The small village of Salford just east of the Kennedy farm had two churches, Methodist and Baptist, and a decided majority of the population identified with one or the other.[13] (As a teenager Aimee Kennedy for a time preferred the propriety of Salford's Methodist Church to the exuberance of the Salvation Army.) The festivals marking the land's productivity, from maple syrup festivals to strawberry festivals to peach socials and apple harvests on to the national day of thanksgiving for the harvest, were sponsored by the churches. Civic events and public education always had religious components. The parts of the public calendar not tied explicitly to the land were defined by the churches – especially celebrations of Christmas and Easter and regular rounds of revival meetings in Salford and Ingersoll churches.

The ethos was Protestant but not denominational. In Ingersoll and Salford, Baptist, Presbyterian, and Methodist pastors readily exchanged pulpits and, as need dictated, congregations shared facilities. Every few years one of the pastors left for a new charge, and a new family moved into one of the parsonages. Most were remarkably unremarkable. Each was highly regarded, but the strength of the Protestant churches lay not in their pastors but in their members and in their role in defining and nurturing the culture.

The institutions that sustained the social order, then, fused religion, land, and civic duty. These were closely linked, and what affected one affected all. The churches were evangelical, but they seldom disturbed the comfortable rhythms of life of the solid and upright citizens, their members. To be sure, revival embers just beneath the surface awaited periodic fanning to burst into flame and warm souls to renewed zeal. But then things settled again, to await the next rekindling. In this regard, the Salvation Army worked at being an exception; McPherson built her career on its example. More than the churches, the Army disrupted life's routines and reordered priorities. Army faithful regarded religion as something that happened to people all the time: their Christianity was intense, emotional, expressive, joyful, all-consuming. If their vigour waned, they worried. Aimee Kennedy learned that lesson well.

How the Army, the churches, and southern Ontario culture related and the assumptions and values each transmitted defined Aimee Semple McPherson. Her idiom and organization; her determination to involve everyone and to keep everyone busy; her sensitivity to social outcasts; her famous forays into red-light districts, dives, and dance halls; her creative use of drama, costume, music; her penchant for parades, bands, uniforms, flags, banners, and symbols; her marketing abilities; her sense that denominational affiliation mattered far less than common values and piety; her willingness to work with everyone to accomplish a task; her blending of the civic and the religious – all these and more can be traced to the early Canadian Salvation Army and to the Protestant subculture of her southern Ontario upbringing. The religious and social ethos of rural southern Ontario is indispensable to understanding McPherson.

Also indispensable is early Ontario Pentecostalism.

394 Women, Spirituality, and the Evangelical Impulse

EARLY PENTECOSTALISM

Aimee Kennedy first encountered Pentecostalism late in the fall of 1907, when she was 17. Rumours about tongues speech, dancing and "falling under the power" in small house meetings and a store-front mission in Ingersoll prompted her to visit. She went to ridicule, but she found herself unexpectedly captivated by the evening's evangelist, Robert Semple. His earnestness and Irish lilt got her attention, but, as she later told it, it was his tongues speech that convinced her that God was present among the Pentecostals and that she wanted what they had.[14]

Over the next few weeks she acted impulsively on the religious impressions awakened by her encounter with Ingersoll's handful of Pentecostals. She threw herself into their cottage prayer meetings and religious services until she too received the baptism with the Holy Spirit and spoke in tongues. In a Salvation Army ceremony in August 1908, Aimee Kennedy and Robert Semple were married. They spent a brief honeymoon among Toronto Pentecostals and then moved into rented rooms in Stratford to help establish that city's Pentecostal mission. Robert supported them by working for the Grand Trunk Railroad. They looked forward to missionary work in China.

Aimee Kennedy Semple's turn to Pentecostalism brought her into a network that radiated outward from Toronto, extended informally by people associated with one or more separate but cooperating Toronto missions. Enthusiastic men and women who spoke in tongues in Toronto carried testimonies about the restoration of New Testament spiritual gifts first to acquaintances, former colleagues, or relatives. Pentecostalism, then, generally infiltrated (or erupted within) existing networks. A brief consideration of some of the Toronto missions in which Pentecostal impulses flourished provides an illuminating glimpse into the radical evangelical ethos that shaped Aimee Semple McPherson's understanding of Pentecostalism. It also reveals how Ontario Pentecostals like the Semples were linked to the larger Pentecostal world and suggests ways in which early Toronto Pentecostalism differed from its American counterparts.

The Toronto Pentecostal story begins in the fall of 1906. Monday, 19 November 1906, was a gloomy day, with light rain and snow showers. The *Globe* reported that in the evening a city official threw a switch, current flowed, and light dispelled Toronto's gloom. In "a most impressive scene," Niagara power electrified Toronto.[15] The press speculated on the potential of a vast power source.

In a nondescript three-story building just east of downtown Toronto, entirely unnoticed by the press, a small group of people speculated about another power that flowed that night: it was said that Pentecost came to Toronto on 19 November 1906. It had, in fact, been coming for several days to a faith mission on Queen Street in the person of mission co-founder Ellen Hebden and her explanations of her unusual religious impressions and experiences.[16] At about the same time Pentecost pressed into the city from other sources as well, manifesting itself in scattered, unrelated missions.

Several features of this nascent Pentecostalism should be noted. First, it did not disrupt or even disturb Toronto's religious establishment. Second, from its inception Toronto Pentecostalism was linked to the United States through networks established earlier by people and movements active on both sides of the border. The Semples' ties to these extended networks later enabled Aimee Semple McPherson to establish herself independently in the United States. Third, the early Toronto Pentecostal subculture that nurtured the Semples flourished for less than four years. By 1911 it had virtually vanished. The fact that it existed for such a short time underscores a few of its features: Pentecostals were mobile and restless; strong personalities clashed; an anti-organizational bias prevailed.

More than any other individuals, James and Ellen Hebden influenced the immediate character of the Pentecostal world Aimee Kennedy entered in 1908. Lay Christian workers from Yorkshire, the Hebdens arrived in Toronto in 1904, purchased property on Queen Street, and in 1906 opened a combination mission and faith home variously known as the East End Mission, the Hebden Mission, and the Church of God. The two had strong affinities for "deeper" or "higher" Christian life teaching. They also practised prayer for the sick and "faith living." On 19 November 1906 Ellen Hebden publicly spoke in tongues. She insisted that the experience was part of her personal spiritual pilgrimage, surprising even to her and unrelated to reports she soon heard of similar happenings elsewhere.

The Hebden mission now began attracting people interested in tongues and other spiritual gifts. Within a few weeks Albert S. Copley, an American minister affiliated with the Evangelical Association who was in Toronto to preach at the Evangelical Church, heard of the unusual happenings at the Hebden Mission. He visited the mission, then recounted his impressions in a letter to John Martin Pike, Methodist editor of *The Way of Faith*, a weekly South Carolina holiness publication with national circulation. Pike printed Copley's letter, and the Azusa Street Mission publication, *The Apostolic Faith*, reprinted it in January 1907.[17] And so popular publications put the Hebden Mission onto the map of North American Pentecostalism.

It is difficult to order the events between November and February in the winter of 1906 in which Pentecostalism emerged in Toronto. Simultaneous and apparently unrelated outbursts of tongues occurred in settings superficially different but indirectly linked. Together they created a fragile Pentecostal subculture that blended various popular evangelical streams.

It must be noted that first-hand reports of tongues speech in the United States reached Toronto by late fall 1906.[18] And reports of tongues speech anywhere prompted a surprising number of responses from people who had already spoken in tongues or knew someone who had.[19] To a greater extent than is generally recognized, the Pentecostal movement linked people who had exercised spiritual gifts before they actually heard of Pentecostalism. It offered them a way to understand their experiences.

In January 1907 Toronto evangelicals whose interest in speaking in tongues had been heightened in the past six weeks by rumours, periodicals, testimonies, and protracted meetings at the Hebden Mission had their first opportunity to gather and consider the broader meaning of what was happening. The occasion was a series of meetings led by the indefatigable "progenitor" of American Pentecostalism, Charles Fox Parham. Parham came to Toronto at the invitation of Eugene Brooks, an elder in John Alexander Dowie's Zion who led Zion's Toronto mission on Concord Avenue.[20]

In January 1901 in Topeka Parham had linked the baptism with the Holy Spirit and speaking in tongues, first articulating what became the Pentecostal distinctive. In the fall of 1906 Parham had brought his Pentecostal message to Zion, Illinois, in perhaps his most successful campaign ever. Pentecostalism had spread rapidly through Zion's far-flung outposts until it reached Toronto.[21]

Parham arrived directly from Zion in January 1907. His message and demeanour favourably impressed Eugene Brooks and his Canadian wife, Sarah Leggett Brooks. After a week at the Zion mission, they moved the services to Wolesley Hall, a second-floor auditorium near the corner of Yonge and Gerrard Streets. The advertisement they placed in a Toronto newspaper outlined the content of Parham's presentations: "Faith once for all delivered ... Christ's soon coming. Conviction – deep and pungent. Repentance – to God and man. Salvation – real conversion. Healing – prayer of faith. Sanctification – lived and possessed. Baptism – of Holy Ghost evidenced by recipient speaking in tongues."[22] Brooks enlisted the cooperation of the Hebdens and other missions where people were also eager to be part of the revival for daily afternoon and evening services.[23] (It is noteworthy that just six weeks after

Ellen Hebden spoke in tongues, Brooks readily identified six missions that would cooperate to sponsor Parham.)

When the meetings ended, Parham recommended that his converts be gathered in a new mission. The cooperating congregations agreed, and Parham invited Henry and Martha Robinson to take charge. Both were ordained ministers of Dowie's Zion. English-born Henry Robinson was a Canadian citizen, and he gladly returned to Canada. Parham, then, was directly responsible for one new Pentecostal mission and for the "pentecostalization" of the Zion outpost in Toronto.[24] He also influenced the start of monthly union meetings among the missions supportive of Pentecostalism (which cooperated informally as the United Pentecostal Missions of Toronto.)[25]

One of these was associated with the Holiness Movement Church, led in Toronto by George A. Christie. The Holiness Movement Church taught an experience of baptism of the Holy Ghost "as distinct and separate from entire sanctification, or holiness."[26] The group also celebrated an annual Feast of Pentecost. But until early 1907, Christie noted that summer, "only occasionally ha[d] anyone spoken in tongues."[27]

Christie welcomed the Pentecostal message, but it was Herbert Randall who became the first Holiness Movement Church leader to experience the baptism with the Holy Spirit.[28] Randall, who established the Holiness Movement Church mission in Egypt in 1900, was on furlough in Toronto in 1907.[29] He had already heard about Pentecostalism from several sources – *The Apostolic Faith* from Azusa Street, a friend in Los Angeles, and colleagues in Toronto – before he made his way to the Hebden Mission with "heart longing," as he put it, "for something, I couldn't tell what."[30] On 6 March 1907 he was baptized in the Holy Spirit. He immediately set out to penetrate southern Ontario with the Pentecostal message. His travels took him to Wingham, Simcoe, and Stratford. In the summer he was one of several Canadians at the Pentecostal camp meeting in Alliance, Ohio. The camp's leader, Quaker-turned-Pentecostal evangelist Levi Lupton, sent him with A.S. Copley (who as noted had reported from Toronto in December 1906) to "battle for Pentecost" in Lupton, Michigan. (Lupton also commissioned two women as missionaries to Toronto.)[31] Ever restless, Randall was back in Canada in the fall. In October he came to Ingersoll where he gathered those among whom Aimee Kennedy soon found her husband and her calling.

The Christian and Missionary Alliance also intersected strategically with this emerging Pentecostalism, chronologically first through the efforts of George and Annie Murray. Scottish by birth, the Murrays settled in Toronto in 1904 for an extended furlough following twelve years of missionary service in Palestine. George Murray was lame, his wife blind, but by all accounts physical challenges did not impede their operation of a small girls' school or their relief work among the destitute in Hebron.[32] In the fall of 1906 – during a visit among her Alliance friends in Pittsburgh – Annie Murray received the baptism with the Holy Spirit and spoke in tongues.[33] By January 1907 the Murrays were in touch with other Toronto tongues speakers. They introduced into this Toronto group their Alliance friends from western Pennsylvania and Ohio who spoke in tongues.[34] During the next few years the Murrays at one time or another assisted at two of the Toronto missions identified with the Pentecostal movement.[35] George Murray served as secretary of the United Pentecostal Missions, but though he diligently sought the experience, he never spoke in tongues.[36]

In June 1907, Annie Murray's efforts inclined Canadian Alliance patriarch John Salmon and his congregation, Bethany Chapel, towards Pentecostal experience.[37] Also a native of Scotland, Salmon was thoroughly networked in the Toronto's popular Protestant subculture and aware of reports of Pentecostal revival in the United States. Annie Murray prodded him to seek a deeper Christian experience.[38] In July 1907 at the Alliance's Beulah Park Convention in Collinwood, Ohio, Salmon (a vice-president of the Alliance) – along with numerous Alliance personalities – spoke in tongues.[39]

Some adherents of the Christian Workers Church also blended easily into Pentecostalism. The Christian Workers Church had emerged out of unrest within Canadian Salvationist ranks, and over the years some of its workers forged Alliance ties.[40] One such was George Fisher who had resigned from the Salvation Army's Soul Saving Troupe in October 1892.[41] Another, John Craig, had left the Army about the same time. Craig and Fisher associated their efforts with the city's Pentecostal network.[42]

With hindsight it is easy to identify as well the significance for the Semples of other people who passed through Toronto between 1907 and 1910. The genial Anglican rector Alexander Boddy visited often from England. Until World War I Boddy's parish in Sunderland was the nerve centre of English Pentecostalism. Boddy's associates would sponsor the Semples in Britain (en route to Hong Kong) in 1910 and would later mobilize on behalf of Aimee Semple McPherson. During her campaigns in the South in the World War I era, McPherson benefited from well-established relationships between Canadians, the holiness movement and holiness Pentecostalism. The most important links for Toronto Pentecostals reached to God's Bible School in Cincinnati and its widely circulated publication, *God's Revivalist*, and especially to the

Fire Baptized Holiness Association and the leader who brought that association into the Pentecostal movement, Joseph H. King.[43]

Personal interaction between Toronto and American Pentecostals often corresponded with easy rail and ferry connections. Lake Ontario ferries provided regular service to Rochester, New York, where the style of the Pentecostal work supervised by the Duncan sisters and known as Elim drew Toronto Pentecostals.[44] Pentecostals from both sides of the border travelled to Alliance, Ohio (Levi Lupton), and several Ohio Christian and Missionary Alliance camp meetings. Railroad routing made Zion City and Chicago (the North Avenue Mission and the Stone Church) readily accessible. Railroads and cheap publications played an incalculable role in networking, nurturing, and extending Pentecostalism.

This, then, was the Semples' world, defined by straightforward premises rooted in persuasions about the end-times, restorationism, spiritual gifts, and religious experience. Driven by the certainty of the imminent end of time, the faithful bent every effort to "know God in his fullness" and bring others to that knowledge too. A simple text they often tacked to mission walls aptly summarized the common faith: "Jesus Christ, the same yesterday, today, and forever" (Heb. 13:8). The most visible difference between Pentecostals and others who shared most of their convictions was their emphasis on the so-called utterance gifts – tongues, interpretation of tongues, prophecy.

These early Pentecostals believed the baptism with the Holy Spirit was "enduement with power for service." They seemed driven to spread their message, travelling tirelessly and moving often, sustained by the conviction that God would provide. After all, if Pentecostalism was God's last message to the world, then Pentecostals had the awesome, pressing task of making sure the message was proclaimed.

The Semples' Pentecostal world was charged with supernaturalism. Pentecostalism functioned as a way of life, a reality as well as a manner of perceiving reality. The radical faith Pentecostals espoused had a solution to every problem. Whatever their needs, they prayed: healing, money, and guidance for everyday decisions became subjects of intense supplication. "We must demand and have a Pentecost today which will tally in every essential with the original pattern," J.E. Sanders (who led a Toronto mission) wrote from Toronto in 1907. "Demons must be cast out, those of all tongues must be addressed in their own language, sick must be healed, the unbelieving must see signs and know of a truth 'this is that' ... We must be filled with all the fulness of God."[45]

The Semples' experiences in this Toronto network not only shaped their assumptions about the essence of Pentecostalism but also influenced their views on form and procedure. The first Toronto Pentecostals resisted organizing as a formal network and were disinclined to use the title "reverend" or to form churches. (Even later, there were missions, chapels, tabernacles, and temples, but seldom churches.) Expressions of spiritual gifts flourished, sometimes featuring actions unusual even by early Pentecostal standards.[46] In the schedule-free style of the early Quakers, these people longed to be open to the Spirit, for none knew in advance what God might have in mind. Their services continued indefinitely – after all, the anointing to preach, prophesy, testify, or sing could hardly be confined to a schedule. The Toronto missions also affirmed females in public ministries. (In three of the Toronto missions run by couples, the wife's ministry generally took precedence over her husband's.)

Aimee and Robert Semple moved in this mobile and fluid world, with its transient workers, its global consciousness, its supernaturalism, and its intricate and overlapping networks and international connections. Its piety blended themes from Keswick, the Christian and Missionary Alliance, holiness movements, Dowie's Zion. Its devotional classics came from the pens of Brother Lawrence, Madame Guyon, and John Wesley. It valued physical healing, faith living, Christ-centred devotion, religious experience, spiritual gifts, congregational polity, Quaker-like spontaneity, spiritual disciplines like fasting, and silent "waiting on God."

In the fluid, non-dogmatic pietistic ethos of this Toronto Pentecostal subculture, views that permanently fractured American Pentecostalism coexisted without apparent problem. For example, the Chicago Pentecostal William Durham created a deep and permanent rift in the United States when he challenged Wesleyan views on instantaneous sanctification. In contrast, Toronto Pentecostals readily wove Durham's emphasis on "the finished work of Calvary" with Wesleyan calls to heart purity. They seemed to understand what a few Americans unsuccessfully tried to say: Durham and his holiness opponents were not so far apart after all.[47] For Toronto Pentecostals, organizational relationships posed a more troubling challenge than did doctrine. The issue loomed when British Pentecostals attempted (unsuccessfully) to organize a Toronto branch of the Pentecostal Missionary Union. These Canadians did not argue about doctrine, but they adamantly resisted structure, affirming radical congregationalism. All the while their extensive and layered networks in effect tended toward inchoate organization.

Like most Pentecostal workers, the Semples had few worldly possessions, and they did not stay long in one place. In the first four months following their marriage, they supervised the Pentecostal mission in Stratford and then moved to London for a few weeks to assist in the house meetings that introduced Pentecostalism to that city. Since "the anointing" vindicated their ministry, the Semples needed no formal training, but they chose to associate in January 1909 in an apprentice relationship with William Durham, a well-known Pentecostal Chicago mission pastor, editor, and evangelist.

In January 1910 the Semples prepared to move on again, this time to China. Durham accompanied them from Chicago to Toronto for a convention at the Hebden Mission sponsored by the city's United Pentecostal Missions. They stopped first in Berlin (now Kitchener), then in London for a few weeks of well-publicized meetings in the home of a wealthy manufacturer and prominent Methodist, William Wortman.[48] Durham lingered in London, and the Semples went on to Toronto for "ten wonderful days" of convention at the Hebden Mission. The religious intensity heightened with Durham's arrival, but a crowd of well-wishers nonetheless took time out to give the Semples a memorable send-off.

At every port during their long journey, the Semples met Pentecostals and learned of the progress of the revival. They had a strong sense of kinship with these people, deeper perhaps than they felt with their own flesh and blood. In many ways Pentecostals seemed to devalue the nuclear family, cultivating instead an extended family that reached around the globe.

When the Semples left in February 1910, the Toronto Pentecostal world they knew was in flux, despite its apparent vitality, and their farewell to Toronto was more final than anyone anticipated. In August 1910 Robert Semple was buried in a Hong Kong cemetery known as Happy Valley. Aimee returned, only to discover that the leaders and congregations that had moulded her had either vanished or relocated. James Hebden heeded a "call" to Algiers; the Robinsons and the Brookses left in 1911 to establish Pentecostal faith homes in Zion, Illinois; John Salmon retired to his daughter's home in California; George Murray died, and Annie Murray sailed for a mission station in Bombay; William Durham moved from Chicago to Los Angeles, where he died prematurely in 1912; Herbert Randall was on the road, en route to Egypt. What continuities remained did not effectively replicate the early phase of Toronto Pentecostalism.

The impulses that shaped early Toronto Pentecostalism survived best in people like Aimee Semple McPherson who adapted them and mediated them to another generation. Formed during a unique moment in Canadian Pentecostal history, McPherson always stood somewhat apart from organized Pentecostalism in the United States and Canada.

In summary, the outcome of McPherson's story is different if one starts where she always did – in southern Ontario. The ethos of the earliest forms of Canadian Salvationism and Pentecostalism defined for her certain lifelong commitments. The Canadian Salvation Army fired her imagination and Toronto-based Pentecostalism empowered her faith.

Both influenced her assumptions, practice, and style. McPherson exploited overlapping and layered radical evangelical circles that ignored national borders and denominational boundaries and linked Canadian and American evangelicals in a common quest for spiritual experience. Canadian journalist Gordon Sinclair put it well: McPherson may have been "Hollywood's hot gospeler," but she was "Canada's gift to the sawdust trail."[49]

25 Beyond the Congregation: Women and Canadian Evangelicalism Reconsidered

SHARON ANNE COOK

For those interested in charting the contours of the Canadian evangelical experience, the last few years have been stimulating ones. A good deal of current scholarship has been due to the long-standing research interests of such celebrated and, frankly, pioneering historians as John Webster Grant and George Rawlyk. From Goldwin French's 1968 article surveying "The Evangelical Creed in Canada" and Richard Allen's *The Social Passion* in 1971, little had been written in this province about evangelicalism until John Webster Grant's important 1988 study of Ontario religion, *A Profusion of Spires*.[1] Several works have since explored essential evangelical principles and behaviours, as well as the rise, hegemony, and dissolution of the evangelical consensus in Ontario during the last half of the nineteenth century. George Rawlyk had begun to investigate the Maritime religious culture somewhat earlier; and his ground-breaking analyses of Henry Alline and the Maritime Baptist movement and more recent studies of revivalism and fundamentalism raised new questions and offered suggestive models for the next generation of religious historians.

Several important books have significantly carried the field forward. William Westfall has deftly charted the development of a distinctive Protestant Ontario culture which he has termed "romantic evangelicalism."[2] Michael Gauvreau's highly perceptive analysis of the forces that weakened evangelicalism in Canada[3] has helped to distinguish between the disintegrating effects of Darwinianism, Higher Criticism, historical scholarship, and the disturbing insights and implications of the new social sciences. David Marshall's 1992 study evaluates the Canadian

Protestant clergy's response in this period to the "crisis of plausibility" confronting Christianity and its struggle to find a "preachable gospel."[4] His discussion of the continuities and ruptures in the evangelical tradition aid in plotting the progress of secularism.

Curiously, and also strikingly, only Rawlyk's work on Canadian evangelicalism provides more than passing reference to the role of women. Indeed, the historical record of women's religious thought and activities has been obscured by a triple screen: first, studies of evangelicalism, where women's contribution was considerable, tend to under-examine women's contribution; secondly, the larger Protestant tradition, of which evangelicalism is an important component, has considered women's position only sporadically, and usually in relation to major institutions such as the Sunday school or women's missionary societies; and thirdly, until recently women as central actors have received far less treatment than men in mainstream Canadian history. In this they share a similar fate with most religious subjects. While we cannot hope that Canadian history will become much more respectful of religious issues than the general populace is of religion generally, we certainly can – and should – address the gap in evangelical scholarship on women.

The past five years have seen a parallel flowering of research on various manifestations of religion in women's lives, but rarely have those women been evangelicals. Much of the new scholarship has emerged from women's history,[5] a good deal concerns women's missionary activities both at home[6] and abroad,[7] and recently a sizeable literature has developed on women in the ministry.[8] All of these valuable works, however, are concerned primarily with elucidating women's stories in each, often difficult, instance in which they found themselves. The emphasis is placed on structures developed, challenges to their authority overcome, and women empowered through necessity and will. Only rarely are the women's religious ideas plumbed, possibly because they are not often discussed by those women. And even more rarely are women in the evangelical tradition treated as central to historical analysis.

In a recent critique of the "persistent pattern of avoidance" in Canadian history to engage topics of women and religion, Ruth Compton Brouwer notes that historians have taken notice of religious women only if they have been involved in some form of social activism: "[T]here has been a noticeable tendency to 'approve of' women's religious zeal only when and as it has seemed to serve as a way-station on the road to feminist consciousness."[9] She suggests that the result has been a devaluation of women's spiritual life and development and of the work of historians who address women's spirituality directly. The focus on religious women as activists has been on what women *did*; only rarely has there been any treatment of the religious beliefs underpinning women's actions.[10] Clearly, we have yet to heed Caroline Gifford's suggestion that women's involvement in religion be contextualized in other terms than feminist scholarship or studies of social activism, and that it be treated for what it is: "expressions of strong religious belief and commitment."[11] To take this imprecation seriously, historians should look at the intellectual as well as the spiritual basis for evangelical women's actions within the context of their own time, beliefs, ideas, and possibilities. Above all, historians must avoid the error of Canadian historiography from the 1930s to the 1950s: inventing a "Whig interpretation" of the past that blesses only those figures, events, and movements that show steady progress towards the issues and agenda of today, and which curses or ignores those figures, events, and movements that seem "unprogressive" or "old fashioned." Women in all their rich manifestations are the stuff of her-story, including religious and spiritual ones.

A few studies do explore the evangelical woman's religious beliefs and actions. In her fine analysis of the working-class "Hallelujah Lasses" of the Salvation Army, Lynne Marks shows that the Army's rhetoric reinforcing a dominant family ideology was undermined by women's determination to play active public roles within the organization, and if necessary, to defy male authority if service to God required their independence.[12] Two outstanding contributions are made by Ruth Compton Brouwer and Rosemary Gagan in their studies of single evangelical women missionaries who exercised their "conviction that help such as [they] could give was needed in the Lord's Vineyards abroad."[13] George Rawlyk has uncovered the revolutionary ideas of such evangelical women as Charlotte Prescott and Nancy DeWolf.[14] My own work has focused on the evangelical ideas of the members of the Ontario Woman's Christian Temperance Union, including their notions of atonement, their on-going dependence on biblical authority and their early emphasis on personal and familial conversion.[15] Finally, and very importantly, Marguerite Van Die's detailed biography of Nathaniel Burwash emphasizes the importance of his devoted and determined evangelical mother, Anne Taylor, in shaping his faith.[16] Aside from these, however, there has been little serious examination of Canadian evangelical women's religious beliefs, of their contribution to evangelicalism in the late nineteenth century, and in turn, of evangelicalism's shaping of women's views and culture.

There are several possible reasons for this lack of attention to evangelical women's religious ideas. First, it has been repeatedly noted that evangelicalism was less a "theological system" than "a way of life": "It did not present itself to its adherents as a logical set of beliefs but rather as a series of vivid and compelling personal experiences."[17] In Brian McKillop's useful phrase, evangelicalism was "not a program: it was a temper, a disposition,"[18] but this of course does not suggest that there were no definable patterns of thought within the evangelical temperament. After reading recent Canadian and American works on evangelicalism,[19] no one could seriously suggest that this religion of the heart was lacking in consistent and complex ideas as nineteenth-century evangelicals struggled to reconcile their religiosity with secular culture. Still, it is more difficult to uncover the ideas of some evangelical adherents than others, and the unfamiliar historical sources for women's ideas may have led some historians to believe that women did not care about such matters. It does seem possible that women's ideas have not been examined because of a lingering suspicion that women were largely unaware or uninterested in religious ideas, or that their ideas were never recorded. An examination of the voluminous records and hundreds of publications of the Woman's Christian Temperance Union demonstrates the error of all of these suspicions. The members of the WCTU, especially those in Ontario local unions, regularly evinced their interest in, and knowledge about, evangelical principles as they strove to make theirs a living religion.

A second possible explanation for women's shadowed representation in current evangelical historical writings resides in assumptions about whose ideas deserve to be examined. There is a certain hierarchical approach to most historical research: first the leadership of any movement is studied, then institutional outlines are delineated, and finally, prevailing arguments held by participants are presented and evaluated. We seem still to be at an early stage where many historians of religion assume that the only ideas worth considering are those of the clergy or clergy-professors. As Norman Knowles has observed, "much Canadian church history has been written with the underlying assumption that the clergy are the church."[20] Although David Marshall, for example, posits that "the religious ideas and worship practices of men and women in the churches are central" to understanding the intricate relationship between the sacred and the secular,[21] womean's ideas or worship practices are rarely treated in this otherwise quite nuanced book. How aware were female (or male) parishioners, as contrasted with professor-clergy or congregational leaders, of the profound changes occurring in evangelicalism in the last quarter of the nineteenth century and the early decades of the twentieth? Did female parishioners understand the loss of the evangelical consensus through the combined forces of urbanization, higher criticism, secularization, and consumerism differently from males?

If the WCTU were consulted, one would find that many members of that organization were quite aware of divisions within evangelicalism, particularly by the late 1890s and certainly by the First World War.

These women rarely made statements about their religious anxiety to the general public, but they assiduously recorded their thoughts at national, provincial, and most particularly, local union meetings. This is one type of record, then, that historians must consult to produce a more representative picture of evangelicalism.

Finally, the administrative bias of much historical writing and the denominational bias of much religious history remain obvious; ideas that are apolitical, that touch only tangentially on the political or are not attached to a particular denomination, tend to be disregarded. It could be argued, however, that non-denominational organizations like the WCTU or the National Council of Women of Canada (NCWC) were forced to debate basic principles that much more energetically in order to gain some kind of consensus. When the non-denominational groups were also evangelical, as in the case of the WCTU, it would suggest that the deliberations would likely be even more revealing of ideas, contested and settled.

Whatever the explanation for why women are so rarely a focus in scholarly evangelical history, it is obvious that all dimensions of the record would be enriched by including women's ideas and activities. There is insufficient space to discuss in any detail even the major ideas of evangelical women on the public events of the day. A more reasonable objective, one that was central to the development of personal spirituality in every individual, is the elucidation of ideas associated with "Christian nurture."[22]

It is generally accepted that the strength and persistence of the nineteenth-century evangelical ethic was due in no small part to the primacy of the evangelical home and of mothers within that space to undertake the essential task of Christian nurture. The "Victorian conundrum," Brian McKillop argues, was "the attempt to strike a balance between material and moral progress."[23] The interpretation, inculcation, and monitoring of morality was the evangelical woman's greatest life task. Yet we remain unclear about many components of this undertaking. A good portion of the limited literature on evangelical women's ideas concerns single and often young women rather than evangelical mothers.[24] We know little of the parameters of "Christian nurture" for all evangelical women in this period, how this primary task of motherhood was taught to women, how mothers attempted to accomplish this within the home, and the implications for women and other members of the evangelical family, both within that setting and when family members took their mother-taught evangelical attitudes to the wider spheres of church, society, nation, and Empire.

It is important to try to examine this main facet of the evangelical mother's role as it was prescribed for and defined by these women themselves, and to consider as well the influence of Christian nurture on women's status within the community. Rather than using records of individual mothers or wives of notable evangelicals, subjects for this study have been chosen from a less illustrious but perhaps more representative group: the rank-and-file members of the largest evangelical women's group and, except for the Women's Institute, the largest non-denominational women's organization in late nineteenth-century Canada, the Woman's Christian Temperance Union.

The WCTU was founded in 1874 at the height of Canadian evangelicalism. In this avowedly evangelical organization, the women of local unions, provincial organizations, and the national conventions struggled with many of the challenges facing prominent evangelicals in this era.[25] The WCTU was committed not only to a personal religiosity that called for particular behaviours within the privacy of the home but also to a powerful agenda of social activism. These included, of course, abstinence from both alcohol and tobacco in an age of increasing leisure, consumerism, and narcissism, as well as running refuges for abandoned mothers, reforming prostitutes, and the indigent aged. Also on the agenda were literacy education, Bible study programs and youth clubs for working- and middle-class boys and girls, kindergartens, "Mothers Meetings," a young and single women's sector, and a wide range of self-instruction courses on everything from how to run an efficient meeting to family nutrition to organizing a successful gospel temperance revival. The Canadian WCTU represented the rural, small town, and urbanizing middle-class Protestant woman of late nineteenth-century Canada.[26] Especially at the local level where a network of neighbours, sisters, and mother/daughter teams worked together for decades, the ideas of women were reflected through recording secretaries in carefully maintained union minute books. For many of these unions the cast of characters over the years remained largely set, making the record of their ideas and decisions like a group biography. Statements by the WCTU membership also provide a glimpse of the requirements and process of Christian nurture within the home, and missionizing and social service without. In their attempts to modernize some of their views and retain others, in particular their evangelicalism, the WCTU spilled much ink in journal articles, letters to members, resolutions to legislators, and careful minutes of their fierce debates about the religious and social issues of their day. Amongst these debates can be found much evidence that the women of the WCTU tried to define and then refine their notions of what the evangelical woman should believe, how she should act, and with whom she should join forces in the joint activities of Christian nurture and social evangelism. Caution must be exercised in accepting the prescriptive statements generated by the WCTU as accurate reflections of women's behaviours. However, it must also be remembered that this code was created largely by the WCTU membership in the context of evangelical norms for the period. The organization's journals carried advice from women for women across Canada and beyond.

There exists one study of Canadian evangelical nurture – a compelling portrait of Anne Taylor, mother of Nathaniel Burwash. Marguerite Van Die describes a woman so focused on her sons' "ethical" education that she had "but few hours to spare for society."[27] To what degree was Taylor's interpretation typical of other evangelical mothers of her era, or of those later in the century? One might early be persuaded of Taylor's singularity in the depth of her religiosity and intelligence; she had enough formal education to be a teacher, and was exceedingly well grounded in Scripture and the Shorter Catechism. However, without other contextualized case studies of commonplace evangelical motherhood in this period (although many tributes from sons to their mothers on precisely this score exist in the literature), it is difficult to assess Anne Taylor's distinctiveness or commonality with other evangelical women.[28] Certainly, the few other available profiles of evangelical women in the late nineteenth century illustrate that Anne Taylor was exceptional in her single-minded domestic pursuits and ideas.[29]

When Anne Taylor died in 1886, writes Marguerite Van Die, she was applauded in her eulogy for having "consecrated herself to one work – the training of her children for Christ," not simply during her children's period of dependency on her but for more than forty years.[30] The scrupulous, invasive attentions of a mother in the spiritual guidance of a child's development were indeed a component of Christian nurture within the evangelical home. The imperative for mothers to carry out Christian nurture, and Anglo-Saxon mothers' apparent unwillingness to challenge the racism implicit within some late nineteenth-century concepts of mothering, has been the basis of a charge of racism levelled against the WCTU.[31] Yet such an accusation disregards the critically important evangelical notion of what was involved in Christian nurture, and worse, misconstrues the Canadian WCTU position on Christian nurture, both within the Anglo-Saxon and non-Anglo-Saxon home. In every instance discussed by WCTU women in their records, they pinned their hopes for societal regeneration on the civilizing influence of mothers.

Katherine McKenna's recent book detailing the life of Anne Murray Powell provides some idea of eighteenth-century mothering practices in Upper Canada. McKenna notes that although Powell was by all accounts a "caring mother," she had no difficulty in leaving behind in England two sons when the family emigrated. At that time, they were four years old and an infant of less than a year. When the family was finally reunited six years later, two of the sons were immediately sent off to boarding school. "[M]aternal concern could only go so far in a man's world," observes McKenna.[32] Powell lived before the evangelical revival of the nineteenth century, and her concept of nurturing was consequently vastly different from evangelical mothers a century later.

In her understanding of Christian nurture, Anne Taylor was consistent with many popular writings designed to direct the nineteenth-century evangelical mother. By organizing the home so that regular and disciplined spiritual introspection, prayer, and Bible study became as natural to the child as habits of cleanliness and decorum, mothers ensured that children were raised in an environment that habituated godly behaviour. While conversion remained the responsibility of the individual through "the work of the Spirit," mothers could prepare the child's conscience so that conversion was a natural progression of spiritual growth. Marguerite Van Die and Michael Gauvreau agree that by mid-century, Canadian evangelicalism was becoming a "family religion. Its future, therefore, lay not in the first place in the hands of itinerant evangelists, preachers, and Sunday school teachers but in the Christian training provided by the mother in the home."[33]

This definition of Christian nurture was fundamentally accepted by evangelical women throughout the nineteenth century; Anne Taylor and the less famous evangelical women of the WCTU would have agreed on the prescription with two major differences. First, as the century wore on and evangelicalism experienced greater pressure to accommodate to the challenges of the new biblical criticism, consumerism, and modernity, the evangelical WCTU woman's definition for Christian nurture became more sex-specific. Of course, all children were to be nurtured in the spiritual garden to carry on and strengthen the evangelical creed, and in aid of this process, WCTU mothers were supported by a network of childhood education materials and groups, all based on an evangelical life-view. But by the last decades of the nineteenth century, the family's adolescent males were increasingly targeted for special nurturing by the evangelical mother. This evolving mission within the home was likely a result of the crisis felt by evangelicals in this disturbing period, the attractions of the imperial doctrine of "muscular Christianity" with its evangelical counterpart of "moral manliness," as Nathaniel Burwash termed it, and the relative loss of confidence by evangelical women that they could effect the social revolution necessary to stave off the excesses of the modern age. The second way in which Anne Taylor and the later-century women of the WCTU differed in their definition of Christian nurture concerned the responsibility of women to extend evangelical nurture beyond the home.

The evangelical women of the WCTU learned the prescriptions of their role as Christian nurturer through a variety of written sources, including denominational writings produced for women's missionary societies, advice literature and fiction in such magazines as the WCTU's *Woman's Journal*, and specially prepared pamphlets and tracts (for example, "Somebody is Praying for You," or "What Can We Do?"). There were also public lectures by itinerant or local authorities, and discussion groups of neighbours, mother/daughter groupings, extended families, or clubs and associations: "Mother's Meetings" or local WCTU meetings, Women's Institute and local [NCWC] council meetings or gatherings of the women's missionary societies.

When evangelical women of the WCTU undertook to exercise the tasks of Christian nurture, the process took different forms in dealing with female as opposed to male children and adolescents, or with husbands, who were very certainly also thought to be subject to female nurturing. The evangelical family had to be made aware of each member's particular duty to apply high moral principle to every question. Beyond the very early years of child nurturance when habits of private spiritual observance were being inculcated, this involved the bold naming of dangerous public behaviours – alcohol and tobacco use, and low-minded company, for example – and the modelling and monitoring of appropriately ethical thought and action. Evangelicalism's aim, said one observer, was "to apply moral truths to practical purposes; to point out their bearings on modern opinions and modern manners; and to deduce from them rules of conduct by which the inhabitants of this country, each in his particular station, may be aided in acquiring the knowledge and encouraged in the performance of their several duties."[34] This would be accomplished, WCTU women determined, through ensuring that "'home is the centre,' not the boundry and let all good go out from that."[35]

Christian nurture as applied to one's daughters involved lovingly but firmly educating them to carry on the mission of civilizing and evangelizing in their future homes. A young woman's moral powers and passions were thought to be so easily excited that a strict regimen of daily spiritual communion including individual reflection, prayer, and study was mandatory. Young women, the WCTU believed, could be captured all too easily by their passionate natures. Disaster could result from eating too much or overly spiced food, since this "deranged bodily functions" especially in young women, producing irritable feelings and peculiar temptations including "an appetite for stronger drink."[36] Women's moral powers, so necessary in supporting friends and nurturing the next generation of children, were delicate enough that even the drinking of Coca-Cola produced the dreadful result that "many are held captive by their animal passions."[37]

Nurturing sons was both more challenging and problematic for the late nineteenth-century evangelical woman. Because adolescent sons were imminently moving beyond the secure private zone of the evangelical home into the dangerous and godless public arena, mothers had to actively quiz their sons to gauge the current state of their spiritual health. This could require a mother, unblemished of spirit and behaviour herself, to witness the distressing crudity of the male world. It also demanded that a mother have her priorities in good order. Mothers who mistakenly placed more importance on a clean home than on creating a spiritual haven for the young man stood to be held partly responsible for his moral lapses. A story in an 1886 issue of *The Woman's Journal* points out the danger of mothers placing cleanliness before spiritual succour in the home:

"There are those banisters all fingers marks again," said Mrs. Curry, as she made haste with a soft linen cloth to polish down the shining oak again. "George," she said as she gave a decided wrench out of the basin of suds, "If you go up those stairs again before bed-time you shall be punished." "I should like to know where I am to go," said George, "I cannot stay in the kitchen I am so much in the way, and I can't go into the parlor for fear I'll muss that up; and now you say I can't go up to my room. I know of a grand place I can go," he added to himself, "boys are never told they are in the way there, and we can have lots of fun. I'll go down to Neil's corner. I can smoke a cigar as well as any boy, if it did make me sick the first time. They shall not laugh at me again about." And so the careful housekeeper virtually drove her son from the door to hang about the steps and sit under the broad, inviting portico of the village grog-shop.[38]

To provide this level of spiritual direction, mothers had to know virtually everything about their sons. To young men indulging in "the secret pleasure" of masturbation, a writer warned: "But you are told that mother must not, under any condition, know of it. O boys, the first effort Satan makes toward your ruin is to interpose himself between you and your mother!"[39] An article in *The Canadian White Ribbon Tidings* had a "noble" young lad assert, "'You may laugh if you want to ... but I've made up my mind never, as long as I live, to do anything I would be ashamed to tell my mother.' We need a thousand boys to talk like that."[40] However, the WCTU goal for the young man went beyond simply informing mother of his most private thoughts and actions to empowering him to reject societal evil on his own. "I have been told by many a fortunate mother that her son indignantly repelled the degradation of the common school-boy talk upon subjects he had learned to regard as sacred by reason of confidences exchanged between himself and her who bore him,"[41] wrote Frances Willard of the American WCTU. This mandate for extended and male-directed "Christian nurture" is dramatically different from the code followed by the eighteenth-century Annie Powell.

As difficult as it was for mothers to carry out this systematic surveillance of their sons' lives, none doubted its importance. If properly and thoroughly influenced, mothers could assume that "when they [sons] grow up they shall be ours in sympathy, ours in pure habits, and ours as the coming leaders of the future in State and philanthropic work."[42] But the greater bonus of this intrusive mothering style, WCTU women were assured, was that their sons would be grateful. The portrayal of the emotionally charged, almost sexually reverential mother-son relationship was common in WCTU literature: "'Oh mother, mother,' he sobbed, 'I wish I had never left you! ... I'll keep as near to you in heart as I can. I wish I hadn't grown away from you so; but I'll get back again if I can!'"[43] Another woman enthused in a WCTU educational pamphlet, "One of the beautiful sights I have seen is a lady and her son walking, arm in arm, from church, Sabbath after Sabbath. He was like a lover in his tenderness. It made no difference who saw him, he was just as considerate as he could have been if she had been radiant with youth and beauty."[44] This romanticized characterization reached its height during the First World War when the enforced separation caused women, and undoubtedly their sons, pain and worry. In the WCTU journals, mothers and sons spent long hours together, "walking to take communion when she had noted the consecrated expression on his young face,"[45] sharing the same opinions, glorying in each other.

Even given the Victorian and Edwardian tendency to describe all relationships in an overblown manner, the idealized mother-son relationship was both unrealistic and unhealthy in its implications for the mother. In his analysis of Victorian "boy culture" in America, Anthony Rotundo points out that by about age six, middle-class boys "cut loose from these social and physical restraints" of mother's world by creating an oppositional play culture in backyards, streets, parks, playgrounds, and vacant lots characterized by free movement, casual hostility, and social sadism.[46] Lynne Marks has argued that young, single (and sometimes married) men were easily enticed into a "convivial masculine culture" that thrived in the hotels and on street corners of Ontario's small towns in this period. The middle-class women of the Ontario WCTU were more strongly motivated, she believes, by fears for their sons' unspeakable fates than by hopes in their developing strength to control their future.[47] In any event, the adolescent male was seen to be especially in need of long-range Christian nurture and monitoring because of the difficult task before him of melding private and public spirituality into a workable standard of behaviour for life.

Where middle-class husbands made any appearance at all in WCTU literature, they were depicted as kind but weak, inept at any domestic skill and with an almost complete lack of facility in meaningful conversation or in facing the power of human emotions. The second prize winner of the *Woman's Journal* fiction contest in 1893 told the story of two men, wise Grandmother Brandon's father-in-law and husband. The young Mrs Brandon is first encountered defying the foolish medical doctor who had suggested that cognac be used to revive her father-in-law who had almost drowned. To the doctor's surprise, Mrs Brandon brought the patient around through the ministrations of scalded milk. Unfortunately, however, Mr Brandon Sr had already tasted alcohol and this "taste for liquor" had been inherited by Mrs Brandon's husband. While drunk one evening, the husband gave baby Frank the wrong medicine and almost killed him. The doctor's reputation was salvaged when he saved child and father; and subsequently Mr Brandon Jr vowed never again to touch liquor.[48] The story illustrated that these men were morally weak through lack of will, miscalculation, and misdeed; their only redeeming quality was that, having seen the error of their behaviour, they determined to discipline their selfish nature through the support of a morally upright woman. The reader's hopes are not brought too high, however. Its subtext, of a ridiculous and self-important doctor whose "knowledge" placed the family in danger, would not have been lost on the Victorian woman reader witnessing the professionalization of a medical community that sought women's exclusion.[49]

Husbands were occasionally criticized, if obliquely, as in an article entitled "Undervalued Work of Wives": "Almost all wives engaged in domestic duties work harder, longer hours, and more productively than any other class of laborers, yet receive, instead of wages, only food, clothing and medicine."[50] It does not require a great leap to assume that the author meant that wives work harder than their husbands and without the respect due to them.

Such bold statements of male inadequacy were framed in contrast to the role of these same women as mothers of sons. The mainly negative portraits of husbands betrayed frustration and bitterness at the social inequities of men and women, while the hopeful discussions of radiant mothers and fair-minded, disciplined, and spiritually alive sons pointed to a future of reformed social roles.[51] But whether or not young men could be counted upon to improve on their fathers' dismal records, the one consistent image in all of these prescriptions of Christian nurture was that of the strong, intelligent, and forthright mother. Thus, the evangelical mandate of Christian nurture by the end of the nineteenth century succeeded in portraying mothers, at least in WCTU literature, as powerful agents of the new era. We know that evangelicals such as Nathaniel Burwash, who as children were exposed to a consistent and affecting Christian nurture through their mothers, were influenced very deeply by that experience. By their own admission Christian nurture became one of the tap roots to the full bloom of the evangelical temperament.

This family-based evangelical culture within which children were to be nurtured, husbands civilized, and women celebrated for their presumably superior moral qualities was one component of evangelical women's role in the last half of the nineteenth century. This private process of Christian nurture generally elevated mother's status within the wider community. But beyond family nurturance, the evangelical woman was abjured to involve her life with other women in a supportive evangelical network which took as its main work the transmission of the faith through childhood and adult education and social service. This social mission was a natural result of Christian nurture. It reflected the evangelical conviction that while individual salvation could only be accomplished through a complete spiritual transformation involving conversion, followed by personal scrutiny through Bible study, prayer, and pure living, this transformation had to be made available to others through the "spread of scriptural holiness."[52] This required that evangelical women organize, evangelize, and educate those within and beyond their families. In the case of the WCTU, this included a broad program of social service all undertaken with a clear sense of the evangelical imperative to evangelize to the wider community. It extended from charitable and philanthropic initiatives such as providing food, clothing, warm bedding, and char services for families where the mother had been taken ill or where extreme poverty or drink had disorganized the family, to demanding new legislation to increase the age of majority, give all adult women the vote, and provide women charged with crimes with female magistrates. In between these two poles, evangelical women agitated for strengthened sabbath observance; the sentencing of men using prostitutes; more humane care of the indigent aged, orphans, and abandoned mothers; teacher education standards; and curricular changes in the public schools. WCTU women personally ran middle-class youth groups (Little White Ribboners for children to age seven; Bands of Hope and Loyal Temperance Legions for boys and girls to age fourteen; the Young Woman's Christian Temperance Union for single women) and working-class groups (Kitchen Gardens, literacy groups, and residences for girls and young working women, Bands of Hope, fitness clubs, and newsboys' groups for boys to about sixteen; Bible-study groups for all ages). When all is considered, the range of their public programs is staggering. Furthermore, the example of the WCTU is persuasive that this daunting social agenda was directly attributable to their definition of Christian nurture, not carried out in spite of it. And yet for the most part, the historical record on this important component of evangelical women's lives is almost silent. Where the evangelical social mission is traced at all, it is largely attributed to male initiatives, and then usually to "liberal" evangelicals firmly on the road to social gospelism. There is no denying that evangelical men accomplished a great deal through social activism, but they were not alone.

If we accept that serious study of evangelical women contributes to our knowledge of that wider society, for example in the importance and exercise of Christian nurture, could the study of female evangelicals contribute to any other dimensions of the present debate of evangelicalism's heritage? When gender is accepted as a category of analysis, several questions present themselves to historians. How will an analysis of a religious ethic that held a view of salvation as being personal and experiential differ when considered from women's perspectives? As George Rawlyk's scholarship has shown the differing effects of revivals on men and women, is it possible that other components of the conversion experience had gender-specific meanings?[53] How did women and men define and exercise moral leadership within the evangelical family unit where mother, the "angel in the house,"[54] must on occasion have held dissenting views with father? In the extension of moral leadership beyond the home, did female networks and social projects such as those taken on by the WCTU act as a buffer against the forces of disintegration in evangelicalism, or did these networks place them on the cutting edge of change because of their exposure to the underside of society? If, as now seems to be accepted, one of the dissoluting forces in evangelicalism's armour was consumerism how did women's control of consumer spending intersect with popular culture and the (by this time) fragile evangelical ethic? Furthermore, since the period during which evangelicalism lost its grip on society was also one characterized by the creation of a Canadian middle class,[55] how did women's involvement in class prescription and moral guidance influence the decline of evangelicalism and the rise of a consumer-oriented middle class?

Evangelical women's roles in nineteenth-century Canada represented more than an extension of male evangelical culture. Women who lived their faith sought ways to nurture the next generation of evangelical citizens within the family unit, and beyond, in a rapidly changing society. To appreciate the full measure of the evangelical heritage, women's particular contribution certainly deserves more scholarly investigation.

26 The Awakened and the Spirit-Moved: The Religious Experiences of Canadian Evangelicals in the 1990s

ANDREW S. GRENVILLE

The critically important role of intense religious experience in the birth and growth of the evangelical movement has been well documented, but the religious experiences of today's evangelicals are not as well understood. To remedy this, an attempt has been made here to explore and map out the depth and rich texture of the religious experience of Canadian evangelicals. The picture that emerges suggests that religious experience is indeed central to Canadian evangelicalism in the 1990s – as it was during its formative "radical evangelical" phase.

Evangelicalism sprang into life in the mid-eighteenth century, powered by religious awakenings and the often intense religious experiences of leaders and lay alike. It has been suggested that if George Whitefield, John Wesley, and Jonathan Edwards "defined the revivals on a large canvas, experiences of countless ordinary men and women in the localities sustained the life of the evangelical awakening."[1] As the evangelical movement took shape, numerous accounts of religious experience were published and publizised, providing many ordinary believers with models of conversion and contact with God. These accounts were rapidly dispersed throughout the English-speaking world, and an "evangelical pattern of intense religious experience was established very quickly."[2]

Descriptions by evangelicals indicated a variety of religious experiences. John Wesley felt his "heart strangely warmed" as he experienced "an assurance ... that he has taken away my sins."[3] Henry Alline was "ravished with a divine ecstasy,"[4] and Abigail Hutchinson was overcome by "a lively sense of the excellency of Christ."[5] At some revivals there were reports of numerous people being "struck down by the mighty power of God."⁶ It is clear that religious experience was an essential element of the early days of evangelicalism. The role of religious experience in today's evangelicalism, however, is far less well understood.

In the mid-1990s the "Toronto Blessing" drew much attention to the more spectacular aspects of religious experience. Services at the Toronto Airport Vineyard Church attracted people from around the world, with thousands being "slain in the Spirit," laughing a "holy laugh," and receiving divine healing. Like a deceptively dormant volcano, the Toronto Blessing erupted onto the staid Canadian religious landscape, allowing us a rare glimpse of powerful forces that churn deep below a seemingly placid surface.

Religious experience is by its very nature private and personal and usually only occurs in the public eye when community expectations change the normal boundaries between public and private.⁷ In the case of charismatic or Pentecostal worship, social boundaries are changed and public religious experiences are encouraged, expected, and facilitated.⁸ Public eruptions of religious experience – such as were observed in Nova Scotia in the 1770s, present-day Ontario in the early nineteenth century, Saskatchewan in the 1970s and, in 1995, at the Toronto Blessing – are important and revealing. But to focus on them is to miss what privately, quietly, and often dramatically occurs far from public view.

I have tried to undertake a preliminary exploration of the depth of the religious experiences of Canadian evangelicals, mapping out both spectacular outbursts and quiet moments of perception of the divine. The information presented here is based on survey research with Canadian evangelicals and particularly three recent Canadian studies on religious beliefs. One of these involved a survey of a cross-section of 6,014 Canadians (including evangelicals).⁹ The other two studies were conducted specifically with evangelicals. One was a follow-up survey of 365 evangelicals identified as part of the general population survey, and the other involved in-depth telephone interviews with a small subset of the same group of evangelicals.¹⁰ These interviews, together with some written accounts, help bring life to the sometimes dry bones of survey data.

In approaching this subject I have used a rather broad definition of religious experience: an experience of "other kinds of reality."¹¹ "Experience" is measured at a number of levels, varying from having the "feeling you were somehow in the presence of God," to having "a moment of sudden religious insight and awakening," and being "slain in the Spirit."¹² These tap into what Abraham Maslow has called "peak experiences" – happenings in which a common characteristic is that the whole universe is perceived as an integrated and unified whole. This is not as simple a happening as one might imagine from the bare words themselves. To have a clear perception (rather than a purely abstract and verbal philosophical acceptance) that the universe is all of a piece and that one has his place in it – one is a part of it, he belongs to it – can be so profound and shaking an experience that it can change the person's character and his [world view] forever after.[13]

This kind of perception-altering experience energized many of those who started the evangelical movement. The same experiences fuel many evangelicals today.

Defining evangelicalism is no simple task. Mark Noll addresses the issue very effectively in *The Scandal of the Evangelical Mind*:

[Evangelicalism] has always been made up of shifting movements, temporary alliances, and the lengthened shadows of individuals. All discussions of evangelicalism, therefore, are always both descriptions of the way things really are as well as efforts within our own minds to provide some order to a multifaceted, complex set of impulses and organizations.

The basic evangelical impulses, however, have been quite clear from the mid-eighteenth century ... In one of the most useful general definitions of the phenomenon, the British historian David Bebbington has identified the key ingredients of evangelicalism as conversionism (an emphasis on the "new birth" as a life-changing religious experience), biblicism (a reliance on the Bible as ultimate religious authority), activism (a concern for sharing the faith) and crucicentrism (a focus on Christ's redeeming work on the cross). But these evangelical impulses have never by themselves yielded cohesive, institutionally compact, easily definable, well-coordinated or clearly demarcated groups of Christians.[14]

Rather than a restrictive (and not always illuminating) denominational definition of evangelicalism, I have used criteria that measure the four "ingredients" outlined by Bebbington: conversionism, activism, biblicism, and crucicentrism. These elements were measured using reaction to ten statements including: "I feel it is important for non-Christians to become Christians," "I have committed my life to Christ and consider myself a converted Christian," and "I feel that through the life, death, and resurrection of Jesus, God provided a way for the forgiveness of my sins." The ten items make up a summated rating scale which has been tested in twenty-four samples and can be considered a valid and reliable measure of evangelicalism.[15] In using this definition and measure of evangelicalism I have traded the restrictiveness of denominational categorization for the inclusiveness of measures of "ingredients" and "impulses." Even though the group is less "clearly demarcated" and the people less readily categorized, I feel much more has been gained than sacrificed in implementing such a strategy.

The use of this measure revealed that 3.4 million adult Canadians (16 per cent of all Canadian adults over age eighteen) hold the defining beliefs of evangelicalism. Included in this are six in ten who identify with conservative churches, and one in seven affiliated with mainline Protestant and (perhaps somewhat controversially) Catholic churches.

The inclusion of Catholic evangelicals – Catho-evangelicals, as George Rawlyk has named them – requires some discussion. The anti-Catholicism of many evangelicals is well known. For example, in 1837 evangelical Nathaniel Cheever wrote of Catholicism as a "soul-ruining, degrading system of idolatry, superstition and ignorance."[16] By the 1990s, however, we find a group of prominent Catholics and evangelical Protestants publishing a statement of "common convictions about Christian faith and mission."[17] We also see the Catholic Keith Fornier authoring a book entitled *Evangelical Catholics* and noting that an "evangelical wave is sweeping Christian churches of every tradition, including my own [Catholic church]."[18] And we discover Notre Dame University social scientists Michael Welch and David Leege studying "evangelically oriented Catholics" and reporting that "a pattern of evangelical-style orientations exists among contemporary Catholic parishioners and that it differentiates Catholics on their political views."[19] Further, research shows that 20 per cent of Canadians who regularly attend church describe themselves as "evangelical Christians."[20]

Things have clearly changed. The "us and them" mentality is fading and some Catholics are becoming, as Welch and Leege would put it, more "evangelically oriented." And while Catho-evangelicals differ from their Protestant brothers and sisters on some issues, they do, by definition, meet the criteria of biblicism, conversionism, activism, and crucicentrism. These developments encouraged us not to exclude the possibility that there are some evangelical Catholics in the Canadian evangelical community.

In this study, an attempt has been made to enumerate the prevalence of each of the religious experiences that were measured and then to present an empirically derived typology of evangelicals and their religious experiences. To provide some context for gauging the importance of religious experience, I also contrast the effects of widespread private religious experience and the relatively limited reach of evangelical leaders and evangelical institutions such as the InterVarsity Christian Fellowship and the Evangelical Fellowship of Canada.

In presenting this data I have tended to focus on evangelicals as a whole, turning to denominational categorizations only as a secondary interpretative lens. I have, however, included data tables that separate the three main denominational branches of evangelicalism. This will allow those whose interests may be more focused to find relevant data.

EVANGELICALS' RELIGIOUS EXPERIENCES

Six types of religious experiences were investigated: feeling in the "presence of God"; "feeling in close contact with something sacred or holy"; experiencing a "sudden insight or awakening"; feeling "very close to a powerful spiritual force that seemed to lift you out of yourself"; speaking in tongues; and being slain in the Spirit. These six cover a wide spectrum of experiences, from the non-specific "other world" feeling of being in the presence of God to the very distinctive speaking in tongues.

The research confirmed that religious experience is common among Canadian evangelicals in the 1990s. Almost every evangelical interviewed (94 per cent) had been touched by at least one of these religious experiences. At a basic level an evangelical's experience of "another reality" could be expected to involve "feeling you were somehow in the presence of God." This feeling of presence is part of most conversion accounts, and our in-depth interviews yielded a useful example of this experience. Feeling the presence of God is "very hard to describe," explained Lillian, a fifty-five-year-old Catholic. She experienced "just a very strong presence of God. It totally takes your attention so that you are almost unaware of what's going on around you ... He's so present to you that this is all you can think of."

Over eight in ten evangelicals (84 per cent) have felt the presence of God, with no significant variation by denominational affiliation (see table 1 for a breakdown of findings by denomination). Of the 3.4 million evangelicals in Canada, over 2.8 million have tasted another reality, feeling the presence of God. A similar but more qualified measure asked respondents if they had ever been in "close contact with something holy or sacred." Seven in ten (69 per cent) – roughly 2.3 million – said yes, they had experienced "close contact" with the sacred.

The classic conversion experiences of early evangelicals featured an "awakening" or "sudden insight," typically, a revelation of the salvation offered by Christ. Experiences of "awakenings" are quite prevalent among present-day evangelicals – over six in ten (62 per cent) have experienced a "sudden religious insight and awakening." Not all of these awakenings would have been conversion experiences, but it seems likely that many evangelicals would have had such insights at a time of conversion.

Given the emphasis some conservative Christian churches place on conversion, it is not surprising that this experience was somewhat more common among evangelicals from the conservative churches than it was

Table 1
Prevalence of Religious Experiences among Canadian Evangelicals:
Percentage Ever Experienced Each Item

Experience	Total (365)	Catho-evangelical (95)	Mainline evangelical (85)	Conservative evangelical (130)
Feeling you were in the presence of God	84	84	78	84
Close contact with something holy or sacred	69	65	67	71
Sudden religious insight or awakening	62	55	53	65
Very close to a powerful spiritual force that lifted you out of yourself	28	35	27	25
Speaking in tongues	18	8	11	28
Slain in the Spirit	10	4	6	15

Note: Fifteen respondents did not identify with any particular denomination.

among mainline evangelicals and Catho-evangelicals. However, a majority in all groups reported having a sudden insight or awakening. Art, a now middle-aged convert from Catholicism to Lutheranism, provides us with a useful description of his sudden insight into another reality. "I came to realize," he related, "and not just in an intellectual way, in fact it wasn't intellectual at all, it was very much an awakening – that God does indeed forgive. That forgiveness is from Christ ... It hit me vividly."

Andrew Greeley, an Irish-American sociologist, novelist, and priest, developed a question that taps into what he calls "ecstasy." The question he posed was "Have you ever felt as through you were very close to a powerful spiritual force that seemed to lift you out of yourself?"[21] Three in ten evangelicals (28 per cent) have sampled this ecstatic experience of the divine. Catho-evangelicals were somewhat more likely than mainline and conservative evangelicals to have experienced this particular transcendence of the physical plane.

Speaking in tongues and being "slain in the Spirit" are set apart from experiences of presence and awakenings by their specificity – and their usually public nature. Nearly one in five evangelicals (18 per cent) have spoken in tongues, the number being higher among the conservative evangelicals than among the mainline and Catho-evangelicals. Ten per cent of evangelicals have been slain in the Spirit, and this experience shows the same denominational patterns as observed with speaking in tongues.

Pentecostal or charismatic experiences represent the more extreme end of the spectrum of religious experience. These types of experiences tend to overlap and encompass many other types of religious experience. For example, two-thirds of those who were slain in the Spirit have also spoken in tongues, and almost all of those who have experienced either one of these also tend to have had a religious awakening and felt the presence of God. This overlap occurs in part because the feelings of presence and insight are often one component of the experience of speaking in tongues or being slain in the Spirit. Let us consider the experiences of "Linda," a young Italian Pentecostal:

The Spirit came upon me slowly. As I raised my hands high to heaven, my arms began to shake rhythmically. I lowered my arms to my waist, still keeping my hands raised. My arms were shaking uncontrollably. I was not interested in making a show, so I tried to stop my arms from shaking ... If I stopped for a second and started to pray again, my arms would start to shake again.

In my prayer I was crying and screaming out to the Lord. I would pray in tongues and almost end up shrieking. I could not think of the words to tell the Lord the anguish I felt for those unsaved loved ones, how much I wanted them to know him.

A lady standing nearby put her arm on my shoulder and was praying softly as I was screaming. I saw in my mind a light and thought "Jesus is hearing my prayers." The Pastor came over and prayed with me. The noise of the others praying around me barely penetrated my mind. In fact, I thought they were all doing the same thing I was doing.

I released my body and fell to the floor. It had crossed my mind earlier that if I wasn't standing I might shake all over. That is exactly what briefly happened. I just cried to God and shook with the powerful desire that I did not want my loved ones to spend eternity in Hell.

There were two ladies quietly praying with me, and I began to pray quietly and relax. I was sighing a little, quite relaxed. The ladies left me alone to rest in the presence of the Lord. I did not feel I could move.[22]

Linda's description touches on four aspects of religious experience: being slain in the Spirit, speaking in tongues or making other so-called "holy noises," experiencing an awakening or insight, and being in the presence of the Lord. Linda reported that, despite being surrounded by others who were praying and being slain in the Spirit, she was so transported that their sounds "barely penetrated" her consciousness. Her insight that "Jesus is hearing my prayers" signals the point at which her experience peaks – soon after, she falls to the floor, writhing in prayer. As the physical experiences of being "slain in the Spirit" ebb away, she is quiet and resting "in the presence of the Lord."

Linda's intense and multi-faceted account is representative of a minority of Canadian evangelicals. But her example sheds light on the process of being slain in the Spirit, and it points out that an evangelical may have numerous experiences – in Linda's case, all at once. This experience is not uncommon; on average, the evangelicals had experienced three of the six religious experiences. As noted earlier, 6 per cent did not have any of these religious experiences; another 15 per cent had one experience; 24 per cent had two; an additional 24 per cent had three, 21 per cent had four; 7 per cent had five and 3 per cent had experienced all six.

The frequent overlap of experiences is both interesting and noteworthy, and the patterns of overlap are fascinating: they reveal much about Canadian evangelicalism in the 1990s.

THE VARIETIES OF EVANGELICAL RELIGIOUS EXPERIENCE: A TYPOLOGY

The patterns of religious experience were sifted using a statistical technique known as cluster analysis, an empirical method for grouping people.[23] In this case, cluster analysis was used to sort people into groups based on their religious experiences.[24] In sorting people, cluster analysis finds a solution that minimizes differences within groups and maximizes differences between groups. The result is a typology – a segmentation. Five distinct types of evangelicals emerged from the analysis: the Spirit-moved, the Holy Force, the Awakened, the Sacred Presence, and the Inexperienced. Each name hints at the religious experiences each group has undergone (see table 2).

The Spirit-moved have spoken in tongues and have had a number of other religious experiences. The Holy Force evangelicals have been "very close to a powerful spiritual force that seems to lift you out of yourself" and have had a sudden religious insight. The Awakened fit a classic model of conversion, having experienced a sudden religious insight and the presence of God. Those of the Sacred Presence group have known the quiet peace of being in the presence of the sacred but have not had a sudden awakening. The Inexperienced segment encompasses a number of people who have only felt the presence of God or experienced just one of the other varieties of religious experience – as well as a small group who have not had any of these religious experiences.

The Spirit-moved are perhaps the most distinct and immediately identifiable of the groups. Of the Pentecostal and charismatic branches of evangelicalism, they generally have spoken in tongues, had a sudden awakening, been in the presence of God, and had close contact with something holy or sacred. Many have been slain in the Spirit. One in five evangelicals (18 per cent) fit into this group. "Linda" would fall into the Spirit-moved group.

Table 2
Prevalence of Religious Experiences among Canadian Evangelicals:
Percentage Ever Experienced Each Item

Experience	Spirit-moved	Holy Force	Awakening	Sacred Presence	Inexperienced
Feeling you were in the presence of God	94	98	85	83	72
Close contact with something holy or sacred	85	100	100	100	0
Sudden religious insight and awakening	92	100	100	0	43
Very close to a powerful spiritual force that lifted you out of yourself	39	100	100	29	5
Speaking in tongues	89	0	0	11	0
Slain in the Spirit	52	0	0	4	1

Holy Force evangelicals are intensely experiential but in a manner very different from their more charismatic Spirit-moved cousins. First, all of them have been "very close to a powerful spiritual force that seems to lift you out of yourself," but none have spoken in tongues or been slain in the Spirit. All have felt the presence of God and been in close contact with something holy or sacred. The experience of a sudden insight and awakening is also common to this group, which encompasses 14 per cent of evangelicals. Their experiences seem rather like those of many nineteenth-century evangelicals who were suddenly awakened and seemingly lifted out of themselves as they were "swallowed up by God."[25]

The Awakened fit a more classic model of conversion experiences. These people have had a sudden awakening or insight, a feeling they were in the presence of God and in close contact with something sacred or holy. They have not had any of the charismatic experiences nor have they been "lifted out of themselves." Their experiences reflect two things characteristic of a classic conversion experience: a feeling of close contact with God and a sudden awakening. Wesley's famous account of his conversion sounds rather like something we might expect to hear from one in the Awakened group. Twenty per cent of evangelicals fall into this category.

Sacred Presence is a label that describes the experiences of another 20 per cent of Canadian evangelicals. People in this group have all experienced "close contact" with something holy or sacred and most have felt the presence of God. But none has had a conversion-like "awakening" or sudden insight. Their experience is a quiet, peaceful awareness of a sacred presence.

Table 3
Denominational Identification of Each Segment

Denomination	Spirit-moved	Holy Force	Awakening	Sacred Presence	Inexperienced
Anglican	8	6	8	4	5
Baptist	12	12	13	17	11
Lutheran	2	2	4	4	8
Pentecostal	26	2	4	8	3
Presbyterian	3	6	6	5	6
Roman Catholic	12	2	4	8	3
United Church	0	10	6	15	7

The Inexperienced are defined by their relative lack of religious experiences. Most have felt the presence of God but have not known many of the other aspects of religious experience. Some have had a sudden awakening and a handful have felt lifted out of themselves. On average, they have had only one religious experience – hence their relative "inexperience." This is the largest single group (28 per cent of evangelicals), and it includes the 6 per cent who reported not having had any of the six religious experiences that were measured.

This typology helps us to map out the patterns of religious experience, and the pieces fit together in ways that seem to make sense. It would be intriguing to attempt to locate a variety of late eighteenth- and nineteenth-century Canadian evangelicals in these groups.

It is noteworthy that these patterns of experience do not correspond with neat denominational groupings (see table 3). With the exception of the Spirit-moved, roughly one quarter or more of each group are Catho-evangelicals. Baptists are also spread evenly throughout, accounting for roughly one in ten of each group. Anglicans, Lutherans, and Presbyterians are also found in all the groups, and the United Church is represented in all groups except the Spirit-moved. The Spirit-moved are a little different denominationally in that one quarter are Pentecostals, but the remainder come from other, often mainline, denominations. These experiences obviously transcend denominational borders.

WHAT DOES IT MATTER?

As noted, Abraham Maslow stated that religious experiences are sometimes so profound that they change a person's outlook forever. It has been argued that religious experience "sustained" the First and Second Great Awakenings. These are powerful claims, and one has to wonder if they hold true in Canada in the 1990s. An analysis of the effects of

Table 4
Effects of Religious Experience (percentages)

	Spirit-moved	Holy Force	Awakened	Sacred Presence	Inexperienced
Share faith weekly	64	70	55	49	55
Pray twice or more a day	78	82	75	67	67
Read the Bible daily	62	42	44	32	36
Strongly agree "God speaks to me directly though the Holy Spirit"	82	78	75	52	58
Strongly agree "God speaks to me directly through the Bible"	80	84	76	59	61

religious experience suggests that it has lost none of its power among evangelical Canadians.

Interviews with Canadian evangelicals in the 1990s indicate that religious experience encourages evangelism today just as it did when the movement began. Statistical analysis revealed that feeling the presence of God, having had a sudden religious insight or awakening, feeling you were somehow lifted out of yourself by a powerful spiritual force, and being slain in the Spirit are all directly related to how frequently you share your faith with others.[26] In other words, religious experience fuels evangelism (see table 4).

Given the relationship between experience and evangelism, it is not surprising that some of the groups described earlier are more or less frequently involved in sharing their faith. The people of the Holy Force group were most likely to share their faith once a week or more, followed closely by the Spirit-moved.

Further evidence of the power of religious experience comes from a harmonious relationship between experience and two of the other four "ingredients" of evangelicalism: activism and biblicism.[27] Prayer and feelings about communication with God are aspects of activism or personal piety. Those who have had religious experiences tend to pray more often and for longer periods of time.[28]

The feeling that "God speaks to me directly, through the Holy Spirit" is another aspect of personal piety that is influenced by religious experience. Five of the six religious experiences are associated with a greater depth of belief by respondents that God speaks to them directly through the Holy Spirit. The strongest relationship is with having a "sudden religious insight and awakening."[29] Those evangelicals who fall into the groups that had the greatest number of religious experiences – the Spirit-moved and the Holy Force – showed more obvious patterns of frequent prayer and a more widespread belief that God speaks to them through the Holy Spirit.

Acceptance of the Bible as religious authority is also linked to some religious experiences. Frequency of reading the Bible and believing that "God speaks to me directly through the Bible" are associated with having had a "sudden religious insight and awakening." Speaking in tongues and being slain in the Spirit are also linked with reading the Bible more frequently.[30] The Awakened, the Holy Force, and the Spirit-moved all showed tendencies toward deeper acceptance of the Bible as authority.

Religious experience obviously matters a great deal to Canadian evangelicals in the 1990s. It encourages sharing the faith and strengthens personal piety and biblicism, two key elements of evangelicalism. Before considering some possible implications, it is necessary to provide some context by briefly contrasting the widespread and influential nature of religious experience with the role of evangelical leaders and organizations.

The evangelical experience can arguably be divided into two realms: the public and the private.[31] The public aspect encompasses the actions of evangelical organizations such as InterVarsity Fellowship [IVCF] and Evangelical Fellowship of Canada [EFC], the tasks of denominations and congregations, as well as missionary and relief efforts. In short, it is the social face of evangelicalism. The private aspect encompasses such things as an individual's beliefs, private behaviours, and relationship with God. Religious experiences are in the realm of the private, and, as we have seen, they influence some private (personal piety) and public (evangelism) practices.

Religious experiences are much more prevalent than contact with organizations such as the EFC and IVCF (see table 5). Further, a lack of recognizable leadership suggests that the influence of religious elites is very limited in Canada in the 1990s. The EFC has had contact (either written or personal) with over 500,000 evangelicals (16 per cent) and the IVCF has also touched almost 900,000 evangelicals (26 per cent). As might be expected, there is denominational variation in this contact, with Catho-evangelicals displaying roughly one-tenth the level of contact of their Protestant cousins.

There is, however, considerable overlap in these contacts. Two in ten evangelicals (20 per cent) have had contact with one of these organizations, and an additional one in ten (11 per cent) have had contact with both. Together, these two groups have reached a total of roughly 1.1 million Canadian evangelicals. This is impressive, but it pales in

Table 5
Evangelical Institutions and Leaders (in percentages)

	Total (365)	Catho-evangelical (95)	Mainline evangelical (130)	Conservative evangelical (85)
Had contact with:				
Evangelical Fellowship of Canada	16	4	11	19
InterVarsity Fellowship of Canada	26	3	22	36
Most Influential Evangelical Leader:				
No one	79	85	83	73
David Mainse	5	0	6	6
Brian Stiller	2	0	1	4
Billy Graham	5	1	6	8

comparison to the fact 3.2 million have had religious experiences. Further, as noted earlier, religious experience fuels evangelism. The same analysis also revealed that contact with these organizations has no relationship with the urge to evangelize.[32]

Asked who they would consider to be "Canada's most important evangelical leader," a stunning 79 per cent said "no one." Only a handful mentioned such public figures as *100 Huntley Street*'s David Mainse (5 per cent) and the EFC's Brian Stiller (2 per cent). If we accept that the leadership of people such as Whitefield, Wesley, and Edwards were important to the birth of evangelicalism, we have to conclude that today's leaders play a less central role in Canadian evangelicalism.

This thin slice of information on the penetration of evangelical organizations and leaders provides us with some useful contexts for understanding the importance of religious experience. It is clear that religious experience is more widespread and more influential than evangelical leaders and organizations such as EFC and IVCF.[33]

This analysis provides us with a snapshot of the religious experiences of Canadian evangelicals in the 1990s. The snapshot is a bit grainy and the contrast may be a little too high, yet it is very revealing. From it one can argue credibly that intimate contact with the divine is a crucial aspect of the evangelical experience, an aspect considerably more important than the pronouncements and actions of legions of contemporary leaders.

The snapshot also supports the decision to include Catho-evangelicals. Their patterns of religious experience are remarkably similar to both mainline and conservative Protestant evangelicals, indicating a greater commonality than some might have expected. That Catho-evangelicals are found in all of the segments described in the typology highlights the fact that Catho-evangelicals are a diverse group, shattering any notions that Catholics should be treated as a monolithic presence in the Canadian religious landscape.

A snapshot can provide a reliable record of one instant of time, but it can only hint at the forces that have shaped the scene we actually see. And significant questions remain. The most important area of inquiry has to do with the constancy of religious experience: we know it played a considerable role in the First and Second Great Awakenings, but little is understood about its function in quieter times. It is quite possible that, as social conditions pushed and pulled evangelicals in different directions, there has been considerable variation in both the prevalence and manifestations of religious experience. The temptation is to draw a straight line between our two data points – the 1780s and the 1990s – and assume that everything in between fits the same pattern. This approach assumes too much. And while we wait to see if historical research reveals a variation in the role of religious experience, it seems likely there has been considerable change within this two-hundred-year period.

If we consider the context in which this snapshot was taken, we can entertain one culture-specific explanation for the depth of religious experience in the 1990s. If interest in the experiential side of religion varies with the times, it is quite possible that the situation we see today is in part a product of the sum of the trends we have seen in religion in Canada. Research over the past fifty years has confirmed impressions of a precipitous decline in church attendance and a general loss of attachment to organized religion. At the same time, research also tells us that Canadians' belief in God has remained constant and at exceptionally high levels (see table 6).[34] Further, over six in ten Canadians – including many who never attend church – say that their religious beliefs are very important in their day-to-day lives and that their sins are forgiven because of Christ's life, death, and resurrection.[35] Additionally, eight in ten self-identified Christians (79 per cent), including 54 per cent of evangelicals, "don't think you need to go to church services in order to be a good Christian."[36] These pieces of evidence suggest a trend towards faith apart from organizational support. The information presented earlier on the limited reach of institutions and the lack of leadership among evangelicals supports this conclusion. The fact that 75 per cent of Christians and 70 per cent of evangelicals agree that "my private beliefs about Christianity are more important to me than what is taught by any church" only confirms that Christian belief in the 1990s is a predominately private, personal affair. (This situation, it should be

Table 6
Church Attendance "in the Past Seven Days" and Belief in God (percentages)

	1946	1949	1955	1960	1965	1969	1970	1975	1980	1985	1990
Church attendance	67	–	58	56	55	–	44	41	35	32	27
Belief in God	–	95	–	–	–	92	–	88	–	87	86

noted, is not necessarily inevitable or irreversible. Religion has been more or less private or public at different times in different cultures.)

In a circumstance of privatized belief, where the focus is on the individual rather than the group, it is probable that people would be more open to religious experience than they would be at times when the organizational aspect of belief was dominant. Even if the prevalence of some of the more elemental experiences have remained constant, it is quite likely that they would have a more powerful effect today than they would have had at times when less weight was given to personal experience. It is notable that the situation today in some ways parallels those of the early days of evangelicalism. Writing about religious experience of the mid-1700s, Noll, Bebbington, and Rawlyk note that "Such experiences were not unique to English-speaking Protestants, for a turn to inwardness characterized European religion of the eighteenth century among Roman Catholics as well as Protestants, Jews as well as Christians."[37] If a link existed between an inward focus and religious experience in Europe in the eighteenth century, perhaps it is not surprising that the two appear together in Canada at the close of the twentieth century. David Reed of Wycliffe College may be right in proposing that the Toronto Blessing is a symptom of a church and a society in transition. And perhaps there is something to the claim that the Toronto Blessing signals a "softening up" of the saints and a "revival in embryo."[38]

Clearly, much awaits investigation, and much remains to be seen. Yet based on the research presented here, it seems reasonable to conclude that religious experience shapes and sustains the character of evangelicalism and is a tremendously important aspect of the Canadian evangelical experience in the 1990s.

Notes

INTRODUCTION

1 G.A. Rawlyk to contributors, 30 July 1992, Queen's University Archives [hereafter QUA].
2 Bebbington, *Evangelicalism*, 3.
3 Rawlyk to contributors, 30 July 1992, QUA.
4 In organizing the conference I was assisted by a planning committee consisting of Dr Ian Rennie, Ontario Theological Seminary; Professor Phyllis Airhart, Emmanuel College; Professor Marguerite Van Die, Queen's Theological College; Dr John Stackhouse Jr, Religion Department, University of Manitoba; Professor Mark Noll, Wheaton College; and Mr David Plaxton, History Department, Queen's University.
5 Lyman A. Kellstedt, "The Meaning and Measurement of Evangelicalism: Problems and Prospects," in *Religion and Political Behavior in the United States*, ed. T.G. Jelen (New York: Praeger, 1989), 5.
6 Curtis Johnson, *Redeeming America: Evangelicals and the Road to Civil War* (Chicago: Ivan Dee, 1993), 8. See also Rawlyk, *Canada Fire*.
7 Rawlyk, *Canada Fire*, 185–206.
8 Johnson, *Redeeming America*, 7.
9 Rawlyk, *Canada Fire*, 3–161.
10 Ibid., 121–3.
11 This is the central argument of my "'A Total Revolution in Religious and Civil Government,'" in Noll, Bebbington, and Rawlyk, eds., *Evangelicalism: Comparative Studies*.
12 See Gauvreau, *Evangelical Century*.

13 Goldwin French, "The Evangelical Creed in Canada," in *The Shield of Achilles*, ed. W.L. Morton (Toronto: McClelland & Stewart, 1968).
14 Goldwin French, "The Impact of Christianity on Canadian Culture and Society before 1867," *Theological Bulletin* (McMaster Divinity College), 3 (January 1968): 29.
15 French, "Evangelical Creed," 16.
16 Airhart, *Serving the Present Age*, 144.
17 Charles Johnston, *McMaster University: The Toronto Years* (Toronto: University of Toronto Press, 1976), vol. 1, 72.
18 See Rawlyk, "A.L. McCrimmon, H.P. Whidden, T.T. Shields," in Rawlyk, ed., *Canadian Baptists and Christian Higher Education*.
19 See for example Airhart, *Serving the Present Age*; Marshall, *Secularizing the Faith*.
20 See Marshall, *Secularizing the Faith*; Gauvreau, *Evangelical Century*.
21 W.R. Hutchison, *The Modernist Impulse in American Protestantism*, 2nd ed. (New York: Oxford University Press, 1982).
22 Rawlyk and Noll, eds., *Amazing Grace*, 19.
23 See Grenville, "Christian Evangelicalism Scale."
24 For a pointed critique of this thesis, see Christie and Gauvreau, "A Full-Orbed Christianity."

CHAPTER ONE

1 Quotations from Strachan and Ryerson in this paragraph are from Westfall, *Two Worlds*, 24–6. I also follow Westfall's account of Anglican-Methodist convergence. On the coach ride, see Grant, *Profusion of Spires*, 93.
2 Stackhouse, *Canadian Evangelicalism*, 165–73. See also Stackhouse, "National Association of Evangelicals."
3 For regional studies, see Scobie and Grant, eds., *Contribution of Methodism*; Burkinshaw, "Conservative Evangelicalism in the Twentieth-Century 'West,'" in Rawlyk and Noll, eds., *Amazing Grace* and *Pilgrims in Lotus Land*. There is also some attention to regional differences in: Rawlyk, ed., *Canadian Protestant Experience*; Bibby, *Fragmented Gods*; *Unknown Gods*; and *Mosaic Madness*. It is, however, hard to complain about lack of serious attention to Canada's regions when the much larger tribe of American religious historians pays almost no attention to the question, with the exception of a long-standing interest in the South.
4 See especially Dayton and Johnston, eds., *The Variety of American Evangelicalism*.
5 For a start, see the essays on various denominational traditions in Vander-Vennen, ed., *Church and Canadian Culture* (sponsored by the EFC and the Institute for Christian Studies in Toronto).

6 Rawlyk, *Canada Fire*; Christie, "'In These Times of Democratic Rage and Delusion,'" in Rawlyk, ed., *Canadian Protestant Experience*.
7 Airhart, "'As Canadian as Possible,'"; Blumhofer, *Everybody's Sister*; Burkinshaw, *Pilgrims in Lotus Land*; Elliott, "Knowing No Borders," in Rawlyk and Noll, eds., *Amazing Grace*; Rennie, "Fundamentalism and the Varieties of North Atlantic Evangelicalism," in Noll, Bebbington, and Rawlyk, eds., *Evangelicalism: Comparative Studies*; and William Westfall, "Voices from the Attic: Canada and the Narratives of American Religion," in *Retelling U.S. Religious History*, ed. Thomas Tweed (Berkeley: University of California Press, forthcoming 1997), on the de-centring of American religious history.
8 Fred Matthews, review of Seymour Martin Lipset's *Continental Divide*, *Journal of Interdisciplinary History* 21 (Spring 1991): 719-21. For a related but more pointed criticism that Lipset overstates Anglican at the expense of evangelical experience in discussing Canadian religion, see Rawlyk, "Religion in Canada," 142, 24n.
9 In addition to references in note 6, see Errington and Rawlyk, "Creating a British-American Community."
10 For a recent survey see *Christian Week*, 31 January 1995, 10-12.
11 William Christian, *George Grant: A Biography* (Toronto: University of Toronto Press, 1994).
12 Roberton Davies, *The Cunning Man* (New York: Viking, 1994), 468. See also Farley Mowat, *The Dog Who Wouldn't Be* (1957), on growing up in Saskatchewan; or *And No Birds Sang* (1979), on Canadian soldiers in the Italian campaign. Robertson Davies's three trilogies – Salterton, Deptford, and Cornish – are cosmopolitan, but the main external influences are British and European rather than American. His two most recent novels – *Murthering Spirits* and *The Cunning Man* – are even more British.
13 Michael Bliss, "Northern Wealth: Economic Life in the 20th Century," *The Beaver*, December 1994/January 1995 (75th anniversary issue), 9.
14 The pioneer and still most trenchant student of such comparisons is Robert T. Handy, *A History of the Churches in the United States and Canada* (New York: Oxford University Press, 1977); "Trends in Canadian and American Theological Education, 1880-1980," *Theological Education* 28 (Spring 1982).
15 Noll, "Revolution and the Rise of Evangelical Social Influence in North Atlantic Societies," in Noll, Bebbington, and Rawlyk, eds., *Evangelicalism: Comparative Studies*.
16 Daniel Walker Howe, "Religion and Politics in the Antebellum North," in Noll, ed., *Religion and American Politics*.
17 Some black-white comparisons are well worked out in Albert J. Raboteau, *Slave Religion* (New York: Oxford University Press, 1978); Milton

C. Sernett, *Black Religion and American Evangelicalism ... 1787–1865* (Methuchen, NJ: Scarecrow, 1975); and Donald G. Mathews, *Religion in the Old South* (Chicago: University of Chicago Press, 1977). But there is far less for the post-bellum period.

18 Bebbington, *Evangelicalism*, 2–17.
19 Westfall, *Two Worlds*, 84.
20 Allan Greer's *The Patriots and the People: The Rebellion of 1837 in Rural Lower Canada* (Toronto: University of Toronto Press, 1993) revises existing historiography, but it does not have to contend with powerful regnant myths in the way that every new book on the American Revolution must.
21 Seymour Martin Lipset, *Continental Divide: The Values and Institutions of the United States and Canada* (New York: Routledge, 1990), 8.
22 Ibid., 116.
23 See the essays, with references, on Protestant-Catholic tensions by Barbara Welter, Jay Dolan, and Mark Noll, in *Uncivil Religion: Interreligious Hostility in America*, ed. Robert N. Bellah and Frederick E. Greenspahn (New York: Crossroad, 1987).
24 Paul Laverdure, "The Redemptorist Mission in Canada, 1865–1885," in *Canadian Society of Church History Papers* (1993), ed. Bruce L. Guenther (n.p.: Canadian Society of Church History, 1993), 86–7.
25 The most powerful statement is Hatch, *The Democratization of American Christianity*. See also Robert H. Wiebe, *The Opening of American Society from the Adoption of the Constitution to the Era of Disunion* (New York: Knopf, 1984); Gordon S. Wood, *The Radicalism of the American Revolution* (New York: Knopf, 1992).
26 George Parkin Grant, *Lament for a Nation: The Defeat of Canadian Nationalism* (Toronto: McClelland & Stewart, 1965).
27 Carwardine, "Evangelicals, Politics, and the Coming of the American Civil War," in Noll, Bebbington, and Rawlyk, eds., *Evangelicalism: Comparative Studies*, 212. See also Carwardine, *Evangelicals and Politics in Antebellum America* (New Haven: Yale University Press, 1993).
28 Michael Gauvreau, manuscript research proposal, "The Voluntary Empire: Evangelicalism, Liberalism, and the Formation of Colonial Society in British North America, 1775–1870."
29 U.S. figures are from J. Guth et al., "Evangelicals and God's Own Party," *Christian Century*, 17 February 1993, as supplemented by information from Lyman Kellstedt. Canadian figures are from the Angus Reid Group, courtesy of Andrew Grenville and George Rawlyk.
30 Grant, *Profusion of Spires*.
31 Westfall, *Two Worlds*.
32 Gauvreau, *Evangelical Century*.
33 Vaudry, *Free Church*.

34 Van Die, *An Evangelical Mind*.
35 On Grant, see Mack, "Of Canadian Presbyterians and Guardian Angels," in Rawlyk and Noll, eds., *Amazing Grace*; Vissers, "Recovering the Reformation Conception of Revelation," in Klempa, ed., *The Burning Bush*; and on McNichol, see Stackhouse, *Canadian Evangelicalism*, 56–67.
36 Airhart, *Serving the Present Age*.
37 Blumhofer, *Everybody's Sister*.
38 Rawlyk, *Champions of the Truth*, ch. 3.
39 Burkinshaw, *Pilgrims in Lotus Land*.
40 Stackhouse, *Canadian Evangelicalism*.
41 Phyllis Airhart's suggestion – that the entrance of American evangelical patterns derailed a delicate balance between liberal and conservative forces within Ontario Methodism – probably needs to be set in a larger context (i.e. with respect to other factors in Canada and to influences from Britain), yet it is still a thought-provoking idea. See Airhart, *Serving the Present Age*, and also "'What Must I Do to Be Saved.'"
42 All three quotations are from N.K. Clifford, "His Dominion: A Vision in Crisis," *Sciences Religieuses/Studies in Religion* 2 (1973): 317, 319. The quotations are put to use by Robert Choquette, "Christ and Culture during 'Canada's Century,'" in *New Dimensions in American Religious History*, ed. Jay P. Dolan and James P. Wind (Grand Rapids: Eerdmans, 1993), 88, but Choquette draws much more drastic conclusions about the decrepit quality of Canadian Christianity than any observer from the United States (who knows what real religious racism looks like) could ever do.

CHAPTER TWO

1 Christie, "'In These Times of Democratic Rage and Delusion,'" in Rawlyk, ed., *Canadian Protestant Experience*, 11.
2 Stackhouse, "More Than a Hyphen," in Rawlyk and Noll, eds., *Amazing Grace*.
3 Henry Hussey, *More Than Half a Century of Colonial Life and Christian Experience, with Notes of Travel, Lectures, Publications etc.* (Adelaide: Hussey and Gillingham, 1897), 203.
4 Grant, *Profusion of Spires*, 42.
5 Ibid.
6 Burkinshaw, "Conservative Evangelicalism in the Twentieth-Century 'West,'" in Rawlyk and Noll, eds., *Amazing Grace*, 318.
7 It was this parallelism that made it possible for people like the British-born W.H. Griffith Thomas and T.T. Shields, and the Canadian A.B. Simpson to play important roles in American fundamentalist circles, and for American revivalists like Moody and Torrey to have an impact on the rise of organizations like the InterVarsity Christian Fellowship in Britain.

8 Grant, *Profusion of Spires*, 44.
9 Ibid., 30.
10 See the section on religion in R.C. Gourlay, *A Statistical Account of Upper Canada. Compiled with a View to a Grand System of Emigration* (London: Simkin and Marshall, 1822).
11 E. Campion, *Australian Catholics* (Ringwood: Penguin, 1988).
12 Grant, *Profusion of Spires*, 38–9, 42.
13 See entry on Lang in B.J. Bridges, *Ministers, Licentiates and Catechists of the Presbyterian Churches in New South Wales, 1823–1865* (Melbourne: Ward, 1989).
14 Kenneth Cable and Stephen Judd, *Sydney Anglicans: A History of the Diocese* (Sydney: Anglican Information Office, 1987), 291.
15 Grant, *Profusion of Spires*, 34.
16 Ibid.
17 Ibid., 33.
18 Quoted in D.W.A. Baker, *Days of Wrath: A Life of John Dunmore Lang* (Carlton, Victoria: Melbourne University Press, 1985), 31.
19 Ibid., 119.
20 Grant, *Profusion of Spires*, 33.
21 Ibid., 35.
22 Ibid., 3.
23 Ibid., 28.
24 Douglas Pike, *Paradise of Dissent: South Australia, 1829–1857* (London: Longman Green, 1957), 48–9.
25 Ibid., 48.
26 Grant, *Profusion of Spires*, 28.
27 Knaplund, *James Stephen and the British Colonial System*, as quoted in A.G. Austin, *Australian Education, 1788–1900: Church, State and Public Education in Colonial Australia* (Melbourne: Sir Isaac Pitman and Sons, 1965), 2nd ed., 22–3.
28 Ibid., 25.
29 J.M. Ward, *James Macarthur: Colonial Conservative, 1798–1867* (Sydney: Sydney University Press, 1981), 55.
30 C. Fry, *"Can You Find Me?" A Family History* (Oxford: Oxford University Press, 1978). The Mackay brothers' contribution can be found in the letters of the Presbyterian Church Association, Knox College, University of Toronto.
31 C.W. White, *The Challenge of the Years: A History of the Presbyterian Church in New South Wales* (Sydney: Angus and Robertson, 1951), 22.
32 Conversation with Dr Ian Rennie of Ontario Bible College, 23 April 1992. A four-volume history of the New Hebrides Mission is apparently being written.
33 Ibid.; *Christian Advocate* and *Wesleyan Record*, vol. 2, 1 March 1860 and 1 April 1965.

34 *Christian Advocate* and *Wesleyan Record*, vol. 2, 1 March 1860.
35 Interview with David Michel, Overseas Missionary Fellowship [OMF] Ontario Office, 12 November 1992.
36 C.S. Woods to P. White, 28 October 1944, InterVarsity Fellowship [IVF] Archives, held at the Centre for the Study of Australian Christianity [hereafter CSAC].
37 C.S. Woods to P. White, 20 November 1945, IVF Archives, CSAC.
38 C.S. Woods to P. White, 24 January 1949, IVF Archives, CSAC.
39 C.H. Troutman to H.W. Sutherland, 5 February 1957 and 20 February 1961, IVF Archives, CSAC. The "Tyndale House model" refers to student action resource centres, situated on or near university campuses, which provide inputs for visiting scholars, seminar series, and such-like scholarly endeavour with an evangelical flavour. In theory such centres act to support evangelical scholarship both in and out of the university world.
40 *Presbyterian Record* 6 (June 1925).
41 Quoted in Richard Ely, "The First Anzac Day: Invented or Discovered?" *Journal of Australian Studies* 17 (November 1985): 49.
42 Jack Granatstein and W.L. Morton, *A Nation Forged in Fire: Canadians and the Second World War, 1935–1945* (Toronto: Lester and Orpen Dennys, 1989).

CHAPTER THREE

1 Hatch, *The Democratization of American Christianity*.
2 Rawlyk, *Canada Fire*, 121.
3 Stackhouse, *Canadian Evangelicalism*, 190.
4 Christie, "'In These Times of Democratic Rage and Delusion,'" in Rawlyk, ed., *Canadian Protestant Experience*, xv, 123.
5 Alexander Sutherland, *Methodism in Canada: Its Work and Its Story* (London: Charles H. Kelly, 1903), 152.
6 *The Baptist Magazine*, January 1850, 26 (F[rederick] Bosworth).
7 James Lumsden, *The Skipper Parson* (London: Charles H. Kelly, 1905), 109.
8 Donald Gee, *Wind and Flame* (Croydon: Assemblies of God Publishing House, 1967), 123.
9 John S. Moir, *The Church in the British Era* (Toronto: McGraw-Hill Ryerson, 1972); Grant, *Church in the Canadian Era*.
10 Rawlyk, ed., *Henry Alline*.
11 See in particular Gauvreau, *Evangelical Century*, esp. 11–12.
12 Stackhouse, "More Than a Hyphen," in Rawlyk and Noll, eds., *Amazing Grace*, 383n.
13 Ibid., 393–4; Gauvreau, *Evangelical Century*, 11, 269. See also Bebbington, "Martyrs for the Truth."
14 *Church Missionary Record*, December 1872, 392.

15 E.L. Langston, *Bishop Taylor Smith* (London: Marshall, Morgan & Scott, n.d.), 266.
16 *Canadian Methodist Magazine* 20 (1884): 245, quoted by Doug Owram, *Promise of Eden: The Canadian Expansionist Movement and the Idea of the West, 1856–1900* (Toronto: University of Toronto Press, 1980), 147.
17 Moir, *Enduring Witness*, 222.
18 Brian Underwood, *Faith at the Frontiers: Anglican Evangelicals and Their Countrymen Overseas*, 69.
19 Joan Bayldon, *Cyril Bardsley: Evangelist* (London: Society for Promoting Christian Knowledge, 1942), 183.
20 G.G. Findlay and W.W. Holdsworth, *The History of the Wesleyan Missionary Society*, 5 vols. (London: Epworth Press, 1921), 1: 460.
21 *Baptist Magazine*, January 1850, 27 (Bosworth).
22 *Supplement to the First Annual Report of the Society in Glasgow ... Containing a Reply to the Memorial of Dr Macculloch ...* (Glasgow: Andrew Young, 1826), 30.
23 *Minutes of Methodist Conferences* 15 (London: John Mason, 1865), 137.
24 *Proceedings of the Church Missionary Society*, 1881–82 (London: Church Missionary Society, [1882]), 216.
25 Underwood, *Faith at the Frontiers*, 49–50.
26 Findlay and Holdsworth, *Wesleyan Missionary Society*, 1: 454.
27 Underwood, *Faith at the Frontiers*, 49.
28 Vaudry, *Free Church*, 43.
29 Ibid., 56–9.
30 Rawlyk, "The Holiness Movement and Canadian Maritime Baptists," and Burkinshaw, "Conservative Evangelicalism in the Twentieth-Century 'West,'" in Rawlyk and Noll, eds., *Amazing Grace*, 332.
31 Grant, *Profusion of Spires*, 215.
32 Marshall, *Secularizing the Faith*, ch. 2.
33 Alan Hayes, "The Principalship of R.B. McElheran," in *The Enduring Word: A Centennial History of Wycliffe College*, ed. Arnold Edinborough (Toronto: University of Toronto Press, 1978), 50–1.
34 J.R. Miller, "Anti-Catholic Thought in Victorian Canada," *Canadian Historical Review* 66 (1985).
35 Philip Carrington, *The Anglican Church in Canada* (Toronto: Collins, 1963), 143.
36 *A Text Book for British Protestants* (n.p., n.d.). I am grateful to Bruce Hindmarsh for this item.
37 D.C. Masters, "Anglican Evangelicals in Toronto, 1870–1900," *Journal of the Canadian Church Historical Society* 20 (1978): 52.
38 J. Ewing Ritchie, *To Canada with the Emigrants* (London: T. Fisher Unwin, 1885), 74–5.

39 Masters, "Anglican Evangelicals," 61.
40 Airhart, *Serving the Present Age*, esp. 77.
41 Richard W. Moss, *The Rev. W.B. Pope, D.D.: Theologian and Saint* (London: Robert Culley, [1909]), 10, 20.
42 R. Gordon Balfour, *Presbyterianism in the Colonies* (Edinburgh: Macniven & Wallace, 1899), 49.
43 Ernest Graham Ingham and Clement L. Burrows, *Sketches in Western Canada* (London: Hodder and Stoughton, [1913]), 16, 98.
44 Robert Finch, "The Principalship of Ramsay Armitage," in Edinborough, ed., *Enduring Word*, 77.
45 One who made an impact in Britain was Egerton Young. *Minutes of Several Conversations ... of the People called Methodists*, 1890 (London: Wesleyan Book Room), 389.
46 For example, Thomas R. Millman, "The Principalship of T.R. O'Meara," in Edinborough, ed., *Enduring Word*, 24; William A. Wood, *Something from Our Hands* (Hudson Heights, PQ: Wood Family Archives, 1988), 127–36.
47 Stackhouse, "More Than a Hyphen," 376–7; Elliott, "Knowing No Borders," in Rawlyk and Noll, eds., *Amazing Grace*, 369–71.
48 Patrick Dixon, *Signs of Revival* (Eastbourne, Sussex: Kingsway, 1994), ch. 1.
49 Helen I. Cowan, *British Immigration before Confederation* (Ottawa: Canadian Historical Association, 1978), 16.
50 Marjory Harper, *Emigration from North-East Scotland*, 2 vols. (Aberdeen: Aberdeen University Press, 1988), 2: 13.
51 Margaret Barlow, ed., *The Life of William Hagger Barlow, D.D.* (London: George Allen and Sons, 1910), 171–9.
52 Robert S. Wilson, "British Influence in the Nineteenth Century," in *Baptists in Canada: Search for Identity amidst Diversity*, ed. Jarold K. Zeman (Burlington: Welch, 1980), 34. I am grateful to Jonathan Wilson for this reference.
53 Vaudry, *Free Church*, 50.
54 Margaret Pawley, *Donald Coggan: Servant of Christ* (London: Society for Promoting Christian Knowledge, 1987), esp. 59.
55 Wilson, "British Influence," 29.
56 *Minutes of the Methodist Conferences* 15 (1865), 164.
57 W.Y. Fullerton, *F.B. Meyer: A Biography*, 2nd ed. (London: Marshall, Morgan & Scott, n.d.), 201.
58 *Minutes of the Methodist Conferences* 15, 352.
59 Elizabeth A.K. McDougall and John S. Moir, eds., *Selected Correspondence of the Glasgow Colonial Society, 1825–1840* (Toronto: Champlain Society, 1994), xiv; *Proceedings of the Church Missionary Society, 1851–52* (London: for the Society), 188.

60 *The Home and Foreign Missionary Record for the Free Church of Scotland*, June 1850, 339.
61 Finch, "Ramsay Armitage," 78–9.
62 W.S. Shepperson, *British Emigration to North America: Projects and Opinions in the Early Victorian Period* (Oxford: Basil Blackwell, 1957), 258–9; Dudley Baines, *Migration in a Mature Economy: Emigration and Internal Migration in England and Wales, 1861–1900* (Cambridge: Cambridge University Press, 1985), 62–5.
63 Grant, *Profusion of Spires*, 49.
64 McDougall and Moir, eds., *Glasgow Colonial Society*, xlix.
65 *Church Missionary Record*, December 1830, 281; Underwood, *Faith at the Frontiers*, ch. 2.
66 T.W. Acheson, "Methodism and the Problem of Methodist Identity in Nineteenth-Century New Brunswick," in Scobie and Grant, eds., *Contribution of Methodism*, 115.
67 Andrew Reed and James Matheson, *A Narrative of the Visit to the American Churches by the Deputation from the Congregational Union of England & Wales*, 2 vols. (London: Jackson and Walford, 1835), 340–70.
68 Francis A. Cox and James Hoby, eds., *The Baptists in America* (London: T. Ward & Co., 1836), 244.
69 Baines, *Migration*, 65.
70 *The Free Church of Scotland Monthly*, March 1900, 56–7; *Report to the General Assembly by the Colonial Committee*, 25 May 1894, 9.
71 *The Baptist Times*, 21 October 1904, 764; 10 March 1904, 305. I am grateful for these references to Rosemary Chadwick.
72 Underwood, *Faith at the Frontiers*, 73.
73 Ingham and Burrows, *Sketches in Western Canada*, 6–7.
74 Bayldon, *Bardsley*, 58.
75 Ingham and Burrows, *Sketches in Western Canada*, 6–7.
76 Ibid., 23.
77 *Proceedings of the Church Missionary Society, 1881–82*, 215.
78 *Home and Foreign Missionary Record for the Free Church of Scotland*, March 1846, 323 (William Hamilton).
79 Frederic W. Macdonald, *The Life of William Morley Punshon, LL.D.* (London: Hodder and Stoughton, 1887), 306.
80 *Baptist Magazine*, January 1850, 26.
81 *The Missionary Register*, December 1835, 571.
82 Reed and Matheson, *Narrative*, 345.
83 Bebbington, "Revival and Enlightenment," 28–31.
84 John Fairbairn to Robert Burns, 29 July 1834, in *Glasgow Colonial Society*, 75.

85 Underwood, *Faith at the Frontiers*, 22–8.
86 Alan P.F. Sell, "Harley College and Its Congregational Alumni," in *Commemorations: Studies in Christian Thought and History* (Calgary: University of Calgary Press, 1993), 292.
87 Macdonald, *Punshon*, 370n.
88 Underwood, *Faith at the Frontiers*, 75.
89 Moir, *Enduring Witness*, 39.
90 Diary of the Reverend William Proudfoot, 19 September 1832, as quoted in Stewart D. Gill, *The Rev. William Proudfoot and the United Secession Mission in Canada*, Studies in the History of Missions, 7 (Queenston, ON: Edwin Mellen Press, 1991), 125; ibid., 52.
91 *Report of the Committee of the General Assembly of the Church of Scotland for Promoting the Religious Interests of Scottish Presbyterians in the Colonies*, May 1866 (Edinburgh: Thomas Paton, 1866), 14.
92 *Second Report of the Baptist Colonial Missionary Society*, 1840 (n.p.), 10; Underwood, *Faith at the Frontiers*, 51–2.
93 Wilson, "British Influence," 23–7.
94 Underwood, *Faith at the Frontiers*, 106.
95 Elliott, "Knowing No Borders," 356–8.
96 Wilson, "British Influence," 30–1.
97 Mack, "Of Canadian Presbyterians and Guardian Angels," in Rawlyk and Noll, eds., *Amazing Grace*, esp. 280.
98 Margaret Prang, *N.W. Rowell: Ontario Nationalist* (Toronto: University of Toronto Press, 1975), 70–88.
99 Renfree, *Heritage and Horizon*, 221–4.
100 Bebbington, "The Persecution of George Jackson"; Clyde Binfield, *Pastors and People: The Biography of a Baptist Church: Queen's Road, Coventry* (Coventry: Queen's Road Baptist Church, 1984), 182–90.
101 Mark Sorrell, *The Peculiar People* (Exeter: Paternoster Press, 1979); Roger Homan, "The Society of Dependents: A Case Study in the Rise and Fall of Rural Peculiars," *Sussex Archaeological Collections* 119 (1981).
102 George Herod, *Biographical Sketches of Some of those Preachers Whose Labours Contributed to the Origination and Early Extension of the Primitive Methodist Connexion* (London: T. King, [1855]), 251; Julia S. Werner, *The Primitive Methodist Connexion: Its Background and Early History* (Madison: University of Wisconsin Press, 1984).
103 C.B. Sissons, *Egerton Ryerson: His Life and Letters*, 2 vols. (Toronto: Clarke, Irwin, 1937), 1: 178.
104 Moir, *Enduring Witness*, 46, 60.
105 *Supplement to the First Annual Report*, 28.
106 Vaudry, *Free Church*, ch. 2.

107 Grant, *Profusion of Spires*, 77.
108 *Minutes of Several Conversations*, 1894, 418.
109 Donald E. Meek, "Aspects of the Role of Dissenting Evangelicalism in Highland Emigration," in *Proceedings of the First North American Congress of Celtic Studies*, ed. Gordon W. MacLennan (Ottawa: University of Ottawa, 1988), 23.
110 Harper, *Emigration from North-East Scotland*, 1: 211.
111 Meek, "Dissenting Evangelicalism."
112 Grant, *Profusion of Spires*, 32.
113 Robert F. Burns, *The Life and Times of the Rev. Robert Burns, D.D.* (Toronto: James Campbell & Son, 1872), 291–2; see also Rawlyk, *Canada Fire*, ch. 11.
114 John Webster Grant, "Brands from Blazing Heather: Canadian Religious Revival in the Highland Tradition," Canadian Society of Presbyterian History, *Papers*, 1991, cited by Van Die, "'The Double Vision,'" in Noll, Bebbington, and Rawlyk, eds., *Evangelicalism: Comparative Studies*, 257.
115 Robert Sandall, *The History of the Salvation Army*, vol. 2 (London: Thomas Nelson and Sons, 1952), 255–6.
116 Lawrence Kitzan, "The London Missionary Society in Upper Canada," *Ontario History* 59 (1967): 40.
117 Rennie, "Fundamentalism and the Varieties of North Atlantic Evangelicalism," in Noll, Bebbington, and Rawlyk, eds., *Evangelicalism: Comparative Studies*, 342–5.
118 Thomas N. Turnbull, *What God Hath Wrought: A Short History of the Apostolic Church* (Bradford: Puritan Press, 1959), ch. 11.
119 Grant, *Profusion of Spires*, 161.
120 John Hawthorn, *Alexander Marshall: Evangelist, Author and Pioneer* (London: Pickering & Inglis, n.d.), 72, 52. See also Airhart, "'What Must I Do to Be Saved?'"
121 Henry Varley, *Henry Varley's Life-Story* (London: Alfred Holness, n.d.), 114–15. The four evangelical denominations of Brantford, however, admitted a total of only 167 converts following Varley's campaign. I am grateful for this information to Marguerite Van Die.
122 *The Advent Witness*, October 1927, 158. I am grateful for this reference to Rev. Ian Randall.
123 Langston, *Taylor Smith*, 238.
124 Rawlyk, *Canada Fire*.
125 Thomas Coke, *An Address to the Pious and Benevolent proposing an Annual Subscription for the Support of the Missionaries ...*, quoted in John Vickers, *Thomas Coke: Apostle of Methodism* (Nashville: Abingdon Press, 1969), 148.

CHAPTER FOUR

The author gratefully acknowledges the comments of Bob Burkinshaw, Nancy Christie, Gordon Harland, and George Rawlyk, and the support of the Social Sciences and Humanities Research Council of Canada, in the preparation of this paper.

1 Quoted in Leonard Schapiro, *The Russian Revolutions of 1917: The Origins of Modern Communism* (New York: Basic Books, 1984), 213.
2 For example, see Marsden, "Evangelical Denomination," viii–xvi; Bebbington, *Evangelicalism*, 2–17; Dayton and Johnston, eds., *American Evangelicalism*; and Stackhouse, *Canadian Evangelicalism*, 6–12.
3 Some evangelicals believe that such a relationship must begin at a determinate point in one's life. (One recent example is Stanley J. Grenz, *Revisioning Evangelical Theology: A Fresh Agenda for the 21st Century* [Downers Grove, IL: InterVarsity Press, 1993], 37–59.) Others believe that such a particular beginning is not necessary for true piety but rather that true piety can be "grown into" as one matures in a Christian setting. On this question see Stackhouse, "Billy Graham."
4 Prohibition was enacted first in Prince Edward Island in 1901, and in the rest of Canada during World War I. Quebec rejected it first, in 1919, and PEI gave it up last, in 1930. The Lord's Day Act, for another example, was passed in 1907. It must be noted, though, that not all evangelicals were in favour of prohibition, and that it is always problematic to assume that evangelicals are of one mind on any particular social issue.
5 Allen, *Social Passion*.
6 Donald A. Wicks, "T.T. Shields and the Canadian Protestant League, 1941–50" (M.A. thesis, University of Guelph, 1971); Brent Reilly, "Baptists and Organized Opposition to Roman Catholicism, 1941–1962," in *Costly Vision: The Baptist Pilgrimage in Canada*, ed. Jarold K. Zeman (Burlington: Welch, 1988).
7 On Prairie Bible Institute and Toronto Bible College, see Stackhouse, *Canadian Evangelicalism*.
8 Guenther, "Bible School Movement," 135–73.
9 Stackhouse, *Canadian Evangelicalism*, discusses this *en passant* particularly in terms of Toronto/Ontario Bible College and Prairie Bible Institute. See also idem, "Respectfully Submitted."
10 Little research has been undertaken as yet into these recent developments. For introductions to Trinity Western University and its context, see Burkinshaw, *Pilgrims in Lotus Land* and Stackhouse, *Canadian Evangelicalism*.
11 ICS is discussed in Stackhouse, "Respectfully Submitted."
12 Wuthnow, *Restructuring of American Religion*, esp. ch. 6.

13 For introductions to the EFC, see Stackhouse, *Canadian Evangelicalism*, ch. 12; and Mark Chapman, "Rebuilding the Broken Wall: The EFC and Canadian Evangelicals" (M.A. thesis, Wilfrid Laurier University, 1994).
14 Harry J. Kits, "World Views and Social Involvement: A Proposal for Classification of Canadian Neo-Calvinist Social Involvement, 1945–1980" (Master of Philosophical Foundations thesis, Institute for Christian Studies, Toronto, 1988); idem, "25 Years of Public Witness," *The Catalyst* 12 (February 1989): 1, 11.
15 Some introductory Centre for Renewal of Public Policy materials are in the author's possession. Some evangelical Christians mobilized in explicitly religious political organizations like evangelist Ken Campbell's Renaissance International and the Christian Heritage Party. But these small groups remained on the fringes even of evangelical support.
16 An extraordinary case of evangelicals both affecting a government and being affected by it is that of the notorious Padlock Laws and other contraventions of civil rights of Protestants, Jehovah's Witnesses, and others under the Duplessis regime in Quebec.
17 This issue is explored briefly in Stackhouse, "Women in Public Ministry."
18 On the origins of the charismatic movement among mainline Protestants, see P.D. Hocken, "Charismatic Movement," in *Dictionary of Pentecostal and Charismatic Movements*, ed. Stanley M. Burgess, Gary B. McGee, and Patrick H. Alexander (Grand Rapids: Zondervan, 1988); and Richard Quebedeaux, *The New Charismatics: The Origins, Development, and Significance of Neo-Pentecostalism* (Garden City, NY: Doubleday, 1976).
19 Kydd, "Pentecostals, Charismatics"; Al Reimers, *God's Country: Charismatic Renewal* (Toronto: Welch, 1979).
20 George Egerton, ed., *Anglican Essentials: Reclaiming Faith within the Anglican Church of Canada* (Toronto: Anglican Book Centre, 1995).
21 Hillis, "The Evangel and Evangelicalism."
22 Grant, *Profusion of Spires*; Gauvreau, *Evangelical Century*; and Westfall, *Two Worlds*.
23 Bibby, *Fragmented Gods* and *Unknown Gods*; see the cover story and related stories in *Maclean's*, 12 April 1993, 32–50.
24 Electronic mail message to the author, responding to an earlier draft of this paper, 3 May 1995.
25 J.M. Bumsted, "Becoming Canadian," *The Beaver*, December 1994.
26 Ibid., 61.
27 J.M. Bumsted, *The Peoples of Canada*, 2 vols. (Toronto: Oxford University Press, 1992).
28 Robert Bothwell, Ian Drummond, and John English, *Canada 1900–1945* (Toronto: University of Toronto Press, 1987); and idem, *Canada since 1945: Power, Politics, and Provincialism* (Toronto: University of Toronto Press, 1981).

29 Bothwell, Drummond, and English, *Canada since 1945*, 452.
30 R. Cook, *The Regenerators*; J.M. Bumsted, *Henry Alline* (Toronto: University of Toronto Press, 1971).
31 Take, for example, two distinguished historians writing in the ambitious Canadian Centenary Series. J.L. Granatstein ignores religion in *Canada 1957–1967: The Years of Uncertainty and Innovation* (Toronto: McClelland & Stewart, 1986). In *The Forked Road: Canada 1939–1957* (Toronto: McClelland & Stewart, 1976), 28, Donald Creighton pays attention to religion, but his discussion of evangelicalism is fraught with words like "narrow," "puritanical," and "repressive."
32 Allen, *Social Passion*; R. Cook, *The Regenerators*.
33 Airhart, *Serving the Present Age*; Westfall, *Two Worlds*.
34 Bibby, *Unknown Gods*, 6, table 1.1.
35 Reported in Robert Marshall, "The Gamut of Belief: The Poll Defines the Faithful," *Maclean's*, 12 April 1993, 46. George Rawlyk's forthcoming report on this poll apparently will revise such figures slightly (personal communication to the author).
36 Bothwell, Drummond, and English, *Canada 1900–1945*, 13.
37 Bob Burkinshaw pays careful attention to evangelicals in British Columbian politics in his *Pilgrims in Lotus Land*. Such study is lacking for every other region of Canada for the twentieth century, with the exception of William Aberhart's regime in Alberta.
38 In this section I have in mind the analysis of American culture offered in Noll, Hatch, and Marsden, *The Search for Christian America*. I have considered these issues briefly in an even larger context in "Whose Dominion?"
39 Lois Sweet, "That Cross Everyone's Bearing Is Only for Fashion or Is It?" *Toronto Star*, 22 February 1994, B4.
40 Bibby, *Unknown Gods*, 127, table 5.3.
41 Martin E. Marty's ground-breaking study of secularization in France, England, and the United States, *The Modern Schism: Three Paths to the Secular* (Evanston and New York: Harper & Row, 1969), indicates that in each of these three societies, at least, the "hump" of significant secularization was traversed in the nineteenth century. It may be that, as Gauvreau has begun to sketch it in *Evangelical Century*, Canadian nineteenth-century evangelicals simply went to work in politics according to "evident" principles that were "just there," in the same way scientists were presumed to study a natural world that was "just there." This Baconian presumption of the seamless complementarity of reason and revelation has forestalled consideration of the possible influence of unconscious non-Christian presuppositions or the possible importance of conscious Christian presuppositions upon political (or scientific) pursuits. The intellectual culture of Canadian evangelicalism remains a rich and underexplored field.

42 Gauvreau's book is particularly helpful here, but see also McKillop, *A Disciplined Intelligence*; Masters, *Protestant Church Colleges*; and Van Die, *An Evangelical Mind*.
43 So the firestorms of protest ignited in 1992 and 1993 when groups across the country placed advertisements entitled "In Defense of a Little Virginity" (developed by Focus on the Family) in a number of Canadian newspapers.
44 Robert Wright, *A World Mission: Canadian Protestantism and the Quest for a New International Order, 1918–1939* (Montreal and Kingston: McGill-Queen's University Press, 1991); Marshall, *Secularizing the Faith*, ch. 4.
45 Grant, *Church in the Canadian Era*, 180.
46 For examples see Brian C. Stiller, *Critical Options for Evangelicals* (Markham: Faith Today, 1991); Donald C. Posterski, *True to You: Living Our Faith in Our Multi-Minded World* (Winfield, BC: Wood Lake Books, 1995); Aileen Van Ginkel, ed., *Shaping a Christian Vision for Canada* (Markham: Faith Today, 1992); and essays in VanderVennen, ed., *Church and Canadian Culture*.
47 Stackhouse, "National Association of Evangelicals."
48 Noll, *Scandal of the Evangelical Mind*.

CHAPTER FIVE

1 George Cornish, ed., *Cyclopedia of Methodism in Canada*, 2 vols. (Toronto: Methodist Book and Publishing House, 1881), 1:19.
2 Nathan O. Hatch, "The Puzzle of American Methodism," *Church History* 63,2 (1994).
3 See, for example, Marshall, *Secularizing the Faith*.
4 R.D. Gidney and W.P.J. Millar, *Professional Gentlemen: The Professions in Nineteenth-Century Ontario* (Toronto: University of Toronto Press, 1994), 281–2.
5 Hatch, "The Puzzle of American Methodism," 189.
6 For a recent description see Rawlyk, *Canada Fire*, 143–61.
7 Quoted in Rawlyk, ed., *Canadian Protestant Experience*, 12. The date has been corrected.
8 Harriet Phelps Youmans, *Grimsby Park: Historical and Descriptive* (Toronto: William Briggs, 1900).
9 A. Gregory Schneider, *The Way of the Cross Leads Home: The Domestication of American Methodism* (Bloomington: Indiana University Press, 1993), 196–208; Russell E. Richey, *Early American Methodism* (Bloomington: Indiana University Press 1991), xii–xiii, 21–32.
10 Rawlyk, *Canada Fire*, 208.

11 Abraham Joshua Heschel, *The Sabbath: Its Meaning for Modern Man* (New York: Strauss, Farrar and Giroux, 1951), 75–6.
12 Schmidt, "Time, Celebration, and the Christian Year," in Noll, Bebbington, and Rawlyk, eds., *Evangelicalism: Comparative Studies*, 104.
13 Deborah M. Valenze, *Prophetic Sons and Daughters: Female Preaching and Popular Religion in Industrial England* (Princeton: Princeton University Press, 1985); E.P. Thompson, "Time, Work-Discipline, and Industrial Capitalism," *Past and Present* 38 (1967).
14 Schmidt, "Time, Celebration, and the Christian Year," 102.
15 A Journal of a Voyage from England to America Kept by W. Peters, National Archives of Canada [hereafter NAC], 1830.
16 Letter from William Peters, Immigrant, 29 September 1831, NAC.
17 An Account of the Voyage from England to America in 1831 by Elizabeth Peters, NAC, 23.
18 George Pashley Journal 1833–4, NAC.
19 A Short Journey of the Travels of George Pashley, NAC, 26–7.
20 John Macdonald, "Recollections of British Methodism in Toronto, from 1842 to the Union with the Canadian Methodists in 1848, and of St. Andrew's Church (Presbyterian), from 1840 to the Disruption," *Methodist Magazine* 30 (1889): 229.
21 Ibid., 232.
22 Valenze, *Prophetic Sons and Daughters*, 219–26.
23 William H. Pearson, *Recollections and Records of Toronto of Old* (Toronto: William Briggs, 1914), 312–15.
24 Douglas McCalla, *Planting the Province: The Economic History of Upper Canada, 1780–1870* (Toronto: University of Toronto Press, 1993); Jacob Spelt, *Urban Development in South-Central Ontario* (Toronto: McClelland & Stewart, 1972); Westfall, *Two Worlds*.
25 T.W. Acheson, "Methodism and the Problem of Methodist Identity in Nineteenth-Century New Brunswick," in Scobie and Grant, eds., *Contribution of Methodism*, 119.
26 For Canada in 1871 see A. Gordon Darroch and Michael D. Ornstein, "Ethnicity and Occupational Structure in Canada in 1871: The Vertical Mosaic in Historical Perspective," *Canadian Historical Review* 61,3 (1980).
27 Gidney and Millar, *Professional Gentlemen*, 117.
28 Westfall, *Two Worlds*, 68–73; Neil Semple, "The Impact of Urbanization on the Methodist Church in Central Canada, 1854–1884" (Ph.D. diss., University of Toronto, 1979), ch. 3.
29 Westfall, *Two Worlds*, 129.
30 See for example "Dr. Taylor's Lecture at Farmersville," *Christian Guardian*, 13 April 1870; "The Laying of the Cornerstone of the Wesleyan

Methodist Centenary Church in Stanstead Plain," *Christian Guardian*, 21 November 1866.
31 Westfall, *Two Worlds*, ch. 3.
32 Wesleyan Methodist Church in Canada, *Minutes ... of Twelve Annual Conferences ... from 1846 to 1857 Inclusive* (Toronto: Anson Green, 1863), 239.
33 Ibid., 359.
34 Robert W. Burtner and Robert E. Chiles, *John Wesley's Theology: A Collection from His Works* (Nashville: Abingdon, 1982), 245.
35 Henry D. Rack, *Reasonable Enthusiast: John Wesley and the Rise of Methodism*, 2nd ed. (London: Epworth Press, 1992), 370.
36 Allen B. Robertson, "'Give All You Can': Methodists and Charitable Causes in Nineteenth-Century Nova Scotia," in Scobie and Grant, eds., *Contribution of Methodism*, 93.
37 Alexander Sutherland, *Methodism in Canada* (Toronto: Methodist Mission Rooms, 1904), 332–3.
38 Cornish, *Cyclopedia*, 1:32, 455. Methodist Episcopal membership showed a similar influx, from 4,090 to 8,588. *Minutes of the Annual Bay of Quinte and Niagara Conferences of the Methodist Episcopal Church in Canada* (1850), 5; (1859), 6.
39 Wesleyan Methodist Church, *Minutes of Several Conversations at the Yearly Conference of the People Called Methodist* (London: Wesleyan Conference Office, 1850), 110–11; Cornish, *Cyclopedia*, 1:372. In the fall of 1858, Dr and Mrs Phoebe Palmer engaged in extensive revivalism in major centres in the Maritimes (*Christian Guardian*, 22 September 1858).
40 From $7,360.25 to $17,1190.22 (Cornish, *Cyclopedia*, 1:33).
41 See, for example, "The Good Work Prospering," *Christian Guardian*, 25 April 1856.
42 Van Die, *An Evangelical Mind*, 78–87; Peter George Bush, "James Caughey, Phoebe and Walter Palmer and the Methodist Revival Experience in Canada West, 1850–1858" (M.A. thesis, Queen's University, 1985).
43 Bush, "James Caughey, Phoebe and Walter Palmer," 82; Alden Aikens, "Christian Perfection in Central Canadian Methodism, 1828–1884" (Ph.D. diss., McGill University, 1987).
44 A.W. Nicolson, *Memories of James Bain Morrow* (Toronto and Halifax: Methodist Book Room, 1881), 39.
45 Nathanael Burwash, "Jane Clement Jones," *Canadian Methodist Magazine* 42 (1895); J. William Lamb, *Bridging the Years: A History of Bridge Street United/Methodist Church, Belleville, 1815–1990* (Winfield, BC: Woodlake Books, 1990), 112–13.
46 *Christian Guardian*, 26 October 1857.
47 Gidney and Millar, *Professional Gentlemen*, ch. 12.

48 Wesleyan Methodist Church in Canada, *Minutes* (1855), 302; (1857), 407. This was well before the 1874 union between the Wesleyan and New Connexion Methodists made provision for lay delegates to attend the quadrennial general conference. Methodist Church of Canada, *Journal of the Proceedings of the First General Conference* (Toronto: Samuel Rose, 1874), 50.
49 Curtis Johnson, *Islands of Holiness: Rural Religion in Upstate New York, 1790–1860* (Ithaca and London: Cornell University Press, 1989), 169.
50 See for example Diary of William Coates 1865, Archives of Ontario [hereafter AO]; Diary of John Wesley Hopkins, Stoney Creek 1868, United Church of Canada/Victoria University Archives [hereafter UCA]; Minutes of the Quarterly Board, New Wesleyan Methodist Church, Stanstead, PQ, 15 September 1871, Eastern Townships Research Centre, Bishop's University, Lennoxville, PQ.
51 Wellington Street Wesleyan Methodist Church, Brantford, Circuit Register 1855–1882. Names for the "Dumfries Street Class" were matched with census records, 1851 and 1861.
52 [Maria Noble], *Golden Jubilee 1871–1921 Brant Avenue Methodist Church* (Brantford: n.p., n.d.), 7.
53 *Christian Guardian*, 31 March 1858.
54 In 1858 the membership increased from 41,927 to 49,231, but the number of new members declined from 2,646 in 1859 to 1,965 in 1860 to a loss of 70 in 1861 (Cornish, *Cyclopedia*, 1:32).
55 Nicolson, *James Bain Morrow*, 161.
56 Lamb, *Bridging the Years*, 114–16.
57 *Christian Guardian*, 5 January 1864.
58 Neil Semple, "'The Nurture and Admonition of the Lord': Nineteenth-Century Canadian Methodism's Response to Childhood," *Histoire Sociale/Social History* 14 (1981).
59 Wesleyan Methodist Church in Canada, *Minutes* (1857), 412–13.
60 See William Watson, Diaries, 3 vols., UCA, and "A Brief Sketch of the Life of William Watson by His Son, William Gladstone Watson ... 1940," UCA.
61 See Harry A. Stout and Catherine A. Brekus, "Declension, Gender and the 'New Religious History,'" and Terry D. Bilhartz, "Sex and the Second Great Awakening: The Feminization of American Religion Reconsidered," in *Belief and Behavior: Essays in the New Religious History*, ed. Philip R. Vandermeer and Robert P. Swierenga (New Brunswick: Rutgers University Press, 1991).
62 Lane, "Wife, Mother, Sister, Friend." Membership records for Wellington Street Methodist Church, Brantford, reveal that women consistently formed a majority, ranging from 58 per cent in 1855 to 70 per cent in 1890.

63 See, for example, Circuit Register, Metropolitan Methodist Church, Toronto 1877–1883, UCA, where 10 of 28 classes in 1877 were entirely female. All had female leaders, with the exception of the largest, consisting of 51 women, taught by the minister.
64 Susan Juster, *Sexual Politics & Evangelicalism in Revolutionary New England* (Ithaca and London: Cornell University Press, 1994), 108–44, 180–208; Clyde Griffen, "Reconstructing Masculinity from the Evangelical Revival to the Waning of Progressivism: A Speculative Synthesis," in *Meanings for Manhood: Constructions of Masculinity in Victorian America*, ed. Mark C. Carnes and Clyde Griffen (Chicago: University of Chicago Press, 1990), 188–9.
65 See, for example, "Revivals in the Churches," *Christian Guardian*, 17 February 1875.
66 Mrs. Jones' Mutual Improvement Class 1872–1878, 2 vols., OA.
67 Richard Bushman, *The Refinement of America: Persons, Houses, Cities* (New York: Vintage, 1993), 313–52.
68 For Punshon's impact on Canadians, see Frederic W. Macdonald, *The Life of Morley Punshon* (London: Hodder & Stoughton, 1887), ch. 11–15.
69 Toronto Metropolitan Church, First Annual Report of the McGill Square Association 1870, UCA.
70 Bushman, *Refinement of America*, 352.
71 For an example of congregations differentiating themselves by socio-economic status, see Doris O'Dell, "The Class Character of Church Participation in Late Nineteenth-Century Belleville, Ontario" (Ph.D. diss., Queen's University, 1990).
72 Pearson, *Recollections and Records*, 252.
73 David G. Burley, *A Particular Condition in Life: Self-Employment and Social Mobility in Mid-Victorian Brantford* (Montreal and Kingston: McGill-Queen's University Press, 1994), 76–8; Michael B. Katz, *The People of Hamilton, Canada West: Family and Class in a Mid-Nineteenth-Century City* (Cambridge: Harvard University Press, 1975), 27–8, 355; Acheson, "Problem of Methodist Identity," 122, 32n.
74 Gordon Darroch and Lee Soltow, *Property and Inequality in Victorian Ontario: Structural Patterns and Cultural Communities in the 1871 Census* (Toronto: University of Toronto Press, 1994), 97.
75 "Letter from Grimsby Camp Grounds," *Brantford Daily Expositor*, 30 August 1875.
76 "Correspondence," ibid., 1 September 1875.
77 Steven D. Cooley, "Applying the Vagueness of Language: Poetic Strategies and Campmeeting Piety in the Mid-Nineteenth Century," *Church History* 63,2 (1994): 578.

CHAPTER SIX

1 *Christian Guardian*, 22 October 1919, 17. Much of the campaign publicity appeared in all the regional papers. *The Wesleyan*, for example, carried an identical item on the same date.
2 *Christian Guardian*, 2 June 1920.
3 William Bridges, *Managing Transitions: Making the Most of Change* (Reading, MA: Addison-Wesley, 1991), 35–7.
4 I have explored the changing understanding of the conversion experience along with other characteristic aspects of Methodist piety in *Serving the Present Age*.
5 Salem Goldworth Bland fonds, 86.037, file 711a, "After Sixty Years," 15 September 1940, United Church of Canada, Victoria University Archives [hereafter UCA], 4.
6 Nathan O. Hatch, "The Puzzle of American Methodism," *Church History* 63,2 (1994): 188.
7 Michael Bliss, *Northern Enterprise: Five Centuries of Canadian Business* (Toronto: McClelland & Stewart, 1987), 335–42.
8 Craig Dykstra and James Hudnut-Beumler, "The National Organizational Structures of Protestant Denominations: An Invitation to a Conversation," in *The Organizational Revolution: Presbyterians and American Denominationalism*, ed. Milton Coalter, John M. Mulder, and Louis Weeks (Louisville: Westminster-John Knox Press, 1992), argue that this metaphor fits the mainstream Protestant denominations until the 1960s when the organizational characteristics of the "regulatory agency" come into play.
9 Ibid., 314.
10 Ibid., 316–18.
11 See John Thomas, "'A Pure and Popular Character': Case Studies in the Development of the Methodist 'Organizational' Church, 1884–1925" (Ph.D. diss., York University, 1991), for case studies of the leaders who helped to set Canadian Methodism on a new organizational course. The rise of what he describes as the "institutional" church is another term for the incorporation described by Dykstra and Hudnut-Beumler. Also see Wuthnow, *Restructuring of American Religion*, 20–9; and William McGuire King, "Denominational Modernization and Religious Identity: The Case of the Methodist Episcopal Church," *Methodist History* 20 (1982). The incompatibility of corporate organization and Methodist piety has been noted by A. Gregory Schneider, *The Way of the Cross Leads Home: The Domestication of American Methodism* (Bloomington and Indianapolis: University of Indiana Press, 1993), 196–208.
12 Peter F. Drucker, "The Age of Social Transformation," *Atlantic Monthly*, November 1994, 55–6.

13 Ibid., 59. For an indication of the impact of these changes in the Canadian labour force, see Kenneth Buckley, "Capital Formation in Canada, 1896–1930," in *Approaches to Canadian Economic History*, ed. W.T. Easterbrook and M.H. Watkins (Ottawa: Carleton University Press, 1986), esp. 178–9.
14 Ibid., 74.
15 "The Coming Convention," editorial, *Pioneer*, 20 January 1903, 2.
16 A.D. Weeks, "Letter to the Editor," ibid., 11 July 1902, 3.
17 "Church vs. Bar-room," editorial, ibid., 16 November 1906, 2. See also "The Church and Temperance," editorial, ibid., 11 January 1907, 2.
18 "The Boys and Girls," editorial, ibid., 8 November 1907, 2.
19 A similar move towards a more bureaucratic approach to Christian education is evident. See Lucille Marr, "Hierarchy, Gender and the Goals of the Religious Educators in the Canadian Presbyterian, Methodist and United Churches, 1919–39," *Studies in Religion* 20 (1991).
20 Samuel Dwight Chown fonds, 86.019C, box 11, file 287, "Anniversary Address, Quebec Branch Dominion Alliance," 26 February 1903, UCA, 7.
21 "The Methodist National Campaign," *Journal of the Methodist General Conference* [1922], 297. The report provides a good comparison of the goals and "spiritual objectives," and, the actual statistics for 1920 (295–301), indicating that the campaign fell far short.
22 For example, at least 12 of the 16 secretaries listed in the United Church *Yearbook* for 1927 had committee experience with the Inter-Church movement, generally chairing a committee in the same area of responsibility. Of the 4 who did not, 1 was the Women's Missionary Society secretary.
23 Methodists, Presbyterians, and Anglicans initially were allowed to send twenty representatives each; Congregationalists fifteen, and Baptists ten. No smaller denominations were represented on the Advisory Council.
24 National Survey Commission fonds, 78.116C, box 1, file 4, "Report," 27 May 1921, UCA, 1. (All subsequent references to conference meetings come from this collection unless noted.) The executive committee gave instructions that Bryce "should, at a time suiting his convenience, visit the Inter-Church Headquarters in the United States and consider their methods of survey" in order to prepare for his task. Minutes of the Methodist National Executive, 21 May 1920.
25 Bay of Quinte Rural Conference meeting (ministers), 17 November 1920, 90. Some meetings were organized for ministers, others for lay men, women, youth, etc. Hereafter, the notes will indicate the composition.
26 London meeting (ministers), 3 November 1920, 24.
27 London meeting (lay men), 1 November 1920, 4.
28 Ibid.
29 Bay of Quinte Rural Conference (lay men and women), 19 November 1920, 101.

30 Ibid.
31 London meeting (women), 4 November 1920, 30.
32 Ibid.
33 Montreal meeting (ministers), 30 November 1920, 145.
34 Ibid., 149.
35 Bay of Quinte Rural Conference (lay men and women), 19 November 1920, 101.
36 London meeting, (lay men), 5 November 1920, 33.
37 Woodstock Rural Conference (ministers), 11 and 12 November 1920, 56.
38 Bay of Quinte Rural Conference (ministers), 17 November 1920, 90.
39 London meeting (ministers), 3 November 1920, 23; Bay of Quinte Rural Conference (lay men and women), 17 November 1920, 99. At the Montreal meeting (ministers, 30 November 1920, 145) Rose was reported as remarking that the YMCA was "doing a lot of work which is being accepted as a substitute for the spiritual work."
40 Stratford Rural Conference (lay men and women), 25 November 1920, 122-3; Chatham Rural Conference, 6 December 1920, 170-1.
41 Woodstock Rural Conference (ministers), 11 and 12 November 1920, 57.
42 London meeting (ministers), 3 November 1920, 24.
43 Montreal meeting (ministers), 30 November 1920, 145-8.
44 Chatham Rural Conference, 6 December 1920, 162.
45 London meeting (lay men), 1 November 1920, 1.
46 Montreal meeting (lay men), 137; see also Bay of Quinte Rural Conference (lay men and women), 19 November 1920, 97.
47 Bay of Quinte Rural Conference (men and women), 19 November 1920, 97.
48 Stratford Rural Conference (men and women), 25 November 1920, 109.
49 London meeting (young people), 2 November 1920, 18.
50 Woodstock Rural Conference (ministers), 11 and 12 November 1920, 45.
51 "Report," 7-8.
52 Ibid., 32. The other notable silence in the report was "women's work."
53 While multiple charges sharing one minister was recognized as a serious problem and closing congregations conceded as a solution, little time was spent discussing the implications. Union with the Presbyterians and Congregationalists (which eventually provided the occasion for consolidation) was mentioned so rarely that one wonders how seriously these local congregations took the proposal – and how well their leaders were preparing them for yet another transition.
54 Bay of Quinte Rural Conference, 17 November 1920, 76. Ironically, the results of the salary review, which he lauded, had come as part of an effort to encourage weekly giving of a pledged amount – a method of congregational fundraising that found only lukewarm support in rural areas. The weekly offering envelopes had not been successful, suggested

one minister, because of "the different methods in which the farmer handles his money. The farmer does not want to pay 25¢ or 50¢ a week – but would rather pay quarterly or annually in one lump sum." Monthly support from some farmers corresponded with the arrival of the milk cheque. The Survey Commission, on the other hand, enthusiastically recommended weekly giving. See "Report," 21–2.

55 The dissatisfaction with amalgamation of small charges was a problem in many areas after church union. See Mann, *Sect, Cult and Church*, 94–112. New religious movements grew in rural areas in part because of a willingness to be served by preachers who earned a portion of their living by farming, teaching, or other part-time employment. For an interesting comparison of the rejection of ecumenism in rural areas of the United States, see Roger Finke and Rodney Stark, *The Churching of America: Winners and Losers in Our Religious Economy* (New Brunswick: Rutgers University Press, 1992), 202–18. The ecumenical vision and reform agenda of the Federal Council of Churches presents another opportunity to explore parallels with the church union and social gospel movements in Canada. See Robert T. Handy, "Reflections on the Federal Council of Churches, the United Church of Canada, and the Social Gospel in the 1930s" (paper presented at a conference on Christianizing the Social Order, Emmanuel College, University of Toronto, March 1992); and Robert Schneider, "Voice of Many Waters: Church Federation in the Twentieth Century," in *Between the Times: The Travail of the Protestant Establishment in America, 1900–1960*, ed. William R. Hutchison (Cambridge: Harvard University Press, 1989).

56 London meeting (lay men), 5 November 1920, 32. Whether this agenda was as much an expression of the social gospel as Allen suggests in *Social Passion* is open to question. For example, he implies that Charles Stelzle was selected as national director of the Methodist National Campaign because of his social gospel credentials (138). It is far more likely that he was selected because he was by that time operating a successful church advertising agency – on Madison Avenue! See Susan Curtis, *A Consuming Faith: The Social Gospel and Modern American Culture* (Baltimore: Johns Hopkins University Press, 1991), 254–65. Stelzle proved to be a disappointment; the minutes of the secretarial cabinet of 16 December 1919 raised questions about his supervision, regretting that "he has given so little time to the work of the Campaign in Canada" (Methodist National Campaign fonds, 78.121C, box 1, file 1, UCA). As Curtis notes, the Social Service Council is an interesting case to consider; operating outside the emerging network of denominational executives, it found it increasingly difficult to arrange for funding through the Inter-Church Advisory Council (239–49).

57 Methodist National Survey, London meeting (lay men), 5 November 1920, 32.

58 Methodist National Campaign fonds, minutes of the National Executive Committee, 78–121C, box 1, file 1; Women's Missionary Society to the Executive Committee, 26 February 1920, UCA.
59 Ibid., box 4, file 2, Minutes of the Executive Committee, 6 May 1920, UCA.
60 For a summary of the final disbursements, see the Joint Committee on Church Union, "The Methodist National Campaign," in *First General Council of the United Church of Canada* (1925): 150–1; Methodist National Campaign fonds; and Financial Records, file 6, "Methodist National Campaign Daily Balance Sheet," 20 January 1920, UCA.
61 C.E. Silcox, *Church Union in Canada: Its Causes and Consequence* (New York: Institute of Social and Religious Research, 1933), 88.

CHAPTER SEVEN

The author acknowledges with gratitude the financial assistance of the School of Graduate Studies, Queen's University at Kingston; the Social Sciences and Humanities Research Council of Canada, and the Pew Charitable Trusts.

1 David Wilson, "Minister Wins Law Suit against United Church," *United Church Observer*, August 1988, 9.
2 Ibid.
3 See for example Marshall, *Secularizing the Faith*, 181–6; and Stackhouse, *Canadian Evangelicalism*, 184. For a different take on the evangelical roots of the United Church, see John Webster Grant, "The United Church and Its Heritage in Evangelism," *Touchstone* 1,3 (October 1983), and "Unauthoritative Reflections on the United Church's History," *Touchstone* 12,1 (January 1994).
4 Stackhouse, *Canadian Evangelicalism*, 184–5.
5 Gauvreau, *Evangelical Century*, 5.
6 William R. Hutchison, ed., *Between the Times: The Travail of the Protestant Establishment in America, 1900–1960* (Cambridge: Cambridge University Press, 1989), viii.
7 Bebbington, *Evangelicalism*, 212.
8 George Campbell Pidgeon Papers, box 32, file 523, "The New Birth," United Church of Canada Central Archives [hereafter UCCA].
9 For example, Pidgeon Papers, box 41, file 1179, "The Essence of Christianity"; box 41, file 1116, "Risen With Christ or, The Symbolism of Christ's Death and Resurrection in Christian Experience"; box 44, file 1404, "The Spiritual Background and Ideal of the United Church of Canada," UCCA.
10 Marshall, *Secularizing the Faith*, 150.
11 Pidgeon Papers, box 38, file 943, "Christianity in Life's Relationships," UCCA.

12 Ibid., box 39, file 996, "The Spiritual and the Practical in the Church's Life," UCCA, 1.
13 Ibid.
14 Ibid., 14–15.
15 See for example Allen, *Social Passion*; Airhart, *Serving the Present Age*; Van Die, *An Evangelical Mind*.
16 T. Albert Moore, "The Mission of the Church in Personal Evangelism and Social Service," *New Outlook* 1,1 (1925): 23.
17 See Grant, *Church in the Canadian Era*, ch. 7.
18 David R. Elliot, "Hugh Wesley Dobson (1879–1956): Regenerator of Society," *Canadian Methodist Historical Society Papers*, vol. 9 (1991–92) (Toronto, 1993), 37.
19 Hugh Wesley Dobson Papers, box B18b, file Mc(2)B, letter to D.N. McLachlan, 16 February 1931, United Church of Canada, British Columbia Conference Archives [hereafter UCBCA].
20 Hugh W. Dobson in "Annual Reports of Secretaries," United Church of Canada Board of Evangelism and Social Service [hereafter UCC-BESS], *Annual Report 1930*, 14.
21 Ibid., *Annual Report 1932*, 19.
22 Dobson Papers, box 18B, file Mc(2)B, letter to D.N. McLachlan, 5 February 1932, UCBCA. See Marshall, *Secularizing the Faith*, 227.
23 Marshall, *Secularizing the Faith*, 207.
24 Dobson Papers, box B4, file L, UCBCA, handwritten report to the General Board of Evangelism and Social Service, 1925.
25 Ibid. From a document entitled "For the General Board of Evangelism and Social Service." A note written on the original document indicates that this letter was written in 1923.
26 Marshall, *Secularizing the Faith*, 225–6.
27 For a clear argument that the Oxford Group Movement represented an evangelical revival that tapped into the mainstream belief in conversionism, see "The United Church and the Revival of Personal Religion," in Christie and Gauvreau, *"A Full-Orbed Christianity."*
28 Wright, "The Canadian Protestant Tradition 1914–1945," in Rawlyk, ed., *Canadian Protestant Experience*, 176.
29 *The Statement on Evangelism* (Toronto: The Board of Evangelism and Social Service of the United Church of Canada, n.d.).
30 Ibid., 2, 8. See Robert G. Stewart, "Radiant Smiles in the Dirty Thirties: History and Ideology of the Oxford Group Movement in Canada, 1932–1936" (M.Div. thesis, Vancouver School of Theology, 1974).
31 *The Statement on Evangelism*, 7–8.
32 G.C. Pidgeon, "The Challenge of Jesus to Canadian Life," *The Western Recorder* 12,2 (August 1936): 1. See also, in the same issue, Hugh Dobson, "Evangelism and Social Service," 4.

33 Dobson Papers, box B28, file M, letter, Dobson to J.R. Mutchmor, 29 December 1938, UCBCA.
34 See Airhart, *Serving the Present Age*.
35 R.B.Y. Scott and Gregory Vlastos, eds., *Towards the Christian Revolution* (1936; reprint, Kingston: Ronald P. Frye & Company, 1989).
36 Grant, "Unauthoritative Reflections," 9.
37 Dobson Papers, box B22, file P4, letter, Dobson to Rev. Harry Heathfield, 27 June 1940, UCBCA.
38 *Church, Nation and World Order: A Report of the Commission on Church, Nation and World Order, Presented to the Eleventh General Council* (Toronto: The United Church of Canada Board of Evangelism and Social Service, 1944), 12.
39 "A Programme for the United Church," editorial, *Quebec Chronicle Telegraph*, 9 May 1944, in Church, Nation and World Order Collection, box 2, file 17, UCCA.
40 Dobson Papers, box B6, file F, "The Task of the Church," from the *Vancouver Sun*, 15 September 1945, UCBCA. Gordon Alfred Sisco Papers, box 1, file 6, "Specific Tasks of the Crusade," UCCA.
41 Dobson Papers, box B33, file C(1), "Facing the Post War Years, The Moderator of the United Church of Canada Calls Ministers and People to a New Crusade for Christ and His Kingdom," UCBCA.
42 Ibid., box B6, file F, "10,000 Attend Opening of 'Crusade For Christ' Rally," from the *Vancouver Sun*, 17 September 1945.
43 Wuthnow, *Restructuring of American Religion*, 16, 138–45.
44 George W. Birtch, "Evangelizing Evangelism," in UCC-BESS, *Annual Report 1959*, 11–12.
45 Wuthnow, *Restructuring of American Religion*, 60–1; James R. Mutchmor, *Mutchmor: The Memoirs of James Ralph Mutchmor* (Toronto: Ryerson Press, 1965), 107–19.
46 Mutchmor, *Memoirs*, 116.
47 Ibid., 117. Charles Templeton, *Charles Templeton: An Anecdotal Memoir* (Toronto: McClelland & Stewart, 1983), 84–90.
48 Mutchmor, *Memoirs*, 115.
49 E.L. Homewood, "Billy Graham and Evangelism," *United Church Observer*, 15 October 1963, 13.
50 Ibid., 13–14.
51 See letters to the editor concerning the Church's relationship with Billy Graham in *United Church Observer*, 15 November 1963, 2; 1 December 1963, 6; 15 December 1963, 2.
52 Mutchmor, *Memoirs*, 117–18.
53 Grant, "Unauthoritative Reflections," 6–7.
54 *Small Voice* was the official publication of the Renewal Fellowship. Vol. 1, no. 1 appeared in spring 1967.

55 W. Clarke MacDonald, "Total Evangelism – Now," UCC-BESS, *Annual Report 1971*, 7.
56 Ibid., 11. The emphasis is MacDonald's.
57 Rawlyk, *"Is Jesus Your Personal Saviour,"* 86.
58 Ibid., 99.
59 Ibid., 129.
60 Ibid., 114.

CHAPTER EIGHT

1 For example, see Klempa, ed., *The Burning Bush*.
2 Goldwin French, "The Evangelical Creed in Canada," in *The Shield of Achilles: Aspects of Canada in the Victorian Age*, ed. W.L. Morton (Toronto: McClelland & Stewart, 1968). See also Masters, *Protestant Church Colleges*.
3 See Gauvreau, *Evangelical Century*; Allen, *Social Passion*; McKillop, *A Disciplined Intelligence*; Brian Fraser, *The Social Uplifters: Presbyterian Progressives and the Social Gospel in Canada, 1975–1915* (Waterloo: Wilfrid Laurier University Press, 1988); Klempa, "History of Presbyterian Theology in Canada to 1875," in Klempa, ed., *The Burning Bush*.
4 Gauvreau, *Evangelical Century*, 2–12, 20–3, 32–45, 58–66, 71–83, 91–104, 139–60. See also Bebbington, "Evangelicalism in Modern Britain and America," in Rawlyk and Noll, eds., *Amazing Grace*, 183–92.
5 R. Cook, *The Regenerators*; Marshall, *Secularizing the Faith*.
6 Marshall, *Secularizing the Faith*, 4–10, 21–3, 25–40, 57–64.
7 Ibid., 43–4, 80–3, 104–6; Gauvreau, *Evangelical Century*, 155–60.
8 Mack, "George Grant."
9 Bebbington, *Evangelicalism*, esp. ch. 2.
10 Mack, "George Grant," 50–69, 70–89.
11 Ibid., 16–18, 46–9, 65, 114, 121–2, 191–3.
12 Ibid., 135–6; also 3–18, 38, 52, 127, 192. See also his "Of Canadian Presbyterians and Guardian Angels," in Rawlyk and Noll, eds., *Amazing Grace*.
13 Mack, "George Grant," 177, 195, 206–7; 135–8, 142–8, 160–5.
14 Gauvreau, *Evangelical Century*, 9–10. Most of Marshall's evidence in *Secularizing the Faith*, 8–9, comes from Methodism: he refers to only a handful, mostly of later (1870s) Presbyterians, and he does not give much treatment or credit to the influence of Secessionists, Carlyle, Luther, or revivals in Grant's career.
15 Reid, "Jesus Only."
16 See John S. Moir, "Who Pays the Piper," in Klempa, ed., *The Burning Bush*; and *Enduring Witness*; Moir with Elizabeth McDougall, *Selected Correspondence of the Glasgow Colonial Society* (Toronto: Champlain

Society, 1994); Moir, "To Fertilise the Wilderness," *Canadian Society of Presbyterian History* [hereafter CSPH], *Papers*, 1992. Also see his "The Quay of Greenock," *Scottish Tradition* 5 (1975). On Cape Breton, see Laurie Stanley, *The Well-Watered Garden* (Sydney: University College of Cape Breton Press, 1983).

17 Moir, *Enduring Witness*, 144.
18 Vaudry, *Free Church*. On the prominent role of Free Churchmen in Canada and the cause of black rights, see Allen Stouffer, *The Light of Nature and the Law of God* (Montreal and Kingston: McGill-Queen's University Press, 1992). See also Vaudry, "Peter Brown."
19 Vaudry, *Free Church*, 17–18, 43–4, 70–7.
20 See Iain Maciver, "The Evangelical Party and the Eldership in the General Assembly," *Records of the Scottish Church History Society* 20,1 (1978).
21 Stanley, *Well-Watered Garden*, esp. ch. 7. Another account of a similar celebration in the Highlander-dominated Zorra settlement can be found in C.W. Gordon, *Life of James Robertson* (Toronto: Westminster, 1908), ch. 3.
22 Leigh Eric Schmidt, *Holy Fairs: Scottish Communions and American Revivals in the Early Modern Period* (Princeton: Princeton University Press, 1989); and his "Time, Celebration and the Christian Year," in Noll, Bebbington, and Rawlyk, eds., *Evangelicalism: Comparative Studies*.
23 See Rawlyk, *Canada Fire*, ch. 11; and John Webster Grant, "Brands from the Blazing Heather: Canadian Religious Revival in the Highland Tradition," CSPH, *Papers*, 1991. See also "Burning Bushes: Flames of Revival in the Nineteenth Century Canadian Presbyterianism," *Canadian Society of Church History*, *Papers*, 1991.
24 Robert Gordon, "The Attitude of the Clergy to Highland Settlers in Upper Canada," CSPH, *Papers*, 1993.
25 Harry John Bridgman, "Three Scots Presbyterians in Upper Canada" (Ph.D. diss., Queen's University, 1978). For a slightly different emphasis, see Peter Russell, "Church of Scotland Clergy in Upper Canada," *Ontario History* 73,2 (June 1981).
26 Stewart Gill, "A Scottish Divine on the Frontier of Upper Canada" (Ph.D. diss., University of Guelph, 1984).
27 Royce MacGillivray and Ewan Ross, *A History of Glengarry* (Belleville: Mika, 1979); and Donald MacMillan, *The Kirk in Glengarry* (Private, 1984). See also *Wee Kirks and Stately Steeples: A History of the Presbytery of Hamilton, Presbyterian Church in Canada, 1800–1990*, ed. Thomas Melville Bailey (Burlington: Eagle Press, 1990).
28 Ralph Connor (C.W. Gordon), *The Man From Glengarry* (McClelland & Stewart, 1963), 70; MacMillan, *The Kirk in Glengarry*, 389–94, 453.
29 For an early foray into kirk session discipline, see Crerar, "Church and Community."

30 For example, see Alexander Hill, *The Practice of the Several Judicatories of the Church of Scotland* (Edinburgh: J. Waugh, 1830); David King, *The Ruling Eldership of the Christian Church* (Edinburgh: Oliphaunt 1846); J. Lorimer, *The Eldership of the Church of Scotland* (Glasgow: Collins, 1842). For a Belfast evangelical version that was transmitted to Canada, see *The Canadian Christian Examiner and Presbyterian Magazine* II (January/February, 1839), published in Niagara, Upper Canada. On the new type of parishioner zeal and democratic tensions emerging from the revivals in the Highlands, and brought to the New World, see Stanley, *Well-Watered Garden*, ch. 1 and 7.

31 Maciver, "The Evangelical Party and the Eldership," 12–13.

32 First Presbyterian Church, Perth, Upper Canada, Session Minutes, 1817–1857 (author's copy). In 1836, when the congregation entered the Church of Scotland, its constitution forbade members "to go to law" against each other without first submitting their dispute to session arbitration. For other very early Secessionist disciplinary examples, see Scarborough Presbyterian (Secessionist) Church, Extracts of Session Minutes, United Church Archives, Toronto, 1818ff. (All subsequent church minutes mentioned are held at this archives unless noted.)

33 First Presbyterian Church, Perth, Upper Canada, Session Minutes, 1817–1857, 4 January, 1 February, 17 December 1818; also 1 September 1833, 1 January 1836.

34 In 1836, when a woman was suspended for quarrelling and violent acts against her family, and attempted suicide, her emotional state was so unstable that a few minutes before the meeting closed the husband returned and "said that his wife refused to go home with him, and was afraid she might be driven to extremity of despair – but thought that she would be pacified, and would live quietly with him, if she knew that he was punished as well as her. He therefore requested the Session to suspend him as well as her in the meantime. This, in the painful circumstances of the case, was agreed to." Almonte United Church, "Auld Kirk," Ramsay, Minutes of Session, 1834–1867, 16 December 1836 (in possession of local congregation). See also, Minutes of the Synod of the Presbyterian Church of Canada in Connection with the Church of Scotland, 1843, 8–17; Presbytery of Bathurst Minutes, January–June 1843. See also, Beckwith-Franktown-Black's Corners Presbyterian Churches, Minutes of Session, 1844–1867, whose activity has been cited by Peter Ward, *Courtship, Love and Marriage in Nineteenth-Century English Canada* (Montreal and Kingston: McGill-Queen's University Press, 1990), 26–7. For a more generous assessment of the pastoral nature of discipline, see Allan Farris, "Mark Young Stark: Pioneer Missionary Statesmen," in *The Tide of Time: Historical Essays by the Late Allan L. Farris*, ed. John S. Moir (Toronto: Knox College, 1978), 90–1.

35 Perth United Church, Free Church, Minutes of Session, 1844–1867.
36 Canada Presbyterian Church, *Minutes of Synod*, 1862, (Toronto: various publishers, 1862). Osgoode Presbyterian Church, Session Minutes, October 1854 to 31 May 1862, Presbyterian Church in Canada Archives, Toronto. Significantly, the record of this uprising was heavily censored by an Ottawa Presbytery delegation in 1862, which simply glued pages of the session book together and razored out offensive paragraphs.
37 The Glengarry elders bore themselves much as did those of the Zorra Church at Embro, where elders took turns sitting in the balcony to watch out for any levity among the youth during service. London Conference, Presbyterian Church of Embro (also known as Zorra), Minutes of Session, 14 July 1851, 13 December 1852. Unlike Gordon's kirk, however, the Zorra session never permitted anything but sung Psalms to adorn their worship.
38 Connor, *The Man From Glengarry*; MacMillan, *The Kirk in Glengarry*, 177–86.
39 Van Die, "Revivalism, Gender and Community" and "Recovering Religious Experience." See also Ruth Compton Brouwer, *New Women for God: Canadian Presbyterian Women and India Missions, 1876–1914* (Toronto: University of Toronto Press, 1990).
40 Zorra Presbyterian Church, Session Minutes, 1–16 July; November 1871. On the appeal of the Brethren to Presbyterians, see Westfall, *Two Worlds*, 167–9, 175.
41 William Bell Papers, Journals, 2 (1825), Queen's University Archives, 175.

CHAPTER NINE

1 G.M. Grant, "The Religious Condition of Canada," *Christianity Practically Applied: The Discussions of the International Christian Conference, held in Chicago, October, 1893* (New York: The Baker and Taylor Co., 1894).
2 See Brian Fraser, *The Social Uplifters: Presbyterian Progressives and the Social Gospel in Canada, 1875–1915* (Waterloo: Wilfrid Laurier Press, 1988), 176.
3 Grant Papers, vol. 31, J.L. Grant to G.M. Grant, 22 November 1893, Public Archives of Canada [hereafter PAC].
4 Ibid., vol. 2, Charles Macdonald to G.M. Grant [1878], 406, PAC.
5 Ibid., vol. 32, A. Pollock to G.M. Grant, 11 January 1895, PAC.
6 William MacLaren, *Sixty Year Retrospect* (Toronto: Armac Press, 1907), 9.
7 Ibid., 13.
8 K. Clifford, *The Resistance to Church Union* (Vancouver: University of British Columbia Press, 1985), 40.

9 Cited in Gordon Harland, "John Mark King: First Principal of Manitoba College," in *Prairie Spirit*, ed. Dennis Butcher et al. (Winnipeg: University of Manitoba Press, 1985), 182.
10 Clifford, *Resistance to Church Union*, 16.
11 *Acts and Proceedings of the General Assembly, Presbyterian Church in Canada* [hereafter A&P] (1911), 266.
12 A&P (1912), 337–8; see Gandier Papers, box 2, C.W. Gordon to Gandier, 8 August 1910, and box 2, reply to Gordon's letter, n.d., United Church of Canada Archives; Daniel Strachan, "That Interview with Ralph Connor," 19 March 1914, 359.
13 B.J. Fraser, *Church, College and Clergy: A History of Theological Education at Knox College, Toronto, 1844–1994* (Montreal and Kingston: McGill-Queen's University Press, 1995), 12.
14 Fraser, *Social Uplifters*, 175.
15 J.A. Macdonald, "The Christianization of Our Civilization," *Canada's Missionary Congress* (Toronto, 1909), 119, cited in Moir, *Enduring Witness*, 184.
16 Rosalind Goforth, *Goforth of China* (Toronto: McClelland & Stewart, 1937), 205.
17 In Gordon's case, the impact was also intensely personal. During his postgraduate year in Scotland in 1887–8, Gordon attended Drummond's evangelistic meeting for students in Edinburgh. His diary is full of references to Drummond's Sunday evening talks. In a twelve-page eulogy he recalls his first "vision of Henry Drummond. 'Vision' is the word, for even then as I looked at him and listened to him, there was something so rare, so unique, that on coming away I had the feeling of having been in the presence of an atmosphere not quite of our common world, and now seen through this midst of years, the face and form of the speaker of that evening glow with the luminous radiance of a vision ... Tall, slight, full of grace and perfectly at ease he stood before the audience looking straight and steady into us out of his large, clear blue eyes ... His manner was frank, manly, natural, and perfectly respectful. Naturalness was the key note of Drummond's religion. You felt he could say what he was saying on that Sabbath evening ... just as forcibly in the cold light of next Monday morning ... Henry Drummond's speaking gave you thought, but in a series of visions. It was the most luminous and light giving speaking I ever listened to." Gordon also recalled, walking on the mountains around Banff, "we paced up and down while he braced me with his brave words and drew me with his sympathetic silence. Drummond could say more with his silence than most men with speech." See the opening description of Barry Dunbar in *Sky Pilot in No Man's Land* (New York: Grosset and Dunlap, 1919), 9–11.

18 C.W. Gordon Papers, "Christianity, as presented by the Church as a Religious System ...," Elizabeth Dafoe Library Archives, University of Manitoba, 2.
19 G.M. Grant, "The Marvels of Scientific Logic," *Rose Belford's Canadian Monthly and National Review* 5 (October 1880). See also Grant, "The Relations of Religion to Secular Life," in *Presbyterian Alliance: Report of the Second General Council of the Presbyterian Alliance ...*, ed. John B. Dales and R.M. Patterson (Philadelphia: Presbyterian Journal Company and J.C. McCurdy, 1880), 95.
20 "You will never be able to gauge the reality of spiritual things by the test of the senses, by the yard-stick, the crucible, or the balance. The instruments that faith uses, the evidence that it relies upon, the victories that it gains, have nothing in common with such demonstrations." Grant Papers, Grant to Agnes Maule Machar, 8 November 1876, Queen's University Archives [hereafter QUA].
21 Fraser, *Church, College and Clergy*, 136.
22 James G. Greenlee, *Sir Robert Falconer* (Toronto: University of Toronto Press, 1988), 99, 119.
23 President Falconer worked closely with J.G. Shearer in the establishment of the University of Toronto's Department of Social Work in 1914.
24 See Gordon's address in *Pre-Assembly Congress of the Presbyterian Church in Canada* (Toronto: Presbyterian Church in Canada, [1913]), 85–94.
25 Adam Shortt Papers, box 11, diary entry for Sunday, 17 May 1908, QUA.
26 O.D. Skelton, "The Problem of the City," in *Social Service: A Book for Young Canadians*, ed. W.R. McIntosh (Toronto, 1911), 42.
27 See my "Ralph Connor and the Progressive Vision."
28 Greenlee, *Sir Robert Falconer*, 214.
29 W. Stanford Reid, "The Quebec Trio W.D., A.S., A.D., Reid," in *Called to Witness*, ed. W.S. Reid (Toronto: Committee on History, Presbyterian Church of Canada, 1980).
30 *A&P* (1925), 128.
31 *A&P* (1926), 37. See Stuart C. Parker, *Yet Not Consumed* (Toronto: n.p., 1946), 190ff.
32 Ephraim Scott, *"Church Union" and the Presbyterian Church in Canada* (Montreal, 1928), 132.
33 W.W. Bryden, *Why I Am a Presbyterian* (Toronto: n.p., 1934), 64.
34 Ibid., 80.
35 Ibid., 81.
36 Ibid., 165.
37 See James Smart, "The Evangelist as Theologian," in W.W. Bryden, *Separated unto the Gospel* (Toronto: Burns and MacEachern, 1956); Joseph

C. McLelland, "Walter Bryden: 'By Circumstance and God,'" in *Called to Witness*, ed. W.S. Reid (n.p., 1980); Vissers, "Recovering the Reformation Conception of Revelation," in Klempa, ed., *The Burning Bush*.

38 S. Vernon McCasland, review of *The Christian's Knowledge of God*, in *The Journal of Bible and Religion* (August 1941), 179–80; D.M. MacKinnon, *Scottish Journal of Theology* 2 (1949): 210.

39 Moir, *Enduring Witness*, 238.

40 *A&P* (1936), 104.

41 G.M. Grant, "The Outlook of the Twentieth Century in Theology," *The American Journal of Theology* 6 (January 1902).

42 Fraser, *Church, College and Clergy*, 184–6.

43 Moir, *Enduring Witness*, 2nd ed., 271, 279, 284–5.

44 G.M. Grant, *Ocean to Ocean* (Toronto: Joseph Campbell and Son, 1873), 366.

45 Bryden, *Why I Am a Presbyterian*, 118.

CHAPTER TEN

The author would like to thank David Priestley and George Rawlyk for their comments on earlier versions of this paper.

1 *Huron Synod Journal, 1863*, quoted in A.H. Crowfoot, *This Dreamer: Life of Isaac Hellmuth, Second Bishop of Huron* (Vancouver: Copp Clark, 1963), 26.

2 H.E. Turner, "Isaac Hellmuth," *Dictionary of Canadian Biography* [hereafter DCB], 13: 462; Crowfoot, *This Dreamer*, 26–32.

3 J.D. Bollen, "English Christianity and the Australian Colonies, 1788–1860," *Journal of Ecclesiastical History* 28,4 (October 1977): 385.

4 D.H. Akenson, *The Irish in Ontario: A Study in Rural History* (Montreal and Kingston: McGill-Queen's University Press, 1984), 264.

5 This was applied to extraparliamentary politics in the reign of George III but is, it seems, capable of wider application. John Brewer, *Party Ideology and Popular Politics at the Accession of George III* (Cambridge: Cambridge University Press, 1976).

6 Philip Carrington, *The Anglican Church in Canada* (Toronto: Collins, 1963), 13.

7 T.R. Millman, "Beginnings of the Synodical Movement in Colonial Anglican Churches with Special Reference to Canada," *Journal of the Canadian Church Historical Society* [hereafter JCCHS] 21 (1979): 14.

8 A.B. McKillop's recent study of the university in Ontario, *Matters of Mind: The University in Ontario 1791–1951* (Toronto: University of Toronto Press, 1994), 36, completely misunderstands the evangelical tradition within Anglicanism by identifying Huron College as a "Broad Church" alternative to Trinity College, Toronto. One of the notable exceptions to

this neglect of Anglican evangelicals was found in the work of D.C. Masters, *The Rise of Toronto 1850–1890* (Toronto: University of Toronto Press, 1947), and "Anglican Evangelicals in Toronto, 1870–1900," *JCCHS* 20 (1978). Masters's personal commitments and his espousal of "metropolitanism" allowed him to see beyond the characterization of evangelicalism as sectarian, common to the work of S.D. Clark and Fred Landon, and to see it as a subject of importance in its own right. On the destructive effects of S.D. Clark's church-sect model to the study of Canadian evangelicalism, see Ian Rennie's comments, *Canadian Evangelical Review* 10 (Spring 1995): 6. Curtis Fahey's *In His Name: The Anglican Experience in Upper Canada, 1791–1854* (Ottawa: Carleton University Press, 1991) recognizes many of the divisions between evangelicals and high churchmen, but insists on referring to evangelicals as "low churchmen." Intellectual and cultural historians tend to perpetuate this consensus paradigm by stressing *longue durée* philosophical continuities among evangelicals or by insisting on the emergence of a unitary Protestant culture in Ontario. See Gauvreau, *Evangelical Century*; Westfall, *Two Worlds*.

9 Phillip Buckner, "Whatever Happened to the British Empire," *Journal of the Canadian Historical Association*, New Series, vol. 4, 1993.

10 Quoted in Donald C. Masters and Marjorie W. Masters, *Ten Rings on the Oak: 1947–1856 Mountain-Nicolls Family Story* (Lennoxville: Bishop's University, 1987), 99.

11 Isaac Hellmuth, *A Reply to a Letter of the Right Rev. The Lord Bishop of Montreal* ... (Quebec: Middleton & Dawson, 1862).

12 Ibid. It seems likely that the Hellmuth/Fulford controversy gave a greater sense of urgency to the need for English evangelicals to support Huron College, and may have led directly to the Peache Endowment. See "Hellmuth," *DCB*, 13: 462.

13 See "Fulford," *DCB*, 9; T.R. Millman, "A Sketch of the Life of Francis Fulford," *JCCHS* 17 (December 1975).

14 Francis Fulford, *A Letter ... to the Bishops and Clergy*, 9, 13 (appended to Hellmuth, *Reply*).

15 Isaac Hellmuth, *Reply to a Third Letter of the Right Rev. the Lord Bishop of Montreal* ... (Quebec: Middleton & Dawson, 1862).

16 Christopher Nicholl, *Bishop's University 1843–1970*, (Montreal and Kingston: McGill-Queen's University Press, 1994), 35–7.

17 "Hellmuth," *DCB*, 13: 462.

18 Ibid., 461; Crowfoot, *This Dreamer*, 3–6.

19 Rennie, "Fundamentalism and the Varieties of North Atlantic Evangelicalism," in Noll, Bebbington, and Rawlyk, eds., *Evangelicalism: Comparative Studies*, 335. For McNeile in Liverpool, see Frank Neal, *Sectarian Violence: The Liverpool Experience 1819–1914* (Manchester: Manchester University Press, 1988), esp. ch. 2.

20 Donald M. Lewis, *Lighten Their Darkness: The Evangelical Mission to Working-Class London, 1828–1860* (Westport, CT: Greenwood Press, 1986), 14.
21 Rennie, "Fundamentalism," 334.
22 Peter Toon, *Evangelical Theology 1833–1845: A Response to Tractarianism* (London: Marshall, Morgan & Scott, 1979), 5.
23 Toon, *Evangelical Theology*, 5. For a similar definition of generic evangelicalism, see Bebbington, *Evangelicalism*, 2–17.
24 Owen Chadwick, *The Mind of the Oxford Movement* (London: Adam and Charles Black, 1963), 21–2. This section on high and low churchmanship owes much to the discussion in Chadwick, and to Stephen Neil, *Anglicanism*, 4th ed. (Oxford: Mowbray, 1977). On the later Caroline divines and the doctrine of justification, see Alister E. McGrath, *Iustitia Dei: A History of the Christian Doctrine of Justification, vol. 2, From 1500 to the Present Day* (Cambridge: Cambridge University Press, 1986).
25 See A.W. Mountain, *Memoir of George J. Mountain* (Montreal, 1866), 250, for Mountain's comments concerning low churchmen.
26 "Hellmuth," DCB, 13: 464.
27 Cronyn daughters were married to Samuel Hume Blake and Edward Blake, and Cronyn's son married Samuel Hume Blake's sister Sophy. See A.H. Crowfoot, *Benjamin Cronyn: First Bishop of Huron* (London, ON: 1957); J.J. Talman, "Benjamin Cronyn," DCB, 10: 205–10.
28 "Hellmuth," DCB, 13; Crowfoot, *This Dreamer*.
29 See Ian S. Rennie, "Charles James Stewart," in *Dictionary of Christianity in America*, ed. Daniel G. Reid et al. (Downers Grove, IL: InterVarsity Press, 1990), 1133–4.
30 T.R. Millman, *The Life of the Right Reverend, the Honourable Charles James Stewart, D.D., Oxon., Second Anglican Bishop of Quebec* (London, ON: Huron College, 1953). See Millman, "Charles James Stewart," DCB, 7: 825–9.
31 Ashton Oxenden, *The History of My Life: An Autobiography* (London: 1891), 61–2.
32 Ibid., 62–4.
33 Ibid., 64.
34 Carrington, *Anglican Church*, 143.
35 Oxenden, *History of My Life*, 86.
36 J.I. Cooper, *The Blessed Communion: The Origins and History of the Diocese of Montreal 1760–1960* (Montreal: Diocese of Montreal, 1960), 94.
37 For these judgments see Eugene R. Fairweather, "A Tractarian Patriarch: John Medley of Fredericton," *Canadian Journal of Theology* 6 (1960); Millman, "Francis Fulford"; Clive Clapson, "John Travers Lewis: An Irish High Churchmen in Canada West," JCCHS 22 (October 1980); articles on Fulford, Feild, Bethune in DCB, 10, 11. The sources on Strachan

469 Notes to pages 163-7

are too numerous to list but see one of the more recent treatments in Fahey, *In His Name*. On Stanser and Inglis see Judith Fingard, *The Anglican Design in Loyalist Nova Scotia 1783–1816* (London: SPCK Press, 1972).

38 *The Judgments of the Canadian Bishops, on the Documents Submitted to Them by the Corporation of Trinity College* ... (Toronto: 1863). See *The Protest of the Minority of Trinity College* ... (London, 1864).
39 Carrington, *Anglican Church*, 144.
40 S.W. Horrall, "The Clergy and the Election of Bishop Cronyn," *Ontario History* 58 (December 1966): 215.
41 Ibid., 218.
42 Cooper, *Blessed Communion*, 91; Carrington, *Anglican Church*, 143.
43 Clapson, "John Travers Lewis," 22.
44 H.E. Turner, "Protestantism and Progress: The Church Association in the Diocese of Toronto 1873–1879," *JCCHS*, 22 (April 1980): 9.
45 Masters, "Anglican Evangelicals"; H.E. Turner, "Protestantism and Progress"; Alan L. Hayes, "The Struggle for the Rights of the Laity in the Diocese of Toronto 1850–1879," *JCCHS* 26 (April 1984).
46 *The Church*, 22 January 1842; 25 November 1842.
47 R.M. Black, "Anglicans and French-Canadian Evangelism 1839–1848," *JCCHS* 26 (April 1984).
48 T.C.F. Stunt, "Evangelical Cross-Currents in the Church of Ireland, 1820–1833," in *The Churches, Ireland and the Irish*, Studies in Church History, vol. 25, ed. W.J. Shiels and Diane Wood (Oxford: Blackwell, 1989), 217; Fahey, *In His Name*, 256–7, makes a similar point; Lewis, *Lighten Their Darkness*, ch. 1.
49 John Webster Grant has also drawn attention to this trend towards establishing alternative institutions in *Profusion of Spires*, 128, 209.
50 Fahey, *In His Name*, 260.
51 Not unlike the Cronyn/Blake family nexus in Upper Canada.
52 S.M. Trofimenkoff, *The Dream of Nation: A Social and Intellectual History of Quebec* (Toronto: Gage, 1983), esp. ch. 8. For the application of this to the Anglican Church in Lower Canada, see Black, "Anglicans and French-Canadian Evangelism."
53 Gilbert Percy, *A Letter to the Right Rev., the Lord Bishop of Quebec on Subjects Connected with Tractarianism in the Church* (Quebec, 1858), 3.
54 See Diarmaid MacCulloch, "The Myth of the English Reformation," *Journal of British Studies* 30 (January 1991).
55 Carrington, *Anglican Church*, 95–6; *Report ... of the Montreal Association in Aid of the Colonial Church and School Society of London* (Montreal: John Lovell, 1851).
56 *A Statement of the Constitution and Objects of the Colonial Church and School Society* ... (Quebec, 1859), 4.

57 *Report ... Montreal Association in Aid of CCSS; Mission to the Free Colored Population in Canada,* vol. 9, Occasional Paper, October 1855 (West London Branch of the Colonial Church and School Society).
58 *A Short Explanation of Circumstances Preventing Coalition with the Colonial Church and School Society,* by G.J. Mountain, D.D., D.C.L., Lord Bishop of Quebec. (Quebec, 1859), 10.
59 *Address to the Laity of the Diocese of Quebec, from the Church of England Lay Association.* 2d. ed. (Quebec: Middleton & Dawson, 1859).
60 Ibid.; *Proceedings of the Synod of the United Church of England and Ireland, in the Diocese of Quebec ... 1859* (Quebec, 1859), 8.
61 Quebec *Gazette,* 27 April 1959.
62 George J. Mountain, *A Letter Address to the Clergy and Laity of the Diocese of Quebec ...* (Quebec, 1858).
63 Westfall, *Two Worlds,* 120.

CHAPTER ELEVEN

Funding for this essay was provided by Queen's University, the Social Sciences and Humanities Research Council of Canada, and the Pew Charitable Trusts.
1 William Hockin, "New Birth amidst New Realities," *Christian Week,* 20 September 1994, 11.
2 Quoted in *Christian Week,* 20 September 1994, 8.
3 For the "Montreal Declaration," see *Anglican Essentials,* ed. George Egerton (Toronto: Anglican Book Centre, 1995), 310. Also see David Neff, "Anglicans Refocus on Essentials," *Christianity Today,* September 1994, 49.
4 *Christian Week,* 20 September 1994, 8.
5 For a more complete account, see Dyson Hague, "The History of Wycliffe College," *The Jubilee Volume of Wycliffe College* (Toronto: University of Toronto Press, 1927), and Jacob Jocz, "The Principalship of James Paterson Sheraton," in *The Enduring Word: A Centennial History of Wycliffe College,* ed. Arnold Edinborough (Toronto: University of Toronto Press, 1978). This paper will have a heavy Toronto bias; limits of space and research time necessitate this.
6 Hague, "History of Wycliffe College."
7 Sweatman, in ibid., 28–9. Also see C.W. Vernon, *The Old Church in the New Dominion* (London: SPCK Press, 1929) and Alan Hayes, "Repairing the Walls: Church Reform and Social Reform, 1867–1939," in *By Grace Co-workers,* ed. Alan Hayes (Toronto: Anglican Book Centre, 1989).
8 Meeting, 27 January 1881, Book I.A. Trustees and Board of Management, 11 July 1879 – 25 May 1892, Wycliffe Council [hereafter WC] Minutes, box 1 (1-B), Wycliffe College Archives [hereafter WCA].

9 Protestant Episcopal Divinity School [hereafter PEDS] calender, 1885, 11, 13, Wycliffe Calenders, box 1, WCA.
10 Cody Papers, MU4952, Frederick J. Steen to Cody, 20 February 1895, Ontario Archives [hereafter OA].
11 See T.C.B. Boon, *The Anglican Church from the Bay to the Rockies* (Toronto: Ryerson Press, 1962).
12 See WC Minutes 1907–1916, box 4(1-B), WCA.
13 Report, WC Meetings, 24 September 1907, 31 May 1910; box 4(1-B), WCA.
14 Memorandum to the Council, 23 November 1909, WC Minutes, box 4(1-B), WCA.
15 See the Annual Report to the Trustees, 31 May 1910, WC Minutes, 1907–1916, box 4(1-B), WCA.
16 William Armitage, *The Story of the Canadian Revision of the Prayer Book* (Toronto: McClelland & Stewart, 1922), 141, 150–1, 180, 186, 240–3. See also Hague, *The Story of the English Prayer Book* (London: Longmans, Green, 1926).
17 "I Object," *Canadian Churchman*, 27 February 1908, 148–9.
18 Cody Papers, MU4954, Armitage to Cody, 27 September 1909, OA.
19 Ibid., Matheson to Cody, 1 March 1911.
20 See Minutes, Trustee and Council Meeting, 19 May 1919, box 3(1-B), WCA.
21 Armitage to O'Meara, 12 November 1919, WC Minutes, 6 April 1920, box 3(1-B), WCA.
22 See Joan Bayldon, *Cyril Beardsley: Evangelist* (London: SPCK Press, 1942), 183.
23 In part, this decline in number of students may have been a result of the post-war decline of missions. Many of Wycliffe's students, over the years, had been motivated by missions.
24 Acting Principal's Report, 1929–30, Appendix to Minutes, Council and Trustees Meetings (1927–40), WCA.
25 See Calender for 1927, 14, Wycliffe Calenders, box 2, WCA.
26 Principal's Report, 22 May 1931, Minutes of Council and Trustees (1927–40), WCA.
27 Principal's Report on His Eastern Trip, 1932, ibid.
28 Hague to McElheran, 29 June 1934, ibid.
29 Minutes, Trustees Annual Meeting, 28 May 1937, box 5(1-B), WCA.
30 Cody Papers, MU4962, C. Venn Pilcher to Cody, 29 January 1937, OA.
31 Ibid., Elmore M[?] to Cody, 29 December 1933.
32 Ibid., James Nicholson, Esq., to Cody, 9 January 1933.
33 Noll, *History of Christianity*, 276.
34 WC Minutes, 12 January 1940, box 5(1-B), WCA.
35 Principal's Report, Trustees Annual Meeting, 6 June 1944, box 5(1-B), WCA.

36 Ibid., 30 May 1941.
37 Ibid., 30 May 1946.
38 Ibid., 7 June 1951, box 6(1-B), WCA.
39 See WC Minutes, Council Meeting, 7 June 1951, ibid.
40 Minutes, Trustees Annual Meeting, 12 June 1953, ibid.
41 Ibid., 31 May 1954.
42 Robin Guinness, "A Short History of God's Work in the Anglican Church in Montreal (1950–1985)" (unpublished), author's copy.
43 Note that there is less of a drop-off in the census data where people claim religious affiliation. Attendance and membership have fallen off more radically than the simple cultural claim to being an Anglican made for the census. See Bibby, *Fragmented Gods*, 14–15, 47.
44 Pierre Berton, *The Comfortable Pew* (Toronto: McClelland & Stewart, 1965), 30.
45 I owe this detail to David Lyon, who has written a history of St James'.
46 WC Minutes, 26 November 1968, box 6(1-B), WCA.
47 Minutes, Annual Meeting of Trustees, 9 June 1970, ibid.
48 David Lyon and Bishop Peter Mason from the Diocese of Ontario have been helpful with some details on Desmond Hunt and St James' Church. On the history of Anglicans in Montreal, see Robin Guinness's short paper.
49 See Bibby, *Fragmented Gods*.
50 According to Bibby, evangelicals were suffering too, but less so than other varieties of Christians.
51 This estimate is based on a conversation with Peter Mason in March 1995. Because a number of bishops in the Arctic and North-West are evangelicals, the percentage of evangelical bishops is higher than the percentage of evangelical members. That proportion is probably one-fifth or less evangelical. These bishops represent the variety of evangelicals in the ACC: conservative, liberal, charismatic, and Prayer Book evangelicals.
52 George Egerton, "Anglican Charismatics after Three Decades," *INCOURAGE*, Winter 1992/93, 12–13, a report on research done by Wycliffe's David Reed.
53 See Wuthnow, *Restructuring of American Religion*.
54 According to Bibby only one-fifth of this 720,000 is active (regular attendance, etc.). See *Unknown Gods*.
55 Marsden, "Evangelical Denomination"; Bebbington, *Evangelicalism*, 2–17; and Robert K. Johnston, "American Evangelicalism: An Extended Family," in Dayton and Johnston, eds., *American Evangelicalism*.
56 High/low church refers to both style and principle. Like Roman Catholics, high church Anglicans use ornate liturgies ("smells and bells") and have "high" theologies that stress the Church as the means of grace (sacraments) and the guarantee of religious authority (tradition, apostolic

succession). Low church "Protestants" stress the Bible *alone* as ultimately authoritative, and focus on the individual's relationship to God as the means of grace. I thus use Protestant and low church as virtual synonyms (though Lutherans and some Reformed Christians have "high church" tendencies). Note also that evangelicals clearly have their own deeply embedded, authoritative (if unconsciously so) traditions.

57 My argument is not new. See Jay P. Dolan, *Catholic Revivalism: The American Experience, 1830–1900* (Notre Dame: University of Notre Dame Press, 1978).

58 The statement was entitled "Evangelicals and Catholics Together" (published in *First Things*). Signers include J.I. Packer, Charles Colson, and John Richard Neuhaus. It has caused controversy among many evangelicals; note letters to the editor in *Christianity Today* in 1995.

59 Reported in Allan Swift, "A nation of private Christians?" *Faith Today*, July/August 1993, 20–8. For the report on Rawlyk's findings, see "God Is Alive: Canada is a Nation of Believers," *Maclean's*, 12 April 1993, 32–50.

60 Dayton, "Some Doubts About the Usefulness of the Category 'Evangelical,'" in Dayton and Johnston, eds., *American Evangelicalism*, 250–1.

61 See Leonard Sweet, "Wise As Serpents, Innocent As Doves," *Journal of the Academy of American Religion* 56 (Fall 1988); and Douglas Sweeney, "The Essential Evangelicalism Dialectic: The Historiography of the Early Neo-Evangelical Movement and the Observer-Participant Dilemma," *Church History* 60 (1991). Note that James Turner and others have referred to these historians as "the evangelical mafia." See Turner, "Forward," in *Reckoning with the Past*, ed. D.G. Hart (Grand Rapids: Baker, 1995), 7.

62 See my "Gospel and Party."

63 Rt Rev. John R. Sperry, Bishop of the Arctic (retired), letter to the author, 25 April 1993.

64 A good example of this kind of analysis is Charles Hambrick-Stowe's *The Practice of Piety: Puritan Devotional Disciplines in Seventeenth-Century New England* (Chapel Hill: University of North Carolina Press, 1982). He argues that Puritanism was a devotional movement that took much of its devotional literature from arch-enemies like the Roman Catholics.

CHAPTER TWELVE

1 I.E. Bill, *Fifty Years with the Baptist Ministers and Churches of the Maritime Provinces of Canada* (Saint John: Barnes and Co., 1880), vii.

2 Figures are from Airhart, "Ordering a New Nation," in Rawlyk, ed., *Canadian Protestant Experience*, 102–3.

3 The literature on Alline and the Great Awakening is extensive. See the helpful review by David G. Bell, "All Things New: The Transformation

of Maritime Baptist Historiography," *Nova Scotia Historical Review* 4 (1984). An important recent analysis of the radical evangelical tradition in early British North America is Rawlyk, *Canada Fire*.
4 Rawlyk, *Ravished by the Spirit*, 71–106.
5 G.E. Levy, *The Baptists of the Maritime Provinces: 1753–1946* (Saint John: Barnes-Hopkins, 1946), 69–86.
6 Rawlyk, *Canada Fire*, 163.
7 Charles W. Deweese, "Church Covenants and Church Discipline Among Baptists in the Maritime Provinces, 1778–1878," in *Repent and Believe: The Baptist Experience in Maritime Canada*, ed. Barry M. Moody (Hantsport, NS: Lancelot Press, 1980).
8 Christie, "'In These Times of Democratic Rage and Delusion,'" in Rawlyk, ed., *Canadian Protestant Experience*, 41–2.
9 Philip [Griffin-]Allwood, "First Baptist Church, Halifax: Its Origins and Early Years" (M.Div. thesis, Acadia University, 1978).
10 Manning Collection, letter, Alexander Crawford to Edward Manning, 2 October 1813, Acadia University Archives.
11 See David Weale, "The Ministry of the Reverend Donald McDonald on Prince Edward Island, 1826–1867: A Case Study Examination of the Influence and Role of Religion within Colonial Society" (Ph.D. diss., Queen's University, 1976).
12 Rawlyk, *Canada Fire*, 102.
13 For a different view of Baptists in nineteenth-century Ontario, consult William Norman Albert Gillespie, "Ontario's 19th Century Baptist Tradition: Its Roots and Its Development" (Ph.D. diss., University of Waterloo, 1990).
14 The above discussion is taken from Stuart Ivison and Fred Rosser, *The Baptists in Upper and Lower Canada Before 1820* (Toronto: University of Toronto Press, 1956).
15 Renfree, *Heritage and Horizon*, 122–5.
16 George W. Campbell, "Canada Baptist College 1838–1849: The Generation and Demise of a Pioneering Dream in Canadian Theological Education" (M.Th. thesis, Knox College, 1974), 129.
17 Theo T. Gibson, *Robert Alexander Fyfe: His Contemporaries and His Influence* (Burlington: Welch, 1988), 50.
18 See Campbell, "Canada Baptist College," ch. 4–5.
19 Thomas A. Higgins, *The Life of John Mockett Cramp, D.D., 1796–1881* (Montreal: W. Drysdale, 1887), 101–2.
20 Renfree, *Heritage and Horizon*, 77–8.
21 See ibid., 155–68.
22 Westfall, *Two Worlds*, 49.
23 Gibson, *Robert Fyfe*, 264.
24 Ibid., 265.

25 Robert A. Fyfe, *Suggestions to Canadian Baptist Churches, Pastors and Deacons* (Toronto: Canada Baptist Office, 1866), 29-30.
26 Rawlyk, "A.L. McCrimmon, H.P. Whidden, T.T. Shields," in Rawlyk, ed., *Christian Higher Education*, 31-2.
27 Fyfe, *Suggestions*, 39.
28 D.C. Harvey, "The Intellectual Awakening of Nova Scotia," *Dalhousie Review* 13 (1933).
29 See Goodwin, "The Baptismal Controversy."
30 See Moody, "Breadth of Vision, Breadth of Mind," in Rawlyk, ed., *Christian Higher Education*, 13.
31 *Christian Messenger*, 11 February 1863.
32 See Levy, *Baptists of the Maritime Provinces*, 152.
33 See Jonathan Wilson, "'An Excitement Among the People': Richard Burpee, Maritime Baptists, and Foreign Missions 1810-1853" (B.A. Hons. thesis, Acadia University, 1993).
34 J.M. Cramp, *The Future of the Baptists* (Halifax: n.p., 1852), 14.
35 D.G. Bell, "The Allinite Tradition and the New Brunswick Free Christian Baptists 1830-1875," in *An Abiding Conviction: Maritime Baptists and Their World*, ed. Robert S. Wilson (Hantsport, NS: Lancelot Press, 1988), 71.
36 For a discussion of formal, informal, and ecstatic forms of evangelicalism, see Curtis D. Johnson, *Redeeming America: Evangelicals and the Road to Civil War* (Chicago: Ivan Dee, 1993), 7-9.

CHAPTER THIRTEEN

1 I.E. Bill, *Fifty Years with the Baptist Ministers and Churches of the Maritime Provinces of Canada* (Saint John: Barnes and Co., 1880), vii.
2 See the introduction in Noll, Bebbington, and Rawlyk, eds., *Evangelicalism: Comparative Studies*.
3 The provincial breakdown was Prince Edward Island 5.7 per cent; Nova Scotia 19.0 per cent; New Brunswick 25.2 per cent; Quebec .6 per cent; Ontario 5.5 per cent; Manitoba 14.3 per cent; and British Columbia .9 per cent. Statistics from Airhart, "Ordering a New Nation," in Rawlyk, ed., *Canadian Protestant Experience*, 103-4.
4 Mainline Baptists are most commonly referred to in the literature as Regular or Calvinistic Baptists. Those who held to Free doctrines and practices adopted various titles, including Free Baptist, Free Christian Baptist, and Free Will Baptist among others.
5 Stackhouse, *Canadian Evangelicalism*, 9.
6 Grant, *Church in the Canadian Era*, 50.
7 E.R. Fitch, *The Baptists of Canada: A History of Their Progress and Achievements* (Toronto: Standard Publishing Company, 1911), 232-4.

8 Jarold Zeman, "Baptists in Canada," unpublished manuscript, 4. The Baptist Convention of Western Canada was organized in 1907.
9 The "Serving Seven" were W.F. Armstrong, Rufus and Mary Lamont Sanford, George and Matilda Faulkner Churchill, Flora Eaton, and Maria Armstrong.
10 *Maritime Baptist*, 25 April 1909, 8.
11 Ibid., 2 June 1909, 8.
12 Moody, "Breadth of Vision, Breadth of Mind," in Rawlyk, ed., *Christian Higher Education*, 21–4.
13 Margaret Conrad, Elizabeth Rice and Patricia Townsend, *Women at Acadia University: The First Fifty Years, 1884–1934* (Kentville, NS: Kentville Publishing, 1984), 4.
14 Rawlyk, "A.L. McCrimmon, H.P. Whidden, T.T. Shields," in Rawlyk, ed., *Christian Higher Education*, 41.
15 Ibid.
16 Ellis, "What the Times Demand," in Rawlyk, ed., *Christian Higher Education*, 85.
17 Ibid., 86.
18 Wilfred C. Keirstead, "What is Truth," Keirstead Papers, University of New Brunswick Archives.
19 Rawlyk, "J.S. Cramp and W.C. Keirstead," 119.
20 Moody, "Breadth of Vision," 28.
21 Rawlyk, "A.L. McCrimmon, H.P. Whidden, T.T. Shields," 43.
22 Minutes, McMaster University Senate, 29 May 1909, as quoted in ibid.
23 Rawlyk, "A.L. McCrimmon, H.P. Whidden, T.T. Shields," 44.
24 Swedish Baptist churches were established by missionaries who arrived in Quebec in 1892 and in Winnipeg in 1894 via the United States. There were also "pockets" of Ukrainian and Hungarian Baptists on the Prairies. The work among these new ethnic groups was in addition to the Baptists' ongoing evangelical outreach in Quebec and on the Prairies. Most of the mission support and activity in the Maritime Baptist Convention continued to be focused on the India mission field.
25 Airhart, "Ordering a New Nation," 102–4.
26 Stackhouse, *Canadian Evangelicalism*, 23.
27 Shields as quoted in ibid.
28 Stackhouse, *Canadian Evangelicalism*, 26.
29 Initially, thirty churches, including Shields's Jarvis Street Church, left the Convention. By 1940 seventy of 490 churches had left, taking 8,500 of the 60,000 members. A further schism later developed between the "Shieldites" and Regular Baptists.
30 The Convention of Regular Baptists of British Columbia was formed in 1927, and the Prairie Regular Baptist Missionary Fellowship was created in 1930 as a result of schisms within the British Columbia and Western

Conferences. These kinds of tensions between hardline and mainline adherents led to the secularization of Brandon College in 1939.
31 Rawlyk, *Champions of the Truth*, 56.
32 Ibid., 70.
33 Renfree, *Heritage and Horizon*, 340–2.
34 Stackhouse, *Canadian Evangelicalism*, 202.
35 Ibid.
36 For Maritime Baptist women's participation in the missionary enterprise, see, for example, H. Miriam Ross, "Matrimonial Matters: Maritime Baptist Women and 'Single Lady Missionaries' Commissioned for Burma/India 1867–1920," and "'Sisters' in the Homeland: Vision for Mission Among Maritime Baptist Women, 1867–1920," in *A Fragile Stability: Definition and Redefinition of Maritime Baptist Identity*, ed. David T. Priestley (Hantsport, NS: Lancelot Press, 1994); and Coops, "Not A Romantic Notion."
37 *Maritime Baptist*, 5 October 1910, 8.
38 Administration of all mission fields in India was turned over to native Christians in 1947, at which time the missionaries became advisors to the newly formed India Conference. See Orville E. Daniel, *Moving with the Times* (Toronto: Canadian Baptist Overseas Mission Board, 1973).
39 Linda Eaton, "The Issue of Female Ordination in the Maritime Baptist Convention 1929–1954" (B.A. Hons. thesis, Mount Allison University, 1989), 1.
40 *Baptist Year Book* (1987), 31, as quoted in ibid., 2.
41 *Baptist Year Book* (1988), 33, as quoted in ibid., 5.
42 In 1993, three-quarters of all Baptists were members of the Canadian Baptist Federation, whose membership was 129,720 with 1,124 pastors serving 1,165 churches across Canada. The groups within the Federation that have shown the most growth in recent decades tend to represent particular ethnic communities – for example, the Union D'Eglises Baptistes Francaises au Canada, Estonian Baptist congregations in Toronto in the 1970s, and Asian Baptists on the West Coast and in Toronto in the 1980s. See *Yearbook of American and Canadian Churches, 1993*, ed. Kenneth Bedell (Nashville: Abingdon Press, 1993).
43 These represent "splinter groups" formed during the Shields fundamentalist split.
44 The Fellowship of Evangelical Baptist Churches in Canada presence is strongest in Ontario and Quebec. In 1993 there were 484 churches with a membership of 57,780. Bedell, *Yearbook*.
45 Bedell, *Yearbook*. As of 1990, the Canadian Convention of Southern Baptists membership was 6,001 attending 104 churches. The North American Baptist General Conference (German) for 1992 had 18,125 members in 120 churches and the Baptist General Conference (Swedish)

6,066 members in 70 churches. The latter two groups exert a strong conservative presence in Western Canada.
46 Stackhouse, *Canadian Evangelicalism*.

CHAPTER FOURTEEN

1 See comments by James Urry cited by David Arnason, "A History of Turnstone Press," in *Acts of Concealment: Mennonite Writing in Canada* (Waterloo: University of Waterloo Press, 1992), 214.
2 Ted Regehr, *Mennonites in Canada, 1939-1970: A People Transformed* (Toronto: University of Toronto Press, forthcoming).
3 Wes Michaelson, "Evangelicalism and Radical Discipleship," in *Evangelicals and Anabaptism*, ed. C. Norman Kraus (Scottdale, PA: Herald Press, 1979).
4 John Friesen, "Four Influences in the GC Mosaic," *The Mennonite*, 14 May 1985, 221.
5 "Mennonite: Neither Liberal nor Evangelical," *Direction* 20 (Spring 1991): 38.
6 F. Wiens, "This We Believe," *Gospel Tidings* 9 (August 1969): 1.
7 Bebbington, *Evangelicalism*, 1-19.
8 A delineation of the differences can be found in Kraus, "Evangelicalism: A Mennonite Critique," in Dayton and Johnston, eds., *American Evangelicalism*.
9 Frank Epp, *Mennonites in Canada, 1920-1940: A People's Struggle for Survival* (Toronto: Macmillan, 1982), 505.
10 It was stated: "Whereas there are ... Mennonites ... who have but one thing in common with the MBC church, namely 'non-resistance,' and have many things which are quite objectionable, both to citizenship and spirituality on account of which the name Mennonite has brought disrepute, thus becoming a great barrier ... to aggressive evangelism and church extension." Everek Richard Storms, *History of the United Missionary Church* (Elkhart, IN: Bethel Publishing Company, 1958), 70.
11 Frank Epp, *Mennonites in Canada, 1786-1920: The History of a Separate People* (Toronto: Macmillan, 1974), 244.
12 Phoebe Sanders, "A Tribute to C.F. Derstine," *Canadian Mennonite*, 28 June 1966, 23.
13 *Gospel Herald*, 28 January 1929, 898.
14 Bender's influential essay "The Anabaptist Vision," *Mennonite Quarterly Review* 18 (April 1944) reaffirmed a unique theological identity for North-American Mennonites in the face of the encroaching influence of evangelicalism and the loss of many ethnic and cultural distinctives.
15 In 1921 a resolution encouraged Mennonite Conference of Ontario churches to support Toronto Bible College, but in 1954 Ontario Mennonite Bible School and Institute publicity made a frontal attack by declaring,

"Students in our Bible Institute avoid exposure to Militarism, Calvinism, Dispensationalism, and lack of Biblicism ... Don't expose yourself to a watered down, emaciated, powerless, popular, easy discipleship, cheap grace kind of Christianity. Get your Bible training ... where all the Bible doctrines receive their proper balanced emphasis." J. Martin and N. Gingrich, *Mission Completed* (St Jacobs: St Jacob's Printery, 1969), 147.

16 Harry Loewen, "Ambivalence in Mennonite Brethren Self-Understanding," *Direction* 23,2 (Fall 1994): 15.

17 Gerald Ediger, "*Deutsch und Religion*: Ethnicity, Religion and Canadian Mennonite Brethren, 1940–1970" (Th.D diss., Toronto School of Theology, 1993), 16–17. Ediger documents the transition from a unilingual German religious community in the early twentieth century into a multilingual, multi-ethnic denomination in the 1990s. Although he does not often highlight the connections, there are correlations between the process of acculturation experienced by the Mennonite Brethren, their missionary impulse, the Bible school movement, and evangelicalism. See also Benjamin Redekop, "The German Identity of Mennonite Brethren Immigrants in Canada, 1930–1960" (M.A. thesis, University of British Columbia, 1990).

18 Peter Penner, *No Longer at Arms Length: Mennonite Brethren Church Planting in Canada, 1883–1983* (Winnipeg: Kindred Press, 1987), 22, 151.

19 Ibid., 32.

20 See J. Howard Kauffman and Leland Harder, *Anabaptists Four Centuries Later: A Profile of Five Mennonite and Brethren in Christ Denominations* (Scottdale, PA: Herald Press, 1975), 341–2.

21 John H. Redekop, "Ethnicity and the Mennonite Brethren: Issues and Responses," *Direction* 17 (Spring 1988): 4.

22 For a discussion of stratification, class structure, and distribution of power within Old Colony society, see Calvin Redekop, *Old Colony Mennonites: Dilemmas of Ethnic Minority Life* (Baltimore: Johns Hopkins Press, 1969), 93–102.

23 Others attended Mennonite schools like Rosthern Bible School, Tabor Bible School, and Elim Bible Institute. In 1966 the Rudnerweider formally became a part of Steinbach Bible Institute. A decade later they started their own school in Aylmer, Ontario.

24 Jack Heppner, *Search for Renewal: The Story of the Rudnerweider/ Evangelical Mennonite Mission Conference, 1937–1987* (Altona, MB: Friesen Printers, 1987), 255.

25 For a detailed analysis, see my "'In the World but Not of It.'"

26 See Timothy Weber, *Living in the Shadow of the Second Coming: American Premillennialism 1875–1925* (New York: Oxford University Press, 1979), 67.

27 Redekop, *Old Colony Mennonites*, 228.

28 This coincides with the idea that evangelicalism was both "a part of the Americanization process and part of the resistance to Americanization." Paul Toews, "Fundamentalist Conflict in Mennonite Colleges"; Theron Schlabach, "Paradoxes of Mennonite Separatism," *Pennsylvania Mennonite Heritage* 2 (1979).
29 See Robert Webber, "To Recover Our Apostolic Roots," *The New Oxford Review* (January 1978): 13; and Jon Johnson, *Will Evangelicalism Survive Its Own Popularity?* (Grand Rapids: Zondervan, 1978), 71.
30 Rodney Sawatsky, "Mennonite Ethnicity: Medium, Message and Mission," *Journal of Mennonite Studies* 9 (1991): 116–17.
31 "Theological Reflections," *Direction* 14 (Fall 1985).
32 Rodney J. Sawatsky, "Where in the World? Mennonite Colleges and Nonconformity" (paper presented at a conference on Mennonite Higher Education: Experience and Vision, Bluffton College, June 1992), 3–4.
33 Paul Toews, "Recent Interpretations of Evangelical Pluralism," *Direction* 20 (Spring 1991): 24.

CHAPTER FIFTEEN

1 Historians of Canadian church history are often hard pressed to identify Lutheranism with Canadian evangelical history. For example, in outlining the growth of the Canadian evangelical network, Stackhouse does not mention Lutherans in "The Protestant Experience in Canada since 1945," in Rawlyk, ed., *Canadian Protestant Experience*, and includes only one paragraph in his more recent *Canadian Evangelicalism* (185) on the similar concerns of evangelicals and the Lutheran Church–Missouri Synod.
2 The Lutheran Church–Canada has been autonomous since 1988. However, it is still closely tied to the Lutheran Church–Missouri Synod in terms of doctrine and administration.
3 In 1993 there were only 961 members in seven Canadian churches. See *Yearbook of American & Canadian Churches, 1995*, ed. Kenneth B. Bedell (Nashville: Abingdon Press, 1995), 262.
4 E. Clifford Nelson, *The Rise of World Lutheranism: An American Perspective* (Philadelphia: Fortress Press, 1982), 26.
5 Ellingsen, "Lutheranism," in Dayton and Johnston, eds., *American Evangelicalism*, 222.
6 The following scholars and Lutherans list the Lutheran Church–Missouri Synod as "evangelical": Richard Quebedeaux, *The Worldly Evangelicals* (New York: Harper & Row, 1978), 38–40; Marsden, "Fundamentalism and American Evangelicalism," in Dayton and Johnston, eds., *American Evangelicalism*, 22; Noll, "The Lutheran Difference," 36; David Luecke, *Evangelical Style and Lutheran Substance* (St Louis: Concordia Publishing House, 1988), 50; Milton L. Rudnick,

Fundamentalism and the Missouri Synod: A Historical Study of their Interaction and Mutual Influence (St Louis: Concordia Publishing House, 1966).
7 Ellingsen, "Lutheranism," 222.
8 Kenn Ward, *This Evangelical Church of Ours* (Winfield, BC: Wood Lake Books, 1994), 10.
9 Nelson, *Rise of World Lutheranism*, 19.
10 Ibid.
11 Ibid., 24.
12 Ibid.
13 *The Book of Concord: The Confessions of the Evangelical Lutheran Church*, ed. Theodore G. Tappert (Philadelphia: Fortress Press, 1959), 32.
14 Nelson, *Rise of World Lutheranism*, 30–3.
15 Ibid., 32–4.
16 Carl Raymond Cronmiller, *A History of the Lutheran Church in Canada* (n.p.: Evangelical Lutheran Synod of Canada, 1961), 13–20.
17 Noll, "Children of the Reformation." See also Mark Ellingsen, "Common Sense Realism: The Cutting Edge of Evangelical Identity," *Dialog* 24 (Summer 1985); and David O. Moberg, "Fundamentalists and Evangelicals in Society," in *The Evangelicals: What They Believe, Who They Are, Where They Are Changing*, ed. David F. Wells and John D. Woodbridge (Nashville: Abingdon Press, 1975), 160.
18 Norman Threinen, "Pivotal Points in Early Canadian Church History," *Consensus: A Canadian Lutheran Journal of Theology* 13,2 (1987).
19 Cronmiller, *A History*, 13–20; E. Theodore Bachman and Mercia Brenne Bachmann, *Lutheran Churches in the World: A Handbook* (Minneapolis: Augsburg Fortress, 1989), 557.
20 E. Clifford Nelson, *The Lutherans in North America* (Philadelphia: Fortress Press, 1975), 365; also Noll, "The Lutheran Difference," 32.
21 Ellingsen, "Common Sense Realism," 202. At the May Conference which provided the basis of this volume, John Stackhouse suggested that, as a former state religion, Lutheranism was "suspect" from the perspective of other voluntaristic denominations which otherwise might have sought cooperation with such an established, trusted tradition.
22 Noll, "The Lutheran Difference," 32–3. It should also be noted that Lutheranism, while informed by an eschatological ethic, is neither pre- nor post-millennialistic, as evangelicals may or may not be! If anything, Lutheranism is amillennialistic, and is "But about that day or hour no one knows" (Mark 13:32). See Paul Kuenning, "Pietism: A Lutheran Resource for Dialogue with Evangelicalism," *Dialog* 24 (Fall 1985): 289.
23 Joseph A. Burgess, ed., *Lutherans in Ecumenical Dialogue: A Reappraisal* (Minneapolis: Augsburg Fortress, 1990), 76. See also Kuenning, "Pietism," 285–92, and *The Rise and Fall of American Lutheran Pietism:*

The Rejection of an Activist Heritage (Macon: Mercer University Press, 1988).
24 Harold O.J. Brown, "Evangelicalism in America," *Dialog* 24 (Summer 1985).
25 Nelson, *Lutherans in North America*, 63.
26 Ibid., 63–4.
27 Walter O. Forster, *Zion on the Mississippi: The Settlement of the Saxon Lutherans in Missouri, 1839–1841* (St Louis: Concordia Publishing House, 1953), 532.
28 Peter C. Erb, ed., *Pietists Selected Writings* (New York: Paulist Press, 1983), 21; Dale Brown, *Understanding Pietism* (Grand Rapids: Eerdmans, 1978), 158. Both D. Brown, ibid., and H. Brown, "Evangelicalism," 189, note that the Moravian Brethren made a profound impact on John Wesley on his return to the United States.
29 Kuenning, "Pietism," 89.
30 Nelson, *Lutherans in North America*, 63–5.
31 John Pless, "The Evangelization of Missouri," *Lutheran Forum* 23,2 (1989): 30–1; Carter Lindberg, "Pietism and the Church Growth Movement in a Confessional Lutheran Perspective," *Concordia Theological Quarterly*, July/August 1988.
32 F. Ernest Stoeffler, *The Rise of Evangelical Pietism* (Leiden: E.J. Brill, 1965), 235.
33 Theodore G. Tappert, trans., *Pia Desideria: or Heartfelt Desires for a God-pleasing Improvement of the True Protestant Church* (Philadelphia: Fortress Press, 1964).
34 F. Ernest Stoeffler, *German Pietism during the Eighteenth Century* (Leiden: E.J. Brill, 1973), ix.
35 H. Brown, "Evangelicalism," 190.
36 Walter Freitag, "Lutheran Tradition in Canada," in *The Churches and the Canadian Experience*, ed. John Webster Grant (Toronto: Ryerson Press, 1963), 99.
37 Walter Freitag, "Fundamentalism and Canadian Lutheranism," *Consensus* 13,1 (1987): 30.
38 Two Lutheran Bible institutes were established: Outlook Bible College in 1911 and Canadian Lutheran Bible Institute at Camrose in 1932. See George Evenson, *Adventuring for Christ: The Story of the Evangelical Lutheran Church of Canada* (Calgary: Foothills Lutheran Press, 1974), 77–8, 122–3.
39 The author is indebted to Dr Ian Rennie, president of Ontario Theological Seminary, for this reference.
40 Nelson, *Lutherans in North America*, 482.
41 Noll, *Between Faith and Criticism*, 100.

42 Information obtained from WorldCat Database, a service of the University of Regina FirstSearch system.
43 Noll, "Children of the Reformation," 177.
44 Lindberg, "Pietism and the Church Growth Movement," 130.
45 David Luecke, *Evangelical Style*. Mark Hutchinson of the Centre for the Study of Australian Christianity cites the example of Charles Troutman, an American Lutheran clergyman, who conducted evangelistic revival meetings in Canada as well as in the United States during the first half of the twentieth century.
46 Noll, "Children of the Reformation"; H. Brown, "Evangelicalism"; Ellingsen, "Lutheranism"; John H. Gerstner, "The Theological Boundaries of Evangelical Faith," in Wells and Woodbridge, eds., *The Evangelicals*; George Marsden, *Understanding Fundamentalism and Evangelicalism* (Grand Rapids: Eerdmans, 1991), 12; Noll, "The Lutheran Difference," 38.
47 For one of the clearer analyses of the various types of evangelicalism, see Richard Quebedeaux, *The Young Evangelicals: Revolution in Orthodoxy* (New York: Harper & Row, 1974), 18–45, 53–4.
48 Bebbington, *Evangelicalism*, 1–17.
49 Carl E. Braaten, *Principles of Lutheran Theology* (Philadelphia: Fortress Press, 1983), 71.
50 Gustaf Aulen, *Christus Victor* (New York: Macmillan, 1969).
51 Carl Braaten and Robert Jenson, eds., *Christian Dogmatics I* (Minneapolis: Augsburg Fortress Press, 1984), 95.
52 Braaten, *Principles*, 3–27.
53 Hillis, *Can Two Walk Together*, 45–98.
54 Braaten, *Principles*, 23.
55 Eric W. Gritsch, *Fortress Introduction to Lutheranism* (Minneapolis: Fortress Press, 1994), 130–3; Ward, *This Evangelical Church*, 81.
56 Erwin Buck, "The Place of the New Testament in the Neo-Conservative Movement," *Consensus* 13,1 (1987).
57 Since the 1974 schism, the Lutheran Church–Missouri Synod and Lutheran Church–Canada have become resistant to any sort of historical criticism, claiming the inerrancy of scripture. This and the related issue of women's ordination are cited as the reasons for the Lutheran Church–Canada not joining the Evangelical Lutheran Church in Canada in 1985, even though it took part in the negotiations until late in the process. See William Hordern, "A Partially Achieved Dream: Theological Issues in Recent Canadian Lutheran History," *Consensus* 13,2 (1987).
58 Martin Luther, "The Smalcald Articles," in *The Book of Concord*, 311.
59 Ward, *This Evangelical Church*, 37; Gritsch, *Lutheranism*, 108; Noll, "The Lutheran Difference," 40.

60 Braaten, *Principles*, 87–107.
61 According to the *1991 Directory of Lutheran Churches in Canada*, there are only five individuals and five married couples acting as missionaries for the Canadian Lutheran denominations.
62 Roland E. Miller, *The Sending of God: Essays on the Mission of God and His People* (Calgary: Concord Canada, 1980), 23–4.
63 Noll, "The Lutheran Difference," 38.
64 William Hordern, "Political Theology," in *Political Theology in the Canadian Context*, ed. Benjamin G. Smillie (Waterloo: Wilfrid Laurier University Press, 1982).
65 Hordern, "Conservative Theology with Radical Politics," *Consensus* 13,1 (1987): 77ff. There are others now, as noted by Oscar L. Arnal in "An Agenda for Canadian Lutherans: The Search for Prophetic Soil," *Consensus* 13,2 (1987).
66 Freitag, "Fundamentalism," 23, is not reflective of all North American Lutheranism. He sees no difference between evangelicalism and fundamentalism. See Martin E. Marty, "Tensions with Contemporary Evangelicalism: A Critical Appraisal," in Wells and Woodbridge, eds., *The Evangelicals*; and Walter Koehler, "A Look at the Positive Side of Neo-Evangelicalism," *Consensus* 13,1 (1987).
67 Freitag, "Fundamentalism," 27–30. The pronouncements were made before Canadian Lutheran synods became autonomous from the American parent churches.
68 Ibid., 30–2.
69 Ibid., 33–4.
70 Moberg, "Fundamentalists and Evangelicals," 155–6.
71 Koehler, "A Look at the Positive Side," 82.
72 Ibid., 85–6.
73 Ibid., 88.
74 Noll, "Children of the Reformation," 179–80; "The Lutheran Difference," 31–40.
75 David Scaer, "How Do Lutherans Approach the Doing of Theology Today," in *Doing Theology in Today's World*, ed. John D. Woodbridge and Thomas E. McComiskey (Grand Rapids: Zondervan, 1991), 198ff; William Lazareth and Peri Rasolondraibe, eds., *Lutheran Identity and Mission: Evangelical and Evangelistic* (Minneapolis: Fortress Press, 1994), 15–30.
76 Braaten, *Principles*, 87–105; Gritsch, *Lutheranism*, 131–3; and Ward, *This Evangelical Church*, 35–50.
77 Pless, "Evangelization of Missouri," 30–1.
78 Robert Kelly states stridently that while pietism may be enjoying something of a revival in Lutheranism, it is still not quite Lutheran enough.

"True Repentance and Sorrow: Johann Arndt's Doctrine of Justification," *Consensus* 16,2 (1990): 66.
79 Koehler, "A Look at the Positive Side," 88.

CHAPTER SIXTEEN

1 Albert Mills, diary, 95.064C, 22 November 1903, 37, United Church of Canada Archives [hereafter UCA].
2 Organized in 1879 as the Canada Association for the Promotion of Holiness, in 1895 it became the Christian Association, but it most frequently used the name Canada Holiness Association.
3 For the Keswick movement in Canada, see Airhart, *Serving the Present Age*, 52–3; for the Canadian National Holiness Association (organized in 1910, Rev. J. Melvin Smith, president) see Albert Carman fonds, 86.003C, box 14, files 95, 96; box 20, file 132, UCA.
4 On Nelson Burns and his association, see Ron Sawatsky, "'Unholy Contentions about Holiness': The Canada Holiness Association and the Methodist Church, 1875–1894" (proceedings of the 1982 meeting of the Canadian Society of Church History). On Horner, see Brian R. Ross, "Ralph Cecil Horner: A Methodist Sectarian Deposed, 1887–1895," in *Methodist History* 16,1 (October 1977). See also Harold William Pointen, *The Holiness Movement Church in Canada* (B.D. thesis, Emmanuel College, 1950).
5 Work on the Gospel Workers centres on the holiness group itself and not on ecclesiastical conflict. See R. Gerald Hobbs, "Stepchildren of John Wesley: The Gospel Workers Church of Canada," Papers of the Canadian Methodist Historical Society (1990); Helen G. Hobbs, "'What She Could': Women in the Gospel Workers Church," in *Changing Roles of Women within the Christian Church in Canada*, ed. Elizabeth Gillan Muir and Marilyn Färdig Whiteley (Toronto: University of Toronto Press, 1995).
6 Albert Truax, ed., *Autobiography of the late Rev. Nelson Burns* (Toronto: Christian Association, n.d.), 8.
7 Ibid., 58–9.
8 Canada Association for the Promotion of Holiness/Christian Association fonds, 88.061C, minutes of annual convention business meetings [hereafter CHA Minutes], 1879–1921, 30 December 1879, UCA.
9 *Christian Guardian* [hereafter CG], 14 January 1880, 14.
10 See Airhart, *Serving the Present Age*, 51; Sawatsky, "Unholy Contentions," sec. 4.
11 *Expositor of Holiness*, March 1891, 235.
12 Ibid., April 1892, 257.

13 Ibid., June 1894, 326.
14 CHA Minutes, 1905, 105; c.31 December 1910 – 3 January 1911, 121.
15 Ibid., 1921, 147.
16 Ibid., 1879, 3.
17 *Expositor of Holiness*, December 1892, 155.
18 Truax, *Rev. Nelson Burns*, 69.
19 *Ralph C. Horner, Evangelist; Reminiscences from His Own Pen* (Brockville: A.E. Horner, n.d.), 12, 11.
20 Ibid., 44.
21 For further discussion of this issue, see Whiteley, "Cyclones of Power."
22 *Ralph C. Horner, Evangelist*, 111.
23 CG, 14 June 1893, 373.
24 Evangelists' Examinations, letter of Ella Birdsell and Inda Mason to S.D. Chown, 24 July 1893, Montreal and Ottawa Conference, UCA.
25 CG, 15 August 1894, 520; 24 October 1894, 680.
26 CG, 15 August 1894, 520.
27 *Minutes of the Montreal Annual Conference of The Methodist Church* (Toronto: William Briggs, 1895), 66.
28 Pointen, *Holiness Movement Church in Canada*, 76.
29 See correspondence in the Albert Carman papers, 86.003C, esp. box 6, files 23, 24a, 25, UCA.
30 Holiness Movement Church [hereafter HMC] General Conference Minutes, 1899, 95.065C, UCA.
31 HMC General Conference Minutes, 1920, 326.
32 *Ralph C. Horner, Evangelist*, 14.
33 On Fire-Baptized churches, see Vinson Synan, *The Holiness-Pentecostal Movement in the United States* (Grand Rapids: Eerdmans, 1971), 61–5.
34 R.C. Horner, *Fragments from the Feast, or, 18 Sermons*, ed. E.T. Campbell (Belleville: The "Cruse of Oil" Tract Repository, 1902), 43, 44, 103 includes testimonies from the 1902 Feast.
35 Mills, diary, July 1902, 24, UCA.
36 See, for example, ibid., 4 February 1903, 31–2: "Fred Arthur, Abe, Mary, Emma and Millie Shunk have withdrawn from the Methodist Church. They could not get along harmoniously with the minister and some of the people and felt it about the only thing to do ... These feel that as they gather in their own little meetings they are blest of God while in the church they are only reproached and tongue thrashed."
37 Ibid., review of camp meeting, September 1902, 95.
38 Ibid., 29 August 1902, 56.
39 Ibid., 21 November 1903, 35; 25 February 1904, 94.
40 Ibid., review of camp meeting; and 22 September 1902, 95, 98. See also *Holiness Worker*, March 1907, 4.
41 Ibid., 22 September 1903, 170.

42 Only S.D. Clark, in *Church and Sect in Canada* (Toronto: University of Toronto Press, 1948), 429, has seen it as more than a leadership conflict, suggesting that it was "indicative of increasing strains within the movement as a result of the conflicting claims of the interest in organization and the interest in evangelization." Scattered references to this small denomination appear in Irwin Brown, *Encyclopedia Canadiana*, vol. 9, 394; Earl R. Conley: *Anniversary "Reflections" 1917–1987*; various "Historical Highlights" printed 1986–1988. I am grateful to Earl Conley for providing me with copies of this, and for giving me access to the denomination's paper, the *Christian Standard*.
43 HMC General Conference Special Committee Minutes, May 1914, 196–205.
44 HMC General Conference Minutes, December 1914 – January 1915, 207.
45 Ibid., October – November 1915, 137–8.
46 Ibid., December 1916, 258.
47 HMC Ottawa Conference Minutes, 1918, 213, 231–2.
48 *Christian Standard*, 20 September 1918, 2.
49 Ibid., 6 September 1918, 2.
50 Gospel Workers Church [hereafter GWC], Special Session of Conference Minutes, 18 October 1926, 319, 95.062.C, UCA.
51 Truax, *Rev. Nelson Burns*, 68.
52 HMC, Ottawa Conference Minutes, 1920, 312.
53 Ibid., 1922, 379; 1924, 433.
54 Ibid., 1925–6, 458. At that meeting letters were read from the Gospel Workers and the Church of the Nazarene, and when a Wesleyan minister spoke to the conference about "the need of a still closer union among all Holiness bodies, of Canada," the delegates responded "by standing to their feet" (500).
55 GWC Annual Conference Minutes, December 1925, 297.
56 Interview by the author with W.J. Stonehouse, Perth, Ontario, 10 February 1995.
57 HMC, Ottawa Conference Minutes, 1953, 411.
58 *Christian Standard*, 1 November 1958, 10.
59 HMC, General Conference Minutes, 1924, 435; GWC Special Conference Minutes, 29 September 1956.
60 Malcolm Greenshields, "'Raising Up a Holy People': Holiness History and Culture," *North American Religion* 2 (1993).
61 Ibid., 90–91. Charles Edwin Jones noted of an earlier stage in this development that "Holiness revivalism had become the evangelism of the already convinced." *Perfectionist Persuasion: The Holiness Movement and American Methodism, 1867–1936* (Metuchen, NJ: Scarecrow Press, 1974), 20.
62 GWC Annual Conference Minutes, 29 December 1954, (n.p.).

CHAPTER SEVENTEEN

1 Although the Christian and Missionary Alliance is a small denomination by North American standards, with 370,000 "inclusive members" (members and adherents) gathered in 2,271 churches, its 1,184 missionaries serve a constituency of over two million inclusive members in fifty-four countries. In addition to its widespread publishing and broadcasting endeavours, the Alliance supports thirty college-level educational institutions and 338 education extension centres, three hospitals and 106 clinics, and its relief agency, CAMA services, which maintains operations in ten countries. "C&MA Mission Facts," *Canadian Statistical Report* (Willowdale, ON: C&MA, 1992).
2 Albert was consecrated in infancy by his parents to missionary service by Geddie himself. A.E. Thompson, *A.B. Simpson: His Life and Work* (Harrisburg, PA: Christian Publications, 1920), 118.
3 Henry Grattan Guinness was an evangelist loosely affiliated with the Plymouth Brethren. Through preaching tours in southwest England and Ulster in 1857 and 1858, he had earned a reputation as a Spirit-filled preacher able to sway thousands, and later became known as the herald of the Great Revival of 1859. J. Edwin Orr, *The Fervent Prayer* (Chicago: Moody Press, 1974), 26.
4 "A.B. Simpson: My Own Story," in *Simpson Scrapbook*, ed. Donald McKaig (Nyack, NY: CMA, n.d.), 11.
5 Ibid.
6 See B.J. Fraser, *Church, College and Clergy* (Montreal and Kingston: McGill-Queen's University Press, 1995).
7 In 1864 Simpson won the Prince of Wales Prize, a two-year award for the best essay judged by Dr Robert Burns on the subject "Preparation of the World for the Appearing of the Saviour and the Setting up of His Kingdom." Knox College Senate minutes, 13 January 1864; *Home and Foreign Record*, May 1864, 94.
8 Such an appointment was virtually unheard of in the CPC. The major reason for this move was that for the previous three years Knox's Church had been embroiled in bitter controversies among the elders, and then with the Presbytery and National Synod. Simpson was, in effect, a compromise candidate; two others had been unsuccessfully called before him. An ongoing account of the controversy can be found in the Presbytery of Hamilton minutes, 1863–65.
9 See Reid, "Jesus Only," ch. 4.
10 Born and raised in Massachusetts, Daniel Webster Whittle (1840–1901), under the influence of D.L. Moody, gave up a lucrative career with the Elgin Watch Company in 1874 to become a non-sectarian, full-time evangelist. Known for his earnest, unadorned preaching and hymn writing,

Whittle conducted evangelistic campaigns in nearly all of the United States. His first evangelistic partner, Philip Paul Bliss (1838–1876), had also been encouraged by Moody to take up itinerant evangelism.
11 *Louisville Courier-Journal*, 17 February 1875, 3.
12 A.B. Simpson, *The Gospel of Healing* (Harrisburg, PA: Christian Publications, 1915), 162.
13 Thirteenth Street Presbyterian Church, *Minutes of Session*, 31 October 1881, 476–7.
14 A.B. Simpson, *Word, Work and World* (New York), March 1883, 45.
15 A.B. Simpson, "The Work of the Christian and Missionary Alliance," *The Alliance Weekly* 46 (May 1916): 107.
16 Robert L. Niklaus, John S. Sawin, and Samuel J. Stoesz, *All for Jesus: God at Work in the Christian and Missionary Alliance over One Hundred Years* (Camp Hill: Christian Publications, 1986), 63. Meetings were held in New York, Philadelphia, Boston, Pittsburgh, Buffalo, Detroit, and Chicago.
17 Simpson, *Word, Work and World*, March 1883, 47.
18 Ibid., 94. In its first annual report of 1897 the Christian and Missionary Alliance reported over 300 missionaries overseas and a minimal budget of more than $1,000,000.
19 See Blumhofer, *Assemblies of God*; Charles W. Nienkirchen, *A.B. Simpson and the Pentecostal Movement* (Peabody, MA: Hendrickson, 1992); John S. Sawin, "The Tongues Crisis, 1905–1914: A Bibliography ..." (Colorado Springs: A.B. Simpson Historical Library, 1984).
20 *The World's Crisis*, 28 November 1866, 2.
21 See Ronald G. Sawatsky, "Looking for That Blessed Hope: The Roots of Fundamentalism in Canada, 1875–1914" (Ph.D. diss., University of Toronto, 1986).
22 *Toronto Mail*, 19 December 1882, 8.
23 *Alliance Witness*, 29 December 1917, 198.
24 *Constitution of Bethany Church* (manuscript), September 1891.
25 *Faithful Witness*, November 1893, 178.
26 *Christian Alliance*, August 1889, 26.
27 Between 1889 and 1917 the Methodist, Congregationalist, Presbyterian, and Baptist churches cooperated with Simpson.
28 Reynolds, *Rebirth*, 38.
29 Perhaps the most prominent of these cases was that of William Howland, whose death from pneumonia in 1893 was at least partly attributable to his determination to rely solely on "the efficacy of divine healing." The press depicted his delay in calling in physicians as one of the follies of "Christian Science." *Toronto News*, 12, 13 December 1893, 1, 8.
30 Statistics Canada, *The Nation* (1993), 104. Between 1981 and 1991 membership in Canada has grown by over 90 per cent, from 33,900 to

almost 60,000, with significant growth among those less than 10–19 years and those 30–39 years.

31 Smith held to a Keswick doctrine of gradual and never fully realized sanctification; he had not yet established a view on divine healing and had not been baptized by immersion. Moreover, Smith held strongly dispensational and separatist views.

32 See, for example, "Tearful Scores Give Testimony," *Toronto Globe*, 11 May 1921, 13: "For a time at Massey Hall last night it looked as though, with a modern setting, the miracle of Pentecost would be repeated, when under the preaching of Rev. F.F. Bosworth over one hundred people sought salvation, while hundreds were seekers after a deeper spiritual life ... Hundreds also sought healing last night, and there were scores of testimonies of bodily healing having been experienced."

33 *Toronto Star*, 18 April 1921, 22.

34 See criticisms of Rev. Roland Bingham, founder of the Sudan Interior Mission, and a former pastoral assistant at Bethany Church, *Evangelical Christian*, July 1921, 199ff.

35 Reynolds, *Rebirth*, 113–14. Among the first missionaries were four single women, sent out on horseback in the summer of 1923. Concerned for their safety, Alliance officials cancelled this innovation after the first year.

36 *The Canadian Alliance*, September 1924, 3.

37 Mann, *Sect, Cult and Church*, 121.

38 Christian and Missionary Alliance in Canada, "President's Report: General Services," 1994, 2.

39 Niklaus, Sawin and Stoesz, *All for Jesus*, xii.

40 This growth shows little sign of abating. Consisting of 376 churches and 86,330 inclusive members in 1994, the CMA in Canada supports 230 missionaries around the world. Total revenues in 1994 neared $75 million.

41 The catalyst for this inquiry was Reynolds's *Footprints*.

42 David F. Hartzfeld and Charles W. Nienkirchen, *The Birth of a Vision: Essays on the Ministry and Thought of A.B. Simpson* (Regina: Canadian Theological Seminary, 1987).

43 Nienkirchen, *A.B. Simpson and the Pentecostal Movement: A Study in Continuity, Crisis and Change* (Peabody, MA: Hendrickson, 1992). Tozer's revisionism can be found in his popular Simpson biography, *Wingspread: A.B. Simpson, a Study in Spiritual Altitude* (Harrisburg, PA: Christian Publications, 1943).

44 Arnold Cook, "Draw Me Deeper: 1994 President's Address to Elders' Boards" (Willowdale: CMA in Canada, 1994), video.

45 Ibid.

46 Arnold Cook, "Briefing: A Communication from the President to the Churches of the CMA," February 1995.

47 Ibid.

CHAPTER EIGHTEEN

I would like to express my gratitude to the Pew Charitable Trusts and to Dr Edith Blumhofer for a grant which made it possible for me to assemble representatives of eleven out of thirteen Canadian Pentecostal denominations for an unprecedented meeting. This meeting provided useful insights for this paper, and it will continue to bear fruit for years to come. I am also deeply grateful to Sharon Cunningham, who provided invaluable assistance with some of the fundamental research behind this paper.

1 Telephone interview with James MacKnight, 22 March 1995.
2 See S.D. Clark, *Church and Sect in Canada* (Toronto: University of Toronto Press, 1948), 14, 93, 160; H.H. Walsh, *The Christian Church in Canada* (Toronto: Ryerson, 1956), 117, 134; J.S. Moir, "Sectarian Tradition in Canada," in *The Churches and the Canadian Experience*, ed. J.W. Grant (Toronto: Ryerson, 1963), 124–6.
3 The Independent Assemblies of God International of Canada had ties to Sweden (Harry Nunn, Sr to R. Kydd, 19 October 1981), and Global Missions/Sharon arose out of a split from another Pentecostal group. See G.H. Warnock, then secretary of Sharon Orphanage and Schools, to C.J. Jaenen, 26 August 1949, C.J. Jaenen, M.A. Papers, Purdie Archives, Central Pentecostal College, Saskatoon, SK, [hereafter Jaenen Papers].
4 C.W. Conn, *Like a Mighty Army*, rev. ed. (Cleveland, TN: Pathway, 1977), 153.
5 P.H. Walker, State Overseer, West Virginia Church of God, to W.L. Roset, Pastor of the Pentecostal Assemblies of Canada Church in Morden, Manitoba, 5 April 1950, Jaenen Papers; Darrell Lindsay to Deanna McAffee, n.d. (Personal papers of Deanna McAffee, Moose Jaw, SK); and Deanna McAffee to R. Kydd, 22 January 1982.
6 Burton K. Janes, *The Lady Who Stayed* (St John's: Good Tidings Press, 1983), 143; Luigi Zucchi, *The Italian Pentecostal Church of Canada* (Montreal: The Italian Pentecostal Church of Canada, 1987), 10–11.
7 See Blumhofer, *Restoring the Faith*, 113–41.
8 The "Jesus Only" question: Franklin Small, "Historical and Valedictory Account of the Origin of the Water Baptism in Jesus' Name Only and the Doctrine of the Fullness of God in Christ, in Pentecostal Circles in Canada," *Living Waters*, April 1941, 1; and interview with John Paterson, a participant in these events, Montreal, 16 November 1981.
9 Taped interview with W.E. McAlister, participant in events, 1974; interview with Mervil Jackson, Spruce Lake, SK, May 1974; Minutes of the Second Annual Meeting of the Pentecostal Assemblies of Canada, 20 November 1920, 31, Archives, Pentecostal Assemblies of Canada, Mississauga [hereafter Archives]; Minutes of the Fourth Annual Meeting of the Pentecostal Assemblies of Canada, 11 October 1922, 43, Archives;

"Petition from the PAOC to the Assemblies of God, U.S.A.," 1925, Archives; and General Council Minutes, Assemblies of God, U.S.A., 22 September 1925, copy, Archives.

10 A.D. Urshan, *The Life Story of Andrew Bar David Urshan: An Autobiography*, 2d. ed. (Stockton, CA: WABC Press, 1981), 140.

11 Robert Larden, *Our Apostolic Heritage* (Calgary: Apostolic Church of Pentecost Inc., 1971), 30–2; interview with Paterson; Small, "Historical and Valedictory Account," 1–2.

12 D.W. Breen, then moderator of the Apostolic Church of Pentecost, to R. Kydd, 6 November 1981; also Gil Killam, current Moderator, *Brief Outline of ACOP History* (paper given at a meeting of Canadian Pentecostal Leaders, Mississauga, 24 October 1994), 1. (Hereafter, this meeting is noted as October 1994.)

13 See Barry Buzza, *History of the Foursquare Gospel Church of Canada* (October 1994), 7; Nicholas Murray, *A History of the Pentecostal Holiness Church of Canada*, 2.

14 Interestingly, its pattern does not conform to any of the common career-growth patterns identified by Rodney Stark and W.S. Bainbridge, "American-born Sects: Initial Findings," *Journal for the Scientific Study of Religion* [hereafter, *JSSR*] 20 (1981): 137.

15 The 1911 to 1981 totals are from Canadian census reports. Figures for 1911 to 1941 do not include data from Newfoundland. If they did, the total number of Pentecostals for those reports would be significantly higher, as would the number of Pentecostals per 1,000 of the Canadian plus Newfoundland population. On the other hand, if data from Newfoundland had been present, the growth from 1941 to 1951 would not have been as rapid as it appears. Also, the figure for 1911 is definitely too low, since there were large Pentecostal groups in existence by 1911 in Toronto and Winnipeg, with approximately thirty other small groups located at various places across the country. The 1921 total is also questionable.

16 Interview with Paterson; Larden, *Our Apostolic Heritage*, 169–70.

17 Max Weber, *The Sociology of Religion*, trans. E. Fischoff (Boston: Beacon Press, 1963); Ernst Troeltsch, *The Social Teaching of the Christian Church*, trans. O. Wynn (London: Allen & Unwin, 1956).

18 See Peter L. Berger, "The Sociological Study of Sectarianism," *Social Research* 21 (1954); Benton Johnson, "Church and Sect Revisited," *JSSR* 10 (1971); Laurence R. Iannaccone, "A Formal Model of Church and Sect," *American Journal of Sociology* 94 (1988); David A. Nock, "Differential Ecological Receptivity of Conversionist and Revolutionist Sects: Reconsideration of Stark and Bainbridge," *Sociological Analysis* 50 (1989); Lorne Dawson, "Church/Sect Theory: Getting It Straight," *North American Religion* 1 (1992).

19 See Allan W. Eisler, "Toward a Radical Critique of Church-Sect Typologizing," *JSSR* 6 (1967); and James A. Beckford, "Religious Organizations: A Survey of Some Recent Publications," *Archives de sciences sociales des religions* 57 (1984).
20 See Walter G. Muelder, "From Sect to Church," *Christendom* 10 (1942); J.H. Chamberlayne, "From Sect to Church in British Methodism," *British Journal of Sociology* 15 (1964); Elizabeth Isichei, "From Sect to Denomination among English Quakers," *Patterns of Sectarianism*, ed. B.R. Wilson (London: Heinemann, 1967); Rodney Stark and W.S. Bainbridge, "Of Churches, Sects, and Cults: Preliminary Concepts for a Theory of Religious Movements," *JSSR* 18 (1979).
21 Benton Johnson, "On Church and Sect," *American Sociological Review* 28 (1963).
22 See H. Richard Niebuhr, *The Kingdom of God in America* (New York: Harper, 1937), 167–9; *The Social Sources of Denominationalism* (New York: Meridian Books, 1957), 19; Liston Pope, *Millhands and Preachers* (New Haven: Yale University Press, 1942), 118–20; Calvin Redekop, "A New Look at Sect Development," *JSSR* 13 (1974): 347; Johnson, "Church and Sect Revisited," 129–30. The last two emphasize the way wider societies influence how particular groups institutionalize.
23 Muelder, "From Sect to Church," 454.
24 Bryan R. Wilson, "An Analysis of Sect Development," *Patterns of Sectarianism*, ed. Bryan R. Wilson (London: Heinemann, 1967), 44; Wilson, *Religious Sects* (London: World University Library, 1970), 36–40, 51, 235.
25 With apologies to other Pentecostal groups, I will be drawing most of my illustrative material from the Pentecostal Assemblies of Canada, as I have had most ready access to this group.
26 "Separation," *The Pentecostal Testimony* [hereafter PT], November 1927, 15; G.A. Chambers, "This Age," PT, June 1926, 13–14; G.E. Smith, "Citizenship," PT, January 1927, 16. (Smith implies that Christians should not even vote.) In 1928 the PAOC was officially pacifist. See "A Statement of Fundamental Truths Approved by the Pentecostal Assemblies of Canada," PT, October 1928, 5.
27 "Evangelism the Supreme Mission of the Church," PT, March 1929, 16–17.
28 *The Promise*, March 1910, 1.
29 A.G. Ward to J.W. McKillop, 18 December 1935, Archives.
30 D.N. Buntain, "Workers Together with God!" PT, February 1937, 23.
31 E.N.O. Kulbeck, "Separation or Isolation," PT, September 1957, 2.
32 See "Rev. P.A. Gaglardi, Appointed Works Minister in Bennett's Cabinet," PT, 15 September 1952, 11; "Surprise Vote: Pastor Sam Boilermakers Head," PT, April 1955, 26.

33 Bruce Reed, *Dynamics of Religion: Process and Movement in Christian Churches* (London: Darton, Longman and Todd, 1978), 32.
34 Ibid., 15, 32.
35 A further stratum may soon be added as Pentecostals embrace the "Toronto Blessing," which began in 1994.
36 Rawlyk, *Canada Fire*, xiv.
37 *The Good Report*, May 1911, 4.
38 G.A. Chambers, "Fifty Years Ago," PT, May 1956, 6. Another early Pentecostal, John C. Ball, had also been associated with that group. Gloria Kulbeck, *What God Hath Wrought: A History of the Pentecostal Assemblies of Canada* (Toronto: PAOC, 1958), 110.
39 A.G. Ward, "Reminiscences of Fifty Years in the Gospel Ministry," PT, 15 February 1950, 4; A.G. Ward, "My Personal Experience of Pentecost," PT, May 1956, 7.
40 Kulbeck, *What God Hath Wrought*, 93.
41 Stackhouse, *Canadian Evangelicalism*, 16.
42 R.E. McAlister, "The Pentecostal Movement," PT, April 1922, 1.
43 See Kydd, "H.C. Sweet: Canadian Churchman."
44 Application for Charter, Archives, Apostolic Church of Pentecost, Calgary. How an ordained Presbyterian played this role in a "Jesus Only" group is open to speculation.
45 See Kydd, "Denominationally-Trained Clergymen."
46 Edward Hildebrandt, "A History of the Winnipeg Bible Institute and College from 1925–1960" (M.Th. thesis, Dallas Theological Seminary, 1965), 37–8.
47 See Gordon Atter, "The Pentecostal Movement," PT, 15 April 1930, 10; "Candid Camera," PT, 15 December 1947, 13; H.H. Barber, "What Is an Evangelical?" PT, December 1956, 12; and Brian C. Stiller, "The Evolution of Pentecostalism: From Sectarianism to Denominationalism with Special Reference to the Danforth Gospel Temple 1922–1968" (Master of Religion thesis, Wycliffe College, 1975), 8–10.
48 Interview with Brian C. Stiller, Evangelical Fellowship of Canada, Markham, Ontario, 8 February 1995.
49 For example, "General Conference," PT, 15 October 1944, 4.
50 Interviews with Stiller and Kenneth B. Birch, Pentecostal Assemblies of Canada, Mississauga, 28 February 1995.
51 Interview with J. Harry Faught, Cobden, Ontario, 21 February 1995.
52 Stiller, *Evolution of Pentecostalism*, 44–8.
53 Minutes, Organization Meeting of the EFC, 16 February 1965, People's Church, Toronto, Archives, Evangelical Fellowship of Canada, Markham, Ontario [hereafter Archives, EFC].
54 Ibid. This policy was later amended to admit evangelical denominations and evangelical denominational fellowships to membership.

55 See Stackhouse, *Canadian Evangelicalism*, 196.
56 Interview with Faught.
57 Minutes, Biennial Meeting, EFC, February 1983, Archives, EFC.
58 Interview with Stiller. Stiller says Pentecostals have become "insular by institution."

CHAPTER NINETEEN

1 Martin E. Marty and R. Scott Appleby, *The Glory and the Power: The Fundamentalist Challenge to the Modern World* (Boston: Beacon Press, 1992), 203n.
2 Stackhouse, *Canadian Evangelicalism*, 6–17.
3 See Michael S. Hamilton, "The Fundamentalist Harvard: Wheaton College, and the Continuing Vitality of American Evangelicalism, 1919–1965" (Ph.D. diss., University of Notre Dame, 1994), introduction.
4 See James Opp, "'Culture of the Soul': Fundamentalism and Evangelism in Canada, 1921–1940" (M.A. thesis, University of Calgary, 1994).
5 William E. Curtis, *The Chicago Record Herald* (1911), quoted in Alan Artibise, *Winnipeg: An Illustrated History* (Toronto: Lorimer, 1977), 23.
6 Paul Voisey, "The Urbanization of the Canadian Prairies, 1871–1916," in *The Prairie West: Historical Readings*, ed. R. Douglas Francis and Howard Palmer (Edmonton: Pica Press, 1985); Gerald Friesen, *The Canadian Prairies: A History* (Toronto: University of Toronto Press, 1984), 274–80.
7 The phenomenal growth may be traced in *Westminster Church, 1892–1992* (Winnipeg: privately printed, 1992), 6–8; and Minutes of Session Book, Westminster United Church, 6 September 1893 – 2 June 1916, United Church Archives, University of Winnipeg.
8 Entry for 15 February 1911, Minutes of Session Book, 1893–1916. See also Clarence MacKinnon, *Reminiscences* (Toronto: Ryerson Press, 1938), 154–75.
9 See Gertrude E. McCance and Gordon Smith, *Elim Chapel: Seventy-Fifth Anniversary, 1910–1985* (Winnipeg: privately printed, 1985); McCance, Transcript of Address on the History of Elim Chapel, 20 June 1976, Elim Chapel Church Archives, Winnipeg [hereafter EC Archives].
10 "Elim Chapel Unique" (c.1914), undated clipping, EC Archives.
11 Advertisements, EC Archives.
12 McCance, Transcript of Address, 2.
13 Arno C. Gaebelein, *Half a Century: The Autobiography of a Servant* (n.p., 1930), 178.
14 "Elim Chapel Is Big Factor" (c.1917), undated clipping, EC Archives.
15 See "John Bellingham, Superintendent, Elim Chapel, Dies Tuesday," *Winnipeg Free Press*, 12 July 1937; obituary and funeral notices, EC Archives.

16 As a result of a fire in 1974, only one minute book remains, Elim Chapel Record Book of Minutes of Meetings of Managers and Directors, 1928–1941, EC Archives.
17 On American fundamentalism, see George Marsden, *Fundamentalism and American Culture: The Shaping of Twentieth-Century Evangelicalism, 1870–1925* (Oxford: Oxford University Press, 1980).
18 On this mediating tradition, see Gauvreau, *Evangelical Century*, 268–71; Mack, "Of Canadian Presbyterians and Guardian Angels," in Rawlyk and Noll, eds., *Amazing Grace*.
19 The Fundamentals of the Faith and Application Blank, Elim Chapel, Winnipeg, Canada, copy dated January 1918, EC Archives.
20 See undated obituary, "Sidney T. Smith, Grain Head, Dies"; Paterson, "Elim Chapel"; and other articles, EC Archives.
21 Tricia Howison, "Elim Chapel and Sidney T. Smith: A Case Study in Canadian Fundamentalism" (Seminary paper, Regent College, 1979). The question of Smith's alleged sexual infidelity is currently being researched by David Elliot.
22 Rennie, "Fundamentalism and the Varieties of North Atlantic Evangelicalism," in Noll, Bebbington, and Rawlyk, eds., *Evangelicalism: Comparative Studies*, 344.
23 McCance, Transcript of Address, 2.
24 See "Visiting Ministers"; "Some Distinguished Missionary Visitors"; other clippings and articles, EC Archives.
25 "Elim Chapel Is Big Factor" (c.1917), undated newspaper clipping, EC Archives.
26 Gaebelein, *Half a Century*, 180.
27 H.H. Hildebrand, telephone interview by author, tape recording and transcript, 31 March 1995.
28 See Reynolds, *Rebirth*.
29 See Minute Book of Winnipeg Bible Training School, 6 September 1926 – 23 April 1931, Providence College and Theological Seminary, Otterburne, Manitoba; Edward Hildebrandt, "A History of the Winnipeg Bible Institute" (M.Th. thesis, Dallas Theological Seminary, 1965).
30 See Minute Book of the Canadian Sunday School Mission, Winnipeg, transcribed by C.L. Johnston, secretary, 8 March 1927 – 29 April 1929, Canadian Sunday School Mission, National Office, Winnipeg; John Anderson Barbour, *They That Be Wise: The Story of the Canadian Sunday School Mission* (Winnipeg: Hull Printing [1962]); Judith P. Funk, *Explosion of the Ordinary: The Ongoing Story of the Canadian Sunday School Mission* (Winnipeg: CSSM Press, 1992).
31 McCance, Transcript of Address, 6; "Elim Chapel Outreach," typed document, EC Archives.
32 On Millar's break with T.T. Shields over dispensationalism, see Opp, "Culture of the Soul," 34n, 91; Orville Swenson, interview by author,

tape recording and transcript, 31 March 1995. On Millar and the Moose Jaw Bible Institute, see *Links of Gold* (privately printed, 1982).

33 Simon E. Forsberg, "Information on Mr. Forsberg," autobiographical typescript, Montana Bible College, Bozeman.

34 See Dick Bohrer, *Lion of God: A Biography of John G. Mitchell, D.D.* (Portland, OR: Multnomah Bible College, 1994); and ibid.

35 H.H. Hildebrand, interview by author, 31 March 1995; Walter Aikenhead (son of D.R. Aikenhead), interview by author, tape recording and transcript, 4 April 1995; Brokenshell History Committee, *Browsing Through Brokenshell* (Trossachs, SK: privately printed, 1983), 45–9.

36 See Kydd, "H.C. Sweet: Canadian Churchman."

37 Mr and Mrs Wesley Affleck, telephone interview by author, tape recording and transcript, and follow-up conversation, 3 April 1995.

38 Henry Hildebrand, *In His Loving Service* (Caronport, SK: Briercrest Bible College, 1985), 34–5; Hildebrand, interview by author, 31 March 1995.

39 See board minutes from July 1930 to 16 January 1931, Minute Book of Winnipeg Bible Training School; Hildebrandt, History of the Winnipeg Bible Institute, 36–8; Opp, "Culture of the Soul," 97–8.

40 See board minutes, 22 April 1930, Minute Book of Winnipeg Bible Training School; 5 September 1931, Minutes of the Board of the Winnipeg Bible College, 8 June 1931 – 15 December 1932, Loose-leaf binder, Providence College and Theological Seminary, Otterburne, Manitoba. See also statement of faith, Moose Jaw Bible Institute (under Millar and Forsberg), 1929, in *Links of Gold*, 7.

41 Swenson, interview by author, 31 March 1995; Hildebrandt, "History of Winnipeg Bible Institute," 44. Moose Jaw Bible Institute had the same motto in 1931. See *Links of Gold*, 9.

42 See board minutes, 4 February, 4 April, and 20 September 1932, Minutes of the Board of the Winnipeg Bible College.

43 Hildebrand, interview by author, 31 March 1995.

44 See Hildebrand, *In His Loving Service*, 13–63.

45 The Winnipeg fundamentalist network may yet be seen to have been one of the most powerful, if inadvertent, engines of ethnic assimilation, in an age when so many of the mainline churches and social gospel missions struggled with that task as a central preoccupation. In *In His Loving Service*, 48, Hildebrand describes the ethnic composition of the Briercrest Gospel Assembly. See also Forsberg's "Principal's Report to the Board of Trustees" for 4 February 1932, which likewise breaks down the student numbers by country of origin (Minutes of the Board of the Winnipeg Bible College, 1931–1942, Providence College and Theological Seminary, Otterburne, Manitoba).

46 See Gerald L. Wright, "In Bigger Business," *Moody Monthly*, January 1956, 22–3, 55–6.

47 See Bernard and Marjorie Palmer, *Beacon on the Prairies* (Caronport: Briercrest Bible Institute, 1970); Henry Budd, *Wind in the Wheatfields* (Caronport: privately printed, 1985).
48 Hildebrand, interview by author, 31 March 1995.
49 See Opp, "Culture of the Soul," 91–2.
50 It should be noted that out of the Winnipeg fundamentalist network also came George Blackett, one-time principal of Winnipeg Bible Institute and later founder of the Christian and Missionary Alliance school, Canadian Bible Institute, in Regina (Reynolds, *Rebirth*, 345ff). R. Wesley Affleck, who has been noted for his association with fundamentalist clusters in Saskatoon and Winnipeg and who went on from his principalship at Winnipeg Bible Institute to found Burrard Inlet Bible Institute, later moved to Kelowna and renamed the Okanagan Bible Institute.
51 Al Hiebert, interview by author, tape recording and transcript, 5 April 1995, Otterburne, Manitoba; letter to the author from Myrna Friesen, librarian, Steinbach Bible College, 17 April 1995.
52 Voisey, "Urbanization," 388.
53 Bohrer, *Lion of God*, 110.
54 Meredith B. Banting, *Early History of Saskatchewan Churches (Grassroots)*, 2 vols (Regina: Banting Publishers [1975]).
55 Elim Chapel advertised itself as interdenominational. Advertisement for Mass Meeting at Walker Theatre, 20 January 1918, EC Archives.
56 This was George Blackett, who graduated in 1915 (Reynolds, *Rebirth*, 80).
57 David Phillips, "The History of the Inter-Varsity Christian Fellowship in Western Canada" (M.C.S. thesis, Regent College, Vancouver, 1976), 71.
58 Stackhouse, *Canadian Evangelicalism*, 49–108
59 Friesen, *Canadian Prairies*, 304, 320.

CHAPTER TWENTY

1 *United Church of Canada London Conference*, 1934, Hugh T. Crossley and John E. Hunter Personal Papers, Archives of the United Church of Canada, Toronto [hereafter AUCC]. The "Newspaper Clippings File [hereafter File]," a scrap-book compiled by Hunter, contains articles describing their various revivals. Many of these articles have no date, location, or title. To organize the material, page references are given.
2 Quoted in William J. Lamb, *Bridging the Years* (Winfield, BC: Wood Lake Books, 1990), 182.
3 *Christian Guardian*, 29 February 1888.
4 File, 63.
5 Ibid., 14.
6 John A. Macdonald, Personal Papers, National Archives of Canada, M.F. 1085.

7 File, 72.
8 *Belleville Daily Intelligencer*, 3 March 1888, 3.
9 *New Outlook*, 24 October 1934, 947.
10 File, 7.
11 Grant, *Profusion of Spires*, 175.
12 Quoted in *Christian Guardian*, 2 February 1887, 68.
13 File, 23.
14 Ibid., 16.
15 Ibid., 72.
16 Ibid., 23.
17 Ibid., 21.
18 Ernest Crossley Hunter and Frank Chamberlain, "Old-Time Evangelism," *United Church Observer*, 24, Crossley and Hunter Personal Papers, AUCC.
19 File, 32.
20 Ibid., 21.
21 Crossley Hunter, "Old-Time Evangelism," 26.
22 *Christian Guardian*, 17 October 1888, 660.
23 John E. Hunter, *Pay-Pray-Prosper* (Toronto: William Briggs, 1896).
24 File, 46.
25 Ibid., 8.
26 Ibid., 113.
27 Crossley Hunter, "Old-Time Evangelism," 26.
28 File, 53.
29 *Daily Intelligencer*, 17 April 1888, 3.
30 File, 115.
31 Ibid., 39.
32 Ibid., 113.
33 Ibid., 78.
34 Ibid., 104.
35 Ibid.
36 Ibid., 111.
37 Ibid., 63.
38 Ibid., 114.
39 Ibid., 110.
40 Quoted in *Christian Guardian*, 7 March 1888, 153.
41 File, 88.
42 Ibid., 100.
43 Quoted in Airhart, *Serving the Present Age*, 25.
44 *Daily Intelligencer*, 11 March 1908, 3.
45 Hugh T. Crossley, *Practical Talks on Important Themes* (Toronto: William Briggs, 1895), 165.
46 Ibid., 163.
47 Ibid., 171.

48 Ibid., 176.
49 File, 72.
50 Ibid., 99.
51 Ibid., 101.
52 Crossley, *Practical Talks*, 298.
53 Airhart, "Ordering a New Nation," in Rawlyk, ed., *Canadian Protestant Experience*, 109.
54 Grant, *Profusion of Spires*, 211.
55 Crossley, *Practical Talks*, 256.
56 Ibid., 259.
57 Ibid., 321–2.
58 *Daily Intelligencer*, 16 March 1908, 7.
59 Crossley, *Practical Talks*, 323–4.
60 Ibid., 121.
61 Ibid., 258.
62 Ibid., 261.
63 Ibid., emphasis mine.
64 File, 41.
65 *Daily Intelligencer*, 19 March 1888, 3.
66 Crossley, *Practical Talks*, 252.
67 Grant, *Profusion of Spires*, 179.
68 *Kingston Daily British Whig*, 6 November 1889, 1.
69 File, 113.
70 Ibid., 123.
71 Ibid., 77.
72 Ibid., 62.
73 *Daily Intelligencer*, 16 March 1888, 3.
74 File, 105.
75 Ibid., 84.
76 Ibid., 65.
77 Ibid.
78 Evidence suggests that the evangelists and some railroad barons were remarkably close. After they delivered a sobriety message to one group of railwaymen, Crossley and Hunter were taken on a short holiday tour, compliments of the thankful owners.
79 File, 59, emphasis mine.

CHAPTER TWENTY-ONE

1 Robert S. Kenny Collection, MS. 179, box 33, A.E. Smith to Dear Sir, 3 May 1946, University of Toronto, Thomas Fisher Rare Books Library. On the appeal of evangelism to the "common people," see Rev. John

Maclean Papers, box 3, file 62, A.E. Smith to Maclean, 12 March 1919; Maclean to C.W. Morrow, 13 March 1919, United Church Archives.
2 Maclean Papers, box 3, A.E. Smith to Rev. M.C. Flatt, 13 June 1919.
3 See Craig Heron, "Labourism and the Canadian Working Class," *Labour/Le travail* 13 (Spring 1984), 63–4; Gregory S. Kealey, "1919: The Canadian Labour Revolt," *Labour/Le travail* 13 (Spring 1984). Working-class hostility to religion has also become paradigmatic among American labour historians. See Bruce C. Nelson, "Revival and Upheaval: Religion, Irreligion, and Chicago's Working Class in 1886," *Journal of Social History* 25,2 (Winter 1991).
4 Allen, *Social Passion*, 93; A. Ross McCormack, *Reformers, Rebels and Revolutionaries: The Western Canadian Radical Movement, 1899–1919* (Toronto: University of Toronto Press, 1977); David Jay Bercuson, *Confrontation at Winnipeg: Labour, Industrial Relations and the General Strike* (Montreal and London: McGill-Queen's University Press, 1974).
5 "Delegation Will Invite Sunday to Winnipeg," *Winnipeg Free Press* [hereafter *FP*], 5 May 1914.
6 P.W.L., "Billy Sunday," *FP*, 28 April 1914.
7 *FP*, An Ex-Yankee, "Billy Sunday," 25 April 1914; Dr A.G. Sinclair, "Tributes Paid to 'Billy' Sunday by City Ministers," 15 June 1914; P.W.L., "Billy Sunday," 28 April 1914.
8 "If Billy Sunday Comes, What Will He Do to Winnipeg?" *FP*, 20 April 1914.
9 Horace Westwood, All Soul's Unitarian Church, "A Protest Against Billy Sunday's Visit," *FP*, 6 May 1914.
10 "Tributes Paid to 'Billy' Sunday by City Ministers," *FP*, 15 June 1914.
11 Ibid.; *FP*, "Resignation of Dr J.L. Gordon Duly Accepted," 21 May 1914; W.J. McIvor, "Letter to Editor," 13 May 1914.
12 According to Emmanuel Evans in "Defends Billy Sunday," *FP*, 30 April 1914, church membership in Winnipeg in 1914 was approximately 25,000. By applying the formula established by George Rawlyk (*Canada Fire*, 228, 97n) that church attendance was between five- and eight-fold that of actual membership, the church attendance of Winnipeg was about 125,000 in a population estimated between 150–200,000. This extremely high church affiliation accords with the statistics offered by Alan Artibise in *Winnipeg: A Social History of Urban Growth, 1874–1914* (Montreal and London: McGill-Queen's University Press, 1975), 142–3. The two largest Methodist congregations in Canada were in Winnipeg, at Grace Church and Young Church. See Maclean Papers, box 11, file 14, "Diary 1919, Aug.–Sept."
13 *FP*, McIvor, "Letter to Editor," 13 May 1914. See also J.C., "Billy Sunday," 4 May 1914; A.W. Lee, "Is Baseball a Sin?" 6 May 1914.

14 *FP*, "Visiting Clergy in City Churches," 21 September 1914; "Bible Conference to Open Monday," and "Mass Meeting for Men Province Theatre," 19 September 1914; J.A.M., "Took Kindly to Dr. J.L. Gordon," 3 December 1914; "Will Hold Social Reform Campaign – Charles Stelzle Apostle of Working Classes Here for Eight Day Series of Meetings," 11 April 1914.
15 W.F. Osborne, University of Manitoba, "Opposed to Visit of Sunday," *FP*, 1 May 1914.
16 *FP*, "Much Interest in Coming Missions," 23 October 1915; "'Win One' Campaign Launched in City," 26 October 1915. For a longer discussion of this issue, see Christie and Gauvreau, *"A Full-Orbed Christianity."*
17 *FP*, "'La Marechale' Mrs Catherine Booth-Clibborn," 2 May 1914; "Evangelist Talks to Big Audience," 11 May 1914.
18 *FP*, J.R. Hugg, "As to the Value of Revivals," 9 May 1914; S.C. Mulhall, "Letter to Editor," 14 May 1914; "Rev. J.L. Gordon Will Enter New Field of Work," 12 May 1914; "St. Stephen's W.H.M.S. Holds Last Meeting," 2 April 1914.
19 "Explains Reasons for Inviting Sunday," *FP*, 18 May 1914.
20 *FP*, J.W. Bengough, "Says Protection is Anti-Christian," 6 April 1915; "Anniversary at St. James' Church," 11 March 1918; "Woman's Place to See Wars Occur No More," 3 May 1919; "Anniversary of Rev. Dr. Christie," 13 December 1915; Henry E. Wilson, "Criticizes Mr. Hugg's Letter," 16 May 1914; "Minimum Wage Law Workers' Safeguard," 26 April 1918.
21 *FP*, "Church Notices," 1 May 1915; "Winnipeg Church News," 26 January 1918; "People's Forum Closes Season," 18 March 1918, Christie speaking on similar themes; S.G. Bland, "Notes and Impressions of a Visitor to the States," 19 April 1918, speaking about the Winnipeg-born leader of the American Federation of Labor, Frank Morrison; "Socialism Failed," 1 March 1915.
22 *FP*, "Says Protection is Anti-Christian," 6 April 1915; "Friendly Debate on Socialism," 16 April 1915; "Character without Christ an Illusion," 29 November 1915.
23 Osborne, "Opposed to Visit from Sunday."
24 *FP*, "Winnipeg United City Mission"; "Dominion Theatre – Great Mass Meeting – Is There an Atonement? – Soldiers Especially Invited"; "St. Stephen's Church Brotherhood," 26 February 1916.
25 Much historical writing on early twentieth-century Winnipeg has dwelt upon the differences between the "North End" (north of the CPR tracks at Main and Higgins) and the rest of Winnipeg. While this area did contain the bulk of the non-Anglo-Saxon immigrant population, it was still 38.9 per cent British in ethnic origin in 1916. According to one historian, the area between Portage Avenue and Notre Dame Avenue contained a

large number of moderate structures "that differed but little from that carried out in the North End." It was here that the Anglo-Saxon working class was concentrated. The exclusively middle-class section of Winnipeg lay south of the Assiniboine River. See Artibise, *Winnipeg: A Social History of Urban Growth*, 163, 168–9.

26 "Church News" and "Pastor Queried as to Beliefs," FP, 17 February 1917.
27 "News of City Churches," FP, 12 January 1918.
28 Robert S. Kenny Collection, box 37, folder 2, A.E. Smith, "The Passing Shadow," incomplete and unpublished typescript, n.d., ch. I, 2–7; ch. II, 3.
29 Maclean Papers, box 3, file 71, Maclean to Rev. Dr J.W. Saunby, 18 February 1920; box 2, file 50, V.H. Rust to Maclean, 13 June 1916.
30 Allen, *Social Passion*, 16–17; R. Cook, *The Regenerators*, 228–32.
31 Maclean Papers, box 3, file 62, A.E. Smith to Maclean, 12 March 1919. It has become commonplace to view Smith as a liberal in terms of theology because he was a radical in terms of labour politics. However, just prior to the Winnipeg General Strike he was hoping to take over the pastorship of Zion Methodist Church, where he planned to undertake community work among its working-class congregation. His disagreement with the Methodist church revolved not around theological issues but over his conviction that the church needed to adopt new methods of helping the underprivileged. See ibid., C.W. Morrow to Maclean, 9 March 1919; 13 March 1919. Smith did not eschew traditional evangelism as long as it functioned in tandem with practical help for the working classes. See Kenny Collection, box 33, Smith to Rev. William Ivens, 7 July 1917.
32 Maclean Papers, box 11, file 16, "Diary," 27 November 1919; box 41, file 551, John Maclean, "Why Is the Pulpit Silent on the Live Questions of Vital Interest to the Masses?" *Halifax Herald*, 16 May 1907.
33 Maclean Papers, box 2, file 48, "One Day at Bethel," circular, 12 April 1915; box 11, file 10, "Diary 1916–1917," entries for 20, 21, 24 December 1916; box 11, file 12, "Diary," entry for 14 July 1919; box 3, file 76, Maclean to Joseph Clark, 8 November 1920.
34 Ibid., box 11, file 15, "Diary," 5 November 1919; box 11, file 12, 11 July 1919.
35 Ibid., box 3, file 58, Will Gibben to Maclean, 21 November 1918; box 3, file 76, Maclean to Mr George Evans, 20 November 1920; box 3, file 72, M.E. Wiley to Maclean, 29 March 1920; box 3, file 58, J.B. Nicholson to Maclean, 23 November 1918.
36 Ibid., box 3, file 63, Fred C. Franklin to My dear Pastor, 8 July 1919; box 11, file 12, "Diary," 9 July 1919.
37 Ibid., box 2, file 48, W. Prince to Maclean, 6 March 1915.
38 FP, "Church News," 12 February 1916; "Church News," 6 November 1915, where it stated that Maclean would preach: "In the evening there

will be a real old gospel service, of the evangelistic type as usual, the sermon being on 'Almost a Christian.'"

39 For the working-class character of these churches, "Combined Congregation Give Farewell to Rev. W. Wyman"; "St. Giles Church Outing," *FP*, 10 July 1919. Over 1,000 attended St. Giles's annual outing to Winnipeg Beach.
40 *FP*, "Church News," 13 April 1918; "Hand of God Seen in the Great War," 9 August 1915.
41 Maclean Papers, box 3, file 59, "Broadway Methodist Church," n.d.; *FP*, "Church Notes," 6 November 1915; "Church News," 9 August 1915.
42 "Church Notices," *FP*, 20 March 1915.
43 *FP*, "Advertisement," 21 August 1915; "Sunday Church Services," 5 June 1915; "Advertisement," 17 March 1915.
44 "Elim Chapel is Big Factor in Religious Life," *FP*, 19 January 1918.
45 *FP*, "Advertisement," 25 September 1915; "Successful Meeting," 15 November 1915.
46 *FP*, "Church Notices," 5 December 1915; "The Incarnation," 18 December 1915.
47 *FP*, "Sunday Church Services," June 5, 1915; "A Course of Lectures on the Second Coming of Christ," 29 May 1915.
48 *FP*, "Mission Preacher – Dr. Gaebelein Giving Three Addresses on Sunday," 5 February 1916; "Church News," 13 September 1919.
49 Maclean Papers, box 11, file 10, "Diary," 19 December 1916.
50 Ibid., box 11, file 16, "Diary," November 1919.
51 Allen in *Social Passion*, 52–3, suggests that Ivens's radical views assured him of the complete support of the working class members of his congregation.
52 "Plain Talking in Defence of Christian Church," *FP*, 15 February 1915. Interestingly, Hughson was the pastor at Grace Methodist which had once been J.S. Woodsworth's pulpit.
53 Maclean Papers, box 11, file 16, "Diary," 26 November 1919. For Ivens's typical sermons, see "Church News," *FP*, 3 May 1919, when he spoke on "The Significance of the One Big Union"; *FP*, 18 May 1918; 20 May 1918.
54 "Church Notes," *FP*, 29 January 1916.
55 "Revival Meetings," Old Knox Church, *FP*, 5 January 1918. J.E. Rea has noted that the railway workers constituted the hard core of labour political strength in municipal elections throughout the 1920s and 1930s. See "The Politics of Class: Winnipeg City Council, 1919–1945," in *The West and the Nation: Essays in Honour of W.L. Morton*, ed. C. Berger and R. Cook (Toronto: McClelland & Stewart, 1976), 236.
56 *FP*, "Evangelist at Broadway Baptist Church," 15 April 1918; "Evangelist Ross Draws Big Crowd," 16 April 1918.

57 *FP*, "Winnipeg Church News," 16 March 1918; "Dr. Burns Delivers Strong Addresses," 8 April 1918; "Rev. Charles W. Ross On Forgiveness," 24 April 1918; Ross spoke at Home Street Baptist on "The Great Salvation."
58 *FP*, "Winnipeg Church News," 16 February 1918; "Revival Work at Zion Church," 4 March 1918; "Oliver's Winnipeg Evangelistic Campaign," 27 May 1918.
59 Bercuson, *Confrontation at Winnipeg*; McCormack, *Reformers, Rebels, and Revolutionaries*; Kealey, "1919: The Canadian Labour Revolt."
60 Allen, *Social Passion*, 82.
61 "Church News," *FP*, 19 July 1919.
62 Maclean Papers, box 11, file 12, "Diary," 14 July 1919.
63 Ibid., box 11, file 12, "Diary," 6 July 1919; box 11, file 14, "Diary," 15 September 1919.
64 Kenny Collection, box 33, Billie Hill to A.E. Smith, 16 February 1924; Hill to Smith, 9 April 1924; Maclean Papers, box 11, file 14, "Diary," 15 September 1919.
65 Kenny Collection, box 37, folder 51, "Lectures Delivered at the Labor Temple, Toronto, 1923." Smith himself desired to return to the "old church" in 1924 when he realized that the Labor Temples were a failure. See box 33, Smith to Hill, 28 November 1924; Hill to Smith, 19 December 1924.
66 Ibid., box 33, Rev. R. Lorne McTavish to Smith, September 1920; John Potsula to Smith, 25 January 1924; Allen, *Social Passion*, 83.
67 Maclean Papers, box 11, file 12, "Diary," 23 June 1919.
68 Kenny Collection, box 33, Hill to Smith, 16 February 1924.
69 Maclean Papers, box 11, file 16, "Diary," 23, 30 November 1919.
70 Ibid., box 11, file 17, "Diary," 1 December 1919.
71 Ibid., box 11, file 15, "Diary," 17 November 1919.
72 Ibid., box 11, file 14, "Diary," 22 September 1919.
73 Ibid., box 11, file 17, "Diary," 6 December 1919; "Church News," *FP*, 7 February 1920.
74 Maclean Papers, box 11, file 15, "Diary," 8 November 1919.
75 Ibid., box 11, file 17, "Diary," 1, 3, 8 December 1919.
76 *FP*, "Real Gypsy Smith is Coming Sunday," 27 September 1919; "Gypsy Smith Makes a Deep Impression," 29 September 1919, front page; "Many Answer Appeal of Famous Evangelist," 30 September 1919; "Afternoon Meeting Remarks of Special Interest to Women," 1 October 1919; "Church Needs Another Pentacost Says Gypsy," and "Triumphs of Cross Among the Soldiers," 2 October 1919. There were 900 conversions at the last meeting: "Gypsy Smith Finishes Great Campaign Here," 13 October 1919.
77 "Gypsy Smith Finishes Great Campaign Here," *FP*, 13 October 1919. On McPherson's revival, see *FP*, "To Open Campaign," and "She's Here for

the Big Revival," 14 February 1920. For a discussion of McPherson's Winnipeg activities, see Blumhofer, *Everybody's Sister*, 150-1.
78 FP, "Church News," 20, 27 May, 1918; 7 June 1919; 28 June 1919; 26 July 1919; "Presbyterians Urge Reform in Economics," 12 June 1919; "Mr. Dobson Outlines Reconstruction Work," 18 June 1919; "Ivens and Smith Cases Puzzling," 14 June 1919.
79 "Manitoba Methodist Conference Opens," FP, 12 June 1919.
80 FP, "Church News," 12, 28 July 1919; "Dr. Stauffer's Views on the Recent Strike," 30 June 1919.
81 Maclean Papers, box 3, file 72, Methodist Ministerial Association, Grace Church, 15 March 1920.
82 Ibid., box 47, file 33, "Premillennialism," 1922.
83 Christie and Gauvreau, *"A Full-Orbed Christianity,"* ch. 2.
84 Kenny Collection, box 33, Ivens to Smith, 11, 31 March 1920.

CHAPTER TWENTY-TWO

1 Henry Frost, *The Days That Are Past* (hereafter cited as HWF, *Memoirs*), typescript, Overseas Missionary Fellowship Archives, Toronto (hereafter OMF Archives), 522.
2 Dr and Mrs Howard Taylor, *Hudson Taylor and the China Inland Mission*, vol. 2, *The Growth of a Work of God* [cited as *Growth of a Work*] (London: CIM, 1918), 437-8.
3 Dr and Mrs Howard Taylor, *"By Faith ...": Henry W. Frost and the China Inland Mission* (Philadelphia: CIM, 1938), 88.
4 A.J. Broomhall, *Hudson Taylor and China's Open Century* (Sevenoaks: OMF, 1989), book 7, 82-3.
5 Taylor, *By Faith*, 88.
6 Taylor, *Growth of a Work*, 449.
7 HWF, *Memoirs*, 570.
8 Ibid., 698-9.
9 Ibid., 649-51.
10 *China's Millions*, April 1925, 52.
11 Broomhall, *Hudson Taylor 6, Assault on the Nine* (Sevenoaks: OMF, 1988), 375. The quote refers to F.W. Baller, the language school principal, and several of the Cambridge Seven.
12 Sara Jeannette Duncan, *The Imperialist* (1903; reprint, Toronto: McClelland & Stewart, 1984), 60-1.
13 Ernest Sandeen, *The Roots of Fundamentalism: British and American Millenarianism 1800-1930* (Chicago: University of Chicago Press, 1970). The quote is one American's description of the Niagara conferences.
14 Moira Jane McKay, *Faith and Facts in the History of the China Inland Mission 1832-1905* (M.Litt. diss., University of Aberdeen, 1981), 92.

15 Marshall Broomhall, *Jubilee Story of the China Inland Mission* (London: CIM, 1915), 30.
16 Eugene Stock, *The History of the Church Missionary Society: Its Environment, Its Men and Its Work*, vol. 3 (London: CMS, 1899), 20.
17 *China's Millions*, November 1876, 215.
18 Taylor, *Growth of a Work*, 378.
19 Taylor, *By Faith*, 90.
20 Broomhall, *Hudson Taylor* 7, 89.
21 Grattan Guinness, founder of many evangelical institutions, happened to be in Canada at the height of the 1859 revival and was one of those who took it back to England. One convert he made at that time was the young A.B. Simpson. Guinness's East London Missionary Training School sent out 1,500 foreign missionaries before 1900. Mrs Howard Taylor, the official historian of the CIM, was his daughter, Geraldine Guinness.
22 Sandeen, *Roots of Fundamentalism*, 132.
23 *China's Millions*, June 1890, 78.
24 For example, G.W. Clarke was one famous pioneer itinerant in China, who died in 1919 after 45 years service. See Broomhall, *Hudson Taylor* 6, 39–40.
25 Wallace played another role in the CIM: after Agnes's death, he married Hudson Taylor's "favourite niece," Edith Broomhall, daughter of Benjamin Broomhall, Taylor's brother-in-law and secretary of the CIM in England. Her brother Marshall became English secretary, and her sister Agnes married D.E. Hoste, Taylor's successor as general director. Wallace's marriage cemented the transatlantic CIM family.
26 HWF, *Memoirs*, 217.
27 Ian Rennie, "Gratitude for the Past," *Ontario Bible College Recorder*, Spring 1984.
28 HWF, *Memoirs*, 307. The Christian Institute figures prominently in Reynolds, *Footprints*.
29 HWF, *Memoirs*, 273.
30 Ibid., 310–11.
31 Ibid., 390.
32 Ibid., HWF to J Howard Taylor, 29 May 1891, 390.
33 Ibid., 397.
34 A former pastor of the Moody church in Chicago, W.J. Erdman was reputed to possess "the best knowledge of theology and the Bible among all the ministers who taught at Niagara." His son Charles Erdman convinced Frost to move to Philadelphia in 1901, where he remained active on the American council.
35 O'Meara to HWF, 4 April 1910, in O'Meara Papers, Wycliffe College Archives.
36 Ibid., 1 June 1915.

37 Margaret Brown, *History of the Honan (North China) Mission of the United Church of Canada, Originally a Mission of the Presbyterian Church in Canada, 1887–1951* (typescript in Anglican and United Church Archives [hereafter UCA]), 9: 5.
38 Goforth joined the CIM in mass evangelistic efforts during the 1907–08 revival. His obituary in *China's Millions*, March 1938, 43–4, noted: "No missionary not actually a member of the mission was ever more akin to it in spirit or more closely associated with it in actual service." The Anglican mission in Kaifeng also ran into the CIM ambitions, when Bishop William C. White built a hospital near the CIM "dispensary." See Austin, *Saving China*, 134–5. The Methodists in West China had a similar confrontation when they expanded their territory in 1907.
39 Brown, *History of the Honan Mission*, 24: 20–2.
40 Airhart, *Serving the Present Age*, 42.
41 CIM application record 43, Application log book, 1888–1915, OMF Archives; A. Sutherland to Virgil Hart, 30 January 1897, West China correspondence, 8, UCA.
42 Reynolds, *Footprints*, 71.
43 Maggie Scott's Alliance connection is not mentioned in the CIM records; her application lists her as Presbyterian. See Reynolds, *Footprints*, 71–3, 488–90; HWF, *Memoirs*, 411–13.
44 Henry Frost, *Miraculous Healing: A Personal Testimony and Biblical Study* (London: Evangelical Press, 1951), 28–30. See also minutes of Toronto Council, July 1904, April 1906, September 1906; Minutes of China Council, July 1906.
45 Marcus Wood, London Council, to HWF, 3 May 1904, in the Archives of the Billy Graham Center, Wheaton College, collection 215 and allied collections. After 1893 the Toronto applications note whether the candidate had been vaccinated.
46 HWF, *Memoirs*, 757–58.
47 Frost, *Miraculous Healing*, 11–14.
48 J.H. Hunter, *A Flame of Fire: The Life and Work of R.V. Bingham, D.D.* (Toronto: SIM, 1961), 65. The first SIM missionaries sent out by Bingham, between 1899 and 1903, had a high death toll.
49 Reynolds, *Rebirth*, 64.
50 HWF, *Memoirs*, 894. See also Austin, "Blessed Adversity," 53.
51 HWF, *Memoirs*, 431–2.
52 Reynolds, *Footprints*, 193–5.
53 Minutes of Toronto Bible Training School [TBTS] board, 14 May 1894.
54 Reynolds calls TBTS "the Toronto Bible School of Baptist association." *Footprints*, 195.
55 One of them was Anna Wood, later Mrs William E. Tyler, mother of Dr William W. Tyler, Canadian home director from 1947 to 1975.

56 The information in the applications is meagre: name, address, parents, denomination, living in the CIM home, dates of acceptance, sailing, and retirement. Some list occupation, vaccination, baptism, deceased parents, etc., OMF Archives.
57 HWF, *Memoirs*, 559–61; application 667, OMF Archives.
58 Application 626, OMF Archives.
59 HWF, *Memoirs*, 523.
60 Ibid., 637.
61 Ibid., 638.
62 Ibid., 579.
63 Burkinshaw, *Pilgrims in Lotus Land*.
64 HWF, *Memoirs*, 900.

CHAPTER TWENTY-THREE

1 Guenther, "Bible School Movement," 136–7.
2 Mann, *Sect, Cult and Church*, 83, Table IV. According to A.J. Klassen, ed., *The Bible School Story, 1913–1963: Fifty Years of Mennonite Brethren Bible Schools in Canada* (Clearbrook, BC: Canadian Board of Education, 1963), inclusion of the Mennonite schools would have added over 400 to Mann's total in 1947.
3 A.S. Witmer, "Report on Canadian Bible Institutes and Bible Colleges," at Conference of Christian Educators of Alberta, Saskatchewan & Manitoba, 31 May – 2 June 1960.
4 *Faith Alive*, March 1984, 9–13 and November 1985, 31–54.
5 *Faith Today*, January/February 1992, 34–45.
6 Guenther, "Bible School Movement," 135.
7 *Faith Alive*, November 1985, 31–54.
8 See Stackhouse, *Canadian Evangelicalism*, 271, 22n.
9 Donald Goertz, "The Development of a Bible Belt: The Socio-Religious Interaction in Alberta between 1925 and 1938" (M.C.S. thesis, Regent College, 1980), 223–4; Calvin B. Hanson, *From Hardship to Harvest: The Development of the Evangelical Free Church of Canada* (Edmonton: Evangelical Free Church of Canada, 1984), 97–104.
10 Eighteen of some twenty Fellowship of Gospel Churches, most founded by PBI graduates, merged with the EFC in 1957, bringing the total number of EFC congregations in the Prairies at the time to forty-three. See Hanson, *From Hardship to Harvest*, 117–23; interviews with Rev. David Enarson, moderator of the Fellowship of Gospel Churches at the time, 25, 27 January 1983.
11 Enarson interviews, 25, 27 January 1983; 11 June 1987.
12 Muriel Hanson, *Fifty Years and Seventy Places* (Minneapolis: Free Church Publications, 1967), 74.

13 Klassen, *The Bible School Story*.
14 Bruce Guenther, "Ethnicity and the Origin of the Bible School Movement in Western Canada: The Role of the Mennonites" (paper presented to the Canadian Evangelical Theological Association, 1992), 29–31.
15 Gerald C. Ediger, "Deutsch und Religion: Ethnicity, Religion and Canadian Mennonite Brethren, 1940–1970" (Th.D. thesis, Emmanuel College of Victoria University and the University of Toronto, 1993), 16–17, 27, 46, 65–6.
16 Interview, A.J. Klassen, Clearbrook, 25 June 1987; Henry C. Born, "Evangelism and Social Action: A Study of a Mennonite Brethren Church" (M.C.S. thesis, Regent College, 1982), 114–16.
17 From the late 1930s onward, Mennonites consistently made up 25–35 per cent of the enrolment at PBI and Briercrest (Guenther, "Ethnicity," 30).
18 Ibid.; Klassen interview, Clearbrook, 25 June 1987; and Peter Penner, *Reaching the Otherwise Unreached* (Clearbrook, BC: West Coast Children's Mission of British Columbia, 1959), 23–4.
19 Interview, Paul Magnus, Caronport, SK, 1 June 1994; interview, H. Hildebrand, Abbotsford, BC, 13 October 1994.
20 *Sunday School Times*, 11 November 1950.
21 Joel E. Harris, *The Baptist Union of Western Canada: A Centennial History* (Saint John: Lingley Printing, 1976), 107, 129; interview, Mr and Mrs George Davies, Vancouver, 29 November 1983.
22 Interview, Mel Ralston, White Rock, BC, 26 January 1995.
23 The founding and first decades of development are told in Stewart J. Lewis, "Christian Higher Education in the Christian Churches of the Maritime Provinces – Past, Present and Future" (Masters thesis, Cincinnati Christian Seminary, 1986). Interviews with Ken Norris, past-president of the college, 5 October 1993 and Stewart J. Lewis, president, 4 October 1993, provided information on the orientation of the churches.
24 Mann, *Sect, Cult and Church*, 52–90.
25 John M. Badertscher, Gordon Harland, and Roland E. Miller, *Religious Studies in Manitoba and Saskatchewan: A State-of-the-Art Review*, The Study of Religion in Canada, vol. 4 (Waterloo: Wilfred Laurier University Press for the Canadian Corporation for Studies in Religion, 1993), 140–1.
26 New Brunswick Legislature, "An Act to Incorporate the New Brunswick Bible Institute," 1947; *Religious Studies in Manitoba and Saskatchewan*, 138–40; Vancouver Bible Training School, council minutes, 17 May 1918.
27 See Rawlyk, "Protestant Colleges in Canada," 278–302.
28 Stackhouse, *Canadian Evangelicalism*, 64–5.
29 See Noll, "Revolution and the Rise of Evangelical Social Influence," in Noll, Bebbington, and Rawlyk, eds., *Evangelicalism: Comparative Studies*.

30 G. Ronald Neufeld and Allen Steven, *Stay in School Initiatives: A Summary of Research on School Dropouts and Implications for Special Education* (Kingston: The Canadian Council for Exceptional Children, 1992), 2.
31 Hildebrand interview, 13 October 1994.
32 Witmer, "Report," 2.
33 Stackhouse, *Canadian Evangelicalism*, 53–70.
34 "Constitution of the Mennonite Bible School 'Peniel'" at Winkler, MB, 1928 (translated), cited in G.D. Pries, *A Place Called Peniel: Winkler Bible Institute, 1925–1975* (Altona, MB: Friesens & Sons, 1975), 73.
35 Registrars' records of various institutions often recorded more women than men. Virginia Brereton notes the same situation at most American Bible schools. *Training God's Army: The American Bible School, 1880–1940* (Bloomington: Indiana University Press, 1990), 69.
36 See, for example, Stackhouse, "Women in Public Ministry."
37 *Holding Forth the Word of Life ... The Peace River Bible Institute, 1933–1977* (Altona, MB: Friesens, 1977), 10–12.
38 Providence College, *Catalogue*, 1993–5, 10.
39 Interview, Rev. Larry Lindoff, academic dean, Northwest Bible College, Edmonton, 14 June 1994.
40 Reynolds, *Rebirth*, 342–53.
41 Joel Carpenter, "Fundamentalist Institutions and the Rise of Evangelical Protestantism, 1929–1942," *Church History* 49 (March 1980), 67.
42 Neufeld and Steven, *Stay in School Initiatives*, 2.
43 Edward Hildebrandt, "A History of the Winnipeg Bible College and School of Theology from 1925–1960" (Th.M. thesis, Dallas Theological Seminary, 1965), 106–20.
44 Stackhouse, *Canadian Evangelicalism*, 66–8.
45 Al Hiebert, "How Differences in the Canadian and American Environments Affect Bible College Education: A Canadian Perspective" (unpublished AABC workshop paper, 1994), 4–5; S.A. Witmer, "AABC, A Service Agency for Canadian Institutions" (paper presented to Canadian Conference of Christian Educators, Regina, 1961), 8–10.
46 Canadian Bible College, "Self-Evaluation Report," 1961, and *Calendar*, 1953–1960; Ruth Martin, "The Canadian Bible College – History from 1941 to 1962" (M.A. thesis, Winona Lake School of Theology, 1962), 42–5, 87–98.
47 Stackhouse, "Respectfully Submitted," 61–2; *Religious Studies in Manitoba and Saskatchewan*, 37–9.
48 Badertscher, Harland, and Miller, *Religious Studies in Manitoba and Saskatchewan*, 39–40.
49 Hildebrand interview, 13 October 1994.
50 See, for example, Paul Bartel, "Changing Entrance Requirements to Foreign Lands for Missionaries" (minutes of presentation at Conference of

Christian Educators of Alberta, Saskatchewan & Manitoba, Regina, 1960), 7–8; Stackhouse, *Canadian Evangelicalism*, 66–8.

51 Alvin Martin, "The Distinctive Features of Higher Education in Canada and the Goals of Canadian Bible College in Light of Them" (unpublished report, Canadian Bible College, 1968), 4–5.

52 Burkinshaw, in *Pilgrims in Lotus Land*, makes this clear for British Columbia.

53 By the 1960s all of the older, church-related Protestant colleges had been completely, or virtually, secularized. See Masters, *Protestant Church Colleges*; Robert S. Wilson, "Atlantic Baptists Survive the Turbulent Sixties" (paper presented to the Baptist Heritage Conference, Toronto, 1993), 8–12; Rawlyk, "Protestant Colleges in Canada"; Goldwin S. French, "The United Church of Canada and Higher Education in Canada," in Proceedings of the Conference, "Educating for the Kingdom? Church Related Colleges in English-Speaking Canada," University of St Jerome's College and Conrad Grebel College, Waterloo, ON, 1990.

54 See Stackhouse, *Canadian Evangelicalism*, 145–54; Burkinshaw, *Pilgrims in Lotus Land*, 209–15.

55 Robert S. Wilson, "Why Would Maritime Baptists Found a College in 1949?" (paper presented to Baptist Heritage Conference, Edmonton, 1990); Atlantic Baptist College, 1991–92 *Calendar*, 7; interview, Ralph Richardson, president, Atlantic Baptist College, Moncton, 28 September 1993.

56 For a less optimistic view see Rawlyk, "Protestant Colleges in Canada," 299.

57 Despite strong liberal arts offerings and a highly qualified faculty, Redeemer has been unable to break an Ontario tradition whereby the provincial universities possess an exclusive monopoly on the granting of arts degrees. Consequently it can only offer a degree in Bachelor of Christian Studies. Still, it has attracted about the same number of students as King's, nearly 500 in the early 1990s, largely because its students gain transfer credits to many public universities and admission into graduate programs throughout North America. "Tenth Anniversary of Redeemer College," *Redeemer Reflections* 12,1 (September 1992); interview with Henry de Bolster, president, 3 June 1993; The King's College, "Self-Study," vol. 1 (1992), 1–4.

58 Wilson, "Atlantic Baptists Survive the Turbulent Sixties."

59 See Stackhouse, *Canadian Evangelicalism*, 154–64; Burkinshaw, *Pilgrims in Lotus Land*, 215–22.

60 Canadian Theological College, *Calendar*, 1969–70.

61 Providence Theological Seminary, *Catalogue*, 1994–96, 11; Edmonton Baptist Seminary, *Catalogue*, 1994–96, 14–5.

62 Stackhouse, *Canadian Evangelicalism*, 125-130; interview, Dr Charlotte Bates, 8 June 1994, Three Hills, AB.
63 Magnus interview, 1 June 1994.
64 Association of Theological Seminaries, *Fact Book on Theological Education*, 1993-94.
65 The figures presented here have been adjusted based on figures from *Faith Alive*, March 1984, 9-14, which included colleges and seminaries that are not explicitly evangelical.
66 *Faith Today*, January/February 1992, 32-49.
67 Kenneth Gangel, "The Bible College: Past, Present and Future," *Christianity Today*, 7 November 1980, 34-6. This article was cited to me in numerous interviews in 1994 with Bible college leaders.
68 Stackhouse, *Canadian Evangelicalism*, 125. The University of Waterloo began granting transfer credits to Bible College students as early as the 1970s.
69 Badertscher, Harland, and Miller, *Religious Studies in Manitoba and Saskatchewan*, 58; William R. Eichhorst, president, Winnipeg Bible College and Theological Seminary, to supporters, March 1991.
70 For example, Providence College featured its transfer agreements with the University of Manitoba in its student recruitment advertisements in the early 1990s.
71 Interview, Ray Friesen, principal, Swift Current Bible Institute, Swift Current, 2 June 1994.
72 Prairie Bible College, "PBC Programme Rationale," draft document, 1992, 5.
73 Daryl Busby, "Future Will Call for Best in Bible Colleges," *Christian Week*, 21 January 1992; Lindoff interview, 14 June 1994.
74 Interview, Walter Unger, president, Columbia Bible College, Clearbrook, 2 February 1995.
75 Walter Unger, "Building Better Bible Colleges," *Christian Week*, 21 January 1992; Albert Hiebert, "Where Is Providence College Going?" unpublished paper, 1993.
76 "Evangelical Higher Education in Canada: No Small Thing," *Faith Alive*, March 1984, 13.
77 Stackhouse, "What *Should* Christians Want from Higher Education?" *Christian Week*, 18 February 1992, 14; *Canadian Evangelicalism*, 192.
78 Interview, Charles Fordham, director, Capenwray Harbour Centre, Thetis Island, BC, 10 November 1994.
79 "The hindrances to making disciples," 1995 Christian Higher Education Supplement to *Christian Info News*, 12.
80 Karl H. Mueller, "An Evaluation of Youth With a Mission's North American Discipleship Training Schools" (M.A. Miss. thesis, Fuller Theological

Seminary, 1990); interviews with Mueller, former YWAM leader, Kelowna, 7 October 1994; Don Neufeld, director DTS, Winfield, BC, 7 October 1994.
81 Interview, Jay Gurnett, president, Mount Carmel Bible School, Edmonton, 16 June 1994.
82 Statistics Canada, *Canada Yearbook 1992* (Ottawa, 1991), 124; *Canada Yearbook 1994* (Ottawa, 1993), 170.
83 Stackhouse, *Canadian Evangelicalism*, 192, notes the striking similarity in the adjustments of Bible colleges.

CHAPTER TWENTY-FOUR

1 Sarah Comstock, "Aimee Semple McPherson: Prima Donna of Revivalism," *Harper's Monthly Magazine*, December 1927, 11.
2 Joseph Henry Steele, "Sister Aimee: Bernhardt of the Sawdust Trail," *Vanity Fair*, March 1933, 42.
3 William G. McLoughlin, "Aimee Semple McPherson: 'Your Sister in the King's Glad Service,'" *Journal of Popular Culture* 6 (Winter 1967): 193.
4 R.G. Moyles, *The Blood and Fire in Canada* (Toronto: Peter Martin Associates, 1977), 7–9.
5 "The Salvation Army," *The Canadian Post*, 27 July 1883.
6 Ibid.
7 "The Salvation Army," *The Canadian Post*, 3 August 1883.
8 Ibid., 2 September 1883.
9 Blumhofer, *Everybody's Sister*, 31–8.
10 Brother Barraclough, "Ingersoll for Jesus," *War Cry*, 27 December 1883, reprinted in "A Brief History of the Ingersoll Salvation Army," J.L. Savage, comp., 7.
11 See, for example, "What a Salvation Army Soldier Ought to Do Every Day," *War Cry*, 24 June 1899, 4.
12 See, for example, *War Cry*, 29 December 1994; "The Commandant at London and Ingersoll," *War Cry*, 4 May 1895, 8.
13 Art Williams, "Oxford's Church Making Began Near Bend in Road Now Salford," *Woodstock Sentinel Review*, 20 October 1962, in Salford United Church File, United Church of Canada Archives, Toronto.
14 Blumhofer, *Everybody's Sister*, 60–8.
15 *Toronto Globe*, 20 November 1906, 1.
16 Ellen Hebden, "How Pentecost Came to Toronto," *The Promise*, May 1907, 1–3.
17 A.S. Copley, "Pentecost in Toronto," *Apostolic Faith*, January 1907, 4.
18 See, for example, ibid., January 1907, 1.
19 See, for example, John Loney, "Snowflake, Manitoba," ibid., December 1906, 3.

20 For Brooks, see *Conflicts in the Narrow Way* (Zion, IL: privately published, 1944).
21 Blumhofer, "Christian Catholic Church."
22 "It's Old Time Religion," *The Evening Telegram*, 19 January 1907, 11; *The Evening Telegram*, 26 January 1907, 12.
23 Gordon Gardiner, *Radiant Glory* (New York: privately published, 1962), 122.
24 Ibid.
25 An unusually full account of one monthly union meeting is in G.A. Murray, "Pentecost in Toronto," *The Pentecost*, April–May 1909, 9. See also George Murray, "Toronto Convention," *Latter Rain Evangel*, November 1908, 2.
26 George A. Christie, "Pentecost at Toronto," *The New Acts*, July–August 1907, 7; Harold W. Pointen, "The Holiness Movement Church in Canada" (B.D. thesis, Emmanuel College, 1950).
27 Christie, "Pentecost," 7.
28 "The Comforter Has Come to Herbert E. Randall," *The Promise*, June 1907, 1.
29 Pointen, *Holiness Movement Church*, 111.
30 "The Comforter Has Come," 1.
31 "Fields This Side the Sea," *The New Acts*, July–August 1907, 1.
32 For example, "Report from Palestine," *The Christian and Missionary Alliance*, 10 June 1899, 34; "Alliance Work in the Home Field: The Canadian District," *The Christian and Missionary Alliance*, 26 May 1906, 324–5.
33 Murray, *Latter Rain Evangel*, August 1910, 20.
34 See, for example, Murray, "Toronto Convention," 2.
35 J.H. King, *Yet Speaketh: Memoirs of the Late Bishop Joseph H. King* (Franklin Springs, GA: Publishing House of the Pentecostal Holiness Church, 1949), 173; "The Use of Tongues," *Pentecost*, November 1908, 6.
36 King, *Yet Speaketh*, 173.
37 For Salmon's life, see Reynolds, *Footprints*.
38 John Salmon, "My Enduement," *Christian and Missionary Alliance*, 26 October 1907, 54–5; *Triumphs of Faith*, December 1907, 269–71.
39 "Beulah Park Convention," *Christian and Missionary Alliance*, 14 September 1907, 128. In an editorial in the *Christian and Missionary Alliance* (6 July 1907, 313), Alliance founder A.B. Simpson commented, "The work in Toronto has passed through the new movement in connection with the gift of tongues without serious strain."
40 Reynolds, *Footprints*, 171ff.
41 Career sketch of George E. Fisher, "A Roll 258," Salvation Army Archives, George Scott Railton Heritage Centre, Toronto.

42 Frank Bartleman, *How Pentecost Came to Los Angeles*, 3rd ed. (Los Angeles: privately published, n.d.), 117.
43 King, *Yet Speaketh*, 98–9.
44 See Susan A. Duncan, *Trials and Triumphs of a Faith Life* (Rochester, NY: Elim Publishing House, 1910).
45 J.E. Sanders, "The Pentecostal Standard," *Bridegroom's Messenger*, 15 December 1907, 4.
46 Ellen Hebden claimed the Holy Spirit inspired her to paint landscapes and then provided interpretations of the paintings; Martha Robinson said the Spirit moved her to automatic writing; participants craved being "under the power of the Spirit all the time" (Copley, "Pentecost in Toronto," 4). See Martha Robinson's journal, in Gardiner, *Radiant Glory*, 140, 131.
47 See, for example, E.N. Bell's endorsement of J.M. Pike, "The Second Blessing," *Word and Witness*, 20 December 1913, 2.
48 "Londoners (Led by Chicago Missionary) Claim the Gift of Tongues," *Evening Free Press*, 1 February 1910, 1; "32 People Now Claim to Have 'Gift of Tongues' at Pentecost Meeting," ibid., 2 February 1910, 1; "Pentecostal Meetings Likely to Be Resumed But Secretly This Time," ibid., 11 February 1910, 1.
49 Gordon Sinclair, "Sister Aimee Still Insists Kidnapping No Idle Dream," *Toronto Daily Star*, 6 September 1934, 1.

CHAPTER TWENTY-FIVE

The author wishes to thank Terry Cook, George Rawlyk, and Marguerite Van Die for their comments and suggestions on an earlier draft of this paper.
1 Grant, *Profusion of Spires*.
2 Westfall, *Two Worlds*.
3 Gauvreau, *Evangelical Century*.
4 Marshall, *Secularizing the Faith*, 4–5.
5 See for example, Wendy Mitchinson, "Canadian Women and Church Missionary Societies in the Nineteenth Century: A Step towards Independence," *Atlantis* 2,2 (Spring 1977): part 2; Diana Pedersen, "The Young Woman's Christian Association in Canada, 1870–1920: A Movement to Meet a Spiritual, Civic and National Need" (Ph.D. diss., Carleton University, 1987); Lane, "'Wife, Mother, Sister, Friend,'" in Guildford and Morton, eds., *Separate Spheres*.
6 For example, see Paul R. Dekar, "Canadian Baptist Women Missionaries as Peacemakers," in *Costly Vision: The Baptist Pilgrimage in Canada*, ed. Jarold K. Zeman (Burlington: Welch, 1988); Whiteley, "Modest, Retiring, and Fully Consecrated"; Vera K. Fast, "Eva Hasell and the Caravan

Mission," in *The Anglican Church and the World of Western Canada, 1820–1970*, ed. Barry Ferguson (Regina: Canadian Plains Research Centre, 1991).

7 For example, see Ruth Compton Brouwer, "'Far Indeed from the Meekest of Women': Marion Fairweather and the Canadian Presbyterian Mission in Central India, 1873–1880," in *Canadian Protestant and Catholic Missions, 1820s–1960s; Historical Essays in Honour of John Webster Grant*, ed. John S. Moir and C.T. McIntire (New York: Peter Lang, 1988); Geoffrey Johnson, "The Road to Winsome Womanhood: The Canadian Presbyterian Mission among East Indian Women and Girls in Trinidad, 1868–1939," in ibid.; Katherine Ridout, "A Woman of Mission: The Religious and Cultural Odyssey of Agnes Wintemute Coates," *Canadian Historical Review* 71,2 (1990).

8 For example, see Mary Hallett, "Ladies – We Give You the Pulpit!" *Touchstone* 4,1 (January 1986); Valerie J. Korinek, "No Women Need Apply: The Ordination of Women in the United Church, 1918–65," *Canadian Historical Review* 74, 4 (December 1993); Elizabeth Gillan Muir, *Petticoats in the Pulpit: The Story of Early Nineteenth-Century Methodist Women Preachers in Upper Canada* (Toronto: United Church Publishing House, 1991).

9 Ruth Compton Brouwer, "Transcending the 'Unacknowledged Quarantine': Putting Religion into English-Canadian Women's History," *Journal of Canadian Studies/Revue d'etudes canadiennes* 27,3 (Fall 1992).

10 One highly interesting exception to underrating religious belief, albeit not with evangelicalism, is Cecilia Morgan, "Gender, Religion and Rural Society: Quaker Women in Norwich, Ontario, 1820–1880," *Ontario History* 82,4 (December 1990).

11 Caroline DeSwart Gifford, "Sisterhoods of Service and Reform: Organized Methodist Women in the Late Nineteenth Century: An Essay on the State of the Research" (paper presented to the Canadian Methodist Historical Society, Toronto, June 1985), as cited in Rosemary R. Gagan, *A Sensitive Independence: Canadian Methodist Women Missionaries in Canada and the Orient, 1881–1925* (Montreal and Kingston: McGill-Queen's University Press, 1992), 14.

12 Lynne Marks, "The 'Hallelujah Lasses': Working-Class Women in the Salvation Army in English Canada, 1882–92," in *Gender Conflicts: New Essays in Women's History*, ed. Franca Iacovetta and Mariana Valverde (Toronto: University of Toronto Press, 1992).

13 Brouwer, *New Women for God: Canadian Presbyterian Women and India Missions, 1876–1914* (Toronto: University of Toronto Press, 1990); Gagan, *A Sensitive Independence*, 26.

14 Rawlyk, *Canada Fire*, 64–6 and esp. ch. 6.

15 S. Cook, *"Through Sunshine and Shadow."*

16 Van Die, *An Evangelical Mind*, esp. 20–6. See also her "A Woman's Awakening: Evangelical Belief and Female Spirituality in Mid-Nineteenth Century Canada" (paper presented at the Canadian Historical Association Meeting, Queen's University, 1991).
17 Ian Bradley, *The Call to Seriousness* (London: 1976), 22.
18 A.B. McKillop, *Matters of Mind: The University in Ontario, 1791–1951* (Toronto: University of Toronto Press, 1994), 96.
19 See, for example, Noll, *Between Faith and Criticism*; Bebbington, *Evangelicalism*.
20 Norman Knowles, review of Elizabeth Muir's *Petticoats in the Pulpit* and Gagan's *A Sensitive Independence*, in *Journal of the Canadian Church Historical Society* 35, 2 (October 1993): 147.
21 Marshall, *Secularizing the Faith*, 8.
22 Gauvreau, "Protestantism Transformed," in Rawlyk, ed., *Canadian Protestant Experience*, 64.
23 McKillop, *Matters of Mind*, 94.
24 See for example, journal of Eliza Ann Chapman, in *No Place Like Home: Diaries and Letters of Nova Scotia Women, 1771–1938*, ed. Margaret Conrad, Toni Laidlaw, and Donna Smyth (Halifax: Formac, 1988); Eliza Bentley, *Precious Stones for Zion's Wall: A Record of Personal Experience in Things Connected with the Kingdom of God on Earth* (Toronto: Wm. Briggs, 1897); S. Cook, "'A Gallant Little Band.'"
25 See S. Cook, *"Through Sunshine and Shadow."*
26 On the issue of class position, see Lynne Marks, "Ladies, Loafers, Knights and 'Lasses': The Social Dimension of Religion and Leisure in Late Nineteenth-Century Small Town Ontario" (Ph.D. diss., York University, 1992).
27 Van Die, *An Evangelical Mind*, 22.
28 Van Die notes, ibid., 24, that such luminaries as Egerton Ryerson, Hart Massey, and Joseph Flavelle all acknowledged their mothers' deep religious influence on their lives. None can be considered an average Canadian of his period, however.
29 See, for example, S. Cook, "Letitia Youmans"; Van Die, "A Woman's Awakening." This is not a plea to extend the literature of "women worthies." Biographical studies do serve an important function, however. See Natalie Zemon Davis, "Women's History in Transition: The European Case," *Feminist Studies* 3, 3–4 (1976); Dianne M. Hallman, Introduction, *Ontario History* 84, 4 (1992).
30 Van Die, *An Evangelical Mind*, 22.
31 Mariana Valverde, "'When the Mother of the Race is Free': Race, Reproduction, and Sexuality in First-Wave Feminism," in Iacovetta and Valverde, eds., *Gender Conflicts*. See also Valverde, *The Age of Light, Soap and Water: Moral Reform in English Canada, 1885–1925* (Toronto: McClelland & Stewart, 1991).

32 Katherine M.J. McKenna, *A Life of Propriety: Anne Murray Powell and Her Family, 1755–1849* (Kingston and Montreal: McGill-Queens University Press, 1994), 130. See esp. part 2.
33 Van Die, *An Evangelical Mind*, 25.
34 McKillop, *Matters of Mind*, 95.
35 WCTU Collection [hereafter WCTU], MU 8422, Minute Book of the Newmarket WCTU, 2 November 1915, Archives of Ontario.
36 WCTU, *The Canadian White Ribbon Tidings*, August 1910.
37 WCTU, Minutes of the Annual Meeting of the Ontario WCTU, 1887.
38 WCTU, *The Woman's Journal*, December 1886.
39 WCTU, Lucy A. Scott, "Personal Purity," The White Cross Series No. 11.
40 *The Canadian White Ribbon Tidings*, April 1910.
41 WCTU, Frances Willard, "Safety for School Children."
42 *The Woman's Journal*, 1 January 1901.
43 Ibid., October 1890.
44 WCTU, Lucy A. Scott, "Real Chivalry," The White Cross Series No. 12.
45 *The Canadian White Ribbon Tidings*, September 1915.
46 Anthony Rotundo, "Boy Culture: Middle-Class Boyhood in Nineteenth-Century America," in *Meanings For Manhood: Constructions of Masculinity in Victorian America*, ed. Mark C. Carnes and Clyde Griffen (Chicago: University of Chicago Press, 1990).
47 Marks, "Ladies, Loafers, Knights and 'Lasses,'" iv–v, 237–40.
48 *The Canadian White Ribbon Tidings*, January 1893.
49 Wendy Mitchinson, *The Nature of Their Bodies: Women and Their Doctors in Victorian Canada* (Toronto: University of Toronto Press, 1990).
50 *The Canadian White Ribbon Tidings*, February 1910.
51 See also Nancy Garner, "Molding and Making the Next Generation of Men: The Kansas Woman's Christian Temperance Union and the Loyal Temperance Legion, 1890–1935" (paper presented at the Meeting of the Association for the Study of Alcohol, London, Ontario, 1992), 7–8.
52 Van Die, *An Evangelical Mind*, 10. See also Gauvreau, "Protestantism Transformed," 50–7; Rawlyk, *Champions of the Truth*, esp. 32–6.
53 See Rawlyk, *Champions of the Truth*, esp. 26–8.
54 Deborah Gorham, *The Victorian Girl and the Feminine Ideal* (Bloomington: Indiana University Press, 1982).
55 See Valverde, *The Age of Light, Soap and Water*.

CHAPTER TWENTY-SIX

1 Noll, Bebbington, and Rawlyk, eds., *Evangelicalism: Comparative Studies*, 3.
2 Ibid., 4.
3 Nehemiah Curnock, ed., *The Journal of John Wesley*, 8 vols. (London: Charles H. Kelly, 1909), 1: 475–6.

4 H. Alline, *The Life and Journal* (Boston: Gilbert and Dean, 1806), 35.
5 C.C. Goen, ed., *The Works of Jonathan Edwards*, vol. 4, *The Great Awakening* (New Haven: n.p., 1972), 193.
6 A. Stevens, *Life and Times of Nathan Bangs* (New York: Carleton and Porter, 1863), 148, quoted in Rawlyk, *Canada Fire*, 150.
7 See Rawlyk and his discussion of public/private space in the Hay Bay Camp-meeting, *Canada Fire*, ch. 9.
8 Even though these types of religious experiences generally occur in public settings, they are still personal, private experiences. For example, "Linda," whose account of being slain in the Spirit is related later, stated emphatically, "I do not crave attention in my times of prayer. It is just a time between the Lord and me." Copies of the account provided by "Linda" are in the possession of the author.
9 During January, February, March, and April 1993, 6,014 people were interviewed by telephone, roughly 1500 at a time. The questions regarding religious beliefs were included on the National Angus Reid Poll, a public affairs omnibus. The survey samples for the National Angus Reid Polls were stratified by province and by census division. Individual households were selected using a modified random digit dialling procedure. This ensures all numbers – both listed and unlisted – have an equal chance of being selected. See *Maclean's*, 12 April 1993, "God Is Alive: Canada Is a Nation of Believers," for some preliminary results.
10 The surveys conducted with 6,014 randomly selected adult Canadians included interviews with over 900 evangelicals, as identified using a version of the Christian Evangelicalism Scale (CES) (see note 15). Then using the telephone numbers and demographic information of the identified evangelicals, interviewers from the Angus Reid Group placed calls during the summer of 1993 to all available numbers asking to speak to persons who fitted the demographic profile we possessed. All respondents were re-screened using questions from the CES. Those who met the CES criteria were included in the final sample of 365 used for the follow-up survey. Copies of the basic tabular results of this survey are in the possession of the author. In-depth interviews by telephone were conducted with 38 people who were randomly selected from the same sample of evangelicals. Interviews were completed only with English-speaking respondents. Copies of the transcripts of these interviews are in the possession of the author.
11 This definition builds on the approach of David Hay and Ann Morisy, "Reports of Ecstatic, Paranormal, or Religious Experience in Great Britain and the United States – A Comparison on Trends," *Journal for the Scientific Study of Religion* 17 (1978).
12 Many of the questions were adapted from those used in previous investigations of religious experience; and all questions sought "yes" or "no" responses. The questions and the sources they were adapted from were:

(1) "Have you ever, as an adult, had the feeling you were somehow in the presence of God?" from R. Stark, "Social Contexts and Religious Experience," *Review of Religious Research* 6 (1965); (2) "Have you ever felt you were in close contact with something holy or sacred?" from R. Wuthnow, "Peak Experience," *Journal of Humanistic Psychology* 18 (1978); (3) "Would you say you have ever had a 'religious or mystical experience,' that is, a moment of sudden religious insight and awakening?" from K. Back and L. Bourque, "Can Feelings Be Enumerated?," *Behavioral Science* 15 (1970); (4) "Have you ever felt as though you were very close to a powerful spiritual force that seemed to lift you out of yourself?" from Andrew Greeley, *Ecstasy* (Englewood Cliffs: Prentice Hall, 1974); (5) "Have you ever spoken in tongues?"; (6) "Have you ever been slain in the Spirit?"

13 Abraham H. Maslow, *Religions, Values and Peak Experiences* (New York: Penguin, 1976), 59.
14 Noll, *Scandal of the Evangelical Mind*, 8.
15 The questions that make up the scale are as follows (* indicates items that are reverse scored): Please indicate whether you agree or disagree, moderately or strongly with each of the following statements: (1) The concept of God is an old superstition that is no longer needed to explain things in these modern times.* (2) I feel that through the life, death and resurrection of Jesus, God provided a way for the forgiveness of my sins. (3) In my view, Jesus Christ was not the divine son of God.* (4) Man/woman is not a special creature made in the image of God, he/she is simply a recent development in the process of animal evolution.* (5) I believe Jesus was crucified, died and was buried but was resurrected to eternal life. (6) I feel the Bible is God's word, and is to be taken literally, word for word. (7) I have committed my life to Christ and consider myself to be a converted Christian. (8) I feel it is very important to encourage non-Christians to become Christians. (9) Please indicate whether you never, occasionally, weekly, or daily read the Bible or other religious material. Choose the category which comes closest to describing your activity. (10) Which of the following best describes how often you attend religious services? I never, or almost never, attend religious services; I attend religious services on occasion; I attend religious services about once a month or so; I attend religious services once a week or so.

The agree/disagree statements were scored as follows: agree strongly = 4, agree moderately = 3, disagree moderately = 2, disagree strongly = 1. Frequency of Bible reading was scored as follows: daily = 4, weekly = 3, occasionally = 2, never = 1. Frequency of church attendance was scored in a similar manner: weekly = 4, monthly = 3, occasionally = 2, never = 1.

It should be noted that this is a theological rather than a sociological measure of evangelicalism. For details of the psychometric properties of

the scale, see Grenville, *Christian Evangelicalism Scale*. For details on the use of the scale to identify evangelicals, see Grenville, *Counting the Sheep*. Copies of both papers are available from the author.
16 Quoted in Wolffe, "Anti-Catholicism and Evangelical Identity in Britain and the United States," in Noll, Bebbington, and Rawlyk, eds., *Evangelicalism: Comparative Studies*, 179. See also Stackhouse, "More than a Hyphen," in Rawlyk and Noll, eds., *Amazing Grace*.
17 See C. Colson, Fr J. Diaz-Vilar et al., "Evangelicals & Catholics Together: the Christian Mission in the Third Millennium," *First Things*, May 1994. It should be noted that the switch from "I" to "we" in this section serves to acknowledge that this investigation was initiated at the request of Dr G.A. Rawlyk and was conducted in close cooperation with him.
18 Keith A. Fornier, *Evangelical Catholics* (Nashville: Thomas Nelson, 1990), 11.
19 Michael R. Welch and David C. Leege, "Dual Reference Groups and Political Orientations: An Examination of Evangelically Oriented Catholics," *American Journal of Political Science* 35 (1991): 45.
20 This measure is based on agreement with the statement "I consider myself to be an evangelical Christian." Fourteen per cent of all Canadian Catholics consider themselves to be evangelicals, a figure similar to the approximately 10 per cent observed in the United States by Gallup and reported in Welch and Leege, ibid.
21 Greeley, *Ecstasy*.
22 Copies of the account provided by "Linda" are in the possession of the author.
23 Cluster analysis is a technique for grouping subjects that places no a priori assumptions on the data, and the data (in this case, the experiences of evangelicals) are allowed to dictate the patterns.
24 Ward's method of hierarchical clustering was used to develop this solution. Between groups, linkages were calculated using squared Euclidean distances. The most important factor in the development of a cluster solution is the selection of the items for inclusion. Five religious experiences were included (adapted from the items enumerated in note 12).

This cluster solution was chosen (from among hundreds of alternatives which were run using different sets of inputs and clustering techniques) because it had the greatest validity and reliability. It reproduced exceptionally well in random sub-samples of as few as 60 per cent of respondents – an excellent result considering the relatively small sample size. Those interested in cluster analysis and an example of its role in developing typologies in the study of religion are referred to C. Kirk Hadaway, "Identifying American Apostates: A Cluster Analysis," *Journal for the Scientific Study of Religion* 29 (1989).

523   Notes to pages 425–8

25 S. Juster, *Disorderly Women* (Ithaca: Cornell University Press, 1994), 65.
26 This analysis was conducted using multiple regression analysis. Included in the analysis were all six measures of religious experience. Also included were variables measuring whether one had been in contact with IVCF and/or EFC, because those who had had religious experiences were more likely to have been in touch with them. The analysis shows that contact with these organizations is completely unrelated to frequency of evangelism, while three of the religious experiences were related to frequency. The following table shows the results of the analysis. The independent variables were all coded to 1 = "yes" (experienced/been in contact), and 0 = "no" (no contact). The dependent variable – frequency of evangelism – was coded as follows: 1 = daily, 2 = weekly, 3 = monthly, 4 = occasionally, 5 = never.

Variables	Beta	Significance
Presence of God	.14	.01
Lifted out of yourself	.12	.03
Awakening	.10	.08
Slain in the Spirit	.11	.08
Speaking in tongues	.05	not sig.
Sacred presence	.04	not sig.
EFC	.03	not sig.
IVCF	.09	not sig.
Adjusted R-squared	.06	.0006

27 In suggesting that religious experience is one of the "other" ingredients of evangelicalism, I have assumed that experience, particularly when measured as a "sudden religious insight or awakening," comes under Bebbington's category of conversionism.
28 The Pearson correlations for frequency of prayer and each of the religious experiences were all between .14 and .19. All were significant at a 99 per cent confidence interval, using a two-tailed T-test.
29 The Pearson correlations ranged from .11 for speaking in tongues and having felt lifted out of yourself, to .24 for sudden religious insight. Five of the six correlations were significant at 95 per cent or greater confidence interval. Having been in close contact with something holy or sacred did not show any link to feeling God speaks directly to you through the Holy Spirit.
30 Pearson correlations showed significant relationships between frequency of Bible reading and having had a sudden religious insight (.18), speaking in tongues (.20), and being slain in the Spirit (.16). All were significant at the 99 per cent confidence interval. The other experiences did not show a significant relationship with frequency of Bible reading. The experiences

which were correlated with "feeling God speaks directly through the Bible" were "having had a sudden religious insight" (.19) and "having felt lifted out of yourself" (.11). Both were significant at a 95 per cent confidence level. The other experiences did not show a significant relationship with this belief. It is worth noting that the two statements about God speaking directly through the Holy Spirit and/or the Bible were not measuring a single underlying construct. The correlation between the two was significant (.27) but not high enough to suggest that they are, in essence, the same idea.

31 See Jose Casanova, *Public Religions in the Modern World* (Chicago and London: University of Chicago Press, 1994), ch. 2.
32 See note 26 for details on the relationship between contact with these organizations, religious experience, and frequency of evangelism.
33 The lack of contact with institutions and leaders that is observed here is in keeping with a general social trend toward alienation from social institutions, including organized religion. Data collected by Gallup Canada reveals that the percentage of people who have "a great deal" or "quite a bit" of respect and confidence in organized religion declined from 60 per cent in 1979 to 41 per cent in 1993. The same figures for confidence in political parties were 30 per cent in 1979 and 9 per cent in 1991.
34 See table 6, highlights of relevant data collected by Gallup Canada. The level of belief in God that Gallup reports for Canada in 1990 (86 per cent) is slightly lower than 1991 ISSP figures for the US (96 per cent); the same as that measured in Italy (85 per cent); and higher than those observed in Britain and New Zealand (both 70 per cent), West Germany (67 per cent), and the Netherlands (50 per cent). See Andrew M. Greeley, "Religion Around the World" (paper presented to the May 1993 meeting of the International Social Survey Program).
35 Sixty-one per cent of Canadians agreed with the statement "I feel that through the life, death, and resurrection of Jesus, God provided a way for the forgiveness of my sins." And 66 per cent of Canadians agreed that "My religious faith is very important to me in my day-to-day life."
36 In the survey in which this particular data was collected, 71 per cent of Canadians said they were Christians.
37 Noll, Bebbington, and Rawlyk, *Evangelicalism: Comparative Studies*, 5.
38 David A. Reed, "The Toronto Mixed Blessing" (lecture presented at Praxis '95, Toronto, April 1995). In this piece Reed draws on systems theory to provide an intriguing perspective on the Toronto Blessing on the Charismatic Revival. He likens this movement to a child who is "acting out" on behalf of an angst-ridden church family.

Selected Bibliography

Airhart, Phyllis D. "'As Canadian as Possible under the Circumstances': Reflections on the Study of Protestantism in North America." In *New Perspectives in American Religious American History*, ed. Harry S. Stout and D.G. Hart. New York: Oxford University Press, forthcoming.
- *Serving the Present Age: Revivalism, Progressivism, and the Methodist Tradition in Canada*. Montreal and Kingston: McGill-Queen's University Press, 1992.
- "'What Must I Do to Be Saved?': Two Paths to Evangelical Conversion in Late Victorian Canada." *Church History* 59 (September 1990): 372–85.

Allen, Richard. *The Social Passion: Religion and Social Reform in Canada, 1914–1928*. Toronto: University of Toronto Press, 1971.

Austin, Alvyn. "Blessed Adversity: Henry W. Frost and the China Inland Mission." In *Earthen Vessels: American Evangelicals and Foreign Missions 1880–1980*, ed. Joel A. Carpenter and Wilbert R. Shenk. Grand Rapids: Eerdmans, 1990.
- *Saving China: Canadian Missionaries in the Middle Kingdom, 1888–1959*. Toronto: University of Toronto Press, 1986.

Bebbington, David W. *Evangelicalism in Modern Britain: A History from the 1730s to the 1980s*. London: Unwin Hyman, 1989.
- "Martyrs for the Truth: Fundamentalists in Britain." In *Martyrs and Martyrologies*, Studies in Church History, 30, ed. Diana Wood. Oxford: Basil Blackwell, 1993.
- "The Persecution of George Jackson: A British Fundamentalist Controversy." In *Persecution and Toleration*, Studies in Church History, 21, ed. W.J. Sheils. Oxford: Basil Blackwell, 1984.

- "Revival and Enlightenment in Eighteenth-Century England." In *Modern Christian Revivals*, ed. Edith L. Blumhofer and Randall Balmer. Urbana: University of Illinois Press, 1993.
Bibby, Reginald W. *Fragmented Gods: The Poverty and Potential of Religion in Canada*. Toronto: Irwin, 1987.
- *Mosaic Madness: The Poverty and Potential of Life in Canada* Toronto: Stoddart, 1990.
- *Unknown Gods: The Ongoing Story of Religion in Canada*. Toronto: Stoddart, 1993.
Blumhofer, Edith L. *Aimee Semple McPherson: Everybody's Sister*. Grand Rapids: Eerdmans, 1993.
- *The Assemblies of God: A Chapter in the Story of American Pentecostalism*. 2 vols. Springfield, MO: Gospel Publishing House, 1989.
- "The Christian Catholic Church and the Apostolic Faith." In *Charismatic Experiences in History*, ed. Cecil M. Robeck. Peabody, MA: 1986.
- *Restoring the Faith: The Assemblies of God, Pentecostalism, and American Culture*. Urbana and Chicago: University of Illinois Press, 1993.
Burkinshaw, Robert K. *Pilgrims in Lotus Land: Conservative Protestantism in British Columbia, 1917–1981*. Montreal and Kingston: McGill-Queen's University Press, 1995.
Christie, Nancy and Michael Gauvreau. *"A Full-Orbed Christianity": Protestantism, the Social Sciences and the Welfare State in Canada, 1900–1940*. Forthcoming.
Cook, Ramsay. *The Regenerators: Social Criticism in Late Victorian English Canada*. Toronto: University of Toronto Press, 1985.
Cook, Sharon Anne. "'A Gallant Little Band': Bertha Wright and the Late Nineteenth-Century Evangelical Woman." *Journal of Canadian Church Historical Society* 37,1 (April 1995): 3–21.
- "Letitia Youmans: Ontario's Nineteenth-Century Temperance Educator." *Ontario History* 34,4 (December 1992): 329–42.
- *"Through Sunshine and Shadow": The Woman's Christian Temperance Union, Evangelicalism and Reform in Ontario, 1874–1930*. Montreal and Kingston: McGill-Queen's University Press, 1995.
Coops, P. Lorraine. "Not A Romantic Notion: Single Women Missionaries From the Maritime Baptist Convention Who Served in the Telugu Fields in India, 1880–1912." M.A. thesis, Queen's University, 1992.
Crerar, Duff. "Church and Community: The Presbyterian Kirk-Session in the District of Bathurst, Upper Canada." M.A. thesis, University of Western Ontario, 1979.
Dayton, Donald W. and Robert K. Johnston, eds. *The Variety of American Evangelicalism*. Downers Grove, IL: InterVarsity Press; 1991.
Errington, Jane and G.A. Rawlyk. "Creating a British-American Community: The Federalist-Loyalist Alliance in Upper Canada." In *Loyalists and Community in*

North America, ed. R.M. Calhoon, T.M. Barnes, and G.A. Rawlyk. Westport, CT: Greenwood, 1994.

Gauvreau, Michael. *The Evangelical Century: College and Creed in English Canada from the Great Revival to the Great Depression.* Montreal and Kingston: McGill-Queen's University Press, 1991.

Goodwin, Daniel C. "The Baptismal Controversy, 1811–1848, as the Religious Dimension of the Intellectual Awakening in Nova Scotia." M.Div. thesis, Acadia University, 1989.

Grant, John Webster. *The Church in the Canadian Era.* Toronto: McGraw-Hill Ryerson, 1972.

– *A Profusion of Spires: Religion in Nineteenth-Century Ontario.* Toronto: University of Toronto Press, 1988.

Grenville, Andrew S. *Counting the Sheep: Using the Christian Evangelicalism Scale to Identify Evangelicals.* Angus Reid Group, 1995.

– *Development of the Christian Evangelicalism Scale.* Angus Reid Group, 1995.

Guenther, Bruce. "The Origin of the Bible School Movement in Western Canada: An Ethnic Interpretation." Canadian Society of Church History, *Papers*, 1993.

– "'In the World but Not of It': Old Colony Mennonites, Evangelicalism and Contemporary Canadian Culture – A Case Study of Osler Mission Chapel (1974–94)." *Journal of Mennonite Studies.* Forthcoming.

Hatch, Nathan O. *The Democratization of American Christianity.* New Haven: Yale University Press, 1989.

Hillis, Bryan V. *Can Two Walk Together Unless They Be Agreed?: American Religious Schisms in the 1970s.* New York: Carlson, 1991.

– "The Evangel and Evangelicalism: A Lutheran Perspective." *Canadian Evangelical Theological Association Newsletter* 6 (Spring 1993): 1–4.

Katerberg, William. "Gospel and Party: The Varied Course of Evangelicalism in the Anglican Communion in North America, 1880–1950." Ph.D. diss., Queen's University, 1995.

Klempa, William, ed. *The Burning Bush and a Few Acres of Snow: The Presbyterian Contribution to Canadian Life and Culture.* Toronto: University of Toronto Press, 1994.

Kydd, Ronald. "The Contribution of Denominationally-Trained Clergymen to the Emerging Pentecostal Movement in Canada." *Pneuma* 5 (1983): 17–33.

– "H.C. Sweet: Canadian Churchman." *Journal of the Canadian Church Historical Society* 20 (1978): 19–30.

– "Pentecostals, Charismatics and the Canadian Denominations." *Eglise et Théologie* 13 (1982), 211–31.

Lane, Hannah M. "'Wife, Mother, Sister, Friend': Methodist Women in St. Stephen, New Brunswick, 1861–1881." In *Separate Spheres: Women's World in the 19th-Century Maritimes*, ed. Janet Guildford and Suzanne Morton. Fredericton: Acadiensis Press, 1994.

Mack, Barry. "George Monro Grant: Evangelical Prophet." Ph.D. diss., Queen's University, 1992.
– "Ralph Connor and the Progressive Vision." M.A. thesis, Carleton University, 1986.
Mann, W.E. *Sect, Cult and Church in Alberta*. Toronto: University of Toronto Press, 1955.
Marsden, George M. "The Evangelical Denomination." In *Evangelicalism and Modern America*, ed. George M. Marsden. Grand Rapids: Eerdmans, 1984.
Marshall, David B. *Secularizing the Faith: Canadian Protestant Clergy and the Crisis of Belief, 1850–1940*. Toronto: University of Toronto Press, 1992.
Masters, D.C. *The Protestant Church Colleges in Canada*. Toronto: University of Toronto Press, 1966.
McKillop, A.B. *A Disciplined Intelligence: Critical Inquiry and Canadian Thought in the Victorian Era*. Montreal and Kingston: McGill-Queen's University Press, 1979.
Moir, John S. *Enduring Witness: A History of the Presbyterian Church in Canada*. Presbyterian Publications, 1974; 2nd ed., Presbyterian Church in Canada, 1987.
Noll, Mark A. *Between Faith and Criticism: Evangelicals, Scholarship, and the Bible in America*. San Francisco: Harper & Row, 1986.
– "Children of the Reformation: Why American Evangelicals Differ from Lutheran Evangelicals." *Dialog* 24 (Summer 1985): 176–80.
– *A History of Christianity in the United States and Canada*. Grand Rapids: Eerdmans, 1992.
– "The Lutheran Difference." *First Things* 20 (February 1992): 31–40.
– *The Scandal of the Evangelical Mind*. Grand Rapids: Eerdmans; Leicester, England: InterVarsity Press, 1994.
–, Nathan O. Hatch, and George M. Marsden, *The Search for Christian America*, expanded ed. Colorado Springs: Helmers & Howard, 1989.
–, ed. *Religion and American Politics from the Colonial Period to the 1980s*. New York: Oxford University Press, 1990.
–, David W. Bebbington, and George A. Rawlyk, eds. *Evangelicalism: Comparative Studies of Popular Protestantism in North America, The British Isles, and Beyond, 1770–1990*. New York and Oxford: Oxford University Press, 1994.
Rawlyk, George A. *The Canada Fire: Radical Evangelicalism in British North America, 1775–1812*. Montreal and Kingston: McGill-Queen's University Press, 1994.
– *Champions of the Truth: Fundamentalism, Modernism, and the Maritime Baptists*. Montreal and Kingston: McGill-Queen's University Press, 1990.
– "Is Jesus Your Personal Saviour": *In Search of Canadian Evangelicalism in the 1990s*. Montreal and Kingston: McGill-Queen's University Press, 1996.

- "J.S. Cramp and W.C. Keirstead: The Response of Two Late Nineteenth Century Baptist Sermons to Science." In *Science and Society in the Maritimes Prior to 1914*, ed. Paul A. Bogaard. Fredericton: Acadiensis Press, 1990.
- "Protestant Colleges in Canada: Past and Future." In *The Secularization of the Academy*, ed. George Marsden and Bradley Longfield. New York and Oxford: Oxford University Press, 1992.
- *Ravished by the Spirit: Religious Revivals, Baptists, and Henry Alline*. Montreal and Kingston: McGill-Queen's University Press, 1984.
- "Religion in Canada: A Historical Overview." *Annals*, AAPSS 538 (March 1995).
-, ed. *Canadian Baptists and Christian Higher Education*. Montreal and Kingston: McGill-Queen's University Press, 1988.
-, ed. *The Canadian Protestant Experience 1760-1990*. Burlington: Welch, 1990.
-, ed. *Henry Alline: Selected Writings*. New York: Paulist Press, 1987.
- and Mark A. Noll, eds. *Amazing Grace: Evangelicalism in Australia, Britain, Canada, and the United States*. Montreal and Kingston: McGill-Queen's University Press, 1994.

Reid, Darrel R. "Jesus Only: The Early Life and Presbyterian Ministry of Albert Benjamin Simpson, 1843-1881." Ph.D. diss., Queen's University, 1994.

Renfree, Harry A. *Heritage and Horizon: The Baptist Story in Canada*. Mississauga: Canadian Baptist Federation, 1988.

Reynolds, Lindsay. *Footprints: The Beginnings of the Christian and Missionary Alliance in Canada*. Willowdale: Christian and Missionary Alliance in Canada, 1982.
- *Rebirth: The Redevelopment of the Christian and Missionary Alliance in Canada, 1919-1983*. Willowdale: Christian and Missionary Alliance in Canada, 1992.

Scobie, Charles H.H. and John Webster Grant, eds. *The Contribution of Methodism to Atlantic Canada*. Montreal and Kingston: McGill-Queen's University Press, 1992.

Stackhouse, Jr, John G. "Billy Graham and the Nature of Conversion: A Paradigm Case." *Studies in Religion/Sciences religeuses* 21, 3 (1992): 337-50.
- *Canadian Evangelicalism in the Twentieth Century: An Introduction to Its Character*. Toronto: University of Toronto Press, 1993.
- "The National Association of Evangelicals, the Evangelical Fellowship of Canada, and the Limits of Evangelical Cooperation." *Christian Scholar's Review*. Forthcoming.
- "Respectfully Submitted for American Consideration: Canadian Options in Christian Higher Education." *Faculty Dialogue* 17 (Spring 1992): 51-71.
- "Whose Dominion? Christianity and Canadian Culture Historically Considered." *Crux* 28 (June 1992): 29-35.

- "Women in Public Ministry in Twentieth-Century Canadian and American Evangelicalism: Five Models." *Studies in Religion/Sciences religeuses* 17 (Fall 1988): 471–85.
Underwood, Brian. *Faith at the Frontiers: Anglican Evangelicals and Their Countrymen Overseas*. London: Commonwealth and Continental Church Society, 1974.
VanderVennen, Robert E., ed. *Church and Canadian Culture*. Lanham, MD: University Press of America, 1991.
Van Die, Marguerite. *An Evangelical Mind: Nathanael Burwash and the Methodist Tradition in Canada, 1839–1918*. Montreal and Kingston: McGill-Queen's University Press, 1989.
- "Recovering Religious Experience: Some Reflections on Methodology." Canadian Society of Church History, *Papers*, 1992.
- "Revivalism, Gender and Community in 19th Century Ontario Congregationalism, a Case Study." Canadian Society of Presbyterian History, *Papers*, 1994.
Vaudry, Richard W. *The Free Church in Victorian Canada, 1844–1861*. Waterloo: Wilfrid Laurier University Press, 1989.
- "Peter Brown, the *Toronto Banner*, and the Evangelical Mind in Victorian Toronto." *Ontario History* 87,1 (March 1985): 3–18.
Westfall, William. *Two Worlds: The Protestant Culture of Nineteenth-Century Ontario*. Montreal and Kingston: McGill-Queen's University Press, 1989.
Whiteley, Marilyn Färdig. "Cyclones of Power/Noisy Display: The Holiness Conflict in the Methodist Church." Papers of the Canadian Methodist Historical Society, 1995.
- "Modest, Retiring, and Fully Consecrated: Lady Evangelists in Canadian Methodism, 1884–1900." Papers of the Canadian Methodist Historical Society, 1987.
Wuthnow, Robert. *The Restructuring of American Religion*. Princeton: Princeton University Press, 1988.

Index

Aberhardt, William 16, 64, 286, 303, 304
aboriginal peoples, 41, 48
Acadia Divinity College 221, 380
Acadia University 204, 212
Accrediting Association of Bible Colleges (AABC) 378
activism xiii, xiv, 56, 66, 165, 208–9, 251, 419, 427
Adventists 279
Affleck, R. Wesley 311, 312, 498n50
African-Americans 11
African Industrial Mission 362
Aglukark, Susan 66
Aikenhead, D.R. 311, 314
Aikens, Alden 82
Airhart, Phyllis xx–xxi, 8, 18
Akenson, D.H. 154
alcoholism 334–5
Allen, Richard 63, 337, 340, 403
Alline, Henry xv, 8, 26, 67, 186, 192–3, 207, 417
American Baptist Missionary Union (ABMU) 211, 212
American evangelicalism. *See* United States
Anabaptists 57, 229
Anderson, David 160
Andrews, Frederick 164
Anglicans: as formalists xv; as distinct from evangelical churches xvi; and evangelicalism xxi, 44, 60, 165–66, 180–5, 426; rivalry with Methodists 22–3, 26; early years in Canada and Australia 29; Church Association 43; education 48, 49; membership (1911) 147, (1990s) 186; ties with England 154–5, 156; politics 155; and historiography 155–6; Recordite tradition 158; "Irish channels" 158, 165; mid-Victorian definition of "evangelicals" 158–9; high/low differentiation 158–60, 472n56; synodical controversy (1858–9) 164, 167–9; activism 165; high church opposition to "dissent" 165; in Lower Canada 166–69; in colonial culture 169; divisions in mid–19th century 170; Montreal conference (1994) 171–2, 185, 186; and PEDS 173–4; founding of colleges 175; and WWI 177; Book of Common Prayer and hymn book revision 176–7; interwar years 178; blurring of past lines 186–7. *See also* Church of England
Angus Reid Group xviii, 12, 61

Anti-Burgher Secessionist Presbyterians 51
anti-Catholicism 14, 42–3, 57, 158, 166, 167, 420
antinomianism 193
Apostolic Church of Pentecost 52, 290, 291
Argue, A.H. 296
Armitage, Ramsay 176–7, 177–8, 181–2, 183
arts 66
Asbury, Francis 4
Assemblies of God (USA) 290, 298
Associated Canadian Theological Schools (ACTS) 380
Association of Foreign Mission Societies 362
Atwood, Margaret 66
Aulen, Gustaf 250
Austin, Alvyn xxiv, 23
Australia xix, 21–37
Avison, Margaret 66

Baldwin, M.S. 163
Bangs, Nathan 74–5, 196
baptism 193–4, 251
Baptist Canadian Missionary Society (U.K.) 198
Baptist Colonial Missionary Society 46
Baptist General Conference 380
Baptist Home Mission Board 19

Baptist Leadership Training Centre 383
Baptist Missionary Convention 200
Baptist New Brunswick Seminary 212
Baptists: in Maritimes xxii, 192–5, 202–6, 207; as radical evangelists xiv–xv; conservative revival xxii; British influence 44; 19th-century theological debate 49; education 49, 198–9, 212–13; regional variations 191–2; on Prince Edward Island 195–6; in Upper Canada 196–99; membership and growth (1881) 197, 209–10, 217, (1991) 217; 19th-century societies and divisions 198–200; missionary work 200–1, 205, 210–12; immersion controversy 203; Sunday schools 205; as formal evangelicalism 206–7; emphasis on conversionism and activism 208–9; Calvinistic views 209; associationalism 209; and "evangelical consensus" 209–10; response to science and technology 214–16; challenge of immigration 216–17; core beliefs today 219–20; gender roles and treatment of women 220–1; Atlantic convention (1986) 221; merger of organizations 222; and Convention Baptists 222; and divine healing 360; and CIM 363, 364; and Acadia Divinity College 380; and contemporary evangelical experience 426; categories 475n4, ethnic groupings 476n24. See also Regular Baptists
Baptist Union of Ontario and Quebec 383
Baptist Union of Western Canada (BUWC) 372
Bardsley, Cyril 41
Barnabas Anglican Ministries 185
Barnardo, Dr Thomas 353, 355, 356
Barth, Karl 150
Basis of Union 104, 106
Beaver, William 42
Beaver magazine 62

Bebbington, David xiii, xx, 108, 125, 249, 250, 253, 419
Beecher, Lyman 14
Bell, William 130, 132, 135–6
Bellingham, John 305, 306, 309, 319
Bender, H.S. 228, 229
Bengough, J.W. 340
Bentom, Clark 52
Bercuson, David 337
Berger, W.T. 355
Berry, Dr William 119
Bertermann, Eugene Rudolph 248
Berton, Pierre 183–4
Bestvater, William J. 231
Bethany Church 280, 283, 398
Bethell, Rev. T.G. 341
Bethel Mission (Winnipeg) 341, 342–3, 344
Bethune, Bishop Alexander Neil 158, 163, 172–3
Bibby, Reginald 61
Bible Christians 77
Bible colleges and institutes. See Bible schools
Bible schools xxiv, 57–8, 276, 363, 369–84; and CIM 354; numerical significance 369–70; influence on churches 370–3; reasons for success 373–4; admission to 374–6; faculties 375–6; compared to traditional theological colleges 376–7; 1950s–1960s changes in 377–8; accreditation of 378–9; new liberal arts colleges 379–80; establishment of seminaries 380; "progressive colleges" 381; new directions 381–3; Torchbearer Capenwray Bible School 383; need for diversity 384
biblicism xiii, xiv, xvii, 56, 65–6, 208, 250–1, 427; biblical experientialism 10–11; criticism as liberal tendency 42; early 20th-century controversies 49–50; bibliocentrism 253; biblical sanction 330
Bickersteth, Bishop Robert 160
Bilbrough, Ellen Agnes 356
Bill, I.E. 191, 208
Bingham, Rowland V. 57, 308, 361–2

Birch, Dr Kenneth 299
Birtch, George 118–19
Black, William 26
Blackett, George 498n50
black evangelicals 11
Blake, Samuel Hoyles 160, 164, 173, 359
Bland, Rev. Salem 92, 93, 338, 340
Bliss, P.P. 274
Bloor, Joseph 83
Blumhofer, Edith xxiv, 8, 18
Boardman, William 274
Boddy, Alexander 398
Bollen, J.D. 154
Bompas, W. Carpenter 40
Bond, William Bennett 163
Booth, Catherine 391
Booth, Evangeline 392
Booth, Herbert 391
Booth, General William 388, 391, 392
Booth-Clibborn, Mrs Catherine 339
Boreham, F.W. 35
Bosworth, Frederick 47
Bosworth, F.F. and B.B. 283–4
Bourke, Richard 31
Brandon College 213–14, 218
Brayton, Mary 365
Breadalbane Baptist Church 51
Bridgman, Henry 129, 130–1
Briercrest Bible Institute 314, 374, 376, 379, 380, 381, 382
Brigden, Beatrice 348
Britain: influences on Canada 8–10, 38–9, 44–5, 47–54; emigration to Australia 29; emigration to Canada 29, 44, 45, 46; financial contributions 41; missions to Canadian provinces 46–7; civilizing mission 48; CIM in 353
broadcasting. See religious broadcasting
Broadway Tabernacle Presbyterian Church 274
Brooks, Eugene 396–7, 401
Brooks, Sarah Leggett 396, 401
Broomhall, Benjamin 507n25
Broomhall, Edith 507n25
Brouwer, Ruth Compton 404, 405
Brown, Harold 246, 247–8
Brownlee, Edgar A. 362, 365
Browns (of Toronto) 128
Bryan, William Jennings 16

533 Index

Bryce, Peter 98
Bryden, Walter W. 17, 149–51, 153
Buchanan, Isaac 129
Buck, Dr Erwin 250–1
Buckner, Phillip 156
Bumsted, J.M. 62–63
Buntain, D.N. 297, 376
Burgher Secessionist Presbyterians 51
Burkholder, Oscar 227, 228
Burkinshaw, Robert xxiv, 8, 18, 25, 61, 367
Burns, Nelson xxii-xxiii, 257, 259–61, 263, 267
Burns, Robert 129, 131, 132
Burpee, Rev. Richard E. 205, 210–11
Burwash, Nathaniel 409, 410, 414
Bush, Peter 82
Buzza, Rev. Barry 292

Caird, John and Edward 145
Calhoun, Lieutenant Mattie 390
Calvinism 42
Calvinistic Baptists 205–6, 209
Calvinists, 42, 242
Campbell, Don 34
Campion, E. 26
Campus Crusade for Christ 61
Canada: links with U.S. 7–8; British influence and links 8–10, 41–4; trade with U.S. 9; compared with U.S. 11–12; French-English social tensions 11–12; founding myths 13–15; Charter of Rights 14; links with Australia 24–5, 31–3, 34, 35; impact of immigration 25; Irish and Scottish immigration 26; and New Zealanders 33
Canada Baptist College (Montreal) 198–9
Canada Baptist Union 200
Canada Holiness Association 257, 259, 260, 268, 269
Canada Presbyterian Church (CPC) 273
Canadian Alliance 281, 282, 287–8
Canadian Baptist 218
Canadian Baptist Federation 222
Canadian Baptist Missionary Federation 198, 199

Canadian Bible College (Regina) 286, 377, 378, 379, 380
Canadian Bible Institute. See Canadian Bible College
Canadian Churchman 176
Canadian Convention of Southern Baptists 222
Canadian Evangelical Free Church: See Evangelical Free Church
Canadian Free Churchmen 128
Canadian InterVarsity Fellowship (IVF) 33, 34. See also InterVarsity Christian Fellowship
Canadian Lutheran Bible Institutes 248
Canadian Mennonite Bible College 378–9
Canadian Mennonite Brethren 360; supporters of transdenominational evangelicalism 230; Bible schools 230–3; influx of *Russländers* 231–2; missionary activity 232–3; ambivalence towards evangelicalism 233; involvement in EFC 233; and CIM 358
Canadian Nazarene College 379
Canadian Protestant League 57
Canadian Salvation Army. See Salvation Army
Canadian Sunday School Mission (CSSM) 232–3, 304, 308–10, 311, 315, 317
Canadian Theological Seminary 380
Carlyle, Thomas 125
Carmichael, J. 163
Carpenter, Joel 377
Carrington, Philip 155, 163
Carroll, John 259–60
Carwardine, Richard 15
Case, William 196
Catherine Booth College 379
Catho-evangelicals xxiv, 420, 422, 426, 428, 429–30. See also Roman Catholic Church
Catholic Church. See Roman Catholic Church
Caughey, James 82, 331, 355
Caven, William 142, 143, 144
Central Europeans 46
Centre for Renewal of Public Policy 59

Chafer, Lewis Sperry 308
Chalmers, R.C. 119
Chambers, G.A. 296
charismatic movement xiv, 295, 300, 422–4. See also Pentecostalism
Cheever, Nathaniel 420
China 359–60
China Inland Mission (CIM) xxiv, 32, 351–68
China's Millions 362–3, 365, 366, 367
Chown, S.D. 19, 96
Christian Alliance (CA) 260, 276, 281, 282. See also Christian and Missionary Alliance
Christian and Missionary Alliance (CMA) xxii-xxiii, 357; formed from merger 277, 282; organizational tensions 278; shift to fundamentalism 284–5; push to West 285–6; mobile ministry 285; use of broadcasting 286; Bible schools 286; membership growth 286–7; re-examination of 287–8; founded (1889) 361; takes over Toronto Missionary Training Institute 363; launches Canadian Bible Institute 377; and Canadian Bible College 379; and Pentecostalism 397–8, 400
Christian colleges. See Bible schools
Christian Institute 357
Christian Messenger, The 44
Christian (Plymouth) Brethren 383
Christian Reformed churches 5, 58, 59, 379–80
Christian universities. See Bible schools; universities
Christian Week 12, 68
Christian Workers Church 258, 398
Christie, Rev. David 340
Christie, George A. 397
Christie, Nancy xxiii-xxiv, 7–8, 22, 194
Church Association of the Diocese of Toronto 172–3
Churches of Christ/Christian Churches 372–3
Church Growth Movement 249
Church Missionary Society (CMS) 26, 41, 45, 168, 172

Church of England: clerically dominated in Australia 27; relations with state 29–30; Latitudinarians 159; "high" and "low" 159–60; Evangelical Association 172; and CIM 358–9. *See also* Anglicans; Lay Association of the Church of England
Church of God 290, 291–2
Church of God of Prophecy 291–2
Church of Scotland (or Kirk) 29, 45, 51, 133, 134
Church of the Lutheran Brethren 242
Church of the Nazarene 258, 268, 269
church-sect model 292–3
Citizens for Public Justice 5, 59, 68
Clarke, G.W. 507n24
Clarkson, Margaret 8
class 88, 89, 94, 333–4, 335–50, 415
Clifford, Keith 143, 148
Clyde, Alexander 210
Cockburn, Bruce 66
Cody, Henry John 174, 177, 180
Coffman, Samuel F. 227, 228
Coggan, F.D. 181
Cokelers 50
Colonial and Continental Church Society 49
Colonial Church and School Society (CCSS) 46, 157, 167
Colonial Missionary Society 46
Columbia Bible College 382
Comfortable Pew, The (Berton) 183–4
Congregationalists 26, 52, 97, 135, 192–3, 279
Congregational Union of Ontario and Quebec 279
Connor, Ralph. *See* Gordon, Rev. C.W.
Conrad Grebel College (Waterloo) 229
consumerism xvii
Convention Baptists 222
conversionism 66–7, 251, 254, 419; introduced by Bebbington xiii; as central defining moment xiv; downplayed in late 19th century xvi; shift to ethics 99–100; in mainline Protestantism 108–10; Dobson's 1938

position 115–16; and United Church 118–19, 121; and Baptists 208–9; in Pentecostalism 293; experiences in 1990s 421–2
Cook, Arnold 287
Cook, Ramsay 62, 63, 337
Cook, Sharon xxiv
Cooper, J.I. 163
Cooperative Commonwealth Federation (CCF) 16
Coops, Lorraine xxii
Copeland, Joseph 32
Copley, Albert S. 395, 397
corporatism 93–4
Counter, John 83
Craig, John 398
Cramp, John Mockett 198–9, 204, 205
Craven, Vincent 34
Crawford, Alexander 195–6
Crawley, E.A. 195, 203, 207
Crerar, Duff xxi
Cronyn, Bishop Benjamin 158, 160, 161, 163, 167, 172
Crooks, John 26
Cross. *See* crucicentrism
Crossley, Hugh T. 320–36. *See also* Crossley-Hunter team
Crossley-Hunter team xxiii, 320–36
Crossthwaite, Isabella 360
crucicentrism xiii, xiv, xvii, 56, 65, 208, 250, 419
Cumberland Presbyterians 366

Daggett, Rev. J.B. 219
dancing 329–30
Dannhauer, Johann 247
Darby, John Nelson 53, 355
Darbyite Brethren 355
Darroch, Gordon 88
Davies, Dr Benjamin 198
Davies, John 34
Davies, Robertson 9, 66
Dayton, D.W. xiii, 187
Deck, Northcote 34
Decade of Evangelism 60
"Deeper Life" movement 280
de Long, P.R. 361
demographics xv, xviii, 8, 63, 94, 185
Derstine, Clayton 227, 228
DesBarres, T.C. 359, 364
Dewart, E.H. 329
DeWolf, Nancy 405
Disciples of Christ 372
Disruption, the 127, 130
Dissenters 51–2

divine healing 275, 276, 280, 281, 282, 360–2
Dixon, F.J. 340
Dobson, Hugh Wesley 111–12, 113, 114, 115–16, 117, 120
Dominion Auxiliary 281, 282
Donald, Melvin 34
Douglas, Tommy 16
Dowie, John Alexander 396, 397
Dowie's Zion 400
Draper, William Henry 164
Drucker, Peter 94, 95
Drummond, Henry 124, 145, 146
Duncan, Sara Jeannette 354
Durham, William 400, 401
Dutaud, R.L. 296
Dykstra, Craig 93–4

Eakin, Thomas 149
Eastern British America Methodist Conference 45
Eastman, David 48
Eby, Solomon 226
ecumenism 97, 104
education 58. *See also* Bible schools; universities
Edwards, Rev. John 197
Edwards, Jonathan 246, 417
Elder, William 203
Elim Chapel (Winnipeg) xxiii, 143, 304–8, 309, 315, 317, 345
Elim Tabernacle. *See* Elim Chapel
Ellice Avenue Mission. *See* Elim Chapel
Ellingsen, Mark 242, 245–6
Elliott, David 8
Ellis, Walter 213–14, 376
Emmanuel College (Saskatchewan) 41, 175
End Days, the 277
Erdman, Charles 507n34
Erdman, William J. 358, 364
Essentials '94 Conference (Montreal) 171–2, 185, 186
Estonian Evangelical Lutheran Church 241
Evangelical Alliance. *See* Evangelical Missionary Alliance
"Evangelical Christian Church" 243
Evangelical Churches of Pentecost 291
Evangelical Churchman 173, 174–5
Evangelical Fellowship of Canada (EFC) 58, 59, 68,

104, 428; sponsors *Cross Currents* 5; founding inspired by NAE 6; and United Church 61; and Mennonite Brethren 233; organizational meeting 298; Pentecostal involvement in 299; and PBI 370; expansion in BC 370–1
Evangelical Free Church (EFC) 370, 379, 380
evangelicalism: definitions xiii, 55–6, 186–8, 249, 250, 419–20; beginnings in Canada xiv; history in Canada xiv–xix; Canadian compared with U.S. xv, 17–18; and liberal consensus xvii; re-emerges as force in late 20th century xviii; in 1990s xviii–xix, 420; leadership xix–xx, 429; diversity 7; characteristics of 10, 56, 104; environmental influences 11; liberal 17–18, 97; early ministers 26–7; early colonial difficulties 27–8; international influences 35–37; influences on Canada 38–9, 60–7, 69; geophysical influences 40; early 20th-century controversies 49–50; standard commitments 56; social influences 56–9; decline in effects of preaching 98–9; influences on in 1950s 119; studies of experience 403–4; as "family religion" 410; early period 417–18; types of experience 421–4; cluster analysis 424–6; effects of experience in 1990s 426–8; organizational contacts 428–9. *See also* formal evangelicalism; neo-evangelicals
Evangelical Lutheran Church in Canada 241, 242. *See also* Lutherans
Evangelical Lutheran Church of America 246
Evangelical Mennonite Missionary Church (EMMC) 235–7
Evangelical Missionary Alliance (EMA) xvi, 104, 273, 276–7, 281, 282
Evangelical Union Church 42
Evans, William 308
evolution 42

faith healing. *See* divine healing
Faith Today 68
Falconer, Robert 143, 146, 148
Faught, Dr J. Harry 298–9
Faunce, W.H.P. 218
Feild, Edward 163
Feller, Henrietta 199
Fellowship Baptist 380
Fellowship for a Christian Social Order 116
Fellowship of Evangelical Baptist Churches in Canada 222
Ferguson, John 195
Fire Baptized Holiness Association 399
First Church of the Christian Association 260
First Great Awakening 26, 192–3, 207, 426, 430
Fisher, George 398
Fletcher, Lionel 35
Focus on the Family 59
Ford, Leighton 8
formal evangelicalism xv, xvi
Fornier, Keith 420
Forsberg, Simon E. 310–13, 314, 316
Forsyth, James Bell 164
Fourfold Gospel 280
Foursquare Gospel Church of Canada 292
Francke, Herman 246
Franklin, Fred 343
Fraser, Brian 144, 145, 147
Fraser, Donald 43
Fraser, William 197
Free Christian Baptists 193, 206, 209
Free Church in Canada 127–8, 133–4, 144, 273
Free Church of Scotland 29, 42, 44
Free Communion Baptists 198
Free Methodist Church 258, 268, 269
Freethinking Christians 50
Free Will Baptists 198
Freitag, Walter 248, 251–2
French, Goldwin xvi, 124, 403
French Canadian Missionary Society 165
Friesen, Gerald 318
Frost, Henry W. 352–3, 356–8, 360–8
Fulford, Francis 154–5, 157, 163, 167
Fuller Theological Seminary 246, 249

Full Gospel Bible Institute 383–4
fundamentalism 25; avoidance by Canadian evangelicalism 198; compared to evangelicalism 252; and mainline evangelicalism 303; Winnipeg network 303–19; Bible institute 315; on Canadian Prairies 316; relations with mainline churches 317; and working-class piety 349; and CIM 367
Furness, Grace 314
Fyfe, Robert Alexander 201, 202

Gaebelein, Dr Arno C. 308, 346
Gagan, Rosemary 405
Gagliardi, Phil 64
Gandier, Alfred 143
Gangel, Kenneth 381
Garber, John 229
Garrettson, Freeborn xv
Garrigus, Alice 289
Gauvreau, Michael xxiii–xxiv, 15–16, 17, 25, 66, 107, 124, 125, 126–7, 410
Geddie, Rev. James 272
Geddie, John 32
gender 135. *See also* women
Gibson, Theo T. 198
Gifford, Caroline 405
Gifford, W.A. 99
Gill, Stewart 129–30
Gilmour, John 197
Glasgow Colonial Society 45
Global Missions/Sharon 290, 291
Glover, Robert H. 308
Gnosticism 260
Goderich, Lord 30
God's Bible School (Cincinnati) 398
Goff, Frank xxii–xxiii, 257–8, 259, 264–5, 267
Goforth, Jonathan 145, 359–60, 508n38
Gooderham, William 357, 360
Goodwin, Dan xxii
Gordon, Rev. C.W. (Ralph Connor) 19, 66, 131, 134–5, 143, 144, 145–8, 339
Gospel Tabernacle 275–6
Gospel Workers Church in Canada 257, 264–5, 269
Gourlay, R.C. 26
Graham, Billy 119, 183, 248, 429

536 Index

Graham, Lady Catherine 161
Grand Ligue Mission 199
Grant, David 34
Grant, George Monro, 17, 49, 125–6, 128, 139–40, 152; on state of Protestantism (1893) 137; as preacher 142; death 143; attacks positivism 146; and evangelical centre 151
Grant, George Parkin 9, 15
Grant, J.L. (Mrs G.M.) 139
Grant, John Webster 17, 27, 39, 108, 111, 116, 128–9, 403
Granville Street Baptist Church (Halifax) 194–5
Great Awakening 246. *See also* First Great Awakening; Second Great Awakening
Great Glengarry Revival 135–6
Greeley, Andrew 422
Greenman, W.R. 347
Greenshields, Malcolm 269
Grenville, Andrew xviii, xxiv
Griffen, Clyde 86
Griffen Thomas, William Henry 175, 176, 177, 359
Grimsby Park Campground 75–6, 88–9
Guenther, Bruce xxii, 369, 370
Guiness, Howard 317
Guinness, Henry Grattan 272, 355, 507n21
Gundy, J.H. 98, 101
Gunson, Neil 26

Hague, Dyson 42, 176–7, 179, 180
Haldane, Robert and James 195, 197
Hale, Jeffrey 164, 168, 169
Hall, Justice Emmett 297
Hall, George 164
Hallesby, Dr Ole 248
Hammond, Carrie 220
Harms, John F. 230–1
Harnack, Adolf von 146
Harris, Rev. Elmore 215, 363, 364
Harris, J.E. 372
Hartz, Louis 24
Harvey, D.C. 202–3
Hatch, Ellen 282
Hatch, Nathan xv, 38, 73, 74, 93
Hay, David 151
"Heavenly Railroad, The" 321, 324–5

Hebden, Ellen 289, 293, 395, 397, 516n46
Hebden, James 289, 293, 395, 401
Hellmuth, Isaac 154–5, 156–8, 160, 161, 164
Helmer, J.S. 366
Henan, China 359–60
Henry, Carl 248, 298
Herbert Bible School 230–1
Heschel, Abraham Joshua 76
Higgins, Walter V. 211–12
Higher Christian Life, The 274
Hildebrand, Henry H. 309, 312, 313–14, 377, 379
Hildebrandt, Edward 297
Hill, Billie 348
Hillis, Bryan xxii
Hindmarsh, Bruce xxiii
historiography 7, 8–9, 62–3, 155–6
Hobart, John Henry 4
Hockin, Rev. William 171
Hoffman, Dr Oswald 249
Holiness Gospel Workers. *See* Gospel Workers Church in Canada
holiness movement xxii–xxiii, 42; main emphases 258; issue of plain dress 263; leadership problems 267; reconciliation attempts 268; in Methodism 331; and Pentecostalism 398, 400. *See also* Hornerite holiness movement; Keswick holiness movement
Holiness Movement Church 257–8, 397; founded 263; foreign missions 263; characteristics of 263–4; Egypt mission 263, 265; compared to Gospel Workers Church 265; split in 265–7; membership 268; merges with Free Methodist Church 269
Holmes, Arthur 9–10
Horan, Benjamin W. 42, 180
Hordern, William 251
Horner, Ralph xxii–xxiii, 259, 261–3, 264, 265–7, 270, 331, 332
Hornerite holiness movement 35, 349
Horsch, J. 228
Howard family (Tottenham, England) 335
Howe, Daniel Walker 10
Howland, William 279, 356, 357, 489n29

Howlett, M.A. 346
Hoyles, N.W. 176
Hudnut-Beumler, James 93–4
Hughson, Rev. J.E. 346
Hunt, A. Clarke 309, 312
Hunt, Desmond 184
Hunt, Leslie 184
Hunter, Ernest Crossley 324, 325
Hunter, J. Lloyd 309, 310, 314, 316
Hunter, John E. 320–36. *See also* Crossley-Hunter team
Huntington, Bishop 29
Huron College (London, ON) 157, 160, 172
Hussey, Henry 23
Hutchinson, Abigail 417
Hutchinson, Mark xix–xx
Hutchinson, William 107
hymns 8

immigration 25, 44, 46, 77–9, 216–7
Independent Assemblies of God International of Canada 290
Ingersoll, ON 390, 391–2
Ingham, Bishop 43
Inglis, Bishop Charles 162, 193
Inglis, John 162
Institute for Christian Studies (Toronto) 58
institutionalization 292–3
Inter-Church Advisory Council 97, 104
Inter-Church Forward Movement 90, 97–8, 104
Inter-Church National Campaign 97
Interdenominational Foreign Missions Committee 362
InterVarsity Christian Fellowship (IVCF) 61, 228, 248, 297–8, 317, 353, 354, 428. *See also* Canadian InterVarsity Fellowship
Ironside, Harry 308
Irvine, Rev. G.O. 346
Italian Pentecostal Church of Canada 290
Ivens, Rev. William 337, 346, 347, 348, 350

Jackson, George 49–50
Jackson, Rain 35
Jantz, Harold 233
Jenkins, William 130
Jensen, Rev. Rasmus 244
Jensen, Richard 249

537 Index

John-Paul II, Pope 186–7
Johnson, Curtis 83
Johnson, Richard 27
Johnston, C.L. 310
Johnston, R.K. xiii
Johnstone, James and Lewis 194
Johnstone, Laleah 210–11
Jones, Jane Clement 82, 84–5, 86
Jones, Stephen and Margaret 83
Juster, Susan 86

Katerberg, Will xxi
Kee, Kevin xxiii
Keirstead, Wilfred Currier 214
Kennedy, James 388, 390
Kennedy, Minnie Pearce 388, 389–90
Keswick holiness movement 25, 42, 258, 353, 355, 400, 490n31
Kilpatrick, T.B. 143
King, John Mark 141, 143
King, Joseph H. 399
King, Phyllis 34
King, William Lyon Mackenzie 139
King's College (Edmonton). *See* University College
Knaplund, Paul 30
Knox, Constance 34
Knox College (Toronto) 140–1, 146, 273
Knox's Church (Hamilton, ON) 273
Koehler, Walter 252–3, 254
Kulbeck, E.N.O. 293
Kydd, Ron xxiii

Labor Churches 347–8
Lamarckianism 11
Lang, John Dunmore 27, 28
Langford, Fred 99
Latimer College (Vancouver) 175
Latter Rain Pentecostalism 35
Latto, T.T. 297
Latvian Evangelical Lutheran Church in America 241
Laurence, Margaret 66
Lay Association of the Church of England 164, 168–9, 170
Lazareth, William 253
Lee, Rev. F.W. 349
Leege, David 420
Leeson, M. 321
Lenin, Vladimir Ilych 55, 69
Lewis, John Travers 163, 164

Liberal Evangelical Group Movement 180
Lindberg, Carter 246
Lippe, Michael 221
Lipset, Seymour Martin 8, 13–15
Little, Lieutenant Mercy 390
Lloyd, Rev. George E. 46, 48, 175
Loane, Marcus 34
Lockhart, Grace Annie 213
Lupton, Levi 397, 399
Luther, Martin 125
Lutheran Church–Canada 242, 246, 249, 252
Lutheran Church–Missouri Synod (MS) 242, 246
Lutheran Evangelistic Movement 248
Lutherans xxii; and evangelicalism 61, 246–9, 252–4, 426; and term "evangelical" 241–4; early history in Europe 242–4; and confessionalism 244, 252, 254; first Canadian service 244; pivotal historical moments 245; ethnic origins 245; pietistic origins 247–8; World Mission Prayer League 248; compared to evangelicals 249–50; and social activism 251; confessionalism 252; sacramental emphasis 253–4
Lyon, Robert 132

McAlister, R.E. 296
McCaw, Rev. Ronald 106
McClung, Nellie 340
McClure, W.J. 346
McCulloch, Thomas 41, 126
MacDonald, Alexander 210
Macdonald, Charles 139
Macdonald, J.A. 143, 145
Macdonald, John 78–9, 83
Macdonald, Sir John A. 320–1, 325, 327, 336
MacDonald, W. Clarke 121
McDonaldites 196
Macdonell, Alexander 25
Macdonnell, D.J. 125
Macdonnell heresy trial (1875–7) 140, 149
Mcdougall, Elizabeth 127
McElheran, Rev. Robert 179–80
MacFadgen, John Edgar 141
MacGillivray, Donald 360
McGregor, James 126
Machar, Agnes Maule 146

Machen, J. Gresham 148–9
Machray, Robert 160
McIvor, W.J. 339
Mack, Barry xxi, 125, 126
McKay, A.C. 215
MacKay, Leslie 143
MacKay, R.P. 358, 360
McKenna, Katherine 409–10
Mackenzie, Alexander 201, 320
McKillop, J.W. 297
MacLaren, William 140–1, 142, 143
Maclean, Rev. John 342, 344, 346, 348–9
McLeod, Ezekiel 206
McLeod, Norman 125
McLoughlin, William 387
McMaster, William 201–2, 213, 216
McMaster University 212, 213, 215–16, 218
MacMillan, Donald 131
Macmillan, Rev. J.W. 340
McNeile, Hugh 158
McNichol, Rev. John 18, 364
McPherson, Aimee Semple xxiv, 8, 349, 387–402
MacPherson, Annie 356
MacVicar, Donald Harvey 142, 143, 144
Magic Methodists 50
Mainse, David 429
Mann, W.E. 369, 373
Manning, Edward 196
Manning, Ernest 64
Manning, Preston 64
Marchmount Homes 356
Marion, James 348
Maritime Baptists 214, 215, 218–19
Maritime Christian College of Charlottetown 372–3
Marks, Lynne 405, 413
Marsden, Samuel 22, 27
Marshall, Alexander 53
Marshall, Clara Belle 213
Marshall, David 112–13, 124–5, 126–7, 403–4, 406
Marshall, Lawrence 50
Marshall, Walter 272
Martin, Abraham 226
Martin, Alvin 379
Martin, Jessie 227, 228, 229
Maslow, Abraham 418–19, 426
Matheson, S.P. 175, 177
Matthews, Fred 8
Matthews, I.G. 215–16
Maxwell, L.E. 304, 318, 377
media. *See* religious broadcasting

538 Index

Medley, John 163
Mennonite Brethren in Christ (MBC): influence, 12; origins 226, 229, 230; compared to Mennonite Church 226–7; Bible schools 226, 371; in EFC 233; Home Missions Committee 371
Mennonite Conference of Ontario (MCO) 226, 227, 229
Mennonites xxii; influence, 12; Bible schools 57, 369; origins in Canada 223; makeup and membership 223; diversity 223–4; and evangelicalism 224–5, 239–40; Swiss 225–27; Old Order groups 226; Sunday school movement 227; Alberta-Saskatchewan Conference 227; key traditions 228; peace theology 228–9; denounce dispensationalism 228–9; Anabaptist vision 229; Old Colony and Sommerfelders 234–5; schisms 235–6; case of Osler Mission Chapel 237–9. *See also* Mennonite Brethren in Christ
Merry, Mrs 356
Methodism: omitted by historiography 7; and Anglicanism 26, 29; and revivalism 80, 84; growth (1851–81) 87; and conversion 92, 102; adopts corporate structure 94; effect of social mobility 94–5; shift to religion of service 99–100; concern for youth 100; and ministry candidates 101–2; religion linked with service 101; meaning of "evangelical" 103–4; Crossley-Hunter revivalism 320–36; and evangelicalism 325–6, 349; sanctification 331–2
Methodist Episcopal Church. *See* Methodists
Methodist Episcopal Church (U.S.) 39
Methodist Foreign Missionary Society 360
Methodists: radical evangelists xiv–xv; denounced by Strachan 3; use of circuit system 25; early education for clergy 25; links with Britain 43; divisions in Canada West 51; membership (1792, 1884) 73, 81, (1911) 147, (1881) 197; social and individual reform 73, 329; camp meetings 74–77, 87, 88–9, 196–7; in New Brunswick and Ontario 79–80; and wealth 83–4; youth and women 84–87; and middle class 89; class meetings 99; "connexional" work 102–3; missionary societies 103, 360; disbursement of funds (1920) 103; holiness tradition 258–9; and Horner 261–2; grant licences to evangelists 262; 1886 "Footnote" 329, 336; appeal to bourgeois norms 335–6; impact of Winnipeg General Strike 350; and CIM 360. *See also* Free Methodist Church; Magic Methodists; Primitive Methodists; Wesleyan Methodist Connection; Wesleyan Methodists
Methodist Survey Commission (1920) 98–103, 104
Meyer, F.B. 45, 53
Michel, David 32–3
middle class. *See* class
Millar, W.J. 311
Millar College of the Bible 383–4
Miller, Roland 373
Millman, T.R. 155
Mills, Albert xxiii, 257, 264–5, 270,
Milner, Isaac 161
missionary movement 32, 93–4
Missionary Training Institute 276
Missionary Training School (MTS, Toronto) 280–1
Missionary Union for the Evangelization of the World 276
Mitchell, John 311, 316
Moir, John 39, 127
Moody, Barry 204, 212, 213, 214–15, 274
Moody, D.L. 124, 306, 322, 351, 353
Moody Bible Institute 339, 351, 363
Moody Church in Chicago 366
Moody revivals. *See* Moody, D.L.
Moore, Josephine Kinley 221
Moore, T. Albert 111
Moore, Major Thomas 388–9
Morgan, G. Campbell 308
Morison, James 42
Morphett, John 30
Morris, Alexander 132
Morris, William 129
Morrow, James Bain 82, 84–5
Morse, Asahel 27–28
Morse, Dr Reginald 211–12
Mountain, Armine 156
Mountain, George Jehoshaphat 160, 163, 164, 166, 167–70
Mountain, Bishop Jacob 161, 162
Mount Carmel School (Edmonton) 383
Mowat, Farley 9
Mowll, Howard K. 35, 175, 359
Muelder, Walter 292
Muhlenberg, Henry Melchior 246
Muller, George 355
Muller, Julius 141
Mulroney, Brian 64
multiculturalism 68
Munck, Jens 244
Murphy, Maurice 34
Murray, Annie and George 397–8, 401
Mutchmor, J.R. 115, 119, 120

National Association of Evangelicals (NAE) 6, 242, 298
National Council of Women (NCWC) 407
Navigators 61
Nazarenes. *See* Church of the Nazarene
Nelson, E. Clifford 242
neo-evangelicals 187, 253
"neutral zone" xx, 92
New Birth xiv, xvii, 108–10. *See also* conversionism
New Brunswick Bible Institute 383–4
New Connexion church 77
New Democratic Party (NDP) 16
New Dispensation 192
Newfoundland and British North American School Society 45–6, 167
New Light revivalism 24, 42, 67, 192, 193, 205
Newman, John Henry 163

Index

Niagara-on-the-Lake, ON 355
Nicolls, Harriet 156
Nicolls, Jasper Hume 156
Niebuhr, H. Richard 292
Nienkirchen, Charles 287
Nipawin Bible Institute (SK) 383–4
Nixon, Richard 311–12
Noll, Mark 68, 244–5, 253, 289, 419
Norris, Hannah Maria 220
Norris, Ken 373
North American Baptist Divinity School 380
Northwest Baptist Theology College 382
Northwest Bible College (Edmonton) 376
Nova Scotia 202–3
Nutting, J.W. 194–5

Oke, Janette 66
O'Leary, Captain Annie 390
Oliver, Dr French 347
O'Meara, Thomas R. 175, 176, 359
Ontario Bible College (and Seminary) 57–8, 218, 281, 380, 381. *See also* Toronto Bible College
Ontario Mennonite Bible School and Institute (Berlin/Kitchener, ON) 227, 229
Ontario Theological Seminary (Toronto) 58, 380
Ontario Woman's Christian Temperance Union 405
Open Air Campaigners Movement 35
Osborne, W.F. 341
Osler Mission Chapel (SK) 235
Ottawa Gospel Tabernacle 284
Overseas Missionary Fellowship (OMF) 32, 33
Oxenden, Ashton 161–2
Oxford Group Movement (United Church) 113–14, 162, 163, 167, 169

Packer, J.I. 172
Palmer, Phoebe 82–3, 258, 259, 331, 355
Palmer, Walter 331
Parham, Charles Fox 396–7
Parkdale Tabernacle (Toronto) 283–4
Parsons, Rev. Dr Henry Martyn 358, 364
Pashley, George 78
Passing Shadow, The 342
Patrick, William 143

Peace River Bible Institute 375
Pearce, Mary 389
Pearce, Minnie. *See* Kennedy, Minnie Pearce
Pearson, William 85
Peculiar People of Essex 50
Peden, Robert 42
Pennefather, William 355
Pentecostal Assemblies of Canada (PAOC) 290, 291, 293, 294, 297, 298, 299
Pentecostal Assemblies of Newfoundland 290
Pentecostalism, xxii–xxiii, 222, 277; origins in Canada 289–90; U.S. influence 290–1; growth in Canada 291–2; church-sect model 292–3; extra-dependence/intra-dependence model 294–5; strata 295; and youth 298; style of worship 299–300; emerges in Toronto 394–5, 399–400; and Aimee Semple McPherson 394, 395; early links 397–9; early beliefs and practices 399–401; women in ministries 400
Pentecostal Missionary Union 400
Pentecostal Testimony, The 297
Peoples Church (Toronto) 35, 43
Percy, Rev. Gilbert 164, 166–8, 169
Peters, Elizabeth 77, 78
Peters, F.C. 233
Peters, William 77–8
Pidgeon, George 108–10, 113, 114, 115, 120, 143
Pidgeon, Rev. Leslie 341
Pierson, A.T. 367
pietism 10, 81, 254, 445n3
Pike, John Martin 395
Pilcher, Charles Venn 35, 175, 180
Plaxton, David xxi
Pless, John 246
Polding, J.B. 25
political behaviour 15–16, 63–4, 68–9. *See also* social activism; social gospel movement
Pollard, Richard 27
Pollock, Allan 139
Pope, Richard 164
Pope, W.B. 43
populist communalism 16
Powell, Anne Murray 409–10, 412

Practical Talks on Important Themes (Crossley) 329, 332
Prairie Bible College 382. *See also* Prairie Bible Institute
Prairie Bible Institute (PBI, Three Hills, AB) 57, 317, 318–19, 370–1, 380, 381–2
premillennialism 42, 276, 345–6, 349
Prendergast, Ross 183
Presbyterians xxi; as formalists xv; as distinct from evangelical churches xvi; early development in Canada and Australia 27, 29; and church union 40, 148–50; moderating influence of George Grant 49; beliefs and practices 52, 126, 127, 131–4; emblem and motto 123; early thinkers 124; and evangelicalism 125, 129, 141, 145, 147, 426; in Maritime provinces 126; as largest Protestant denomination 127, 146; Princeton Old School 127–8; historical studies of 128; "Long Communion" 128–9, 194; indigenization 129–30; voluntarism 130; in Upper Canada 131–6; in early 20th century 138–9, 141; 19th-century growth 140; Westminster Standards 140, 141, 149, 151; leadership 141–2, 143–4, 148–9; and social criticism 142–3; Board of Moral and Social Reform 144; Boards of Home and Foreign Missions 144; education 144–5; Progressives 144–5, 147; and 1930s Depression 150–1; Committee on Evangelism and Church Life and Work 151; in post-war era 151; social activism 151; compared to United Church 152; in 1990s 152; membership (1926 and 1990s) 152; and McDonaldites 196; impact of Winnipeg General Strike 350; and CIM 358, 359–60
Prescott, Charlotte 405
Primitive Methodists 50, 77
Prince, W. 344
Progressive Conservative Party 64

prohibition 445n4
Protestant Episcopal Divinity School (PEDS) 173, 174, 175. *See also* Wycliffe College
Protestantism xvi, 104, 107–8
Protestant Truth Society 43
Proudfoot, William 48, 129–30
Providence College (Winnipeg) 381, 382. *See also* Winnipeg Bible College
"Prussian Union Church" 243
Pryor, John 195
Punshon, Rev. Morley 32, 47, 48, 87
Purdie, J.E. 296, 376

quadrilateral ideology xiii, xiv, 295. *See also* Bebbington
Quakers 400
Queen's University (Kingston, ON) Theological Alumni conferences 142

racial stereotyping 19
radical evangelicalism xiv–xv, xvi, xvii, 53, 54
radio. *See* religious broadcasting
Ralston, Mel 372
Randall, Herbert 397, 401
Rawlyk, George 403, 416; on border crossings 7–8; public opinion research 12; history of Maritime Baptists 18; work on "New Light" revivalism 24; on religion in Maritimes 39; and early radical evangelicals 54; research on Presbyterians 128–9; survey of evangelicalism 187; on Maritime Baptists 214, 215; and "accommodating spirit" 221; and role of women 404, 405
Redeemer College (Ancaster, ON) 58, 380, 512n57
Redekop, David E. 233
Redekop, John H. 233
Redemptive Homes for Women 115
Redpath, John 128
Reed, Bruce 294, 300
Reed, David 431
Reekie, Archibald B. 211
Reformed (or Holiness) Baptists 258
Reformed churches. *See* Christian Reformed churches

Reform Party 16
Regent College (Vancouver) 185, 380
Regular Baptist Mission and Education Society 218
Regular Baptists 193, 194, 199, 203–4, 206
Reid, Darrel xxiii, 127
Reid, Peter 383
Reid, Rev. S.J. 341, 345
Reid, W.D. 148
Reimer, Ben D. 315
religion: as historically socialized 28–29; and civil society 29; church and state relationships in early Canada and Australia 29–31; reform movement 30; church leadership 33–4; theological education 48–9, 100; early 19th-century democratization 50; influence of evangelicalism 60–1; music 61; role in Canadian society 65; use of Bible 65–6; disestablishment of 93; theological liberalism; 149–50 definition of experience 418–19; in 1990s 430–1
religious broadcasting 61, 286, 318, 370, 371, 373
Renfree, Henry 219
Renison, Robert 180
Rennie, Ian 8
Republican Party (U.S.) 16
revivalism 50, 55, 81–83, 261–2, 333–5, 338, 339–40, 350
Reynolds, Lindsay 281–2, 287
Riley, W.B. 228, 308, 309
Robertson, James 46, 141–2, 143
Robinson, Donald 34
Robinson, Rev. Harry 171, 172
Robinson, Henry and Martha 397, 401, 516n46
Robinson, Tom 185
Roe, Rev. Henry 166–8
Roman Catholic Church, xviii, xxiv, 60, 166, 186–7, 420, 426. *See also* Catho-evangelicals
Ross, Britton 347
Rotundo, Anthony 413
Roussy, Louis 199
Rudnerweider Mennonite Church. *See* Evangelical Mennonite Missionary Church

Runnells, Rev. 99
Ryan, Henry 196
Ryerson, Egerton 3–4, 50

sabbatarianism 43
sacraments 253
St John's College (Winnipeg) 175
St Stephen's University (New Brunswick) 379
Salmon, Rev. John xxiii, 278–81, 282, 285, 362, 363, 398, 401
Salvation Army 18, 52, 260, 379, 388–93, 398, 401–2
sanctification 276, 331–2
Sanders, J.E. 399
Sandham, Alfred 279, 356, 357, 363
"Saskatchewan 60" 46
Saunders, Alexander 367
Sawatsky, Rodney 240
Sawatsky, Ronald 363
Scaer, David 253
Schindel, Rev. A.C. 297–8
Schmidt, Leigh Eric 76, 77, 128
Schmucker, Samuel 246
Scott, Christina 361
Scott, Daniel 361
Scott, Dr E. 36
Scott, Ephraim 149
Scott, Maggie 282, 361
Scott, Rev. (of Winnipeg) 350
Scott, T.H. 28
Scott, Sir Walter 131
Scottish Brethren 53
Scriven, Joseph 8
Scroggie, Graham 308
Seceders 29, 125, 126
Secessionist churches 132
Secessionist-Free Church. *See* Free Church in Canada
Secessionist United Presbytery 129
Second Great Awakening 28, 426, 430
sectarianism xxii, 29, 50, 67, 296
secularization xviii
Semple, Robert 394, 401
Sewell, E.W. 164
Shearer, John 143
Sheraton, Rev. James Paterson 173
Shields, Thomas Todhunter 18, 50, 52, 57, 216, 217–18, 219, 303, 307, 311
Shortt, Adam 139, 142, 147
Sidey, John James 218–19

Simpson, A.B. xxiii, 8, 127, 271–8, 280, 281, 285, 288, 353, 357
Sinclair, Gordon 402
Skelton, O.D. 147
"slain in the Spirit" 422–3, 424, 428
Small, Franklin 290
Smith, Rev. A.E. 340, 342, 343, 344, 348, 503n31
Smith, George Adam 141
Smith, Gypsy 349
Smith, Oswald J. 35, 43–4, 283–4
Smith, Robert Pearsall 274
Smith, Rev. Sidney T. 305, 306, 307–8, 316, 319, 350
Smith, Bishop Taylor 40
social activism 59, 110–11, 116, 118–19
social Christianity. *See* social gospel movement
Social Credit Party 16, 64
social gospel movement 87, 96–7, 337, 340–1. *See also* social activism
socialism 340
Society for the Propagation of the Gospel in Foreign Parts (SPG) 26, 29, 161, 167
Soltow, Lee 88
Sommerfelder Mennonite Church 235
Southcottians 50
Southern Baptist Convention 7
South Seas Evangelical Mission (Australia) 32
Soward, R.H. 184
speaking in tongues 394, 395, 396, 398, 422, 423, 424, 428
Speer, Robert 355
Spener, Philip Jacob 247
Sperry, John R. 187
Stackhouse, John xx, 18, 23, 107, 187, 222, 303, 317, 383
Standard Church of America 258, 265, 267, 269
Stanley-Blackwell, Laurie 127, 128–9
Stanser, Robert 162
Stansfield, Dr Joshua 339
Steen, Frederick J. 174–5
Stelzle, Charles 339
Stephen, James 30
Stewart, Rev. Charles 344
Stewart, Charles James 161
Stiller, Brian 5, 12, 33, 299, 383, 429
Stiller, Rev. C.H. 297

Stonehouse, W.J. 268
Strachan, John 3–4, 28, 163, 167
Stuart, Andrew 164
Stuart, George Okill 164, 168
Stuart, John 28
Student Volunteer Movement for Foreign Missions 351
Sudan Interior Mission (SIM, Toronto) 32, 357, 361, 362, 364
Sullivan, Edward 163
Sunday, Billy 338–9
Sweatman, Archdeacon Arthur 173–4
Swedenborgians 50
Sweet, Henry Charles 296, 297, 312
Suteras (evangelical twins) 286
Sutherland, Wilbur 34
Swift Current Bible Institute 381

Taylor, Anne 409, 410
Taylor, Hudson 351–2, 353, 354, 355–6, 359–60, 363
Taylor, Muriel 309, 310
Taylor, W.E. 178
Taylor Smith, John 53
Telfer, E.G. 35
temperance 43, 95–96. *See also* Ontario Woman's Christian Temperance Union; Woman's Christian Temperance Union
Templeton, Charles 119
Theological Alumni conferences (Queen's University) 142
Tholuck, Friedrich 141
Thomas, W.H. Griffith 49
Thompson (CCSS missionary) 164
Thompson, Charles P. 31
Thompson, Robert 64
Threinen, Norman 245
Timpany, Jane Bates 211
Toews, John E. 240
Toon, Peter 158–9
Torchbearer Capenwray Bible schools 383
Toronto, ON 352, 356–7
Toronto Bible College 18, 58, 317, 354, 376, 378. *See also* Ontario Bible College (and Seminary); Toronto Bible Training Centre
Toronto Bible School. *See* Ontario Bible College (and Seminary)

Toronto Bible Training School (TBTS) 363–4
Toronto Blessing (1994) 44, 418, 431
Toronto Missionary Training Institute 363
Toronto Mission Union 279–80
Torrey, R.A. 228
Tozer, A.W. 287
Tractarianism 156, 157, 158, 162, 163, 168, 169
Treaty of Westphalia 243
Trinity College (Toronto) 176
Trinity Western University (Langley, BC) 58, 379, 380, 382
Troeltsch, Ernst 292
Troutman, Charles 34
Truax, Albert 259, 260
Trudeau, Pierre 65
Trumbull, Charles 367
Tupper, Charles 196, 203
Turner, H.E. 164
Turner, Harry L. 309
Tyler, Dr William W. 508n55
Tyndale House model 439n39

Unger, Walter 382
Union of Regular Baptist Churches of Ontario 218
United Baptist Bible Training School (Moncton) 379
United Church of Canada: and evangelicalism xxi, 14–15, 60–1, 106–7, 114–15, 120–2, 426; and homosexuality 61; founding 97, 108; anti-evangelicalism 106; founding emphases 110; social activism 110–11, 116, 118–9; history 110–19; Board of Evangelism and Social Service 111, 121; Commission on Church, Nation and World Order 117; emphasis on conversionism 118–9, 121; "Crusade For Christ and His Kingdom" 118, 119; and Billy Graham 119–20; action in Depression 150–1; and TBTS 364. *See also* Oxford Group Movement
United Church Renewal Fellowship 121
United Pentecostal Missions of Toronto 397, 398
United Presbyterians 127
United (Secessionist) Presbyterians 271

United States: evangelicalism in xv, 6; romanticized view of Canada 8; influences on Canada 9, 38–9; trade with Canada 9; main social tension 11; founding myths 13–15; evangelical divisions 18
universities 58, 379–80
University College (Edmonton) 58, 379–80
University of Western University 160
Unruh, A.H. 232, 371
urban tabernacles 283–5
Urshan, Andrew 290

Vance, W.H. 175
Vanderzande, Gerald 5
Van Die, Marguerite xx, 17, 405, 409, 410
Varley, Henry 53
Vaudry, Richard xxi, 17, 127–8
Vespucius, Americus 211
Vickers, Maria Ann 32
Victoria College (Toronto) 4, 100
voluntarism 93
von Zinzendorf, Nicholas 246

Wallace, Rev. Robert 356, 507n25
Walther, C.F.W. 246
Ward, A.G. 293, 296
Ward, Kenn 242
Ward, Peter 133
Wardrope, Thomas 358, 359
Warren, A.T. 266
War of 1812 xv, xvi, 9, 194
Wass, Captain Charles 389
Watson, John 137, 145
Weber, Max 292
Welch, Michael 420
Wenger, J.C. 228
Wentworth, W.C. 30
Wesley, John 80, 81, 88, 92, 258, 259, 417
Wesleyan Conference (U.K.) 39
Wesleyan Female College (Hamilton, ON) 45
Wesleyanism 26, 77, 400
Wesleyan Methodist Connection 263
Wesleyan Methodists 46, 79–80, 268, 269
Wesleyan Missionary Society 26

Wesleyan Sabbath School Committee 85
West, John 26
Western Bible College (Winnipeg) 312
Western University 160
Westfall, William 8, 12–13, 17, 25, 169, 200
Westminster Confessions. *See* Presbyterians, Westminster Standards
Westwood, Horace 338–9
Whitaker, Provost 163, 167
White, Paul 33–4
Whitefield, George 26, 161, 338, 417
Whiteley, Marilyn xxii
Whiting, Rev. 341
Whittaker, Sinclair 314
Whittle, Daniel Webster 274, 488n10
Why I Am a Presbyterian (1934) 149–50
Wiebe, Jake 237–8
Wiens, Delbert 224
Wilberforce, William 161
Willard, Frances 412
Williams, Rev. Eliezer 161
Williams, Rev. John 272
Wilson, Bryan R. 292–3
Wilson, Daniel 164
Wilson, John 132
Wilson, Rev. T.C. 132
Winchester, A.B. 308
Winnipeg, MB xxiii–xxiv, 303–19, 337–50
Winnipeg Bible College. *See* Winnipeg Bible Institute
Winnipeg Bible Institute (WBI) and College of Theology 304, 308–10, 312–13, 317, 375, 378, 380, 381. *See also* Providence College
Winnipeg Bible Training School (WBTS) 296, 297
Winnipeg General Strike 337, 347–50
Winter, Ralph 289
Wisconsin Lutheran Synod 7
Witmer, S.A. 369
Woman's Christian Temperance Union (WCTU) xxiv, 95–6, 406–7, 408–9, 410–15, 415–16
women: religious experiences xx; in evangelicalism xxiv; in 19th-century Methodism 85–6; as temperance workers 95–6; in Presbyterianism 134–5; in Baptist church 212–13, 220–1; in missionary work 220–1; and ordination 221; and Crossley-Hunter revivals 327–8; at Bible schools 375; in Pentecostalism 400; and Canadian evangelical studies 404–7; and "Christian nurture" 407–15; and social mission 415–16; and evangelical roles 416
Woman's Journal 411, 412
Women's Missionary Society (WMS) 103
Wood, Alice 289
Wood, Anna 508n55
Woods, Stacey 33–4
Woodsworth, J.S. 144, 305, 337, 347
Woodward, Rev. John H. 285, 286
Wooster, Hezekiah, xv
working class. *See* class
Wortman, William 401
Wuthnow, Robert 58–9
Wycliffe College (Toronto) xxi, 35, 173, 175–83, 359. *See also* Protestant Episcopal Divinity School

Yates, Rev. Charles 299
Yates, Richard 83
Yonge Street Mission (Toronto) 364
Youmans, Harriet Phelps 75, 76
Young, Irene 34
Young Men's Christian Association (YMCA) 279, 354, 355–6
youth: influence of evangelicalism on 61; in Methodism 84–5, 86–7, 100; in Presbyterian Church 149; in Pentecostalism 298; and postsecondary education 384; males targeted for nurturing 410; WCTU groups 415
Youth for Christ 61, 298
Youth with a Mission 383

Zeidman, Morris 150
Zion 396, 397. *See also* Dowie's Zion